"I've never purchased a better programming book… This book proved to be the most informative, easiest to follow, and had the best examples of any other computer-related book I have ever purchased. The text is very easy to follow!"

—Nick Landman

"…the Sams book by Welling & Thomson is the only one which I have found to be indispensable. The writing is clear and straightforward but never wastes my time. The book is extremely well laid out. The chapters are the right length and chapter titles quickly take you where you want to go."

—Wright Sullivan, President, A&E Engineering, Inc., Greer South Carolina

"I just wanted to tell you that I think the book *PHP and MySQL Web Development* rocks! It's logically structured, just the right difficulty level for me (intermediate), interesting and easy to read, and, of course, full of valuable information!"

—CodE-E, Austria

"There are several good introductory books on PHP, but Welling & Thomson is an excellent handbook for those who wish to build up complex and reliable systems. It's obvious that the authors have a strong background in the development of professional applications and they teach not only the language itself, but also how to use it with good software engineering practices."

—Javier Garcia, senior telecom engineer, Telefonica R&D Labs, Madrid

"I picked up this book two days ago and I am half way finished. I just can't put it down. The layout and flow is perfect. Everything is presented in such a way so that the information is very palatable. I am able to immediately grasp all the concepts. The examples have also been wonderful. I just had to take some time out to express to you how pleased I have been with this book."

—Jason B. Lancaster

"This book has proven a trusty companion, with an excellent crash course in PHP and superb coverage of MySQL as used for Web applications. It also features several complete applications that are great examples of how to construct modular, scalable applications with PHP. Whether you are a PHP newbie or a veteran in search of a better desk-side reference, this one is sure to please!"

—WebDynamic

"The true PHP/MySQL bible, *PHP and MySQL Web Development* by Luke Welling and Laura Thomson, made me realize that programming and databases are now available to the commoners. Again, I know 1/10000th of what there is to know, and already I'm enthralled."

—Tim Luoma, TnTLuoma.com

"Welling and Thomson's book is a good reference for those who want to get to grips with practical projects straight off the bat. It includes webmail, shopping cart, session control, and web-forum/weblog applications as a matter of course, and begins with a sturdy look at PHP first, moving to MySQL once the basics are covered."

—twilight30 on Slashdot

"This book is absolutely excellent, to say the least.... Luke Welling and Laura Thomson give the best in-depth explanations I've come across on such things as regular expressions, classes and objects, sessions etc. I really feel this book filled in a lot of gaps for me with things I didn't quite understand.... This book jumps right into the functions and features most commonly used with PHP, and from there it continues in describing real-world projects, MySQL integration, and security issues from a project manager's point of view. I found every bit of this book to be well organized and easy to understand."

—notepad on codewalkers.com

"A top-notch reference for programmers using PHP and MySQL. Highly recommended."

—*The Internet Writing Journal*

"This book rocks! I am an experienced programmer, so I didn't need a lot of help with PHP syntax; after all, it's very close to C/C++. I don't know a thing about databases, though, so when I wanted to develop a book review engine (among other projects) I wanted a solid reference to using MySQL with PHP. I have O'Reilly's *mSQL and MySQL* book, and it's probably a better pure-SQL reference, but this book has earned a place on my reference shelf...Highly recommended."

—Paul Robichaux

"One of the best programming guides I've ever read."

—jackofsometrades from Lahti, Finland

"This is a well-written book for learning how to build Internet applications with two of the most popular open-source Web development technologies.... The projects are the real jewel of the book. Not only are the projects described and constructed in a logical, component-based manner, but the selection of projects represents an excellent cross-section of common components that are built into many web sites."

—Craig Cecil

"The book takes an easy, step-by-step approach to introduce even the clueless programmer to the language of PHP. On top of that, I often find myself referring back to it in my Web design efforts. I'm still learning new things about PHP, but this book gave me a solid foundation from which to start and continues to help me to this day."

—Stephen Ward

"This book is one of few that really touched me and made me 'love' it. I can't put it in my bookshelf; I must put it in a touchable place on my working bench as I always like to refer from it. Its structure is good, wordings are simple and straight forward, and examples are clear and step by step. Before I read it, I knew nothing of PHP and MySQL. After reading it, I have the confidence and skill to develop any complicated Web application."

—Power Wong

"This book is God.... I highly recommend this book to anyone who wants to jump in the deep end with database driven Web application programming. I wish more computer books were organized this way."

—Sean C Schertell

PHP and MySQL
Web Development

Second Edition

Luke Welling
Laura Thomson

DEVELOPER'S
LIBRARY

Sams Publishing, 201 West 103rd Street, Indianapolis, Indiana 46290

PHP and MySQL Web Development
Second Edition

Copyright © 2003 by Sams Publishing

International Standard Book Number: 0-672-32525-X

Library of Congress Catalog Card Number: 2002115573

Printed in the United States of America

First Printing: February 2003

06   05   04   03   4   3

Trademarks

Warning and Disclaimer

Acquisitions Editor
Shelley Johnston

Development Editor
Scott Meyers

Managing Editor
Charlotte Clapp

Copy Editors
Seth Kerney
Rhonda Tinch-Mize

Indexers
Kelly Castell
Mandie Frank

Proofreader
Suzanne Thomas

Technical Editor
Chris Newman

Media Specialist
Dan Scherf

Cover Design
Alan Clements

Production
Michelle Mitchell

❖

To our Mums and Dads

❖

Overview

Table of Contents

III E-commerce and Security

12 Running an E-commerce Site   261

26 Building a Content Management System 555

VI Appendixes

A Installing PHP and MySQL   789

About the Authors

Laura Thomson is a lecturer in the School of Computer Science and Information Technology at RMIT University in Melbourne, Australia. She is also a partner in the award-winning Web-development firm Tangled Web Design. Laura has previously worked for Telstra and the Boston Consulting Group. She holds a Bachelor of Applied Science (Computer Science) degree and a Bachelor of Engineering (Computer Systems Engineering) degree with honors, and is currently completing her Ph.D. in Adaptive Web Sites. In her spare time, she enjoys sleeping. Laura can be reached via email at laura@tangledweb.com.au.

Luke Welling is a lecturer in the School of Computer Science and Information Technology at RMIT University in Melbourne, Australia. He is also a partner in Tangled Web Design. He holds a Bachelor of Applied Science (Computer Science) degree and is currently completing a master's degree in Genetic Algorithms for Communication Network Design. In his spare time, he attempts to perfect his insomnia. Luke can be reached via email at luke@tangledweb.com.au.

About the Contributors

Israel Denis, Jr. is a freelance consultant working on e-commerce projects throughout the world. He specializes in integrating ERP packages such as SAP and Lawson with custom Web solutions. When he is not busy designing software or writing books, Israel enjoys traveling to Italy, a place he considers home. Israel obtained a master's degree in Electrical Engineering from Georgia Tech in Atlanta, Georgia, in 1998. He is the author of numerous articles about Linux, Apache, PHP, and MySQL. He has worked for companies such as GE and Procter & Gamble with mainly Unix-based computer systems. Israel can be reached via email at idenis@ureach.com.

Chris Newman is a consultant programmer specializing in the development of dynamic Internet applications. He has extensive commercial experience using PHP and MySQL to produce a wide range of applications for an international client base. A graduate of Keele University, Chris lives in Stoke-on-Trent, England, where he runs Lightwood Consultancy Ltd., the company he founded in 1999 to further his interest in Internet development. Chris became fascinated with the potential of the Internet while at the university, and is thrilled to be working with cutting-edge technology. More information on Lightwood Consultancy Ltd. can be found at http://www.lightwood.net, and Chris can be contacted at chris@lightwood.net.

Acknowledgments

We would like to thank the team at Sams for all their hard work. In particular, we would like to thank Shelley Johnston without whose dedication and patience this book would not have been possible. We would also like to thank Israel Denis Jr. and Chris Newman for their valuable contributions.

We appreciate immensely the work done by the PHP and MySQL development teams. Their work has made our lives easier for a number of years now, and continues to do so on a daily basis.

We thank Adrian Close at eSec for saying "You can build that in PHP" back in 1998. He said we would like PHP, and it seems he was right.

Finally, we would like to thank our family and friends for putting up with us while we have been antisocial for the better part of a year. Specifically, thank you for your support to our family members: Julie, Robert, Martin, Lesley, Adam, Paul, James, Archer, and Barton.

We Want to Hear from You!

As the reader of this book, *you* are our most important critic and commentator. We value your opinion and want to know what we're doing right, what we could do better, what areas you'd like to see us publish in, and any other words of wisdom you're willing to pass our way.

You can email or write me directly to let me know what you did or didn't like about this book—as well as what we can do to make our books stronger.

Please note that I cannot help you with technical problems related to the topic of this book, and that due to the high volume of mail I receive, I might not be able to reply to every message.

When you write, please be sure to include this book's title and author as well as your name and phone or email address. I will carefully review your comments and share them with the author and editors who worked on the book.

Email: opensource@samspublishing.com

Mail: Mark Taber
            Associate Publisher
            Sams Publishing
            201 West 103rd Street
            Indianapolis, IN 46290 USA

Reader Services

For more information about this book or others from Sams Publishing, visit our Web site at www.samspublishing.com. Type the ISBN (excluding hyphens) or the title of the book in the Search box to find the book you're looking for.

For a list of known errors and any updates to the book's source code please check www.lukelaura.com.

Introduction

Welcome to *PHP and MySQL Web Development*. Within its pages, you will find distilled knowledge from our experiences using PHP and MySQL, two of the hottest Web development tools around.

In this introduction, we'll cover

- Why you should read this book
- What you will be able to achieve using this book
- What PHP and MySQL are and why they're great
- An overview of the latest features of PHP 4
- How this book is organized

Let's get started.

Why You Should Read This Book

This book will teach you how to create interactive Web sites from the simplest order form to complex secure e-commerce sites. What's more, you'll learn how to do it using Open Source technologies.

This book is aimed at readers who already know at least the basics of HTML and have done some programming in a modern programming language before, but have not necessarily programmed for the Internet or used a relational database. If you are a beginning programmer, you should still find this book useful, but it might take you a little longer to digest. We've tried not to leave out any basic concepts, but we do cover them at speed. The typical reader of this book is someone who wants to master PHP and MySQL for the purpose of building a large or commercial Web site. You might already be working in another Web development language; if so, this book should get you up to speed quickly.

We wrote this book because we were tired of finding books on PHP that were basically a function reference. These books are useful, but they don't help when your boss or client has said "Go build me a shopping cart." We have done our best to make every example useful. Many of the code samples can be directly used in your Web site, and many others can be used with minor modifications.

What You Will Be Able to Achieve Using This Book

Reading this book will enable you to build real-world, dynamic Web sites. If you've built Web sites using plain HTML, you will realize the limitations of this approach. Static content from a pure HTML Web site is just that—static. It stays the same unless you physically update it. Your users can't interact with the site in any meaningful fashion.

Using a language such as PHP and a database such as MySQL allows you to make your sites dynamic: to have them be customizable and contain real-time information.

We have deliberately focused this book on real-world applications, even in the introductory chapters. We'll begin by looking at a simple online ordering system, and work our way through the various parts of PHP and MySQL.

We will then discuss aspects of electronic commerce and security as they relate to building a real-world Web site, and show you how to implement these aspects in PHP and MySQL.

In the final section of this book, we will talk about how to approach real-world projects, and take you through the design, planning, and building of the following eight projects:

- User authentication and personalization
- Shopping carts
- Content management systems
- Web-based email
- Mailing list managers
- Web forums
- Document generation
- Connecting to Web services with XML

Any of these projects should be usable as is, or can be modified to suit your needs. We chose them because we believe they represent eight of the most common Web-based applications built by programmers. If your needs are different, this book should help you along the way to achieving your goals.

What Is PHP?

PHP is a server-side scripting language designed specifically for the Web. Within an HTML page, you can embed PHP code that will be executed each time the page is visited. Your PHP code is interpreted at the Web server and generates HTML or other output that the visitor will see.

PHP was conceived in 1994 and was originally the work of one man, Rasmus Lerdorf. It was adopted by other talented people and has gone through three major rewrites to bring us the broad, mature product we see today. As of October 2002, it was in use on more than nine million domains worldwide, and this number is growing rapidly. You can see the current number at http://www.php.net/usage.php.

PHP is an Open Source product. You have access to the source code. You can use it, alter it, and redistribute it all without charge.

PHP originally stood for *Personal Home Page*, but was changed in line with the GNU recursive naming convention (GNU = Gnu's Not Unix) and now stands for *PHP Hypertext Preprocessor*.

The current major version of PHP is 4. This version has seen some major improvements to the language, discussed in the next section.

The home page for PHP is available at http://www.php.net.

The home page for Zend—the company whose founders designed PHP4—is at http://www.zend.com.

What's New in PHP Version 4.3?

If you have used PHP before, you will notice a few important improvements in version 4.3.

- Most I/O functions now use a unified stream approach, meaning they can easily open files, as well as HTTP, HTTPS and FTP connections.
- PEAR is out of beta and has a user-friendly installer.
- The GD graphic library is now bundled with PHP.
- Apache 2 support is still considered experimental, but is getting better all the time.
- An executable intended for use with command line scripts is now built by default when you install PHP.

What Is MySQL?

MySQL (pronounced *My-Ess-Que-Ell*) is a very fast, robust, *relational database management system (RDBMS)*. A database enables you to efficiently store, search, sort, and retrieve data. The MySQL server controls access to your data to ensure that multiple users can work with it concurrently, to provide fast access to it, and ensure that only authorized users can obtain access. Hence, MySQL is a multi-user, multi-threaded server. It uses *SQL (Structured Query Language)*, the standard database query language worldwide. MySQL has been publicly available since 1996, but has a development history going back to 1979. It has now won the *Linux Journal* Readers' Choice Award on a number of occasions.

MySQL is now available under an Open Source license, but commercial licenses are also available if required.

Why Use PHP and MySQL?

When setting out to build an e-commerce site, there are many different products that you could use.

You will need to choose the following:

- Hardware for the Web server
- An operating system
- Web server software
- A database management system
- A programming or scripting language

Some of these choices will be dependent on the others. For example, not all operating systems will run on all hardware, not all scripting languages can connect to all databases, and so on.

In this book, we do not pay much attention to your hardware, operating system, or Web server software. We don't need to. One of the nice features of PHP is that it is available for Microsoft Windows, for many versions of Unix, and with any fully functional Web server. MySQL is similarly versatile.

To demonstrate this, the examples in this book have been written and tested on two popular setups:

- Linux using the Apache Web server
- Microsoft Windows 2000 using Microsoft Internet Information Server (IIS)

Whatever hardware, operating system, and Web server you choose, we believe you should seriously consider using PHP and MySQL.

Some of PHP's Strengths

Some of PHP's main competitors are Perl, Microsoft Active Server Pages (ASP), Java Server Pages (JSP), and Allaire ColdFusion.

In comparison to these products, PHP has many strengths, including the following:

- High performance
- Interfaces to many different database systems
- Built-in libraries for many common Web tasks
- Low cost
- Ease of learning and use
- Portability
- Availability of source code

A more detailed discussion of these strengths follows.

Performance

PHP is very efficient. Using a single inexpensive server, you can serve millions of hits per day. Benchmarks published by Zend Technologies (http://www.zend.com) show PHP outperforming its competition.

Database Integration

PHP has native connections available to many database systems. In addition to MySQL, you can directly connect to PostgreSQL, mSQL, Oracle, dbm, filePro, Hyperwave, Informix, InterBase, and Sybase databases, among others.

Using the *Open Database Connectivity Standard (ODBC)*, you can connect to any database that provides an ODBC driver. This includes Microsoft products, and many others.

Built-in Libraries

Because PHP was designed for use on the Web, it has many built-in functions for performing many useful Web-related tasks. You can generate GIF images on-the-fly, connect to other network services, send email, work with cookies, and generate PDF documents, all with just a few lines of code.

Cost

PHP is free. You can download the latest version at any time from http://www.php.net for no charge.

Learning PHP

The syntax of PHP is based on other programming languages, primarily C and Perl. If you already know C or Perl, or a C-like language such as C++ or Java, you will be productive using PHP almost immediately.

Portability

PHP is available for many different operating systems. You can write PHP code on the free Unix-like operating systems such as Linux and FreeBSD, commercial Unix versions such as Solaris and IRIX, or on different versions of Microsoft Windows.

Your code will usually work without modification on a different system running PHP.

Source Code

You have access to the source code of PHP. Unlike commercial, closed-source products, if there is something you want modified or added to the language, you are free to do this.

You do not need to wait for the manufacturer to release patches. You don't need to worry about the manufacturer going out of business or deciding to stop supporting a product.

Some of MySQL's Strengths

Some of MySQL's main competitors are PostgreSQL, Microsoft SQL Server, and Oracle. MySQL has many strengths, including the following:

- High performance
- Low cost
- Easy to configure and learn
- Portable
- The source code is available

A more detailed discussion of these strengths follows.

Performance

MySQL is undeniably fast. You can see the developers' benchmark page at the mysql.com Web site. Many of these benchmarks show MySQL to be orders of magnitude faster than the competition.

Low Cost

MySQL is available at no cost, under an Open Source license, or at low cost under a commercial license if required for your application.

Ease of Use

Most modern databases use SQL. If you have used another RDBMS, you should have no trouble adapting to this one. MySQL is also easier to set up than many similar products.

Portability

MySQL can be used on many different Unix systems as well as under Microsoft Windows.

Source Code

As with PHP, you can obtain and modify the source code for MySQL.

How Is This Book Organized?

This book is divided into five main sections.

Part I, "Using PHP," gives an overview of the main parts of the PHP language with examples. Each of the examples will be a real-world example used in building an e-commerce site, rather than "toy" code. We'll kick this section off with Chapter 1, "PHP Crash Course." If you've already used PHP, you can whiz through this section. If you are new to PHP or new to programming, you might want to spend a little more time on it.

Part II, "Using MySQL," discusses the concepts and design involved in using relational database systems such as MySQL, using SQL, connecting your MySQL database to the world with PHP, and advanced MySQL topics, such as security and optimization.

Part III, "E-commerce and Security," covers some of the general issues involved in developing an e-commerce site using any language. The most important of these issues is security. We then discuss how you can use PHP and MySQL to authenticate your users and securely gather, transmit, and store data.

Part IV, "Advanced PHP Techniques," offers detailed coverage of some of the major built-in functions in PHP. We have selected groups of functions that are likely to be useful when building an e-commerce site. You will learn about interaction with the server, interaction with the network, image generation, date and time manipulation, and session variables.

Part V, "Building Practical PHP and MySQL Projects," deals with practical real-world issues such as managing large projects and debugging, and provides sample projects that demonstrate the power and versatility of PHP and MySQL.

Finally

We hope you enjoy this book, and enjoy learning about PHP and MySQL as much as we did when we first began using these products. They are really a pleasure to use. Soon, you'll be able to join the thousands of Web developers who use these robust, powerful tools to easily build dynamic, real-time Web sites.

Barnes & Noble Bookseller
45 Gosling Road
Newington, NH 03801
(603) 422-7733
12-09-03 S02988 R008

CUSTOMER RECEIPT COPY

PHP and MySQL Web Develo   49.99N
G67232525X

SUB TOTAL   49.99
TOTAL   49.99
AMOUNT TENDERED
VISA   49.99
CARD #:   ***********6788
AMOUNT   49.99
AUTH CODE   175020

TOTAL PAYMENT   49.99
Thank you for Shopping at
Barnes & Noble Booksellers
Shop online 24 hours a day www.bn.com
#146336 12-09-03 05:49P Eileen

I

Using PHP

1

PHP Crash Course

THIS CHAPTER GIVES YOU A QUICK overview of PHP syntax and language constructs. If you are already a PHP programmer, it might fill some gaps in your knowledge. If you have a background using C, ASP, or another programming language, it will help you get up to speed quickly.

In this book, you'll learn how to use PHP by working through lots of real world examples, taken from our experience in building e-commerce sites. Often programming textbooks teach basic syntax with very simple examples. We have chosen not to do that. We recognize that often what you want to do is get something up and running, to understand how the language is used, rather than plowing through yet another syntax and function reference that's no better than the online manual.

Try the examples out—type them in or load them from the CD-ROM, change them, break them, and learn how to fix them again.

In this chapter, we'll begin with the example of an online product order form to learn how variables, operators, and expressions are used in PHP. We will also cover variable types and operator precedence. You will learn how to access form variables and how to manipulate them by working out the total and tax on a customer order.

We will then develop the online order form example by using our PHP script to validate the input data. We'll examine the concept of Boolean values and give examples of using if, else, the ?: operator, and the switch statement.

Finally, we'll explore looping by writing some PHP to generate repetitive HTML tables.

Key topics you will learn in this chapter include

- Embedding PHP in HTML
- Adding dynamic content
- Accessing form variables
- Identifiers
- User declared variables
- Variable types

- Assigning values to variables
- Constants
- Variable scope
- Operators and precedence
- Expressions
- Variable functions
- Making decisions with `if`, `else`, and `switch`
- Iteration: `while`, `do`, and `for` loops

Using PHP

In order to work through the examples in this chapter and the rest of the book, you will need access to a Web server with PHP installed. To get the most from the examples and case studies, you should run them and try changing them. To do this, you'll need a test-bed where you can experiment.

If PHP is not installed on your machine, you will need to begin by installing it, or getting your system administrator to install it for you. You can find instructions for doing so in Appendix A, "Installing PHP 4 and MySQL." Everything you need to install PHP under UNIX or Windows NT can be found on the accompanying CD-ROM.

Sample Application: Bob's Auto Parts

One of the most common applications of any server side scripting language is processing HTML forms. You'll start learning PHP by implementing an order form for Bob's Auto Parts, a fictional spare parts company. All the code for the Bob's examples used in this chapter is in the directory called chapter1 on the CD-ROM.

The Order Form

Right now, Bob's HTML programmer has gotten as far as setting up an order form for the parts that Bob sells. The order form is shown in Figure 1.1. This is a relatively simple order form, similar to many you have probably seen while surfing. The first thing Bob would like to be able to do is know what his customer ordered, work out the total of the customer's order, and how much sales tax is payable on the order.

Part of the HTML for this is shown in Listing 1.1. There are two important things to notice in this code.

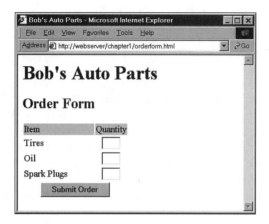

Figure 1.1   Bob's initial order form only records products and quantities.

Listing 1.1   **orderform.html—HTML for Bob's Basic Order Form**

```
<form action="processorder.php" method=post>
<table border=0>
<tr bgcolor=#cccccc>
  <td width=150>Item</td>
  <td width=15>Quantity</td>
</tr>
<tr>
  <td>Tires</td>
  <td align="center"><input type="text" name="tireqty" size="3"
    maxlength="3"></td>
</tr>
<tr>
  <td>Oil</td>
  <td align="center"><input type="text" name="oilqty" size="3" maxlength="3"></td>
</tr>
<tr>
  <td>Spark Plugs</td>
  <td align="center"><input type="text" name="sparkqty" size="3"
    maxlength="3"></td>
</tr>
<tr>
  <td colspan="2" align="center"><input type="submit" value="Submit Order"></td>
</tr>
</table>
</form>
```

The first thing to notice is that we have set the form's action to be the name of the PHP script that will process the customer's order. (We'll write this script next.) In general, the value of the ACTION attribute is the URL that will be loaded when the user presses the submit button. The data the user has typed in the form will be sent to this URL via the method specified in the METHOD attribute, either GET (appended to the end of the URL) or POST (sent as a separate packet).

The second thing you should notice is the names of the form fields—tireqty, oilq-ty, and sparkqty. We'll use these names again in our PHP script. Because of this, it's important to give your form fields meaningful names that you can easily remember when you begin writing the PHP script. Some HTML editors will generate field names like field23 by default. These are difficult to remember. Your life as a PHP programmer will be easier if these names reflect the data that is typed into the field.

You might want to consider adopting a coding standard for field names so that all field names throughout your site use the same format. This makes it easier to remember whether, for example, you abbreviated a word in a field name, or put in underscores as spaces.

Processing the Form

To process the form, we'll need to create the script mentioned in the ACTION attribute of the FORM tag called processorder.php. Open your text editor and create this file. Type in the following code:

```
<html>
<head>
  <title>Bob's Auto Parts - Order Results</title>
</head>
<body>
<h1>Bob's Auto Parts</h1>
<h2>Order Results</h2>
</body>
</html>
```

Notice, how everything we've typed so far is just plain HTML. It's now time to add some simple PHP code to our script.

Embedding PHP in HTML

Under the <h2> heading in your file, add the following lines:

```
<?php
  echo '<p>Order processed.</p>';
?>
```

Save the file and load it in your browser by filling out Bob's form and clicking the Submit Order button. You should see something similar to the output shown in Figure 1.2.

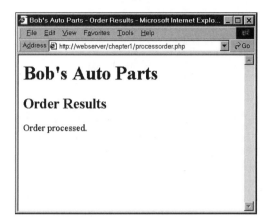

Figure 1.2   Text passed to PHP's echo construct is echoed to the browser.

Notice how the PHP code we wrote was embedded inside a normal-looking HTML file. Try viewing the source from your browser. You should see this code:

```
<html>
<head>
  <title>Bob's Auto Parts - Order Results</title>
</head>
<body>
<h1>Bob's Auto Parts</h1>
<h2>Order Results</h2>
<p>Order processed.</p></body>
</html>
```

None of the raw PHP is visible. This is because the PHP interpreter has run through the script and replaced it with the output from the script. This means that from PHP we can produce clean HTML viewable with any browser—in other words, the user's browser does not need to understand PHP.

This illustrates the concept of server-side scripting in a nutshell. The PHP has been interpreted and executed on the Web server, as distinct from JavaScript and other client-side technologies that are interpreted and executed within a Web browser on a user's machine.

The code that we now have in this file consists of four things:

- HTML
- PHP tags
- PHP statements
- Whitespace

We can also add

- Comments

Most of the lines in the example are just plain HTML.

Using PHP Tags

The PHP code in the previous example began with `<?php` and ended with `?>`. This is similar to all HTML tags because they all begin with a less than (<) symbol and end with a greater than (>) symbol. These symbols are called PHP tags that tell the Web server where the PHP code starts and finishes. Any text between the tags will be interpreted as PHP. Any text outside these tags will be treated as normal HTML. The PHP tags allow us to *escape* from HTML.

Different tag styles are available. Let's look at this in more detail.

PHP Tag Styles

There are actually four different styles of PHP tags we can use. Each of the following fragments of code is equivalent.

- XML style

```
<?php echo '<p>Order processed.</p>'; ?>
```

  This is the tag style that will be used in this book. It is the preferred tag style to use with PHP 3 and 4. The server administrator cannot turn it off, so you can guarantee it will be available on all servers. This style of tag can be used with XML (Extensible Markup Language) documents. If you plan to serve XML on your site, you should definitely use this style of tag.

- Short style

```
<? echo '<p>Order processed.</p>'; ?>
```

  This style of tag is the simplest and follows the style of an SGML (Standard Generalized Markup Language) processing instruction. To use this type of tag—which is the shortest to type—you either need to enable short_tags in your config file, or compile PHP with short tags enabled. You can find more information on installation in Appendix A.

- SCRIPT style

```
<script language='php'> echo '<p>Order processed.</p>'; </script>
```

  This style of tag is the longest and will be familiar if you've used JavaScript or VBScript. It can be used if you are using an HTML editor that gives you problems with the other tag styles.

- ASP style

```
<% echo '<p>Order processed.</p>'; %>
```

This style of tag is the same as used in Active Server Pages (ASP). It can be used if you have enabled the asp_tags configuration setting. You might want to use this style of tag if you are using an editor that is geared toward ASP or if you already program in ASP.

PHP Statements

We tell the PHP interpreter what to do by having PHP statements between our opening and closing tags. In this example, we used only one type of statement:

```
echo '<p>Order processed.</p>';
```

As you have probably guessed, using the echo construct has a very simple result; it prints (or echoes) the string passed to it to the browser. In Figure 1.2, you can see the result is that the text "Order processed." appears in the browser window.

You will notice that a semicolon appears at the end of the echo statement. This is used to separate statements in PHP much like a period is used to separate sentences in English. If you have programmed in C or Java before, you will be familiar with using the semicolon in this way.

Leaving the semicolon off is a common syntax error that is easily made. However, it's equally easy to find and to correct.

Whitespace

Spacing characters such as new lines (carriage returns), spaces, and tabs are known as whitespace. As you probably already know, browsers ignore whitespace in HTML. So does the PHP engine. Consider these two HTML fragments:

```
<h1>Welcome to Bob's Auto Parts!</h1><p>What would you like to order today?</p>
```

and

```
<h1>Welcome           to Bob's
Auto Parts!</h1>
<p>What would you like
 to order today?</p>
```

These two snippets of HTML code produce identical output because they appear the same to the browser. However, you can and are encouraged to use whitespace in your HTML as an aid to humans—to enhance the readability of your HTML code. The same is true for PHP. There is no need to have any whitespace between PHP statements, but it makes the code easier to read if we put each statement on a separate line. For example,

```
echo 'hello ';
echo 'world';
```

and

```
echo 'hello ';echo 'world';
```

are equivalent, but the first version is easier to read.

Comments

Comments are exactly that: Comments in code act as notes to people reading the code. Comments can be used to explain the purpose of the script, who wrote it, why they wrote it the way they did, when it was last modified, and so on. You will generally find comments in all but the simplest PHP scripts.

The PHP interpreter will ignore any text in a comment. Essentially the PHP parser skips over the comments that are equivalent to whitespace.

PHP supports C, C++, and shell script style comments.

This is a C-style, multiline comment that might appear at the start of our PHP script:

```
/* Author: Bob Smith
   Last modified: April 10
   This script processes the customer orders.
*/
```

Multiline comments should begin with a /* and end with */. As in C, multiline comments cannot be nested.

You can also use single line comments, either in the C++ style:

```
echo '<p>Order processed.</p>'; // Start printing order
```

or in the shell script style:

```
echo '<p>Order processed.</p>'; # Start printing order
```

With both of these styles, everything after the comment symbol (# or //) is a comment until we reach the end of the line or the ending PHP tag, whichever comes first.

Adding Dynamic Content

So far, we haven't used PHP to do anything we couldn't have done with plain HTML.

The main reason for using a server-side scripting language is to be able to provide dynamic content to a site's users. This is an important application because content that changes according to a user's needs or over time will keep visitors coming back to a site. PHP allows us to do this easily.

Let's start with a simple example. Replace the PHP in processorder.php with the following code:

```
<?php
  echo '<p>Order processed at ';
  echo date('H:i, jS F');
  echo '</p>';
?>
```

In this code, we are using PHP's built-in `date()` function to tell the customer the date and time when his order was processed. This will be different each time the script is run. The output of running the script on one occasion is shown in Figure 1.3.

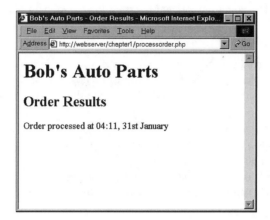

Figure 1.3   PHP's `date()` function returns a formatted date string.

Calling Functions

Look at the call to `date()`. This is the general form that function calls take. PHP has an extensive library of functions you can use when developing Web applications. Most of these functions need to have some data passed to them and return some data.

Look at the function call:

```
date('H:i, jS F')
```

Notice that we are passing a string (text data) to the function inside a pair of parentheses. This is called the function's argument or parameter. These arguments are the input used by the function to output some specific results.

The date() Function

The `date()` function expects the argument you pass it to be a format string, representing the style of output you would like. Each of the letters in the string represents one part of the date and time. H is the hour in a 24-hour format, i is the minutes with a leading zero where required, j is the day of the month without a leading zero, S represents the ordinal suffix (in this case "th"), and F is the full name of the month.

(For a full list of formats supported by `date()`, see Chapter 18, "Managing the Date and Time.")

Accessing Form Variables

The whole point of using the order form is to collect the customer order. Getting the details of what the customer typed in is very easy in PHP, but the exact method depends on the version of PHP you are using and a setting in your php.ini file.

Form Variables

Within your PHP script, you can access each of the form fields as a PHP variable whose name relates to the name of the form field. You can recognize variable names in PHP because they all start with a dollar sign ($). (Forgetting the dollar sign is a common programming error.)

Depending on your PHP version and setup, there are three ways of accessing the form data via variables. These methods do not have official names, so we have nicknamed them short, medium, and long style. In any case, each form field on a page that is submitted to a PHP script is available in the script.

You can access the contents of the field tireqty in the following ways:

```
$tireqty                         // short style
$_POST['tireqty']                // medium style
$HTTP_POST_VARS['tireqty']       // long style
```

In this example, and throughout this book, we have used the long style for referencing form variables, but we create short versions of the variables for ease of use. This is a convenient, secure way of handling data that will work on all systems regardless of version or settings.

For your own code, you might decide to use a different approach, but you should make an informed choice, so we will cover the different methods now.

In brief:

- Short style is convenient, but requires the register_globals configuration setting to be on. (By default, whether it is on or off depends on the version of PHP.) This style also allows you to make errors that could make your code insecure.

- Medium style is fairly convenient, but only came into existence with PHP 4.1.0, so it will not work on older installations.

- Long style is the most verbose, but is the only style that is guaranteed at present to work on every server, regardless of the configuration. Note, however, that it is deprecated and is therefore likely to be removed in the long term.

We want the sample code in the book to work without alteration on as many readers' systems as possible, which is why we have chosen the long style, but your decision will probably be different.

When using short style, the names of the variables in the script are the same as the names of the form fields in the HTML form. You don't need to declare the variables or take any action to create these variables in your script. They are passed into your script, essentially as arguments are passed to a function. If you are using this style, you can just use a variable like $tireqty. The field tireqty in the form creates the variable $tireqty in the processing script.

Using short style requires that a setting called register_globals is turned on in your php.ini configuration file. In PHP from version 4.2.0 onward it is off by default. In older versions it is on by default.

Such convenient access to variables is appealing, but before simply turning register_globals on, it is worth considering why the PHP development team sets it to off.

Having direct access to variables like this is very convenient, but it does allow you to make programming mistakes that could compromise the security of your scripts. With form variables automatically turned into global variables like this, there is no obvious separation between variables that you have created, and untrusted variables that have come directly from the user.

If you are not careful to give all your own variables a starting value, then users of your scripts can pass variables and values as form variables that will be mixed with your own. If you choose to use the convenient short style of accessing variables, you need to be careful to give all your own variables a starting value.

Medium style involves retrieving form variables from one of the arrays $_POST, $_GET, and $_REQUEST. One of $_GET or $_POST arrays will hold the details of all the form variables. Which array is used depends on whether the method used to submit the form was POST or GET, respectively. In addition, all data submitted via POST or GET will be available through $_REQUEST.

If the form was submitted via the POST method, then the data entered in the tireqty box will be stored in $_POST['tireqty']. If the form was submitted via GET, then the data will be in $_GET['tireqty']. In either case, the data will be available in $_REQUEST['tireqty'].

These arrays are some of the new so-called superglobals. We will revisit the super-globals when we talk about variable scope.

If you are using an older version of PHP, you might not have access to $_POST or $_GET. Prior to version 4.1.0, this information was stored in arrays named $HTTP_POST_VARS and $HTTP_GET_VARS. We are calling this long style. This style can be used with new or old versions of PHP, but has been deprecated so may not work with all future versions. There is no equivalent of $_REQUEST in this style.

If you are using long style, you can access the user's response through $HTTP_POST_VARS['tireqty'] or $HTTP_GET_VARS['tireqty'].

Throughout the book, we have tried to remember to point out where examples might not work with older versions, but the examples in the book were tested with PHP version 4.3 and will sometimes be incompatible with versions of PHP prior to version 4.1.0. We recommend that, where possible, you use the current version.

You might have noticed that we don't, at this stage, check the variable contents to make sure that sensible data has been entered in each of the form fields. Try entering deliberately wrong data and observing what happens. After you have read the rest of the chapter, you might want to try adding some data validation to this script.

Let's look at an example.

Because the long style variable names are somewhat cumbersome, and rely on a variable type known as arrays, which we will not cover properly until Chapter 3, "Using Arrays," we will start by creating easier-to-use copies.

To copy the value of one variable into another, you use the assignment operator, which in PHP is an equal sign (=). The following line of code will create a new variable named $tireqty and copy the contents of $HTTP_POST_VARS['tireqty'] into the new variable:

```
$tireqty = $HTTP_POST_VARS['tireqty'];
```

Place the following block of code at the start of the processing script. All other scripts in this book that handle data from a form will contain a similar block at the start. As it will not produce any output, it makes no difference whether you place this above or below the <html> and other HTML tags that start your page. We are generally placing this block at the very start of the script to make it easy to find.

```php
<?php
  //create short variable names
  $tireqty = $HTTP_POST_VARS['tireqty'];
  $oilqty = $HTTP_POST_VARS['oilqty'];
  $sparkqty = $HTTP_POST_VARS['sparkqty'];
?>
```

This code is creating three new variables, $tireqty, $oilqty, and $sparkqty, and setting them to contain the data that was sent via the POST method from the form. To make the script start doing something visible, add the following lines to the bottom of your PHP script:

```
echo '<p>Your order is as follows: </p>';
echo $tireqty.' tires<br />';
echo $oilqty.' bottles of oil<br />';
echo $sparkqty.' spark plugs<br />';
```

If you now load this file in your browser, the script output should resemble what is shown in Figure 1.4. The actual values shown will, of course, depend on what you typed into the form.

A couple of interesting things to note in this example are discussed in the following subsections.

String Concatenation

In the script, we used echo to print the value the user typed in each of the form fields, followed by some explanatory text. If you look closely at the echo statements, you will see that the variable name and following text have a period (.) between them, such as this:

```
echo $tireqty.' tires<br />';
```

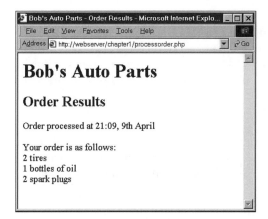

Figure 1.4   The form variables typed in by the user are easily accessible in processorder.php.

This is the string concatenation operator and is used to add strings (pieces of text) together. You will often use it when sending output to the browser with `echo`. This is used to avoid having to write multiple `echo` commands.

For any non-array variables you can also place the variable inside a double-quoted string to be echoed. (Arrays are a little more complicated so we will look at combining arrays and strings in Chapter 4, "String Manipulation and Regular Expressions.")

For example:

```
echo "$tireqty tires<br />";
```

This is equivalent to the first statement. Either format is valid, and which one you use is a matter of personal taste. Note that this is only a feature of double-quoted strings. You cannot place variable names inside a single-quoted string in this way. Running the following line of code

```
echo '$tireqty tires<br />';
```

will send "`$tireqty tires<br />`" to the browser. Within double quotes, the variable name will be replaced with its value. Within single quotes, the variable name, or any other text will be sent unaltered.

Variables and Literals

The variable and string we concatenate together in each of the `echo` statements are different types of things. Variables are a symbol for data. The strings are data themselves. When we use a piece of raw data in a program like this, we call it a literal to distinguish it from a variable. `$tireqty` is a variable, a symbol which represents the data the customer typed in. On the other hand, `' tires<br />'` is a literal. It can be taken at face value.

Well, almost. Remember the second example previously? PHP replaced the variable name $tireqty in the string with the value stored in the variable.

Remember there are two kinds of strings in PHP—ones with double quotes and ones with single quotes. PHP will try and evaluate strings in double quotes, resulting in the behavior we saw earlier. Single quoted strings will be treated as true literals.

Identifiers

Identifiers are the names of variables. (The names of functions and classes are also identifiers—we'll look at functions and classes in Chapters 5, "Reusing Code and Writing Functions," and 6, "Object-Oriented PHP.") There are some simple rules about identifiers:

- Identifiers can be of any length and can consist of letters, numbers, underscores, and dollar signs. However, you should be careful when using dollar signs in identifiers. You'll see why in the section called, "Variable Variables."

- Identifiers cannot begin with a digit.

- In PHP, identifiers are case sensitive. $tireqty is not the same as $TireQty. Trying to use these interchangeably is a common programming error. Function names are an exception to this rule—their names can be used in any case.

- A variable can have the same name as a function. This is confusing however, and should be avoided. Also, you cannot create a function with the same name as another function.

User Declared Variables

You can declare and use your own variables in addition to the variables you are passed from the HTML form.

One of the features of PHP is that it does not require you to declare variables before using them. A variable will be created when you first assign a value to it—see the next section for details.

Assigning Values to Variables

You assign values to variables using the assignment operator, =, as we did when copying one variable's value to another. On Bob's site, we want to work out the total number of items ordered and the total amount payable. We can create two variables to store these numbers. To begin with, we'll initialize each of these variables to zero.

Add these lines to the bottom of your PHP script:

```
$totalqty = 0;
$totalamount = 0.00;
```

Each of these two lines creates a variable and assigns a literal value to it. You can also assign variable values to variables, for example:

```
$totalqty = 0;
$totalamount = $totalqty;
```

Variable Types

A variable's type refers to the kind of data that is stored in it.

PHP's Data Types

PHP supports the following data types:

- Integer—Used for whole numbers
- Double—Used for real numbers
- String—Used for strings of characters
- Boolean—Used for true or false values
- Array—Used to store multiple data items of the same type (see Chapter 3)
- Object—Used for storing instances of classes (see Chapter 6)

PHP 4 added three extra types—Boolean, NULL, and resource. Variables that have not been given a value, have been unset, or have been given the specific value NULL are of type NULL. Certain built-in functions (such as database functions) return variables that have the type resource. You will almost certainly not directly manipulate a resource variable.

PHP also supports the `pdfdoc` and `pdfinfo` types if it has been installed with PDF (Portable Document Format) support. We will discuss using PDF in PHP in Chapter 30, "Generating Personalized Documents in Portable Document Format (PDF)."

Type Strength

PHP is a very weakly typed language. In most programming languages, variables can only hold one type of data, and that type must be declared before the variable can be used, as in C. In PHP, the type of a variable is determined by the value assigned to it.

For example, when we created `$totalqty` and `$totalamount`, their initial types were determined, as follows:

```
$totalqty = 0;
$totalamount = 0.00;
```

Because we assigned 0, an integer, to `$totalqty`, this is now an integer type variable. Similarly, `$totalamount` is now of type double.

Strangely enough, we could now add a line to our script as follows:

```
$totalamount = 'Hello';
```

The variable $totalamount would then be of type string. PHP changes the variable type according to what is stored in it at any given time.

This ability to change types transparently on-the-fly can be extremely useful. Remember PHP "automagically" knows what data type you put into your variable. It will return the data with the same data type once you retrieve it from the variable.

Type Casting

You can pretend that a variable or value is of a different type by using a type cast. These work identically to the way they work in C. You simply put the temporary type in brackets in front of the variable you want to cast.

For example, we could have declared the two variables above using a cast.

```
$totalqty = 0;
$totalamount = (double)$totalqty;
```

The second line means "Take the value stored in $totalqty, interpret it as a double, and store it in $totalamount." The $totalamount variable will be of type double. The cast variable does not change types, so $totalqty remains of type integer.

Variable Variables

PHP provides one other type of variable—the variable variable. Variable variables enable us to change the name of a variable dynamically.

(As you can see, PHP allows a lot of freedom in this area—all languages will let you change the value of a variable, but not many will allow you to change the variable's type, and even fewer will let you change the variable's name.)

The way these work is to use the value of one variable as the name of another. For example, we could set

```
$varname = 'tireqty';
```

We can then use $$varname in place of $tireqty. For example, we can set the value of $tireqty:

```
$$varname = 5;
```

This is exactly equivalent to

```
$tireqty = 5;
```

This might seem a little obscure, but we'll revisit its use later. Instead of having to list and use each form variable separately, we can use a loop and a variable to process them all automatically. There's an example illustrating this in the section on for loops.

Constants

As you saw previously, we can change the value stored in a variable. We can also declare constants. A constant stores a value such as a variable, but its value is set once and then cannot be changed elsewhere in the script.

In our sample application, we might store the prices for each of the items on sale as constants. You can define these constants using the define function:

```
define('TIREPRICE', 100);
define('OILPRICE', 10);
define('SPARKPRICE', 4);
```

Add these lines of code to your script.

You will notice that the names of the constants are all in uppercase. This is a convention borrowed from C that makes it easy to distinguish between variables and constants at a glance. This convention is not required but will make your code easier to read and maintain.

We now have three constants that can be used to calculate the total of the customer's order.

One important difference between constants and variables is that when you refer to a constant, it does not have a dollar sign in front of it. If you want to use the value of a constant, use its name only. For example, to use one of the constants we have just created, we could type:

```
echo TIREPRICE;
```

As well as the constants you define, PHP sets a large number of its own. An easy way to get an overview of these is to run the `phpinfo()` command:

```
phpinfo();
```

This will provide a list of PHP's predefined variables and constants, among other useful information. We will discuss some of these as we go along.

Variable Scope

The term scope refers to the places within a script where a particular variable is visible. The four types of scope in PHP are as follows:

- Built-in superglobal variables are visible everywhere within a script.
- Global variables declared in a script are visible throughout that script, but *not inside functions*.
- Variables used inside functions are local to the function.
- Variables used inside functions that are declared as global refer to the global variable of the same name.

In PHP 4.2 onwards, the arrays `$_GET` and `$_POST` and some other special variables have their own scope rules. These are known as superglobals and can be seen everywhere, both inside and outside functions.

The complete list of superglobals is as follows:

- $GLOBALS, an array of all global variables
- $_SERVER, an array of server environment variables
- $_GET, an array of variables passed to the script via the GET method
- $_POST, an array of variables passed to the script via the POST method
- $_COOKIE, an array of cookie variables
- $_FILES, an array of variables related to file uploads
- $_ENV, an array of environment variables
- $_REQUEST, an array of all user input variables
- $_SESSION, an array of session variables

We will come back to each of these throughout the book as they become relevant. We will cover scope in more detail when we discuss functions. For the time being, all the variables we use will be global by default.

Operators

Operators are symbols that you can use to manipulate values and variables by performing an operation on them. We'll need to use some of these operators to work out the totals and tax on the customer's order.

We've already mentioned two operators: the assignment operator, =, and ., the string concatenation operator. Now we'll look at the complete list.

In general, operators can take one, two, or three arguments, with the majority taking two. For example, the assignment operator takes two—the storage location on the left-hand side of the = symbol, and an expression on the right-hand side. These arguments are called operands; that is, the things that are being operated upon.

Arithmetic Operators

Arithmetic operators are very straightforward—they are just the normal mathematical operators. The arithmetic operators are shown in Table 1.1.

Table 1.1 **PHP's Arithmetic Operators**

Operator	Name	Example
+	Addition	$a + $b
-	Subtraction	$a - $b
*	Multiplication	$a * $b
/	Division	$a / $b
%	Modulus	$a % $b

With each of these operators, we can store the result of the operation. For example,

```
$result = $a + $b;
```

Addition and subtraction work as you would expect. The result of these operators is to add or subtract, respectively, the values stored in the $a and $b variables.

You can also use the subtraction symbol, -, as a unary operator (that is, an operator that takes one argument or operand) to indicate negative numbers; for example:

```
$a = -1;
```

Multiplication and division also work much as you would expect. Note the use of the asterisk as the multiplication operator, rather than the regular multiplication symbol, and the forward slash as the division operator, rather than the regular division symbol.

The modulus operator returns the remainder of dividing the $a variable by the $b variable. Consider this code fragment:

```
$a = 27;
$b = 10;
$result = $a%$b;
```

The value stored in the $result variable is the remainder when we divide 27 by 10; that is, 7.

You should note that arithmetic operators are usually applied to integers or doubles. If you apply them to strings, PHP will try and convert the string to a number. If it contains an "e" or an "E" it will be converted to a double, otherwise it will be converted to an int. PHP will look for digits at the start of the string and use those as the value—if there are none, the value of the string will be zero.

String Operators

We've already seen and used the only string operator. You can use the string concatenation operator to add two strings and to generate and store a result much as you would use the addition operator to add two numbers.

```
$a = "Bob's ";
$b = 'Auto Parts';
$result = $a.$b;
```

The $result variable will now contain the string "Bob's Auto Parts".

Assignment Operators

We've already seen =, the basic assignment operator. Always refer to this as the assignment operator, and read it as "is set to." For example,

```
$totalqty = 0;
```

This should be read as "$totalqty is set to zero". We'll talk about why when we discuss the comparison operators later in this chapter.

Returning Values from Assignment

Using the assignment operator returns an overall value similar to other operators. If you write

```
$a + $b
```

the value of this expression is the result of adding the $a and $b variables together. Similarly, you can write:

```
$a = 0;
```

The value of this whole expression is zero.
This enables you to do things such as

```
$b = 6 + ($a = 5);
```

This will set the value of the $b variable to 11. This is generally true of assignments: The value of the whole assignment statement is the value that is assigned to the left-hand operand.

When working out the value of an expression, parentheses can be used to increase the precedence of a subexpression as we have done here. This works exactly the same way as in mathematics.

Combination Assignment Operators

In addition to the simple assignment, there is a set of combined assignment operators. Each of these is a shorthand way of doing another operation on a variable and assigning the result back to that variable. For example,

```
$a += 5;
```

This is equivalent to writing:

```
$a = $a + 5;
```

Combined assignment operators exist for each of the arithmetic operators and for the string concatenation operator.

A summary of all the combined assignment operators and their effects is shown in Table 1.2.

Table 1.2 **PHP's Combined Assignment Operators**

Operator	Use	Equivalent to
+=	$a += $b	$a = $a + $b
-=	$a -= $b	$a = $a - $b
*=	$a *= $b	$a = $a * $b
/=	$a /= $b	$a = $a / $b
%=	$a %= $b	$a = $a % $b
.=	$a .= $b	$a = $a . $b

Pre- and Post-Increment and Decrement

The pre- and post- increment (++) and decrement (--) operators are similar to the +=
and -= operators, but with a couple of twists.

All the increment operators have two effects—they increment and assign a value.
Consider the following:

```
$a=4;
echo ++$a;
```

The second line uses the pre-increment operator, so called because the ++ appears before
the $a. This has the effect of first, incrementing $a by 1, and second, returning the incremented value. In this case, $a is incremented to 5 and then the value 5 is returned and
printed. The value of this whole expression is 5. (Notice that the actual value stored in
$a is changed: We are not just returning $a + 1.)

However, if the ++ is after the $a, we are using the post-increment operator. This has
a different effect. Consider the following:

```
$a=4;
echo $a++;
```

In this case, the effects are reversed. That is, first, the value of $a is returned and printed,
and second, it is incremented. The value of this whole expression is 4. This is the value
that will be printed. However, the value of $a after this statement is executed is 5.

As you can probably guess, the behavior is similar for the -- operator. However, the
value of $a is decremented instead of being incremented.

References

A new addition in PHP 4 is the reference operator, & (ampersand), which can be used in
conjunction with assignment. Normally when one variable is assigned to another, a copy
is made of the first variable and stored elsewhere in memory. For example,

```
$a = 5;
$b = $a;
```

These lines of code make a second copy of the value in $a and store it in $b. If we sub-
sequently change the value of $a, $b will not change:

```
$a = 7; // $b will still be 5
```

You can avoid making a copy by using the reference operator, &. For example,

```
$a = 5;
$b = &$a;
$a = 7; // $a and $b are now both 7
```

Comparison Operators

The comparison operators are used to compare two values. Expressions using these operators return either of the logical values `true` or `false` depending on the result of the comparison.

The Equals Operator

The equals comparison operator, `==` (two equal signs), enables you to test if two values are equal. For example, we might use the expression

```
$a == $b
```

to test if the values stored in `$a` and `$b` are the same. The result returned by this expression will be `true` if they are equal, or `false` if they are not.

It is easy to confuse this with `=`, the assignment operator. This will work without giving an error, but generally will not give you the result you wanted. In general, non-zero values evaluate to `true` and zero values to `false`. Say that you have initialized two variables as follows:

```
$a = 5;
$b = 7;
```

If you then test `$a = $b`, the result will be `true`. Why? The value of `$a = $b` is the value assigned to the left-hand side, which in this case is 7. This is a non-zero value, so the expression evaluates to `true`. If you intended to test `$a == $b`, which evaluates to `false`, you have introduced a logic error in your code that can be extremely difficult to find. Always check your use of these two operators, and check that you have used the one you intended to use.

This is an easy mistake to make, and you will probably make it many times in your programming career.

Other Comparison Operators

PHP also supports a number of other comparison operators. A summary of all the comparison operators is shown in Table 1.3.

One to note is the new identical operator, `===`, introduced in PHP 4, which returns `true` only if the two operands are both equal and of the same type.

Table 1.3 **PHP's Comparison Operators**

Operator	Name	Use
`==`	equals	`$a == $b`
`===`	identical	`$a === $b`
`!=`	not equal	`$a != $b`
`<>`	not equal	`$a <> $b`
`<`	less than	`$a < $b`

Table 1.3   **Continued**

Operator	Name	Use
>	greater than	`$a > $b`
<=	less than or equal to	`$a <= $b`
>=	greater than or equal to	`$a >= $b`

Logical Operators

The logical operators are used to combine the results of logical conditions. For example, we might be interested in a case where the value of a variable, $a, is between 0 and 100. We would need to test the conditions $a >= 0 and $a <= 100, using the AND operator, as follows

```
$a >= 0 && $a <=100
```

PHP supports logical AND, OR, XOR (exclusive or), and NOT.

The set of logical operators and their use is summarized in Table 1.4.

Table 1.4   **PHP's Logical Operators**

Operator	Name	Use	Result
!	NOT	`!$b`	Returns `true` if $b is `false` and vice versa
&&	AND	`$a && $b`	Returns `true` if both $a and $b are `true`; otherwise `false`
||	OR	`$a || $b`	Returns `true` if either $a or $b or both are `true`; otherwise `false`
and	AND	`$a and $b`	Same as &&, but with lower precedence
or	OR	`$a or $b`	Same as ||, but with lower precedence

The `and` and `or` operators have lower precedence than the `&&` and `||` operators. We will cover precedence in more detail later in this chapter.

Bitwise Operators

The bitwise operators enable you to treat an integer as the series of bits used to represent it.

You probably will not find a lot of use for these in PHP, but a summary of bitwise operators is shown in Table 1.5.

Table 1.5 **PHP's Bitwise Operators**

Operator	Name	Use	Result
&	bitwise AND	$a & $b	Bits set in $a and $b are set in the result
|	bitwise OR	$a | $b	Bits set in $a or $b are set in the result
~	bitwise NOT	~$a	Bits set in $a are not set in the result and vice versa
^	bitwise XOR	$a ^ $b	Bits set in $a or $b but not in both are set in the result
<<	left shift	$a << $b	Shifts $a left $b bits
>>	right shiftt	$a >> $b	Shifts $a right $b bits

Other Operators

In addition to the operators we have covered so far, there are a number of others.

The comma operator, , ,is used to separate function arguments and other lists of items. It is normally used incidentally.

Two special operators, new and ->, are used to instantiate a class and to access class members respectively. These will be covered in detail in Chapter 6.

The array element operators, [], enable us to access array elements. We also use the => operator in some array contexts. These will be covered in Chapter 3.

There are three others that we will discuss briefly here.

The Ternary Operator

This operator, ?:, works the same way as it does in C. It takes the form

```
condition ? value if true : value if false
```

The ternary operator is similar to the expression version of an if-else statement, which is covered later in this chapter.

A simple example is

```
($grade > 50 ? 'Passed' : 'Failed');
```

This expression evaluates student grades to 'Passed' or 'Failed'.

The Error Suppression Operator

The error suppression operator, @, can be used in front of any expression, that is, anything that generates or has a value. For example,

```
$a = @(57/0);
```

Without the @ operator, this line will generate a divide-by-zero warning (try it). With the operator included, the error is suppressed.

If you are suppressing warnings in this way, you should write some error handling code to check when a warning has occurred. If you have PHP set up with the `track_errors` feature enabled, the error message will be stored in the global variable `$php_errormsg`.

The Execution Operator

The execution operator is really a pair of operators: a pair of backticks (` `` `) in fact. The backtick is not a single quote—it is usually located on the same key as the ~ (tilde) symbol on your keyboard.

PHP will attempt to execute whatever is contained between the backticks as a command at the command line of the server. The value of the expression is the output of the command.

For example, under UNIX-like operating systems, you can use:

```
$out = `ls -la`;
echo '<pre>'.$out.'</pre>';
```

Or, equivalently on a Windows server

```
$out = `dir c:`;
echo '<pre>'.$out.'</pre>';
```

Either of these versions will obtain a directory listing and store it in `$out`. It can then be echoed to the browser or dealt with in any other way.

There are other ways of executing commands on the server. We will cover these in Chapter 16, "Interacting with the File System and the Server."

Using Operators: Working Out the Form Totals

Now that you know how to use PHP's operators, you are ready to work out the totals and tax on Bob's order form.

To do this, add the following code to the bottom of your PHP script:

```
$totalqty = 0;
$totalqty = $tireqty + $oilqty + $sparkqty;
echo 'Items ordered: '.$totalqty.'<br />';

$totalamount = 0.00;

define('TIREPRICE', 100);
define('OILPRICE', 10);
define('SPARKPRICE', 4);

$totalamount = $tireqty * TIREPRICE
             + $oilqty * OILPRICE
             + $sparkqty * SPARKPRICE;
```

```
echo 'Subtotal: $'.number_format($totalamount,3).'<br />';

$taxrate = 0.10;  // local sales tax is 10%
$totalamount = $totalamount * (1 + $taxrate);
echo 'Total including tax: $'.number_format($totalamount,2).'<br />';
```

If you refresh the page in your browser window, you should see output similar to Figure 1.5.

Figure 1.5   The totals of the customer's order have been calculated, formatted, and displayed.

As you can see, we've used several operators in this piece of code. We've used the addition (+) and multiplication (*) operators to work out the amounts, and the string concatenation operator (.) to set up the output to the browser.

We also used the number_format() function to format the totals as strings with two decimal places. This is a function from PHP's Math library.

If you look closely at the calculations, you might ask why the calculations were performed in the order they were. For example, consider this statement:

```
$totalamount = $tireqty * TIREPRICE
          + $oilqty * OILPRICE
          + $sparkqty * SPARKPRICE;
```

The total amount seems to be correct, but why were the multiplications performed before the additions? The answer lies in the precedence of the operators, that is, the order in which they are evaluated.

Precedence and Associativity: Evaluating Expressions

In general, operators have a set precedence, or order, in which they are evaluated.

Operators also have an associativity, which is the order in which operators of the same precedence will be evaluated. This is generally left to right (called left for short), right to left (called right for short), or not relevant.

Table 1.6 shows operator precedence and associativity in PHP.

In this table, the lowest precedence operators are at the top, and precedence increases as you go down the table.

Table 1.6 **Operator Precedence in PHP**

Associativity	Operators
left	,
left	or
left	xor
left	and
right	print
left	= += -= *= /= .= %= &= |= ^= ~= <<= >>=
left	? :
left	||
left	&&
left	|
left	^
left	&
n/a	== != ===
n/a	< <= > >=
left	<< >>
left	+ - .
left	* / %
right	! ~ ++ -- (int) (double) (string) (array) (object) @
right	[]
n/a	new
n/a	()

Notice that the highest precedence operator is one we haven't covered yet: plain old parentheses. The effect of these is to raise the precedence of whatever is contained within them. This is how we can work around the precedence rules when we need to.

Remember this part of the last example:

```
$totalamount = $totalamount * (1 + $taxrate);
```

If we had written

```
$totalamount = $totalamount * 1 + $taxrate;
```

the multiplication operator, having higher precedence than the addition operator, would be performed first, giving us an incorrect result. By using the parentheses, we can force the sub-expression 1 + $taxrate to be evaluated first.

You can use as many sets of parentheses as you like in an expression. The innermost set of parentheses will be evaluated first.

Variable Functions

Before we leave the world of variables and operators, we'll take a look at PHP's variable functions. These are a library of functions that enable us to manipulate and test variables in different ways.

Testing and Setting Variable Types

Most of these functions have to do with testing the type of a function.

The two most general are gettype() and settype(). These have the following function prototypes; that is, this is what arguments expect and what they return.

```
string gettype(mixed var);
bool settype (mixed var, string type);
```

To use gettype(), we pass it a variable. It will determine the type and return a string containing the type name, or "unknown type" if it is not one of the standard types; that is, integer, double, string, array, or object.

To use settype(), we pass it a variable that we would like to change the type of, and a string containing the new type for that variable from the previous list.

We can use these as follows:

```
$a = 56;
echo gettype($a).'<br />';
settype($a, 'double');
echo gettype($a).'<br />';
```

When gettype() is called the first time, the type of $a is integer. After the call to settype(), the type will be changed to double.

PHP also provides some specific type testing functions. Each of these takes a variable as argument and returns either true or false. The functions are

- is_array()
- is_double(), is_float(), is_real() (All the same function)

- `is_long()`, `is_int()`, `is_integer()` (All the same function)
- `is_string()`
- `is_object()`

Testing Variable Status

PHP has several ways to test the status of a variable.

The first of these is `isset()`, which has the following prototype:

```
bool isset(mixed var);
```

This function takes a variable name as argument and returns `true` if it exists and `false` otherwise.

You can wipe a variable out of existence by using its companion construct, `unset()`. This has the following prototype:

```
void unset(mixed var);
```

This gets rid of the variable it is passed and returns `true`.

Finally there is `empty()`. This checks to see if a variable exists and has a non-empty, non-zero value and returns `true` or `false` accordingly. It has the following prototype:

```
boolean empty(mixed var);
```

Let's look at an example using these.

Try adding the following code to your script temporarily:

```
echo isset($tireqty);
echo isset($nothere);
echo empty($tireqty);
echo empty($nothere);
```

Refresh the page to see the results.

The variable `$tireqty` should return `true` from `isset()` regardless of what value you entered or didn't enter in that form field. Whether it is `empty()` or not depends on what you entered in it.

The variable `$nothere` does not exist, so it will generate a `false` result from `isset()` and a `true` result from `empty()`.

These can be handy in making sure that the user filled out the appropriate fields in the form.

Re-interpreting Variables

You can achieve the equivalent of casting a variable by calling a function. The three functions that can be useful for this are

```
int intval(mixed var);
float doubleval(mixed var);
string strval(mixed var);
```

Each of these accepts a variable as input and returns the variable's value converted to the appropriate type.

A convention used in this book, and in the php.net documentation is referring to the datatype mixed. There is no such datatype, but because PHP is so flexible with type handling, many functions can take many (or any) datatypes as an argument. Arguments where many types are permitted are shown with the type mixed.

Control Structures

Control structures are the structures within a language that allow us to control the flow of execution through a program or script. You can group them into conditionals (or branching) structures, and repetition structures, or loops. We will consider the specific implementations of each of these in PHP next.

Making Decisions with Conditionals

If we want to sensibly respond to our user's input, our code needs to be able to make decisions. The constructs that tell our program to make decisions are called conditionals.

if Statements

We can use an if statement to make a decision. You should give the if statement a condition to use. If the condition is true, the following block of code will be executed. Conditions in if statements must be surrounded by brackets ().

For example, if we order no tires, no bottles of oil and no spark plugs from Bob, it is probably because we accidentally pressed the Submit button. Rather than telling us "Order processed," the page could give us a more useful message.

When the visitor orders no items, we might like to say, "You did not order anything on the previous page!" We can do this easily with the following if statement:

```
if( $totalqty == 0 )
echo 'You did not order anything on the previous page!<br />';
```

The condition we are using is $totalqty == 0. Remember that the equals operator (==) behaves differently from the assignment operator (=).

The condition $totalqty == 0 will be true if $totalqty is equal to zero. If $totalqty is not equal to zero, the condition will be false. When the condition is true, the echo statement will be executed.

Code Blocks

Often we have more than one statement we want executed inside a conditional statement such as if. There is no need to place a new if statement before each. Instead, we can group a number of statements together as a block. To declare a block, enclose it in curly braces:

```
if( $totalqty == 0 )
{
  echo '<font color=red>';
  echo 'You did not order anything on the previous page!<br />';
  echo '</font>';
}
```

The three lines of code enclosed in curly braces are now a block of code. When the condition is `true`, all three lines will be executed. When the condition is `false`, all three lines will be ignored.

> **Note**
>
> As already mentioned, PHP does not care how you lay out your code. You should indent your code for readability purposes. Indenting is generally used to enable us to see at a glance which lines will only be executed if conditions are met, which statements are grouped into blocks, and which statements are part of loops or functions. You can see in the previous examples that the statement which depends on the `if` statement and the statements which make up the block are indented.

else Statements

You will often want to decide not only if you want an action performed, but also which of a set of possible actions you want performed.

An `else` statement allows you to define an alternative action to be taken when the condition in an `if` statement is `false`. We want to warn Bob's customers when they do not order anything. On the other hand, if they do make an order, instead of a warning, we want to show them what they ordered.

If we rearrange our code and add an `else` statement, we can display either a warning or a summary.

```
if( $totalqty == 0 )
{
  echo 'You did not order anything on the previous page!<br />';
}
else
{
  echo $tireqty.' tires<br />';
  echo $oilqty.' bottles of oil<br />';
  echo $sparkqty.' spark plugs<br />';
}
```

We can build more complicated logical processes by nesting `if` statements within each other. In the following code, not only will the summary only be displayed if the condition `$totalqty == 0` is `true`, but also each line in the summary will only be displayed if its own condition is met.

```
if( $totalqty == 0)
{
  echo 'You did not order anything on the previous page!<br />';
}
else
{
  if ( $tireqty>0 )
    echo $tireqty.' tires<br />';
  if ( $oilqty>0 )
    echo $oilqty.' bottles of oil<br />';
  if ( $sparkqty>0 )
    echo $sparkqty.' spark plugs<br />';
}
```

elseif Statements

For many of the decisions we make, there are more than two options. We can create a
sequence of many options using the elseif statement. The elseif statement is a combination of an else and an if statement. By providing a sequence of conditions, the
program can check each until it finds one that is true.

Bob provides a discount for large orders of tires. The discount scheme works like this:

- Less than 10 tires purchased—no discount

- 10-49 tires purchased—5% discount

- 50-99 tires purchased—10% discount

- 100 or more tires purchased—15% discount

We can create code to calculate the discount using conditions and if and elseif statements. We need to use the AND operator (&&) to combine two conditions into one.

```
if( $tireqty < 10 )
  $discount = 0;
elseif( $tireqty >= 10 && $tireqty <= 49 )
  $discount = 5;
elseif( $tireqty >= 50 && $tireqty <= 99 )
  $discount = 10;
elseif( $tireqty >= 100 )
  $discount = 15;
```

Note that you are free to type elseif or else if—with or without a space are both
correct.

If you are going to write a cascading set of elseif statements, you should be aware
that only one of the blocks or statements will be executed. It did not matter in this
example because all the conditions were mutually exclusive—only one can be true at a

time. If we wrote our conditions in a way that more than one could be true at the same time, only the block or statement following the first true condition would be executed.

switch Statements

The `switch` statement works in a similar way to the `if` statement, but allows the condition to take more than two values. In an `if` statement, the condition can be either `true` or `false`. In a `switch` statement, the condition can take any number of different values, as long as it evaluates to a simple type (integer, string, or double). You need to provide a `case` statement to handle each value you want to react to and, optionally, a default case to handle any that you do not provide a specific `case` statement for.

Bob wants to know what forms of advertising are working for him. We can add a question to our order form.

Insert this HTML into the order form, and the form will resemble Figure 1.6:

```
<tr>
  <td>How did you find Bob's</td>
  <td><select name="find">
        <option value = "a">I'm a regular customer
        <option value = "b">TV advertising
        <option value = "c">Phone directory
        <option value = "d">Word of mouth
     </select>
  </td>
</tr>
```

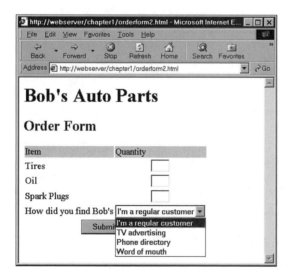

Figure 1.6   The order form now asks visitors how they found Bob's Auto Parts.

This HTML code has added a new form variable whose value will either be "a", "b", "c", or "d". We could handle this new variable with a series of if and elseif statements like this:

```
if($find == 'a')
   echo '<p>Regular customer.</p>';
elseif($find == 'b')
   echo '<p>Customer referred by TV advert.</p>';
elseif($find == 'c')
   echo '<p>Customer referred by phone directory.</p>';
elseif($find == 'd')
   echo '<p>Customer referred by word of mouth.</p>';
```

Alternatively, we could write a switch statement:

```
switch($find)
{
   case 'a' :
     echo '<p>Regular customer.</p>';
     break;
   case 'b' :
     echo '<p>Customer referred by TV advert.</p>';
     break;
   case 'c' :
     echo '<p>Customer referred by phone directory.</p>';
     break;
   case 'd' :
     echo '<p>Customer referred by word of mouth.</p>';
     break;
   default :
     echo '<p>We do not know how this customer found us.</p>';
     break;
}
```

The switch statement behaves a little differently from an if or elseif statement. An if statement affects only one statement unless you deliberately use curly braces to create a block of statements. A switch behaves in the opposite way. When a case in a switch is activated, PHP will execute statements until it reaches a break statement. Without break statements, a switch would execute all the code following the case that was true. When a break statement is reached, the next line of code after the switch statement will be executed.

Comparing the Different Conditionals

If you are not familiar with these statements, you might be asking, "Which one is the best?"

That is not really a question we can answer. There is nothing that you can do with one or more `else`, `elseif`, or `switch` statements that you cannot do with a set of `if` statements. You should try to use whichever conditional will be most readable in your situation. You will acquire a feel for this with experience.

Iteration: Repeating Actions

One thing that computers have always been very good at is automating repetitive tasks. If there is something that you need done the same way a number of times, you can use a loop to repeat some parts of your program.

Bob wants a table displaying the freight cost that will be added to a customer's order. With the courier Bob uses, the cost of freight depends on the distance the parcel is being shipped. The cost can be worked out with a simple formula.

We want our freight table to resemble the table in Figure 1.7.

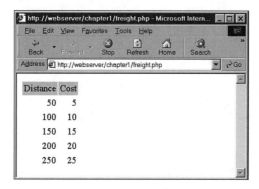

Figure 1.7   This table shows the cost of freight as distance increases.

Listing 1.2 shows the HTML that displays this table. You can see that it is long and repetitive.

Listing 1.2   **freight.html—HTML for Bob's Freight Table**

```
<html>
<body>
<table border="0" cellpadding="3">
<tr>
  <td bgcolor="#CCCCCC" align="center">Distance</td>
  <td bgcolor="#CCCCCC" align="center">Cost</td>
</tr>
<tr>
  <td align="right">50</td>
  <td align="right">5</td>
</tr>
```

Listing 1.2   **Continued**

```
<tr>
  <td align="right">100</td>
  <td align="right">10</td>
</tr>
<tr>
  <td align="right">150</td>
  <td align="right">15</td>
</tr>
<tr>
  <td align="right">200</td>
  <td align="right">20</td>
</tr>
<tr>
  <td align="right">250</td>
  <td align="right">25</td>
</tr>
</table>
</body>
</html>
```

It would be helpful if rather than requiring an easily bored human—who must be paid for his time—to type the HTML, a cheap and tireless computer could do it.
Loop statements tell PHP to execute a statement or block repeatedly.

while Loops

The simplest kind of loop in PHP is the while loop. Like an if statement, it relies on a condition. The difference between a while loop and an if statement is that an if statement executes the following block of code once if the condition is true. A while loop executes the block repeatedly for as long as the condition is true.

You generally use a while loop when you don't know how many iterations will be required to make the condition true. If you require a fixed number of iterations, consider using a for loop.

The basic structure of a while loop is

```
while( condition ) expression;
```

The following while loop will display the numbers from 1 to 5.

```
$num = 1;
while ($num <= 5 )
{
  echo $num."<br />";
  $num++;
}
```

At the beginning of each iteration, the condition is tested. If the condition is `false`, the block will not be executed and the loop will end. The next statement after the loop will then be executed.

We can use a `while` loop to do something more useful, such as display the repetitive freight table in Figure 1.7.

Listing 1.3 uses a `while` loop to generate the freight table.

Listing 1.3   freight.php—Generating Bob's Freight Table with PHP

```
<body>
<table border="0" cellpadding="3">
<tr>
  <td bgcolor="#CCCCCC" align="center">Distance</td>
  <td bgcolor="#CCCCCC" align="center">Cost</td>
</tr>
<?php
$distance = 50;
while ($distance <= 250 )
{
  echo '<tr>  <td align="right">'.$distance.'</td>';
  echo '  <td align="right">'. $distance / 10 .'</td></tr>';
  $distance += 50;
}
?>
</table>
</body>
</html>
```

In order to make the HTML generated by our script readable, it needs to include new lines and spaces. As already mentioned, browsers will ignore this but it is important for human readers. You often need to look at the HTML if your output is not what you were seeking.

In Listing 1.3, you will see \n inside some of the strings. When inside a double-quoted string, this character sequence represents a new line character.

for and foreach Loops

The way that we used the `while` loops previously is very common. We set a counter to begin with. Before each iteration, we tested the counter in a condition. At the end of each iteration, we modified the counter.

We can write this style of loop in a more compact form using a `for` loop.

The basic structure of a `for` loop is

```
for( expression1; condition; expression2)
  expression3;
```

- *expression1* is executed once at the start. Here you will usually set the initial value of a counter.
- The *condition* expression is tested before each iteration. If the expression returns `false`, iteration stops. Here you will usually test the counter against a limit.
- *expression2* is executed at the end of each iteration. Here you will usually adjust the value of the counter.
- *expression3* is executed once per iteration. This expression is usually a block of code and will contain the bulk of the loop code.

We can rewrite the `while` loop example in Listing 1.3 as a `for` loop. The PHP code will become

```php
<?
for($distance = 50; $distance <= 250; $distance += 50)
{
  echo "<tr>\n  <td align='right'>$distance</td>\n";
  echo "  <td align='right'>". $distance / 10 ."</td>\n</tr>\n";
}
?>
```

Both the `while` version and the `for` version are functionally identical. The `for` loop is somewhat more compact, saving two lines.

Both these loop types are equivalent—neither is better or worse than the other. In a given situation, you can use whichever you find more intuitive.

As a side note, you can combine variable variables with a `for` loop to iterate through a series of repetitive form fields. If, for example, you have form fields with names such as name1, name2, name3, and so on, you can process them like this:

```php
for ($i=1; $i <= $numnames; $i++)
{
  $temp= "name$i";
  echo $$temp.'<br />'; // or whatever processing you want to do
}
```

By dynamically creating the names of the variables, we can access each of the fields in turn.

As well as the `for` loop there is a `foreach` loop, designed specifically for use with arrays. We will discuss how to use it in Chapter 3.

do..while Loops

The final loop type we will mention behaves slightly differently. The general structure of a `do..while` statement is

```
do
   expression;
while( condition );
```

A `do..while` loop differs from a `while` loop because the condition is tested at the end. This means that in a `do..while` loop, the statement or block within the loop is always executed at least once.

Even if we take this example in which the condition will be `false` at the start and can never become `true`, the loop will be executed once before checking the condition and ending.

```
$num = 100;
do
{
   echo $num.'<br />';
}
while ($num < 1 );
```

Breaking Out of a Control Structure or Script

If you want to stop executing a piece of code, there are three approaches, depending on the effect you are trying to achieve.

If you want to stop executing a loop, you can use the `break` statement as previously discussed in the section on `switch`. If you use the `break` statement in a loop, execution of the script will continue at the next line of the script after the loop.

If you want to jump to the next loop iteration, you can instead use the `continue` statement.

If you want to finish executing the entire PHP script, you can use `exit`. This is typically useful when performing error checking. For example, we could modify our earlier example as follows:

```
if( $totalqty == 0)
{
   echo 'You did not order anything on the previous page!<br />';
   exit;
}
```

The call to exit stops PHP from executing the remainder of the script.

Next: Saving the Customer's Order

Now you know how to receive and manipulate the customer's order. In the next chapter, we'll look at how to store the order so that it can be retrieved and fulfilled later.

2

Storing and Retrieving Data

NOW THAT WE KNOW HOW TO access and manipulate data entered in an HTML form, we can look at ways of storing that information for later use. In most cases, including the example we looked at in the previous chapter, you'll want to store this data and load it later. In our case, we need to write customer orders to storage so that they can be filled later.

In this chapter we'll look at how you can write the customer's order from the previous example to a file and read it back. We'll also talk about why this isn't always a good solution. When we have large numbers of orders, we should use a database management system such as MySQL.

Key topics you will learn about in this chapter include

- Saving data for later
- Opening a file
- Creating and writing to a file
- Closing a file
- Reading from a file
- File locking
- Deleting files
- Other useful file functions
- Doing it a better way: database management systems
- Further reading

Saving Data for Later

There are basically two ways you can store data: in flat files or in a database.

A flat file can have many formats but, in general, when we refer to a *flat file*, we mean a simple text file. In this example, we'll write customer orders to a text file, one order per line.

This is very simple to do, but also pretty limiting, as we'll see later in this chapter. If you're dealing with information of any reasonable volume, you'll probably want to use a database instead. However, flat files have their uses and there are some situations when you'll need to know how to use them.

Writing to and reading from files in PHP is virtually identical to the way it's done in C. If you've done any C programming or UNIX shell scripting, this will all seem pretty familiar to you.

Storing and Retrieving Bob's Orders

In this chapter, we'll use a slightly modified version of the order form we looked at in the last chapter. We'll begin with this form and the PHP code we wrote to process the order data.

> **Note**
>
> The HTML and PHP scripts used in this chapter can be found in the `chapter2/` folder of this book's CD-ROM.

We've modified the form to include a quick way to obtain the customer's shipping address. You can see this form in Figure 2.1.

Figure 2.1   This version of the order form gets the
customer's shipping address.

The form field for the shipping address is called `address`. This gives us a variable we can access as `$address` when we process the form in PHP, if we have register_globals on, or as $_POST['address'] or $_GET['address'] if register_globals is off (see Chapter 1, "PHP Crash Course," for details).

We'll write each order that comes in to the same file. Then we'll construct a Web interface for Bob's staff to view the orders that have been received.

Overview of File Processing

There are three steps to writing data to a file:

1. Open the file. If the file doesn't already exist, it will need to be created.
2. Write the data to the file.
3. Close the file.

Similarly, there are three steps to reading data from a file:

1. Open the file. If the file can't be opened (for example, if it doesn't exist), we need to recognize this and exit gracefully.
2. Read data from the file.
3. Close the file.

When you want to read data from a file, you have choices about how much of the file to read at a time. We'll look at each of those choices in detail.

For now, we'll start at the beginning by opening a file.

Opening a File

To open a file in PHP, we use the fopen() function. When we open the file, we need to specify how we intend to use it. This is known as the *file mode*.

File Modes

The operating system on the server needs to know what you want to do with a file that you are opening. It needs to know if the file can be opened by another script while you have it open, and to work out if you (the owner of the script) have permission to use it in that way. Essentially, file modes give the operating system a mechanism to determine how to handle access requests from other people or scripts and a method to check that you have access and permission to this particular file.

There are three choices you need to make when opening a file:

1. You might want to open a file for reading only, for writing only, or for both reading and writing.
2. If writing to a file, you might want to overwrite any existing contents of a file or to append new data to the end of the file.
3. If you are trying to write to a file on a system that differentiates between binary and text files, you might want to specify this.

The fopen() function supports combinations of these three options.

Using fopen() to Open a File

Let's assume that we want to write a customer order to Bob's order file. You can open this file for writing with the following:

```
$fp = fopen("$DOCUMENT_ROOT/../orders/orders.txt", "w");
```

When `fopen` is called, it expects two or three parameters. Usually you'll use two, as shown in this code line.

The first parameter should be the file you want to open. You can specify a path to this file as we've done in the previous code—our `orders.txt` file is in the orders directory. We've used the PHP built-in variable `$HTTP_SERVER_VARS['DOCUMENT_ROOT']` but, as with the cumbersome full names for form variables, we have assigned it a shorter name.

This variable points at the base of the document tree on your Web server. We've used the `".."` to mean "the parent directory of the document root directory." This directory is outside the document tree, for security reasons. We do not want this file to be Web accessible except through the interface that we provide. This path is called a relative path as it describes a position in the file system relative to the document root.

As with the short names we are giving form variables, unless register_globals is turned on, we need the following line at the start of our script

```
$DOCUMENT_ROOT = $HTTP_SERVER_VARS['DOCUMENT_ROOT'];
```

to copy the contents of the long style variable to the short style name.

In the same way as there are different ways to access form data, there are different ways to access the predefined server variables. Depending on your server setup you can get at the document root through:

- `$DOCUMENT_ROOT`
- `$_SERVER['DOCUMENT_ROOT']`
- `$HTTP_SERVER_VARS['DOCUMENT_ROOT']`

As with form data, the first style, which we have been calling short style, is only automatically available if you have register_globals turned on. The second style (medium style) cannot be turned off, but is only available in PHP 4.1 and later versions. The long style is available on all systems, but this style is deprecated, so may not be around forever.

You could also specify an absolute path to the file. This is the path from the root directory (/ on a UNIX system and typically `c:\` on a Windows system). On our UNIX server, this would be `/home/book/orders`. The problem with doing this is that, particularly if you are hosting your site on somebody else's server, the absolute path might change. We once learned this the hard way after having to change absolute paths in a large number of scripts when the systems administrators decided to change the directory structure without notice.

If no path is specified, the file will be created or looked for in the same directory as the script itself. This will be different if you are running PHP through some kind of CGI wrapper and will depend on your server configuration.

In a UNIX environment, the slashes in directories will be forward slashes (/). If you are using a Windows platform, you can use forward or backslashes. If you use back slashes, they must be escaped (marked as a special character) for fopen to understand them properly. To escape a character, you simply add an additional backslash in front of it, as shown in the following:

```
$fp = fopen("$DOCUMENT_ROOT\\..\\orders\\orders.txt", 'w');
```

Very few people use backslashes in paths within PHP as it means your code will only work on Windows. If you use forward slashes you can often move your code between Windows and UNIX machines without alteration.

The second parameter of fopen() is the file mode, which should be a string. This specifies what you want to do with the file. In this case, we are passing 'w' to fopen()—this means open the file for writing. A summary of file modes is shown in Table 2.1.

Table 2.1   **Summary of File Modes for fopen**

Mode	Meaning
r	Read mode—Open the file for reading, beginning from the start of the file.
r+	Read mode—Open the file for reading and writing, beginning from the start of the file.
w	Write mode—Open the file for writing, beginning from the start of the file. If the file already exists, delete the existing contents. If it does not exist, try and create it.
w+	Write mode—Open the file for writing and reading, beginning from the start of the file. If the file already exists, delete the existing contents. If it does not exist, try and create it.
a	Append mode—Open the file for appending (writing) only, starting from the end of the existing contents, if any. If it does not exist, try and create it.
a+	Append mode—Open the file for appending (writing) and reading, starting from the end of the existing contents, if any. If it does not exist, try and create it.
b	Binary mode—Used in conjunction with one of the other modes. You might want to use this if your file system differentiates between binary and text files. Windows systems differentiate; UNIX systems do not.

The file mode to use in our example depends on how the system will be used. We have used 'w', which will only allow one order to be stored in the file. Each time a new

order is taken, it will overwrite the previous order. This is probably not very sensible, so
we are better off specifying append mode:

```
$fp = fopen("$DOCUMENT_ROOT/../orders/orders.txt", 'a');
```

The fopen() function has an optional third parameter. You can use it if you want to
search the include_path (set in your PHP configuration—see Appendix A, "Installing
PHP 4 and MySQL") for a file. If you want to do this, set this parameter to 1. If you tell
PHP to search the include_path, you do not need to provide a directory name or path:

```
$fp = fopen('orders.txt', 'a', 1);
```

If fopen() opens the file successfully, a pointer to the file is returned and should be
stored in a variable, in this case $fp. You will use this variable to access the file when you
actually want to read from or write to it.

Opening Files Through FTP or HTTP

As well as opening local files for reading and writing, you can open files via FTP and
HTTP using fopen().

  If the filename you use begins with ftp://, a passive mode FTP connection will be
opened to the server you specify and a pointer to the start of the file will be returned.

  If the filename you use begins with http://, an HTTP connection will be opened to
the server you specify and a pointer to the response will be returned. When using HTTP
mode, you must specify trailing slashes on directory names, as shown in the following:

```
http://www.server.com/
```

not

```
http://www.server.com
```

When you specify the latter form of address (without the slash), a Web server will normally use an HTTP redirect to send you to the first address (with the slash). Try it in
your browser.

  Prior to PHP 4.0.5, the fopen() function did not support HTTP redirects, so you
must specify URLs that refer to directories with a trailing slash.

  As of PHP 4.3.0 you can also open files over SSL as long as you have compiled or
enabled support for OpenSSL and you begin the name of the file with https://.

  Remember that the domain names in your URL are not case sensitive, but the path
and filename might be.

Problems Opening Files

A common error you might make while trying to open a file is trying to open a file you
don't have permission to read or write to. PHP will give you a warning similar to the
one shown in Figure 2.2.

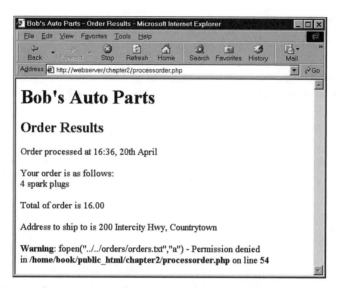

Figure 2.2 PHP will specifically warn you when a file can't be opened.

If you get this error, you need to make sure that the user that the script runs as has permission to access the file you are trying to use. Depending on how your server is set up, the script might be running as the Web server user or as the owner of the directory that the script is in.

On most systems, the script will run as the Web server user. If your script was on a UNIX system in the `~/public_html/chapter2/` directory, you would create a world writeable directory in which to store the order by typing the following:

```
mkdir ~/orders
chmod 777 ~/orders
```

Bear in mind that directories and files that anybody can write to are dangerous. You should not have directories that are accessible directly from the Web as writeable. For this reason, our `orders` directory is two subdirectories back, above the `public_html` directory. We will talk more about security later in Chapter 13, "E-commerce Security Issues."

Incorrect permission settings is probably the most common thing that can go wrong when opening a file, but it's not the only thing. If the file can't be opened, you really need to know this so that you don't try to read data from or write data to it.

If the call to `fopen()` fails, the function will return `false`. You can deal with the error in a more user-friendly way by suppressing PHP's error message and giving your own:

```
@ $fp = fopen("$DOCUMENT_ROOT/../orders/orders.txt", 'a', 1);

  if (!$fp)
  {
    echo '<p><strong> Your order could not be processed at this time.   '
         .'Please try again later.</strong></p></body></html>';
    exit;
  }
```

The @ symbol in front of the call to fopen() tells PHP to suppress any errors resulting from the function call. Usually it's a good idea to know when things go wrong, but in this case we're going to deal with that elsewhere.

This line can also be written as follows

```
$fp = @fopen("$DOCUMENT_ROOT/../orders/orders.txt", "a", 1);
```

but this does tend to make it less obvious that you are using the error suppression operator.

You can read more about error reporting in Chapter 23, "Debugging."

The if statement tests the variable $fp to see if a valid file pointer was returned from the fopen call; if not, it prints an error message and ends script execution. Because the page will finish here, notice that we have closed the HTML tags to give valid HTML.

The output when using this approach is shown in Figure 2.3.

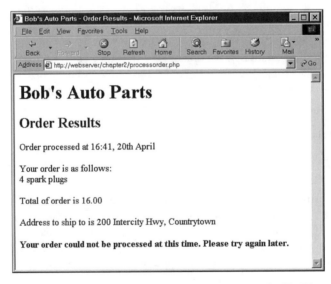

Figure 2.3   Using your own error messages instead of PHP's
can be more user friendly.

Writing to a File

Writing to a file in PHP is relatively simple. You can use either of the functions `fwrite()` (file write) or `fputs()` (file put string); `fputs()` is an alias to `fwrite()`. We call `fwrite()` in the following:

```
fwrite($fp, $outputstring);
```

This tells PHP to write the string stored in `$outputstring` to the file pointed to by `$fp`. We'll discuss `fwrite()` in more detail before we talk about the contents of `$outputstring`.

Parameters for fwrite()

The function `fwrite()` actually takes three parameters but the third one is optional. The prototype for `fwrite()` is

```
int fwrite ( int fp, string string [, int length])
```

The third parameter, *length*, is the maximum number of bytes to write. If this parameter is supplied, `fwrite()` will write *string* to the file pointed to by *fp* until it reaches the end of *string* or has written *length* bytes, whichever comes first.

File Formats

When you are creating a data file like the one in our example, the format in which you store the data is completely up to you. (However, if you are planning to use the data file in another application, you may have to follow that application's rules.)

Let's construct a string that represents one record in our data file. We can do this as follows:

```
$outputstring = $date."\t".$tireqty." tires \t".$oilqty." oil\t"
              .$sparkqty." spark plugs\t\$".$total
              ."\t". $address."\n";
```

In our simple example, we are storing each order record on a separate line in the file. We choose to write one record per line because this gives us a simple record separator in the newline character. Because newlines are invisible, we represent them with the control sequence `"\n"`.

We will write the data fields in the same order every time and separate fields with a tab character. Again, because a tab character is invisible, it is represented by the control sequence `"\t"`. You may choose any sensible delimiter that is easy to read back.

The separator or delimiter character should either be something that will certainly not occur in the input, or we should process the input to remove or escape out any instances of the delimiter. We will look at processing the input in Chapter 4, "String Manipulation and Regular Expressions." For now, we will assume that nobody will place a tab into our order form. It is difficult, but not impossible, for a user to put a tab or newline into a single line HTML input field.

Using a special field separator will allow us to split the data back into separate variables more easily when we read the data back. We'll cover this in Chapter 3, "Using Arrays," and Chapter 4. For the time being, we'll treat each order as a single string.

After processing a few orders, the contents of the file will look something like the example shown in Listing 2.1.

Listing 2.1   **orders.txt—Example of What the Orders File Might Contain**

```
15:42, 20th April 4 tires  1 oil 6 spark plugs  $434.00 22 Short St,   Smalltown
15:43, 20th April 1 tires  0 oil 0 spark plugs  $100.00 33 Main Rd,    Newtown
15:43, 20th April 0 tires  1 oil 4 spark plugs  $26.00  127 Acacia St, Springfield
```

Closing a File

When you've finished using a file, you need to close it. You should do this with the `fclose()` function as follows:

```
fclose($fp);
```

This function will return `true` if the file was successfully closed, or `false` if it wasn't. This is generally much less likely to go wrong than opening a file in the first place, so in this case we've chosen not to test it.

Reading from a File

Right now, Bob's customers can leave their orders via the Web, but if Bob's staff wants to look at the orders, they'll have to open the files themselves.

Let's create a Web interface to let Bob's staff read the files easily. The code for this interface is shown in Listing 2.2.

Listing 2.2   **vieworders.php—Staff Interface to the Orders File**

```php
<?php
  //create short variable name
  $DOCUMENT_ROOT = $HTTP_SERVER_VARS['DOCUMENT_ROOT'];
?>
<html>
<head>
  <title>Bob's Auto Parts - Customer Orders</title>
</head>
<body>
<h1>Bob's Auto Parts</h1>
<h2>Customer Orders</h2>
<?php
```

Listing 2.2 **Continued**

```
@  $fp = fopen("$DOCUMENT_ROOT/../orders/orders.txt", 'r');

   if (!$fp)
   {
     echo '<p><strong>No orders pending.'
         .'Please try again later.</strong></p>';
     exit;
   }

   while (!feof($fp))
   {
     $order= fgets($fp, 999);
     echo $order.'<br />';
   }

   fclose($fp);
?>
</body>
</html>
```

This script follows the sequence we talked about earlier: open the file, read from the file, close the file. The output from this script using the data file from Listing 2.1 is shown in Figure 2.4.

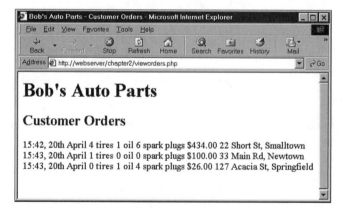

Figure 2.4 The vieworders.php script displays all the orders currently in the orders.txt file in the browser window.

Let's look at the functions in this script in detail.

Opening a File for Reading: fopen()

Again, we open the file using fopen(). In this case we are opening the file for reading only, so we use the file mode 'r':

```
$fp = fopen("$DOCUMENT_ROOT/../orders/orders.txt", 'r');
```

Knowing When to Stop: feof()

In this example, we use a while loop to read from the file until the end of the file is reached. The while loop tests for the end of the file using the feof() function:

```
while (!feof($fp))
```

The feof() function takes a file pointer as its single parameter. It will return true if the file pointer is at the end of the file. Although the name might seem strange, it is easy to remember if you know that feof stands for File End Of File.

In this case (and generally when reading from a file), we read from the file until EOF is reached.

Reading a Line at a Time: fgets(), fgetss(), and fgetcsv()

In our example, we use the fgets() function to read from the file:

```
$order= fgets($fp, 999);
```

This function is used to read one line at a time from a file. In this case, it will read until it encounters a newline character (\n), encounters an EOF, or has read 998 bytes from the file. The maximum length read is the length specified minus one byte.

There are many different functions that can be used to read from files. The fgets() function is useful when dealing with files that contain plain text that we want to deal with in chunks.

An interesting variation on fgets() is fgetss(), which has the following prototype:

```
string fgetss(int fp, int length, string [allowable_tags]);
```

This is very similar to fgets() except that it will strip out any PHP and HTML tags found in the string. If you want to leave any particular tags in, you can include them in the allowable_tags string. You would use fgetss() for safety when reading a file written by somebody else or containing user input. Allowing unrestricted HTML code in the file could mess up your carefully planned formatting. Allowing unrestricted PHP could give a malicious user almost free rein on your server.

The function fgetcsv() is another variation on fgets(). It has the following prototype:

```
array fgetcsv ( int fp, int length [, string delimiter [, string enclosure]])
```

It is used for breaking up lines of files when you have used a delimiting character, such as the tab character as we suggested earlier or a comma as commonly used by spreadsheets and other applications. If we want to reconstruct the variables from the order separately rather than as a line of text, `fgetcsv()` allows us to do this simply. You call it in much the same way as you would call `fgets()`, but you pass it the delimiter you used to separate fields. For example,

```
$order = fgetcsv($fp, 100, "\t");
```

would retrieve a line from the file and break it up wherever a tab (\t) was encountered. The results are returned in an array ($order in this code example). We will cover arrays in more detail in Chapter 3.

The *length* parameter should be greater than the length in characters of the longest line in the file you are trying to read.

The `enclosure` parameter is used to specify what each field in a line is surrounded by. If not specified, it defaults to " (double quote). This parameter was added as of PHP 4.3.0.

Reading the Whole File: readfile(), fpassthru(), file()

Instead of reading from a file a line at a time, we can read the whole file in one go. There are four different ways we can do this.

The first uses `readfile()`. We can replace the entire script we wrote previously with one line:

```
readfile("$DOCUMENT_ROOT/../orders/orders.txt");
```

A call to the `readfile()` function opens the file, echoes the content to standard output (the browser), and then closes the file. The prototype for `readfile()` is

```
int readfile(string filename, int [use_include_path]);
```

The optional second parameter specifies whether PHP should look for the file in the include_path and operates the same way as in `fopen()`. The function returns the total number of bytes read from the file.

Secondly, you can use `fpassthru()`. You need to open the file using `fopen()` first. You can then pass the file pointer as argument to `fpassthru()`, which will dump the contents of the file from the pointer's position onward to standard output. It closes the file when it is finished.

You can replace the previous script with `fpassthru()` as follows:

```
$fp = fopen("$DOCUMENT_ROOT/../orders/orders.txt", 'r');
fpassthru($fp);
```

The function `fpassthru()` returns `true` if the read is successful and `false` otherwise.

The third option for reading the whole file is using the `file()` function. This function is identical to `readfile()` except that instead of echoing the file to standard output, it turns it into an array. We will cover this in more detail when we look at arrays in Chapter 3. Just for reference, you would call it using

```
$filearray = file($fp);
```

This will read the entire file into the array called `$filearray`. Each line of the file is stored in a separate element of the array. Note that this function is not binary-safe.

Finally, as of PHP 4.3.0 you can use the `file_get_contents()` function. This function is identical to `readfile()` except that it returns the content of the file as a string instead of outputting it to the browser. The advantage of this new function is that it is binary-safe, unlike the `file()` function.

Reading a Character: fgetc()

Another option for file processing is to read a single character at a time from a file. You can do this using the `fgetc()` function. It takes a file pointer as its only parameter and returns the next character in the file. We can replace the while loop in our original script with one that uses `fgetc()`:

```
while (!feof($fp))
{
  $char = fgetc($fp);
  if (!feof($fp))
    echo ($char=="\n" ? '<br />': $char);
}
```

This code reads a single character from the file at a time using `fgetc()` and stores it in `$char`, until the end of the file is reached. We then do a little processing to replace the text end-of-line characters, \n, with HTML line breaks, `<br />`. This is just to clean up the formatting. Because browsers don't render a newline in HTML as a newline without this code, the whole file would be printed on a single line. (Try it and see.) We use the ternary operator to do this neatly.

A minor side effect of using `fgetc()` instead of `fgets()` is that it will return the EOF character whereas `fgets()` will not. We need to test `feof()` again after we've read the character because we don't want to echo the EOF to the browser.

It is not generally sensible to read a file character-by-character unless for some reason we want to process it character-by-character.

Reading an Arbitrary Length: fread()

The final way we can read from a file is using the `fread()` function to read an arbitrary number of bytes from the file. This function has the following prototype:

```
string fread(int fp, int length);
```

The way it works is to read up to *length* bytes or to the end of file, whichever comes first.

Other Useful File Functions

There are a number of other file functions we can use that are useful from time-to-time.

Checking Whether a File Is There: file_exists()

If you want to check if a file exists without actually opening it, you can use
file_exists(), as follows:

```
if (file_exists("$DOCUMENT_ROOT/../orders/orders.txt"))
    echo 'There are orders waiting to be processed.';
else
    echo 'There are currently no orders.';
```

Knowing How Big a File Is: filesize()

You can check the size of a file with the filesize() function. It returns the size of a
file in bytes:

```
echo filesize("$DOCUMENT_ROOT/../orders/orders.txt");
```

It can be used in conjunction with fread() to read a whole file (or some fraction of the
file) at a time. We can replace our entire original script with

```
$fp = fopen("$DOCUMENT_ROOT/../orders/orders.txt", 'r');
echo fread( $fp, filesize("$DOCUMENT_ROOT/../orders/orders.txt" ));
fclose( $fp );
```

Deleting a File: unlink()

If you want to delete the order file after the orders have been processed, you can do it
using unlink(). (There is no function called delete.) For example,

```
unlink("$DOCUMENT_ROOT/../orders/orders.txt");
```

This function returns false if the file could not be deleted. This will typically occur if
the permissions on the file are insufficient or if the file does not exist.

Navigating Inside a File: rewind(), fseek(), and ftell()

You can manipulate and discover the position of the file pointer inside a file using
rewind(), fseek(), and ftell().

The rewind() function resets the file pointer to the beginning of the file. The
ftell() function reports how far into the file the pointer is in bytes. For example, we
can add the following lines to the bottom of our original script (before the fclose()
command):

```
echo 'Final position of the file pointer is '.(ftell($fp));
echo '<br />';
```

```
rewind($fp);
echo 'After rewind, the position is '.(ftell($fp));
echo '<br />';
```

The output in the browser will be similar to that shown in Figure 2.5.

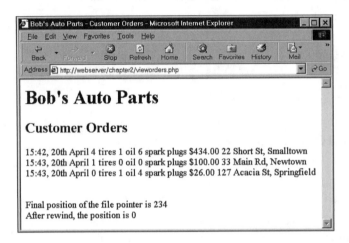

Figure 2.5   After reading the orders, the file pointer points to the end
of the file, an offset of 234 bytes. The call to rewind sets it
back to position 0, the start of the file.

The function fseek() can be used to set the file pointer to some point within the file.
Its prototype is

```
int fseek ( int fp, int offset [, int whence])
```

A call to fseek() sets the file pointer *fp* at a point starting from *whence* and moving *offset*
bytes into the file. The optional *whence* parameter was added in PHP 4.0.0. It defaults to
the value SEEK_SET which is effectively the start of the file. The other possible values are
SEEK_CUR (the current location of the file pointer) and SEEK_END (the end of the file).

The rewind() function is equivalent to calling the fseek() function with an offset
of zero. For example, you can use fseek() to find the middle record in a file or to perform a binary search. Often if you reach the level of complexity in a data file where you
need to do these kinds of things, your life will be much easier if you use a database.

File Locking

Imagine a situation where two customers are trying to order a product at the same time.
(Not uncommon, especially when you start to get any kind of volume of traffic on a
Web site.) What if one customer calls fopen() and begins writing, and then the other

customer calls fopen() and also begins writing? What will be the final contents of the file? Will it be the first order followed by the second order or vice versa? Will it be one order or the other? Or will it be something less useful, like the two orders interleaved somehow? The answer depends on your operating system, but is often impossible to know.

To avoid problems like this, you can use file locking. This is implemented in PHP using the flock() function. This function should be called after a file has been opened, but before any data is read from or written to the file.

The prototype for flock() is

```
bool flock(int fp, int operation [, int &wouldblock])
```

You need to pass it a pointer to an open file and a number representing the kind of lock you require. It returns true if the lock was successfully acquired, and false if it was not.

The possible values of *operation* are shown in Table 2.2. The possible values changed at PHP 4.0.1. Both sets of values are shown in the table.

Table 2.2   **flock() Operation Values**

Value of operation	Meaning
LOCK_SH (formerly 1)	Reading lock. This means the file can be shared with other readers.
LOCK_EX (formerly 2)	Writing lock. This is exclusive. The file cannot be shared.
LOCK_UN (formerly 3)	Release existing lock.
LOCK_NB (formerly 4)	*Adding* 4 to the operation prevents blocking while trying to acquire a lock.

If you are going to use flock(), you will need to add it to all the scripts that use the file; otherwise, it is worthless.

Note that flock() does not work with NFS or other networked file systems. It also does not work with older file systems that do not support locking such as FAT. On some operating systems it is implemented at the process level and will not work correctly if you are using a multithreaded server API.

To use it with this example, you can alter processorder.php as follows:

```
$fp = fopen("$DOCUMENT_ROOT/../orders/orders.txt", 'a');
flock($fp, LOCK_EX); // lock the file for writing
fwrite($fp, $outputstring);
flock($fp, LOCK_UN);  // release write lock
fclose($fp);
```

You should also add locks to vieworders.php:

```
$fp = fopen("$DOCUMENT_ROOT /../orders/orders.txt", 'r');
flock($fp, LOCK_SH);  // lock file for reading
```

```
// read from the file
flock($fp, LOCK_UN);  // release read lock
fclose($fp);
```

Our code is now more robust, but still not perfect. What if two scripts tried to acquire a lock at the same time? This would result in a race condition, where the processes compete for locks but it is uncertain which will succeed, that could cause more problems. We can do better by using a DBMS.

Doing It a Better Way: Database Management Systems

So far all the examples we have looked at use flat files. In the next section of this book we'll look at how you can use MySQL, a relational database management system, instead. You might ask, "Why would I bother?"

Problems with Using Flat Files

There are a number of problems in working with flat files:

- When a file gets large, it can be very slow to work with.
- Searching for a particular record or group of records in a flat file is difficult. If the records are in order, you can use some kind of binary search in conjunction with a fixed-width record to search on a key field. If you want to find patterns of information (for example, you want to find all the customers who live in Smalltown), you would have to read in each record and check it individually.
- Dealing with concurrent access can become problematic. We have seen how you can lock files, but this can cause a race condition as we discussed earlier. It can also cause a bottleneck. With enough traffic on the site, a large group of users may be waiting for the file to be unlocked before they can place their order. If the wait is too long, people will go elsewhere to buy.
- All the file processing we have seen so far deals with a file using sequential processing—that is, we start from the start of the file and read through to the end. If we want to insert records into or delete records from the middle of the file (random access), this can be difficult—you end up reading the whole file into memory, making the changes, and writing the whole file out again. With a large data file, this becomes a significant overhead.
- Beyond the limits offered by file permissions, there is no easy way of enforcing different levels of access to data.

How RDBMSs Solve These Problems

Relational database management systems address all of these issues:

- RDBMSs can provide faster access to data than flat files. And MySQL, the database system we use in this book, has some of the fastest benchmarks of any RDBMS.
- RDBMSs can be easily queried to extract sets of data that fit certain criteria.
- RDBMSs have built-in mechanisms for dealing with concurrent access so that you as a programmer don't have to worry about it.
- RDBMSs provide random access to your data.
- RDBMSs have built-in privilege systems. MySQL has particular strengths in this area.

Probably the main reason for using an RDBMS is that all (or at least most) of the functionality that you want in a data storage system has already been implemented. Sure, you could write your own library of PHP functions, but why reinvent the wheel?

In Part 2 of this book, "Using MySQL," we'll discuss how relational databases work generally, and specifically how you can set up and use MySQL to create database-backed Web sites.

Further Reading

For more information on interacting with the file system, you can go straight to Chapter 16, "Interacting with the File System and the Server." In that section, we'll talk about how to change permissions, ownership, and names of files; how to work with directories; and how to interact with the file system environment.

You may also want to read through the file system section of the PHP online manual at `http://www.php.net/filesystem`.

Next

In the next chapter, we'll discuss what arrays are and how they can be used for processing data in your PHP scripts.

3

Using Arrays

THIS CHAPTER SHOWS YOU HOW TO use an important programming construct—arrays. The variables that we looked at in the previous chapters are *scalar* variables, which store a single value. An *array* is a variable that stores a set or sequence of values. One array can have many elements. Each element can hold a single value, such as text or numbers, or another array. An array containing other arrays is known as a multidimensional array.

PHP supports both numerically indexed and associative arrays. You will probably be familiar with numerically indexed arrays if you've used any programming language, but unless you use PHP or Perl, you might not have seen associative arrays before. Associative arrays let you use more useful values as the index. Rather than each element having a numeric index, they can have words or other meaningful information.

We will continue developing the Bob's Auto parts example using arrays to work more easily with repetitive information such as customer orders. Likewise, we will write shorter, tidier code to do some of the things we did with files in the previous chapter.

Key topics covered in this chapter include

- Numerically indexed arrays
- Associative arrays
- Multidimensional arrays
- Sorting arrays

What Is an Array?

We looked at scalar variables in Chapter 1, "PHP Crash Course." A scalar variable is a named location in which to store a value; similarly, an array is a named place to store a *set* of values, thereby allowing you to group scalars.

Bob's product list will be the array for our example. In Figure 3.1, you can see a list of three products stored in an array format and one variable, called $products, which stores the three values. (We'll look at how to create a variable like this in a minute.)

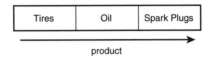

Figure 3.1   Bob's products can be stored in an array.

After we have the information as an array, we can do a number of useful things with it. Using the looping constructs from Chapter 1, we can save work by performing the same actions on each value in the array. The whole set of information can be moved around as a single unit. This way, with a single line of code, all the values can be passed to a function. For example, we might want to sort the products alphabetically. To achieve this, we could pass the entire array to PHP's sort() function.

The values stored in an array are called the array *elements*. Each array element has an associated *index* (also called a *key*) that is used to access the element.

Arrays in most programming languages have numerical indexes that typically start from zero or one. PHP supports this type of array.

PHP also supports *associative* arrays, which will be familiar to Perl programmers. Associative arrays can have almost anything as the array indices, but typically use strings.

We will begin by looking at numerically indexed arrays.

Numerically Indexed Arrays

These arrays are supported in most programming languages. In PHP, the indices start at zero by default, although you can alter this.

Initializing Numerically Indexed Arrays

To create the array shown in Figure 3.1, use the following line of PHP code:

```
$products = array( 'Tires', 'Oil', 'Spark Plugs' );
```

This will create an array called products containing the three values given—'Tires', 'Oil', and 'Spark Plugs'. Note that, like echo, array() is actually a language construct rather than a function.

Depending on the contents you need in your array, you might not need to manually initialize them as in the preceding example.

If you have the data you need in another array, you can simply copy one array to another using the = operator.

If you want an ascending sequence of numbers stored in an array, you can use the range() function to automatically create the array for you. The following line of code will create an array called numbers with elements ranging from 1 to 10:

```
$numbers = range(1,10);
```

If you have the information stored in file on disk, you can load the array contents direct-ly from the file. We'll look at this later in this chapter under the heading "Loading Arrays from Files."

If you have the data for your array stored in a database, you can load the array con-tents directly from the database. This is covered in Chapter 10, "Accessing Your MySQL Database from the Web with PHP."

You can also use various functions to extract part of an array or to reorder an array. We'll look at some of these functions later in this chapter, under the heading "Other Array Manipulations."

Accessing Array Contents

To access the contents of a variable, use its name. If the variable is an array, access the contents using the variable name and a key or index. The key or index indicates which stored values we access. The index is placed in square brackets after the name.

Type `$products[0]`, `$products[1]`, and `$products[2]` to use the contents of the products array.

Element zero is the first element in the array. This is the same numbering scheme as used in C, C++, Java, and a number of other languages, but it might take some getting used to if you are not familiar with it.

As with other variables, array elements' contents are changed by using the = operator. The following line will replace the first element in the array `'Tires'` with `'Fuses'`.

```
$products[0] = 'Fuses';
```

The following line could be used to add a new element—`'Fuses'`—to the end of the array, giving us a total of four elements:

```
$products[3] = 'Fuses';
```

To display the contents, we could type:

```
echo "$products[0] $products[1] $products[2] $products[3]";
```

Note that while PHP's string parsing is pretty clever, you can confuse it. If you are hav-ing trouble with arrays or other variables not being interpreted correctly when embed-ded in a double-quoted string, you can put them outside quotes. The previous echo statement will work correctly, but in many of the more complex examples later in this chapter you will notice that the variables are outside the quoted strings.

Like other PHP variables, arrays do not need to be initialized or created in advance. They are automatically created the first time you use them.

The following code will create the same `$products` array:

```
$products[0] = 'Tires';
$products[1] = 'Oil';
$products[2] = 'Spark Plugs';
```

If $products does not already exist, the first line will create a new array with just one element. The subsequent lines add values to the array.

Using Loops to Access the Array

Because the array is indexed by a sequence of numbers, we can use a for loop to more easily display the contents:

```
for ( $i = 0; $i<3; $i++ )
  echo "$products[$i] ";
```

This loop will give similar output to the preceding code, but will require less typing than manually writing code to work with each element in a large array. The ability to use a simple loop to access each element is a nice feature of numerically indexed arrays. Associative arrays are not quite so easy to loop through, but do allow indexes to be meaningful.

We can also use the foreach loop, specially designed for use with arrays. In this example we could use it as follows:

```
foreach ($products as $current)
  echo $current.' ';
```

This stores each element in turn in the variable $current and prints it out.

Associative Arrays

In the products array, we allowed PHP to give each item the default index. This meant that the first item we added became item 0, the second item 1, and so on. PHP also supports associative arrays. In an associative array, we can associate any key or index we want with each value.

Initializing an Associative Array

The following code creates an associative array with product names as keys and prices as values.

```
$prices = array( 'Tires'=>100, 'Oil'=>10, 'Spark Plugs'=>4 );
```

Accessing the Array Elements

Again, we access the contents using the variable name and a key, so we can access the information we have stored in the prices array as $prices['Tires'], $prices['Oil'], and $prices['Spark Plugs'].

Like numerically indexed arrays, associative arrays can be created and initialized one element at a time.

The following code will create the same $prices array. Rather than creating an array with three elements, this version creates an array with only one element, and then adds two more.

```
$prices = array( 'Tires'=>100 );
$prices['Oil'] = 10;
$prices['Spark Plugs'] = 4;
```

Here is another slightly different, but equivalent piece of code. In this version, we do not explicitly create an array at all. The array is created for us when we add the first element to it.

```
$prices['Tires'] = 100;
$prices['Oil'] = 10;
$prices['Spark Plugs'] = 4;
```

Using Loops with Associative Arrays

Because the indices in this associative array are not numbers, we cannot use a simple counter in a for loop to work with the array. We can use the foreach loop or the list() and each() constructs.

The foreach loop has a slightly different structure when using associative arrays. We can use it exactly as we did in the previous example, or we can incorporate the keys as well:

```
foreach ($prices as $key => $value)
  echo $key.'=>'.$value.'<br />';
```

The following code lists the contents of our $prices array using the each() construct:

```
while( $element = each( $prices ) )
{
  echo $element[ 'key' ];
  echo ' - ';
  echo $element[ 'value' ];
  echo '<br />';
}
```

The output of this script fragment is shown in Figure 3.2.

In Chapter 1, we looked at while loops and the echo statement. The preceding code uses the each() function, which we have not used before. This function returns the current element in an array and makes the next element the current one. Because we are calling each() within a while loop, it returns every element in the array in turn and stops when the end of the array is reached.

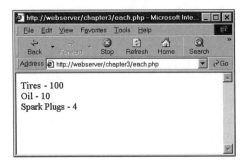

Figure 3.2   An each() statement can be used to loop through arrays.

In this code, the variable $element is an array. When we call each(), it gives us an array with four values and the four indexes to the array locations. The locations key and 0 contain the key of the current element, and the locations value and 1 contain the value of the current element. Although it makes no difference which you choose, we have chosen to use the named locations, rather than the numbered ones.

There is a more elegant and more common way of doing the same thing. The function list() can be used to split an array into a number of values. We can separate two of the values that the each() function gives us like this:

```
$list( $product, $price ) = each( $prices );
```

This line uses each() to take the current element from $prices, return it as an array, and make the next element current. It also uses list() to turn the 0 and 1 elements from the array returned by each() into two new variables called $product and $price.

We can loop through the entire $prices array, echoing the contents using this short script.

```
while ( list( $product, $price ) = each( $prices ) )
  echo "$product - $price<br />";
```

This has the same output as the previous script, but is easier to read because list() allows us to assign names to the variables.

One thing to note when using each() is that the array keeps track of the current element. If we want to use the array twice in the same script, we need to set the current element back to the start of the array using the function reset(). To loop through the prices array again, we type the following:

```
reset($prices);
while ( list( $product, $price ) = each( $prices ) )
  echo "$product - $price<br />";
```

This sets the current element back to the start of the array, and allows us to go through again.

Multidimensional Arrays

Arrays do not have to be a simple list of keys and values—each location in the array can hold another array. This way, we can create a two-dimensional array. You can think of a two dimensional array as a matrix, or grid, with width and height or rows and columns.

If we want to store more than one piece of data about each of Bob's products, we could use a two-dimensional array.

Figure 3.3 shows Bob's products represented as a two-dimensional array with each row representing an individual product and each column representing a stored product attribute.

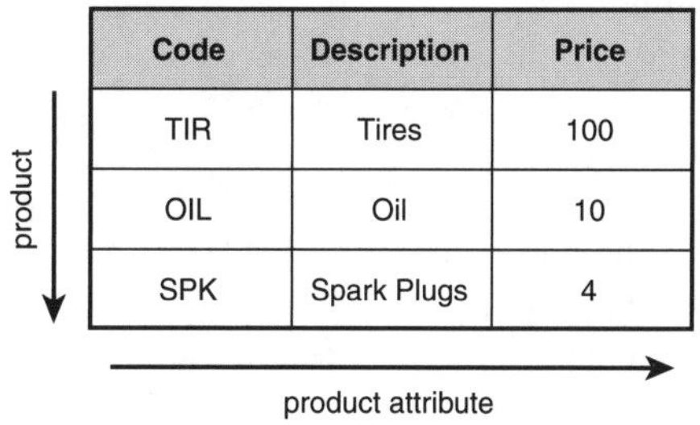

	Code	Description	Price
	TIR	Tires	100
	OIL	Oil	10
	SPK	Spark Plugs	4

product attribute

Figure 3.3   We can store more information about Bob's products in a two- dimensional array.

Using PHP, we would write the following code to set up the data in the array shown in Figure 3.3.

```
$products = array( array( 'TIR', 'Tires', 100 ),
                   array( 'OIL', 'Oil', 10 ),
                   array( 'SPK', 'Spark Plugs', 4 ) );
```

You can see from this definition that our products array now contains three arrays.

To access the data in a one-dimensional array, recall that we need the name of the array and the index of the element. A two-dimensional array is similar, except that each element has two indices—a row and a column. (The top row is row 0 and the far left column is column 0.)

To display the contents of this array, we could manually access each element in order like this:

```
echo '|'.$products[0][0].'|'.$products[0][1].'|'.$products[0][2].'|<br />';
echo '|'.$products[1][0].'|'.$products[1][1].'|'.$products[1][2].'|<br />';
echo '|'.$products[2][0].'|'.$products[2][1].'|'.$products[2][2].'|<br />';
```

Alternatively, we could place a for loop inside another for loop to achieve the same result.

```
for ( $row = 0; $row < 3; $row++ )
{
   for ( $column = 0; $column < 3; $column++ )
   {
      echo '|'.$products[$row][$column];
   }
   echo '|<br />';
}
```

Both versions of this code produce the same output in the browser:

```
|TIR|Tires|100|
|OIL|Oil|10|
|SPK|Spark Plugs|4|
```

The only difference between the two examples is that your code will be shorter if you use the second version with a large array.

You might prefer to create column names instead of numbers as shown in Figure 3.3. To do this, you can use associative arrays. To store the same set of products, with the columns named as they are in Figure 3.3, you would use the following code:

```
$products = array( array( Code => 'TIR',
                          Description => 'Tires',
                          Price => 100
                        ),
                   array( Code => 'OIL',
                          Description => 'Oil',
                          Price => 10
                        ),
                   array( Code => 'SPK',
                          Description => 'Spark Plugs',
                          Price =>4
                        )
                 );
```

This array is easier to work with if you want to retrieve a single value. It is easier to remember that the description is stored in the Description column than to remember that it is stored in column 1. Using associative arrays, you do not need to remember that an item is stored at [x][y]. You can easily find your data by referring to a location with meaningful row and column names.

We do however lose the ability to use a simple for loop to step through each column in turn. Here is one way to write code to display this array:

```
for ( $row = 0; $row < 3; $row++ )
{
```

```
echo '|'.$products[$row]['Code'].'|'.$products[$row]['Description'].
    '|'.$products[$row]['Price'].'|<br />';
}
```

Using a `for` loop, we can step through the outer, numerically indexed `$products` array. Each row in our `$products` array is an associative array. Using the `each()` and `list()` functions in a `while` loop, we can step through the associative arrays. Therefore, we need a `while` loop inside a `for` loop.

```
for ( $row = 0; $row < 3; $row++ )
{
  while ( list( $key, $value ) = each( $products[ $row ] ) )
  {
    echo "|$value";
  }
  echo '|<br />';
}
```

We do not need to stop at two dimensions—in the same way that array elements can hold new arrays, those new arrays in turn can hold more arrays.

A three-dimensional array has height, width, and depth. If you are comfortable thinking of a two-dimensional array as a table with rows and columns, imagine a pile or deck of those tables. Each element will be referenced by its layer, row, and column.

If Bob divided his products into categories, we could use a three-dimensional array to store them. Figure 3.4 shows Bob's products in a three-dimensional array.

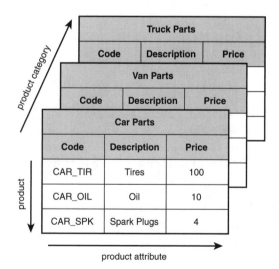

Figure 3.4 This three-dimensional array allows us to
divide products into categories.

From the code that defines this array, you can see that a three-dimensional array is an array containing arrays of arrays.

```
$categories = array( array ( array( 'CAR_TIR', 'Tires', 100 ),
                             array( 'CAR_OIL', 'Oil', 10 ),
                             array( 'CAR_SPK', 'Spark Plugs', 4 )
                           ),
                     array ( array( 'VAN_TIR', 'Tires', 120 ),
                             array( 'VAN_OIL', 'Oil', 12 ),
                             array( 'VAN_SPK', 'Spark Plugs', 5 )
                           ),
                     array ( array( 'TRK_TIR', 'Tires', 150 ),
                             array( 'TRK_OIL', 'Oil', 15 ),
                             array( 'TRK_SPK', 'Spark Plugs', 6 )
                           )
                   );
```

Because this array has only numeric indices, we can use nested `for` loops to display its contents.

```
for ( $layer = 0; $layer < 3; $layer++ )
{
  echo "Layer $layer<br />";
  for ( $row = 0; $row < 3; $row++ )
  {
    for ( $column = 0; $column < 3; $column++ )
    {
      echo '|'.$categories[$layer][$row][$column];
    }
    echo '|<br />';
  }
}
```

Because of the way multidimensional arrays are created, we could create four-, five-, or six-dimensional arrays. There is no language limit to the number of dimensions, but it is difficult for people to visualize constructs with more than three dimensions. Most real-world problems match logically with constructs of three or fewer dimensions.

Sorting Arrays

It is often useful to sort related data stored in an array. Taking a one-dimensional array and sorting it into order is quite easy.

Using sort()

The following code results in the array being sorted into ascending alphabetical order:

```
$products = array( 'Tires', 'Oil', 'Spark Plugs' );
sort($products);
```

Our array elements will now be in the order Oil, Spark Plugs, Tires.

We can sort values by numerical order too. If we have an array containing the prices of Bob's products, we can sort it into ascending numeric order as shown:

```
$prices = array( 100, 10, 4 );
sort($prices);
```

The prices will now be in the order 4, 10, 100.

Note that the sort function is case sensitive. All capital letters come before all lowercase letters. So "A" is less than "Z", but "Z" is less than "a".

Using asort() and ksort() to Sort Associative Arrays

If we are using an associative array to store items and their prices, we need to use different kinds of sort functions to keep keys and values together as they are sorted.

The following code creates an associative array containing the three products and their associated prices, and then sorts the array into ascending price order.

```
$prices = array( 'Tires'=>100, 'Oil'=>10, 'Spark Plugs'=>4 );
asort($prices);
```

The function asort() orders the array according to the value of each element. In the array, the values are the prices and the keys are the textual descriptions. If instead of sorting by price we want to sort by description, we use ksort(), which sorts by key rather than value. This code will result in the keys of the array being ordered alphabetically—Oil, Spark Plugs, Tires.

```
$prices = array( 'Tires'=>100, 'Oil'=>10, 'Spark Plugs'=>4 );
ksort($prices);
```

Sorting in Reverse

You have seen sort(), asort(), and ksort(). These three different sorting functions all sort an array into ascending order. Each of these functions has a matching reverse sort function to sort an array into descending order. The reverse versions are called rsort(), arsort(), and krsort().

The reverse sort functions are used in the same way as the sorting functions. The rsort() function sorts a single dimensional numerically indexed array into descending order. The arsort() function sorts a one-dimensional associative array into descending order using the value of each element. The krsort() function sorts a one-dimensional associative array into descending order using the key of each element.

Sorting Multidimensional Arrays

Sorting arrays with more than one dimension, or by something other than alphabetical or numerical order, is more complicated. PHP knows how to compare two numbers or two text strings, but in a multidimensional array, each element is an array. PHP does not know how to compare two arrays, so you need to create a method to compare them. Most of the time, the order of the words or numbers is fairly obvious—but for complicated objects, it becomes more problematic.

User Defined Sorts

Here is the definition of a two-dimensional array we used earlier. This array stores Bob's three products with a code, a description, and a price for each.

```
$products = array( array( 'TIR', 'Tires', 100 ),
                   array( 'OIL', 'Oil', 10 ),
                   array( 'SPK', 'Spark Plugs', 4 ) );
```

If we sort this array, what order will the values end up in? Because we know what the contents represent, there are at least two useful orders. We might want the products sorted into alphabetical order using the description or by numeric order by the price. Either result is possible, but we need to use the function usort() and tell PHP how to compare the items. To do this, we need to write our own comparison function.

The following code sorts this array into alphabetical order using the second column in the array—the description.

```
function compare($x, $y)
{
  if ( $x[1] == $y[1] )
    return 0;
  else if ( $x[1] < $y[1] )
    return -1;
  else
    return 1;
}

usort($products, 'compare');
```

So far in this book, we have called a number of the built-in PHP functions. To sort this array, we have defined a function of our own. We will examine writing functions in detail in Chapter 5, "Reusing Code and Writing Functions," but here is a brief introduction.

We define a function using the keyword function. We need to give the function a name. Names should be meaningful, so we'll call it compare(). Many functions take parameters or arguments. Our compare() function takes two, one called x and one called y. The purpose of this function is to take two values and determine their order.

For this example, the x and y parameters will be two of the arrays within the main array, each representing one product. To access the Description of the array x, we type $x[1] because the Description is the second element in these arrays, and numbering starts at zero. We use $x[1] and $y[1] to compare the Descriptions from the arrays passed into the function.

When a function ends, it can give a reply to the code that called it. This is called *returning* a value. To return a value, we use the keyword return in our function. For example, the line return 1; sends the value 1 back to the code that called the function.

To be used by usort(), the compare() function must compare x and y. The function must return 0 if x equals y, a negative number if it is less, and a positive number if it is greater. Our function will return 0, 1, or -1, depending on the values of x and y.

The final line of code calls the built-in function usort() with the array we want sorted ($products) and the name of our comparison function (compare()).

If we want the array sorted into another order, we can simply write a different comparison function. To sort by price, we need to look at the third column in the array, and create this comparison function:

```
function compare($x, $y)
{
if ( $x[2] == $y[2] )
  return 0;
else if ( $x[2] < $y[2] )
  return -1;
else
  return 1;
}
```

When usort($products, compare) is called, the array will be placed in ascending order by price.

The "u" in usort() stands for "user" because this function requires a user-defined comparison function. The uasort() and uksort() versions of asort and ksort also require a user-defined comparison function.

Similar to asort(), uasort() should be used when sorting an associative array by value. Use asort if your values are simple numbers or text. Define a comparison function and use uasort() if your values are more complicated objects such as arrays.

Similar to ksort(), uksort() should be used when sorting an associative array by key. Use ksort if your keys are simple numbers or text. Define a comparison function and use uksort() if your keys are more complicated objects such as arrays.

Reverse User Sorts

The functions sort(), asort(), and ksort() all have a matching reverse sort with an "r" in the function name. The user-defined sorts do not have reverse variants, but you can sort a multidimensional array into reverse order. You provide the comparison function, so write a comparison function that returns the opposite values. To sort into reverse order, the function will need to return 1 if x is less than y and -1 if x is greater than y. For example,

```
function reverseCompare($x, $y)
{
if ( $x[2] == $y[2] )
  return 0;
else if ( $x[2] < $y[2] )
  return 1;
else
  return -1;
}
```

Calling usort($products, reverseCompare) would now result in the array being placed in descending order by price.

Reordering Arrays

For some applications, you might want to manipulate the order of the array in other ways. The function shuffle() randomly reorders the elements of your array. The function array_reverse() gives you a copy of your array with all the elements in reverse order.

Using shuffle()

Bob wants to feature a small number of his products on the front page of his site. He has a large number of products, but would like three randomly selected items shown on the front page. So that repeat visitors do not get bored, he would like the three chosen products to be different for each visit. He can easily accomplish his goal if all his products are in an array. Listing 3.1 displays three randomly chosen pictures by shuffling the array into a random order and then displaying the first three.

Listing 3.1 **bobs_front_page.php—Using PHP to Produce a Dynamic Front Page for Bob's Auto Parts**

```
<?php
  $pictures = array('tire.jpg', 'oil.jpg', 'spark_plug.jpg',
                    'door.jpg', 'steering_wheel.jpg',
                    'thermostat.jpg', 'wiper_blade.jpg',
                    'gasket.jpg', 'brake_pad.jpg');

  srand ((float)microtime()*1000000);
  shuffle($pictures);
?>
<html>
<head>
```

Listing 3.1 **Continued**

```
  <title>Bob's Auto Parts</title>
</head>
<body>
  <center>
    <h1>Bob's Auto Parts</h1>
    <table width = 100%>
      <tr>
<?php
  for ( $i = 0; $i < 3; $i++ )
  {
    echo '<td align="center"><img src="';
    echo $pictures[$i];
    echo '"width="100" height="100"></td>';
  }
?>
      </tr>
    </table>
  </center>
</body>
</html>
```

Because the code selects random pictures, it produces a different page nearly every time
you load it, as shown in Figure 3.5.

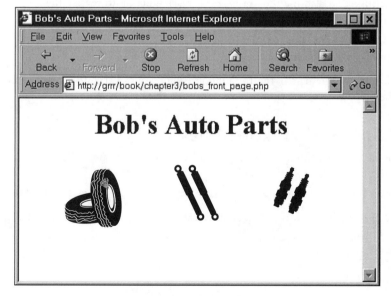

Figure 3.5   The shuffle() function enables us to
feature three randomly chosen products.

Any of the random number functions require that you seed the random number generator first by calling srand().You will see that we did this in Listing 3.1.

The shuffle() function has not had a very illustrious history. In older versions of PHP it does not shuffle very well, giving a result that is not very random. In version 4.2.x on Windows, it does not shuffle at all, giving a result that was exactly what you started with. If it is important to you, test it on your server.

Using array_reverse()

The function array_reverse() takes an array and creates a new one with the same contents in reverse order. For example, there are a number of ways to create an array containing a countdown from ten to one.

Because using range() alone creates an ascending sequence, we must then use rsort() to sort the numbers into descending order. Alternatively, we could create the array one element at a time by writing a for loop:

```
$numbers = array();
for($i=10; $i>0; $i--)
  array_push( $numbers, $i );
```

A for() loop can go in descending order like this.We set the starting value high, and at the end of each loop use the -- operator to decrease the counter by one.

We created an empty array, and then used array_push() for each element to add one new element to the end of an array. As a side note, the opposite of array_push() is array_pop().This function removes and returns one element from the end of an array.

Alternatively, we can use the array_reverse() function to reverse the array created by range().

```
$numbers = range(1,10);
$numbers = array_reverse($numbers);
```

Note that array_reverse() returns a modified copy of the array. Because we did not want the original array, we simply stored the new copy over the original.

Loading Arrays from Files

In Chapter 2, "Storing and Retrieving Data," we stored customer orders in a file. Each line in the file looks something like:

```
15:42, 20th April 4 tires 1 oil 6 spark plugs $434.00 22 Short St, Smalltown
```

To process or fulfill this order, we could load it back into an array. Listing 3.2 displays the current order file.

Listing 3.2 **vieworders.php—Using PHP to Display Orders for Bob**

```php
<?php
//create short variable name
$DOCUMENT_ROOT = $HTTP_SERVER_VARS['DOCUMENT_ROOT'];

$orders= file("$DOCUMENT_ROOT/../orders/orders.txt");

$number_of_orders = count($orders);
if ($number_of_orders == 0)
{
  echo '<p><strong>No orders pending.
      Please try again later.</strong></p>';
}
for ($i=0; $i<$number_of_orders; $i++)
{
  echo $orders[$i].'<br />';
}
?>
```

This script produces almost exactly the same output as Listing 2.2 in the previous chapter, which is shown in Figure 2.4. This time, we are using the function `file()` which loads the entire file into an array. Each line in the file becomes one element of an array.

This code also uses the `count()` function to see how many elements are in an array.

Furthermore, we could load each section of the order lines into separate array elements to process the sections separately or to format them more attractively. Listing 3.3 does exactly that.

Listing 3.3 **vieworders2.php—Using PHP to Separate, Format, and Display Orders for Bob**

```php
<?php
  //create short variable name
  $DOCUMENT_ROOT = $HTTP_SERVER_VARS['DOCUMENT_ROOT'];
?>
<html>
<head>
  <title>Bob's Auto Parts - Customer Orders</title>
</head>
<body>
<h1>Bob's Auto Parts</h1>
<h2>Customer Orders</h2>
<?php
  //Read in the entire file.
  //Each order becomes an element in the array
  $orders= file("$DOCUMENT_ROOT/../orders/orders.txt");
  // count the number of orders in the array
```

Listing 3.3 **Continued**

```
$number_of_orders = count($orders);
if ($number_of_orders == 0)
{
  echo '<p><strong>No orders pending.
        Please try again later.</strong></p>';
}
echo "<table border=1>\n";
echo '<tr><th bgcolor="#CCCCFF">Order Date</th>
        <th bgcolor="#CCCCFF">Tires</th>
        <th bgcolor="#CCCCFF">Oil</th>
        <th bgcolor="#CCCCFF">Spark Plugs</th>
        <th bgcolor="#CCCCFF">Total</th>
        <th bgcolor="#CCCCFF">Address</th>
      <tr>';
for ($i=0; $i<$number_of_orders; $i++)
{
  //split up each line
  $line = explode( "\t", $orders[$i] );
  // keep only the number of items ordered
  $line[1] = intval( $line[1] );
  $line[2] = intval( $line[2] );
  $line[3] = intval( $line[3] );
  // output each order
  echo "<tr><td>$line[0]</td>
            <td align="right">$line[1]</td>
            <td align="right">$line[2]</td>
            <td align="right">$line[3]</td>
            <td align="right">$line[4]</td>
            <td>$line[5]</td>
         </tr>";
}
echo "</table>";
?>
</body>
</html>
```

The code in Listing 3.3 loads the entire file into an array but unlike the example in Listing 3.2, here we are using the function explode() to split up each line, so that we can apply some processing and formatting before printing.

The output from this script is shown in Figure 3.6.

The explode function has the following prototype:

```
array explode(string separator, string string [, int limit])
```

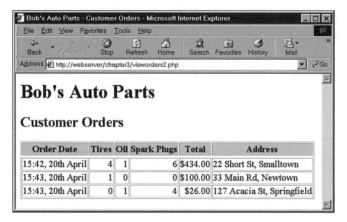

Figure 3.6   After splitting order records with explode, we can put each part of an order in a different table cell for better looking output.

In the previous chapter, we used the tab character as a delimiter when storing this data, so here we called:

```
explode( "\t", $orders[$i] )
```

This "explodes" the passed-in string into parts. Each tab character becomes a break between two elements. For example, the string

```
"15:42, 20th April\t4 tires\t1 oil\t6 spark plugs\t$434.00\t
22 Short St, Smalltown"
```

is exploded into the parts `"15:42, 20th April"`, `"4 tires"`, `"1 oil"`, `"6 spark plugs"`, `"$434.00"`, and `"22 Short St, Smalltown"`.

Note that the optional `limit` parameter can be used to limit the maximum number of parts returned.

We have not done very much processing here. Rather than output tires, oil, and spark plugs on every line, we are only displaying the number of each and giving the table a heading row to show what the numbers represent.

There are a number of ways that we could have extracted numbers from these strings. Here we used the function, `intval()`. As mentioned in Chapter 1, `intval()` converts a `string` to an `integer`. The conversion is reasonably clever and will ignore parts, such as the label in this example, that cannot be converted to an `integer`. We will cover various ways of processing strings in the next chapter.

Other Array Manipulations

So far, we have only covered about half the array processing functions. Many others will be useful from time to time.

Navigating Within an Array: each(), current(), reset(), end(), next(), pos(), and prev()

We mentioned previously that every array has an internal pointer that points to the current element in the array. We indirectly used this pointer earlier when using the each() function, but we can directly use and manipulate this pointer.

If we create a new array, the current pointer is initialized to point to the first element in the array. Calling current($array_name) returns the first element.

Calling either next() or each() advances the pointer forward one element. Calling each($array_name) returns the current element before advancing the pointer. The function next() behaves slightly differently—calling next($array_name) advances the pointer and then returns the new current element.

We have already seen that reset() returns the pointer to the first element in the array. Similarly, calling end($array_name) sends the pointer to the end of the array. The first and last element in the array are returned by reset() and end(), respectively.

To move through an array in reverse order, we could use end() and prev(). The prev() function is the opposite of next(). It moves the current pointer back one and then returns the new current element.

For example, the following code displays an array in reverse order:

```
$value = end ($array);
while ($value)
{
  echo "$value<br />";
  $value = prev($array);
}
```

If $array was declared like this:

```
$array = array(1, 2, 3);
```

The output would appear in a browser as:

```
3
2
1
```

Using each(), current(), reset(), end(), next(), pos(), and prev(), you can write your own code to navigate through an array in any order.

Applying Any Function to Each Element in an Array: array_walk()

Sometimes you might want to work with or modify every element in an array in the same way. The function array_walk() allows you to do this.

The prototype of array_walk() is as follows:

```
int array_walk(array arr, string func, [mixed userdata])
```

Similar to the way we called usort() earlier, array_walk() expects you to declare a function of your own.

As you can see, array_walk() takes three parameters. The first, *arr*, is the array to be processed. The second, *func*, is the name of a user-defined function that will be applied to each element in the array. The third parameter, *userdata*, is optional. If you use it, it will be passed through to your function as a parameter. You'll see how this works in a minute.

A handy user-defined function might be one that displays each element with some specified formatting.

The following code displays each element on a new line by calling the user-defined function myPrint() with each element of $array:

```
function myPrint($value)
{
  echo "$value<br />";
}
array_walk($array, 'myPrint');
```

The function you write needs to have a particular signature. For each element in the array, array_walk takes the key and value stored in the array, and anything you passed as *userdata*, and calls your function like this:

```
Yourfunction(value, key, userdata)
```

For most uses, your function will only be using the values in the array. For some, you might also need to pass a parameter to your function using the parameter *userdata*. Occasionally, you might be interested in the key of each element as well as the value. Your function can, as with MyPrint(), choose to ignore the key and *userdata* parameter.

For a slightly more complicated example, we will write a function that modifies the values in the array and requires a parameter. Note that although we are not interested in the key, we need to accept it in order to accept the third parameter.

```
function myMultiply(&$value, $key, $factor)
{
  $value *= $factor;
}
array_walk(&$array, 'myMultiply', 3);
```

Here we are defining a function, myMultiply(), that will multiply each element in the array by a supplied factor. We need to use the optional third parameter to array_walk() to take a parameter to pass to our function and use it as the factor to multiply by. Because we need this parameter, we must define our function, myMultiply(), to take three parameters—an array element's value ($value), an array element's key ($key), and our parameter ($factor). We are choosing to ignore the key.

A subtle point to note is the way we pass $value. The ampersand (&) before the variable name in the definition of myMultiply() means that $value will be *passed by reference*. Passing by reference allows the function to alter the contents of the array.

We will address passing by reference in more detail in Chapter 5. If you are not familiar with the term, for now just note that to pass by reference, we place an ampersand before the variable name.

Counting Elements in an Array: count(), sizeof(), and array_count_values()

We used the function count() in an earlier example to count the number of elements in an array of orders. The function sizeof() has exactly the same purpose. Both these functions return the number of elements in an array passed to them. You will get a count of one for the number of elements in a normal scalar variable and 0 if you pass either an empty array or a variable that has not been set.

The array_count_values() function is more complex. If you call array_count_values($array), this function counts how many times each *unique* value occurs in the array $array. (This is the set cardinality of the array.) The function returns an associative array containing a frequency table. This array contains all the unique values from $array as keys. Each key has a numeric value that tells you how many times the corresponding key occurs in $array.

For example, the following code

```
$array = array(4, 5, 1, 2, 3, 1, 2, 1);
$ac = array_count_values($array);
```

creates an array called $ac that contains

key	value
4	1
5	1
1	3
2	2
3	1

This indicates that 4, 5, and 3 occurred once in $array, 1 occurred three times, and 2 occurred twice.

Converting Arrays to Scalar Variables: extract()

If we have an associative array with a number of key value pairs, we can turn them into a set of scalar variables using the function extract(). The prototype for extract() is as follows:

```
extract(array var_array [, int extract_type] [, string prefix] );
```

The purpose of extract() is to take an array and create scalar variables with the names of the keys in the array. The values of these variables are set to the values in the array.

Here is a simple example:

```
$array = array( 'key1' => 'value1', 'key2' => 'value2', 'key3' => 'value3');
extract($array);
echo "$key1 $key2 $key3";
```

This code produces the following output:

```
value1 value2 value3
```

The array had three elements with keys: key1, key2, and key3. Using extract(), we created three scalar variables, $key1, $key2, and $key3. You can see from the output that the values of $key1, $key2, and $key3 are 'value1', 'value2', and 'value3', respectively. These values came from the original array.

There are two optional parameters to extract(): *extract_type* and *prefix*. The variable extract_type tells extract() how to handle collisions. These are cases in which a variable already exists with the same name as a key. The default response is to overwrite the existing variable. Four allowable values for extract_type are shown in Table 3.1.

Table 3.1 **Allowed extract_types for extract()**

Type	Meaning
EXTR_OVERWRITE	Overwrites the existing variable when a collision occurs.
EXTR_SKIP	Skips an element when a collision occurs.
EXTR_PREFIX_SAME	Creates a variable named $prefix_key when a collision occurs. You must supply prefix.
EXTR_PREFIX_ALL	Prefixes all variable names with prefix. You must supply prefix.
EXTR_IF_EXISTS	Only extract variables that already exist (that is, fill existing variables with values from the array). This was added at version 4.2.0 and is useful for converting, for example, $_REQUEST to a set of valid variables.
EXTR_PREFIX_IF_EXISTS	Only create a prefixed version if the non-prefixed version already exists. This was added at version 4.2.0.
EXTR_REFS	Extract variables as references. This was added at version 4.3.0.

The two most useful options are the default (EXTR_OVERWRITE) and EXTR_PREFIX_ALL. The other two options might be useful occasionally when you know that a particular collision will occur and want that key skipped or prefixed. A simple example using EXTR_PREFIX_ALL follows. You can see that the variables created are called *prefix*-underscore-*keyname*.

```
$array = array( 'key1' => 'value1', 'key2' => 'value2', 'key3' => 'value3');
extract($array, EXTR_PREFIX_ALL, 'myPrefix');
echo "$myPrefix_key1 $myPrefix_key2 $myPrefix_key3";
```

This code will again produce the output: `value1 value2 value3`.

Note that for `extract()` to extract an element, that element's key must be a valid variable name, which means that keys starting with numbers or including spaces will be skipped.

Further Reading

This chapter covers what we believe to be the most useful of PHP's array functions. We have chosen not to cover all the possible array functions. The online PHP manual available at `http://www.php.net/array` has a brief description of each of them.

Next

In the next chapter, we look at string processing functions. We will cover functions that search, replace, split, and merge strings, as well as the powerful regular expression functions that can perform almost any action on a string.

String Manipulation and Regular Expressions

I N THIS CHAPTER, WE'LL DISCUSS HOW you can use PHP's string functions to format and manipulate text. We'll also discuss using string functions or regular expression functions to search (and replace) words, phrases, or other patterns within a string.

These functions are useful in many contexts. You'll often want to clean up or reformat user input that is going to be stored in a database. Search functions are great when building search engine applications (among other things).

In this chapter, we will cover

- Formatting strings
- Joining and splitting strings
- Comparing strings
- Matching and replacing substrings with string functions
- Using regular expressions

Example Application: Smart Form Mail

In this chapter, we'll look at string and regular expression functions in the context of a Smart Form Mail application. We'll add these scripts to the Bob's Auto Parts site we've been looking at in the last few chapters.

This time, we'll build a straightforward and commonly used customer feedback form for Bob's customers to enter their complaints and compliments, as shown in Figure 4.1. However, our application will have one improvement over many you will find on the Web. Instead of emailing the form to a generic email address like feedback@example.com, we'll attempt to put some intelligence into the process by searching the input for key words and phrases and then sending the email to the appropriate employee at Bob's company. For example, if the email contains the word "advertising," we might send the feedback to the Marketing department. If the email is from Bob's biggest client, it can go straight to Bob.

Figure 4.1 Bob's feedback form asks customers for their name, email address, and comments.

We'll start with the simple script shown in Listing 4.1 and add to it as we go along.

Listing 4.1 **processfeedback.php—Basic Script to Email Forms Contents**

```php
<?php
  //create short variable names
  $name=$HTTP_POST_VARS['name'];
  $email=$HTTP_POST_VARS['email'];
  $feedback=$HTTP_POST_VARS['feedback'];

  $toaddress = 'feedback@example.com';
  $subject = 'Feedback from web site';
  $mailcontent = 'Customer name: '.$name."\n"
               .'Customer email: '.$email."\n"
               ."Customer comments: \n".$feedback."\n";
  $fromaddress = 'From: webserver@example.com';

  mail($toaddress, $subject, $mailcontent, $fromaddress);
?>
<html>
```

Listing 4.1   **Continued**

```
<head>
  <title>Bob's Auto Parts - Feedback Submitted</title>
</head>
<body>
<h1>Feedback submitted</h1>
<p>Your feedback has been sent.</p>
</body>
</html>
```

Note that generally you should check that users have filled out all the required form fields using, for example, isset().We have omitted this from the script and other examples for the sake of brevity.

In this script, you'll see that we have concatenated the form fields together and used PHP's mail() function to email them to feedback@example.com.We haven't yet used mail(), so we will discuss how it works.

Unsurprisingly, this function sends email.The prototype for mail() looks like this:

```
bool mail(string to, string subject, string message,
          string [additional_headers [, string additional_parameters]]);
```

The first three parameters are compulsory and represent the address to send email to, the subject line, and the message contents, respectively.The fourth parameter can be used to send any additional valid email headers.Valid email headers are described in the document RFC822, which is available online if you want more details. (RFCs or Requests for Comment are the source of many Internet standards—we will discuss them in Chapter 17, "Using Network and Protocol Functions.") Here we've used the fourth parameter to add a "From:" address for the mail.You can also use to it add "Reply-To:" and "Cc:" fields, among others. If you want more than one additional header, just separate them by newlines (\n) within the string, as follows:

```
$additional_headers="From: webserver@example.com\n"
                    .'Reply-To: bob@example.com';
```

The optional fifth parameter can be used to pass a parameter to whatever program you have configured to send mail.

In order to use the email() function, set up your PHP installation to point at your mail-sending program. If the script doesn't work for you in its current form, double-check Appendix A, "Installing PHP 4 and MySQL."

Through this chapter, we'll enhance this basic script by making use of PHP's string handling and regular expression functions.

Formatting Strings

You'll often need to tidy up user strings (typically from an HTML form interface) before you can use them.

Trimming Strings: chop(), ltrim(), and trim()

The first step in tidying up is to trim any excess whitespace from the string. Although this is never compulsory, it can be useful if you are going to store the string in a file or database, or if you're going to compare it to other strings.

PHP provides three useful functions for this purpose. We'll use the `trim()` function to tidy up our input data as follows:

```
$name=trim($name);
$email=trim($email);
$feedback=trim($feedback);
```

The `trim()` function strips whitespace from the start and end of a string, and returns the resulting string. The characters it strips by default are newlines and carriage returns (\n and \r), horizontal and vertical tabs (\t and \v), end of string characters (\0), and spaces. You can also pass it a second parameter containing a list of characters to strip instead of this default list. Depending on your particular purpose, you might like to use the `ltrim()` or `chop()` functions instead. They are both similar to `trim()`, taking the string in question as a parameter and returning the formatted string. The difference between these three is that `trim()` removes whitespace from the start and end of a string, `ltrim()` removes whitespace from the start (or left) only, and `chop()` removes whitespace from the end (or right) only.

Formatting Strings for Presentation

PHP has a set of functions that you can use to reformat a string in different ways.

Using HTML Formatting: the nl2br() Function

The `nl2br()` function takes a string as parameter and replaces all the newlines in it with the XHTML `<br />` tag (or the HTML `<br>` tag in versions prior to 4.0.5). This is useful for echoing a long string to the browser. For example, we use this function to format the customer's feedback in order to echo it back:

```
<p>Your feedback (shown below) has been sent.</p>
<p><? echo nl2br($mailcontent); ?> </p>
```

Remember that HTML disregards plain whitespace, so if you don't filter this output through `nl2br()`, it will appear on a single line (except for newlines forced by the browser window). This is illustrated in Figure 4.2.

Formatting a String for Printing

So far, we have used the `echo` language construct to print strings to the browser. PHP also supports a `print()` construct, which does the same thing as echo, but returns a value (true or false, denoting success).

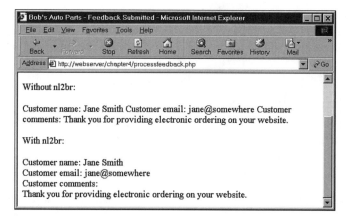

Figure 4.2   Using PHP's nl2br() function improves
the display of long strings within HTML.

Both of these techniques print a string "as is." You can apply some more sophisticated
formatting using the functions printf() and sprintf(). These work basically the same
way, except that printf() prints a formatted string to the browser and sprintf()
returns a formatted string.

If you have previously programmed in C, you will find that these functions are the
same as the C versions. If you haven't, they take getting used to but are useful and powerful.

The prototypes for these functions are

```
string sprintf (string format [, mixed args...])
void printf (string format [, mixed args...])
```

The first parameter passed to both these functions is a format string that describes the
basic shape of the output with format codes instead of variables. The other parameters
are variables that will be substituted in to the format string.

For example, using echo, we used the variables we wanted to print inline, like this:

```
echo "Total amount of order is $total.";
```

To get the same effect with printf(), you would use

```
printf ("Total amount of order is %s.", $total);
```

The %s in the format string is called a conversion specification. This one means "replace
with a string." In this case, it will be replaced with $total interpreted as a string.

If the value stored in $total was 12.4, both of these approaches will print it as 12.4.

The advantage of printf() is that we can use a more useful conversion specification
to specify that $total is actually a floating point number, and that it should have two
decimal places after the decimal point, as follows:

```
printf ("Total amount of order is %.2f", $total);
```

You can have multiple conversion specifications in the format string. If you have n conversion specifications, you will usually have n arguments after the format string. Each conversion specification will be replaced by a reformatted argument in the order they are listed. For example,

```
printf ("Total amount of order is %.2f (with shipping %.2f) ",
        $total, $total_shipping);
```

Here, the first conversion specification will use the variable $total, and the second will use the variable $total_shipping.

Each conversion specification follows the same format, which is

```
%['padding_character] [-] [width] [.precision] type
```

All conversion specifications start with a % symbol. If you actually want to print a % symbol, you will need to use %%.

The *padding_character* is optional. It will be used to pad your variable to the width you have specified. An example of this would be to add leading zeroes to a number like a counter.

The - symbol is optional. It specifies that the data in the field will be left-justified, rather than right-justified, the default.

The *width* specifier tells printf() how much room (in characters) to leave for the variable to be substituted in here.

The *precision* specifier should begin with a decimal point. It should contain the number of places after the decimal point you would like displayed.

The final part of the specification is a type code. A summary of these is shown in Table 4.1.

Table 4.1   **Conversion Specification Type Codes**

Type	Meaning
b	Interpret as an integer and print as a binary number.
c	Interpret as an integer and print as a character.
d	Interpret as an integer and print as a decimal number.
f	Interpret as a double and print as a floating point number.
o	Interpret as an integer and print as an octal number.
s	Interpret as a string and print as a string.
x	Interpret as an integer and print as a hexadecimal number with lowercase letters for the digits a–f.
X	Interpret as an integer and print as a hexadecimal number with uppercase letters for the digits A–F.

As of version 4.0.6 you can use argument numbering, which means that the arguments don't need to be in the same order as the conversion specifications. For example:

```
printf ("Total amount of order is %2\$.2f (with shipping %1\$.2f) ",
        $total_shipping, $total);
```

Just add the argument position in the list directly after the % sign, followed by an escaped $ symbol—in this example 2\$ means "replace with the second argument in the list." This method can also be used to repeat arguments.

Changing the Case of a String

You can also reformat the case of a string. This is not particularly useful for our application, but we'll look at some brief examples.

If we start with the subject string, $subject, which we are using for our email, we can change its case with several functions. The effect of these functions is summarized in Table 4.2. The first column shows the function name, the second describes its effect, the third shows how it would be applied to the string $subject, and the last column shows what value would be returned from the function.

Table 4.2 **String Case Functions and Their Effects**

Function	Description	Use	Value
		$subject	Feedback from web site
strtoupper()	Turns string to uppercase	strtoupper($subject)	FEEDBACK FROM WEB SITE
strtolower()	Turns string to lowercase	strtolower($subject)	feedback from web site
ucfirst()	Capitalizes first character of string if it's alphabetic	ucfirst($subject)	Feedback from web site
ucwords()	Capitalizes first character of each word in the string that begins with an alphabetic character	ucwords($subject)	Feedback From Web Site

Formatting Strings for Storage: AddSlashes() and StripSlashes()

As well as using string functions to reformat a string visually, we can use some of these functions to reformat strings for storage in a database. Although we won't cover actually writing to the database until Part II, "Using MySQL," we will cover formatting strings for database storage now.

Certain characters are perfectly valid as part of a string but can cause problems, particularly when inserting data into a database because the database could interpret these characters as control characters. The problematic ones are quotes (single and double), backslashes (\), and the NUL character.

We need to find a way of marking or *escaping* these characters so that databases such as MySQL can understand that we meant a literal special character rather than a control sequence. To *escape* these characters, add a backslash in front of them. For example, " (double quote) becomes \" (backslash double quote), and \ (backslash) becomes \\ (backslash backslash). (This rule applies universally to special characters, so if you have \\ in your string, you need to replace it with \\\\.)

PHP provides two functions specifically designed for escaping characters. Before you write any strings into a database, you should reformat them with AddSlashes(), for example:

```
$feedback = AddSlashes($feedback);
```

Like many of the other string functions, AddSlashes() takes a string as parameter and returns the reformatted string.

When you use AddSlashes(), the string will be stored in the database with the slashes in it. When you retrieve the string, you will need to remember to take the slashes out. You can do this using the StripSlashes() function:

```
$feedback = StripSlashes($feedback);
```

Figure 4.3 shows the actual effects of using these functions on the string.

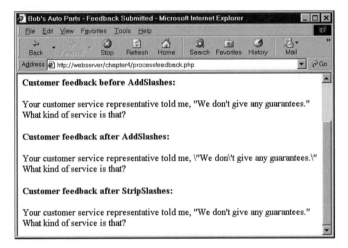

Figure 4.3   After calling the AddSlashes() function, all the quotes have been slashed out. StripSlashes() removes the slashes.

You can also set PHP up to add and strip slashes automatically. This is called using magic quotes. You can read more about magic quotes in Chapter 21, "Other Useful Features."

Joining and Splitting Strings with String Functions

Often, we want to look at parts of a string individually. For example, we might want to look at words in a sentence (say for spellchecking), or split a domain name or email address into its component parts. PHP provides several string functions (and one regular expression function) that allow us to do this.

In our example, Bob wants any customer feedback from `bigcustomer.com` to go directly to him, so we will split the email address the customer typed in into parts to find out if they work for Bob's big customer.

Using explode(), implode(), and join()

The first function we could use for this purpose, `explode()`, has the following proto-type:

```
array explode(string separator, string input [, int limit]);
```

This function takes a string *input* and splits it into pieces on a specified *separator* string. The pieces are returned in an array. You can limit the number of pieces with the optional *limit* parameter, added in PHP 4.0.1.

To get the domain name from the customer's email address in our script, we can use the following code:

```
$email_array = explode('@', $email);
```

This call to `explode()` splits the customer's email address into two parts: the username, which is stored in `$email_array[0]`, and the domain name, which is stored in `$email_array[1]`. Now we can test the domain name to determine the customer's origin, and then send their feedback to the appropriate person:

```
if ($email_array[1]=='bigcustomer.com')
  $toaddress = 'bob@example.com';
else
  $toaddress = 'feedback@example.com';
```

Note if the domain is capitalized, this will not work. We could avoid this problem by converting the domain to all uppercase or all lowercase and then checking:

```
$email_array[1] = strtoupper ($email_array[1]);
```

You can reverse the effects of `explode()` using either `implode()` or `join()`, which are identical. For example,

```
$new_email = implode('@', $email_array);
```

This takes the array elements from `$email_array` and joins them together with the string passed in the first parameter. The function call is very similar to `explode()`, but the effect is opposite.

Using strtok()

Unlike `explode()`, which breaks a string into all its pieces at one time, `strtok()` gets pieces (called tokens) from a string one at a time. `strtok()` is a useful alternative to using `explode()` for processing words from a string one at a time.

The prototype for `strtok()` is

```
string strtok(string input, string separator);
```

The separator can be either a character or a string of characters, but note that the input string will be split on each of the characters in the separator string rather than on the whole separator string (as `explode` does).

Calling `strtok()` is not quite as simple as it seems in the prototype.

To get the first token from a string, you call `strtok()` with the string you want tokenized, and a separator. To get the subsequent tokens from the string, you just pass a single parameter—the separator. The function keeps its own internal pointer to its place in the string. If you want to reset the pointer, you can pass the string into it again.

`strtok()` is typically used as follows:

```
$token = strtok($feedback, ' ');
echo $token.'<br />';
while ($token!='')
{
  $token = strtok(' ');
  echo $token.'<br />';
};
```

As usual, it's a good idea to check that the customer actually typed some feedback in the form, using, for example, `empty()`. We have omitted these checks for brevity.

This prints each token from the customer's feedback on a separate line, and loops until there are no more tokens. Note that prior to version 4.1.0 PHP's `strtok()` didn't work exactly the same as the one in C. If there are two instances of a separator *in a row* in your target string (in this example, two spaces in a row), `strtok()` returns an empty string. You cannot differentiate this from the empty string returned when you get to the end of the target string. Also, if one of the tokens is 0, the empty string will be returned. This made PHP's `strtok()` somewhat less useful than the one in C. The new version works correctly, skipping empty strings.

Using substr()

The `substr()` function enables you to access a substring between given start and end points of a string. It's not appropriate for our example, but can be useful when you need to get at parts of fixed format strings.

The `substr()` function has the following prototype:

```
string substr(string string, int start[, int length] );
```

This function returns a substring copied from within *string*.

We will look at examples using this test string:

```
$test = 'Your customer service is excellent';
```

If you call it with a positive number for *start* (only), you will get the string from the *start* position to the end of the string. For example,

```
substr($test, 1);
```

returns `our customer service is excellent`. Note that the string position starts from 0, as with arrays.

If you call `substr()` with a negative *start* (only), you will get the string from the end of the string minus *start* characters to the end of the string. For example,

```
substr($test, -9);
```

returns `excellent`.

The length parameter can be used to specify either a number of characters to return (if it is positive), or the end character of the return sequence (if it is negative). For example,

```
substr($test, 0, 4);
```

returns the first four characters of the string, namely, `Your`. The following code:

```
echo substr($test, 4, -13);
```

returns the characters between the fourth character and the thirteenth to last character, that is, `customer service`.

Comparing Strings

So far we've just used `==` to compare two strings for equality. We can do some slightly more sophisticated comparisons using PHP. We've divided these into two categories: partial matches and others. We'll deal with the others first, and then get into partial matching, which we will require to further develop the Smart Form example.

String Ordering: strcmp(),strcasecmp(), and strnatcmp()

These functions can be used to order strings. This is useful when sorting data.

The prototype for `strcmp()` is

```
int strcmp(string str1, string str2);
```

The function expects to receive two strings, which it will compare. If they are equal, it will return 0. If `str1` comes after (or is greater than) `str2` in lexicographic order, `strcmp()` will return a number greater than zero. If `str1` is less than `str2`, `strcmp()` will return a number less than zero. This function is case sensitive.

The function `strcasecmp()` is identical except that it is not case sensitive.

The function `strnatcmp()` and its non-case sensitive twin, `strnatcasecmp()`, were added in PHP 4. These functions compare strings according to a "natural ordering," which is more the way a human would do it. For example, `strcmp()` would order the string `"2"` as greater than the string `"12"` because it is lexicographically greater. `strnatcmp()` would do it the other way around. You can read more about natural ordering at

http://www.naturalordersort.org/

Testing String Length with strlen()

We can check the length of a string with the `strlen()` function. If you pass it a string, this function will return its length. For example, `strlen('hello')` returns `5`.

This can be used for validating input data. Consider the email address on our form, stored in `$email`. One basic way of validating an email address stored in `$email` is to check its length. By my reasoning, the minimum length of an email address is six characters—for example, *a@a.to* if you have a country code with no second level domains, a one-letter server name, and a one-letter email address. Therefore, an error could be produced if the address was not at least this length:

```
if (strlen($email) < 6)
{
  echo 'That email address is not valid';
  exit;  // finish execution of PHP script
}
```

Clearly, this is a very simplistic way of validating this information. We will look at better ways in the next section.

Matching and Replacing Substrings with String Functions

It's common to want to check if a particular substring is present in a larger string. This partial matching is usually more useful than testing for equality.

In our Smart Form example, we want to look for certain key phrases in the customer feedback and send the mail to the appropriate department. If we want to send emails talking about Bob's shops to the retail manager, we want to know if the word "shop" (or derivatives thereof) appear in the message.

Given the functions we have already looked at, we could use `explode()` or `strtok()` to retrieve the individual words in the message, and then compare them using the `==` operator or `strcmp()`.

However, we could also do the same thing with a single function call to one of the string matching or regular expression matching functions. These are used to search for a pattern inside a string. We'll look at each set of functions one by one.

Finding Strings in Strings: strstr(), strchr(), strrchr(), stristr()

To find a string within another string you can use any of the functions strstr(), strchr(), strrchr(), or stristr().

The function strstr() is the most generic, and can be used to find a string or character match within a longer string. Note that in PHP, the strchr() function is exactly the same as strstr(), although its name implies that it is used to find a character in a string, similar to the C version of this function. In PHP, either of these functions can be used to find a string inside a string, including finding a string containing only a single character.

The prototype for strstr() is as follows:

```
string strstr(string haystack, string needle);
```

You pass the function a *haystack* to be searched and a *needle* to be found. If an exact match of the *needle* is found, the function returns the *haystack* from the *needle* onward, otherwise it returns false. If the *needle* occurs more than once, the returned string will start from the first occurrence of *needle*.

For example, in the Smart Form application, we can decide where to send the email as follows:

```
$toaddress = 'feedback@example.com';  // the default value

// Change the $toaddress if the criteria are met
if (strstr($feedback, 'shop'))
  $toaddress = 'retail@example.com';
else if (strstr($feedback, 'delivery'))
  $toaddress = 'fulfilment@example.com';
else if (strstr($feedback, 'bill'))
    $toaddress = 'accounts@example.com';
```

This code checks for certain keywords in the feedback and sends the mail to the appropriate person. If, for example, the customer feedback reads "I still haven't received delivery of my last order," the string "delivery" will be detected and the feedback will be sent to fulfilment@example.com.

There are two variants on strstr(). The first variant is stristr(), which is nearly identical but is not case sensitive. This will be useful for this application as the customer might type 'delivery', 'Delivery', or 'DELIVERY'.

The second variant is strrchr(), which is again nearly identical, but will return the *haystack* from the last occurrence of the *needle* onward.

Finding the Position of a Substring: strpos(), strrpos()

The functions strpos() and strrpos() operate in a similar fashion to strstr(), except, instead of returning a substring, they return the numerical position of a *needle* within a *haystack*.

The `strpos()` function has the following prototype:

```
int strpos(string haystack, string needle, int [offset] );
```

The integer returned represents the position of the *first* occurrence of the needle within the haystack. The first character is in position 0 as usual.

For example, the following code will echo the value 4 to the browser:

```
$test = 'Hello world';
echo strpos($test, 'o');
```

In this case, we have only passed in a single character as the needle, but it can be a string of any length.

The optional offset parameter is used to specify a point within the *haystack* to start searching. For example,

```
echo strpos($test, 'o', 5);
```

This code will echo the value 7 to the browser because PHP has started looking for the character o at position 5, and therefore does not see the one at position 4.

The `strrpos()` function is almost identical, but will return the position of the last occurrence of the *needle* in the *haystack*. Unlike `strpos()`, it only works with a single character *needle*. Therefore, if you pass it a string as a *needle*, it will only use the first character of the string to match.

In any of these cases, if the *needle* is not in the string, `strpos()` or `strrpos()` will return `false`. This can be problematic because `false` in a weakly typed language such as PHP is equivalent to 0, that is, the first character in a string.

You can avoid this problem by using the `===` operator to test return values:

```
$result = strpos($test, 'H');
if ($result === false)
  echo 'Not found'
else
  echo 'Found at position 0';
```

Note that this will only work in PHP 4—in earlier versions you can test for `false` by testing the return value to see if it is a string (that is, `false`).

Replacing Substrings: str_replace(), substr_replace()

Find-and-replace functionality can be extremely useful with strings. We have used find and replace in the past for personalizing documents generated by PHP—for example by replacing `<<name>>` with a person's name and `<<address>>` with their address. You can also use it for censoring particular terms, such as in a discussion forum application, or even in the Smart Form application.

Again, you can use string functions or regular expression functions for this purpose.

The most commonly used string function for replacement is `str_replace()`. It has the following prototype:

```
mixed str_replace(mixed needle, mixed new_needle, mixed haystack);
```

This function will replace all the instances of `needle` in `haystack` with `new_needle` and return the new version of the `haystack`.

> **Note**
>
> As of PHP 4.0.5 you can pass all parameters as arrays and the function will work remarkably intelligently. You can pass an array of words to be replaced, an array of words to replace them with (respectively), and an array of strings to apply these rules to. The function will then return an array of revised strings.

For example, because people can use the Smart Form to complain, they might use some colorful words. As programmers, we can prevent Bob's various departments from being abused in that way:

```
$feedback = str_replace($offcolor, '%!@*', $feedback);
```

The function `substr_replace()` is used to find and replace a particular substring of a string based on its position. It has the following prototype:

```
string substr_replace(string string, string replacement, int start,
int [length] );
```

This function will replace part of the string `string` with the string `replacement`. Which part is replaced depends upon the values of the `start` and optional `length` parameters.

The `start` value represents an offset into the string where replacement should begin. If it is 0 or positive, it is an offset from the beginning of the string; if it is negative, it is an offset from the end of the string. For example, this line of code will replace the last character in `$test` with `"X"`:

```
$test = substr_replace($test, 'X', -1);
```

The `length` value is optional and represents the point at which PHP will stop replacing. If you don't supply this value, the string will be replaced from `start` to the end of the string.

If `length` is zero, the replacement string will actually be *inserted* into the string without overwriting the existing string.

A positive `length` represents the number of characters that you want replaced with the new string.

A negative `length` represents the point at which you'd like to stop replacing characters, counted from the end of the string.

Introduction to Regular Expressions

PHP supports two styles of regular expression syntax: POSIX and Perl. The POSIX style of regular expression is compiled into PHP by default, but you can use the Perl style by compiling in the PCRE (Perl-compatible regular expression) library. We'll cover the simpler POSIX style, but if you're already a Perl programmer, or want to learn more about PCRE, read the online manual at `http://php.net`.

> **Note**
> POSIX regular expressions are easier to learn and execute faster, but are not binary-safe.

So far, all the pattern matching we've done has used the string functions. We have been limited to exact match, or to exact substring match. If you want to do more complex pattern matching, you should use regular expressions. Regular expressions are difficult to grasp at first but can be extremely useful.

The Basics

A regular expression is a way of describing a pattern in a piece of text. The exact (or literal) matches we've done so far are a form of regular expression. For example, earlier we were searching for regular expression terms like `"shop"` and `"delivery"`.

Matching regular expressions in PHP is more like a `strstr()` match than an equal comparison because you are matching a string somewhere within another string. (It can be anywhere within that string unless you specify otherwise.) For example, the string `"shop"` matches the regular expression `"shop"`. It also matches the regular expressions `"h"`, `"ho"`, and so on.

We can use special characters to indicate a meta-meaning in addition to matching characters exactly.

For example, with special characters you can indicate that a pattern must occur at the start or end of a string, that part of a pattern can be repeated, or that characters in a pattern must be of a particular type. You can also match on literal occurrences of special characters. We'll look at each of these.

Character Sets and Classes

Using character sets immediately gives regular expressions more power than exact matching expressions. Character sets can be used to match any character of a particular *type*—they're really a kind of wildcard.

First of all, you can use the . character as a wildcard for any other single character except a new line (\n). For example, the regular expression

`.at`

matches the strings `'cat'`, `'sat'`, and `'mat'`, among others.

This kind of wildcard matching is often used for filename matching in operating systems.

With regular expressions, however, you can be more specific about the type of character you would like to match, and you can actually specify a set that a character must belong to. In the previous example, the regular expression matches `'cat'` and `'mat'`, but also matches '#at'. If you want to limit this to a character between a and z, you can specify it as follows:

```
[a-z]
```

Anything enclosed in the special square brace characters [and] is a character class—a set of characters to which a matched character must belong. Note that the expression in the square brackets matches only a *single character*.

You can list a set; for example

```
[aeiou]
```

means any vowel.

You can also describe a range, as we just did using the special hyphen character, or a set of ranges:

```
[a-zA-Z]
```

This set of ranges stands for any alphabetic character in upper- or lowercase.

You can also use sets to specify that a character cannot be a member of a set. For example,

```
[^a-z]
```

matches any character that is *not* between a and z. The caret symbol means *not* when it is placed inside the square brackets. It has another meaning when used outside square brackets, which we'll look at in a minute.

In addition to listing out sets and ranges, a number of predefined *character classes* can be used in a regular expression. These are shown in Table 4.3.

Table 4.3   **Character Classes for Use in POSIX Style Regular Expressions**

Class	Matches
[[:alnum:]]	Alphanumeric characters
[[:alpha:]]	Alphabetic characters
[[:lower:]]	Lowercase letters
[[:upper:]]	Uppercase letters
[[:digit:]]	Decimal digits
[[:xdigit:]]	Hexadecimal digits
[[:punct:]]	Punctuation
[[:blank:]]	Tabs and spaces
[[:space:]]	Whitespace characters
[[:cntrl:]]	Control characters
[[:print:]]	All printable characters
[[:graph:]]	All printable characters except for space

Repetition

Often you want to specify that there might be multiple occurrences of a particular string or class of character. You can represent this using two special characters in your regular expression. The * symbol means that the pattern can be repeated zero or more times, and the + symbol means that the pattern can be repeated one or more times. The symbol should appear directly after the part of the expression that it applied to. For example

```
[[:alnum:]]+
```

means "at least one alphanumeric character."

Subexpressions

It's often useful to be able to split an expression into subexpressions so you can, for example, represent "at least one of these strings followed by exactly one of those." You can do this using parentheses, exactly the same way as you would in an arithmetic expression. For example,

```
(very )*large
```

matches 'large', 'very large', 'very very large', and so on.

Counted Subexpressions

We can specify how many times something can be repeated by using a numerical expression in curly braces ({}). You can show an exact number of repetitions ({3} means exactly 3 repetitions), a range of repetitions ({2, 4} means from 2 to 4 repetitions), or an open ended range of repetitions ({2,} means at least two repetitions).

For example,

```
(very ){1, 3}
```

matches 'very ', 'very very ' and 'very very very '.

Anchoring to the Beginning or End of a String

You can specify if a particular subexpression should appear at the start, the end, or both. This is pretty useful when you want to make sure that only your search term and nothing else appears in the string.

The caret symbol (^) is used at the start of a regular expression to show that it must appear at the beginning of a searched string, and $ is used at the end of a regular expression to show that it must appear at the end.

For example, this matches bob at the start of a string:

```
^bob
```

This matches com at the end of a string:

```
com$
```

Finally, this matches any single character from a to z, in the string on its own:

`^[a-z]$`

Branching

You can represent a choice in a regular expression with a vertical pipe. For example, if we want to match com, edu, or net, we can use the expression:

`(com)|(edu)|(net)`

Matching Literal Special Characters

If you want to match one of the special characters mentioned in this section, such as ., {, or $, you must put a slash (\) in front of it. If you want to represent a slash, you must replace it with two slashes, \\.

Summary of Special Characters

A summary of all the special characters is shown in Tables 4.4 and 4.5. Table 4.4 shows the meaning of special characters outside square brackets, and Table 4.5 shows their meaning when used inside square brackets.

Table 4.4   **Summary of Special Characters Used in POSIX Regular Expressions Outside Square Brackets**

Character	Meaning
\	Escape character
^	Match at start of string
$	Match at end of string
.	Match any character except newline (\n)
|	Start of alternative branch (read as OR)
(	Start subpattern
)	End subpattern
*	Repeat 0 or more times
+	Repeat 1 or more times
{	Start min/max quantifier
{	Start min/max quantifier

Table 4.5   **Summary of Special Characters Used in POSIX Regular Expressions Inside Square Brackets**

Character	Meaning
\	Escape character
^	NOT, only if used in initial position
-	Used to specify character ranges

Putting It All Together for the Smart Form

There are at least two possible uses of regular expressions in the Smart Form application. The first use is to detect particular terms in the customer feedback. We can be slightly smarter about this using regular expressions. Using a string function, we'd have to do three different searches if we wanted to match on 'shop', 'customer service', or 'retail'. With a regular expression, we can match all three:

```
shop|customer service|retail
```

The second use is to validate customer email addresses in our application by encoding the standardized format of an email address in a regular expression. The format includes some alphanumeric or punctuation characters, followed by an @ symbol, followed by a string of alphanumeric and hyphen characters, followed by a dot, followed by more alphanumeric and hyphen characters and possibly more dots, up until the end of the string, which encodes as follows:

```
^[a-zA-Z0-9_\-\.]+@[a-zA-Z0-9\-]+\.[a-zA-Z0-9\-\.]+$
```

The subexpression ^[a-zA-Z0-9_\-\.]+ means "start the string with at least one letter, number, underscore, hyphen, or dot, or some combination of those."

The @ symbol matches a literal @.

The subexpression [a-zA-Z0-9\-]+ matches the first part of the host name including alphanumeric characters and hyphens. Note that we've slashed out the hyphen because it's a special character inside square brackets.

The \. combination matches a literal ..

The subexpression [a-zA-Z0-9\-\.]+$ matches the rest of a domain name, including letters, numbers, hyphens, and more dots if required, up until the end of the string.

A bit of analysis shows that you can produce invalid email addresses that will still match this regular expression. It is almost impossible to catch them all, but this will improve the situation a little. You can refine this expression in many ways. You can, for example, list valid TLDs. Be careful when making things more restrictive though, as a validation function that rejects 1% of valid data is far more annoying than one that allows through 10% of invalid data.

Now that you have read about regular expressions, we'll look at the PHP functions that use them.

Finding Substrings with Regular Expressions

Finding substrings is the main application of the regular expressions we just developed. The two functions available in PHP for matching regular expressions are `ereg()` and `eregi()`.

The `ereg()` function has the following prototype:

```
int ereg(string pattern, string search, array [matches]);
```

This function searches the *search* string, looking for matches to the regular expression in *pattern*. If matches are found for subexpressions of *pattern*, they will be stored in the array *matches*, one subexpression per array element.

The `eregi()` function is identical except that it is not case sensitive.

We can adapt the Smart Form example to use regular expressions as follows:

```
if (!eregi('^[a-zA-Z0-9_\-\.]+@[a-zA-Z0-9\-]+\.[a-zA-Z0-9\-\.]+$', $email))
{
  echo 'That is not a valid email address.  Please return to the'
      .' previous page and try again.';
  exit;
}
$toaddress = 'feedback@example.com';  // the default value
if (eregi('shop|customer service|retail', $feedback))
  $toaddress = 'retail@example.com';
else if (eregi('deliver.*|fulfil.*', $feedback))
  $toaddress = 'fulfilment@example.com';
else if (eregi('bill|account', $feedback))
  $toaddress = 'accounts@example.com';

if (eregi('bigcustomer\.com', $email))
    $toaddress = 'bob@example.com';
```

Replacing Substrings with Regular Expressions

You can also use regular expressions to find and replace substrings in the same way as we used `str_replace()`. The two functions available for this are `ereg_replace()` and `eregi_replace()`. The function `ereg_replace()` has the following prototype:

```
string ereg_replace(string pattern, string replacement, string search);
```

This function searches for the regular expression *pattern* in the *search* string and replaces it with the string *replacement*.

The function `eregi_replace()` is identical, but again, is not case sensitive.

Splitting Strings with Regular Expressions

Another useful regular expression function is `split()`, which has the following prototype:

```
array split(string pattern, string search, int [max]);
```

This function splits the string *search* into substrings on the regular expression *pattern*
and returns the substrings in an array. The *max* integer limits the number of items that
can go into the array.

This can be useful for splitting up domain names or dates. For example,

```
$domain = 'yallara.cs.rmit.edu.au';
$arr = split ('\.', $domain);
while (list($key, $value) = each ($arr))
  echo '<br />'.$value;
```

This splits the host name into its five components and prints each on a separate line.

Comparison of String Functions and Regular Expression Functions

In general, the regular expression functions run less efficiently than the string functions
with similar functionality. If your application is simple enough to use string expressions,
do so.

Further Reading

PHP has many string functions. We have covered the more useful ones in this chapter,
but if you have a particular need (such as translating characters into Cyrillic), check the
PHP manual online to see if PHP has the function for you.

The amount of material available on regular expressions is enormous. You can start
with the man page for `regexp` if you are using UNIX and there are also some terrific
articles at `devshed.com` and `phpbuilder.com`.

At Zend's Web site, you can look at a more complex and powerful email validation
function than the one we developed here. It is called `MailVal()` and is available at
`http://www.zend.com/codex.php?id=88&single=1`.

Regular expressions take a while to sink in—the more examples you look at and run,
the more confident you will be using them.

Next

In the next chapter, we'll discuss several ways you can use PHP to save programming
time and effort and prevent redundancy by reusing pre-existing code.

## 5

Reusing Code and Writing Functions

THIS CHAPTER EXPLAINS HOW REUSING CODE leads to more consistent, reliable, maintainable code, with less effort. We will demonstrate techniques for modularizing and reusing code, beginning with the simple use of `require()` and `include()` to use the same code on more than one page. We will explain why these are superior to server side includes. The example given will cover using include files to get a consistent look and feel across your site.

We will explain how to write and call your own functions using page and form generation functions as examples.

In this chapter, we will cover

- Reusing code
- Using `require()` and `include()`
- Introducing functions
- Defining functions
- Parameters
- Returning values
- Call-by-Reference versus Call-by-Value
- Scope
- Recursion

Why Reuse Code?

One of the goals of software engineers is to reuse code in lieu of writing new code. This is not because software engineers are a particularly lazy group. Reusing existing code reduces costs, increases reliability, and improves consistency. Ideally, a new project is created by combining existing reusable components, with a minimum of development from scratch.

Cost

Over the useful life of a piece of software, significantly more time will be spent maintaining, modifying, testing, and documenting it than was originally spent writing it. If you are writing commercial code, you should be attempting to limit the number of lines that are in use within the organization. One of the most practical ways to achieve this is to reuse code already in use rather than writing a slightly different version of the same code for a new task. Less code means lower costs. If software exists that meets the requirements of the new project, acquire it. The cost of buying existing software is almost always less than the cost of developing an equivalent product. Tread carefully though if there is existing software that almost meets your requirements. It can be more difficult to modify existing code than to write new code.

Reliability

If a module of code is in use somewhere in your organization, it has presumably already been thoroughly tested. Even if it is only a few lines, there is a possibility that if you rewrite it, you will either overlook something that the original author incorporated or something that was added to the original code after a defect was found during testing. Existing, mature code is usually more reliable than fresh, "green" code.

Consistency

The external interfaces to your system, including both user interfaces and interfaces to outside systems, should be consistent. It takes a will and a deliberate effort to write new code that is consistent with the way other parts of the system function. If you are reusing code that runs another part of the system, your functionality should automatically be consistent.

On top of these advantages, reusing code is less work for you, as long as the original code was modular and well written. While you work, try to recognize sections of your code that you might be able to call on again in the future.

Using require() and include()

PHP provides two very simple, yet very useful, statements to allow you to reuse any type of code. Using a `require()` or `include()` statement, you can load a file into your PHP script. The file can contain anything you would normally type in a script including PHP statements, text, HTML tags, PHP functions, or PHP classes.

These statements work similarly to the Server Side Includes offered by many Web servers and #include statements in C or C++.

Using require()

The following code is stored in a file named `reusable.php`:

```php
<?php
  echo 'Here is a very simple PHP statement.<br />';
?>
```

The following code is stored in a file called `main.php`:

```php
<?php
  echo 'This is the main file.<br />';
  require( 'reusable.php' );
  echo 'The script will end now.<br />';
?>
```

If you load `reusable.php`, it probably won't surprise you when "`Here is a very sim-ple PHP statement.`" appears in your browser. If you load `main.php`, something a little more interesting happens. The output of this script is shown in Figure 5.1.

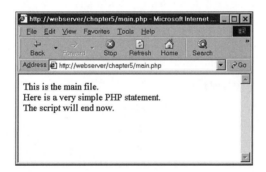

Figure 5.1   The output of main.php shows the result of the require() statement.

A file is needed to use a `require()` statement. In the preceding example, we are using the file named `reusable.php`. When we run our script, the `require()` statement

```php
require( 'reusable.php' );
```

is replaced by the contents of the requested file, and the script is then executed. This means that when we load `main.php`, it runs as though the script were written as follows:

```php
<?php
  echo 'This is the main file.<br />';
  echo 'Here is a very simple PHP statement.<br />';
  echo 'The script will end now.<br />';
?>
```

When using `require()` you need to note the different ways that filename extensions and PHP tags are handled.

File Name Extensions and require()

PHP does not look at the filename extension on the required file. This means that you can name your file whatever you choose as long as you're not going to call it directly. When you use `require()` to load the file, it will effectively become part of a PHP file and be executed as such.

Normally, PHP statements would not be processed if they were in a file called for example, `page.html`. PHP is usually only called upon to parse files with defined extensions such as `.php`. However, if you load this `page.html` via a `require()` statement, any PHP inside it will be processed. Therefore, you can use any extension you prefer for include files, but it would be a good idea to try to stick to a sensible convention, such as `.inc`.

One thing to be aware of is that if files ending in .inc or some other non-standard extension are stored in the Web document tree and users directly load them in the browser, they will be able to see the code in plain text, including any passwords. It is therefore important to either store included files outside the document tree, or use the standard extensions.

PHP Tags and require()

In our example our reusable file (`reusable.php`) was written as follows:

```
<?php
  echo 'Here is a very simple PHP statement.<br />';
?>
```

We placed the PHP code within the file in PHP tags. You will need to do this if you want PHP code within a required file treated as PHP code. If you do not open a PHP tag, your code will just be treated as text or HTML and will not be executed.

Using require() for Web Site Templates

If your company has a consistent look and feel to pages on the Web site, you can use PHP to add the template and standard elements to pages using `require()`.

For example, the Web site of fictional company TLA Consulting has a number of pages all with the look and feel shown in Figure 5.2. When a new page is needed, the developer can open an existing page, cut out the existing text from the middle of the file, enter new text and save the file under a new name.

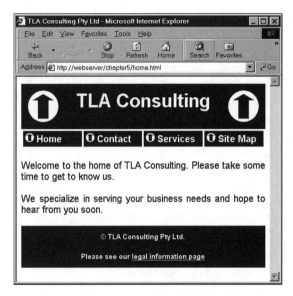

Figure 5.2   TLA Consulting has a standard look
and feel for all their Web pages.

Consider this scenario: The Web site has been around for a while, and there are now tens, hundreds, or maybe even thousands of pages all following a common style. A decision is made to change part of the standard look—it might be something minor, like adding an email address to the footer of each page or adding a single new entry to the navigation menu. Do you want to make that minor change on tens, hundreds, or even thousands of pages?

Directly reusing the sections of HTML that are common to all pages is a much better approach than cutting and pasting on tens, hundreds, or even thousands of pages. The source code for the homepage (home.html) shown in Figure 5.2 is given in Listing 5.1.

Listing 5.1   home.html—The HTML That Produces TLA Consulting's Home Page

```
<html>
<head>
  <title>TLA Consulting Pty Ltd</title>
  <style>
    h1 {color:white; font-size:24pt; text-align:center;
        font-family:arial,sans-serif}
    .menu {color:white; font-size:12pt; text-align:center;
           font-family:arial,sans-serif; font-weight:bold}
    td {background:black}
```

Listing 5.1   **Continued**

```
    p {color:black; font-size:12pt; text-align:justify;
       font-family:arial,sans-serif}
    p.foot {color:white; font-size:9pt; text-align:center;
            font-family:arial,sans-serif; font-weight:bold}
    a:link,a:visited,a:active {color:white}
  </style>
</head>
<body>

  <!-- page header -->
  <table width="100%" cellpadding="12" cellspacing="0" border="0">
  <tr bgcolor="black">
    <td align="left"><img src="logo.gif"></td>
    <td>
        <h1>TLA Consulting</h1>
    </td>
    <td align="right"><img src="logo.gif"></td>
  </tr>
  </table>

  <!-- menu -->
  <table width="100%" bgcolor="white" cellpadding="4" cellspacing="4">
  <tr >
    <td width="25%">
      <img src="s-logo.gif"> <span class="menu">Home</span></td>
    <td width="25%">
      <img src="s-logo.gif"> <span class="menu">Contact</span></td>
    <td width="25%">
      <img src="s-logo.gif"> <span class="menu">Services</span></td>
    <td width="25%">
      <img src="s-logo.gif"> <span class="menu">Site Map</span></td>
  </tr>
  </table>

  <!-- page content -->
  <p>Welcome to the home of TLA Consulting.
  Please take some time to get to know us.</p>
  <p>We specialize in serving your business needs
  and hope to hear from you soon.</p>

  <!-- page footer -->
  <table width="100%" bgcolor="black" cellpadding="12" border="0">
  <tr>
    <td>
      <p class="foot">&copy; TLA Consulting Pty Ltd.</p>
```

Listing 5.1   **Continued**

```
      <p class="foot">Please see our <a href="legal.php">legal information
page</a></p>
    </td>
  </tr>
  </table>
</body>
</html>
```

You can see in Listing 5.1 that a number of distinct sections of code exist in this file. The HTML head contains Cascading Style Sheet (CSS) definitions used by the page. The section labeled "page header" displays the company name and logo, "menu bar" creates the page's navigation bar, and "page content" is text unique to this page. Below that is the page footer. We can usefully split this file and name the parts header.inc, home.php, and footer.inc. Both header.inc and footer.inc contain code that will be reused on other pages.

The file home.php is a replacement for home.html, and contains the unique page content and two require() statements as shown in Listing 5.2.

Listing 5.2   **home.php—The PHP That Produces TLA's Home Page**

```
<?php
  require('header.inc');
?>
  <!-- page content -->
  <p>Welcome to the home of TLA Consulting.
  Please take some time to get to know us.</p>
  <p>We specialize in serving your business needs
  and hope to hear from you soon.</p>
<?php
  require('footer.inc');
?>
```

The require() statements in home.php load header.inc and footer.inc.

As mentioned, the name given to these files does not affect how they are processed when we call them via require(). A common, but entirely optional, convention is to call the partial files that will end up included in other files *something*.inc (here inc stands for include). It is also common, and a good idea, to place your include files in a directory that can be seen by your scripts, but does not permit your include files to be loaded individually via the Web server. This will prevent these files from being loaded individually which will either a) probably produce some errors if the file extension is .php but contains only a partial page or script, or b) allow people to read your source code if you have used another extension.

The file header.inc contains the CSS definitions that the page uses, the tables that display the company name and navigation menus as shown in Listing 5.3.

The file `footer.inc` contains the table that displays the footer at the bottom of each page. This file is shown in Listing 5.4.

Listing 5.3   header.inc—The Reusable Header for All TLA Web Pages

```html
<html>
<head>
  <title>TLA Consulting Pty Ltd</title>
  <style>
    h1 {color:white; font-size:24pt; text-align:center;
        font-family:arial,sans-serif}
    .menu {color:white; font-size:12pt; text-align:center;
           font-family:arial,sans-serif; font-weight:bold}
    td {background:black}
    p {color:black; font-size:12pt; text-align:justify;
       font-family:arial,sans-serif}
    p.foot {color:white; font-size:9pt; text-align:center;
            font-family:arial,sans-serif; font-weight:bold}
    a:link,a:visited,a:active {color:white}
  </style>
</head>
<body>

  <!-- page header -->
  <table width="100%" cellpadding="12" cellspacing="0" border="0">
  <tr bgcolor="black">
    <td align="left"><img src="logo.gif"></td>
    <td>
        <h1>TLA Consulting</h1>
    </td>
    <td align="right"><img src="logo.gif"></td>
  </tr>
  </table>

  <!-- menu -->
  <table width="100%" bgcolor="white" cellpadding="4" cellspacing="4">
  <tr >
    <td width="25%">
      <img src="s-logo.gif"> <span class="menu">Home</span></td>
    <td width="25%">
      <img src="s-logo.gif"> <span class="menu">Contact</span></td>
    <td width="25%">
      <img src="s-logo.gif"> <span class="menu">Services</span></td>
    <td width="25%">
      <img src="s-logo.gif"> <span class="menu">Site Map</span></td>
  </tr>
  </table>
```

Listing 5.4 **footer.inc—The Reusable Footer for All TLA Web Pages**

```
<!-- page footer -->
  <table width="100%" bgcolor="black" cellpadding="12" border="0">
  <tr>
    <td>
      <p class="foot">&copy; TLA Consulting Pty Ltd.</p>
      <p class="foot">Please see our
                    <a href="legal.php">legal information page</a></p>
    </td>
  </tr>
  </table>
</body>
</html>
```

This approach gives you a consistent looking Web site very easily, and you can make a new page in the same style by typing something like:

```
<?php require('header.inc'); ?>
Here is the content for this page
<?php require('footer.inc'); ?>
```

Most importantly, even after we have created many pages using this header and footer, it is easy to change the header and footer files. Whether you are making a minor text change, or completely redesigning the look of the site, you only need to make the change once. We do not need to separately alter every page in the site because each page is loading in the header and footer files.

The example shown here only uses plain HTML in the body, header and footer. This need not be the case. Within these files, we could use PHP statements to dynamically generate parts of the page.

Using auto_prepend_file and auto_append_file

If we want to use require() to add our header and footer to every page, there is another way we can do it. Two of the configuration options in the php.ini file are auto_prepend_file and auto_append_file. By setting these to our header and footer files, we ensure that they will be loaded before and after every page.

For Windows, the settings will resemble the following:

```
auto_prepend_file = "c:/inetpub/include/header.inc"
auto_append_file = "c:/inetpub/include/footer.inc"
```

For UNIX, they will resemble the following:

```
auto_prepend_file = "/home/username/include/header.inc"
auto_append_file = "/home/username/include/footer.inc"
```

If we use these directives, we do not need to type require() statements, but the headers and footers will no longer be optional on pages.

If you are using an Apache Web server, you can change various configuration options like these for individual directories. To do this, your server must be set up to allow its main configuration file(s) to be overridden. To set up auto prepending and appending for a directory, create a file called `.htaccess` in the directory. The file needs to contain the following two lines:

```
php_value auto_prepend_file "/home/username/include/header.inc"
php_value auto_append_file "/home/username/include/footer.inc"
```

Note that the syntax is slightly different from the same option in php.ini, as well as `php_value` at the start of the line: There is no equal sign. A number of other `php.ini` configuration settings can be altered in this way too.

This syntax changed from PHP 3. If you are using an old version, the lines in your .htaccess file should resemble this:

```
php3_auto_prepend_file /home/username/include/header.inc
php3_auto_append_file /home/username/include/footer.inc
```

Setting options in the `.htaccess` file rather than in either php.ini or your Web server's configuration file gives you a lot of flexibility. You can alter settings on a shared machine that only affect your directories. You do not need to restart the Web server, and you do not need administrator access. A drawback to the `.htaccess` method is that the files are read and parsed each time a file in that directory is requested rather than just once at startup, so there is a performance penalty.

Using include()

The statements `require()` and `include()` are almost identical. The only difference between them is that when they fail, the `require()` construct will give a fatal error, while the `include()` construct will only give a warning.

This is a change in the way these constructs work. Prior to PHP 4.0.2, they had some important differences in the way they worked. If you are still using an older version of PHP, the following notes will apply to you:

An `include()` statement is evaluated each time the statement is executed, and not evaluated at all if the statement is not executed. A `require()` statement is executed the first time the statement is parsed, regardless of whether the code block containing it will be executed.

Unless your server is very busy, this will make little difference but it does mean that code with `require()` statements inside conditional statements is inefficient.

```
if($variable == true)
{
  require('file1.inc');
}
else
{
```

```
    require('file2.inc');
}
```

This code will needlessly load both files every time the script is run, but only use one depending on the value of $variable. However, if the code had been written using two include() statements, only one of the files would be loaded and used as in the following version:

```
if($variable == true)
{
    include('file1.inc');
}
else
{
    include('file2.inc');
}
```

Unlike files loaded via a require() statement, files loaded via an include() can return a value. Therefore, we can notify other parts of the program about a success or failure in the included file, or return an answer or result.

We might decide that we are opening files a lot and rather than retyping the same lines of code every time, we want an include file to open them for us. Our include file might be called "openfile.inc" and resemble the following:

```
<?php
@ $fp = fopen($name, $mode);
    if (!$fp)
    {
        echo '<p><strong> Oh No! I could not open the file.</strong></p>';
        return 0;
    }
    else
    {
        return 1;
    }
?>
```

This file will try to open the file named $name using the mode given by $mode. If it fails, it will give an error message and return 0. If it succeeds, it will return 1 and generate no output.

We can call this file in a script as follows:

```
$name = 'file.txt';
$mode = 'r';
$result = include('openfile.php');
if( $result == 1 )
{
```

```
    // do what we wanted to do with the file
    // refer to $fp created in the include file
}
```

Note that we can create variables in the main file or in the included or required file, and the variable will exist in both. This behavior is the same for both `require()` and `include()` statements.

You cannot use `require()` in exactly the way shown here because you cannot return values from `require()` statements. Returning a value can be useful because it enables you to notify later parts of your program about a failure, or to do some self-contained processing and return an answer. Functions are an even better vehicle than included files for breaking code into self-contained modules. We will look at functions next.

If you are wondering why, given the advantages of `include()` over `require()`, you would ever use `require()`, the answer is that it is slightly faster.

As we mentioned before, this behaviour has now changed, so you can simply avoid the issue by upgrading to a newer version of PHP.

Using Functions in PHP

Functions exist in most programming languages. They are used to separate code that performs a single, well-defined task. This makes the code easier to read and allows us to reuse the code each time we need to do the same task.

A function is a self-contained module of code that prescribes a calling interface, performs some task, and optionally returns a result.

You have seen a number of functions already. In preceding chapters, we have routinely called a number of the functions that come built-in to PHP. We have also written a few simple functions but glossed over the details. In this section, we will cover calling and writing functions in more detail.

Calling Functions

The following line is the simplest possible call to a function:

```
function_name();
```

This calls a function named `function_name` that does not require parameters. This line of code ignores any value that might be returned by this function.

A number of functions are called in exactly this way. The function `phpinfo()` is often useful in testing because it displays the installed version of PHP, information about PHP, the Web server set-up, and the values of various PHP and server variables. This function does not take any parameters, and we generally ignore its return value, so a call to `phpinfo()` will resemble the following:

```
phpinfo();
```

Most functions do require one or more parameters—information given to a function when it is called that influences the outcome of executing the function. We pass parameters by placing the data or the name of a variable holding the data inside parentheses after the function name. A call to a function with a parameter resembles the following:

```
function_name('parameter');
```

In this case, the parameter we used was a string containing only the word `parameter`, but the following calls are also fine depending on the function:

```
function_name(2);
function_name(7.993);
function_name($variable);
```

In the last line, `$variable` might be any type of PHP variable, including an array.

A parameter can be any type of data, but particular functions will usually require particular data types.

You can see how many parameters a function takes, what each represents, and what data type each needs to be from the function's *prototype*. We often show the prototype when we describe a function.

This is the prototype for the function `fopen()`:

```
int fopen( string filename, string mode, [int use_include_path] );
```

The prototype tells us a number of things, and it is important that you know how to correctly interpret these specifications. In this case, the word `int` before the function name tells us that this function will return an integer. The function parameters are inside the parentheses. In the case of `fopen()`, three parameters are shown in the prototype. The parameter filename and mode are strings and the parameter is an integer.

The square brackets around `use_include_path` indicate that this parameter is optional. We can provide values for optional parameters or we can choose to ignore them, and the default value will be used.

After reading the prototype for this function, we know that the following code fragment will be a valid call to `fopen()`:

```
$name = 'myfile.txt';
$openmode = 'r';
$fp = fopen($name, $openmode)
```

This code calls the function named `fopen()`. The value returned by the function will be stored in the variable `$fp`. We chose to pass to the function a variable called `$name` containing a string representing the file we want to open, and a variable called `$openmode` containing a string representing the mode in which we want to open the file. We chose not to provide the optional third parameter.

Call to Undefined Function

If you attempt to call a function that does not exist, you will get an error message as
shown in Figure 5.3.

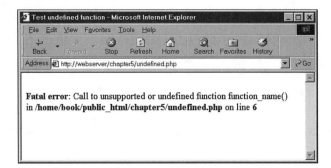

Figure 5.3   This error message is the result of
calling a function that does not exist.

The error messages that PHP gives are usually very useful. This one tells us exactly in
which file the error occurred, in which line of the script it occurred, and the name of
the function we attempted to call. This should make it fairly easy to find and correct.

There are two things to check if you see this error message:

1. Is the function name spelled correctly?

2. Does the function exist in the version of PHP you are using?

It is not always easy to remember how a function name is spelled. For instance, some
two-word function names have an underscore between the words and some do not. The
function `stripslashes()` runs the two words together, whereas the function
`strip_tags()` separates the words with an underscore. Misspelling the name of a function in a function call results in an error as shown in Figure 5.3.

Many functions used in this book do not exist in PHP 3.0 because this book assumes
that you are using at least PHP 4.0. In each new version, new functions are defined and
if you are using an older version, the added functionality and performance justify an
upgrade. To see when a particular function was added, you can check the online manual. Attempting to call a function that is not declared in the version you are running will
result in an error such as the one shown in Figure 5.3.

Case and Function Names

Note that calls to functions are **not** case sensitive, so calling `function_name()`,
`Function_Name()`, or `FUNCTION_NAME()` are all valid and will all have the same result.
You are free to capitalize in any way you find easy to read, but you should aim to be

consistent. The convention used in this book, and most other PHP documentation, is to use all lowercase.

It is important to note that function names behave differently to variable names. Variable names **are** case sensitive, so `$Name` and `$name` are two separate variables, but `Name()` and `name()` are the same function.

In the preceding chapters, you have seen many examples using some of PHP's built-in functions. However, the real power of a programming language comes from being able to create your own functions.

Why Should You Define Your Own Functions?

The functions built in to PHP enable you to interact with files, use a database, create graphics, and connect to other servers. However, in your career there will be many times when you will need to do something that the language's creators did not foresee.

Fortunately, you are not limited to using the built-in functions because you can write your own to perform any task that you like. Your code will probably be a mixture of existing functions combined with your own logic to perform a task for you. If you are writing a block of code for a task that you are likely to want to reuse in a number of places in a script or in a number of scripts, you would be wise to declare that block as a function.

Declaring a function allows you to use your own code in the same way as the built-in functions. You simply call your function and provide it with the necessary parameters. This means that you can call and reuse the same function many times throughout your script.

Basic Function Structure

A function declaration creates or *declares* a new function. The declaration begins with the keyword `function`, provides the function name, the parameters required, and contains the code that will be executed each time this function is called.

Here is the declaration of a trivial function:

```
function my_function()
{
  echo 'My function was called';
}
```

This function declaration begins with `function`, so that human readers and the PHP parser know that what follows will be a user-defined function. The function name is `my_function`. We can call our new function with the following statement:

```
my_function();
```

As you probably guessed, calling this function will result in the text "`My function was called`" appearing in the viewer's browser.

Built-in functions are available to all PHP scripts, but if you declare your own functions, they are only available to the script(s) in which they were declared. It is a good idea to have one file containing your commonly used functions. You can then have a `require()` statement in all your scripts to make your functions available.

Within a function, curly braces enclose the code that performs the task you require. Between these braces, you can have anything that is legal elsewhere in a PHP script including function calls, declarations of new variables or functions, `require()` or `include()` statements, and plain HTML. If we want to exit PHP within a function and type plain HTML, we do it the same way as anywhere else in the script—with a closing PHP tag followed by the HTML. The following is a legal modification of the previous example and produces the same output:

```php
<?php
  function my_function()
  {
?>
My function was called
<?php
  }
?>
```

Note that the PHP code is enclosed within matching opening and closing PHP tags. For most of the small code fragment examples in this book, we do not show these tags. They are shown here because they are required within the example as well as above and below it.

Naming Your Function

The most important thing to consider when naming your functions is that the name should be short but descriptive. If your function creates a page header, `pageheader()` or `page_header()` might be good names.

A few restrictions are as follows:

- Your function cannot have the same name as an existing function.
- Your function name can only contain letters, digits, and underscores.
- Your function name cannot begin with a digit.

Many languages do allow you to reuse function names. This feature is called *function overloading*. However, PHP does not support function overloading, so your function cannot have the same name as any built-in function or an existing user-defined function. Note that although every PHP script knows about all the built-in functions, user-defined functions only exist in scripts where they are declared. This means that you could reuse a function name in a different file, but this would lead to confusion and should be avoided.

The following function names are legal:

```
name()
name2()
name_three()
_namefour()
```

These are illegal:

```
5name()
name-six()
fopen()
```

(The last would be legal if it didn't already exist.)

Parameters

In order to do their work, most functions require one or more parameters. A parameter allows you to pass data into a function. Here is an example of a function that requires a parameter. This function takes a one-dimensional array and displays it as a table.

```
function create_table($data)
{
  echo '<table border="1">';
  reset($data); // Remember this is used to point to the beginning
  $value = current($data);
  while ($value)
  {
     echo "<tr><td>$value</td></tr>\n";
     $value = next($data);
  }
  echo '</table>';
}
```

If we call our `create_table()` function as follows:

```
$my_array = array('Line one.','Line two.','Line three.');
create_table($my_array);
```

we will see output as shown in Figure 5.4.

Passing a parameter allowed us to get data that was created outside the function—in this case, the array `$data`—into the function.

As with built-in functions, user-defined functions can have multiple parameters and optional parameters. We can improve our `create_table()` function in many ways, but one way might be to allow the caller to specify the border or other attributes of the table. Here is an improved version of the function. It is very similar, but allows us to optionally set the table's border width, cellspacing, and cellpadding.

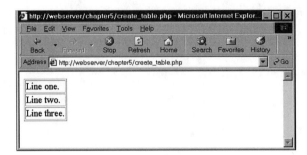

Figure 5.4   This HTML table is the result of calling `create_table()`.

```
function create_table2( $data, $border =1, $cellpadding = 4, $cellspacing = 4 )
{
  echo "<table border='$border' cellpadding = '$cellpadding'"
      ." cellspacing='$cellspacing'>";
  reset($data);
  $value = current($data);
  while ($value)
  {
    echo "<tr><td>$value</td></tr>\n";
    $value = next($data);
  }
  echo '</table>';
}
```

The first parameter for `create_table2()` is still required. The next three are optional because we have defined default values for them. We can create very similar output to that shown in Figure 5.4 with this call to `create_table2()`.

```
create_table2($my_array);
```

If we want the same data displayed in a more spread out style, we could call our new function as follows:

```
create_table2($my_array, 3, 8, 8);
```

Optional values do not all need to be provided—we can provide some and ignore some. Parameters will be assigned from left to right.

Keep in mind that you cannot leave out one optional parameter but include a later listed one. In this example, if you want to pass a value for `cellspacing`, you will have to pass one for `cellpadding` as well. This is a common cause of programming errors. It is also the reason that optional parameters are specified last in any list of parameters.

The following function call:

```
create_table2($my_array, 3);
```

is perfectly legal, and will result in `$border` being set to 3 and `$cellpadding` and `$cellspacing` being set to their defaults.

Scope

You might have noticed that when we needed to use variables inside a required or included file, we simply declared them in the script before the `require()` or `include()` statement, but when using a function, we explicitly passed those variables into the function. This is partly because no mechanism exists for explicitly passing variables to a required or included file, and partly because variable scope behaves differently for functions.

A variable's scope controls where that variable is visible and useable. Different programming languages have different rules that set the scope of variables. PHP has fairly simple rules:

- Variables declared inside a function are in scope from the statement in which they are declared to the closing brace at the end of the function. This is called *function scope*. These variables are called *local variables*.

- Variables declared outside of functions are in scope from the statement in which they are declared to the end of the file, but *not inside functions*. This is called *global scope*. These variables are called *global variables*.

- The special superglobal variables are visible both inside and outside functions. (See Chapter 1, "PHP Crash Course," for a list of these variables.)

- Using `require()` and `include()` statements does not affect scope. If the statement is used within a function, function scope applies. If it is not inside a function, global scope applies.

- The keyword `global` can be used to manually specify that a variable defined or used within a function will have global scope.

- Variables can be manually deleted by calling `unset($variable_name)`. A variable is no longer in scope if it has been unset.

The following examples might help to clarify things.

The following code produces no output. Here we are declaring a variable called `$var` inside our function `fn()`. Because this variable is declared inside a function, it has function scope and only exists from where it is declared, until the end of the function. When we again refer to `$var` outside the function, a new variable called `$var` is created. This new variable has global scope, and will be visible until the end of the file. Unfortunately, if the only statement we use with this new `$var` variable is `echo`, it will never have a value.

```
function fn()
{
  $var = 'contents';
}
echo $var;
```

The following example is the inverse. We declare a variable outside the function, and then try to use it within a function.

```
function fn()
{
  echo 'inside the function, $var = '.$var.'<br />';
  $var = 'contents2';
  echo 'inside the function, $var = '.$var.'<br />';
}
$var = 'contents 1';
fn();
echo 'outside the function, $var = '.$var.'<br />';
```

The output from this code will be as follows:
```
inside the function, $var =
inside the function, $var = contents 2
outside the function, $var = contents 1
```

Functions are not executed until they are called, so the first statement executed is $var = 'contents 1';. This creates a variable called $var, with global scope and the contents "contents 1". The next statement executed is a call to the function fn(). The lines inside the statement are executed in order. The first line in the function refers to a variable named $var. When this line is executed, it cannot see the previous $var that we created, so it creates a new one with function scope and echoes it. This creates the first line of output.

The next line within the function sets the contents of $var to be "contents 2". Because we are inside the function, this line changes the value of the local $var, not the global one. The second line of output verifies that this change worked.

The function is now finished, so the final line of the script is executed. This echo statement demonstrates that the global variable's value has not changed.

If we want a variable created within a function to be global, we can use the keyword global as follows:

```
function fn()
{
  global $var;
  $var = 'contents';
  echo 'inside the function, $var = '.$var.'<br />';
}

fn();
echo 'outside the function, $var = '.$var.'<br />';
```

In this example, the variable $var was explicitly defined as global meaning that after the function is called, the variable will exist outside the function as well. The output from this script will be the following:

```
inside the function, $var = contents
outside the function, $var = contents
```

Note that the variable is in scope from the point in which the line `global $var;` is executed. We could have declared the function above or below where we call it. (Note that function scope is quite different from variable scope!) The location of the function declaration is inconsequential, what is important is where we call the function and therefore execute the code within it.

You can also use the `global` keyword at the top of a script when a variable is first used to declare that it should be in scope throughout the script. This is possibly a more common use of the `global` keyword.

You can see from the preceding examples that it is perfectly legal to reuse a variable name for a variable inside and outside a function without interference between the two. It is generally a bad idea however because without carefully reading the code and thinking about scope, people might assume that the variables are one and the same.

Pass by Reference Versus Pass by Value

If we want to write a function called `increment()` that allows us to increment a value, we might be tempted to try writing it as follows:

```
function increment($value, $amount = 1)
{
  $value = $value +$amount;
}
```

This code will be of no use. The output from the following test code will be "10".

```
$value = 10;
increment ($value);
echo $value;
```

The contents of `$value` have not changed.

This is because of the scope rules. This code creates a variable called `$value` which contains 10. It then calls the function `increment()`. The variable `$value` in the function is created when the function is called. One is added to it, so the value of `$value` is 11 inside the function, until the function ends, and we return to the code that called it. In this code, the variable `$value` is a different variable, with global scope, and therefore unchanged.

One way of overcoming this is to declare `$value` in the function as global, but this means that in order to use this function, the variable that we wanted to increment would need to be named `$value`. A better approach would be to use *pass by reference*.

The normal way that function parameters are called is called *pass by value*. When you pass a parameter, a new variable is created which contains the value passed in. It is a copy of the original. You are free to modify this value in any way, but the value of the original variable outside the function remains unchanged.

The better approach is to use *pass by reference*. Here, when a parameter is passed to a function, rather than creating a new variable, the function receives a reference to the original variable. This reference has a variable name, beginning with a dollar sign, and can be used in exactly the same way as another variable. The difference is that rather than having a value of its own, it merely refers to the original. Any modifications made to the reference also affect the original.

We specify that a parameter is to use pass by reference by placing an ampersand (&) before the parameter name in the function's definition. No change is required in the function call.

The preceding increment() example can be modified to have one parameter passed by reference, and it will work correctly.

```
function increment(&$value, $amount = 1)
{
   $value = $value +$amount;
}
```

We now have a working function, and are free to name the variable we want to increment anything we like. As already mentioned, it is confusing to humans to use the same name inside and outside a function, so we will give the variable in the main script a new name. The following test code will now echo 10 before the call to increment(), and 11 afterwards.

```
$a = 10;
echo $a.'<br />';
increment ($a);
echo $a.'<br />';
```

Returning from Functions

The keyword return stops the execution of a function. When a function ends because either all statements have been executed or the keyword return is used, execution returns to the statement after the function call.

If you call the following function, only the first echo statement will be executed.

```
function test_return()
{
   echo 'This statement will be executed';
   return;
   echo 'This statement will never be executed';
}
```

Obviously, this is not a very useful way to use return. Normally, you will only want to return from the middle of a function in response to a condition being met.

An error condition is a common reason to use a `return` statement to stop execution of a function before the end. If, for instance, you wrote a function to find out which of two numbers was greater, you might want to exit if any of the numbers were missing.

```
function larger( $x, $y )
{
  if (!isset($x)||!isset($y))
  {
    echo 'This function requires two numbers';
    return;
  }
  if ($x>=$y)
    echo $x;
  else
    echo $y;
  echo '<br />';
}
```

The built-in function `isset()` tells you whether a variable has been created and given a value. In this code, we are going to give an error message and return if either of the parameters has not been set with a value. We test this by using `!isset()`, meaning "NOT `isset()`," so the if statement can be read as "if x is not set or if y is not set". The function will return if either of these conditions is true.

If the `return` statement is executed, the subsequent lines of code in the function will be ignored. Program execution will return to the point at which the function was called. If both parameters are set, the function will echo the larger of the two.

The output from the following code:

```
$a = 1;
$b = 2.5;
$c = 1.9;
larger($a, $b);
larger($c, $a);
larger($d, $a);
```

will be as follows:
```
2.5
1.9
This function requires two numbers
```

Returning Values from Functions

Exiting from a function is not the only reason to use `return`. Many functions use `return` statements to communicate with the code that called them. Rather than echoing the result of the comparison in our `larger()` function, our function might have been more useful if we returned the answer. This way, the code that called the function can choose if and how to display or use it. The equivalent built-in function max() behaves in this way.

We can write our larger() function as follows:

```
function larger ($x, $y)
{
  if (!isset($x)||!isset($y))
    return false;
  else if ($x>=$y)
    return $x;
  else
    return $y;
}
```

Here we are returning the larger of the two values passed in. We will return an obviously different value in the case of an error. If one of the numbers is missing, we will return false. The only caveat with this approach is that programmers calling the function must test the return type with === to make sure that false is not confused with 0.

For comparison, the built-in function max() returns nothing if both variables are not set, and if only one was set, returns that one.

The following code:

```
$a = 1; $b = 2.5; $c = 1.9;
echo larger($a, $b)."<br />";
echo larger($c, $a)."<br />";
echo larger($d, $a)."<br />";
```

will produce this output because $d does not exist and *false* is not visible:

```
2.5
1.9
```

Functions that perform some task, but do not need to return a value, often return true or false to indicate if they succeeded or failed. The boolean values true and false can be represented with integer values 1 and 0 respectively, although they are of different types.

Code Blocks

We declare that a group of statements are a block by placing them within curly braces. This does not affect most of the operation of your code, but has specific implications including the way control structures such as loops and conditionals execute.

The following two examples work very differently:

Example Without Code Block

```
for($i = 0; $i < 3; $i++ )
  echo 'Line 1<br />';
echo 'Line 2<br />';
```

Example with Code Block

```
for($i = 0; $i < 3; $i++ )
{
  echo 'Line 1<br />';
  echo 'Line 2<br />';
}
```

In both examples, the `for` loop is iterated through three times. In the first example, only the single line directly below this is executed by the `for` loop. The output from this example is as follows:

```
Line 1
Line 1
Line 1
Line 2
```

The second example uses a code block to group two lines together. This means that both lines are executed three times by the `for` loop. The output from this example is as follows:

```
Line 1
Line 2
Line 1
Line 2
Line 1
Line 2
```

Because the code in these examples is properly indented, you can probably see the difference between them at a glance. The indenting of the code is intended to give readers a visual interpretation of what lines are affected by the `for` loop. However, note that spaces do not affect how PHP processes the code.

In some languages, code blocks affect variable scope. This is not the case in PHP.

Recursion

Recursive functions are supported in PHP. A *recursive function* is one that calls itself. These functions are particularly useful for navigating dynamic data structures such as linked lists and trees.

However, few Web-based applications require a data structure of this complexity, and so we have minimal use for recursion. Recursion can be used instead of iteration in many cases because both of these allow you to do something repetitively. Recursive functions are slower and use more memory than iteration, so you should use iteration wherever possible.

In the interest of completeness, we will look at a brief example shown in Listing 5.5.

Listing 5.5   **recursion.php—It Is Simple to Reverse a String Using Recursion—The Iterative Version Is Also Shown**

```php
function reverse_r($str)
{
    if (strlen($str)>0)
      reverse_r(substr($str, 1));
    echo substr($str, 0, 1);
    return;
}

function reverse_i($str)
{
    for ($i=1; $i<=strlen($str); $i++)
    {
      echo substr($str, -$i, 1);
    }
    return;
}
```

In this listing, we have implemented two functions. Both of these will print a string in reverse. The function `reverse_r()` is recursive, and the function `reverse_i()` is iterative.

The `reverse_r()` function takes a string as parameter. When you call it, it will proceed to call itself, each time passing the second to last characters of the string. For example, if you call

```php
reverse_r('Hello');
```

it will call itself a number of times, with the following parameters:

```php
reverse_r('ello');
reverse_r('llo');
reverse_r('lo');
reverse_r('o');
reverse_r('');
```

Each call the function makes to itself makes a new copy of the function code in the server's memory, but with a different parameter. It is like pretending that we are actually calling a different function each time. This stops the instances of the function from getting confused.

With each call, the length of the string passed in is tested. When we reach the end of the string (`strlen()==0`), the condition fails. The most recent instance of the function (reverse_r('')) will then go on and perform the next line of code, which is to echo the first character of the string it was passed—in this case, there is no character because the string is empty.

Next, this instance of the function returns control to the instance that called it, namely reverse_r('o'). This prints the first character in its string—"o"—and returns control to the instance that called it.

The process continues—printing a character and then returning to the instance of the function above it in the calling order—until control is returned back to the main program.

There is something very elegant and mathematical about recursive solutions. In most cases, however, you are better off using an iterative solution. The code for this is also in Listing 5.5. Note that it is no longer (although this is not always the case with iterative functions) and does exactly the same thing.

The main difference is that the recursive function will make copies of itself in memory and incurs the overhead of multiple function calls.

You might choose to use a recursive solution when the code is much shorter and more elegant than the iterative version, but it will not happen often in this application domain.

Although recursion appears more elegant, programmers often forget to supply a termination condition for the recursion. This means that the function will recur until the server runs out of memory, or until the maximum execution time is exceeded, whichever comes first.

Further Reading

The use of include(), require(), function, and return are also explained in the online manual. To find out more about concepts such as recursion, pass by value/reference, and scope that affect many languages, you can look at a general computer science text book, such as Dietel and Dietel's *C++ How To Program*.

Next

Now that you are using include files, require files, and functions to make your code more maintainable and reusable, the next chapter addresses object oriented software and the support offered in PHP. Using objects allows you to achieve goals similar to the concepts presented in this chapter, but with even greater advantages for complex projects.

## 6

Object-Oriented PHP

This chapter explains concepts of object-oriented development and shows how they can be implemented in PHP.

Key topics in this chapter include

- Object-oriented concepts
- Creating classes, attributes, and operations
- Using class attributes
- Calling class operations
- Inheritance
- Calling class methods
- Designing classes
- Writing the code for your class

Object-Oriented Concepts

Modern programming languages usually support or even require an object-oriented approach to software development. Object-oriented (OO) development attempts to use the classifications, relationships, and properties of the objects in the system to aid in program development.

Classes and Objects

In the context of OO software, an object can be almost any item or concept—a physical object such as a desk or a customer; or a conceptual object that only exists in software, such as a text input area or a file. Generally, we are most interested in conceptual objects including real world objects that need to be represented in software.

Object-oriented software is designed and built as a set of self-contained objects with both attributes and operations that interact to meet our needs. *Attributes* are properties or variables that relate to the object. *Operations* are methods, actions, or functions that the object can perform to either modify itself or for some external effect.

Object-oriented software's central advantage is its capability to support and encourage *encapsulation*—also known as data hiding. Essentially, access to the data within an object is only available via the object's operations, known as the *interface* of the object.

An object's functionality is bound to the data it uses. We can easily alter the details of how the object is implemented to improve performance, add new features, or fix bugs *without having to change the interface*, which can have ripple effects throughout the project.

In other areas of software development, OO is the norm and function oriented software is considered old fashioned. For a number of reasons, most Web scripts are unfortunately still designed and written using an *ad hoc* approach following a function oriented methodology.

A number of reasons for this exist. The majority of Web projects are relatively small and straightforward. You can get away with picking up a saw and building a wooden spice rack without planning your approach and you can successfully complete the majority of Web software projects in the same way because of their small size. However, if you picked up a saw and attempted to build a house without formal planning, you won't get quality results, if you get results at all—the same is true for large software projects.

Many Web projects evolve from a set of hyperlinked pages to a complex application. These complex applications, whether presented via dialog boxes and windows or via dynamically generated HTML pages, need a properly thought out development methodology. Object orientation can help you to manage the complexity in your projects, increase code reusability, and thereby reduce maintenance costs.

In OO software, an object is a unique and identifiable collection of stored data and operations that operate on that data. For instance, we might have two objects that represent buttons. Even if both have a label "OK", a width of 60 pixels, a height of 20 pixels, and any other attributes that are identical, we still need to be able to deal with one button or the other. In software, we have separate variables that act as *handles* (unique identifiers) for the objects.

Objects can be grouped into classes. Classes represent a set of objects that might vary from individual to individual, but must have a certain amount in common. A class contains objects that all have the same operations behaving in the same way and the same attributes representing the same things, although the values of those attributes will vary from object to object.

The noun bicycle can be thought of as a class of objects describing many distinct bicycles with many common features or *attributes*—such as two wheels, a color and a size, and operations, such as move.

My own bicycle can be thought of as an object that fits into the class bicycle. It has all the common features of all bicycles including a move operation that behaves the same as most other bicycles' move—even if it is used more rarely. My bicycle's attributes have unique values because my bicycle is green, and not all bicycles are that color.

Polymorphism

An object-oriented programming language must support *polymorphism*, which means that different classes can have different behaviors for the same operation. If for instance we have a class car and a class bicycle, both can have different move operations. For real-world objects, this would rarely be a problem. Bicycles are not likely to get confused and start using a car's move operation instead. However, a programming language does not possess the common sense of the real world, so the language must support polymorphism in order to know which move operation to use on a particular object.

Polymorphism is more a characteristic of behaviors than it is of objects. In PHP, only member functions of a class can be polymorphic. A real world comparison is that of verbs in natural languages, which are equivalent to member functions. Consider the ways a bicycle can be used in real life. You can clean it, move it, disassemble it, repair it, or paint it, among other things.

These verbs describe generic actions because you don't know what kind of object is being acted on. (This type of abstraction of objects and actions is one of the distinguishing characteristics of human intelligence.)

For example, moving a bicycle requires completely different actions from those required for moving a car, even though the concepts are similar. The verb *move* can be associated with a particular set of actions only once the object acted on is made known.

Inheritance

Inheritance allows us to create a hierarchical relationship between classes using *subclasses*. A subclass inherits attributes and operations from its *superclass*. For example, car and bicycle have some things in common. We could use a class vehicle to contain the things such as a color attribute and a move operation that all vehicles have, and then let our car and bicycle classes inherit from vehicle.

With inheritance, you can build on and add to existing classes. From a simple base class, you can derive more complex and specialized classes as the need arises. This makes your code more reusable, which is one of the important advantages of an object-oriented approach.

Using inheritance might save us work if operations can be written once in a superclass rather than many times in separate subclasses. It might also allow us to more accurately model real-world relationships. If a sentence about two classes makes sense with "is a" between the classes, inheritance is probably appropriate. The sentence "a car is a vehicle" makes sense, but the sentence "a vehicle is a car" does not make sense because not all vehicles are cars. Therefore, car can inherit from vehicle.

Creating Classes, Attributes, Operations in PHP

So far, we have discussed classes in a fairly abstract way. When creating a class in PHP, you must use the keyword `class`.

Structure of a Class

A minimal class definition looks as follows:

```
class classname
{
}
```

In order to be useful, our classes need attributes and operations. We create attributes by declaring variables within a class definition using the keyword var. The following code creates a class called classname with two attributes, $attribute1 and $attribute2.

```
class classname
{
  var $attribute1;
  var $attribute2;
}
```

We create operations by declaring functions within the class definition. The following code will create a class named classname with two operations that do nothing. The operation operation1() takes no parameters and operation2() takes two parameters.

```
class classname
{
  function operation1()
  {
  }
  function operation2($param1, $param2)
  {
  }
}
```

Constructors

Most classes will have a special type of operation called a *constructor*. A *constructor* is called when an object is created, and it also normally performs useful initialization tasks such as setting attributes to sensible starting values or creating other objects needed by this object.

A constructor is declared in the same way as other operations, but has the same name as the class. Though we can manually call the constructor, its main purpose is to be called automatically when an object is created. The following code declares a class with a constructor:

```
class classname
{
  function classname($param)
  {
    echo "Constructor called with parameter $param <br />";
  }
}
```

One thing to remember is that PHP does **not** natively support function overloading, which means that you can only provide one function with any particular name, including the constructor. (This is a feature supported in many OO languages.) There is an experimental extension, which is not terribly useful, that allows overloading of get and set methods.

Instantiation

After we have declared a class, we need to create an object—a particular individual that is a member of the class—to work with. This is also known as creating an instance or instantiating a class. We create an object using the new keyword. We need to specify what class our object will be an instance of, and provide any parameters required by our constructor.

The following code declares a class called classname with a constructor, and then creates three objects of type classname:

```
class classname
{
  function classname($param)
  {
    echo "Constructor called with parameter $param <br />";
  }
}

$a = new classname('First');
$b = new classname('Second');
$c = new classname();
```

Because the constructor is called each time we create an object, this code produces the following output:

```
Constructor called with parameter First
Constructor called with parameter Second
Constructor called with parameter
```

Using Class Attributes

Within a class, you have access to a special variable called $this. If an attribute of your current class is called $attribute, you refer to it as $this->attribute when either setting or accessing the variable from an operation within the class.

The following code demonstrates setting and accessing an attribute within a class:

```
class classname
{
  var $attribute;
  function operation($param)
  {
    $this->attribute = $param
    echo $this->attribute;
  }
}
```

Some programming languages allow you to limit access to attributes by declaring such data private or protected. This feature is not supported by PHP, so all your attributes and operations are visible outside the class (that is, they are all public).

We can perform the same task as previously demonstrated from outside the class, using slightly different syntax.

```
class classname
{
  var $attribute;
}
$a = new classname();
$a->attribute = 'value';
echo $a->attribute;
```

It is not a good idea to directly access attributes from outside a class. One of the advantages of an object-oriented approach is that it encourages encapsulation. Although you cannot **enforce** data hiding in PHP, with a little willpower, you can achieve the same advantages.

If rather than accessing the attributes of a class directly, you write *accessor functions*, you can make all your accesses through a single section of code. When you initially write your accessor functions, they might look as follows:

```
class classname
{
  var $attribute;
  function get_attribute()
  {
    return $this->attribute;
  }
  function set_attribute($new_value)
```

```
  {
    $this->attribute = $new_value;
  }
}
```

This code simply provides functions to access the attribute named $attribute. We have a function named get_attribute() which simply returns the value of $attribute, and a function named set_attribute() which assigns a new value to $attribute.

At first glance, this code might seem to add little or no value. In its present form this is probably true, but the reason for providing accessor functions is simple: We will then have only one section of code that accesses that particular attribute.

With only a single access point, we can implement checks to make sure that only sensible data is being stored. If it occurs to us later that the value of $attribute should only be between zero and one hundred, we can add a few lines of code **once** and check before allowing changes. Our set_attribute() function could be changed to look as follows:

```
function set_attribute($new_value)
{
  if( $new_value >= 0 && $newvalue <= 100 )
    $this->attribute = $new_value;
}
```

This change is trivial, but had we not used an accessor function, we would have to search through every line of code and modify every access to $attribute, a tedious and error-prone exercise.

With only a single access point, we are free to change the underlying implementation. If for some reason, we choose to change the way $attribute is stored, accessor functions allow us to do this and only change the code in one place.

We might decide that rather than storing $attribute as a variable, we will only retrieve it from a database when needed, calculate an up-to-date value every time it is requested, infer a value from the values of other attributes, or encode our data as a smaller data type. Whatever change we decide to make, we can simply modify our accessor functions. Other sections of code will not be affected as long as we make the accessor functions still accept or return the data that other parts of the program expect.

Calling Class Operations

We can call class operations in much the same way that we call class attributes. If we have the following class:

```
class classname
{
  function operation1()
  {
```

```
    }
    function operation2($param1, $param2)
    {
    }
}
```

and create a object of type `classname` called $a as follows:

```
$a = new classname();
```

We then call operations the same way that we call other functions: by using their name and placing any parameters that they need in brackets. Because these operations belong to an object rather than normal functions, we need to specify to which object they belong. The object name is used in the same way as an object's attributes as follows:

```
$a->operation1();
$a->operation2(12, 'test');
```

If our operations return something, we can capture that return data as follows:

```
$x = $a->operation1();
$y = $a->operation2(12, 'test');
```

Implementing Inheritance in PHP

If our class is to be a subclass of another, you can use the `extends` keyword to specify this. The following code creates a class named B that inherits from some previously defined class named A.

```
class B extends A
{
  var $attribute2;
  function operation2()
  {
  }
}
```

If the class A was declared as follows:

```
class A
{
  var $attribute1;
  function operation1()
  {
  }
}
```

all the following accesses to operations and attributes of an object of type B would be valid:

```
$b = new B();
$b->operation1();
$b->attribute1 = 10;
$b->operation2();
$b->attribute2 = 10;
```

Note that because class B extends class A, we can refer to operation1() and $attribute1, although these were declared in class A. As a subclass of A, B has all the same functionality and data. In addition, B has declared an attribute and an operation of its own.

It is important to note that inheritance only works in one direction. The subclass or child inherits features from its parent or superclass, but the parent does not take on features of the child. This means that the last two lines in this code are wrong:

```
$a = new A();
$a->operation1();
$a->attribute1 = 10;
$a->operation2();
$a->attribute2 = 10;
```

The class A does not have an operation2() or an attribute2.

Overriding

We have shown a subclass declaring new attributes and operations. It is also valid and sometimes useful to redeclare the same attributes and operations. We might do this to give an attribute in the subclass a different default value to the same attribute in its superclass, or to give an operation in the subclass different functionality to the same operation in its superclass. This is called *overriding*.

For instance, if we have a class A:

```
class A
{
  var $attribute = 'default value';
  function operation()
  {
    echo 'Something<br />';
    echo "The value of \$attribute is $this->attribute<br />";
  }
}
```

and want to alter the default value of $attribute and provide new functionality for operation(), we can create the following class B, which overrides $attribute and operation():

```
class B extends A
{
  var $attribute = 'different value';
```

```
   function operation()
   {
     echo 'Something else<br />';
     echo "The value of \$attribute is $this->attribute<br />";
   }
}
```

Declaring B does not affect the original definition of A. Consider the following two lines
of code:

```
$a = new A();
$a -> operation();
```

We have created an object of type A and called its operation() function. This will produce

```
Something
The value of $attribute is default value
```

proving that creating B has not altered A. If we create an object of type B, we will get different output.

This code

```
$b = new B();
$b -> operation();
```

will produce

```
Something else
The value of $attribute is different value
```

In the same way that providing new attributes or operations in a subclass does not affect
the superclass, overriding attributes or operations in a subclass does not affect the superclass.

A subclass will inherit all the attributes and operations of its superclass, unless you
provide replacements. If you provide a replacement definition, this takes precedence and
overrides the original definition.

Unlike some other OO languages, PHP does not allow you to override a function
and still be able to call the version defined in the parent.

Inheritance can be many layers deep. We can declare a class imaginatively called C,
that extends B and therefore inherits features from B and from B's parent A. The class C
can again choose which attributes and operations from its parents to override and
replace.

Multiple Inheritance

Some OO languages support multiple inheritance, but PHP does not. This means that
each class can only inherit from one parent. No restrictions exist for how many children
can share a single parent.

It might not seem immediately clear what this means. Figure 6.1 shows three different ways that three classes named A, B, and C can inherit.

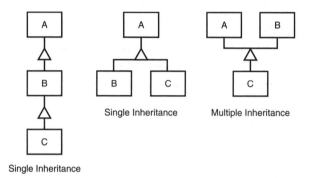

Figure 6.1   PHP does not support multiple inheritance.

The left combination shows class C inheriting from class B, which in turn inherits from class A. Each class has at most one parent, so this is a perfectly valid single inheritance in PHP.

The center combination shows class B and C inheriting from class A. Each class has at most one parent, so again this is a valid single inheritance.

The right combination shows class C inheriting from both class A and class B. In this case, class C has two parents, so this is multiple inheritance and is invalid in PHP.

Designing Classes

Now that you know some of the concepts behind objects and classes and the syntax to implement them in PHP, it is time to look at how to design useful classes.

Many classes in your code will represent classes or categories of real-world objects. Classes you might use in Web development might include pages, user interface components, shopping carts, error handling, product categories, or customers.

Objects in your code can also represent specific instances of the previously mentioned classes, for example, the home page, a particular button, or the shopping cart in use by Fred Smith at a particular time. Fred Smith himself can be represented by an object of type customer. Each item that Fred purchases can be represented as an object, belonging to a category or class.

In the previous chapter, we used simple include files to give our fictional company, TLA Consulting, a consistent look and feel across the different pages of their Web site. Using classes and the timesaving power of inheritance, we can create a more advanced version of the same site.

We want to be able to quickly create pages for TLA that look and behave in the same way. Those pages should be able to be modified to suit the different parts of the site.

We are going to create a `Page` class. The main goal of this class is to limit the amount of HTML needed to create a new page. It should allow us to alter the parts that change from page to page, while automatically generating the elements that stay the same.

The class should provide a flexible framework for creating new pages and should not compromise our freedom.

Because we are generating our page from a script rather than with static HTML, we can add any number of clever things including functionality to enable the following:

- Enable us to only alter page elements in one place. If we change the copyright notice or add an extra button, we should only need to make the change in a single place.
- Have default content for most parts of the page, but be able to modify each element where required, setting custom values for elements such as the title and metatags.
- Recognize which page is being viewed and alter navigation elements to suit— there is no point in having a button that takes you to the home page located on the home page.
- Allow us to replace standard elements for particular pages. If for instance, we want different navigation buttons in sections of the site, we should be able to replace the standard ones.

Writing the Code for Your Class

Having decided what we want the output from our code to look like, and a few features we would like for it, how do we implement it?

We will talk later in the book about design and project management for large projects. For now, we will concentrate on the parts specific to writing object-oriented PHP.

Our class will need a logical name. Because it represents a page, it will be called `Page`. To declare a class called `Page`, we type

```
class Page
{
}
```

Our class needs some attributes. We will set elements that we might want changed from page to page as attributes of our class. The main contents of the page, which will be a combination of HTML tags and text, will be called `$content`. We can declare the content with the following line of code within the class definition:

```
var $content;
```

We can also set attributes to store the page's title. We will probably want to change this to clearly show what particular page our visitor is looking at. Rather than have blank titles, we will provide a default title with the following declaration:

```
var $title = 'TLA Consulting Pty Ltd';
```

Most commercial Web pages include metatags to help search engines index them. In order to be useful, metatags should probably change from page to page. Again, we will provide a default value:

```
var $keywords = 'TLA Consulting, Three Letter Abbreviation,
                 some of my best friends are search engines';
```

The navigation buttons shown on the original page in Figure 5.2 (see the previous chapter) should probably be kept the same from page to page to avoid confusing people, but in order to change them easily, we will make them an attribute too. Because there might be a variable number of buttons, we will use an array, and store both the text for the button and the URL it should point to.

```
var $buttons = array( 'Home'     => 'home.php',
                      'Contact'  => 'contact.php',
                      'Services' => 'services.php',
                      'Site Map' => 'map.php'
                    );
```

In order to provide some functionality, our class will also need operations. We can start by providing accessor functions to set and get the values of the attributes we defined. These all take a form like this:

```
function SetContent($newcontent)
{
  $this->content = $newcontent;
}
```

Because it is unlikely that we will be requesting any of these values from outside the class, we have elected not to provide a matching collection of Get functions.

The main purpose of this class is to display a page of HTML, so we will need a function. We have called ours Display(), and it is as follows:

```
function Display()
  {
    echo "<html>\n<head>\n";
    $this -> DisplayTitle();
    $this -> DisplayKeywords();
    $this -> DisplayStyles();
    echo "</head>\n<body>\n";
    $this -> DisplayHeader();
    $this -> DisplayMenu($this->buttons);
    echo $this->content;
    $this -> DisplayFooter();
    echo "</body>\n</html>\n";
  }
```

The function includes a few simple echo statements to display HTML, but mainly consists of calls to other functions in the class. As you have probably guessed from their names, these other functions display parts of the page.

It is not compulsory to break functions up like this. All these separate functions might simply have been combined into one big function. We separated them out for a number of reasons.

Each function should have a defined task to perform. The simpler this task is, the easier writing and testing the function will be. Don't go too far—if you break your program up into too many small units, it might be hard to read.

Using inheritance, we can override operations. We can replace one large Display() function, but it is unlikely that we will want to change the way the entire page is displayed. It will be much better to break up the display functionality into a few self-contained tasks and be able to override only the parts that we want to change.

Our Display function calls DisplayTitle(), DisplayKeywords(), DisplayStyles(), DisplayHeader(), DisplayMenu(), and DisplayFooter(). This means that we need to define these operations. One of the improvements of PHP 4 over PHP 3 is that we can write operations or functions in this logical order, calling the operation or function before the actual code for the function. In PHP 3 and many other languages, we need to write the function or operation before it can be called.

Most of our operations are fairly simple and need to display some HTML and perhaps the contents of our attributes.

Listing 6.1 shows the complete class, which we have saved as page.inc to include or require into other files.

Listing 6.1   **page.inc—Our Page Class Provides an Easy Flexible Way to Create TLA Pages**

```php
<?php
class Page
{
  // class Page's attributes
  var $content;
  var $title = 'TLA Consulting Pty Ltd';
  var $keywords = 'TLA Consulting, Three Letter Abbreviation,
                   some of my best friends are search engines';
  var $buttons = array( 'Home'     => 'home.php',
                        'Contact'  => 'contact.php',
                        'Services' => 'services.php',
                        'Site Map' => 'map.php'
                      );

  // class Page's operations

  function SetContent($newcontent)
  {
```

Listing 6.1   **Continued**

```php
    $this->content = $newcontent;
  }

  function SetTitle($newtitle)
  {
    $this->title = $newtitle;
  }

  function SetKeywords($newkeywords)
  {
    $this->keywords = $newkeywords;
  }

  function SetButtons($newbuttons)
  {
    $this->buttons = $newbuttons;
  }

  function Display()
  {
    echo "<html>\n<head>\n";
    $this -> DisplayTitle();
    $this -> DisplayKeywords();
    $this -> DisplayStyles();
    echo "</head>\n<body>\n";
    $this -> DisplayHeader();
    $this -> DisplayMenu($this->buttons);
    echo $this->content;
    $this -> DisplayFooter();
    echo "</body>\n</html>\n";
  }

  function DisplayTitle()
  {
    echo '<title> $this->title </title>';
  }

  function DisplayKeywords()
  {
    echo "<META name=\"keywords\" content=\"$this->keywords\">";
  }

  function DisplayStyles()
  {
?>
```

Listing 6.1   **Continued**

```php
<style>
   h1 {color:white; font-size:24pt; text-align:center;
       font-family:arial,sans-serif}
   .menu {color:white; font-size:12pt; text-align:center;
          font-family:arial,sans-serif; font-weight:bold}
   td {background:black}
   p {color:black; font-size:12pt; text-align:justify;
      font-family:arial,sans-serif}
   p.foot {color:white; font-size:9pt; text-align:center;
           font-family:arial,sans-serif; font-weight:bold}
   a:link,a:visited,a:active {color:white}
</style>
<?php
   }

   function DisplayHeader()
   {
?>
   <table width="100%" cellpadding ="12" cellspacing ="0" border ="0">
   <tr bgcolor ="black">
     <td align ="left"><img src = "logo.gif"></td>
     <td>
         <h1>TLA Consulting Pty Ltd</h1>
     </td>
     <td align ="right"><img src = "logo.gif"></td>
   </tr>
   </table>
<?php
   }

   function DisplayMenu($buttons)
   {
     echo "<table width='100%' bgcolor='white' cellpadding='4'
                 cellspacing='4'\n";
     echo "   <tr>\n";

     //calculate button size
     $width = 100/count($buttons);

     while (list($name, $url) = each($buttons))
     {
       $this -> DisplayButton($width, $name, $url, !$this->IsURLCurrentPage($url));
     }
     echo "   </tr>\n";
     echo "</table>\n";
   }
```

Listing 6.1   **Continued**

```php
  function IsURLCurrentPage($url)
  {
    if(strpos( $GLOBALS['SCRIPT_NAME'], $url )==false)
    {
      return false;
    }
    else
    {
      return true;
    }
  }

  function DisplayButton($width, $name, $url, $active = true)
  {
    if ($active)
    {
      echo "<td width ='$width%'>
            <a href ='$url'>
            <img src ='s-logo.gif' alt ='$name' border ='0'></a>
            <a href ='$url'><span class='menu'>$name</span></a></td>";
    }
    else
    {
      echo "<td width ='$width%'>
            <img src ='side-logo.gif'>
            <span class='menu'>$name</span></td>";
    }
  }

  function DisplayFooter()
  {
?>
    <table width = "100%" bgcolor ="black" cellpadding ="12" border ="0">
    <tr>
      <td>
        <p class="foot">&copy; TLA Consulting Pty Ltd.</p>
        <p class="foot">Please see our
                  <a href ="">legal information page</a></p>
      </td>
    </tr>
    </table>
<?php
  }
}
?>
```

When reading it, note that `DisplayStyles()`, `DisplayHeader()`, and `DisplayFooter()` need to display a large block of static HTML, with no PHP processing. Therefore, we have simply used an end PHP tag (`?>`), typed our HTML, and then re-entered PHP with an open PHP tag (`<?php`) while inside the functions.

Two other operations are defined in this class. The operation `DisplayButton()` outputs a single menu button. If the button is to point to the page we are on, we are displaying an inactive button instead, which looks slightly different, and does not link anywhere. This keeps the page layout consistent and provides visitors with a visual location.

The operation `IsURLCurrentPage()` determines if the URL for a button points to the current page. Lots of techniques can be used to discover this. We have used the string function `strpos()` to see if the URL given is contained in one of the server set variables. The statement `strpos( $GLOBALS['SCRIPT_NAME'], $url )` will either return a number if the string in `$url` is inside the global variable `SCRIPT_NAME`, or false if it is not.

To use this page class, we need to include `page.inc` in a script and call `Display()`.

The code in Listing 6.2 will create TLA Consulting's home page and give output very similar to that we previously generated in Figure 5.2.

The code in Listing 6.2 does the following:

1. Uses `require` to include the contents of `page.inc`, which contains the definition of the class Page.

2. Creates an instance of the class Page. The instance is called `$homepage`.

3. Calls the operation `SetContent()` within the object `$homepage` and passes some text and HTML tags to appear in the page.

4. Calls the operation `Display()` within the object `$homepage` to cause the page to be displayed in the visitor's browser.

Listing 6.2 **home.php—This Home Page Uses the Page Class to Do Most of the Work Involved in Generating the Page**

```php
<?php
  require ('page.inc');

  $homepage = new Page();

  $homepage -> SetContent('<p>Welcome to the home of TLA Consulting.
                           Please take some time to get to know us.</p>
                           <p>We specialize in serving your business needs
                           and hope to hear from you soon.</p>'
                          );
  $homepage -> Display();
?>
```

You can see in Listing 6.2 that we need to do very little work to generate new pages using this Page class. Using the class in this way means that all our pages need to be very similar.

If we want some sections of the site to use a variant of the standard page, we could simply copy page.inc to a new file called page2.inc and make some changes. This would mean that every time we updated or fixed parts of page.inc, we would need to remember to make the same changes to page2.inc.

A better course of action is to use inheritance to create a new class that inherits most of its functionality from Page, but overrides the parts that need to be different.

For the TLA site, we want to require that the services page include a second navigation bar.

The script shown in Listing 6.3 does this by creating a new class called ServicesPage which inherits from Page. We provide a new array called $row2buttons that contains the buttons and links we want in the second row. Because we want this class to behave in mostly the same ways, we only override the part we want changed—the Display() operation.

Listing 6.3   services.php—The Services Page Inherits from the Page Class but Overrides Display() to Alter the Output

```php
<?php
  require ('page.inc');

  class ServicesPage extends Page
  {
    var $row2buttons = array( 'Re-engineering' => 'reengineering.php',
                              'Standards Compliance' => 'standards.php',
                              'Buzzword Compliance' => 'buzzword.php',
                              'Mission Statements' => 'mission.php'
                            );
    function Display()
    {
      echo "<html>\n<head>\n";
      $this -> DisplayTitle();
      $this -> DisplayKeywords();
      $this -> DisplayStyles();
      echo "</head>\n<body>\n";
      $this -> DisplayHeader();
      $this -> DisplayMenu($this->buttons);
      $this -> DisplayMenu($this->row2buttons);
      echo $this->content;
      $this -> DisplayFooter();
      echo "</body>\n</html>\n";
    }
  }
```

Listing 6.3 **Continued**

```
$services = new ServicesPage();
$content ='<p>At TLA Consulting, we offer a number of services.
           Perhaps the productivity of your employees would
           improve if we re-engineered your business.
           Maybe all your business needs is a fresh mission
           statement, or a new batch of buzzwords.</p>';
$services -> SetContent($content);
$services -> Display();
?>
```

Our overriding `Display()` is very similar, but contains one extra line

```
$this -> DisplayMenu($this->row2buttons);
```

to call `DisplayMenu()` a second time and create a second menu bar.

Outside the class definition, we create an instance of our `ServicesPage` class, set the values for which we want non-default values and call `Display()`.

As shown in Figure 6.2, we have a new variant of our standard page. The only new code we needed to write was for the parts that were different.

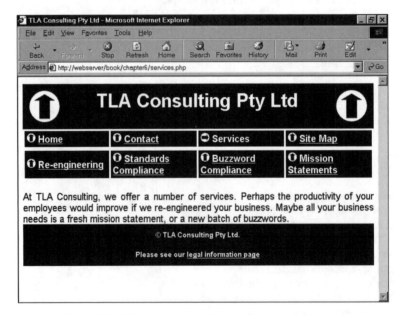

Figure 6.2   The services page is created using inheritance
to reuse most of our standard page.

to reuse most of our standard page.

Creating pages via PHP classes has obvious advantages. With a class to do most of the work for us, we needed to do less work to create a new page. We can update all our pages at once by simply updating the class. Using inheritance, we can derive different versions of the class from our original without compromising the advantages.

As with most things in life, these advantages do not come without cost.

Creating pages from a script requires more computer processor effort than simply loading a static HTML page from disk and sending it to a browser. On a busy site this will be important, and you should make an effort to either use static HTML pages or cache the output of your scripts where possible to reduce the load on the server.

Next

The next section deals with MySQL. We'll talk about how to create and populate a MySQL database, and then link what we've learned to PHP so that you can access your database from the Web.

II

Using MySQL

7

Designing Your Web Database

Now that you are familiar with the basics of PHP, we'll begin looking at integrating a database into your scripts. As you might recall, in Chapter 2, "Storing and Retrieving Data," we talked about the advantages of using a relational database instead of a flat file. They include

- RDBMSs can provide faster access to data than flat files.
- RDBMSs can be easily queried to extract sets of data that fit certain criteria.
- RDBMSs have built-in mechanisms for dealing with concurrent access so that you as a programmer don't have to worry about it.
- RDBMSs provide random access to your data.
- RDBMSs have built-in privilege systems.

In more concrete terms, using a relational database allows you to quickly and easily answer queries about where your customers are from, which of your products is selling the best, or what type of customers spend the most. This information can help you improve the site to attract and keep more users. The database that we will use in this section is MySQL. Before we get into MySQL specifics in the next chapter, we need to discuss

- Relational database concepts and terminology
- Web database design
- Web database architecture

Following chapters cover

- Chapter 8, "Creating Your Web Database," covers the basic configuration you will need in order to connect your MySQL database to the Web.
- Chapter 9, "Working with Your MySQL Database," explains how to query the database and add and delete records, all from the command line.

- Chapter 10, "Accessing Your MySQL Database from the Web with PHP," explains how to connect PHP and MySQL together so that you can use and administer your database from a Web interface.
- Chapter 11, "Advanced MySQL," covers some of the advanced features of MySQL that can come in handy when developing more demanding Web-based applications.

Relational Database Concepts

Relational databases are, by far, the most commonly used type of database. They depend on a sound theoretical basis in relational algebra. You don't need to understand relational theory to use a relational database (which is a good thing), but you do need to understand some basic database concepts.

Tables

Relational databases are made up of relations, more commonly called tables. A table is exactly what it sounds like—a table of data. If you've used an electronic spreadsheet, you've already used a relational table.

Let's look at an example.

In Figure 7.1, you can see a sample table. This contains the names and addresses of the customers of a bookstore, Book-O-Rama.

CUSTOMERS

CustomerID	Name	Address	City
1	Julie Smith	25 Oak Street	Airport West
2	Alan Wong	1/47 Haines Avenue	Box Hill
3	Michelle Arthur	357 North Road	Yarraville

Figure 7.1 Book-O-Rama's customer details are stored in a table.

The table has a name (Customers), a number of columns, each corresponding to a different piece of data, and rows that correspond to individual customers.

Columns

Each column in the table has a unique name and contains different data. Each column has an associated data type. For instance, in the Customers table in Figure 7.1, you can see that CustomerID is an integer and the other three columns are strings. Columns are sometimes called fields or attributes.

Rows

Each row in the table represents a different customer. Because of the tabular format, they all have the same attributes. Rows are also called records or tuples.

Values

Each row consists of a set of individual values that correspond to columns. Each value must have the data type specified by its column.

Keys

We need to have a way of identifying each specific customer. Names usually aren't a very good way of doing this—if you have a common name, you'll probably understand why. Take Julie Smith from the Customers table for example. If I open my telephone directory, there are too many listings of that name to count.

We could distinguish Julie in several ways. Chances are, she's the only Julie Smith living at her address. Talking about "Julie Smith, of 25 Oak Street, Airport West" is pretty cumbersome and sounds too much like legalese. It also requires using more than one column in the table.

What we have done in this example, and what you will likely do in your applications, is assign a unique CustomerID. This is the same principle that leads to you having a unique bank account number or club membership number. It makes storing your details in a database easier. An artificially assigned identification number can be guaranteed to be unique. Few pieces of real information, even if used in combination, have this property.

The identifying column in a table is called the *key* or the *primary key*. A key can also consist of multiple columns. If for example, we had chosen to refer to Julie as "Julie Smith, of 25 Oak Street, Airport West," the key would consist of the Name, Address, and City columns and could not be guaranteed to be unique.

Databases usually consist of multiple tables and use a key as a reference from one table to another. In Figure 7.2, we've added a second table to the database. This one stores orders placed by customers. Each row in the Orders table represents a single order, placed by a single customer. We know who the customer is because we store their CustomerID. We can look at the order with OrderID 2, for example, and see that the customer with CustomerID 1 placed it. If you then look at the Customers table, you can see that CustomerID 1 refers to Julie Smith.

The relational database term for this relationship is *foreign key*. CustomerID is the primary key in Customers, but when it appears in another table, such as Orders, it is referred to as a foreign key.

You might wonder why we chose to have two separate tables—why not just store Julie's address in the Orders table? We'll explore this in more detail in the next section.

CUSTOMERS

CustomerID	Name	Address	City
1	Julie Smith	25 Oak Street	Airport West
2	Alan Wong	1/47 Haines Avenue	Box Hill
3	Michelle Arthur	357 North Road	Yarraville

ORDERS

OrderID	CustomerID	Amount	Date
1	3	27.50	02-Apr-2000
2	1	12.99	15-Apr-2000
3	2	74.00	19-Apr-2000
4	4	6.99	01-May-2000

Figure 7.2   Each order in the Orders table refers to a
customer from the Customers table.

Schemas

The complete set of the table designs for a database is called the database *schema*. It is
akin to a blueprint for the database. A schema should show the tables along with their
columns, the data types of the columns and indicate the primary key of each table and
any foreign keys. A schema does not include any data, but you might want to show sample data with your schema to explain what it is for. The schema can be shown as it is in
the diagrams we are using, in entity relationship diagrams (which are not covered in this
book), or in a text form, such as

Customers(CustomerID, Name, Address, City)

Orders(OrderID, CustomerID, Amount, Date)

Underlined terms in the schema are primary keys in the relation in which they are
underlined. Dotted underlined terms are foreign keys in the relation in which they
appear with a dotted underline.

Relationships

Foreign keys represent a relationship between data in two tables. For example, the link
from Orders to Customers represents a relationship between a row in the Orders table
and a row in the Customers table.

Three basic kinds of relationships exist in a relational database. They are classified
according to the number of things on each side of the relationship. Relationships can be
either one-to-one, one-to-many, or many-to-many.

A one-to-one relationship means that there is one of each thing in the relationship.
For example, if we had put addresses in a separate table from Customers, there would be
a one-to-one relationship between them. You could have a foreign key from Addresses to
Customer or the other way around (both are not required).

In a one-to-many relationship, one row in one table is linked to many rows in another table. In this example, one Customer might place many Orders. In these relationships, the table that contains the many rows will have a foreign key to the table with the one row. Here, we have put the CustomerID into the Order table to show the relationship.

In a many-to-many relationship, many rows in one table are linked to many rows in another table. For example, if we had two tables, Books and Authors, you might find that one book had been written by two coauthors, each of whom had written other books, on their own or possibly with other authors. This type of relationship usually gets a table all to itself, so you might have Books, Authors, and Books_Authors. This third table would only contain the keys of the other tables as foreign keys in pairs, to show which authors have been involved with which books.

How to Design Your Web Database

Knowing when you need a new table and what the key should be can be something of an art. You can read huge reams of information about entity relationship diagrams and database normalization, which are beyond the scope of this book. Most of the time, however, you can follow a few basic design principles. Let's consider these in the context of Book-O-Rama.

Think About the Real World Objects You Are Modeling

When you create a database, you are usually modeling real-world items and relationships and storing information about those objects and relationships.

Generally, each class of real-world objects you model will need its own table. Think about it: We want to store the same information about all our customers. If there is a set of data that has the same "shape," we can easily create a table corresponding to that data.

In the Book-O-Rama example, we want to store information about our customers, the books that we sell, and details of the orders. The customers all have a name and address. The orders have a date, a total amount, and a set of books that were ordered. The books have an ISBN, an author, a title, and a price.

This suggests we need at least three tables in this database: Customers, Orders, and Books. This initial schema is shown in Figure 7.3.

At present, we can't tell from the model which books were ordered in each order. We will deal with this in a minute.

Avoid Storing Redundant Data

Earlier, we asked the question: "Why not just store Julie Smith's address in the Orders table?"

If Julie orders from Book-O-Rama on a number of occasions, which we hope she will, we will end up storing her data multiple times. You might end up with an Orders table that looks like the one shown in Figure 7.4.

CUSTOMERS

CustomerID	Name	Address	City
1	Julie Smith	25 Oak Street	Airport West
2	Alan Wong	1/47 Haines Avenue	Box Hill
3	Michelle Arthur	357 North Road	Yarraville

ORDERS

OrderID	CustomerID	Amount	Date
1	3	27.50	02-Apr-2000
2	1	12.99	15-Apr-2000
3	2	74.00	19-Apr-2000
4	4	6.99	01-May-2000

BOOKS

ISBN	Author	Title	Price
0-672-31687-8	Michael Morgan	Java 2 for Professional Developers	34.99
0-672-31745-1	Thomas Down	Installing Debian GNU/Linux	24.99
0-672-31509-2	Pruitt, et al.	Teach Yourself GIMP in 24 Hours	24.99

Figure 7.3   The initial schema consists of Customers, Orders, and Books.

ORDERS

OrderID	Amount	Date	CustomerID	Name	Address	City
12	199.50	25-Apr-2000	1	Julie Smith	28 Oak Street	Airport West
13	43.00	29-Apr-2000	1	Julie Smith	28 Oak Street	Airport West
14	15.99	30-Apr-2000	1	Julie Smith	28 Oak Street	Airport West
15	23.75	01-May-2000	1	Julie Smith	28 Oak Street	Airport West

Figure 7.4   A database design that stores redundant data takes up
extra space and can cause anomalies in the data.

There are two basic problems with this.

The first is that it's a waste of space. Why store Julie's details three times if we only have to store them once?

The second problem is that it can lead to *update anomalies*, that is, situations where we change the database and end up with inconsistent data. The integrity of the data is violated and we no longer know which data is correct and which incorrect. This generally leads to losing information.

Three kinds of update anomalies need to be avoided: modification, insertion, and deletion anomalies.

If Julie moves to a new house while she has pending orders, we will need to update her address in three places instead of one, doing three times as much work. It is easy to overlook this fact and only change her address in one place, leading to inconsistent data in the database (a very bad thing). These problems are called *modification anomalies* because they occur when we are trying to modify the database.

With this design, we need to insert Julie's details every time we take an order, so each time we must check and make sure that her details are consistent with the existing rows in the table. If we don't check, we might end up with two rows of conflicting information about Julie. For example, one row might tell us that Julie lives in Airport West, and another might tell us she lives in Airport. This is called an *insertion anomaly* because it occurs when data is being inserted.

The third kind of anomaly is called a *deletion anomaly* because it occurs (surprise, surprise) when we are deleting rows from the database. For example, imagine that when an order has been shipped, we delete it from the database. When all Julie's current orders have been fulfilled, they are all deleted from the Orders table. This means that we no longer have a record of Julie's address. We can't send her any special offers, and next time she wants to order something from us, we will have to get her details all over again.

Generally you want to design your database so that none of these anomalies occur.

Use Atomic Column Values

This means that in each attribute in each row, we store only one thing. For example, we need to know what books make up each order. There are several ways we could do this. We could add a column to the Orders table which lists all the books that have been ordered, as shown in Figure 7.5.

ORDERS

OrderID	CustomerID	Amount	Date	Books Ordered
1	3	27.50	02-Apr-2000	0-672-31697-8
2	1	12.99	15-Apr-2000	0-672-31745-1, 0-672-31509-2
3	2	74.00	19-Apr-2000	0-672-31697-8
4	3	6.99	01-May-2000	0-672-31745-1, 0-672-31509-2, 0-672-31697-8

Figure 7.5   With this design, the Books Ordered
attribute in each row has multiple values.

This isn't a good idea for a few reasons. What we're really doing is nesting a whole table inside one column—a table that relates orders to books. When you do it this way, it becomes more difficult to answer questions like "How many copies of *Java 2 for Professional Developers* have been ordered?" The system can no longer just count the matching fields. Instead, it has to parse each attribute value to see if it contains a match anywhere inside it.

Because we're really creating a table-inside-a-table, we should really just create that new table. This new table is called Order_Items and is shown in Figure 7.6.

ORDER_ITEMS

OrderID	ISBN	Quantity
1	0-672-31697-8	1
2	0-672-31745-1	2
2	0-672-31509-2	1
3	0-672-31697-8	1
4	0-672-31745-1	1
4	0-672-31509-2	2
4	0-672-31697-8	1

Figure 7.6   This design makes it easier to search for particular books that have been ordered.

This table provides a link between the Orders table and the Books table. This type of table is common when there is a many-to-many relationship between two objects—in this case, one order might consist of many books, and each book can be ordered by many people.

Choose Sensible Keys

Make sure that the keys you choose are unique. In this case, we've created a special key for customers (CustomerID) and for orders (OrderID) because these real-world objects might not naturally have an identifier that can be guaranteed to be unique. We don't need to create a unique identifier for books—this has already been done, in the form of an ISBN. For Order_Item, you can add an extra key if you want, but the combination of the two attributes OrderID and ISBN will be unique as long as more than one copy of the same book in an order is treated as one row. For this reason, the table Order_Items has a Quantity column.

Think About the Questions You Want to Ask the Database

Continuing from the last section, think about what questions you want the database to answer. (Think back to those questions we mentioned at the start of the chapter. For example, what are Book-O-Rama's bestselling books?) Make sure that the database contains all the data required, and that the appropriate links exist between tables to answer the questions you have.

Avoid Designs with Many Empty Attributes

If we wanted to add book reviews to the database, there are at least two ways we could do this. These two approaches are shown in Figure 7.7.

The first way means adding a Review column to the Books table. This way, there is a field for the Review to be added for each book. If many books are in the database, and the reviewer doesn't plan to review them all, many rows won't have a value in this attribute. This is called having a null value.

BOOKS

ISBN	Author	Title	Price	Review
0-672-31687-8	Michael Morgan	Java 2 for Professional Developers	34.99	
0-672-31745-1	Thomas Down	Installing Debian GNU/Linux	24.99	
0-672-31509-2	Pruitt, et al.	Teach Yourself GIMP in 24 Hours	24.99	

BOOK_REVIEWS

ISBN	Review

Figure 7.7   To add reviews, we can either add a Reviews column to the Books table, or add a table specifically for reviews.

Having many null values in your database is a bad idea. It wastes storage space and causes problems when working out totals and other functions on numerical columns. When a user sees a null in a table, they don't know if it's because this attribute is irrelevant, whether there's a mistake in the database, or whether the data just hasn't been entered yet.

You can generally avoid problems with many nulls by using an alternate design. In this case, we can use the second design proposed in Figure 7.7. Here, only books with a review are listed in the Book_Reviews table, along with their review.

Note that this design is based on the idea of having a single in-house reviewer. We could just as easily let customers author reviews. If we wanted to do this, we could add the CustomerID to the Book_Reviews table.

Summary of Table Types

You will usually find that your database design ends up consisting of two kinds of tables:

- Simple tables that describe a real world object. These might also contain keys to other simple objects where there is a one-to-one or one-to-many relationship. For example, one customer might have many orders, but an order is placed by a single customer. Thus, we put a reference to the customer in the order.

- Linking tables that describe a many-to-many relationship between two real objects such as the relationship between Orders and Books. These tables are often associated with some kind of real-world transaction.

Web Database Architecture

Now that we've discussed the internal architecture of your database, we'll look at the external architecture of a Web database system, and discuss the methodology for developing a Web database system.

Architecture

The basic operation of a Web server is shown in Figure 7.8. This system consists of two objects: a Web browser and a Web server. A communication link is required between them. A Web browser makes a request of the server. The server sends back a response. This architecture suits a server delivering static pages well. The architecture that delivers a database backed Web site is a little more complex.

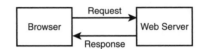

Figure 7.8   The client/server relationship between a Web browser and Web server requires communication.

The Web database applications we will build in this book follow a general Web database structure that is shown in Figure 7.9. Most of this structure should already be familiar to you.

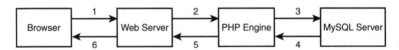

Figure 7.9   The basic Web database architecture consists of the Web browser, Web server, scripting engine, and database server.

A typical Web database transaction consists of the following stages, which are numbered in Figure 7.9. We will examine the stages in the context of the Book-O-Rama example.

1. A user's Web browser issues an HTTP request for a particular Web page. For example, she might have requested a search for all the books at Book-O-Rama written by Laura Thomson, using an HTML form. The search results page is called results.php.

2. The Web server receives the request for results.php, retrieves the file, and passes it to the PHP engine for processing.

3. The PHP engine begins parsing the script. Inside the script is a command to connect to the database and execute a query (perform the search for books). PHP opens a connection to the MySQL server and sends on the appropriate query.

4. The MySQL server receives the database query and processes it, and sends the results—a list of books—back to the PHP engine.

5. The PHP engine finishes running the script, which will usually involve formatting the query results nicely in HTML. It then returns the resulting HTML to the Web server.

6. The Web server passes the HTML back to the browser, where the user can see the list of books she requested.

The process is basically the same regardless of which scripting engine or database server you use. Often the Web server software, the PHP engine, and the database server all run on the same machine. However, it is also quite common for the database server to run on a different machine. You might do this for reasons of security, increased capacity, or load spreading. From a development perspective, this will be much the same to work with, but it might offer some significant advantages in performance.

Further Reading

In this chapter, we covered some guidelines for relational database design. If you want to delve into the theory behind relational databases, you can try reading books by some of the relational gurus like C.J. Date. Be warned, however, that the material can get pretty theoretical and might not be immediately relevant to a commercial Web developer. Your average Web database tends not to be that complicated.

Next

In the next chapter, we'll start setting up your MySQL database. First you'll learn how to set up a MySQL database for the Web, how to query it, and then how to query it from PHP.

8

Creating Your Web Database

IN THIS CHAPTER WE'LL TALK ABOUT how to set up a MySQL database for use on a Web site.

We'll cover

- Creating a database
- Users and Privileges
- Introduction to the privilege system
- Creating database tables
- Column types in MySQL

In this chapter, we'll follow through with the Book-O-Rama online bookstore application discussed in the last chapter. As a reminder, here is the schema for the Book-O-Rama application:

Customers(<u>CustomerID</u>, Name, Address, City)
Orders(<u>OrderID</u>, CustomerID, Amount, Date)
Books(<u>ISBN</u>, Author, Title, Price)
Order_Items(<u>OrderID, ISBN</u>, Quantity)
Book_Reviews(<u>ISBN</u>, Reviews)

Remember that primary keys are underlined and foreign keys have a dotted underline.

In order to use the material in this section, you must have access to MySQL. This usually means that you

- Have completed the basic install of MySQL on your Web server. This includes
  - Installing the files
  - Setting up a user for MySQL to run as

- Setting up your path
- Running `mysql_install_db`, if required
- Setting the root password
- Deleting the anonymous user and the test database
- Starting the MySQL server and setting it up to run automatically

If you've done all those things, you can go right ahead and read this chapter. If you haven't, you can find instructions on how to do these things in Appendix A, "Installing PHP 4 and MySQL."

If you have problems at any point in this chapter, it might be because your MySQL system is not set up correctly. If that happens, refer back to this list and Appendix A to make sure that your setup is correct.

- Have access to MySQL on a machine that you do not administer such as a Web hosting service, a machine at your workplace, and so on.

If this is the case, in order to work through the examples or to create your own database, you'll need to have your administrator set up a user and database for you to work with and tell you the username, password, and database name they have assigned to you.

You can either skip the sections of this chapter that explain how to set up users and databases or read them in order to better explain what you need to your system administrator. As a normal user, you won't be able to execute the commands to create users and databases.

The examples in this chapter were all built and tested with MySQL version 3.23.52. Some earlier versions of MySQL have less functionality. You should install or upgrade to the most current stable release at the time of reading. You can download the current release from the MySQL site at `http://mysql.com`.

A Note on Using the MySQL Monitor

You will notice that the MySQL examples in this chapter and the next end each command with a semicolon (;). This tells MySQL to execute the command. If you leave off the semicolon, nothing will happen. This is a common problem for new users.

This also means that you can have new lines in the middle of a command. We have used this to make the examples easier to read. You will see where we have done this because MySQL provides a continuation symbol. It's an arrow that looks like this:

```
mysql> grant select
    ->
```

This means MySQL is expecting more input. Until you type the semicolon, you will get these characters each time you press Enter.

Another point to note is that SQL statements are not case sensitive, but database and table names can be—more on this later.

How to Log in to MySQL

To do this, go to a command line interface on your machine and type the following:

```
mysql -h hostname -u username -p
```

Your command prompt might look different depending on the operating system and shell you are using.

The `mysql` command invokes the MySQL monitor. This is a command line client that connects you to the MySQL server.

The `-h` switch is used to specify the host to which you want to connect; that is, the machine on which the MySQL server is running. If you're running this command on the same machine as the MySQL server, you can leave out this switch and the `hostname` parameter. If not, you should replace the hostname parameter with the name of the machine where the MySQL server is running.

The `-u` switch is used to specify the `username` you want to connect as. If you do not specify, the default will be the username you are logged into the operating system as.

If you have installed MySQL on your own machine or server, you will need to log in as `root` and create the database we'll use in this section. Assuming that you have a clean install, `root` is the only user you'll have to begin with.

If you are using MySQL on a machine administered by somebody else, use the username they gave you.

The `-p` switch tells the server you want to connect using a password. You can leave it out if a password has not been set for the user you are logging in as.

If you are logging in as `root` and have not set a password for `root`, I strongly recommend that you visit Appendix A and do so right now. Without a `root` password, your system is insecure.

You don't need to include the password on this line. The MySQL server will ask you for it. In fact, it's better if you don't. If you enter the password on the command line, it will appear as plain text on the screen, and will be quite simple for other users to discover.

After you have entered the previous command, you should get a response something like this:

```
Enter password: ****
```

(If this hasn't worked, verify that the MySQL server is running, and the `mysql` command is somewhere in your path.)

You should enter your password. If all goes well, you should see a response something like this:

```
Welcome to the MySQL monitor.  Commands end with ; or \g.
Your MySQL connection id is 5 to server version: 3.23.52-nt
Type 'help;' or '\h' for help. Type '\c' to clear the buffer.
mysql>
```

On your own machine: If you don't get a response similar to this, make sure that you have run `mysql_install_db` if required, you have set the root password, and you've typed it in correctly.

If it isn't your machine, make sure that you typed in the password correctly.

You should now be at a MySQL command prompt, ready to create the database.

If you are using your own machine, follow the guidelines in the next section.

If you are using somebody else's machine, this should already have been done for you. You can jump ahead to the "Using the Right Database" section. You might want to read the intervening sections for general background, but you won't be able to run the commands specified there. (Or at least you shouldn't be able to!)

Creating Databases and Users

The MySQL database system can support many different databases. You will generally have one database per application. In our Book-o-Rama example, the database will be called `books`.

Creating the Database

This is the easiest part. At the MySQL command prompt, type

```
mysql> create database dbname;
```

You should substitute the name of the database you want to create for `dbname`. To begin creating the Book-O-Rama example, you can create a database called `books`.

That's it. You should see a response like

```
Query OK, 1 row affected (0.06 sec)
```

This means everything has worked. If you don't get this response, make sure that you typed the semicolon at the end of the line. A semicolon tells MySQL that you are finished, and it should actually execute the command.

Users and Privileges

A MySQL system can have many users. The root user should generally be used for administration purposes only, for security reasons. For each user who needs to use the system, you will need to set up an account and password. These do not need to be the same as usernames and passwords outside of MySQL (for example, UNIX or NT usernames and passwords). The same principle applies to root. It is a good idea to have different passwords for the system and for MySQL, especially when it comes to the root password.

It isn't compulsory to set up passwords for users, but we strongly recommend that you set up passwords for all the users that you create.

For the purposes of setting up a Web database, it's a good idea to set up at least one user per Web application.

You might ask, "Why would I want to do this?"—the answer lies in privileges.

Introduction to MySQL's Privilege System

One of the best features of MySQL is that it supports a sophisticated privilege system.

A *privilege* is the right to perform a particular action on a particular object, and is associated with a particular user. The concept is very similar to file permissions.

When you create a user within MySQL, you grant her a set of privileges to specify what she can and cannot do within the system.

Principle of Least Privilege

The principle of least privilege can be used to improve the security of any computer system. It's a basic, but very important principle that is often overlooked. The principle is as follows:

A user (or process) should have the lowest level of privilege required in order to perform his assigned task.

It applies in MySQL as it does elsewhere. For example, to run queries from the Web, a user does not need all the privileges to which root has access. We should therefore create another user who only has the necessary privileges to access the database we have just created.

Setting Up Users: The GRANT Command

The GRANT and REVOKE commands are used to give and take away rights to and from MySQL users at four levels of privilege. These levels are

- Global
- Database
- Table
- Column

We'll see in a moment how each of these can be applied.

The GRANT command is used to create users and give them privileges. The general form of the GRANT command is

```
GRANT privileges [columns]
ON item
TO user_name [IDENTIFIED BY 'password']
[WITH GRANT OPTION]
```

The clauses in square brackets are optional. There are a number of placeholders in this syntax.

The first, `privileges`, should be a comma separated list of privileges. MySQL has a defined set of these. They are described in the next section.

The `columns` placeholder is optional. You can use it to specify privileges on a column-by-column basis. You can use a single column name or a comma-separated list of column names.

The `item` placeholder is the database or table to which the new privileges apply.

You can grant privileges on all the databases by specifying `*.*` as the item. This is called granting *global* privileges. You can also do this by specifying `*` alone if you are not using any particular database.

More commonly, you will specify all tables in a database as `dbname.*`, on a single table as `dbname.tablename`, or on specific columns by specifying `dbname.`
`tablename` and some specific columns in the `columns` placeholder. These represent the three other levels of privilege available: *database*, *table*, and *column*, respectively. If you are using a specific database when you issue this command, `tablename` on its own will be interpreted as a table in the current database.

The `user_name` should be the name you want the user to log in as in MySQL. Remember that it does not have to be the same as a system login name. The user_name in MySQL can also contain a hostname. You can use this to differentiate between, say, `laura` (interpreted as `laura@localhost`) and `laura@somewhere.com`. This is quite useful because users from different domains often have the same name. It also increases security because you can specify where users can connect from, and even which tables or databases they can access from a particular location.

The `password` should be the password you want the user to log in with. The usual rules for selecting passwords apply. We will talk more about security later, but a password should not be easily guessable. This means that a password should not be a dictionary word or the same as the username. Ideally, it will contain a mixture of upper- and lower-case and nonalphabetic characters.

The `WITH GRANT OPTION` option, if specified, allows the specified user to grant her own privileges to others.

Privileges are stored in four system tables, in the database called `mysql`. These four tables are called mysql.user, mysql.db, mysql.tables_priv, and mysql.columns_priv, and relate directly to the four levels of privilege mentioned earlier. As an alternative to `GRANT`, you can alter these tables directly. We will discuss this in more detail in Chapter 11, "Advanced MySQL."

Types and Levels of Privilege

Three basic types of privileges exist in MySQL: privileges suitable for granting to regular users, privileges suitable for administrators, and a couple of special privileges. Any user can be granted any of these privileges, but it's usually sensible to restrict the administrator type ones to administrators, according to the principle of least privilege.

You should grant privileges to users only for the databases and tables they need to use. You should not grant access to the mysql database to anyone except an administrator. This is where all the users, passwords, and so on are stored. (We will look at this database in Chapter 11.)

Privileges for regular users directly relate to specific types of SQL commands and whether a user is allowed to run them. We will discuss these SQL commands in detail in the next chapter. For now, we have given a conceptual description of what they do. These privileges are shown in Table 8.1. The items under the Applies To column list the objects to which privileges of this type can be granted.

Table 8.1   **Privileges for Users**

Privilege	Applies To	Description
SELECT	tables, columns	Allows users to select rows (records) from tables.
INSERT	tables, columns	Allows users to insert new rows into tables.
UPDATE	tables, columns	Allows users to modify values in existing table rows.
DELETE	tables	Allows users to delete existing table rows.
INDEX	tables	Allows users to create and drop indexes on particular tables.
ALTER	tables	Allows users to alter the structure of existing tables by, for example, adding columns, renaming columns or tables, and changing data types of columns.
CREATE	databases, tables	Allows users to create new databases or tables. If a particular database or table is specified in the GRANT, they can only CREATE that database or table, which means they will have to DROP it first.
DROP	databases, tables	Allows users to drop (delete) databases or tables.

Most of the privileges for regular users are relatively harmless in terms of system security. The ALTER privilege can be used to work around the privilege system by renaming tables, but it is widely needed by users. Security is always a trade off between usability and safety. You should make your own decision when it comes to ALTER, but it is often granted to users.

In addition to the privileges listed in Table 8.1, a REFERENCES privilege exists that is currently unused, and a GRANT privilege exists that is granted with WITH GRANT OPTION rather than in the *privileges* list.

Table 8.2 shows the privileges suitable for use by administrative users.

Table 8.2 **Privileges for Administrators**

Privilege	Description
RELOAD	Allows an administrator to reload grant tables and flush privileges, hosts, logs, and tables.
SHUTDOWN	Allows an administrator to shut down the MySQL server.
PROCESS	Allows an administrator to view server processes and kill them.
FILE	Allows data to be read into tables from files and vice versa.

It is possible to grant these privileges to nonadministrators, but extreme caution should be used if you are considering doing so. The average user should have no need to use the RELOAD, SHUTDOWN, and PROCESS privileges.

The FILE privilege is a bit different. It is useful for users because loading data from files can save a lot of time re-entering data each time to get it into the database. However, file loading can be used to load any file that the MySQL server can see, including databases belonging to other users and, potentially, password files. Grant it with caution, or offer to load the data for the user.

Two special privileges also exist, and these are shown in Table 8.3.

Table 8.3 **Special Privileges**

Privilege	Description
ALL	Grants all the privileges listed in Tables 8.1 and 8.2. You can also write ALL PRIVILEGES instead of ALL.
USAGE	Grants no privileges. This will create a user and allow her to log on, but it won't allow her to do anything. Usually you will go on to add more privileges later.

The REVOKE Command

The opposite of GRANT is REVOKE. It is used to take privileges away from a user. It is very similar to GRANT in syntax:

```
REVOKE privileges [(columns)]
ON item
FROM user_name
```

If you have given the WITH GRANT OPTION clause, you can revoke this by doing:

```
REVOKE GRANT OPTION
ON item
FROM user_name
```

Examples Using GRANT and REVOKE

To set up an administrator, you can type:

```
mysql> grant all
    -> on *
    -> to fred identified by 'mnb123'
    -> with grant option;
```

This grants all privileges on all databases to a user called Fred with the password mnb123, and allows him to pass on those privileges.

Chances are you don't want this user in your system, so go ahead and revoke him:

```
mysql> revoke all
    -> on *
    -> from fred;
```

Now let's set up a regular user with no privileges:

```
mysql> grant usage
    -> on books.*
    -> to sally identified by 'magic123';
```

After talking to Sally, we know a bit more about what she wants to do, so we can give her the appropriate privileges:

```
mysql> grant select, insert, update, delete, index, alter, create, drop
    -> on books.*
    -> to sally;
```

Note that we don't need to specify Sally's password in order to do this.

If we decide that Sally has been up to something in the database, we might decide to reduce her privileges:

```
mysql> revoke alter, create, drop
    -> on books.*
    -> from sally;
```

And later, when she doesn't need to use the database any more, we can revoke her privileges altogether:

```
mysql> revoke all
    -> on books.*
    -> from sally;
```

Setting Up a User for the Web

You will need to set up a user for your PHP scripts to connect to MySQL. Again we can apply the privilege of least principle: What should the scripts be able to do?

In most cases they'll only need to SELECT, INSERT, DELETE, and UPDATE rows from tables. You can set this up as follows:

```
mysql> grant select, insert, delete, update
    -> on books.*
    -> to bookorama identified by 'bookorama123';
```

Obviously, for security reasons, you should choose a better password than this.

If you use a Web hosting service, you'll usually get access to the other user-type privileges on a database they create for you. They will typically give you the same *user_name* and *password* for command-line use (setting up tables and so on) and for Web script connections (querying the database). This is marginally less secure. You can set up a user with this level of privilege as follows:

```
mysql> grant select, insert, update, delete, index, alter, create, drop
    -> on books.*
    -> to bookorama identified by 'bookorama123';
```

Go ahead and set up this second version of the user as this is what we will need to use in the next section.

Logging Out as root

You can log out of the MySQL monitor by typing **quit**. You should log back in as your Web user to test that everything is working correctly.

Using the Right Database

If you've reached this stage, you should be logged in to a user-level MySQL account ready to test the example code, either because you've just set it up, or because your Web server administrator has set it up for you.

The first thing you'll need to do when you log in is to specify which database you want to use. You can do this by typing

```
mysql> use dbname;
```

where *dbname* is the name of your database.

Alternatively, you can avoid the use command by specifying the database when you log in, as follows:

```
mysql -D dbname -h hostname -u username -p
```

In this example, we'll use the books database:

```
mysql> use books;
```

When you type this command, MySQL should give you a response such as

```
Database changed
```

If you don't select a database before starting work, MySQL will give you an error message such as

```
ERROR 1046: No Database Selected
```

Creating Database Tables

The next step in setting up the database is to actually create the tables. You can do this using the SQL command CREATE TABLE. The general form of a CREATE TABLE statement is

```
CREATE TABLE tablename(columns)
```

You should replace the `tablename` placeholder with the name of the table you want to create, and the `columns` placeholder with a comma-separated list of the columns in your table.

Each column will have a name followed by a datatype.

Here's the Book-O-Rama schema:

Customers(<u>CustomerID</u>, Name, Address, City)

Orders(<u>OrderID</u>, CustomerID, Amount, Date)

Books(<u>ISBN</u>, Author, Title, Price)

Order_Items(<u>OrderID</u>, <u>ISBN</u>, Quantity)

Book_Reviews(<u>ISBN</u>, Review)

Listing 8.1 shows the SQL to create these tables, assuming you have already created the database called books. You can find this SQL on the CD-ROM in the file chapter8/bookorama.sql

You can run an existing SQL file, such as one loaded from the CD-ROM, through MySQL by typing

```
> mysql -h host -u bookorama -D books -p < bookorama.sql
```

(Remember to replace *host* with the name of your host.)

Using file redirection is pretty handy for this because it means that you can edit your SQL in the text editor of your choice before executing it.

Listing 8.1   **bookorama.sql—SQL to Create the Tables for Book-O-Rama**

```
create table customers
( customerid int unsigned not null auto_increment primary key,
  name char(30) not null,
  address char(40) not null,
  city char(20) not null
);
```

Listing 8.1 **Continued**

```
create table orders
( orderid int unsigned not null auto_increment primary key,
  customerid int unsigned not null,
  amount float(6,2),
  date date not null
);

create table books
(  isbn char(13) not null primary key,
   author char(30),
   title char(60),
   price float(4,2)
);

create table order_items
( orderid int unsigned not null,
  isbn char(13) not null,
  quantity tinyint unsigned,

  primary key (orderid, isbn)

);
create table book_reviews
(
   isbn char(13) not null primary key,
   review text
);
```

Each of the tables is created by a separate CREATE TABLE statement. You see that we've created each of the tables in the schema with the columns that we designed in the last chapter. You'll see that each of the columns has a data type listed after its name. Some of the columns have other specifiers, too.

What the Other Keywords Mean

NOT NULL means that all the rows in the table must have a value in this attribute. If it isn't specified, the field can be blank (NULL).

AUTO_INCREMENT is a special MySQL feature you can use on integer columns. It means if we leave that field blank when inserting rows into the table, MySQL will automatically generate a unique identifier value. The value will be one greater than the maximum value in the column already. You can only have one of these in each table. Columns that specify AUTO_INCREMENT must be indexed.

PRIMARY KEY after a column name specifies that this column is the primary key for the table. Entries in this column have to be unique. MySQL will automatically index this column. Notice that where we've used it above with customerid in the customers table we've used it with AUTO_INCREMENT. The automatic index on the primary key takes care of the index required by AUTO_INCREMENT.

Specifying PRIMARY KEY after a column name can only be used for single column primary keys. The PRIMARY KEY clause at the end of the order_items statement is an alternative form. We have used it here because the primary key for this table consists of the two columns together.

UNSIGNED after an integer type means that it can only have a zero or positive value.

Understanding the Column Types

Let's take the first table as an example:

```
create table customers
( customerid int unsigned not null auto_increment primary key,
  name char(30) not null,
  address char(40) not null,
  city char(20) not null
);
```

When creating any table, you need to make decisions about column types.

With the customers table, we have four columns as specified in our schema. The first one, customerid, is the primary key, which we've specified directly. We've decided this will be an integer (data type int) and that these IDs should be unsigned. We've also taken advantage of the auto_increment facility so that MySQL can manage these for us—it's one less thing to worry about.

The other columns are all going to hold string type data. We've chosen the char type for these. This specifies fixed width fields. The width is specified in the brackets, so, for example, name can have up to 30 characters.

This data type will always allocate 30 characters of storage for the name, even if they're not all used. MySQL will pad the data with spaces to make it the right size. The alternative is varchar, which uses only the amount of storage required (plus one byte). It's a small trade off—varchars will use less space but chars are faster.

For real customers with real names and real addresses, these column widths will be far too narrow.

Note that we've declared all the columns as NOT NULL. This is a minor optimization you can make wherever possible.

We'll talk more about optimization in Chapter 11, "Advanced MySQL."

Some of the other CREATE statements have variations in syntax. Let's look at the orders table:

```
create table orders
( orderid int unsigned not null auto_increment primary key,
  customerid int unsigned not null,
  amount float(6,2),
  date date not null
);
```

The `amount` column is specified as a floating point number of type `float`. With most floating point data types, you can specify the display width and the number of decimal places. In this case, the order amount is going to be in dollars, so we've allowed a reasonably large order total (width 6) and two decimal places for the cents.

The `date` column has the data type `date`.

In this particular table, we've specified that all columns bar the amount as NOT NULL. Why? When an order is entered into the database, we'll need to create it in `orders`, add the items to `order_items`, and then work out the amount. We might not know the amount when the order is created, so we've allowed for it to be NULL.

The `books` table has some similar characteristics:

```
create table books
(   isbn char(13) not null primary key,
    author char(30),
    title char(60),
    price float(4,2)
);
```

In this case, we don't need to generate the primary key because ISBNs are generated elsewhere. We've left the other fields NULL because a bookstore might know the ISBN of a book before they know the `title`, `author`, or `price`.

The `order_items` table demonstrates how to create multicolumn primary keys:

```
create table order_items
( orderid int unsigned not null,
  isbn char(13) not null,
  quantity tinyint unsigned,

  primary key (orderid, isbn)
);
```

We've specified the quantity of a particular book as a TINYINT UNSIGNED, which holds an integer between 0 and 255.

As we mentioned before, multicolumn primary keys need to be specified with a special primary key clause. This is used here.

Lastly, if you consider the `book_reviews` table:

```
create table book_reviews
(
  isbn char(13) not null primary key,
  review text
);
```

This uses a new data type, text, which we have not yet discussed. It is used for longer text, such as an article. There are a few variants on this, which we'll discuss later in this chapter.

To understand creating tables in more detail, let's discuss column names and identifiers in general, and then the data types we can choose for columns. First though, let's look at the database we've created.

Looking at the Database with SHOW and DESCRIBE

Log in to the MySQL monitor and use the books database. You can view the tables in the database by typing

```
mysql> show tables;
```

MySQL will display a list of all the tables in the database:

```
+-----------------+
| Tables in books |
+-----------------+
| book_reviews    |
| books           |
| customers       |
| order_items     |
| orders          |
+-----------------+
5 rows in set (0.06 sec)
```

You can also use show to see a list of databases by typing

```
mysql> show databases;
```

You can see more information about a particular table, for example, books, using DESCRIBE:

```
mysql> describe books;
```

MySQL will display the information you supplied when creating the database:

```
+--------+------------+------+-----+---------+-------+
| Field  | Type       | Null | Key | Default | Extra |
+--------+------------+------+-----+---------+-------+
| isbn   | char(13)   |      | PRI |         |       |
| author | char(30)   | YES  |     | NULL    |       |
| title  | char(60)   | YES  |     | NULL    |       |
| price  | float(4,2) | YES  |     | NULL    |       |
+--------+------------+------+-----+---------+-------+
4 rows in set (0.05 sec)
```

These commands are useful to remind yourself of a column type, or to navigate a database that you didn't create.

MySQL Identifiers

There are four kinds of identifiers in MySQL—databases, tables, and columns, which we're familiar with, and aliases, which we'll cover in the next chapter.

Databases in MySQL map to directories in the underlying file structure, and tables map to files. This has a direct effect on the names you can give them. It also affects the case sensitivity of these names—if directory and filenames are case sensitive in your operating system, database and table names will be case sensitive (for example, in UNIX), otherwise they won't (for example, under Windows). Column names and alias names are not case sensitive, but you can't use versions of different cases in the same SQL statement.

As a side note, the location of the directory and files containing the data will be wherever it was set in configuration. You can check the location on your system by using the mysqladmin facility as follows:

```
mysqladmin variables
```

You are looking for the `datadir` variable.

A summary of possible identifiers is shown in Table 8.4. The only additional exception is that you cannot use ASCII(0), ASCII(255), or the quoting character in identifiers (and to be honest, I'm not sure why you'd want to).

Table 8.4 **MySQL Identifiers**

Type	Max Length	Case Sensitive?	Characters Allowed
Database	64	same as O/S	Anything allowed in a directory name in your O/S except the /, \, and . characters
Table	64	same as O/S	Anything allowed in a filename in your O/S except the / and . characters
Column	64	no	Anything
Alias	255	no	Anything

These rules are extremely open.

As of MySQL 3.23.6, you can even have reserved words and special characters of all kinds in identifiers, the only limitation being that if you use anything weird like this, you have to put it in back quotes (located under the tilde key on the top left of most keyboards). For example,

```
create database `create database`;
```

The rules in versions of MySQL (prior to 3.23.6) are more restrictive, and don't allow you to do this.

Of course, you should apply common sense to all this freedom. Just because you *can* call a database `create database`, it doesn't that mean that you *should*. The same principle applies as in any other kind of programming—use meaningful identifiers.

Column Data Types

The three basic column types in MySQL are: numeric, date and time, and string. Within each of these categories are a large number of types. We'll summarize them here, and go into more detail about the strengths and weaknesses of each in Chapter 11.

Each of the three types comes in various storage sizes. When choosing a column type, the principle is generally to choose the smallest type that your data will fit into.

For many data types, when you are creating a column of that type, you can specify the maximum display length. This is shown in the following tables of data types as M. If it's optional for that type, it is shown in square brackets. The maximum value you can specify for M is 255.

Optional values throughout these descriptions are shown in square brackets.

Numeric Types

The numeric types are either integers or floating point numbers. For the floating point numbers, you can specify the number of digits after the decimal place. This is shown in this book as D. The maximum value you can specify for D is 30 or M-2 (that is, the maximum display length minus two—one character for a decimal point and one for the integral part of the number), whichever is lower.

For integer types you can also specify if you want them to be UNSIGNED, as shown in Listing 8.1.

For all numeric types, you can also specify the ZEROFILL attribute. When values from a ZEROFILL column are displayed, they will be padded with leading zeroes. If you specify a column as ZEROFILL, it will automatically also be UNSIGNED.

The integral types are shown in Table 8.5. Note that the ranges shown in this table show the signed range on one line and the unsigned range on the next.

Table 8.5 **Integral Data Types**

Type	Range	Storage (bytes)	Description
TINYINT[(M)]	–127..128 or 0..255	1	Very small integers
BIT			Synonym for TINYINT
BOOL			Synonym for TINYINT
SMALLINT[(M)]	–32768..32767 or 0..65535	2	Small integers

Table 8.5 **Continued**

Type	Range	Storage (bytes)	Description
MEDIUMINT [(M)]	−8388608.. 8388607 or 0..16777215	3	Medium sized integers
INT [(M)]	$-2^{31}..2^{31}-1$ or $0..2^{32}-1$	4	Regular integers
INTEGER [(M)]			Synonym for INT
BIGINT [(M)]	$-2^{63}..2^{63}-1$ or $0..2^{64}-1$	8	Big integers

The floating point types are shown in Table 8.6.

Table 8.6 **Floating Point Data Types**

Type	Range	Storage (bytes)	Description
FLOAT (*precision*)	depends on precision	varies	Can be used to specify single or double precision floating point numbers.
FLOAT [(M,D)]	±1.175494351E−38 ±3.402823466E+38	4	Single precision floating point number. These are equivalent to FLOAT(4), but with a specified display width and number of decimal places.
DOUBLE [(M,D)]	±1. 7976931348623157E +308 ±2.2250738585072014E −308	8	Double precision floating point number. These are equivalent to FLOAT(8) but with a specified display width and number of decimal places.
DOUBLE PRECISION [(M,D)]	as above		Synonym for DOUBLE [(M, D)].
REAL [(M,D)]	as above		Synonym for DOUBLE [(M, D)].
DECIMAL [(M[,D])]	varies	M+2	Floating point number stored as char. The range depends on M, the display width.
NUMERIC [(M,D)]	as above		Synonym for DECIMAL.
DEC [(M,D)]	as above		Synonym for DECIMAL.

Date and Time Types

MySQL supports a number of date and time types. These are shown in Table 8.7. With all these types, you can input data in either a string or numerical format. It is worth noting that a TIMESTAMP column in a particular row will be set to the date and time of the most recent operation on that row if you don't set it manually. This is useful for transaction recording.

Table 8.7   **Date and Time Data Types**

Type	Range	Description
DATE	1000-01-01 9999-12-31	A date. Will be displayed as YYYY-MM-DD.
TIME	-838:59:59 838:59:59	A time. Will be displayed as HH:MM:SS. Note that the range is much wider than you will probably ever want to use.
DATETIME	1000-01-01 00:00:00 9999-12-31 23:59:59	A date and time. Will be displayed as YYYY-MM-DD HH:MM:SS.
TIMESTAMP[(M)]	1970-01-01 00:00:00	A timestamp, useful for transaction reporting. The display format depends on the value of M (see Table 8.8, which follows).
	Sometime in 2037	The top of the range depends on the limit on UNIX timestamps.
YEAR[(2|4)]	70–69 (1970–2069) 1901–2155	A year. You can specify 2 or 4 digit format. Each of these has a different range, as shown.

Table 8.8 shows the possible different display types for TIMESTAMP.

Table 8.8   **TIMESTAMP Display Types**

Type Specified	Display
TIMESTAMP	YYYYMMDDHHMMSS
TIMESTAMP(14)	YYYYMMDDHHMMSS
TIMESTAMP(12)	YYMMDDHHMMSS
TIMESTAMP(10)	YYMMDDHHMM
TIMESTAMP(8)	YYYYMMDD
TIMESTAMP(6)	YYMMDD
TIMESTAMP(4)	YYMM
TIMESTAMP(2)	YY

String Types

String types fall into three groups. First, there are plain old strings, that is, short pieces of text. These are the CHAR (fixed length character) and VARCHAR (variable length character) types. You can specify the width of each. Columns of type CHAR will be padded with spaces to the maximum width regardless of the size of the data, whereas VARCHAR columns vary in width with the data. (Note that MySQL will strip the trailing spaces from CHARs when they are *retrieved*, and from VARCHARs when they are *stored*.) There is a space versus speed trade off with these two types, which we will discuss in more detail in Chapter 11.

Second, there are TEXT and BLOB types. These come in various sizes. These are for longer text or binary data, respectively. BLOBs are *binary large objects*. These can hold anything you like, for example, image or sound data.

In practice, BLOB and TEXT columns are the same except that TEXT is case sensitive and BLOB is not. Because these column types can hold large amounts of data, they require some special considerations. We will discuss this in Chapter 11.

The third group has two special types, SET and ENUM. The SET type is used to specify that values in this column must come from a particular set of specified values. Column values can contain more than one value from the set. You can have a maximum of 64 things in the specified set.

ENUM is an enumeration. It is very similar to SET, except that columns of this type can have only one of the specified values or NULL, and that you can have a maximum of 65,535 things in the enumeration.

We've summarized the string data types in Tables 8.9, 8.10, and 8.11. Table 8.9 shows the plain string types.

Table 8.9 **Regular String Types**

Type	Range	Description
[NATIONAL] CHAR(M) [BINARY]	0 to 255 characters	Fixed length string of length M, where M is between 0 and 255. The NATIONAL keyword specifies that the default character set should be used. This is the default in MySQL anyway, but is included as it is part of the ANSI SQL standard. The BINARY keyword specifies that the data should be treated as not case insensitive. (The default is case sensitive.)
CHAR	1	Synonym for CHAR(1)
[NATIONAL] VARCHAR(M) [BINARY]	1 to 255 characters	Same as above, except they are variable length.

Table 8.10 shows the TEXT and BLOB types. The maximum length of a TEXT field in characters is the maximum size in bytes of files that could be stored in that field.

Table 8.10 **TEXT and BLOB Types**

Type	Maximum Length (characters)	Description
TINYBLOB	2^8 -1 (that is, 255)	A tiny binary large object (BLOB) field
TINYTEXT	2^8 -1 (that is, 255)	A tiny TEXT field
BLOB	2^{16} -1 (that is, 65,535)	A normal sized BLOB field
TEXT	2^{16} -1 (that is, 65,535)	A normal sized TEXT field
MEDIUMBLOB	2^{24}-1 (that is, 16,777,215)	A medium sized BLOB field
MEDIUMTEXT	2^{24}-1 (that is, 16,777,215)	A medium sized TEXT field
LONGBLOB	2^{32}-1 (that is, 4,294,967,295)	A long BLOB field
LONGTEXT	2^{32}-1 (that is, 4,294,967,295)	A long TEXT field

Table 8.11 shows the ENUM and SET types.

Table 8.11 **SET and ENUM Types**

Type	Maximum Values in Set	Description
ENUM('value1', 'value2',...)	65,535	Columns of this type can only hold *one* of the values listed or NULL.
SET('value1', 'value2',...)	64	Columns of this type can hold a set of the specified values or NULL.

Further Reading

For more information, you can read about setting up a database at the MySQL online manual at http://www.mysql.com/.

Next

Now that you know how to create users, databases, and tables, you can concentrate on interacting with the database. In the next chapter, we'll look at how to put data in the tables, how to update and delete it, and how to query the database.

9

Working with Your MySQL Database

IN THIS CHAPTER, WE'LL DISCUSS Structured Query Language (SQL) and its use in querying databases. We'll continue developing the Book-O-Rama database by seeing how to insert, delete, and update data, and how to ask the database questions.

Topics we will cover include

- What is SQL?
- Inserting data into the database
- Retrieving data from the database
- Joining tables
- Updating records from the database
- Altering tables after creation
- Deleting records from the database
- Dropping tables

We'll begin by talking about what SQL is and why it's a useful thing to understand.

If you haven't set up the Book-O-Rama database, you'll need to do that before you can run the SQL queries in this chapter. Instructions for doing this are in Chapter 8, "Creating Your Web Database."

What Is SQL?

SQL stands for *Structured Query Language*. It's the standard language for accessing *relational database management systems (RDBMS)*. SQL is used to store and retrieve data to and from a database. It is used in database systems such as MySQL, Oracle, PostgreSQL, Sybase, and Microsoft SQL Server among others.

There's an ANSI standard for SQL, and database systems such as MySQL generally strive to implement this standard. There are some subtle differences between standard SQL and MySQL's SQL. Some of these are planned to become standard in future versions of MySQL, and some are deliberate differences. We'll point out the more important ones as we go. A complete list of the differences between MySQL's SQL and ANSI SQL at any given version can be found in the MySQL online manual. You can find this page at this URL and in many other locations:

```
http://www.mysql.com/doc/en/Compatibility.html
```

You might have heard the phrases *Data Definition Languages (DDL)*, used for defining databases, and *Data Manipulation Languages (DML)*, used for querying databases. SQL covers both of these bases. In Chapter 8, we looked at data definition (DDL) in SQL, so we've already been using it a little. You use DDL when you're initially setting up a database.

You will use the DML aspects of SQL far more frequently because these are the parts that we use to store and retrieve real data in a database.

Inserting Data into the Database

Before you can do a lot with a database, you need to store some data in it. The way you will most commonly do this is with the SQL INSERT statement.

Recall that RDBMSs contain tables, which in turn contain rows of data organized into columns. Each row in a table normally describes some real-world object or relationship, and the column values for that row store information about the real-world object. We can use the INSERT statement to put rows of data into the database.

The usual form of an INSERT statement is

```
INSERT [INTO] table [(column1, column2, column3,...)] VALUES
(value1, value2, value3,...);
```

For example, to insert a record into Book-O-Rama's Customers table, you could type

```
insert into customers values
  (NULL, "Julie Smith", "25 Oak Street", "Airport West");
```

You can see that we've replaced `table` with the name of the actual table we want to put the data in, and the `values` with specific values. The values in this example are all enclosed in double quotes. Strings should always be enclosed in pairs of single or double quotes in MySQL. (We will use both in this book.) Numbers and dates do not need quotes.

There are a few interesting things to note about the INSERT statement.

The values we specified will be used to fill in the table columns in order. If you want to fill in only some of the columns, or if you want to specify them in a different order, you can list the specific columns in the columns part of the statement. For example,

```
insert into customers (name, city) values
("Melissa Jones", "Nar Nar Goon North");
```

This approach is useful if you have only partial data about a particular record, or if some fields in the record are optional. You can also achieve the same effect with the following syntax:

```
insert into customers
set name="Michael Archer",
    address="12 Adderley Avenue",
    city="Leeton";
```

You'll also notice that we specified a NULL value for the customerid column when adding Julie Smith and ignored that column when adding the other customers. You might recall that when we set the database up, we created customerid as the primary key for the Customers table, so this might seem strange. However, we specified the field as AUTO_INCREMENT. This means that, if we insert a row with a NULL value or no value in this field, MySQL will generate the next number in the autoincrement sequence and insert it for us automatically. This is pretty useful.

You can also insert multiple rows into a table at once. Each row should be in its own set of brackets, and each set of brackets should be separated by a comma.

We've put together some simple sample data to populate the database. This is just a series of simple INSERT statements that use this multirow insertion approach. The script that does this can be found on the CD accompanying this book in the file \chapter9\book_insert.sql. It is also shown in Listing 9.1.

Listing 9.1   book_insert.sql—SQL to Populate the Tables for Book-O-Rama

```
use books;

insert into customers values
   (NULL, "Julie Smith", "25 Oak Street", "Airport West"),
   (NULL, "Alan Wong", "1/47 Haines Avenue", "Box Hill"),
   (NULL, "Michelle Arthur", "357 North Road", "Yarraville");

insert into orders values
   (NULL, 3, 69.98, "2000-04-02"),
   (NULL, 1, 49.99, "2000-04-15"),
   (NULL, 2, 74.98, "2000-04-19"),
   (NULL, 3, 24.99, "2000-05-01");

insert into books values
   ("0-672-31697-8", "Michael Morgan", "Java 2 for Professional Developers",
34.99),
   ("0-672-31745-1", "Thomas Down", "Installing Debian GNU/Linux", 24.99),
   ("0-672-31509-2", "Pruitt, et al.", "Teach Yourself GIMP in 24 Hours", 24.99),
   ("0-672-31769-9", "Thomas Schenk", "Caldera OpenLinux System Administration
```

Listing 9.1 **Continued**

```
    Unleashed", 49.99);

insert into order_items values
    (1, "0-672-31697-8", 2),
    (2, "0-672-31769-9", 1),
    (3, "0-672-31769-9", 1),
    (3, "0-672-31509-2", 1),
    (4, "0-672-31745-1", 3);

insert into book_reviews values
    ("0-672-31697-8", "Morgan's book is clearly written and goes well beyond
                    most of the basic Java books out there.");
```

You can run this script by piping it through MySQL as follows:

```
>mysql -h host -u bookorama -p < book_insert.sql
```

Retrieving Data from the Database

The workhorse of SQL is the SELECT statement. It's used to retrieve data from a database by selecting rows that match specified criteria from a table. There are a lot of options and different ways to use the SELECT statement.

The basic form of a SELECT is

```
SELECT items
FROM tables
[ WHERE condition ]
[ GROUP BY group_type ]
[ HAVING where_definition ]
[ ORDER BY order_type ]
[ LIMIT limit_criteria ] ;
```

We'll talk about each of the clauses of the statement. First of all, though, let's look at a query without any of the optional clauses, one that selects some items from a particular table. Typically, these items are columns from the table. (They can also be the results of any MySQL expressions. We'll discuss some of the more useful ones later in this section.) This query lists the contents of the name and city columns from the Customers table:

```
select name, city
from customers;
```

This query has the following output, assuming that you've entered the sample data from Listing 9.1 and the other two sample INSERT statements:

```
+-----------------+--------------------+
| name            | city               |
+-----------------+--------------------+
| Julie Smith     | Airport West       |
| Alan Wong       | Box Hill           |
| Michelle Arthur | Yarraville         |
| Melissa Jones   | Nar Nar Goon North |
| Michael Archer  | Leeton             |
+-----------------+--------------------+
```

As you can see, we've got a table which contains the items we selected—name and city—from the table we specified, Customers. This data is shown for all the rows in the Customer table.

You can specify as many columns as you like from a table by listing them out after the select keyword. You can also specify some other items. One useful one is the wildcard operator, *, which matches all the columns in the specified table or tables. For example, to retrieve all columns and all rows from the order_items table, we would use

```
select *
from order_items;
```

which will give the following output:

```
+---------+----------------+----------+
| orderid | isbn           | quantity |
+---------+----------------+----------+
|       1 | 0-672-31697-8  |        2 |
|       2 | 0-672-31769-9  |        1 |
|       3 | 0-672-31769-9  |        1 |
|       3 | 0-672-31509-2  |        1 |
|       4 | 0-672-31745-1  |        3 |
+---------+----------------+----------+
```

Retrieving Data with Specific Criteria

In order to access a subset of the rows in a table, we need to specify some selection criteria. You can do this with a WHERE clause. For example,

```
select *
from orders
where customerid = 3;
```

will select all the columns from the orders table, but only the rows with a customerid of 3. Here's the output:

The WHERE clause specifies the criteria used to select particular rows. In this case, we have selected rows with a customerid of 3. The single equal sign is used to test equality—note that this is different from PHP, and it's easy to become confused when you're using them together.

In addition to equality, MySQL supports a full set of comparison operators and regular expressions. The ones you will most commonly use in WHERE clauses are listed in Table 9.1. Note that this is not a complete list—if you need something not listed here, check the MySQL manual.

Table 9.1 **Useful Comparison Operators for WHERE Clauses**

Operator	Name (If Applicable)	Example	Description
=	equality	customerid = 3	Tests whether two values are equal
>	greater than	amount > 60.00	Tests whether one value is greater than another
<	less than	amount < 60.00	Tests whether one value is less than another
>=	greater than or equal	amount >= 60.00	Tests whether one value is greater than or equal to another
<=	less than or equal	amount <= 60.00	Tests whether one value is less than or equal to another
!= or <>	not equal	quantity != 0	Tests whether two values are not equal
IS NOT NULL	n/a	address is not null	Tests whether field actually contains a value
IS NULL	n/a	address is null	Tests whether field does not contain a value
BETWEEN	n/a	amount between 0 and 60.00	Tests whether a value is greater than or equal to a minimum value and less than or equal to a maximum value
IN	n/a	city in ("Carlton", "Moe")	Tests whether a value is in a particular set
NOT IN	n/a	city not in ("Carlton", "Moe")	Tests whether a value is not in a set
LIKE	pattern match	name like ("Fred %")	Checks whether a value matches a pattern using simple SQL pattern matching
NOT LIKE	pattern match	name not like ("Fred %")	Checks whether a value doesn't match a pattern
REGEXP	regular expression	name regexp	Checks whether a value matches a regular expression

The last three lines in the table refer to LIKE and REGEXP. These are both forms of pattern matching.

LIKE uses simple SQL pattern matching. Patterns can consist of regular text plus the %
(percent) character to indicate a wildcard match to any number of characters and the _
(underscore) character to wildcard match a single character.

The REGEXP keyword is used for regular expression matching. MySQL uses POSIX
regular expressions. Instead of REGEXP, you can also use RLIKE, which is a synonym.
POSIX regular expressions are also used in PHP. You can read more about them in
Chapter 4, "String Manipulation and Regular Expressions."

You can test multiple criteria in this way and join them with AND and OR. For
example,

```
select *
from orders
where customerid = 3 or customerid=4;
```

Retrieving Data from Multiple Tables

Often, to answer a question from the database, you will need to use data from more than
one table. For example, if you wanted to know which customers placed orders this
month, you would need to look at the Customers table and the Orders table. If you also
wanted to know what, specifically, they ordered, you would also need to look at the
Order_Items table.

These items are in separate tables because they relate to separate real-world objects.
This is one of the principles of good database design that we talked about in Chapter 7,
"Designing Your Web Database."

To put this information together in SQL, you must perform an operation called a
join. This simply means joining two or more tables together to follow the relationships
between the data. For example, if we want to see the orders that customer Julie Smith
has placed, we will need to look at the Customers table to find Julie's CustomerID, and
then at the Orders table for orders with that CustomerID.

Although joins are conceptually simple, they are one of the more subtle and complex
parts of SQL. Several different types of join are implemented in MySQL, and each is
used for a different purpose.

Simple Two-Table Joins

Let's begin by looking at some SQL for the query about Julie Smith we just talked
about:

```
select orders.orderid, orders.amount, orders.date
from customers, orders
where customers.name = 'Julie Smith'
and customers.customerid = orders.customerid;
```

The output of this query is

```
+----------+--------+-------------+
| orderid  | amount | date        |
+----------+--------+-------------+
|        2 |  49.99 | 2000-04-15  |
+----------+--------+-------------+
```

There are a few things to notice here.

First of all, because information from two tables is needed to answer this query, we have listed both tables.

We have also specified a type of join, possibly without knowing it. The comma between the names of the tables is equivalent to typing INNER JOIN or CROSS JOIN. This is a type of join sometimes also referred to as a *full join*, or the *Cartesian product* of the tables. It means, "Take the tables listed, and make one big table. The big table should have a row for each possible combination of rows from each of the tables listed, whether that makes sense or not." In other words, we get a table, which has every row from the Customers table matched up with every row from the Orders table, regardless of whether a particular customer placed a particular order.

That doesn't make a lot of sense in most cases. Often what we want is to see the rows that really do match, that is, the orders placed by a particular customer matched up with that customer.

We achieve this by placing a *join condition* in the WHERE clause. This is a special type of conditional statement that explains which attributes show the relationship between the two tables. In this case, our join condition was

```
customers.customerid = orders.customerid
```

which tells MySQL to only put rows in the result table if the CustomerId from the Customers table matches the CustomerID from the Orders table.

By adding this join condition to the query, we've actually converted the join to a different type, called an *equi-join*.

You'll also notice the dot notation we've used to make it clear which table a particular column comes from, that is, customers.customerid refers to the customerid column from the Customers table, and orders.customerid refers to the customerid column from the Orders table.

This dot notation is required if the name of a column is ambiguous, that is, if it occurs in more than one table.

As an extension, it can also be used to disambiguate column names from different databases. In this example, we have used a table.column notation. You can specify the database with a database.table.column notation, for example, to test a condition such as

```
books.orders.customerid = other_db.orders.customerid
```

You can, however, use the dot notation for all column references in a query. This can be a good idea, particularly after your queries begin to become complex. MySQL doesn't require it, but it does make your queries much more human readable and maintainable.

You'll notice that we have followed this convention in the rest of the previous query, for example, with the use of the condition

```
customers.name = 'Julie Smith'
```

The column name only occurs in the table customers, so we do not need to specify this, but it does make it clearer.

Joining More Than Two Tables

Joining more than two tables is no more difficult than a two-table join. As a general rule, you need to join tables in pairs with join conditions. Think of it as following the relationships between the data from table to table to table.

For example, if we want to know which customers have ordered books on Java (perhaps so we can send them information about a new Java book), we need to trace these relationships through quite a few tables.

We need to find customers who have placed at least one order that included an order_item that is a book about Java. To get from the Customers table to the Orders table, we can use the customerid as we did previously. To get from the Orders table to the Order_Items table, we can use the orderid. To get from the Order_Items table to the specific book in the Books table, we can use the ISBN. After making all those links, we can test for books with Java in the title, and return the names of customers who bought any of those books.

Let's look at a query that does all those things:

```
select customers.name
from customers, orders, order_items, books
where customers.customerid = orders.customerid
and orders.orderid = order_items.orderid
and order_items.isbn = books.isbn
and books.title like '%Java%';
```

This query will return the following output:

```
+-----------------+
| name            |
+-----------------+
| Michelle Arthur |
+-----------------+
```

Notice that we traced the data through four different tables, and to do this with an equi-join, we needed three different join conditions. It is generally true that you need one join condition for each pair of tables that you want to join, and therefore a total of join conditions one less than the total number of tables you want to join. This rule of thumb can be useful for debugging queries that don't quite work. Check off your join conditions and make sure you've followed the path all the way from what you know to what you want to know.

Finding Rows That Don't Match

The other main type of join that you will use in MySQL is the left join.

In the previous examples, you'll notice that only the rows where there was a match between the tables were included. Sometimes we specifically want the rows where there's no match—for example, customers who have never placed an order, or books that have never been ordered.

The easiest way to answer this type of question in MySQL is to use a left join. A left join will match up rows on a specified join condition between two tables. If there's no matching row in the right table, a row will be added to the result that contains NULL values in the right columns.

Let's look at an example:

```
select customers.customerid, customers.name, orders.orderid
from customers left join orders
on customers.customerid = orders.customerid;
```

This SQL query uses a left join to join Customers with Orders. You will notice that the left join uses a slightly different syntax for the join condition—in this case, the join condition goes in a special ON clause of the SQL statement.

The result of this query is

```
+------------+-------------------+---------+
| customerid | name              | orderid |
+------------+-------------------+---------+
|          1 | Julie Smith       |       2 |
|          2 | Alan Wong         |       3 |
|          3 | Michelle Arthur   |       1 |
|          3 | Michelle Arthur   |       4 |
|          4 | Melissa Jones     |    NULL |
|          5 | Michael Archer    |    NULL |
+------------+-------------------+---------+
```

This output shows us that there are no matching orderids for customers Melissa Jones and Michael Archer because the orderids for those customers are NULLs.

If we want to see only the customers who haven't ordered anything, we can do this by checking for those NULLs in the primary key field of the right table (in this case orderid) as that should not be NULL in any real rows:

```
select customers.customerid, customers.name
from customers left join orders
using (customerid)
where orders.orderid is null;
```

The result is

```
+------------+----------------+
| customerid | name           |
+------------+----------------+
|          4 | Melissa Jones  |
|          5 | Michael Archer |
+------------+----------------+
```

You'll also notice that we used a different syntax for the join condition in this example. Left joins support either the ON syntax we used in the first example, or the USING syntax in the second example. Notice that the USING syntax doesn't specify the table from which the join attribute comes—for this reason, the columns in the two tables must have the same name if you want to use USING.

Using Other Names for Tables: Aliases

It is often handy and occasionally essential to be able to refer to tables by other names. Other names for tables are called *aliases*. You can create these at the start of a query and then use them throughout. They are often handy as shorthand. Consider the huge query we looked at earlier, rewritten with aliases:

```
select c.name
from customers as c, orders as o, order_items as oi, books as b
where c.customerid = o.customerid
and o.orderid = oi.orderid
and oi.isbn = b.isbn
and b.title like '%Java%';
```

As we declare the tables we are going to use, we add an AS clause to declare the alias for that table. We can also use aliases for columns, but we'll return to this when we look at aggregate functions in a minute.

We need to use table aliases when we want to join a table to itself. This sounds more difficult and esoteric than it is. It is useful, if, for example, we want to find rows in the same table that have values in common. If we want to find customers who live in the same city—perhaps to set up a reading group— we can give the same table (Customers) two different aliases:

```
select c1.name, c2.name, c1.city
from customers as c1, customers as c2
where c1.city = c2.city
and c1.name != c2.name;
```

What we are basically doing is pretending that the table Customers is two different tables, c1 and c2, and performing a join on the city column. You will notice that we also need the second condition, c1.name != c2.name—this is to avoid each customer coming up as a match to herself.

Summary of Joins

The different types of joins we have looked at are summarized in Table 9.2. There are a few others, but these are the main ones you will use.

Table 9.2 **Join Types in MySQL**

Name	Description
Cartesian product	All combinations of all the rows in all the tables in the join. Used by specifying a comma between table names, and not specifying a `WHERE` clause.
Full join	Same as preceding.
Cross join	Same as above. Can also be used by specifying the `CROSS JOIN` keywords between the names of the tables being joined.
Inner join	Semantically equivalent to the comma. Can also be specified using the `INNER JOIN` keywords. Without a `WHERE` condition, equivalent to a full join. Usually, you will specify a `WHERE` condition as well to make this a true inner join.
Equi-join	Uses a conditional expression with an = to match rows from the different tables in the join. In SQL, this is a join with a `WHERE` clause.
Left join	Tries to match rows across tables and fills in nonmatching rows with `NULL`s. Use in SQL with the `LEFT JOIN` keywords. Used for finding missing values. You can equivalently use `RIGHT JOIN`.

Retrieving Data in a Particular Order

If you want to display rows retrieved by a query in a particular order, you can use the `ORDER BY` clause of the `SELECT` statement. This feature is handy for presenting output in a good human-readable format.

The `ORDER BY` clause is used to sort the rows on one or more of the columns listed in the `SELECT` clause. For example,

```
select name, address
from customers
order by name;
```

This query will return customer names and addresses in alphabetical order by name, like this:

```
+-----------------+---------------------+
| name            | address             |
+-----------------+---------------------+
| Alan Wong       | 1/47 Haines Avenue  |
| Julie Smith     | 25 Oak Street       |
| Melissa Jones   |                     |
| Michael Archer  | 12 Adderley Avenue  |
| Michelle Arthur | 357 North Road      |
+-----------------+---------------------+
```

(Notice that in this case, because the names are in firstname, lastname format, they are alphabetically sorted on the first name. If you wanted to sort on last names, you'd need to have them as two different fields.)

The default ordering is ascending (a to z or numerically upward). You can specify this if you like using the ASC keyword:

```
select name, address
from customers
order by name asc;
```

You can also do it in the opposite order using the DESC (descending) keyword:

```
select name, address
from customers
order by name desc;
```

You can sort on more than one column. You can also use column aliases or even their position numbers (for example, 3 is the third column in the table) instead of names.

Grouping and Aggregating Data

We often want to know how many rows fall into a particular set, or the average value of some column—say, the average dollar value per order. MySQL has a set of aggregate functions that are useful for answering this type of query.

These aggregate functions can be applied to a table as a whole, or to groups of data within a table.

The most commonly used ones are listed in Table 9.3.

Table 9.3   **Aggregate Functions in MySQL**

Name	Description
AVG(*column*)	Average of values in the specified column.
COUNT(*items*)	If you specify a column, this will give you the number of non-NULL values in that column. If you add the word DISTINCT in front of the column name, you will get a count of the distinct values in that column only. If you specify COUNT(*), you will get a row count regardless of NULL values.
MIN(*column*)	Minimum of values in the specified column.
MAX(*column*)	Maximum of values in the specified column.
STD(*column*)	Standard deviation of values in the specified column.
STDDEV(*column*)	Same as STD(*column*).
SUM(*column*)	Sum of values in the specified column.

Let's look at some examples, beginning with the one mentioned earlier. We can calculate the average total of an order like this:

```
select avg(amount)
from orders;
```

The output will be something like this:

```
+-------------+
| avg(amount) |
+-------------+
|   54.985002 |
+-------------+
```

In order to get more detailed information, we can use the GROUP BY clause. This enables us to view the average order total by group—say, for example, by customer number. This will tell us which of our customers place the biggest orders:

```
select customerid, avg(amount)
from orders
group by customerid;
```

When you use a GROUP BY clause with an aggregate function, it actually changes the behavior of the function. Rather than giving an average of the order amounts across the table, this query will give the average order amount for each customer (or, more specifically, for each customerid):

```
+------------+-------------+
| customerid | avg(amount) |
+------------+-------------+
|          1 |   49.990002 |
|          2 |   74.980003 |
|          3 |   47.485002 |
+------------+-------------+
```

One thing to note when using grouping and aggregate functions: In ANSI SQL, if you use an aggregate function or GROUP BY clause, the only things that can appear in your SELECT clause are the aggregate function(s) and the columns named in the GROUP BY clause. Also, if you want to use a column in a GROUP BY clause, it must be listed in the SELECT clause.

MySQL actually gives you a bit more leeway here. It supports an *extended syntax*, which enables you to leave items out of the SELECT clause if you don't actually want them.

In addition to grouping and aggregating data, we can actually test the result of an aggregate using a HAVING clause. This comes straight after the GROUP BY clause and is like a WHERE that applies only to groups and aggregates.

To extend our previous example, if we want to know which customers have an average order total of more than $50, we can use the following query:

```
select customerid, avg(amount)
from orders
group by customerid
having avg(amount) > 50;
```

Note that the HAVING clause applies to the groups. This query will return the following output:

```
+------------+-------------+
| customerid | avg(amount) |
+------------+-------------+
|          2 |   74.980003 |
+------------+-------------+
```

Choosing Which Rows to Return

One clause of the SELECT statement that can be particularly useful in Web applications is the LIMIT clause. This is used to specify which rows from the output should be returned. It takes two parameters: the row number from which to start and the number of rows to return.

This query illustrates the use of LIMIT:

```
select name
from customers
limit 2, 3;
```

This query can be read as, "Select name from customers, and then return 3 rows, starting from row 2 in the output." Note that row numbers are zero indexed—that is, the first row in the output is row number zero.

This is very useful for Web applications, such as when the customer is browsing through products in a catalog, and we want to show 10 items on each page.

Updating Records in the Database

In addition to retrieving data from the database, we often want to change it. For example, we might want to increase the prices of books in the database. We can do this using an UPDATE statement.

The usual form of an UPDATE statement is

```
UPDATE tablename
SET column1=expression1,column2=expression2,...
[WHERE condition]
[LIMIT number]
```

The basic idea is to update the table called *tablename*, setting each of the columns named to the appropriate expression. You can limit an UPDATE to particular rows with a WHERE clause, and limit the total number of rows to affect with a LIMIT clause.

Let's look at some examples.

If we want to increase all the book prices by 10%, we can use an UPDATE statement without a WHERE clause:

```
update books
set price=price*1.1;
```

If, on the other hand, we want to change a single row—say, to update a customer's address—we can do it like this:

```
update customers
set address = '250 Olsens Road'
where customerid = 4;
```

Altering Tables After Creation

In addition to updating rows, you might want to alter the structure of the tables within your database. For this purpose you can use the flexible ALTER TABLE statement. The basic form of this statement is

```
ALTER TABLE tablename alteration [, alteration ...]
```

Note that in ANSI SQL you can make only one alteration per ALTER TABLE statement, but MySQL allows you to make as many as you like. Each of the alteration clauses can be used to change different aspects of the table.

The different types of alteration you can make with this statement are shown in Table 9.4.

Table 9.4 **Possible Changes with the ALTER TABLE Statement**

Syntax	Description
ADD [COLUMN] `column_description` [FIRST | AFTER `column`]	Add a new column in the specified location (if not specified, then the column goes at the end). Note that `column_descriptions` need a name and a type, just as in a CREATE statement.
ADD [COLUMN] (`column_description`, `column_description`,...)	Add one or more new columns at the end of the table.
ADD INDEX [`index`] (`column`,...)	Add an index to the table on the specified column or columns.
ADD PRIMARY KEY (`column`,...)	Make the specified column or columns the primary key of the table.
ADD UNIQUE [`index`] (`column`,...)	Add a unique index to the table on the specified column or columns.
ALTER [COLUMN] `column` {SET DEFAULT `value` | DROP DEFAULT}	Add or remove a default value for a particular column.

Table 9.4   **Continued**

Syntax	Description
CHANGE [COLUMN] `column new_column _description`	Change the column called `column` so that it has the description listed. Note that this can be used to change the name of a column because a `column_description` includes a name.
MODIFY [COLUMN] `column_description`	Similar to CHANGE. Can be used to change column types, not names.
DROP [COLUMN] `column`	Delete the named column.
DROP PRIMARY KEY	Delete the primary index (but not the column).
DROP INDEX `index`	Delete the named index.
RENAME [AS] `new_table_name`	Rename a table.

Let's look at a few of the more common uses of ALTER TABLE.

One thing that comes up frequently is the realization that you haven't made a particular column "big enough" for the data it has to hold. For example, in our Customers table, we have allowed names to be 30 characters long. After we start getting some data, we might notice that some of the names are too long and are being truncated. We can fix this by changing the data type of the column so that it is 45 characters long instead:

```
alter table customers
modify name char(45) not null;
```

Another common occurrence is the need to add a column. Imagine that a sales tax on books is introduced locally, and that Book-O-Rama needs to add the amount of tax to the total order, but keep track of it separately. We can add a tax column to the Orders table as follows:

```
alter table orders
add tax float(6,2) after amount;
```

Getting rid of a column is another case that comes up frequently. We can delete the column we just added as follows:

```
alter table orders
drop tax;
```

Deleting Records from the Database

Deleting rows from the database is very simple. You can do this using the DELETE statement, which generally looks like this:

```
DELETE FROM table
[WHERE condition] [LIMIT number]
```

If you write

```
DELETE FROM table;
```

on its own, all the rows in a table will be deleted, so be careful! Usually, you want to delete specific rows, and you can specify the ones you want to delete with a WHERE clause. You might do this, if, for example, a particular book were no longer available, or if a particular customer hadn't placed any orders for a long time, and you wanted to do some housekeeping:

```
delete from customers
where customerid=5;
```

The LIMIT clause can be used to limit the maximum number of rows that are actually deleted.

Dropping Tables

At times you may want to get rid of an entire table. You can do this with the DROP TABLE statement. This is very simple, and it looks like this:

```
DROP TABLE table;
```

This will delete all the rows in the table and the table itself, so be careful using it.

Dropping a Whole Database

You can go even further and eliminate an entire database with the DROP DATABASE statement, which looks like this:

```
DROP DATABASE database;
```

This will delete all the rows, all the tables, all the indexes, and the database itself, so it goes without saying that you should be somewhat careful using this statement.

Further Reading

In this chapter, we have given an overview of the day-to-day SQL you will use when interacting with a MySQL database. In the next two chapters, we will look at how to connect MySQL and PHP so that you can access your database from the Web. We'll also explore some advanced MySQL techniques.

If you want to know more about SQL, you can always fall back on the ANSI SQL standard for a little light reading. It's available from:

```
http://www.ansi.org/
```

For more detail on the MySQL extensions to ANSI SQL, you can look at the MySQL Web site:

```
http://www.mysql.com
```

Next

In Chapter 10, "Accessing Your MySQL Database from the Web with PHP," we'll cover how you can make the Book-O-Rama database available over the Web.

10

Accessing Your MySQL Database from the Web with PHP

PREVIOUSLY, IN OUR WORK WITH PHP, we used a flat file to store and retrieve data. When we looked at this in Chapter 2, "Storing and Retrieving Data," we mentioned that relational database systems make a lot of these storage and retrieval tasks easier, safer, and more efficient in a Web application. Now, having worked with MySQL to create a database, we can begin connecting this database to a Web-based front end.

In this chapter, we'll explain how to access the Book-O-Rama database from the Web using PHP. You'll learn how to read from and write to the database, and how to filter potentially troublesome input data.

Overall, we'll look at

- How Web database architectures work
- The basic steps in querying a database from the Web
- Setting up a connection
- Getting information about available databases
- Choosing a database to use
- Querying the database
- Retrieving the query results
- Disconnecting from the database
- Putting new information in the database
- Other useful PHP—MySQL functions
- Using a generic database interface: PEAR DB
- Other PHP-database interfaces

How Web Database Architectures Work

In Chapter 7, "Designing Your Web Database," we outlined how Web database architectures work. Just to remind you, here are the steps again:

1. A user's Web browser issues an HTTP request for a particular Web page. For example, the user might have requested a search for all the books written by Michael Morgan at Book-O-Rama, using an HTML form. The search results page is called results.php.

2. The Web server receives the request for results.php, retrieves the file, and passes it to the PHP engine for processing.

3. The PHP engine begins parsing the script. Inside the script is a command to connect to the database and execute a query (perform the search for books). PHP opens a connection to the MySQL server and sends on the appropriate query.

4. The MySQL server receives the database query, processes it, and sends the results— a list of books—back to the PHP engine.

5. The PHP engine finishes running the script that will usually involve formatting the query results nicely in HTML. It then returns the resulting HTML to the Web server.

6. The Web server passes the HTML back to the browser, where the user can see the list of books she requested.

Now we have an existing MySQL database, so we can write the PHP code to perform the previous steps. We'll begin with the search form. This is a plain HTML form. The code for the form is shown in Listing 10.1.

Listing 10.1   **search.html—Book-O-Rama's Database Search Page**

```
<html>
<head>
  <title>Book-O-Rama Catalog Search</title>
</head>

<body>
  <h1>Book-O-Rama Catalog Search</h1>

  <form action="results.php" method="post">
    Choose Search Type:<br />
    <select name="searchtype">
      <option value="author">Author</option>
      <option value="title">Title</option>
      <option value="isbn">ISBN</option>
    </select>
    <br />
    Enter Search Term:<br />
```

Listing 10.1 **Continued**

```
    <input name="searchterm" type="text">
    <br />
    <input type="submit" value="Search">
  </form>

</body>
</html>
```

This is a pretty straightforward HTML form. The output of this HTML is shown in Figure 10.1.

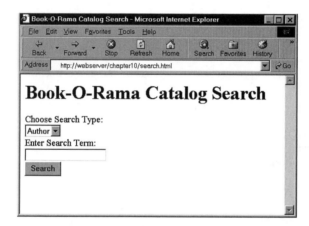

Figure 10.1   The search form is quite general, so you can search
for a book on its title, author, or ISBN.

The script that will be called when the Search button is pressed is results.php. This is listed in full in Listing 10.2. Through the course of this chapter, we will discuss what this script does and how it works.

Listing 10.2   **results.php—Retrieves Search Results from Our MySQL Database
and Formats Them for Display**

```
<html>
<head>
  <title>Book-O-Rama Search Results</title>
</head>
<body>
<h1>Book-O-Rama Search Results</h1>
<?php
  // create short variable names
  $searchtype=$HTTP_POST_VARS['searchtype'];
  $searchterm=$HTTP_POST_VARS['searchterm'];
```

Listing 10.2   **Continued**

```php
$searchterm= trim($searchterm);

if (!$searchtype || !$searchterm)
{
    echo 'You have not entered search details.  Please go back and try again.';
    exit;
}

$searchtype = addslashes($searchtype);
$searchterm = addslashes($searchterm);

@ $db = mysql_pconnect('localhost', 'bookorama', 'bookorama123');

if (!$db)
{
    echo 'Error: Could not connect to database.  Please try again later.';
    exit;
}

mysql_select_db('books');
$query = "select * from books where ".$searchtype." like '%".$searchterm."%'";
$result = mysql_query($query);

$num_results = mysql_num_rows($result);

echo '<p>Number of books found: '.$num_results.'</p>';

for ($i=0; $i <$num_results; $i++)
{
    $row = mysql_fetch_array($result);
    echo '<p><strong>'.($i+1).'. Title: ';
    echo htmlspecialchars(stripslashes($row['title']));
    echo '</strong><br />Author: ';
    echo stripslashes($row['author']);
    echo '<br />ISBN: ';
    echo stripslashes($row['isbn']);
    echo '<br />Price: ';
    echo stripslashes($row['price']);
    echo '</p>';
}
?>

</body>
</html>
```

Figure 10.2 illustrates the results of using this script to perform a search.

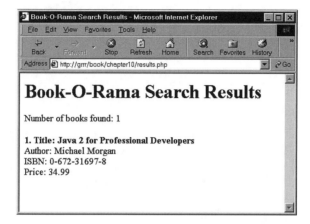

Figure 10.2   The results of searching the database for books about Java are presented in a Web page using the results.php script.

The Basic Steps in Querying a Database from the Web

In any script used to access a database from the Web, you will follow some basic steps:

1. Check and filter data coming from the user.
2. Set up a connection to the appropriate database.
3. Query the database.
4. Retrieve the results.
5. Present the results back to the user.

These are the steps we have followed in the script results.php, and we will go through each of them in turn.

Checking and Filtering Input Data

We begin our script by stripping any whitespace that the user might have inadvertently entered at the beginning or end of his search term. We do this by applying the function trim() to $searchterm.

```
$searchterm=trim($searchterm);
```

Our next step is to verify that the user has entered a search term and search type. Note that we check he entered a search term after trimming whitespace from the ends of $searchterm. Had we arranged these lines in the opposite order, we could get situations where a user's search term was not empty, so it did not create an error message, but it was all whitespace, so it was deleted by `trim()`:

```
if (!$searchtype || !$searchterm)
{
    echo 'You have not entered search details.  Please go back and try again.';
    exit;
}
```

You will notice that we've checked the `$searchtype` variable even though in this case it's coming from an HTML `SELECT`. You might ask why we bother checking data that has to be filled in. It's important to remember that there might be more than one interface to your database. For example, Amazon has many affiliates who use their search interface. Also, it's sensible to screen data in case of any security problems that can arise because of users coming from different points of entry.

Also, when you are going to use any data input by a user, it is important to filter it appropriately for any control characters. As you might remember, in Chapter 4, "String Manipulation and Regular Expressions," we talked about the functions `addslashes()` and `stripslashes()`. You need to use `addslashes()` when submitting any user input to a database such as MySQL and `stripslashes()` when returning output to the user who has had control characters slashed out.

In this case we have used `addslashes()` on the search terms:

```
$searchterm = addslashes($searchterm);
```

We have also used `stripslashes()` on the data coming back from the database. None of the data we have entered by hand into the database has any slashes in it—however, it also doesn't have any control characters in it. The call to `stripslashes()` will have no effect. As we build a Web interface for the database, chances are we will want to enter new books in it, and some of the details entered by a user might contain these characters. When we put them into the database, we will call `addslashes()`, which means that we must call `stripslashes()` when taking the data back out. This is a sensible habit to get into.

We are using the function `htmlspecialchars()` to encode characters that have special meanings in HTML. Our current test data does not include any ampersands (&), less than (<), greater than (>), or double quote (") symbols, but many fine book titles contain an ampersand. By using this function, we can eliminate future errors.

Setting Up a Connection

We use this line in our script to connect to the MySQL server:

```
@ $db = mysql_pconnect('localhost', 'bookorama', 'bookorama123');
```

We have used the `mysql_pconnect()` function to connect to the database. This function has the following prototype:

```
resource mysql_pconnect( [string host [:port] [:/socketpath]  [,
                string user [, string password]]] );
```

Generally speaking, you will pass it the name of the host on which the MySQL server is running, the username to login as, and the password of that user. All of these are optional, and if you don't specify them, the function uses some sensible defaults—localhost for the host, the username that the PHP process runs as, and a blank password.

The function returns a link identifier to your MySQL database on success (which you ought to store for further use) or false on failure. The result is worth checking as none of the rest of code will work without a valid database connection. We have done this using the following code:

```
if (!$db)
{
    echo 'Error: Could not connect to database.  Please try again later.';
    exit;
}
```

An alternative function that does almost the same thing as `mysql_pconnect()` is `mysql_connect()`. The difference is that `mysql_pconnect()` returns a *persistent* connection to the database.

A normal connection to the database will be closed when a script finishes execution, or when the script calls the `mysql_close()` function. A persistent connection remains open after the script finishes execution and cannot be closed with the `mysql_close()` function.

You might wonder why we would want to do this. The answer is that making a connection to a database involves a certain amount of overhead and therefore takes some time. When `mysql_pconnect()` is called, before it tries to connect to the database, it will automatically check if there is a persistent connection already open. If so, it will use this one rather than opening a new one. This saves time and server overhead.

It is also worth noting that persistent connections don't persist if you are running PHP as a CGI. (Each call to a PHP script starts a new instance of PHP and closes it when the script finishes execution. This also closes any persistent connections.)

Bear in mind that there is a limit to the number of MySQL connections that can exist at the same time. The MySQL parameter `max_connections` determines what this limit is. The purpose of this parameter and the related Apache parameter `MaxClients` is to tell the server to reject new connection requests rather than allowing machine resources to be all used at busy times or when software has crashed.

You can alter both of these parameters from their default values by editing the configuration files. To set `MaxClients` in Apache, edit the httpd.conf file on your system. To set `max_connections` for MySQL, edit the file `my.conf`.

If you use persistent connections and nearly every page in your site involves database access, you are likely to have a persistent connection open for each Apache process. This can cause a problem if you leave these parameters set to their default values. By default, Apache allows 150 connections, but MySQL only allows 100. At busy times, there might not be enough connections to go around. Depending on the capabilities of your hardware, you should adjust these so that each Web server process can have a connection.

Choosing a Database to Use

You will remember that when we are using MySQL from a command line interface, we need to tell it which database we plan to use with a command such as

```
use books;
```

We also need to do this when connecting from the Web. We perform this from PHP with a call to the `mysql_select_db()` function, which we have done in this case as follows:

```
mysql_select_db('books');
```

The `mysql_select_db()` function has the following prototype:

```
bool mysql_select_db(string database, [resource database_connection] );
```

It will try to use the database called *database*. You can also optionally include the database link you would like to perform this operation on (in this case $db), but if you don't specify it, the last opened link will be used. If you don't have a link open, the default one will be opened as if you had called `mysql_connect()`.

Querying the Database

To actually perform the query, we can use the `mysql_query()` function. Before doing this, however, it's a good idea to set up the query you want to run:

```
$query = "select * from books where ".$searchtype." like '%".$searchterm."%'";
```

In this case, we are searching for the user-input value ($searchterm) in the field the user specified ($searchtype). You will notice that we have used like for matching rather than equal—it's usually a good idea to be more tolerant in a database search.

> **Tip**
> It's important to realize that the query you send to MySQL does not need a semicolon on the end of it, unlike a query you type into the MySQL monitor.

We can now run the query:

```
$result = mysql_query($query);
```

The `mysql_query()` function has the following prototype:

```
resource mysql_query(string query, [resource database_connection] );
```

You pass it the query you want to run, and optionally, the database link (again, in this case $db). If not specified, the function will use the last opened link. If there isn't one, the function will open the default one as if you had called `mysql_connect()`.

This function returns a result identifier (that allows you to retrieve the query results) on success and false on failure. You should store this (as we have in this case in `$result`) so that you can do something useful with it.

Retrieving the Query Results

A variety of functions are available to break the results out of the result identifier in different ways. The result identifier is the key to accessing the zero, one, or more rows returned by the query.

In our example, we have used two of these: `mysql_num_rows()` and `mysql_fetch_array()`.

The function `mysql_num_rows()` gives you the number of rows returned by the query. You should pass it the result identifier, like this:

```
$num_results = mysql_num_rows($result);
```

It's useful to know this—if we plan to process or display the results, we know how many there are and can now loop through them:

```
for ($i=0; $i <$num_results; $i++)
{
  // process results
}
```

In each iteration of this loop, we are calling `mysql_fetch_array()`. The loop will not execute if no rows are returned. This is a function that takes each row from the resultset and returns the row as an associative array, with each key an attribute name and each value the corresponding value in the array:

```
$row = mysql_fetch_array($result);
```

Given the associative array `$row`, we can go through each field and display them appropriately, for example:

```
    echo '<br />ISBN: ';
    echo stripslashes($row['isbn']);
```

As previously mentioned, we have called `stripslashes()` to tidy up the value before displaying it.

There are several variations on getting results from a result identifier. Instead of an associative array, we can retrieve the results in an enumerated array with `mysql_fetch_row()`, as follows:

```
$row = mysql_fetch_row($result);
```

The attribute values will be listed in each of the array values `$row[0]`, `$row[1]`, and so on.

You could also fetch a row into an object with the `mysql_fetch_object()` function:

```
$row = mysql_fetch_object($result);
```

You can then access each of the attributes via `$row->title`, `$row->author`, and so on.

Each of these approaches fetches a row at a time. The other approach is to access a field at a time using `mysql_result()`. For this, you must specify the row number (from zero to the number of rows[ms]1) as well as the field name. For example,

```
$row = mysql_result($result, $i, 'title');
```

You can specify the field name as a string (either in the form `"title"` or `"books.title"`) or as a number (as in `mysql_fetch_row()`). You shouldn't mix use of `mysql_result()` with any of the other fetching functions.

The row-oriented fetch functions are far more efficient than `mysql_result()`, so in general you should use one of those.

Disconnecting from the Database

You can use

```
mysql_close(database_connection);
```

to close a nonpersistent database connection. This isn't strictly necessary because they will be closed when a script finishes execution anyway.

Putting New Information in the Database

Inserting new items into the database is remarkably similar to getting items out of the database. You follow the same basic steps—make a connection, send a query, and check the results. In this case, the query you send will be an INSERT rather than a SELECT. Although this is all very similar, it can sometimes be useful to look at an example. In Figure 10.3, you can see a basic HTML form for putting new books into the database. The HTML for this page is shown in Listing 10.3.

Listing 10.3 **newbook.html—HTML for the Book Entry Page**

```
<html>
<head>
  <title>Book-O-Rama - New Book Entry</title>
</head>

<body>
  <h1>Book-O-Rama - New Book Entry</h1>

  <form action="insert_book.php" method="post">
    <table border="0">
      <tr>
        <td>ISBN</td>
```

Listing 10.3 **Continued**

```
        <td><input type="text" name="isbn" maxlength="13" size="13"><br /></td>
      </tr>
      <tr>
        <td>Author</td>
        <td> <input type="text" name="author" maxlength="30" size="30"><br /></td>
      </tr>
      <tr>
        <td>Title</td>
        <td> <input type="text" name="title" maxlength="60" size="30"><br></td>
      </tr>
      <tr>
        <td>Price $</td>
        <td><input type="text" name="price" maxlength="7" size="7"><br /></td>
      </tr>
      <tr>
        <td colspan="2"><input type="submit" value="Register"></td>
      </tr>
    </table>
  </form>
</body>
</html>
```

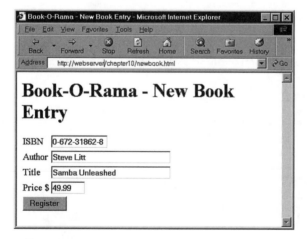

Figure 10.3 This interface for putting new books into the
database could be used by Book-O-Rama's staff.

The results of this form are passed along to `insert_book.php`, a script that takes the
details, performs some minor validations, and attempts to write the data into the database. The code for this script is shown in Listing 10.4.

Listing 10.4   **insert_book.php—This Script Writes New Books into the Database**

```
<html>
<head>
  <title>Book-O-Rama Book Entry Results</title>
</head>
<body>
<h1>Book-O-Rama Book Entry Results</h1>
<?php
  // create short variable names
  $isbn=$HTTP_POST_VARS['isbn'];
  $author=$HTTP_POST_VARS['author'];
  $title=$HTTP_POST_VARS['title'];
  $price=$HTTP_POST_VARS['price'];

  if (!$isbn || !$author || !$title || !$price)
  {
     echo 'You have not entered all the required details.<br />'
          .'Please go back and try again.';
     exit;
  }

  $isbn = addslashes($isbn);
  $author = addslashes($author);
  $title = addslashes($title);
  $price = doubleval($price);

  @ $db = mysql_pconnect('localhost', 'bookorama', 'bookorama123');

  if (!$db)
  {
     echo 'Error: Could not connect to database.  Please try again later.';
     exit;
  }

  mysql_select_db('books');
  $query = "insert into books values
            ('".$isbn."', '".$author."', '".$title."', '".$price."')";
  $result = mysql_query($query);
  if ($result)
     echo  mysql_affected_rows().' book inserted into database.';
?>

</body>
</html>
```

The results of successfully inserting a book are shown in Figure 10.4.

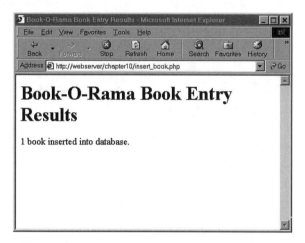

Figure 10.4   The script completes successfully and reports that the book has been added to the database.

If you look at the code for insert_book.php, you will see that much of it is similar to the script we wrote to retrieve data from the database. We have checked that all the form fields were filled in, and we formatted them correctly for insertion into the database with addslashes():

```
$isbn = addslashes($isbn);
$author = addslashes($author);
$title = addslashes($title);
$price = doubleval($price);
```

As the price is stored in the database as a float, we don't want to put slashes into it. We can achieve the same effect of filtering out any odd characters on this numerical field by calling doubleval(), which we discussed in Chapter 1, "PHP Crash Course." This will also take care of any currency symbols that the user might have typed in the form.

Again, we have connected to the database using mysql_pconnect(), and set up a query to send to the database. In this case, the query is an SQL INSERT:

```
$query = "insert into books values
        ('".$isbn."', '".$author."', '".$title."', '".$price."')";
$result = mysql_query($query);
```

This is executed on the database in the usual way by calling mysql_query().

One significant difference between using INSERT and SELECT is in the use of mysql_affected_rows():

```
echo  mysql_affected_rows()." book inserted into database.";
```

In the previous script, we used `mysql_num_rows()` to determine how many rows were returned by a `SELECT`. When you write queries that change the database such as `INSERT`s, `DELETE`s, and `UPDATE`s, you should use `mysql_affected_rows()` instead.

This covers the basics of using MySQL databases from PHP. We'll just briefly look at some of the other useful functions that we haven't talked about yet.

Other Useful PHP-MySQL Functions

There are some other useful PHP-MySQL functions, which we will discuss briefly.

Freeing Up Resources

If you are having memory problems while a script is running, you might want to use `mysql_free_result()`. This has the following prototype:

```
bool mysql_free_result(resource result);
```

You call it with a result identifier, like this:

```
mysql_free_result($result);
```

This has the effect of freeing up the memory used to store the result. Obviously you wouldn't call this until you have finished working with a resultset.

Creating and Deleting Databases

To create a new MySQL database from a PHP script, you can use `mysql_create_db()`, and to drop one, you can use `mysql_drop_db()`.

These functions have the following prototypes:

```
bool mysql_create_db(string database, [resource database_connection] );
bool mysql_drop_db(string database, [resource database_connection] );
```

Both these functions take a database name and an optional connection. If no connection is supplied, the last open one will be used. They will attempt to create or drop the named database. Both functions return true on success and false on failure.

Other PHP-Database Interfaces

PHP supports libraries for connecting to a large number of databases including Oracle, Microsoft SQL Server, mSQL, and PostgreSQL.

In general, the principles of connecting to and querying any of these databases are much the same. The individual function names vary, and different databases have slightly different functionality, but if you can connect to MySQL, you should be able to easily adapt your knowledge to any of the others.

If you want to use a database that doesn't have a specific library available in PHP, you can use the generic ODBC functions. ODBC stands for *Open Database Connectivity* and is a standard for connections to databases. It has the most limited functionality of any of the function sets, for fairly obvious reasons. If you have to be compatible with everything, you can't exploit the special features of anything.

In addition to the libraries that come with PHP, database abstraction classes such as Metabase or PEAR::DB are available that allow you to use the same function names for each different type of database.

Using a Generic Database Interface: PEAR DB

We will look at a brief example using the PEAR DB abstraction layer. This is one of the core components of PEAR, and probably the most widely used of all the PEAR components. If you have PEAR installed, then you should already have DB. If not, please refer to the "PEAR Installation" section in Appendix A.

For comparative purposes, let's look at how we would have written our search results script differently using DB.

Listing 10.5   **results_generic.php—Retrieves Search Results from our MySQL Database and Formats Them for Display**

```
<html>
<head>
  <title>Book-O-Rama Search Results</title>
</head>
<body>
<h1>Book-O-Rama Search Results</h1>
<?php
  // create short variable names
  $searchtype=$HTTP_POST_VARS['searchtype'];
  $searchterm=$HTTP_POST_VARS['searchterm'];

  $searchterm= trim($searchterm);

  if (!$searchtype || !$searchterm)
  {
    echo 'You have not entered search details.  Please go back and try again.';
    exit;
  }

  $searchtype = addslashes($searchtype);
  $searchterm = addslashes($searchterm);

  // set up for using PEAR DB
  require('DB.php');
  $user = 'bookorama';
  $pass = 'bookorama123';
  $host = 'localhost';
```

Listing 10.5 **Continued**

```php
$db_name = 'books';

// set up universal connection string or DSN
$dsn = "mysql://$user:$pass@$host/$db_name";

// connect to database
$db = DB::connect($dsn, true);

// check if connection worked
if (DB::isError($db))
{
  echo $db->getMessage();
  exit;
}

// perform query
$query = "select * from books where ".$searchtype." like '%".$searchterm."'";
$result = $db->query($query);
// check that result was ok
if (DB::isError($result))
{
  echo $db->getMessage();
  exit;
}

// get number of returned rows
$num_results = $result->numRows();

// display each returned row
for ($i=0; $i <$num_results; $i++)
{
    $row = $result->fetchRow(DB_FETCHMODE_ASSOC);
    echo '<p><strong>'.($i+1).'. Title: ';
    echo htmlspecialchars(stripslashes($row['title']));
    echo '</strong><br />Author: ';
    echo stripslashes($row['author']);
    echo '<br />ISBN: ';
    echo stripslashes($row['isbn']);
    echo '<br />Price: ';
    echo stripslashes($row['price']);
    echo '</p>';
}

// disconnect from database
$db->disconnect();
```

Listing 10.5   **Continued**

```
?>

</body>
</html>
```

Let's examine what we are doing differently in this script.
To connect to the database we use the line

```
$db = DB::connect($dsn, true);
```

This function accepts a universal connection string that contains all the parameters necessary to connect to the database. You can see this if you look at the format of the connection string:

```
$dsn = "mysql://$user:$pass@$host/$db_name";
```

The second parameter to connect() determines whether the connection will be persistent or not. A value of true will make it persistent.

After this, we check to see if connection was unsuccessful using the isError() method and, if so, print the error message and exit:

```
if (DB::isError($db))
{
  echo $db->getMessage();
  exit;
}
```

Assuming everything has gone well, we then set up a query and execute it as follows:

```
$result = $db->query($query);
```

We can check the number of rows returned:

```
$num_results = $result->numRows();
```

We retrieve each row as follows:

```
$row = $result->fetchRow(DB_FETCHMODE_ASSOC);
```

The generic method fetchRow() can fetch a row in many different formats —the parameter DB_FETCHMODE_ASSOC tells it that we would like the row returned as an associative array.

After outputting the returned rows, we finish by closing the database connection:

```
$db->disconnect();
```

As you can see, this generic example is very similar to our first script.
The advantages of using DB are that we only need to remember one set of database functions and that the code will require minimal changes if we decide to change our database software.

Since this is a MySQL book we will use the MySQL native libraries for a little extra speed and flexibility. You might wish to use the DB package in your projects, however, as there are times when the use of an abstraction layer can be extremely helpful.

Further Reading

For more information on connecting MySQL and PHP together, you can read the appropriate sections of the PHP and MySQL manuals.

For more information on ODBC, visit

```
http://www.webopedia.com/TERM/O/ODBC.html
```

Metabase is available from

```
http://phpclasses.upperdesign.com/browse.html/package/20
```

Next

In the next chapter, we will go into more detail about MySQL administration and discuss how you can optimize your databases.

11

Advanced MySQL

IN THIS CHAPTER, WE'LL COVER SOME more advanced MySQL topics including advanced privileges, security, and optimization.

The topics we'll cover are

- Understanding the privilege system in detail
- Making your MySQL database secure
- Getting more information about databases
- Speeding things up with indexes
- Optimization tips
- Different table types
- Backup and recovery

Understanding the Privilege System in Detail

Previously (in Chapter 8, "Creating Your Web Database") we looked at setting up users and granting them privileges. We did this with the GRANT command. If you're going to administer a MySQL database, it can be useful to understand exactly what GRANT does and how it works.

When you issue a GRANT statement, it affects tables in the special database called mysql. Privilege information is stored in five tables in this database. Given this, when granting privileges on databases, you should be cautious about granting access to the mysql database.

One side note is that the GRANT command is only available from MySQL version 3.22.11 onward.

We can look at what's in the mysql database by logging in as an administrator and typing

```
use mysql;
```

If you do this, you can then view the tables in this database by typing

show tables;

as usual.

The results you get will look something like this:

```
+-----------------+
| Tables_in_mysql |
+-----------------+
| columns_priv    |
| db              |
| func            |
| host            |
| tables_priv     |
| user            |
+-----------------+
```

Each of these tables except for the func table stores information about privileges. (That one stores user defined functions.) They are sometimes called *grant tables*. These tables vary in their specific function but all serve the same general function, which is to determine what users are and are not allowed to do. Each of them contains two types of fields: scope fields, which identify the user, host, and part of a database; and privilege fields, which identify which actions can be performed by that user in that scope.

The user table is used to decide whether a user can connect to the MySQL server and whether she has any administrator privileges. The db and host tables determine which databases the user can access. The tables_priv table determines which tables within a database a user can use, and the columns_priv table determines which columns within tables they have access to.

The user Table

This table contains details of global user privileges. It determines whether a user is allowed to connect to the MySQL server at all, and whether she has any global level privileges; that is, privileges that apply to every database in the system.

We can see the structure of this table by issuing a describe user; statement. The schema for the user table is shown in Table 11.1.

Table 11.1 **Schema of the user Table in the mysql Database**

Field	Type
Host	char(60)
User	char(16)
Password	char(16)
Select_priv	enum('N','Y')
Insert_priv	enum('N','Y')

Table 11.1 **Continued**

Field	Type
Update_priv	enum('N','Y')
Delete_priv	enum('N','Y')
Create_priv	enum('N','Y')
Drop_priv	enum('N','Y')
Reload_priv	enum('N','Y')
Shutdown_priv	enum('N','Y')
Process_priv	enum('N','Y')
File_priv	enum('N','Y')
Grant_priv	enum('N','Y')
References_priv	enum('N','Y')
Index_priv	enum('N','Y')
Alter_priv	enum('N','Y')

Each row in this table corresponds to a set of privileges for a user coming from a host and logging in with the password Password. These are the *scope fields* for this table, as they describe the scope of the other fields, called *privilege fields*.

The privileges listed in this table (and the others to follow) correspond to the privileges we granted using GRANT in Chapter 8. For example, Select_priv corresponds to the privilege to run a SELECT command.

If a user has a particular privilege, the value in that column will be Y. Conversely, if a user has not been granted that privilege, the value will be N.

All the privileges listed in the user table are global, that is, they apply to *all the databases in the system* (including the mysql database). Administrators will therefore have some Ys in there, but the majority of users should have all Ns. Normal users should have rights to appropriate databases, not all tables.

The db and host Tables

Most of your average users' privileges are stored in the tables db and host.

The db table determines which users can access which databases from which hosts. The privileges listed in this table apply to whichever database is named in a particular row.

The host table supplements the db table. If a user is to connect to a database from multiple hosts, no host will be listed for that user in the db table. Instead, she will have a set of entries in the host table, one to specify the privileges for each user-host combination.

The schemas of these two tables are shown in Tables 11.2 and 11.3, respectively.

Table 11.2 **Schema of the db Table in the mysql Database**

Field	Type
Host	char(60)
Db	char(64)
User	char(16)
Select_priv	enum('N','Y')
Insert_priv	enum('N','Y')
Update_priv	enum('N','Y')
Delete_priv	enum('N','Y')
Create_priv	enum('N','Y')
Drop_priv	enum('N','Y')
Grant_priv	enum('N','Y')
References_priv	enum('N','Y')
Index_priv	enum('N','Y')
Alter_priv	enum('N','Y')

Table 11.3 **Schema of the host Table in the mysql Database**

Field	Type
Host	char(60)
Db	char(64)
Select_priv	enum('N','Y')
Insert_priv	enum('N','Y')
Update_priv	enum('N','Y')
Delete_priv	enum('N','Y')
Create_priv	enum('N','Y')
Drop_priv	enum('N','Y')
Grant_priv	enum('N','Y')
References_priv	enum('N','Y')
Index_priv	enum('N','Y')
Alter_priv	enum ('N','Y')

The tables_priv and columns_priv Tables

These two tables are used to store table-level privileges and column-level privileges, respectively. They work like the db table, except that they provide privileges for tables within a specific database and columns within a specific table respectively.

These tables have a slightly different structure to the user, db, and host tables. The schemas for the tables_priv table and the columns_priv table are shown in Tables 11.4 and 11.5, respectively.

Table 11.4   **Schema of the tables_priv Table in the mysql Database**

Field	Type
Host	char(60)
Db	char(64)
User	char(16)
Table_name	char(60)
Grantor	char(77)
Timestamp	timestamp(14)
Table_priv	set('Select', 'Insert', 'Update', 'Delete', 'Create', 'Drop', 'Grant', 'References', 'Index', 'Alter')
Column_priv	set ('Select', 'Insert', 'Update', 'References')

Table 11.5   **Schema of the columns_priv Table in the mysql Database**

Field	Type
Host	char(60)
Db	char(64)
User	char(16)
Table_name	char(64)
Column_name	char(64)
Timestamp	timestamp(14)
Column_priv	set('Select', 'Insert', 'Update', 'References')

The Grantor column in the tables_priv table stores the user who granted this privilege to this user. The Timestamp column in both these tables stores the date and time when the privilege was granted.

Access Control: How MySQL Uses the Grant Tables

MySQL uses the grant tables to determine what a user is allowed to do in a two-stage process:

1. Connection verification. Here, MySQL checks whether you are allowed to connect at all, based on information from the user table, as shown previously. This is based on your username, hostname, and password. If a username is blank, it matches all users. Hostnames can be specified with a wildcard character (%). This can be

used as the entire field—that is, % matches all hosts—or as part of a hostname, for example, %.tangledweb.com.au matches all hosts ending in .tangledweb.com.au. If the password field is blank, then no password is required. It's more secure to avoid having blank users, wildcards in hosts, and users without passwords.

2. Request verification. Each time you enter a request, after you have established a connection, MySQL checks whether you have the appropriate level of privileges to perform that request. The system begins by checking your global privileges (in the user table) and if they are not sufficient, checks the db and host tables. If you still don't have sufficient privileges, MySQL will check the tables_priv table, and, if this is not enough, finally it will check the columns_priv table.

Updating Privileges: When Do Changes Take Effect?

The MySQL server automatically reads the grant tables when it is started, and when you issue GRANT and REVOKE statements.

However, now that we know where and how those privileges are stored, we can alter them manually. When you update them manually, the MySQL server *will not notice that they have changed*.

You need to point out to the server that a change has occurred, and there are three ways you can do this. You can type

```
FLUSH PRIVILEGES;
```

at the MySQL prompt (you will need to be logged in as an administrator to do this). This is the most commonly used way of updating the privileges.

Alternatively you can run either

```
mysqladmin flush-privileges
```

or

```
mysqladmin reload
```

from your operating system.

After this, global level privileges will be checked the next time a user connects; database privileges will be checked when the next use statement is issued; and table and column level privileges will be checked on a user's next request.

Making Your MySQL Database Secure

Security is important, especially when you begin connecting your MySQL database to your Web site. In this section, we'll look at the precautions you ought to take to protect your database.

MySQL from the Operating System's Point of View

It's a bad idea to run the MySQL server (`mysqld`) as root if you are running a UNIX-like operating system. This gives a MySQL user with a full set of privileges the right to read and write files anywhere in the operating system. This is an important point, easily overlooked, which was famously used to hack Apache's Web site. (Fortunately the crackers were "white hats" [good guys], and the only action they took was to tighten up security.)

It's a good idea to set up a MySQL user specifically for the purpose of running `mysqld`. In addition, you can then make the directories (where the physical data is stored) accessible only by the MySQL user. In many installations, the server is set up to run as userid mysql, in the mysql group.

You should also ideally set up your MySQL server behind your firewall. This way you can stop connections from unauthorized machines—check and see whether you can connect from outside to your server on port number 3306. This is the default port that MySQL runs on, and should be closed on your firewall.

Passwords

Make sure that all your users have passwords (especially root!) and that these are well chosen and regularly changed, as with operating system passwords. The basic rule to remember here is that passwords that are or contain words from a dictionary are a bad idea. Combinations of letters and numbers are best.

If you are going to store passwords in script files, then make sure only the user whose password is stored can see that script. The two main places this can arise are

1. In the `mysql.server` script, you might need to use the UNIX root password. If this is the case, make sure only root can read this script.

2. In PHP scripts that are used to connect to the database, you will need to store the password for that user. This can be done securely by putting the login and password in a file called, for example, `dbconnect.php`, that you then include when required. This script can be stored outside the Web document tree and made accessible only to the appropriate user. Remember that if you put these details in a .inc or some other extension file in the Web tree, you must be careful to check that your Web server knows these files must be interpreted as PHP so that the details cannot be viewed in a Web browser.

Don't store passwords in plain text in your database. MySQL passwords are not stored that way, but commonly in Web applications you additionally want to store Web site members' login names and passwords. You can encrypt passwords (one-way) using MySQL's `PASSWORD()` or `MD5()` functions. Remember that if you `INSERT` a password in one of these formats when you run a `SELECT` (to log a user in), you will need to use the same function again to check the password a user has typed.

We will use this functionality when we come to implement the projects in Part V, "Building Practical PHP and MySQL Projects."

User Privileges

Knowledge is power. Make sure that you understand MySQL's privilege system, and the consequences of granting particular privileges. Don't grant more privileges to any user than she needs. You should check this by looking at the grant tables.

In particular, don't grant the PROCESS, FILE, SHUTDOWN, and RELOAD privileges to any user other than an administrator unless absolutely necessary. The PROCESS privilege can be used to see what other users are doing and typing, including their passwords. The FILE privilege can be used to read and write files to and from the operating system (including, say, /etc/password on a Unix system).

The GRANT privilege should also be granted with caution as this allows users to share their privileges with others.

Make sure that when you set up users, you only grant them access from the hosts that they will be connecting from. If you have jane@localhost as a user, that's fine, but plain jane is pretty common and could log in from anywhere—and she might not be the jane you think she is. Avoid using wildcards in hostnames for similar reasons.

You can further increase security by using IPs rather than domain names in your host table. This avoids problems with errors or crackers at your DNS. You can enforce this by starting the MySQL daemon with the --skip-name-resolve option, which means that all host column values must be either IP addresses or localhost.

Another alternative is to start mysqld with the --secure option. This checks resolved IPs to see whether they resolve back to the hostname provided. (This is on by default from version 3.22 onwards.)

You should also prevent non-administrative users from having access to the mysqladmin program on your Web server. Because this runs from the command line, it is an issue of operating system privilege.

Web Issues

When you connect your MySQL database to the Web, it raises some special security issues.

It's not a bad idea to start by setting up a special user just for the purpose of Web connections. This way you can give them the minimum privilege necessary and not grant, for example, DROP, ALTER, or CREATE privileges to that user. You might grant SELECT only on catalog tables, and INSERT only on order tables. Again, this is an illustration of how to use the principle of least privilege.

> **Caution**
> We talked in the last chapter about using PHP's addslashes() and stripslashes() functions to get rid of any problematic characters in strings. It's important to remember to do this, and to do a general data clean up before sending anything to MySQL. You might remember that we used the doubleval() function to check that the numeric data was really numeric. It's a common error to forget this—people remember to use addslashes() but not to check numeric data.

You should always check all data coming in from a user. Even if your HTML form consisted of select boxes and radio buttons, someone might alter the URL to try to crack your script. It's also worth checking the size of the incoming data.

If users are typing in passwords or confidential data to be stored in your database, remember that it will be transmitted from the browser to the server in plaintext unless you use SSL (Secure Sockets Layer). We'll discuss using SSL in more detail later.

Getting More Information About Databases

So far, we've used SHOW and DESCRIBE to find out what tables are in the database and what columns are in them. We'll briefly look at how else they can be used, and at the use of the EXPLAIN statement to get more information about how a SELECT is performed.

Getting Information with SHOW

Previously we had used

```
show tables;
```

to get a list of tables in the database.
The statement

```
show databases;
```

will display a list of available databases. You can then use the SHOW TABLES statement to see a list of tables in one of those databases:

```
show tables from books;
```

When you use SHOW TABLES without specifying a database, it defaults to the one in use.

When you know what the tables are, you can get a list of the columns:

```
show columns from orders from books;
```

If you leave the database parameter off, the SHOW COLUMNS statement will default to the database currently in use. You can also use the table.column notation:

```
show columns from books.orders;
```

One other very useful variation of the SHOW statement can be used to see what privileges a user has. For example, if we run the following, we'll get the output shown in Figure 11.1:

```
show grants for bookorama;
```

The GRANT statements shown are not necessarily the ones that were executed to give privileges to a particular user, but rather summary equivalent statements that would produce the user's current level of privilege.

```
+----------------------------------------------------------------------------+
| Grants for bookorama@%                         |                           |
+----------------------------------------------------------------------------+
|GRANT USAGE ON *.* TO 'bookorama'@'%' IDENTIFIED BY PASSWORD '6a87b6810cb073de' |
|GRANT SELECT, INSERT, UPDATE, DELETE, CREATE, DROP, INDEX, ALTER ON books.* TO 'bookorama'@'%' |
+----------------------------------------------------------------------------+
```

Figure 11.1   The output of the SHOW GRANTS statement.

> **Note**
>
> The SHOW GRANTS statement was added in MySQL version 3.23.4—if you have an earlier version, this statement won't work.

There are many other variations of the SHOW statement. A summary of all the variations is shown in Table 11.6.

Table 11.6 **SHOW Statement Syntax**

Variation	Description
SHOW DATABASES [LIKE database]	Lists available databases, optionally with names like database.
SHOW TABLES [FROM database] [LIKE table]	Lists tables from the database currently in use, or from the database called database if specified, optionally with table names like table.
SHOW COLUMNS FROM table [FROM database] [LIKE column]	Lists all the columns in a particular table from the database currently in use, or from the database specified, optionally with column names like column. You might use SHOW FIELDS instead of SHOW COLUMNS.
SHOW INDEX FROM table [FROM database]	Shows details of all the indexes on a particular table from the database currently in use, or from the database called database if specified. You might use SHOW KEYS instead.
SHOW STATUS [LIKE status_item]	Gives information about a number of system items, such as the number of threads running. The LIKE clause is used to match against the names of these items, so, for example, 'Thread%' matches the items 'Threads_cached', 'Threads_connected', and 'Threads_running'.
SHOW VARIABLES [LIKE variable_name]	Displays the names and values of the MySQL system variables, such as the version number. The LIKE clause can be used to match against these in a fashion similar to SHOW STATUS.
SHOW [FULL] PROCESSLIST	Displays all the running processes in the system, that is, the queries that are currently being executed. Most users will see their own threads but if they have the PROCESS privilege, they can see everybody's processes—including passwords if these are in queries. The queries are truncated to 100 characters by default. Using the optional keyword FULL displays the full queries.

Table 11.6 **Continued**

Variation	Description
SHOW TABLE STATUS [FROM *database*] [LIKE *database*]	Displays information about each of the tables in the database currently being used, or the database called *database* if it is specified, optionally with a wildcard match. This information includes the table type and when each table was last updated.
SHOW GRANTS FOR *user*	Shows the GRANT statements required to give the user specified in *user* his current level of privilege.

Getting Information About Columns with DESCRIBE

As an alternative to the SHOW COLUMNS statement, you can use the DESCRIBE statement, similar to the DESCRIBE statement in Oracle (another RDBMS). The basic syntax for it is

```
DESCRIBE table [column];
```

This will give information about all the columns in the table or a specific column if *column* is specified. You can use wildcards in the column name if you like.

Understanding How Queries Work with EXPLAIN

The EXPLAIN statement can be used in two ways. First, you can use

```
EXPLAIN table;
```

This gives very similar output to DESCRIBE *table* or SHOW COLUMNS FROM *table*.

The second and more interesting way you can use EXPLAIN allows you to see exactly how MySQL evaluates a SELECT query. To use it this way, just put the word explain in front of a SELECT statement.

You can use the EXPLAIN statement when you are trying to get a complex query to work and clearly haven't got it quite right, or when a query's taking a lot longer to process than it should. If you are writing a complex query, you can check this in advance by running the EXPLAIN command before you actually run the query. With the output from this statement, you can rework your SQL to optimize it if necessary. It's also a handy learning tool.

For example, try running the following query on the Book-O-Rama database. It produces the output shown in Figure 11.2.

```
explain
select customers.name
from customers, orders, order_items, books
where customers.customerid = orders.customerid
and orders.orderid = order_items.orderid
and order_items.isbn = books.isbn
and books.title like '%Java%';
```

```
+----------------+---------+---------------+---------+---------+------------------+------+-------------+
| table          | type    | possible_keys | key     | key_len | ref              | rows | Extra       |
+----------------+---------+---------------+---------+---------+------------------+------+-------------+
| orders         | ALL     | PRIMARY       | NULL    | NULL    | NULL             |    4 |             |
| order_items    | ref     | PRIMARY       | PRIMARY |    4    | orders.orderid   |    1 | Using index |
| customers      | ALL     | PRIMARY       | NULL    | NULL    | NULL             |    3 | where used  |
| books          | eq_ref  | PRIMARY       | PRIMARY |   13    | order_items.isbn |    1 | where used  |
+----------------+---------+---------------+---------+---------+------------------+------+-------------+
```

Figure 11.2   The output of the EXPLAIN statement.

This might look confusing at first, but it can be very useful. Let's look at the columns in this table one by one.

The first column, `table`, just lists the tables used to answer the query. Each row in the result gives more information about how that particular table is used in this query. In this case, you can see that the tables used are `orders`, `order_items`, `customers`, and `books`. (We knew this already by looking at the query.)

The `type` column explains how the table is being used in joins in the query. The set of values this column can have is shown in Table 11.7. These values are listed in order from fastest to slowest in terms of query execution. It gives you an idea of how many rows need to be read from each table in order to execute a query.

Table 11.7   **Possible Join Types as Shown in Output from EXPLAIN**

Type	Description
const or system	The table is read from only once. This happens when the table has exactly one row. The type `system` is used when it is a system table, and the type `const` otherwise.
eq_ref	For every set of rows from the other tables in the join, we read one row from this table. This is used when the join uses all the parts of the index on the table, and the index is UNIQUE or is the primary key.
ref	For every set of rows from the other tables in the join, we read a set of rows from this table which all match. This is used when the join cannot choose a single row based on the join condition, that is, when only part of the key is used in the join, or if it is not UNIQUE or a primary key.
range	For every set of rows from the other tables in the join, we read a set of rows from this table that fall into a particular range.
index	The entire index is scanned.
ALL	Every row in the table is scanned.

In the previous example, you can see that one of the tables is joined using `eq_ref` (`books`), and one is joined using `ref` (`order_items`), but the other two (`orders` and `customers`) are joined by using `ALL`; that is, by looking at every single row in the table. The `rows` column backs this up—it lists (roughly) the number of rows of each table that has to be scanned to perform the join. You can multiply these together to get the total number of rows examined when a query is performed. We multiply these numbers because a join is like a product of rows in different tables—check out Chapter 9, "Working with Your MySQL Database," for details. Remember that this is the number of rows examined, not the number of rows returned, and that it is only an estimate—MySQL can't know the exact number without performing the query.

Obviously, the smaller we can make this number, the better. At present we have a pretty negligible amount of data in the database, but when the database starts to increase in size, this query would blow out in execution time. We'll return to this in a minute.

The possible_keys column lists, as you might expect, the keys that MySQL might use to join the table. In this case, you can see that the possible keys are all PRIMARY keys.

The key column is either the key from the table MySQL actually used, or NULL if no key was used. You'll notice that, although there are possible PRIMARY keys for the orders and customers tables, they were not used in this query. We'll look at how to fix this in a minute.

The key_len column indicates the length of the key used. You can use this to tell whether only part of a key was used. This is relevant when you have keys that consist of more than one column. In this case, where the keys were used (order_items and books), the full key was used.

The ref column shows the columns used with the key to select rows from the table.

Finally, the Extra column tells you any other information about how the join was performed. The possible values you might see in this column are shown in Table 11.8.

Table 11.8   Possible Values for Extra Column as Shown in Output from EXPLAIN

Value	Meaning
Not exists	The query has been optimized to use LEFT JOIN.
Range checked for each record	For each row in the set of rows from the other tables in the join, try to find the best index to use, if any.
Using filesort	Two passes will be required to sort the data. (This obviously takes twice as long.)
Using index	All information from the table comes from the index—that is, the rows are not actually looked up.
Using temporary	A temporary table will need to be created to execute this query.
WHERE used	A WHERE clause is being used to select rows.

There are several ways you can fix problems you spot in the output from EXPLAIN. First, check column types and make sure they are the same. This applies particularly to column width. Indexes can't be used to match columns if they have different widths. You can fix this by changing the types of columns to match, or building this in to your design to begin with.

Second, you can tell the join optimizer to examine key distributions and therefore optimize joins more efficiently using the myisamchk utility. You can invoke this by typing

```
myisamchk --analyze pathtomysqldatabase/table
```

You can check multiple tables by listing them all on the command line, or by using

```
myisamchk --analyze pathtomysqldatabase/*.MYI
```

You can check all tables in all databases by running the following, which will produce the output shown in Figure 11.3:

```
myisamchk --analyze pathtomysqldatadirectory/*/*.MYI
```

```
+-------------+-------+--------------+---------+---------+---------------------+------+----------------------------+
| table       | type  | possible_keys| key     | key_len | ref _____ | rows | Extra                      |
+-------------+-------+--------------+---------+---------+---------------------+------+----------------------------+
| books       | ALL   | PRIMARY      | NULL    | NULL    | NULL                | 4    | where used                 |
| order_items | index | PRIMARY      | PRIMARY | 17      | NULL                | 5    | where used; Using index    |
| orders      | eq_ref| PRIMARY      | PRIMARY | 4       | order_items.orderid | 1    |                            |
| customers   | eq_ref| PRIMARY      | PRIMARY | 4       | orders.customerid   | 1    |                            |
+-------------+-------+--------------+---------+---------+---------------------+------+----------------------------+
```

Figure 11.3   This is the output of the EXPLAIN after running myisamchk.

You'll notice that the way the query is evaluated has changed quite a lot. We're now only using ALL the rows in one of the tables (books), which is fine. In particular, we're now using eq_ref for two of the tables and index for the other. MySQL is also now using the whole key for order_items (17 characters as opposed to 4 previously).

You'll also notice the number of rows being used has actually gone up. This is probably caused by the fact that we have little data in the actual database at this point. Remember that the number of rows listed is only an estimate—try performing the actual query and checking this. If these numbers are way off, the MySQL manual suggests using a straight join and listing the tables in your FROM clause in a different order.

Third, you might want to consider adding a new index to the table. If this query is a) slow and b) common, you should seriously consider this. If it's a one-off query that you'll never use again, such as an obscure report requested once, it won't be worth the effort, as it will slow other things down. We'll look at how to do this in the next section.

Speeding Up Queries with Indexes

If you are in the situation mentioned previously, in which the possible_keys column from an EXPLAIN contains some NULL values, you might be able to improve the performance of your query by adding an index to the table in question. If the column you are using in your WHERE clause is suitable for indexing, you can create a new index for it using ALTER TABLE like this:

```
ALTER TABLE table ADD INDEX (column);
```

General Optimization Tips

In addition to the previous query optimization tips, there are quite a few things you can do to generally increase the performance of your MySQL database.

Design Optimization

Basically you want everything in your database to be as small as possible. You can achieve this in part with a decent design that minimizes redundancy. You can also achieve it by using the smallest possible data type for columns. You should also minimize NULLs wherever possible, and make your primary key as short as possible.

Avoid variable length columns if at all possible (like VARCHAR, TEXT, and BLOB). If your tables have fixed-length fields they will be faster to use but might take up a little more space.

Permissions

In addition to using the suggestions mentioned in the previous section on EXPLAIN, you can improve the speed of queries by simplifying your permissions. We discussed earlier the way that queries are checked with the permission system before being executed. The simpler this process is, the faster your query will run.

Table Optimization

If a table has been in use for a period of time, data can become fragmented as updates and deletions are processed. This will increase the time taken to find things in this table. You can fix this by using the statement

```
OPTIMIZE TABLE tablename;
```

or by typing

```
myisamchk -r table
```

at the command prompt.

You can also use the myisamchk utility to sort a table index and the data according to that index, like this:

```
myisamchk --sort-index --sort-records=1 pathtomysqldatadirectory/*/*.MYI
```

Using Indexes

Use indexes where required to speed up your queries. Keep them simple, and don't create indexes that are not being used by your queries. You can check which indexes are being used by running EXPLAIN as shown previously.

Use Default Values

Wherever possible, use default values for columns, and only insert data if it differs from the default. This reduces the time taken to execute the INSERT statement.

Use Persistent Connections

This particular optimization tip applies particularly to Web databases. We've already discussed it elsewhere so this is just a reminder.

Other Tips

There are many other minor tweaks you can make to improve performance in particular situations and when you have particular needs. The MySQL Web site offers a good set of additional tips. You can find it at

```
http://www.mysql.com
```

Different Table Types

One last useful thing to discuss before we leave MySQL for the time being is the existence of different types of tables. You can choose a table type when you create a table, using

```
CREATE TABLE table TYPE=type ....
```

The possible table types are

- MyISAM. This is the default, and what we have used to date. This is based on ISAM, which stands for *Indexed Sequential Access Method*, a standard method for storing records and files.

- ISAM, as described above.

- HEAP. Tables of this type are stored in memory, and their indexes are hashed. This makes HEAP tables extremely fast, but, in the event of a crash, your data will be lost. These characteristics make HEAP tables ideal for storing temporary or derived data. You should specify the MAX_ROWS in the CREATE TABLE statement, or these tables can hog all your memory. Also, they cannot have BLOB, TEXT, or AUTO INCREMENT columns.

- BDB. These tables are transaction safe; that is, they provide COMMIT and ROLL-BACK capabilities. They are slower to use than the MyISAM tables, but obviously give all the advantages of using transactions. These tables are based on the Berkeley DB.

- InnoDB. These are also transaction safe, and the same riders apply as for BDB.

These additional table types can be useful when you are striving for extra speed or transactional safety.

If you want to use the BDB or InnoDB table types, you should use the MySQL-Max binary which came with your MySQL distribution, rather than the regular MySQL binary.

Loading Data from a File

One useful feature of MySQL that we have not yet discussed is the LOAD DATA INFILE statement. This can be used to load table data in from a file. It executes very quickly.

This is a flexible command with many options, but typical usage is something like the following:

```
LOAD DATA INFILE "newbooks.txt" INTO TABLE books;
```

This will read row data from the file newbooks.txt into the table books. By default, data fields in the file must be separated by tabs and enclosed in single quotes, and each row must be separated by a newline (\n). Special characters must be escaped out with a slash (\). All these characteristics are configurable with the various options of the LOAD statement—see the MySQL manual for more details.

To use the LOAD DATA INFILE statement, a user must have the FILE privilege discussed earlier.

Backing Up Your MySQL Database

In MySQL, there are two ways to do a backup.

The first way is to lock the tables while you copy the physical files, using a LOCK TABLES command. This has the syntax:

```
LOCK TABLES table lock_type [, table lock_type ...]
```

Each table should be the name of a table, and the lock type either READ or WRITE. For a backup, you should only need a READ lock. Users and scripts will still be able to run read-only queries while you make your backup. If you have a reasonable volume of queries that alter the database, such as customer orders, this is not a practical solution.

The second, and superior, method is using the mysql_dump command. Typical usage is something such as

```
mysqldump --opt --all-databases > all.sql
```

This will dump a set of all the SQL required to reconstruct the database to the file called all.sql.

You should then stop the mysqld process for a moment and restart it with the --log-update[=logfile] option. The updates stored in the log file will give you the changes made since your dump. (Obviously you should back up the log files in any normal file backup.)

Restoring Your MySQL Database

If you need to restore your MySQL database, there are, again, a couple of approaches.

If the problem is a corrupted table, you can run myisamchk with the -r (repair) option.

If you've used the first method for backup, then you can copy the data files back into the same locations in a new MySQL installation.

If you have used the second method for backup, there are a couple of steps. First, you need to run the queries in your dump file. This will reconstruct the database up to the point where you dumped that file. Second, you will need to update the database to the point stored in the log files. Under UNIX, you can run a command such as

```
ls -1 -t -r hostname.[0-9]* | xargs cat | mysql
```

to process the log files in the correct order.

More information about the process of MySQL backup and recovery can be found at the MySQL Web site:

```
http://www.mysql.org
```

Further Reading

In these chapters on MySQL, we have focused on the uses and parts of the system most relevant to Web development, and to linking MySQL with PHP.

If you want to know more, particularly with regard to non-Web applications, or MySQL administration, you can visit the MySQL Web site at

```
http://www.mysql.com
```

You might also want to consult Paul Dubois' book *MySQL*, available from New Riders Publishing.

Next

We have now covered the fundamentals of PHP and MySQL. In Chapter 12, "Running an E-commerce Site," we will look at the e-commerce and security aspects of setting up database-backed Web sites.

E-commerce and Security

12

Running an E-commerce Site

THIS CHAPTER INTRODUCES SOME OF THE ISSUES involved in specifying, designing, building, and maintaining an e-commerce site effectively. We will examine your plan, possible risks, and some ways to make a Web site pay its own way.

We will cover

- What you want to achieve with your e-commerce site
- Types of commercial Web site
- Risks and threats
- Deciding on a strategy

What Do You Want to Achieve?

Before spending too much time worrying about the implementation details of your Web site, you should have firm goals in mind, and a reasonably detailed plan leading to meeting those goals.

In this book, we make the assumption that you are building a commercial Web site. Presumably then, making money is one of your goals.

There are many ways to take a commercial approach to the Internet. Perhaps you want to advertise your offline services or sell a real-world product online. Maybe you have a product that can be sold and provided online. Perhaps your site is not directly intended to generate revenue, but instead supports offline activities or acts as a cheaper alternative to present activities.

Types of Commercial Web Sites

Commercial Web sites generally perform one or more of the following activities:

- Publish company information through online brochures
- Take orders for goods or services

- Provide services or digital goods
- Add value to goods or services
- Cut costs

Sections of many Web sites will fit more than one of these categories. What follows is a description of each category, and the usual way of making each generate revenue or other benefits for your organization.

The goal of this section of the book is to help you formulate your goals. Why do you want a Web site? How is each feature built in to your Web site going to contribute to your business?

Online Brochures

Nearly all the commercial Web sites in the early 1990s were simply an online brochure or sales tool. This type of site is still the most common form of commercial Web site. Either as an initial foray onto the Web, or as a low-cost advertising exercise, this type of site makes sense for many businesses.

A *brochureware* site can be anything from a business card rendered as a Web page to an extensive collection of marketing information. In any case, the purpose of the site, and its financial reason for existing, is to entice customers to make contact with your business.

This type of site does not generate any income directly, but can add to the revenue your business receives via traditional means.

Developing a site like this presents few technical challenges. The issues faced are similar to those in other marketing exercises. A few of the more common pitfalls with this type of site include

- Failing to provide important information
- Poor presentation
- Not answering feedback generated by the site
- Allowing a site to age
- Not tracking the success of the site

Failing to Provide Important Information

What are visitors likely to be seeking when they visit your site? Depending on how much they already know, they might want detailed product specifications, or they might just want very basic information such as contact details.

Many Web sites provide no useful information, or miss crucial information. At the very least, your site needs to tell visitors what you do, what geographical areas your business services, and how to make contact.

Poor Presentation

"On the Internet, nobody knows you are a dog," or so goes the old saying.[1] In the same way that small businesses, or dogs, can look larger and more impressive when they are using the Internet, large businesses can look small, unprofessional, and unimpressive with a poor Web site.

Regardless of the size of your company, make sure that your Web site is of a high standard. Text should be written and proofread by somebody with a very good grasp of the language being used. Graphics should be clean, clear, and fast to download. On a business site, you should carefully consider your use of graphics and color, and make sure that they fit the image you would like to present. Use animation and sound carefully if at all.

Although you will not be able make your site look the same on all machines, operating systems, and browsers, make sure that it is viewable and does not give errors to the vast majority of users.

Not Answering Feedback Generated by the Web Site

Good customer service is just as vital in attracting and retaining customers on the Web as it is in the outside world. Large and small companies are guilty of putting an email address on a Web page, and then neglecting to check or answer that mail promptly.

People have different expectations of response times to email than to postal mail. If you do not check and respond to mail daily, people will believe that their inquiry is not important to you.

Email addresses on Web pages should usually be generic, addressed to job title or department, rather than a specific person. What will happen to mail sent to `fred.smith@example.com` when Fred leaves? Mail addressed to `sales@example.com` is more likely to be passed to his successor. It could also be delivered to a group of people, which might help ensure that it is answered promptly.

Allowing a Site to Age

You need to be careful to keep your Web site fresh. Content needs to be changed periodically. Changes in the organization need to be reflected on the site. A "cobweb" site discourages repeat visits, and leads people to suspect that much of the information might now be incorrect.

One way to avoid a stale site is to manually update pages. Another is to use a scripting language such as PHP to create dynamic pages. If your scripts have access to up-to-date information, they can constantly generate up-to-date pages.

Not Tracking the Success of the Site

Creating a Web site is all well and good, but how do you justify the effort and expense? Particularly if the site is for a large company, there will come a time when you are asked to demonstrate or quantify its value to the organization.

---

[1] Of course, an "old saying" about the Internet cannot really be very old. This is the caption from a cartoon by Peter Steiner originally published in the July 5, 1993, issue of *The New Yorker*.

For traditional marketing campaigns, large organizations spend tens of thousands of dollars on market research, both before launching a campaign and after the campaign to measure its effectiveness. Depending on the scale and budget of your Web venture, these measures might be equally appropriate to aid in the design and measurement of your site.

Simpler or cheaper options include

Examining Server Logs: Web servers store a lot of data about every request from your server. Much of this data is useless, and its sheer bulk makes it useless in its raw form. To distill your log files into a meaningful summary, you need a log file analyzer. Two of the better-known free programs are Analog, which is available from `http://www.statslab.cam.ac.uk/~sret1/analog`, and Webalizer, available from `http://www.mrunix.net/webalizer/`. Commercial programs such as Summary, available from `http://summary.net`, might be more comprehensive. A log file analyzer will show you how traffic to your site changes over time and what pages are being viewed.

Monitoring Sales: Your online brochure is supposed to generate sales. You should be able to estimate its effect on sales by comparing sales levels before and after the launch of the site. This obviously becomes difficult if other kinds of marketing cause fluctuations in the same period.

Soliciting User Feedback: If you ask them, your users will tell you what they think of your site. Providing a feedback form or email address will gather some useful opinions. To increase the quantity of feedback, you might like to offer a small inducement, such as entry into a prize draw for all respondents.

Surveying Representative Users: Holding focus groups can be an effective technique for evaluating your site, or even a prototype of your intended site. To conduct a focus group, you simply need to gather some volunteers, encourage them to evaluate the site, and then interview them to gauge and record their opinions.

Focus groups can be expensive affairs, conducted by professional facilitators, who evaluate and screen potential participants to try to ensure that they accurately represent the spread of demographics and personalities in the wider community and then skillfully interview participants. Focus groups can also cost nothing, be run by an amateur, and be populated by a sample of people whose relevance to the target market is unknown.

Paying a specialist market research company is one way to get a well-run focus group and useful results, but it is not the only way. If you are running your own focus groups, choose a skilful moderator. The moderator should have excellent people skills and not have a bias or stake in the result of the research. Limit group sizes to six to ten people. The moderator should be assisted by a recorder or secretary to leave the moderator free to facilitate discussion. The result that you get from your groups will only be as relevant as the sample of people you use. If you evaluate your product only with friends and family of your staff, they are unlikely to represent the general community.

Taking Orders for Goods or Services

If your online advertising is compelling, the next logical step is to allow your customers to order while still online. Traditional salespeople know that it is important to get the customer to make a decision now. The more time you give people to reconsider a purchasing decision, the more likely they are to shop around or change their mind. If a customer wants your product, it is in your best interests to make the purchase as quick and easy as possible. Forcing people to hang up their modem and call a phone number or visit a store places obstacles in their way. If you have online advertising that has convinced a viewer to buy, let them buy now, without leaving your Web site.

Taking orders on a Web site makes sense for many businesses. Every business wants orders. Allowing people to place orders online can either provide additional sales, or reduce the workload of your salespeople. There will obviously be costs involved. Building a dynamic site, organizing payment facilities, and providing customer service all cost money. Try to determine whether your products are suitable for an e-commerce site.

Products that are commonly bought using the Internet include books and magazines, computer software and equipment, music, clothing, travel, and tickets to entertainment events.

Just because your product is not in one of these categories, do not despair. Those categories are already crowded with established brands. However, you would be wise to consider some of the factors that make these products big online sellers.

Ideally, an e-commerce product is nonperishable and easily shipped, expensive enough to make shipping costs seem reasonable, yet not so expensive that the purchaser feels compelled to physically examine the item before purchase.

The best e-commerce products are commodities. If you buy an avocado, you will probably want to look at the particular avocado and perhaps feel it. All avocados are not the same. One copy of a book, CD, or computer program is usually identical to other copies of the same title. Purchasers do not need to see the particular item they will purchase.

In addition, e-commerce products should appeal to people who use the Internet. At the time of writing, this audience consists primarily of employed, younger adults, with above-average incomes, living in metropolitan areas.[2] With time, though, the online population is beginning to look more like the whole population.

Some products are never going to be reflected in surveys of e-commerce purchases, but are still a success. If you have a product that appeals only to a niche market, the Internet might be the ideal way to reach buyers.

Some products are unlikely to succeed as e-commerce categories. Cheap, perishable items, such as groceries, seem a poor choice, although this has not deterred companies from trying, mostly unsuccessfully. Other categories suit brochureware sites very well, but not online ordering. Big, expensive items fall into this category—items such as vehicles and real estate that require a lot of research before purchasing, but that are too expensive to order without seeing and impractical to deliver.

[2] Use of Internet by Householders, Australia, Feb 2000 (Cat. No. 8147.0) Australian Bureau of Statistics

There are a number of obstacles to convincing a prospective purchaser to complete an order. These include

- Unanswered questions
- Trust
- Ease of use
- Compatibility

If a user is frustrated by any of these obstacles, she is likely to leave without buying.

Unanswered Questions

If a prospective customer cannot find an immediate answer to one of her questions, she is likely to leave. This has a number of implications. Make sure that your site is well organized. Can a first-time visitor find what she wants easily? Make sure your site is comprehensive, without overloading visitors. On the Web, people are more likely to scan than to carefully read, so be concise. For most advertising media, there are practical limits on how much information you can provide. This is not true for a Web site. For a Web site, the two main limits are the cost of creating and updating information and limits imposed by how well you can organize, layer, and connect information so as not to overwhelm visitors.

It is tempting to think of a Web site as an unpaid, never sleeping, automatic salesperson, but customer service is still important. Encourage visitors to ask questions. Try to provide immediate or nearly immediate answers via phone, email, or some other convenient means.

Trust

If a visitor is not familiar with your brand name, why should he trust you? Anybody can put together a Web site. People do not need to trust you to read your brochureware site, but placing an order requires a certain amount of faith. How is a visitor to know whether you are a reputable organization, or the aforementioned dog?

People are concerned about a number of things when shopping online:

- **What are you going to do with their personal information?** Are you going to sell it to others, use it to send them huge amounts of advertising, or store it somewhere insecurely so that others can gain access to it? It is important to tell people what you will and will not do with their data. This is called a *privacy policy* and should be easily accessible on your site.

- **Are you a reputable business?** If your business is registered with the relevant authority in a particular place, has a physical address and a phone number, and has been in business for a number of years, it is less likely to be a scam than a business that consists solely of a Web site and perhaps a post office box. Make sure that you display these details.

- **What happens if a purchaser is not satisfied with a purchase?** Under what circumstances will you give a refund? Who pays for shipping? Mail order retailers have traditionally had more liberal refund and return policies than traditional shops. Many offer an unconditional satisfaction guarantee. Consider the cost of returns against the increase in sales that a liberal return policy will create. Whatever your policy is, make sure that it is displayed on your site.

- **Should customers entrust their credit card information to you?** The single greatest trust issue for Internet shoppers is fear of transmitting their credit card details over the Internet. For this reason, you need to both handle credit cards securely and be seen as security conscious. At the very least, this means using SSL (Secure Sockets Layer) to transmit the details from the user's browser to your Web server and ensuring that your Web server is competently and securely administered. We will discuss this in more detail later.

Ease of Use

Consumers vary greatly in their computer experience, language, general literacy, memory, and vision. Your site needs to be as easy as possible to use. User interface design fills many books on its own, but here are a few guidelines:

- **Keep your site as simple as possible.** The more options, advertisements, and distractions on each screen, the more likely a user is to get confused.

- **Keep text clear.** Use clear, uncomplicated fonts. Do not make text too small and bear in mind that it will be different sizes on different types of machines.

- **Make your ordering process as simple as possible.** Intuition and available evidence both support the idea that the more mouse clicks users have to make to place an order, the less likely they are to complete the process. Keep the number of steps to a minimum, but note that Amazon.com has a U.S. patent[3] on a process using only one click, which they call 1-Click. This patent is strongly challenged by many Web site owners.

- **Try not to let users get lost.** Provide landmarks and navigational cues to tell users where they are. For example, if a user is within a subsection of the site, highlight the navigation for that subsection.

If you are using a shopping cart metaphor in which you provide a virtual container for customers to accumulate purchases prior to finalizing the sale, keep a link to the cart visible on the screen at all times.

Compatibility

Be sure to test your site in a number of browsers and operating systems. If the site does not work for a popular browser or operating system, you will look unprofessional and lose a section of your potential market.

---

[3]U.S. Patent and Trademark Office Patent Number 5,960,411. Method and system for placing a purchase order via a communications network.

If your site is already operating, your Web server logs can tell you what browsers your visitors are using. As a rule of thumb, if you test your site in the last two versions of Microsoft Internet Explorer and Netscape/Mozilla on a PC running Microsoft Windows, the last two versions of Netscape/Mozilla on a Apple Mac, the current version of Netscape/Mozilla on Linux, and a text-only browser such as Lynx, you will be visible to the majority of users.

Try to avoid features and facilities that are brand-new, unless you are willing to write and maintain multiple versions of the site.

Providing Services and Digital Goods

Many products or services can be sold over the Web and delivered to the customer via a courier. Some services can be delivered immediately online. If a service or good can be transmitted to a modem, it can be ordered, paid for, and delivered instantly, without human interaction.

The most obvious service provided this way is information. Sometimes the information is entirely free or supported by advertising. Some information is provided via subscription or paid for on an individual basis.

Digital goods include e-books and music in electronic formats such as MP3. Stock library images can be digitized and downloaded. Computer software does not always need to be on a CD, inside shrink-wrap. It can be downloaded directly.

Services that can be sold this way include Internet access or Web hosting and some professional services that can be replaced by an expert system.

If you are going to physically ship an item that was ordered from your Web site, you have both advantages and disadvantages over digital goods and services.

Shipping a physical item costs money. Digital downloads are nearly free. This means that if you have something that can be duplicated and sold digitally, the cost to you is very similar whether you sell one item or one thousand items. Of course, there are limits to this—if you have a sufficient level of sales and traffic, you will need to invest in more hardware or bandwidth.

Digital products or services can be easy to sell as impulse purchases. If a person orders a physical item, it will be a day or more before it reaches her. Downloads are usually measured in seconds or minutes. Immediacy can be a burden on merchants. If you are delivering a purchase digitally, you need to do it immediately. You cannot manually oversee the process, or spread peaks of activity through the day. Immediate delivery systems are therefore more open to fraud and are more of a burden on computer resources.

Digital goods and services are ideal for e-commerce, but obviously only a limited range of goods and services can be delivered this way.

Adding Value to Goods or Services

Some successful areas of commercial Web sites do not actually sell any goods or services. Services such as courier companies' (UPS at www.ups.com or Fedex at www.fedex.com) tracking services are not generally designed to directly make a profit. They add value to the existing services offered by the organization. Allowing customers to track their parcels or bank balances can give the company a competitive advantage.

Support forums also fall into this category. There are sound commercial reasons for giving customers a discussion area to share troubleshooting tips about your company's products. Customers might be able to solve their problems by looking at solutions given to others, international customers can get support without paying for long distance phone calls, and customers might be able to answer one another's questions outside your office hours. Providing support in this way can increase your customers' satisfaction at a low cost.

Cutting Costs

One popular use of the Internet is to cut costs. Savings could result from distributing information online, facilitating communication, replacing services, or centralizing operations.

If you currently provide information to a large number of people, you could possibly do the same thing more economically via a Web site. Whether you are providing price lists, a catalog, documented procedures, specifications, or something else, it could be cheaper to make the same information available on the Web instead of printing and delivering paper copies. This is particularly true for information that changes regularly. The Internet can save you money by facilitating communication. Whether this means that tenders can be widely distributed and rapidly replied to, or whether it means that customers can communicate directly with a wholesaler or manufacturer, eliminating middlemen, the result is the same. Prices can come down, or profits can go up.

Replacing services that cost money to run with an electronic version can cut costs. A brave example is Egghead.com. They chose to close their chain of computer stores, and concentrate on their e-commerce activities. Although building a significant e-commerce site obviously costs money, a chain of more than 70 retail stores has much higher ongoing costs. Replacing an existing service comes with risks. At the very least, you will lose customers who do not use the Internet.

Centralization can cut costs. If you have numerous physical sites, you need to pay numerous rents and overheads, staff at all of them, and the costs of maintaining inventory at each. An Internet business can be in one location, but be accessible all over the world.

Risks and Threats

Every business faces risks, competitors, theft, fickle public preferences, and natural disasters, among other risks. The list is endless. However, many risks that e-commerce companies face are either less of a risk, or not relevant, to other ventures. These risks include

- Crackers
- Failing to attract sufficient business
- Computer hardware failure

- Power, communication, or network failures
- Reliance on shipping services
- Extensive competition
- Software errors
- Evolving governmental policies and taxes
- System-capacity limits

Crackers

The best-publicized threat to e-commerce comes from malicious computer users known as *crackers*. All businesses run the risk of becoming targets of criminals, but high profile e-commerce businesses are bound to attract the attention of crackers with varying intentions and abilities.

Crackers might attack for the challenge, for notoriety, to sabotage your site, to steal money, or to gain free goods or services.

Securing your site involves a combination of

- Keeping backups of important information
- Having hiring policies that attract honest staff and keep them loyal—the most dangerous attacks can come from within
- Taking software-based precautions, such as choosing secure software and keeping it up-to-date
- Training staff to identify targets and weaknesses
- Auditing and logging to detect break-ins or attempted break-ins

Most successful attacks on computer systems take advantage of well-known weaknesses such as easily guessed passwords, common misconfigurations, and old versions of software. A few sensible precautions can turn away nonexpert attacks and ensure that you have a backup if the worst happens.

Failing to Attract Sufficient Business

Although attacks by crackers are widely feared, most e-commerce failures relate to traditional economic factors. It costs a lot of money to build and market a major e-commerce site. Companies are willing to lose money in the short term, based on assumptions that after the brand is established in the market place, customer numbers and revenue will increase.

At the time of writing, Amazon.com, arguably the Web's best-known retailer, has traded at a loss for five consecutive years, losing $99 million (U.S.) in the first quarter of 2000. The string of high-profile failures includes European boo.com, which ran out of money and changed hands after burning $120 million in six months. It was not that Boo did not make sales; it was just that they spent far more than they made.

Computer Hardware Failure

It almost goes without saying that if your business relies on a Web site, the failure of a critical part of one of your computers will have an impact.

Busy or crucial Web sites justify having multiple redundant systems so that the failure of one does not affect the operation of the whole system. As with all threats, you need to determine whether the chance of losing your Web site for a day while waiting for parts or repairs justifies the expense of redundant equipment.

Power, Communication, Network, or Shipping Failures

If you rely on the Internet, you are relying on a complex mesh of service providers. If your connection to the rest of the world fails, you can do little other than wait for your supplier to reinstate service. The same goes for interruptions to power service, and strikes or other stoppages by your delivery company.

Depending on your budget, you might choose to maintain multiple services from different providers. This will cost you more, but will mean that, if one of your providers fails, you will still have another. Brief power failures can be overcome by investing in an uninterruptible power supply.

Extensive Competition

If you are opening a retail outlet on a street corner, you will probably be able to make a pretty accurate survey of the competitive landscape. Your competitors will primarily be businesses that sell similar things in surrounding areas. New competitors will open occasionally. With e-commerce, the terrain is less certain.

Depending on shipping costs, your competitors could be anywhere in the world, and subject to different currency fluctuations and labor costs. The Internet is fiercely competitive and evolving rapidly. If you are competing in a popular category, new competitors can appear every day.

There is little that you can do to eliminate the risk of competition, but, by staying abreast of developments, you can ensure that your venture remains competitive.

Software Errors

When your business relies on software, you are vulnerable to errors in that software.

You can reduce the likelihood of critical errors by selecting software that is reliable, allowing sufficient time to test after changing parts of your system, having a formal testing process, and not allowing changes to be made on your live system without testing elsewhere first.

You can reduce the severity of outcomes by having up-to-date backups of all your data, keeping known working software configurations when making a change, and monitoring system operation to quickly detect problems.

Evolving Governmental Policies and Taxes

Depending on where you live, legislation relating to Internet-based businesses might be nonexistent, in the pipeline, or immature. This is unlikely to last. Some business models might be threatened, regulated, or eliminated by future legislation. Taxes might be added.

You cannot avoid these issues. The only way to deal with them is to keep up-to-date with what is happening and keep your site in line with the legislation. You might want to consider joining any appropriate lobby groups as issues arise.

System Capacity Limits

One thing to bear in mind when designing your system is growth. Your system will hopefully get busier and busier. It should be designed in such a way that it will scale to cope with demand.

For limited growth, you can increase capacity by simply buying faster hardware. There is a limit to how fast a computer you can buy. Is your software written so that after you reach this point, you can separate parts of it to share the load on multiple systems? Can your database handle multiple concurrent requests from different machines?

Few systems cope with massive growth effortlessly, but if you design it with scalability in mind, you should be able to identify and eliminate bottlenecks as your customer base grows.

Deciding on a Strategy

Some people believe that the Internet changes too fast to allow effective planning. We would argue that it is this very changeability that makes planning crucial. Without setting goals and deciding on a strategy, you will be left reacting to changes as they occur, rather than being able to act in anticipation of change.

Having examined some of the typical goals for a commercial Web site, and some of the main threats, you hopefully have some strategies for your own.

Your strategy will need to identify a business model. The model will usually be something that has been shown to work elsewhere, but is sometimes a new idea that you have faith in. Will you adapt your existing business model to the Web, mimic an existing competitor, or aggressively create a pioneering service?

Next

In the next chapter, we will look specifically at security for e-commerce, providing an overview of security terms, threats, and techniques.

13

E-commerce Security Issues

THIS CHAPTER DISCUSSES THE ROLE OF SECURITY in e-commerce. We will discuss who might be interested in your information and how they might try to obtain it, the principles involved in creating a policy to avoid these kinds of problems, and some of the technologies available for safeguarding the security of a Web site including encryption, authentication, and tracking.

Topics include

- How important is your information?
- Security threats
- Creating a security policy
- Balancing usability, performance, cost, and security
- Authentication principles
- Using authentication
- Encryption basics
- Private key encryption
- Public key encryption
- Digital signatures
- Digital certificates
- Secure Web servers
- Auditing and logging
- Firewalls
- Backing up data
- Physical security

How Important Is Your Information?

When considering security, the first thing you need to evaluate is the importance of what you are protecting. You need to consider its importance both to you and to potential crackers.

It might be tempting to believe that the highest possible level of security is required for all sites at all times, but protection comes at a cost. Before deciding how much effort or expense your security warrants, you need to decide how much your information is worth.

The value of the information stored on the computer of a hobby user, a business, a bank, and a military organization obviously varies. The lengths to which an attacker would be likely to go in order to obtain access to that information vary similarly. How attractive would the contents of your machines be to a malicious visitor?

Hobby users will probably have limited time to learn about or work towards securing their systems. Given that information stored on their machines is likely to be of limited value to anyone other than its owner, attacks are likely to be infrequent and involve limited effort. However, all network computer users should take sensible precautions. Even the computer with the least interesting data still has significant appeal as an anonymous launching pad for attacks on other systems.

Military computers are an obvious target for both individuals and foreign governments. As attacking governments might have extensive resources, it would be wise to invest personnel and other resources to ensure that all practical precautions are taken in this domain.

If you are responsible for an e-commerce site, its attractiveness to crackers presumably falls somewhere between these two extremes.

Security Threats

What is at risk on your site? What threats are out there?

We discussed some of the threats to an e-commerce business in Chapter 12, "Running an E-commerce Site." Many of these relate to security.

Depending on your Web site, security threats might include

- Exposure of confidential data
- Loss or destruction of data
- Modification of data
- Denial of service
- Errors in software
- Repudiation

Let's run through each of these threats.

Exposure of Confidential Data

Data stored on your computers, or being transmitted to or from your computers, might be confidential. It might be information that only certain people are intended to see such as wholesale price lists. It might be confidential information provided by a customer, such as his password, contact details, and credit card number.

Hopefully you are not storing information on your Web server that you do not intend anyone to see. A Web server is the wrong place for secret information. If you were storing your payroll records or your plan for world domination on a computer, you would be wise to use a computer other than your Web server. The Web server is inherently a publicly accessible machine, and should only contain information that either needs to be provided to the public or has recently been collected from the public.

To reduce the risk of exposure, you need to limit the methods by which information can be accessed and limit the people who can access it. This involves designing with security in mind, configuring your server and software properly, programming carefully, testing thoroughly, removing unnecessary services from the Web server, and requiring authentication.

Design, configure, code, and test carefully to reduce the risk of a successful criminal attack and, equally important, to reduce the chance that an error will leave your information open to accidental exposure.

Remove unnecessary services from your Web server to decrease the number of potential weak points. Each service you are running might have vulnerabilities. Each one needs to be kept up-to-date to ensure that known vulnerabilities are not present. The services that you do not use might be more dangerous. If you never use the command rcp, why have the service installed?[1] If you tell the installer that your machine is a network host, the major Linux distributions and Windows NT install a large number of services that you do not need and should remove.

Authentication means asking people to prove their identity. When the system knows who is making a request, it can decide whether that person is allowed access. There are a number of possible methods of authentication, but only two commonly used forms—passwords and digital signatures. We will talk a little more about both later.

CD Universe offers a good example of the cost both in dollars and reputation of allowing confidential information to be exposed. In late 1999, a cracker calling himself Maxus reportedly contacted CD Universe, claiming to have 300,000 credit card numbers stolen from their site. He wanted a $100,000 (U.S.) ransom from the site to destroy the numbers. They refused and found themselves in embarrassing coverage on the front pages of major newspapers as Maxus doled out numbers for others to abuse.

Data is also at risk of exposure while it traverses a network. Although TCP/IP networks have many fine features that have made them the *de facto* standard for connecting diverse networks together as the Internet, security is not one of them. TCP/IP works by

---

[1] Even if you do currently use rcp, you should probably remove it and use scp (secure copy) instead.

chopping your data into packets and then forwarding those packets from machine to machine until they reach their destination. This means that your data is passing through numerous machines on the way, as illustrated in Figure 13.1. Any one of those machines could view your data as it passes by.

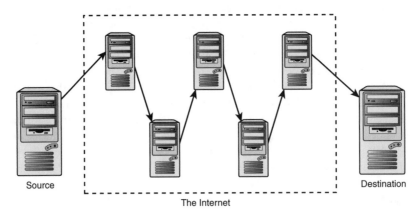

Source   Destination

The Internet

Figure 13.1   Transmitting information via the Internet sends your
information via a number of potentially untrustworthy hosts.

To see the path that data takes from you to a particular machine, you can use the command `traceroute` (on a Unix machine). This command will give you the addresses of the machines that your data passes through to reach that host. For a host in your own country, data is likely to pass through 10 different machines. For an international machine, there can be more than 20 intermediaries. If your organization has a large and complex network, your data might pass through five machines before it even leaves the building.

To protect confidential information, you can encrypt it before it is sent across a network, and decrypt it at the other end. Web servers often use Secure Socket Layer (SSL), developed by Netscape, to accomplish this as data travels between Web servers and browsers. This is a fairly low-cost, low-effort way of securing transmissions, but because your server needs to encrypt and decrypt data rather than simply sending and receiving it, the number of visitors-per-second that a machine can serve drops dramatically.

Loss or Destruction of Data

It can be more costly for you to lose data than to have it revealed. If you have spent months building up your site, gathering user data and orders, how much would it cost you, in time, reputation, and dollars to lose all that information? If you had no backups of any of your data, you would need to rewrite the Web site in a hurry and start from scratch.

It is possible that crackers *will* break into your system and format your hard drive. It is fairly likely that a careless programmer or administrator *will* delete something by accident, and it is almost certain that you *will* occasionally lose a hard disk drive. Hard disk drives rotate thousands of times per minute, and, occasionally, they fail. Murphy's Law would tell you that the one that fails will be the most important one, long after you last made a backup.

You can take various measures to reduce the chance of data loss. Secure your servers against crackers. Keep the number of staff with access to your machine to a minimum. Hire only competent, careful people. Buy good quality drives. Use RAID so that multiple drives can act like one faster, more reliable drive.

Regardless of the cause, there is only one real protection against data loss—backups. Backing up data is not rocket science. On the contrary, it is tedious, dull, and hopefully useless, but it is vital. Make sure that your data is regularly backed up, and make sure that you have tested your backup procedure to be certain that you can recover. Make sure that your backups are stored away from your computers. Although it is unlikely that your premises will burn down or suffer some other catastrophic fate, storing a backup offsite is a fairly cheap insurance policy.

Modification of Data

Although the loss of data could be damaging, modification could be worse. What if somebody obtained access to your system and modified files? Although wholesale deletion will probably be noticed and can be remedied from your backup, how long will it take you to notice modification?

Modifications to files could include changes to data files or executable files. A cracker's motivation for altering a data file might be to graffiti your site or to obtain fraudulent benefits. Replacing executable files with sabotaged versions might give a cracker who has gained access once a secret backdoor for future visits.

You can protect data from modification as it travels over the network by computing a signature. This does not stop somebody from modifying the data, but if the recipient checks that the signature still matches when the file arrives, he will know whether the file has been modified. If the data is being encrypted to protect it from unauthorized viewing, this will also make it very difficult to modify en route without detection.

Protecting files stored on your server from modification requires that you use the file permission facilities your operating system provides and protect the system from unauthorized access. Using file permissions, users can be authorized to use the system, but not be given free rein to modify system files and other users' files. The lack of a proper permissions system is one of the reasons that Windows 95 and 98 are not suitable as server operating systems.

Detecting modification can be difficult. If at some point you realize that your system's security has been breached, how will you know whether important files have been modified? Some files, such as the data files that store your databases, are intended to change over time. Many others are intended to stay the same from the time you install them, unless you deliberately upgrade them. Modification of both programs and data can be insidious, but although programs can be reinstalled if you suspect modification, you cannot know which version of your data was "clean."

File integrity assessment software, such as Tripwire, records information about important files in a known safe state, probably immediately after installation, and can be used at a later time to verify that files are unchanged. You can download commercial or conditional free versions from

```
http://www.tripwire.com
```

Denial of Service

One of the most difficult threats to guard against is denial of service. *Denial of Service (DoS)* occurs when somebody's actions make it difficult or impossible for users to access a service, or delay their access to a time-critical service.

Early in the year 2000, there was a famous spate of *Distributed Denial of Service (DDoS)* attacks against high profile Web sites. Targets included Yahoo!, eBay, Amazon, E-Trade, and Buy.com. Sites such as these are accustomed to traffic levels that most of us can only dream of, but are still vulnerable to being shut down for hours by a DoS attack. Although crackers generally have little to gain from shutting down a Web site, the proprietor might be losing money, time, and reputation.

One of the reasons that these attacks are so difficult to guard against is that there are a huge number of ways of carrying them out. Methods could include installing a program on a target machine that uses most of the system's processor time, reverse spamming, or using one of the automated tools. A *reverse spam* involves somebody sending out fake spam with the target listed as the sender. This way, the target will have thousands of angry replies to deal with.

Automated tools exist to launch distributed DoS attacks on a target. Without needing much knowledge, somebody can scan a large number of machines for known vulnerabilities, compromise a machine, and install the tool. Because the process is automated, an attacker can install the tool on a single host in under five seconds. When enough machines have been co-opted, all are instructed to flood the target with network traffic.

Guarding against DoS attacks is difficult in general. With a little research, you can find the default ports used by the common DDoS tools and close them. Your router might provide mechanisms such as limiting the percentage of traffic that uses particular protocols such as ICMP. Detecting hosts on your network being used to attack others is easier than protecting your machines from attack. If every network administrator could be relied on to vigilantly monitor his own network, DDoS would not be such a problem.

Because there are so many possible methods of attack, the only really effective defense is to monitor normal traffic behavior and have a pool of experts available to take countermeasures when abnormal things occur.

Errors in Software

It is possible that the software you have bought, obtained, or written has serious errors in it. Given the short development times normally allowed to Web projects, it is highly likely that this software has some errors. Any business that is highly reliant on computerized processes is vulnerable to buggy software.

Errors in software can lead to all sorts of unpredictable behavior including service unavailability, security breaches, financial losses, and poor service to customers.

Common causes of errors that you can look for include poor specifications, faulty assumptions made by developers, and inadequate testing.

Poor Specifications

The more sparse or ambiguous your design documentation is, the more likely you are to end up with errors in the final product. Although it might seem superfluous to you to specify that when a customer's credit card is declined, the order should not be sent to the customer, at least one big-budget site had this bug. The less experience your developers have with the type of system they are working on, the more precise your specification needs to be.

Assumptions Made by Developers

The designers and programmers of a system need to make many assumptions. Hopefully, they will document their assumptions and usually be right. Sometimes though, people make poor assumptions. These might include assumptions that input data will be valid, will not include unusual characters, or will be less than a particular size. It could also include assumptions about timing such as the likelihood of two conflicting actions occurring at the same time or that a complex processing task will always take more time than a simple task.

Assumptions like these can slip through because they are usually true. A cracker could take advantage of a buffer overrun because a programmer assumed a maximum length for input data, or a legitimate user could get confusing error messages and leave because it did not occur to your developers that a person's name might have an apostrophe in it. These sort of errors can be found and fixed with a combination of good testing and detailed code review.

Historically, the operating system or application level weaknesses exploited by crackers have usually related either to buffer overflows or race conditions.

Poor Testing

It is rarely possible to test for all possible input conditions, on all possible types of hardware, running all possible operating systems with all possible user settings. This is even more true than usual with Web-based systems.

What is needed is a well-designed test plan that tests all the functions of your software on a representative sample of common machine types. A well-planned set of tests should aim to test every line of code in your project at least once. Ideally, this test suite should be automated so that it can be run on your selected test machines with little effort.

The greatest problem with testing is that it is unglamorous and repetitive. Although some people enjoy breaking things, few people enjoy breaking the same thing over and over again. It is important that people other than the original developers are involved in testing. One of the major goals of testing is to uncover faulty assumptions made by the developers. A fresh person is much more likely to have different assumptions. In addition to this, professionals are rarely keen to find flaws in their own work.

Repudiation

The final risk we will consider is repudiation. *Repudiation* occurs when a party involved in a transaction denies having taken part. E-commerce examples might include a person ordering goods off a Web site and then denying having authorized the charge on his credit card, or a person agreeing to something in email and then claiming that somebody else forged the email.

Ideally, financial transactions should provide the peace of mind of nonrepudiation to both parties. Neither party could deny their part in a transaction, or, more precisely, both parties could conclusively prove the actions of the other to a third party, such as a court. In practice, this rarely happens.

Authentication provides some surety about whom you are dealing with. If issued by a trusted organization, digital certificates of authentication can provide greater confidence.

Messages sent by each party also need to be tamperproof. There is not much value in being able to demonstrate that Corp Pty Ltd sent you a message if you cannot also demonstrate that what you received was exactly what they sent. As mentioned previously, signing or encrypting messages makes them difficult to surreptitiously alter.

For transactions between parties with an ongoing relationship, digital certificates together with either encrypted or signed communications are an effective way of limiting repudiation. For one-off transactions, such as the initial contact between an e-commerce Web site and a stranger bearing a credit card, they are not so practical.

An e-commerce company should be willing to hand over proof of its identity and a few hundred dollars to a certifying authority such as VeriSign (http://www.verisign.com/) or Thawte (http://www.thawte.com/) in order to assure visitors of the company's bona fides. Would that same company be willing to turn away every customer who was not willing to do the same in order to prove his identity? For small transactions, merchants are generally willing to accept a certain level of fraud or repudiation risk rather than turn away business.

An alliance between VISA, a number of financial organizations, and software companies, has been promoting a standard called Secure Electronic Transaction since 1997. One component of the SET system is that cardholders can obtain digital certificates from their card issuers. If SET takes off, it could reduce the risk of repudiation and other credit card fraud in Internet transactions.

Unfortunately, although the specification has existed for many years, there seems to be little push from banks to issue SET-compliant certificates to their cardholders. No retailers seem willing to reject all customers without SET software, and there is little enthusiasm from consumers to adopt the software. There is very little reason for consumers to queue up at their local bank and spend time installing digital wallet software on their machines unless retailers are going to reject their customers without such software.

Balancing Usability, Performance, Cost, and Security

By its very nature, the Web is risky. It is designed to allow numerous anonymous users to request services from your machines. Most of those requests will be perfectly legitimate requests for Web pages, but connecting your machines to the Internet will allow people to attempt other types of connections.

Although it can be tempting to assume that the highest possible level of security is appropriate, this is rarely the case. If you wanted to be really secure, you would keep all your computers turned off, disconnected from all networks, in a locked safe. In order to make your computers available and usable, some relaxation of security is required.

There is a trade-off to be made between security, usability, cost, and performance. Making a service more secure can reduce usability by, for instance, limiting what people can do or requiring them to identify themselves. Increasing security can also reduce the level of performance of your machines. Running software to make your system more secure—such as encryption, intrusion detection systems, virus scanners, and extensive logging—uses resources. It takes a lot more processing power to provide an encrypted session, such as an SSL connection to a Web site, than to provide a normal one. These performance losses can be countered by spending more money on faster machines or hardware specifically designed for encryption.

You can view performance, usability, cost, and security as competing goals. You need to examine the trade-offs required and make sensible decisions to come up with a compromise. Depending on the value of your information, your budget, how many visitors you expect to serve, and what obstacles you think legitimate users will be willing to put up with, you can come up with a compromise position.

Creating a Security Policy

A security policy is a document that describes

- The general philosophy towards security in your organization
- What is to be protected—software, hardware, data
- Who is responsible for protecting these items
- Standards for security and metrics, which measure how well those standards are being met

A good guideline for writing your security policy is that it's like writing a set of functional requirements for software. The policy shouldn't talk about specific implementations or solutions, but instead about the goals and security requirements in your environment. It shouldn't need to be updated very often.

You should keep a separate document that sets out guidelines for how the requirements of the security policy are met in a particular environment. You can have different guidelines for different parts of your organization. This is more along the lines of a design document or a procedure manual that documents what is actually done in order to ensure the level of security that you require.

Authentication Principles

Authentication attempts to prove that somebody is actually who she claims to be. There are many possible ways to provide authentication, but as with many security measures, the more secure methods are more troublesome to use.

Authentication techniques include passwords, digital signatures, biometric measures such as fingerprint scans, and measures involving hardware such as smart cards. Only two are in common use on the Web: passwords and digital signatures.

Biometric measures and most hardware solutions involve special input devices and would limit authorized users to specific machines with these attached. This might be acceptable, or even desirable, for access to an organization's internal systems, but takes away much of the advantage of making a system available over the Web.

Passwords are simple to implement, simple to use, and require no special input devices. They provide some level of authentication, but might be not be appropriate on their own for high security systems.

A password is a simple concept. You and the system know your password. If a visitor claims to be you, and knows your password, the system has reason to believe he is you. As long as nobody else knows or can guess the password, this is secure. Passwords on their own have a number of potential weaknesses and do not provide strong authentication.

Many passwords are easily guessed. If left to choose their own passwords, around 50% of users will choose an easily guessed password. Common passwords that fit this description include dictionary words or the username for the account. At the expense of usability, you can force users to include numbers or punctuation in their passwords, but this will cause some users to have difficulty remembering their passwords. Educating users to choose better passwords can help, but even when educated, around 25% of users will still choose an easily guessed password. You could enforce password policies that stop users from choosing easily guessed combinations by checking new passwords against a dictionary, or requiring some numbers or punctuation symbols or a mixture of uppercase and lowercase letters. One danger is that strict password rules will lead to passwords that many legitimate users will not be able to remember.

Hard to remember passwords increase the likelihood that users will do something unsecure such as write "username fred password rover" on a note taped to their monitors.

Users need to be educated not to write down their passwords or to do other silly things like give them to people over the phone who ring up claiming to be working on the system.

Passwords can also be captured electronically. By running a program to capture keystrokes at a terminal or using a packet sniffer to capture network traffic, crackers can—and do—capture useable pairs of login names and passwords. You can limit the opportunities to capture passwords by encrypting network traffic.

For all their potential flaws, passwords are a simple and relatively effective way of authenticating your users. They provide a level of secrecy that might not be appropriate for national security, but is ideal for checking on the delivery status of a customer's order.

Using Authentication

Authentication mechanisms are built in to the most popular Web browsers and Web servers. Web servers might require a username and password for people requesting files from particular directories on the server.

When challenged for a login name and password, your browser will present a dialog box looking something like the one shown in Figure 13.2.

Figure 13.2   Web browsers prompt users for authentication when they attempt to visit a restricted directory on a Web server.

Both the Apache Web server and Microsoft's IIS enable you to very easily protect all or part of a site in this way. Using PHP or MySQL, there are many other ways we can achieve the same effect. Using MySQL is faster than the built-in authentication. Using PHP, we can provide more flexible authentication or present the request in a more attractive way.

We will see some authentication examples in Chapter 14, "Implementing Authentication with PHP and MySQL."

Encryption Basics

An *encryption algorithm* is a mathematical process to transform information into a seemingly random string of data.

The data that you start with is often called *plain text*, although it is not important to the process what the information represents—whether it is actually text, or some other sort of data. Similarly, the encrypted information is called *ciphertext*, but rarely looks anything like text. Figure 13.3 shows the encryption process as a simple flowchart. The plain text is fed to an encryption engine, which might have been a mechanical device, such as a World War II Engima machine, once upon a time, but is now nearly always a computer program. The engine produces the ciphertext.

Figure 13.3   Encryption takes plain text and transforms it into seemingly random ciphertext.

To create the protected directory whose authentication prompt is shown in Figure 13.2, we used Apache's most basic type of authentication. (You'll see how to use this in the next chapter.) This encrypts passwords before storing them. We created a user with the password `password`. This was encrypted and stored as `aWDuA3X3H.mc2`. You can see that the plain text and ciphertext bear no obvious resemblance to each other.

This particular encryption method is not reversible. Many passwords are stored using a one-way encryption algorithm. In order to see whether an attempt at entering a password is correct, we do not need to decrypt the stored password. We can instead encrypt the attempt and compare that to the stored version.

Many, but not all encryption processes can be reversed. The reverse process is called *decryption*. Figure 13.4 shows a two-way encryption process.

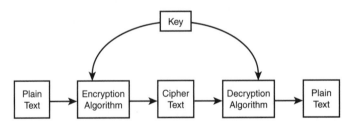

Figure 13.4   Encryption takes plain text and transforms it into seemingly random ciphertext. Decryption takes the ciphertext and transforms it back into plain text.

Cryptography is nearly 4000 years old, but came of age in World War II. Its growth since then has followed a similar pattern to the adoption of computer networks, initially only being used by military and finance corporations, being more widely used by companies starting in the 1970s, and becoming ubiquitous in the 1990s. In the last few years, encryption has gone from a concept that ordinary people only saw in World War II movies and spy thrillers to something that they read about in newspapers and use every time they purchase something with their Web browsers.

Many different encryption algorithms are available. Some, like DES, use a secret or private key; some, like RSA, use a public key and a separate private key.

Private Key Encryption

Private key encryption relies on authorized people knowing or having access to a key. This key must be kept secret. If the key falls into the wrong hands, unauthorized people can also read your encrypted messages. As shown in Figure 13.4, both the sender (who encrypts the message) and the recipient (who decrypts the message) have the same key.

The most widely used secret key algorithm is the Data Encryption Standard (DES). This scheme was developed by IBM in the 1970s and adopted as the American standard for commercial and unclassified government communications. Computing speeds are orders of magnitudes faster now than in 1970, and DES has been obsolete since at least 1998.

Other well-known secret key systems include RC2, RC4, RC5, triple DES, and IDEA. Triple DES is fairly secure.[2] It uses the same algorithm as DES, applied three times with up to three different keys. A plain text message is encrypted with key one, decrypted with key two, and then encrypted with key three.

One obvious flaw of secret key encryption is that, in order to send somebody a secure message, you need a secure way to get the secret key to him. If you have a secure way to deliver a key, why not just deliver the message that way?

Fortunately, there was a breakthrough in 1976, when Diffie and Hellman published the first public key scheme.

Public Key Encryption

Public key encryption relies on two different keys, a public key and a private key. As shown in Figure 13.5, the public key is used to encrypt messages, and the private key to decrypt them.

The advantage to this system is that the public key, as its name suggests, can be distributed publicly. Anybody to whom you give your public key can send you a secure message. As long as only you have your private key, then only you can decrypt the message.

---

[2] Somewhat paradoxically, triple DES is twice as secure as DES. If you needed something three times as strong, you could write a program to implement a quintuple DES algorithm.

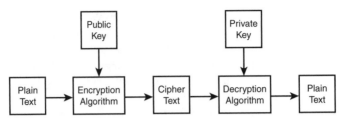

Figure 13.5   Public key encryption uses separate keys for encryption and decryption.

The most common public key algorithm is RSA, developed by Rivest, Shamir, and Adelman at MIT and published in 1978. RSA was a proprietary system, but the patent expired in September 2000.

The capability to transmit a public key in the clear and not need to worry about it being seen by a third party is a huge advantage, but secret key systems are still in common use. Often, a hybrid system is used. A public key system is used to transmit the key for a secret key system that will be used for the remainder of a session's communication. This added complexity is tolerated because secret key systems are around 1000 times faster than public key systems.

Digital Signatures

Digital signatures are related to public key cryptography, but reverse the role of public and private keys. A sender can encrypt and digitally sign a message with her secret key. When the message is received, the recipient can decrypt it with the sender's public key. As the sender is the only person with access to the secret key, the recipient can be fairly certain from whom the message came and that it has not been altered.

Digital signatures can be really useful. They let the recipient be sure that the message has not been tampered with, and they make it difficult for the sender to repudiate, or deny sending, the message.

It is important to note though that although the message has been encrypted, it can be read by anybody who has the public key. Although the same techniques and keys are used, the purpose of encryption here is to prevent tampering and repudiation, not to prevent reading.

As public key encryption is fairly slow for large messages, another type of algorithm, called a *hash function*, is usually used to improve efficiency.

The hash function calculates a message digest or hash value for any message it is given. It is not important what value the algorithm produces. It is important that the output is deterministic, that is, that the output is the same each time a particular input is used, that the output is small, and that the algorithm is fast.

The most common hash functions are MD5 and SHA.

A hash function generates a message digest that matches a particular message. If you have a message and a message digest, you can verify that the message has not been tampered with, as long as you are sure that the digest has not been tampered with.

To this end, the usual way of creating a digital signature is to create a message digest for the whole message using a fast hash function, and then encrypt only the brief digest using a slow public key encryption algorithm. The signature can now be sent with the message via any normal unsecure method.

When a signed message is received, it can be checked. The signature is decrypted using the sender's public key. A hash value is generated for the message using the same method that the sender used. If the decrypted hash value matches the hash value you generated, then the message is from the sender and has not been altered.

Digital Certificates

It is good to be able to verify that a message has not been altered and that a series of messages all come from a particular user or machine. For commercial interactions, it would be even better to be able to tie that user or server to a real legal entity such as a person or company.

A digital certificate combines a public key and an individual's or organization's details in a signed digital format. Given a certificate, you have the other party's public key, in case you want to send an encrypted message, and you have that party's details, which you know have not been altered.

The problem here is that the information is only as trustworthy as the person who signed it. Anybody can generate and sign a certificate claiming to be anybody he likes. For commercial transactions, it would be useful to have a trusted third party verify the identity of participants and the details recorded in their certificates.

These third parties are called *Certifying Authorities (CAs)*. Certifying Authorities issue digital certificates to individuals and companies subject to identity checks. The two best known CAs are VeriSign (http://www.verisign.com/) and Thawte (http://www.thawte.com/), but there are a number of other authorities. VeriSign and Thawte are both owned by the same company, and there is little practical difference between them. Some of the lesser-known authorities, like Equifax Secure (www.equifaxsecure.com), are significantly cheaper.

The authorities sign a certificate to verify that they have seen proof of the person or company's identity. It is worth noting that the certificate is not a reference or statement of credit worthiness. It does not guarantee that you are dealing with somebody reputable. What it does mean is that if you are ripped off, you have a pretty good chance of having a real physical address and somebody to sue.

Certificates provide a network of trust. Assuming you choose to trust the CA, you can then choose to trust the people they choose to trust and then trust the people the certified party chooses to trust.

Figure 13.6 shows the certificate path that Internet Explorer displays for a particular certificate. From this, you can see that `www.equifaxsecure.com` has a certificate issued by Equifax Secure E-Business Certifying Authority. This CA, in turn, has a certificate issued by Thawte Server Certifying Authority.

Figure 13.6   The certificate path for `www.equifaxsecure.com`
shows the network of trust that enables us to trust this site.

The most common use for digital certificates is to provide an air of respectability to an e-commerce site. With a certificate issued by a well-known CA, Web browsers can make SSL connections to your site without bringing up warning dialogs. Web servers that enable SSL connections are often called secure Web servers.

Secure Web Servers

You can use the Apache Web server, Microsoft IIS, or any number of other free or commercial Web servers for secure communication with browsers via Secure Sockets Layer. Using Apache enables you to use a UNIX-like operating system, which will almost certainly be more reliable, but is harder to set up than IIS. You can also, of course, choose to use Apache on a Windows platform.

Using SSL on IIS involves simply installing IIS, generating a key pair, and installing your certificate. Using SSL on Apache requires installing three different packages: Apache, Mod_SSL, and OpenSSL.

You can also have your cake and eat it too by purchasing Stronghold. Stronghold is a commercial product available from `www.c2.net` for around $1000 (U.S.). It is based on Apache, but comes as a self-installing binary preconfigured with SSL. This way you get the reliability of UNIX, as well as an easy-to-install product with technical support from the vendor.

Installation instructions for the two most popular Web servers, Apache and IIS, are in Appendix A, "Installing PHP 4 and MySQL." You can begin using SSL immediately by generating your own digital certificate, but visitors to your site will be warned by their Web browsers that you have signed your own certificate. In order to use SSL effectively, you will also need a certificate issued by a certifying authority.

The exact process to get this varies between CAs, but in general, you will need to prove to a CA that you are some sort of legally recognized business with a physical address and that the business in question owns the relevant domain name.

You need to generate a Certificate Signing Request. The process for this will vary from server to server. Instructions are on the Web sites of the CAs. Stronghold and IIS provide a dialog box-driven process, whereas Apache requires you to type commands. However, the process is the essentially the same for all servers. The end result is an encrypted certificate signing request (CSR). Your CSR should look something like this:

```
-----BEGIN NEW CERTIFICATE REQUEST-----
MIIBuwIBAAKBgQCLn1XX8faMHhtzStp9wY6BVTPuEU9bpMmhrb6vgaNZy4dTe6VS
84p7wGepq5CQjfOL4Hjda+g12xzto8uxBkCDO98Xg9q86CY45HZk+q6GyGOLZSOD
8cQHwh1oUP65s5Tz018OFBzpI3bHxfO6aYelWYziDiFKp1BrUdua+pK4SQIVAPLH
SV9FSz8Z7IHOg1Zr5H82oQOlAoGAWSPWyfVXPAF8h2GDb+cf97k44VkHZ+Rxpe8G
ghlfBn9L3ESWUZNOJMfDLlny7dStYU98VTVNekidYuaBsvyEkFrny7NCUmiuaSnX
4UjtFDkNhX9j5YbCRGLmsc865AT54KRu31O2/dKHLo6NgFPirijHy99HJ4LRY9Z9
HkXVzswCgYBwBFH2QfK88C6JKW3ah+6cHQ4Deoiltxi627WN5HcQLwkPGn+WtYSZ
jG5tw4tqqogmJ+IP2F/5G6FI2DQP7QDvKNeAU8jXcuijuWo27S2sbhQtXgZRTZvO
jGn89BC0mIHgHQMkI7vz35mx1Skk3VNq3ehwhGCvJlvoeiv2J8X2IQIVAOTRp7zp
En7QlXnXw1s7xXbbuKPO
-----END NEW CERTIFICATE REQUEST-----
```

Armed with a CSR, the appropriate fee, and documentation to prove that you exist, and having verified that the domain name you are using is in the same name as in the business documentation, you can sign up for a certificate with a CA.

When the CA issues your certificate, you need to store it on your system and tell your Web server where to find it. The final certificate is a text file that looks a lot like the CSR shown previously.

Auditing and Logging

Your operating system will let you log all sorts of events. Events that you might be interested in from a security point of view include network errors, access to particular data files such as configuration files or the NT registry, and calls to programs such as su (used to become another user, typically root, on a UNIX system).

Log files can help you detect erroneous or malicious behavior as it occurs. They can also tell you how a problem or break-in occurred if you check them after noticing problems. There are two main problems with log files: size and veracity.

If you set the criteria for detecting and logging problems at their most paranoid, you will end up with massive logs that are very difficult to examine. To help with large log files, you really need to either use an existing tool or derive some audit scripts from your security policy to search the logs for "interesting" events. The auditing process could occur in real-time, or could be done periodically.

Log files are vulnerable to attack. If an intruder has root or administrator access to your system, she is free to alter log files to cover her tracks. Unix provides facilities to log events to a separate machine. This would mean that a cracker would need to compromise at least two machines to cover her tracks. Similar functionality is possible in NT, but not easily.

Your system administrator might do regular audits, but you might like to have an external audit periodically to check the behavior of administrators.

Firewalls

Firewalls in networks are designed to separate your network from the wider world. In the same way that firewalls in a building or a car stop fire from spreading into other compartments, network firewalls stop chaos from spreading into your network.

A *firewall* is designed to protect machines on your network from outside attack. It filters and denies traffic that does not meet its rules. It restricts the activities of people and machines outside the firewall.

Sometimes, a firewall is also used to restrict the activities of those within it. A firewall can restrict the network protocols people can use, restrict the hosts they can connect to, or force them to use a proxy server to keep bandwidth costs down.

A firewall could either be a hardware device, such as a router with filtering rules, or a software program running on a machine. In any case, the firewall needs interfaces to two networks and a set of rules. It monitors all traffic attempting to pass from one network to the other. If the traffic meets the rules, it is routed across to the other network; otherwise, it is stopped or rejected.

Packets can be filtered by their type, source address, destination address, or port information. Some packets will be merely discarded while certain events could trigger log entries or alarms.

Backing Up Data

You cannot underestimate the importance of backups in any disaster recovery plan. Hardware and buildings can be insured and replaced, or sites hosted elsewhere, but if your custom-developed Web software is gone, no insurance company can replace it for you.

You need to back up all the components of your Web site—static pages, scripts, and databases—on a regular basis. Just how often you do this depends on how dynamic your site is. If it is all static, you can get away with backing it up when it's changed. However, the kind of sites we talk about in this book are likely to change frequently, particularly if you are taking orders online.

Most sites of a reasonable size will need to be hosted on a server with RAID (a Redundant Array of Inexpensive Disks), which can support mirroring. This covers the situation in which you might have a hard disk failure. Consider, however, what might happen in a situation where something happens to the entire array, machine, or building.

You should run separate backups at a frequency corresponding to your update volume. These backups should be stored on separate media, and preferably in a safe, separate location, in case of fire, theft, or natural disasters.

Many resources are out there on backup and recovery. We'll concentrate on how you can back up a site built with PHP and a MySQL database.

Backing Up General Files

Backing up your HTML, PHP, images, and other non-database files can be done fairly simply on most systems by using backup software.

The most widely used of the freely available utilities is AMANDA, the Advanced Maryland Automated Network Disk Archiver, developed by the University of Maryland. It ships with many UNIX distributions and can also be used to back up Windows machines via SAMBA. You can read more about AMANDA at

```
http://www.amanda.org/
```

Backing Up and Restoring Your MySQL Database

Backing up a live database is more complicated. You want to avoid copying any table data while the database is in the middle of being changed.

Instructions on how to back up and restore a MySQL database can be found in Chapter 11, "Advanced MySQL."

Physical Security

The security threats we have considered so far relate to intangibles such as software, but you should not neglect the physical security of your system. You need air conditioning, and protection against fire, people (both the clumsy and the criminal), power failure, and network failure.

Your system should be locked up securely. Depending on the scale of your operation, this could mean a room, a cage, or a cupboard. Personnel who do not need access to this machine room should not have it. Unauthorized people might deliberately or accidentally unplug cables or attempt to bypass security mechanisms using a bootable disk.

Water sprinklers can do as much damage to electronics as a fire. In the past, halon fire suppression systems were used to avoid this problem. The production of halon is now banned under the Montreal Protocol on Substances That Deplete the Ozone Layer, so new fire suppression systems must use other, less harmful, alternatives such as argon or carbon dioxide. You can read more about this at

```
http://epa.gov/ozone/title6/snap
```

Occasional brief power failures are a fact of life in most places. In locations with harsh weather and above ground wires, long failures occur regularly. If the continuous operation of your systems is important to you, you should invest in an uninterruptible power supply (UPS). A UPS that will power a single machine for 10 minutes will cost less than $300 (U.S.). Allowing for longer failures, or more equipment, can get expensive. Long power failures really require a generator to run air conditioning as well as computers.

Like power failures, network outages of minutes or hours are out of your control and bound to occur occasionally. If your network is vital, it makes sense to have connections to more than one Internet service provider. It will cost more to have two connections, but should mean that, in case of failure, you have reduced capacity rather than becoming invisible.

These sorts of issues are some of the reasons you might like to consider co-locating your machines at a dedicated facility. Although one medium-sized business might not be able to justify a UPS that will run for more than a few minutes, multiple redundant network connections, and fire suppression systems, a quality facility housing the machines of a hundred similar businesses can.

Next

In Chapter 14, we will look specifically at authentication—allowing your users to prove their identity. We will look at a few different methods, including using PHP and MySQL to authenticate your visitors.

14

Implementing Authentication with PHP and MySQL

THIS CHAPTER WILL DISCUSS HOW TO IMPLEMENT various PHP and MySQL techniques for authenticating a user.

Topics include

- Identifying visitors
- Implementing access control
- Basic authentication
- Using basic authentication in PHP
- Using Apache's .htaccess basic authentication
- Using basic authentication with IIS
- Using mod_auth_mysql authentication
- Creating your own custom authentication

Identifying Visitors

The Web is a fairly anonymous medium, but it is often useful to know who is visiting your site. Fortunately for visitors' privacy, you can find out very little about them without their assistance.

With a little work, servers can find out quite a lot about computers and networks that connect to them. A Web browser will usually identify itself, telling the server what browser, browser version, and operating system you are running. You can determine what resolution and color depth visitors' screens are set to and how large their Web browser windows are.

Each computer connected to the Internet has a unique IP address. From a visitor's IP address, you might be able to deduce a little about her. You can find out who owns an IP and sometimes have a reasonable guess as to a visitor's geographic location. Some addresses will be more useful than others. Generally people with permanent Internet connections will have a permanent address. Customers dialing into an ISP will usually only get the temporary use of one of the ISP's addresses. The next time you see that address, it might be being used by a different computer, and the next time you see that visitor, she will likely be using a different IP address.

Fortunately for Web users, none of the information that their browsers give out identifies them. If you want to know a visitor's name or other details, you will have to ask her.

Many Web sites provide compelling reasons to get users to provide their details. The *New York Times* newspaper (http://www.nytimes.com) provides its content for free, but only to people willing to provide details such as name, sex, and total household income. Nerd news and discussion site Slashdot (http://www.slashdot.org) allows registered users to participate in discussions under a nickname and customize the interface they see. Most e-commerce sites record their customers' details when they make their first order. This means that a customer is not required to type her details every time.

Having asked for and received information from your visitor, you need a way to associate the information with the same user the next time she visits. If you are willing to make the assumption that only one person visits your site from a particular account on a particular machine and that each visitor only uses one machine, you could store a cookie on the user's machine to identify the user. This is certainly not true for all users—frequently, many people share a computer and many people use more than one computer. At least some of the time, you will need to ask a visitor who she is again. In addition to asking who a user is, you will also need to ask a user to provide some level of proof that she is who she claims to be.

As discussed in Chapter 13, "E-commerce Security Issues," asking a user to prove her identity is called *authentication*. The usual method of authentication used on Web sites is asking visitors to provide a unique login name and a password. Authentication is usually used to allow or disallow access to particular pages or resources, but can be optional, or used for other purposes such as personalization.

Implementing Access Control

Simple access control is not difficult to implement. The code shown in Listing 14.1 delivers one of three possible outputs. If the file is loaded without parameters, it will display an HTML form requesting a username and password. This type of form is shown in Figure 14.1.

Figure 14.1   Our HTML form requests that visitors
enter a username and password for access.

If the parameters are present but not correct, it will display an error message. Our error
message is shown in Figure 14.2.

Figure 14.2   When users enter incorrect details, we need to
give them an error message. On a real site, you might
want to give a somewhat friendlier message.

If these parameters are present and correct, it will display the secret content. Our test
content is shown in Figure 14.3.

The code to create the functionality shown in Figures 14.1, 14.2, and 14.3 is shown
in Listing 14.1.

Figure 14.3   When provided with correct details, our
script will display content.

Listing 14.1   **secret.php—PHP and HTML to Provide a Simple Authentication
Mechanism**

```php
<?php
  //create short names for variables
@ $name = $HTTP_POST_VARS['name'];
@ $password = $HTTP_POST_VARS['password'];

  if(empty($name)||empty($password))
  {
    //Visitor needs to enter a name and password
?>
    <h1>Please Log In</h1>
    This page is secret.
    <form method="post" action="secret.php">
    <table border="1">
    <tr>
      <th> Username </th>
      <td> <input type="text" name="name"> </td>
    </tr>
    <tr>
      <th> Password </th>
      <td> <input type="password" name="password"> </td>
    </tr>
    <tr>
      <td colspan="2" align="center">
        <input type="submit" value="Log In">
      </td>
    </tr>
    </table>
    </form>
```

Listing 14.1   **Continued**

```php
<?php
  }
  else if($name=='user'&&$password=='pass')
  {
    // visitor's name and password combination are correct
    echo '<h1>Here it is!</h1>';
    echo 'I bet you are glad you can see this secret page.';
  }
  else
  {
    // visitor's name and password combination are not correct
    echo '<h1>Go Away!</h1>';
    echo 'You are not authorized to view this resource.';
  }
?>
```

The code from Listing 14.1 will give you a simple authentication mechanism to allow authorized users to see a page, but it has some significant problems.

This script

- Has one username and password hard-coded into the script
- Stores the password as plain text
- Only protects one page
- Transmits the password as plain text

These issues can all be addressed with varying degrees of effort and success.

Storing Passwords

There are many better places to store usernames and passwords than inside the script. Inside the script, it is difficult to modify the data. It is possible, but a bad idea to write a script to modify itself. It would mean having a script on your server, which gets executed on your server, but is writable or modifiable by others. Storing the data in another file on the server will let you more easily write a program to add and remove users and to alter passwords.

Inside a script or another data file, there is a limit to the number of users you can have without seriously affecting the speed of the script. If you are considering storing and searching through a large number of items in a file, you should consider using a database instead, as previously discussed. As a rule of thumb, if you want to store and search through a list of more than 100 items, they should be in a database rather than a flat file.

Using a database to store usernames and passwords would not make the script much more complex, but would allow you to authenticate many different users quickly. It would also allow you to easily write a script to add new users, delete users, and allow users to change their passwords.

A script to authenticate visitors to a page against a database is given in Listing 14.2.

Listing 14.2   **secretdb.php—We Have Used MySQL to Improve Our Simple**
                    Authentication Mechanism

```php
<?php
  if(!isset($HTTP_POST_VARS['name'])&&!isset($HTTP_POST_VARS['password']))
  {
    //Visitor needs to enter a name and password
?>
    <h1>Please Log In</h1>
    This page is secret.
    <form method="post" action="secretdb.php">
    <table border="1">
    <tr>
      <th> Username </th>
      <td> <input type="text" name="name"> </td>
    </tr>
    <tr>
      <th> Password </th>
      <td> <input type="password" name="password"> </td>
    </tr>
    <tr>
      <td colspan="2" align="center">
        <input type="submit" value="Log In">
      </td>
    </tr>
    </table>
    </form>
<?php
  }
  else
  {
    // connect to mysql
    $mysql = mysql_connect( 'localhost', 'webauth', 'webauth' );
    if(!$mysql)
    {
      echo 'Cannot connect to database.';
      exit;
    }
    // select the appropriate database
    $mysql = mysql_select_db( 'auth' );
    if(!$mysql)
    {
      echo 'Cannot select database.';
```

Listing 14.2   **Continued**

```
      exit;
  }

  // query the database to see if there is a record which matches
  $query = "select count(*) from auth where
            name = '$name' and
            pass = '$password'";

  $result = mysql_query( $query );
  if(!$result)
  {
    echo 'Cannot run query.';
    exit;
  }

  $count = mysql_result( $result, 0, 0 );

  if ( $count > 0 )
  {
    // visitor's name and password combination are correct
    echo '<h1>Here it is!</h1>';
    echo 'I bet you are glad you can see this secret page.';
  }
  else
  {
    // visitor's name and password combination are not correct
    echo '<h1>Go Away!</h1>';
    echo 'You are not authorized to view this resource.';
  }
 }
?>
```

The database we are using can be created by connecting to MySQL as the MySQL root user and running the contents of Listing 14.3.

Listing 14.3   **createauthdb.sql—These MySQL Queries Create the auth Database, the
              auth Table, and Two Sample Users**

```
create database auth;

use auth;

create table auth (
        name            varchar(10) not null,
        pass            varchar(30) not null,
        primary key     (name)
```

Listing 14.3 **Continued**

```
);

insert into auth values
  ('user', 'pass');

insert into auth values
  ( 'testuser', password('test123') );

grant select, insert, update, delete
on auth.*
to webauth@localhost
identified by 'webauth';
```

Encrypting Passwords

Regardless of whether we store our data in a database or a file, it is an unnecessary risk to store the passwords as plain text. A one-way hashing algorithm can provide a little more security with very little extra effort.

The PHP function `crypt()` provides a one-way cryptographic hash function. The prototype for this function is

```
string crypt (string str [, string salt])
```

Given the string `str`, the function will return a pseudo-random string. For example, given the string `"pass"` and the salt `"xx"`, `crypt()` returns `"xxkT1mYjlikoII"`. This string cannot be decrypted and turned back into `"pass"` even by its creator, so it might not seem very useful at first glance. The property that makes `crypt()` useful is that the output is deterministic. Given the same string and salt, `crypt()` will return the same result every time it is run.

Rather than having PHP code like

```
if( $username == 'user' && $password == 'pass' )
{
  //OK passwords match
}
```

we can have code like

```
if( $username == 'user' && crypt($password,'xx') == 'xxkT1mYjlikoII' )
{
  //OK passwords match
}
```

We do not need to know what `'xxkT1mYjlikoII'` looked like before we used `crypt()` on it. We only need to know if the password typed in is the same as the one that was originally run through `crypt()`.

As already mentioned, hard-coding our acceptable usernames and passwords into a script is a bad idea. We should use a separate file or a database to store them.

If we are using a MySQL database to store our authentication data, we could either use the PHP function crypt() or the MySQL function PASSWORD(). These functions do not produce the same output, but are intended to serve the same purpose. Both crypt() and PASSWORD() take a string and apply a non-reversible hashing algorithm.

To use PASSWORD(), we could rewrite the SQL query in Listing 14.2 as

```
select count(*) from auth where
       name = '$name' and
       pass = password('$password')
```

This query will count the number of rows in the table auth that have a name value equal to the contents of $name and a pass value equal to the output given by PASSWORD() applied to the contents of $password. Assuming that we force people to have unique usernames, the result of this query will be either 0 or 1.

If you look back at Listing 14.3 you will see that we have created one user ('user') with an unencrypted password and another user with an encrypted one ('testuser') to illustrate the two possible approaches.

Protecting Multiple Pages

Making a script like this protect more than one page is a little harder. Because HTTP is stateless, there is no automatic link or association between subsequent requests from the same person. This makes it harder to have data, such as authentication information that a user has entered, carry across from page to page.

The easiest way to protect multiple pages is to use the access control mechanisms provided by your Web server. We will look at these shortly.

To create this functionality ourselves, we could include parts of the script shown in Listing 14.1 in every page that we want to protect. Using auto_prepend_file and auto_append_file, we can automatically prepend and append the code required to every file in particular directories. The use of these directives was discussed in Chapter 5, "Reusing Code and Writing Functions."

If we use this approach, what happens when our visitors go to multiple pages within our site? It would not be acceptable to require them to re-enter their names and passwords for every page they want to view.

We could append the details they entered to every hyperlink on the page. As usernames might have spaces, or other characters that are not allowed in URLs, we should use the function urlencode() to safely encode these characters.

There would still be a few problems with this approach though. Because the data would be included in Web pages sent to the user and the URLs they visit, the protected pages they visit will be visible to anybody who uses the same computer and steps back through cached pages or looks at the browser's history list. Because we are sending the password back and forth to the browser with every page requested or delivered, this sensitive information is being transmitted more often than necessary.

There are two good ways to tackle these problems: HTTP basic authentication and sessions. Basic authentication overcomes the caching problem, but the browser still sends the password to the browser with every request. Session control overcomes both of these problems. We will look at HTTP basic authentication now, and examine session control in Chapter 20, "Using Session Control in PHP," and in more detail in Chapter 24, "Building User Authentication and Personalization."

Basic Authentication

Fortunately, authenticating users is a common task, so there are authentication facilities built in to HTTP. Scripts or Web servers can request authentication from a Web browser. The Web browser is then responsible for displaying a dialog box or similar device to get required information from the user.

Although the Web server requests new authentication details for every user request, the Web browser does not need to request the user's details for every page. The browser generally stores these details for as long as the user has a browser window open and automatically resends them to the Web server as required without user interaction.

This feature of HTTP is called *basic authentication*. You can trigger basic authentication using PHP, or using mechanisms built in to your Web server. We will look at the PHP method, the Apache method, and the IIS method.

Basic authentication transmits a user's name and password in plain text, so it is not very secure. HTTP 1.1 contains a somewhat more secure method known as *digest authentication*, which uses a hashing algorithm (usually MD5) to disguise the details of the transaction. Digest authentication is supported by many Web servers, but is not supported by a significant number of Web browsers. Digest authentication has been supported by Microsoft Internet Explorer from version 5.0. At the time of writing, it is not supported by any version of Netscape or Mozilla.

In addition to being poorly supported by installed Web browsers, digest authentication is still not very secure. Both basic and digest authentication provide a low level of security. Neither gives the user any assurance that she is dealing with the machine she intended to access. Both might permit a cracker to replay the same request to the server. Because basic authentication transmits the user's password as plain text, it allows any cracker capable of capturing packets to impersonate the user for making any request.

Basic authentication provides a (low) level of security similar to that commonly used to connect to machines via telnet or ftp, transmitting passwords in plaintext. Digest authentication is a little more secure, encrypting passwords before transmitting them. Using SSL and digital certificates, all parts of a Web transaction can be protected by strong security.

If you want strong security, you should read the next chapter, Chapter 15, "Implementing Secure Transactions with PHP and MySQL." However, for many situations, a fast, but relatively insecure, method such as basic authentication is appropriate.

Basic authentication protects a named realm and requires users to provide a valid username and password. Realms are named so that more than one realm can be on the same server. Different files or directories on the same server can be part of different realms, each protected by a different set of names and passwords. Named realms also let you group multiple directories on the one host or virtual host as a realm and protect them all with one password.

Using Basic Authentication in PHP

PHP scripts are generally cross-platform, but using basic authentication relies on environment variables set by the server. In order for an HTTP authentication script to run on Apache using PHP as an Apache Module or on IIS using PHP as an ISAPI module, it needs to detect the server type and behave slightly differently. The script in Listing 14.4 will run on both servers, but unlike most of the scripts in this book, it relies on your php.ini file having register_globals turned on.

Listing 14.4   http.php—PHP Can Trigger HTTP Basic Authentication

```php
<?php

// if we are using IIS, we need to set $PHP_AUTH_USER and $PHP_AUTH_PW
if (substr($SERVER_SOFTWARE, 0, 9) == 'Microsoft' &&
    !isset($PHP_AUTH_USER) &&
    !isset($PHP_AUTH_PW) &&
    substr($HTTP_AUTHORIZATION, 0, 6) == 'Basic '
   )
{
  list($PHP_AUTH_USER, $PHP_AUTH_PW) =
    explode(':', base64_decode(substr($HTTP_AUTHORIZATION, 6)));
}

// Replace this if statement with a database query or similar
if ($PHP_AUTH_USER != 'user' || $PHP_AUTH_PW != 'pass')
{
  // visitor has not yet given details, or their
  // name and password combination are not correct

  header('WWW-Authenticate: Basic realm="Realm-Name"');
  if (substr($SERVER_SOFTWARE, 0, 9) == 'Microsoft')
    header('Status: 401 Unauthorized');
  else
    header('HTTP/1.0 401 Unauthorized');

  echo '<h1>Go Away!</h1>';
  echo 'You are not authorized to view this resource.';
}
```

Listing 14.4   **Continued**

```
else
{
  // visitor has provided correct details
  echo '<h1>Here it is!</h1>';
  echo '<p>I bet you are glad you can see this secret page.</p>';
}
?>
```

The code in Listing 14.4 acts in a very similar way to the previous listings in this chapter. If the user has not yet provided authentication information, it will be requested. If she has provided incorrect information, she is given a rejection message. If she provides a matching name-password pair, she is presented with the contents of the page.

The user will see an interface somewhat different from the previous listings. We are not providing an HTML form for login information. The user's browser will present her with a dialog box. Some people see this as an improvement; others would prefer to have complete control over the visual aspects of the interface. The login dialog box that Internet Explorer provides is shown in Figure 14.4.

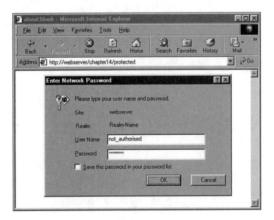

Figure 14.4   The user's browser is responsible for the appearance of the dialog box when using HTTP authentication.

Because the authentication is being assisted by features built in to the browser, the browsers choose to exercise some discretion in how failed authorization attempts are handled. Internet Explorer lets the user try to authenticate three times before displaying the rejection page. Netscape will let the user try an unlimited number of times, popping up a dialog box to ask, "Authorization failed. Retry?" between attempts. Netscape only displays the rejection page if the user clicks Cancel.

As with the code given in Listing 14.1 and 14.2, we could include this code in pages we wanted to protect, or automatically prepend it to every file in a directory.

Using Basic Authentication with Apache's .htaccess Files

We can achieve very similar results to the previous script without writing a PHP script.

The Apache Web server contains a number of different authentication modules that can be used to decide the validity of data entered by a user. The easiest to use is mod_auth, which compares name-password pairs to lines in a text file on the server.

In order to get the same output as the previous script, we need to create two separate HTML files, one for the content and one for the rejection page. We skipped some HTML elements in the previous examples, but really should include `<html>` and `<body>` tags when we are generating HTML.

Listing 14.5 contains the content that authorized users see. We have called this file `content.html`. Listing 14.6 contains the rejection page. We have called this `rejection.html`. Having a page to show in case of errors is optional, but it is a nice, professional touch if you put something useful on it. Given that this page will be shown when a user attempts to enter a protected area but is rejected, useful content might include instructions on how to register for a password, or how to get a password reset and emailed if it has been forgotten.

Listing 14.5   **content.html—Our Sample Content**

```
<html><body>
<h1>Here it is!</h1>
<p>I bet you are glad you can see this secret page.</p>
</body></html>
```

Listing 14.6   **rejection.html—Our Sample 401 Error Page**

```
<html><body>
<h1>Go Away!</h1>
<p>You are not authorized to view this resource.</p>
</body></html>
```

There is nothing new in these files. The interesting file for this example is Listing 14.7. This file needs to be called .htaccess, and will control accesses to files and any subdirectories in its directory.

Listing 14.7   **.htaccess—An .htaccess File Can Set Many Apache Configuration Settings, Including Activating Authentication**

```
ErrorDocument 401 /chapter14/rejection.html
AuthUserFile /home/book/.htpass
AuthGroupFile /dev/null
AuthName "Realm-Name"
AuthType Basic
require valid-user
```

Listing 14.7 is an `.htaccess` file to turn on basic authentication in a directory. Many settings can be made in an `.htaccess` file, but the six lines in our example all relate to authentication.

The first line

```
ErrorDocument 401 /chapter14/rejection.html
```

tells Apache what document to display for visitors who fail to authenticate. You can use other `ErrorDocument` directives to provide your own pages for other HTTP errors such as 404. The syntax is

```
ErrorDocument error_number URL
```

For a page to handle error 401, it is important that the URL given is publicly available. It would not be very useful in providing a customized error page to tell people that their authorization failed if the page is locked in a directory in which they need to successfully authenticate to see.

The line

```
AuthUserFile /home/book/.htpass
```

tells Apache where to find the file that contains authorized users' passwords. This is often named `.htpass`, but you can give it any name you prefer. It is not important what this file is called, but it is important where it is stored. It should not be stored within the Web tree—somewhere that people can download it via the Web server. Our sample `.htpass` file is shown in Listing 14.8.

As well as specifying individual users who are authorized, it is possible to specify that only authorized users who fall into specific groups may access resources. We have chosen not to, so the line

```
AuthGroupFile /dev/null
```

sets our `AuthGroupFile` to point to `/dev/null`, a special file on Unix systems that is guaranteed to be null.

Like the PHP example, to use HTTP authentication, we need to name our realm as follows:

```
AuthName "Realm-Name"
```

You can choose any realm name you prefer, but bear in mind that the name will be shown to your visitors. To make it obvious that the name in the example should be changed, ours is named `"Realm-Name"`.

Because a number of different authentication methods are supported, we need to specify which authentication method we are using.

We are using `Basic` authentication as specified by this directive:

```
AuthType Basic
```

We need to specify who is allowed access. We could specify particular users, particular groups, or as we have done, simply allow any authenticated user access.

The line

```
require valid-user
```

specifies that any valid user is to be allowed access.

Listing 14.8   .htpass—The Password File Stores Usernames and Each User's Encrypted Password

```
user1:0nRp9M80GS7zM
user2:nC13sOTOhp.ow
user3:yjQMCPWjXFTzU
user4:LOmlMEi/hAme2
```

Each line in the .htpass file contains a username, a colon, and that user's encrypted password.

The exact contents of your .htpass file will vary. To create it, you use a small program called htpasswd that comes in the Apache distribution.

The htpasswd program is used in one of the following ways:

```
htpasswd [-cmdps] passwordfile username
```

or

```
htpasswd -b[cmdps] passwordfile username password
```

The only switch that you need to use is -c. Using -c tells htpasswd to create the file. You must use this for the first user you add. Be careful not to use it for other users because if the file exists, htpasswd will delete it and create a new one.

The optional m, d, p, or s switches can be used if you want to specify which encryption algorithm (including no encryption) you would like to use.

The b switch tells the program to expect the password as a parameter, rather than prompting for it. This is useful if you want to call htpasswd noninteractively as part of a batch process, but should not be used if you are calling htpasswd from the command line.

The following commands created the file shown in Listing 14.8:

```
htpasswd -bc /home/book/.htpass user1 pass1
htpasswd -b /home/book/.htpass user2 pass2
htpasswd -b /home/book/.htpass user4 pass3
htpasswd -b /home/book/.htpass user4 pass4
```

This sort of authentication is easy to set up, but there are a few problems with using a .htaccess file this way.

Users and passwords are stored in a text file. Each time a browser requests a file that is protected by the .htaccess file, the server must parse the .htaccess file, and then parse the password file, attempting to match the username and password. Rather than using an .htaccess file, we could specify the same things in our httpd.conf file—the main configuration file for the Web server. An .htaccess file is parsed every time a file is requested. The `httpd.conf` file is only parsed when the server is initially started. This will be faster, but means that if we want to make changes, we need to stop and restart the server.

Regardless of where we store the server directives, the password file still needs to be searched for every request. This means that, like other techniques we have looked at that use a flat file, this would not be appropriate for hundreds or thousands of users.

Using Basic Authentication with IIS

Like Apache, IIS supports HTTP authentication. Apache uses the UNIX approach and is controlled by editing text files, and as you might expect, selecting options in dialog boxes controls the IIS setup.

Using Windows 2000, you change the configuration of Internet Information Server 5 (IIS5) using the Internet Services Manager. You can find this utility by choosing Administrative Tools in the Control Panel.

The Internet Services Manager will look something like the picture shown in Figure 14.5. The tree control on the left side shows that on the machine named windows-server, we are running a number of services. The one we are interested in is the default Web site. Within this Web site, we have a directory called `protected`. Inside this directory is a file called `content.html`.

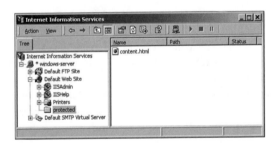

Figure 14.5   The Microsoft Management Console allows us to configure Internet Information Server 5.

To add basic authentication to the `protected` directory, right-click on it and select Properties from the context menu.

The Properties dialog allows us to change many settings for this directory. The two tabs that we are interested in are Directory Security and Custom Errors. One of the options on the Directory Security tab is Anonymous Access and Authentication Control. Pressing this Edit button will bring up the dialog box shown in Figure 14.6.

Figure 14.6   IIS5 allows anonymous access by default,
but allows us to turn on authentication.

Within this dialog, we can disable anonymous access and turn on basic authentication. With the settings shown in Figure 14.6, only people who provide an appropriate name and password can view files in this directory.

In order to duplicate the behavior of the previous examples, we will also provide a page to tell users that their authentication details were not correct. Closing the Authentication methods dialog box will allow us to choose the Custom Errors tab.

The Custom Errors tab, shown in Figure 14.7, associates errors with error messages. Here, we have stored the same rejection file we used earlier, `rejection.html`, shown in Listing 14.6. IIS gives us the ability to provide a more specific error message than Apache does, providing the HTTP error code that occurred and a reason why it occurred. For the error 401, which represents failed authentication, IIS provides five different reasons. We could provide different messages for each, but have chosen to only replace the two that are going to occur in this example with our rejection page.

That is all we need to do to require authentication for this directory using IIS5. Like a lot of Windows software, it is easier to set up than similar UNIX software, but harder to copy from machine to machine or directory to directory. It is also easy to accidentally set it up in a way that makes your machine insecure.

The major flaw with IIS's approach is that it authenticates Web users by comparing their login details to accounts on the machine. If we want to allow a user "john" to log in with the password "password", we need to create a user account on the machine, or on a domain, with this name and password. You need to be very careful when you are creating accounts for Web authentication so that the users only have the account rights they need to view Web pages and do not have other rights such as telnet access.

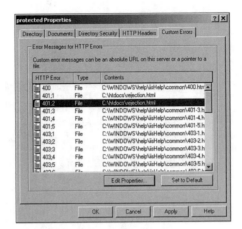

Figure 14.7   The Custom Errors tab lets us associate
custom error pages with error events.

Using mod_auth_mysql Authentication

As already mentioned, using mod_auth with Apache is easy to set up and is effective.
Because it stores users in a text file, it is not really practical for busy sites with large
numbers of users.

Fortunately, you can have most of the ease of mod_auth, and the speed of a database
using mod_auth_mysql. This module works in much the same way as mod_auth, but
because it uses a MySQL database instead of a text file, it can search large user lists
quickly.

In order to use it, you will need to compile and install the module on your system or
ask your system administrator to install it.

Installing mod_auth_mysql

In order to use mod_auth_mysql, you will need to set up Apache and MySQL according
to the instruction in Appendix A, "Installing PHP and MySQL," but add a few extra
steps. There are quite good instructions in the files README and USAGE that are in the distribution, but here is a summary.

1. Obtain the distribution archive for the module. It is on the CD-ROM that came
   with this book, but you can always get the latest version from

   ```
   http://www.mysql.com/doc/en/Contrib.html
   ```

   or alternatively

   ```
   http://www.mysql.com/Downloads/Contrib/
   ```

2. Unzip and untar the source code.

3. Change to the `mod_auth_mysql` directory and run `configure`. You need to tell it where to find your MySQL installation and your Apache source code. To suit the directory structure on my machine, I typed

```
./configure --with-mysql=/var/mysql --with-apache=../src/apache_1.x.xx
```

but your locations might be different.

4. Run `make`, and then `make install`. You will need to add

```
--activate-module=src/modules/auth_mysql/libauth_mysql.a
```

to the parameters you give to `configure` when you configure Apache.

For the setup on my system, I used

```
./configure --enable-module=ssl \
--activate-module=src/modules/php4/libphp4.a \
--enable-module=php4 --prefix=/usr/local/apache --enable-shared=ssl \
--activate-module=src/modules/auth_mysql/libauth_mysql.a
```

5. After following the other steps in Appendix A, you will need to create a database and table in MySQL to contain authentication information. This does not need to be a separate database or table; you can use an existing table such as the auth database from the example earlier in this chapter.

6. Add a line to your `httpd.conf` file to give `mod_auth_mysql` the parameters it needs to connect to MySQL. The directive will look like

```
Auth_MySQL_Info hostname user password
```

Did It Work?

The easiest way to check whether your compilation worked is to see whether Apache will start. To start Apache, if you have SSL support type

```
/usr/local/apache/bin/apachectl startssl
```

If you don't have SSL support you can type

```
/usr/local/apache/bin/apachectl start
```

If it starts with the `Auth_MySQL_Info` directive in the `httpd.conf` file, `mod_auth_mysql` was successfully added.

Using mod_auth_mysql

After you have successfully installed the module, using it is no harder than using `mod_auth`. Listing 14.9 shows a sample `.htaccess` file that will authenticate users with encrypted passwords stored in the database created earlier in this chapter.

Listing 14.9   .htaccess—This .htaccess File Authenticates Users Against a MySQL
Database

```
ErrorDocument 401 /chapter14/rejection.html

AuthName "Realm Name"
AuthType Basic

Auth_MySQL_DB auth
Auth_MySQL_Encryption_Types MySQL
Auth_MySQL_Password_Table auth
Auth_MySQL_Username_Field name
Auth_MySQL_Password_Field pass

require valid-user
```

You can see that much of Listing 14.9 is the same as Listing 14.7. We are still specifying
an error document to display in the case of error 401 (when authentication fails). We
again specify basic authentication and give a realm name. As in Listing 14.7, we will
allow any valid, authenticated user access.

Because we are using mod_auth_mysql and did not want to use all the default settings, we have some directives to specify how this should work. Auth_MySQL_DB,
Auth_MySQL_Password_Table, Auth_MySQL_Username_Field, and
Auth_MySQL_Password_Field specify the name of the database, the table, the username
field, and the password field, respectively.

We are including the directive Auth_MySQL_Encryption_Types to specify that we
want to use MySQL password encryption. Acceptable values are Plaintext, Crypt_DES,
or MySQL. Crypt_DES is the default, and uses standard UNIX DES–encrypted passwords.

From the user perspective, this mod_auth_mysql example will work in exactly the
same way as the mod_auth example. She will be presented with a dialog box by her Web
browser. If she successfully authenticates, she will be shown the content. If she fails, she
will be given our error page.

For many Web sites, mod_auth_mysql is ideal. It is fast, relatively easy to implement,
and allows you to use any convenient mechanism to add database entries for new users.
For more flexibility, and the ability to apply fine-grained control to parts of pages, you
might want to implement your own authentication using PHP and MySQL.

Creating Your Own Custom Authentication

We have looked at creating our own authentication methods including some flaws and
compromises and using built-in authentication methods, which are less flexible than
writing your own code. Later in the book, when we have covered session control, you
will be able to write your own custom authentication with fewer compromises than in
this chapter.

In Chapter 20, "Using Session Control in PHP," we will develop a simple user authentication system that avoids some of the problems we have faced here by using sessions to track variables between pages.

In Chapter 24, "Building User Authentication and Personalization," we apply this approach to a real-world project and see how it can be used to implement a fine grained authentication system.

Further Reading

The details of HTTP authentication are specified by RFC 2617, which is available at

```
http://www.rfc-editor.org/rfc/rfc2617.txt
```

The documentation for mod_auth, which controls basic authentication in Apache, can be found at

```
http://www.apache.org/docs/mod/mod_auth.html
```

The documentation for mod_auth_mysql is inside the download archive. It is a tiny download, so even if you just want to find out more about it, downloading the archive to look at the readme is not silly.

Next

The next chapter explains how to safeguard data at all stages of processing from input, through transmission, and in storage. It includes the use of SSL, digital certificates, and encryption.

15

Implementing Secure Transactions with PHP and MySQL

Ｉ N THIS CHAPTER, WE WILL EXPLAIN HOW to deal with user data securely from input, through transmission, and in storage. This will allow us to implement a transaction between us and a user securely from end to end. Topics include

- Providing secure transactions
- Using Secure Sockets Layer (SSL)
- Providing secure storage
- Why are you storing credit card numbers?
- Using encryption in PHP

Providing Secure Transactions

Providing secure transactions using the Internet is a matter of examining the flow of information in your system and ensuring that at each point, your information is secure. In the context of network security, there are no absolutes. No system is ever going to be impenetrable. By secure we mean that the level of effort required to compromise a system or transmission is high compared to the value of the information involved.

If we are to direct our security efforts effectively, we need to examine the flow of information through all parts of our system. The flow of user information in a typical application, written using PHP and MySQL, is shown in Figure 15.1.

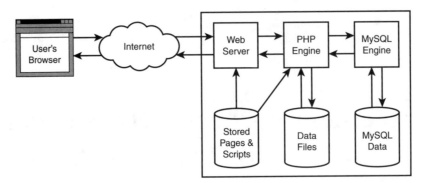

Figure 15.1   User information is stored or processed by the following elements of a typical Web application environment.

The details of each transaction occurring in your system will vary, depending both on your system design and on the user data and actions that triggered the transaction. You can examine all of these in a similar way. Each transaction between a Web application and a user begins with the user's browser sending a request through the Internet to the Web server. If the page is a PHP script, the Web server will delegate processing the page to the PHP engine.

The PHP script might read or write data to disk. It might also include() or require() other PHP or HTML files. It will also send SQL queries to the MySQL daemon and receive responses. The MySQL engine is responsible for reading and writing its own data on disk.

This system has three main parts:

- The user's machine
- The Internet
- Your system

We will look at security considerations for each separately, but obviously the user's machine and the Internet are largely out of your control.

The User's Machine

From our point of view, the user's machine is running a Web browser. We have no control over other factors such as how securely the machine is set up. We need to bear in mind that the machine might be very insecure or even a shared terminal at a library, school, or café.

Many different browsers are available, each having slightly different capabilities. If we only consider recent versions of the most popular two browsers, most of the differences between them only affect how HTML will be rendered and displayed, but there are security or functionality issues that we need to consider.

You should note that some people will disable features that they consider a security or privacy risk, such as Java, cookies, or JavaScript. If you use these features, you should either test that your application degrades gracefully for people without these features, or consider providing a less feature rich interface that allows these people to use your site.

Users outside the United States and Canada might have Web browsers that only support 40-bit encryption. Although the U.S. Government changed the law in January 2000 to allow export of strong encryption (to non-embargoed countries) and 128-bit versions are now available to most users, some of them will not have upgraded. Unless you are making guarantees of security to users in the text of your site, this need not concern you overly as a Web developer. SSL will automatically negotiate for you to enable your server and the user's browser to communicate at the most secure level that they both understand.

We cannot be sure that we are dealing with a Web browser connecting to our site through our intended interface. Requests to our site might be coming from another site stealing images or content, or from a person using software such as cURL to bypass safety measures.

We will look at the cURL library, which can be used to simulate connections from a browser, in Chapter 17, "Using Network and Protocol Functions." This is useful to us as developers, but can also be used maliciously.

Although we cannot change or control the way that our users' machines are set up, we do need to bear it in mind. The variability of user machines might be a factor in how much functionality we provide via server-side scripting (such as PHP) and how much we provide via client-side scripting (such as JavaScript).

Functionality provided by PHP can be compatible with every user's browser, as the end result is merely an HTML page. Using anything but very basic JavaScript will involve taking into account the different capabilities of individual browser versions.

From a security perspective, we are better off using server-side scripting for such things as data validation because, that way, our source code will not be visible to the user. If we validate data in JavaScript, users will be able to see the code and perhaps circumvent it.

Data that needs to be retained can be stored on our own machines, as files or database records, or on our users' machines as cookies. We will look at using cookies for storing some limited data (a session key) in Chapter 20, "Using Session Control in PHP."

The majority of data we store should reside on the Web server, or in our database. There are a number of good reasons to store as little information as possible on the user's machine. If the information is outside your system, you have no control over how securely it is stored, you cannot be sure that the user will not delete it, and you cannot stop the user from modifying it in an attempt to confuse your system.

The Internet

Like the user's machine, you have very little control over the characteristics of the Internet, but, like the user's machine, this does not mean that you can ignore these characteristics when designing your system.

The Internet has many fine features, but it is an inherently insecure network. When sending information from one point to another, you need to bear in mind that others could view or alter the information you are transmitting, as we discussed in Chapter 13. With this in mind, you can decide what action to take.

Your response might be to

- Transmit the information anyway, knowing that it might not be private.

- Encrypt or sign the information before transmitting it to keep it private or protect it from tampering.

- Decide that your information is too sensitive to risk any chance of interception and find another way to distribute your information.

The Internet is also a fairly anonymous medium. It is difficult to be certain whether the person you are dealing with is who they claim to be. Even if you can assure yourself about a user to your own satisfaction, it might be difficult to prove this beyond a sufficient level of doubt in a forum such as a court. This causes problems with repudiation, which we discussed in Chapter 13, "E-commerce Security Issues."

In summary, privacy and repudiation are big issues when conducting transactions over the Internet.

There are at least two different ways you can secure information flowing to and from your Web server through the Internet:

- SSL (Secure Sockets Layer)
- S-HTTP (Secure Hypertext Transfer Protocol)

Both these technologies offer private, tamper resistant messages and authentication, but SSL is readily available and widely used whereas S-HTTP has not really taken off. We will look at SSL in detail later in this chapter.

Your System

The part of the universe that you do have control over is your system. Your system is represented by the components within the rectangular box as shown previously in Figure 15.1. These components might be physically separated on a network, or all exist on the one physical machine.

It is fairly safe to not worry about the security of information while the various third-party products that we use to deliver our Web content are handling it. The authors of those particular pieces of software have probably given them more thought than you have time to give them. As long as you are using an up-to-date version of a well-known product, you will be able to find any well-known problems by judicious application of Google or your favorite Web search engine. You should make it a priority to keep up-to-date with this information.

If installation and configuration are part of your role, you do need to worry about the way software is installed and configured. Many mistakes made in security are a result of not following the warnings in the documentation, or involve general system administration issues that are topics for another book. Buy a good book on administering the operating system you intend to use, or hire an expert system administrator.

One specific thing to consider when installing PHP is that it is generally more secure, as well as much more efficient, to install PHP as a SAPI module for your Web server than to run it via the CGI interface.

The primary thing you need to worry about is what your own scripts do or not do.

What potentially sensitive data does our application transmit to the user over the Internet? What sensitive data do we ask users to transmit to us? If we are transmitting information that should be a private transaction between us and our users or that should be difficult for an intermediary to modify, we should consider using SSL.

We have already talked about using SSL between the user's computer and the server. You should also think about the situation where you are transmitting data from one component of your system to another over a network. A typical example arises when your MySQL database resides on a different machine from your Web server. PHP will connect to your MySQL server via TCP/IP, and this connection will be unencrypted. If these machines are both on a private local area network, you need to ensure that network is secure. If the machines are communicating via the Internet, your system will probably run slowly, and you need to treat this connection in the same way as other connections over the Internet.

It is important that when our users think they are dealing with us, they are dealing with us. Registering for a digital certificate will protect our visitors from spoofing (someone else impersonating our site), allow us to use SSL without users seeing a warning message, and provide an air of respectability to our online venture.

Do our scripts carefully check the data that users enter?

Are we careful about storing information securely?

We will answer these questions in the next few sections of this chapter.

Using Secure Sockets Layer (SSL)

The Secure Sockets Layer protocol suite was originally designed by Netscape to facilitate secure communication between Web servers and Web browsers. It has since been adopted as the unofficial standard method for browsers and servers to exchange sensitive information.

Both SSL version 2 and version 3 are well supported. Most Web servers either include SSL functionality, or can accept it as an add-on module. Internet Explorer and Netscape have both supported SSL from version 3.

Networking protocols and the software that implements them are usually arranged as a stack of layers. Each layer can pass data to the layer above or below, and request services of the layer above or below. Figure 15.2 shows such a protocol stack.

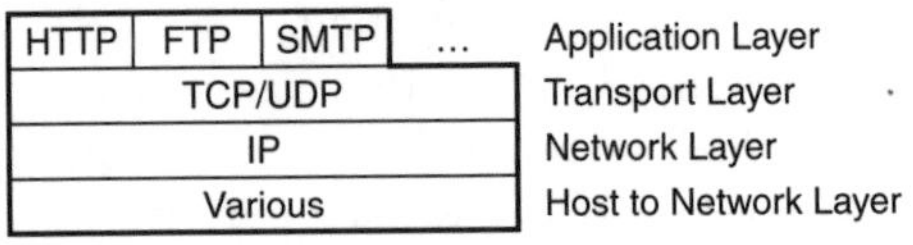

HTTP	FTP	SMTP	...	Application Layer
TCP/UDP				Transport Layer
IP				Network Layer
Various				Host to Network Layer

Figure 15.2 The protocol stack used by an application layer
protocol such as Hypertext Transfer Protocol.

When you use HTTP to transfer information, the HTTP protocol calls on the
Transmission Control Protocol (TCP), which in turn relies on the *Internet Protocol (IP)*. This
protocol in turn needs an appropriate protocol for the network hardware being used to
take packets of data and send them as an electrical signal to our destination.

HTTP is called an application layer protocol. There are many other application layer
protocols such as FTP, SMTP and telnet (as shown in the figure), and others such as
POP and IMAP. TCP is one of two transport layer protocols used in TCP/IP networks.
IP is the protocol at the network layer. The host to network layer is responsible for connecting our host (computer) to a network. The TCP/IP protocol stack does not specify
the protocols used for this layer, as we need different protocols for different types of networks.

When sending data, the data is sent down through the stack from an application to
the physical network media. When receiving data, data travels up from the physical network, through the stack, to the application.

Using SSL adds an additional transparent layer to this model. The SSL layer exists
between the transport layer and the application layer. This is shown in Figure 15.3. The
SSL layer modifies the data from our HTTP application before giving it to the transport
layer to send it to its destination.

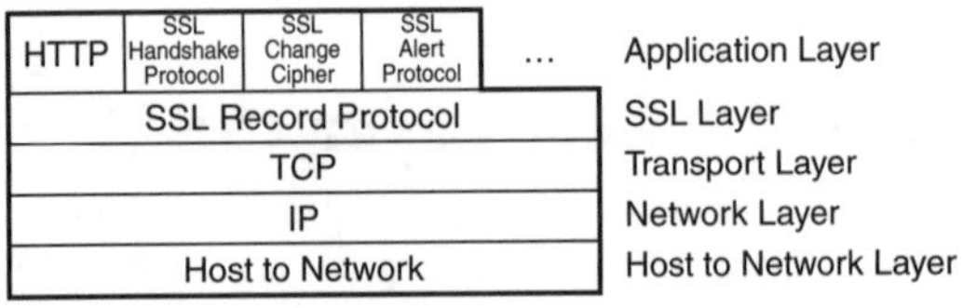

HTTP	SSL Handshake Protocol	SSL Change Cipher	SSL Alert Protocol	...	Application Layer
SSL Record Protocol					SSL Layer
TCP					Transport Layer
IP					Network Layer
Host to Network					Host to Network Layer

Figure 15.3 SSL adds an additional layer to the protocol stack as well as
application layer protocols for controlling its own operation.

SSL is theoretically capable of providing a secure transmission environment for protocols
other than HTTP, but is normally only used for HTTP. Other protocols can be used
because the SSL layer is essentially transparent. The SSL layer provides the same interface
to protocols above it as the underlying transport layer. It then transparently deals with
handshaking, encryption, and decryption.

When a Web browser connects to a secure Web server via HTTP, the two need to
follow a handshaking protocol to agree on things such as authentication and encryption.

The handshake sequence involves the following steps:

1. The browser connects to an SSL enabled server and asks the server to authenticate itself.
2. The server sends its digital certificate.
3. The server might optionally (and rarely) request that the browser authenticate itself.
4. The browser presents a list of the encryption algorithms and hash functions it supports. The server selects the strongest encryption that it also supports.
5. The browser and server generate session keys:

    5.1 The browser obtains the server's public key from its digital certificate and uses it to encrypt a randomly generated number.

    5.2 The server responds with more random data sent in plaintext (unless the browser has provided a digital certificate at the server's request in which case the server will use the browser's public key).

    5.3 The encryption keys for the session are generated from this random data using hash functions.

Generating good quality random data, decrypting digital certificates, and generating keys and using public key cryptography takes time, so this handshake procedure takes time. Fortunately, the results are cached, so if the same browser and server want to exchange multiple secure messages, the handshake process and the required processing time only occur once.

When data is sent over an SSL connection, the following steps occur:

1. It is broken into manageable packets.
2. Each packet is (optionally) compressed.
3. Each packet has a message authentication code (MAC) calculated using a hashing algorithm.
4. The MAC and compressed data are combined and encrypted.
5. The encrypted packets are combined with header information and sent to the network.

The entire process is shown in Figure 15.4.

One thing you might notice from the diagram is that the TCP header is added after the data is encrypted. This means that routing information could still potentially be tampered with, and although snoopers cannot tell what information we are exchanging, they can see who is exchanging it.

The reason that SSL includes compression before encryption is that although most network traffic can be (and often is) compressed before being transmitted across a network, encrypted data does not compress well.

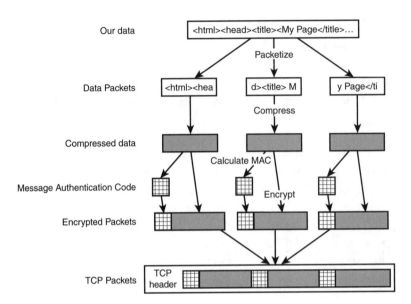

Figure 15.4   SSL breaks up, compresses, hashes, and
encrypts data before sending it.

Compression schemes rely on identifying repetition or patterns within data. Trying to apply a compression algorithm after data has been turned into an effectively random arrangement of bits via encryption is usually pointless. It would be unfortunate if SSL, which was designed to increase network security, had the side effect of dramatically increasing network traffic.

Although SSL is relatively complex, users and developers are shielded from most of what occurs, as its external interfaces mimic existing protocols.

In the future, SSL 3.0 may be replaced by TLS 1.0 (Transport Layer Security), but at the time of writing, TLS is a draft standard and not supported by any servers or browsers. TLS is intended to be a truly open standard, rather than a standard defined by one organization but made available for others. It is based directly on SSL 3.0, but contains improvements intended to overcome weaknesses of SSL.

Screening User Input

One of the principles of building a safe Web application is that you should never trust user input. Always screen user data before putting it in a file or database or passing it through a system execution command.

We've talked in several places throughout this book of techniques you can use to screen user input. We'll list these briefly here as a reference.

- The `addslashes()` function should be used to filter user data before it is passed to a database. This function will escape out characters which might be troublesome to a database. You can use the `stripslashes()` function to return the data to its original form.

- Magic quotes. You can switch on the `magic_quotes_gpc` and `magic_quotes_run-time` directives in your php.ini file. These directives will automatically add and strip slashes for you. The `magic_quotes_gpc` directive will apply this formatting to incoming GET, POST, and cookie variables, and the `magic_quote_runtime` directive will apply it to data going to and from databases.

- The `escapeshellcmd()` function should be used when you are passing user data to a `system()` or `exec()` call or to backticks. This will escape out any metacharacters that can be used to force your system to run arbitrary commands entered by a malicious user.

- You can use the `strip_tags()` function to strip out HTML and PHP tags from a string. This will avoid users planting malicious scripts in user data that you might echo back to the browser.

- You can use the `htmlspecialchars()` function, which will convert characters to their HTML entity equivalents. For example, < will be converted to `&lt;`. This will convert any script tags to harmless characters.

Providing Secure Storage

The three different types of stored data (HTML or PHP files, script related data, and MySQL data) will often be stored in different areas of the same disk, but are shown separately in Figure 15.1. Each type of storage requires different precautions and will be examined separately.

The most dangerous type of data we store is executable content. On a Web site, this usually means scripts. You need to be very careful that your file permissions are set correctly within your Web hierarchy. By this we mean the directory tree starting from htdocs on an Apache server or inetpub on an IIS server. Others need to have permission to read your scripts in order to see their output, but they should not be able to write over or edit them.

The same proviso applies to directories within the Web hierarchy. Only we should be able to write to these directories. Other users, including the user who the Web server runs as, should not have permission to write or create new files in directories that can be loaded from the Web server. If you allow others to write files here, they could write a malicious script and execute it by loading it through the Web server.

If your scripts need permission to write to files, make a directory outside the Web tree for this purpose. This is particularly true for file upload scripts. Scripts and the data that they write should not mix.

When writing sensitive data, you might be tempted to encrypt it first. There is usually little value in this approach though.

We'll put it this way: If you have a file called `creditcardnumbers.txt` on your Web server and a cracker obtains access to your server and can read it, what else can he read? In order to encrypt and decrypt data, you will need a program to encrypt data, a program to decrypt data, and one or more key files. If the cracker can read your data, probably nothing is stopping him from reading your key and other files.

Encrypting data could be valuable on a Web server, but only if the software and key to decrypt the data was not stored on the Web server, but only existed on another machine. One way of securely dealing with sensitive data would be to encrypt it on the server, and then transmit it to another machine, perhaps via email.

Database data is similar to data files. If you set up MySQL correctly, only MySQL can write to its data files. This means that we need only worry about accesses from users within MySQL. We have already discussed MySQL's own permission system, which assigns particular rights to particular usernames at particular hosts.

One thing that needs special mention is that you will often need to write a MySQL password in a PHP script. Your PHP scripts are generally publicly loadable. This is not as much of a disaster as it might seem at first. Unless your Web server configuration is broken, your PHP source will not be visible from outside.

If your Web server is configured to parse files with the extension .php using the PHP interpreter, outsiders will not be able to view the uninterpreted source. However, you should be careful when using other extensions. If you place .inc files in your Web directories, anybody requesting them will receive the unparsed source. You need to either place include files outside the Web tree, configure your server not to deliver files with this extension, or use .php as the extension on these as well.

If you are sharing a Web server with others, your MySQL password might be visible to other users on the same machine who can also run scripts via the same Web server. Depending on how your system is set up, this might be unavoidable. This can be avoided by having a Web server set up to run scripts as individual users, or by having each user run her own instance of the Web server. If you are not the administrator for your Web server (as is likely the case if you are sharing a server), it might be worth discussing this with your administrator and exploring security options.

Why Are You Storing Credit Card Numbers?

Having discussed secure storage for sensitive data, one type of sensitive data deserves special mention. Internet users are paranoid about their credit card numbers. If you are going to store them, you need to be very careful. You also need to ask yourself why you are doing it, and if it is really necessary.

What are you going to do with a card number? If you have a one-off transaction to process and real-time card processing, you will be better off accepting the card number from your customer and sending it straight to your transaction processing gateway without storing it at all.

If you have periodic charges to make, such as the authority to charge a monthly fee to the same card for an ongoing subscription, this might not be an option. In this case, you should think about storing the numbers somewhere other than the Web server.

If you are going to store large numbers of your customers' card details, make sure that you have a skilled and somewhat paranoid system administrator who has enough time to check up-to-date sources of security information for the operating system and other products you use.

Using Encryption in PHP

A simple, but useful, task we can use to demonstrate encryption is sending encrypted email. The *defacto* standard for encrypted email has for many years been PGP, which stands for Pretty Good Privacy. Philip R. Zimmermann wrote PGP specifically to add privacy to email.

Freeware versions of PGP are available, but you should note that this is not Free Software. The freeware version can only legally be used for non-commercial use.

If you are a U.S. citizen in the United States, or a Canadian citizen in Canada, you can obtain the freeware version from `http://web.mit.edu/network/pgp.html`.

If you want to use PGP for commercial use and are in the United States or Canada, you can get a commercial license from Network Associates. See `http://www.pgp.com` for details.

To obtain PGP for use outside the USA and Canada, see the list of international download sites at the international PGP page: `http://www.pgpi.org`.

An Open Source alternative to PGP has recently become available. GPG—Gnu Privacy Guard—is a free (as in beer) and Free (as in speech) replacement for PGP. It contains no patented algorithms, and can be used commercially without restriction.

The two products perform the same task in fairly similar ways. If you intend to use the command line tools it might not matter, but each has different interfaces such as plug-ins for email programs that will automatically decrypt email when it is received.

GPG is available from `http://www.gnupg.org`.

You can use the two products together, creating an encrypted message using GPG for somebody using PGP (as long as it is a recent version) to decrypt. As it is the creation of messages at the Web server we are interested in, we will provide an example here using GPG. Using PGP instead will not require many changes.

As well as the usual requirements for examples in this book, you will need to have GPG available for this code to work. GPG might already be installed on your system. If it is not, do not be concerned: The installation procedure is very straightforward, but the setup can be a bit tricky.

Installing GPG

To add GPG to our Linux machine, we downloaded the appropriate archive file from `www.gnupg.org`. Depending on whether you choose the .tar.gz or .tar.bz2 archive, you will need to use `gunzip` and `tar` or to extract the files from the archive.

To compile and install the program, use the same commands as for most Linux programs:

```
configure (or ./configure depending on your system)
make
make install
```

If you are not the root user, you will need to run the configure script with the `--prefix` option as follows:

```
./configure --prefix=/path/to/your/directory
```

This is because a non-root user will not have access to the default directory for GPG. If all goes well, GPG will be compiled and the executable copied to `/usr/local/bin/gpg` or the directory that you specified. You can change many options. See the GPG documentation for details.

For a Windows server, the process is even easier. Download the zip file, unzip it, and place gpg.exe somewhere in your PATH. (C:\Windows\ or similar will be fine). Create a directory at C:\gnupg. Open a command prompt and type **gpg**.

You also need to install GPG or PGP and generate a key pair on the system that you plan to check mail from.

On the Web server, there are very few differences between the command-line versions of GPG and PGP, so we might as well use GPG as it is free. On the machine that you read mail from, you might prefer to buy a commercial version of PGP in order to have a nicer graphical user interface plug-in to your mail reader.

If you do not already have one, generate a key pair on your mail reading machine. Recall that a key pair consists of a Public Key that other people (and your PHP script) use to encrypt mail before sending it to you, and a Private Key, which you use to either decrypt received messages or sign outgoing mail.

It is important that the key generation is done on your mail reading machine, rather than on your Web server, as your private key should not be stored on the Web server.

If you are using the command-line version of GPG to generate your keys, enter the following command:

```
gpg --gen-key
```

You will be asked a number of questions. Most of them have a default answer that can be accepted. On separate lines, you will be asked for your real name, your email address and a comment, which will be used to name the key.

My key is named `'Luke Welling <luke@tangledweb.com.au>'`. I am sure that you can see the pattern. Had I provided a comment too, it would be between the name and address.

To export the public key from your new key pair, you can use the command:

```
gpg --export > filename
```

This will give you a binary file suitable for importing into the GPG or PGP keyring on another machine. If you want to email this key to people, so they can import it into their key rings, you can instead create an ASCII version like this:

```
gpg --export -a > filename
```

Having extracted the public key, you can upload the file to your account on the Web server. You can do this with FTP.

The following commands assume that you are using UNIX. The steps are the same for Windows, but directory names and system commands will be different.

Log into your account on the Web server and change the permissions on the file so that other users will be able to read it. Type

```
chmod 644 filename
```

You will need to create a keyring so that the user who your PHP scripts get executed as can use GPG. Which user this is depends on how your server is setup. It is often the user 'nobody', but could be something else.

Change to being the Web server user. You will need to have root access to the server to do this. On many systems, the Web server runs as nobody. The following examples assume this. (You can change it to the appropriate user on your system.) If this is the case on your system, type

```
su root
su nobody
```

Create a directory for nobody to store their key ring and other GPG configuration information in. This will need to be in nobody's home directory.

The home directory for each user is specified in /etc/passwd. On many Linux systems, nobody's home directory defaults to /, which nobody will not have permission to write to. On many BSD systems, nobody's home directory defaults to /nonexistent, which, as it doesn't exist, cannot be written to. On our system, nobody has been assigned the home directory /tmp. You will need to make sure your Web server user has a home directory that he can write to.

Type

```
cd ~
mkdir .gnupg
```

The user nobody will need a signing key of her own. To create this, run this command again:

```
gpg --gen-key
```

As your nobody user probably receives very little personal email, you can create a signing only key for them. This key's only purpose is to allow us to trust the public key we extracted earlier.

To import the pubic key we exported earlier, use the following:

```
gpg --import filename
```

To tell GPG that we want to trust this key, we need to edit the key's properties using

```
gpg --edit-key 'Luke Welling <luke@tangledweb.com.au>'
```

On this line, the text in quotes is the name of the key. Obviously, the name of your key will not be `'Luke Welling <luke@tangledweb.com.au>'`, but a combination of the name, comment, and email address you provided when generating it.

Options within this program include `help`, which will describe the available commands—`trust`, `sign`, and `save`.

Type **trust** and tell GPG that you trust your key fully. Type **sign** to sign this public key using nobody's private key. Finally, type **save** to exit this program, keeping your changes.

Testing GPG

GPG should now be set up and ready to use.

Creating a file containing some text and saving it as test.txt will allow us to test it.

Typing the following command (modified to use the name of your key)

```
gpg -a --recipient 'Luke Welling <luke@tangledweb.com.au>' --encrypt test.txt
```

should give you the warning

```
gpg: Warning: using insecure memory!
```

and create a file named `test.txt.asc`. If you open `test.txt.asc` you should see an encrypted message like this:

```
-----BEGIN PGP MESSAGE-----
Version: GnuPG v1.0.3 (GNU/Linux)
Comment: For info see http://www.gnupg.org

hQEOA0DU7hVGgdtnEAQAhr4HgR7xpIBsK9CiELQw85+k1QdQ+p/FzqL8tICrQ+B3
0GJTEehPUDErwqUw/uQLTds0r1oPSrIAZ7c6GVkh0YEVBj2MskT81IIBvdo95OyH
K9PUCvg/rLxJ1kxe4Vp8QFET5E3FdII/ly8VP5gSTE7gAgm0SbFf3S91PqwMyTkD
/2oJEvL6e3cP384s0i81rBbDbOUAAhCjjXt2DX/uX9q6P18QW56UICUOn4DPaW1G
/gnNZCkcVDgLcKfBjbkB/TCWWhpA7o7kX4CIcIh7KlIMHY4RKdnCWQf271oE+8i9
cJRSCMsFIoI6MMNRCQHY6p9bfxL2uE39IRJrQbe6xoEe0nkB0uTYxiL0TG+FrNrE
tvBVMS0nsHu7HJey+oY4Z833pk5+MeVwYumJwlvHjdZxZmV6wz46GO2XGT17b28V
wSBnWOoBHSZsPvkQXHTOq65EixP8y+YJvBN3z4pzdH0Xa+NpqbH7q3+xXmd30hDR
+u7t6MxTLDbgC+NR
=gfQu
-----END PGP MESSAGE-----
```

You should be able to transfer this file to the system where you generated the key initially and run

```
gpg test.txt.asc
```

to see your original text again.

To place the text in a file, rather than output it to the screen, you can use the -o flag and specify an output file like this:

```
gpg -do test.out test.txt.asc
```

If you have GPG set up so that the user your PHP scripts run as can use it from the command line, you are most of the way there. If this is not working, see your system administrator or the GPG documentation.

Listings 15.1 and 15.2 enable people to send encrypted email by using PHP to call GPG.

Listing 15.1   private_mail.php—Our HTML Form to Send Encrypted Email

```php
<html>
<body>
<h1>Send Me Private Mail</h1>

<?php
 // you might need to change this line, if you do not use
 // the default ports, 80 for normal traffic and 443 for SSL
 if($HTTP_SERVER_VARS['SERVER_PORT']!=443)
   echo '<p><font color="red">
           WARNING: you have not connected to this page using SSL.
           Your message could be read by others.</font></p>';
?>

<form method="post" action="send_private_mail.php"><br />
Your email address:<br />
<input type="text" name="from" size"="38"><br />
Subject:<br />
<input type="text" name="title" size"="38"><br />
Your message:<br />
<textarea name="body" cols="30" rows="10">
</textarea><br />
<input type="submit" value="Send!">
</form>
</body>
</html>
```

Listing 15.2   send_private_mail.php—Our PHP Script to Call GPG and Send Encrypted Email

```php
<?php
 //create short variable names
 $from = $HTTP_POST_VARS['from'];
 $title = $HTTP_POST_VARS['title'];
 $body = $HTTP_POST_VARS['body'];
```

Listing 15.2 **Continued**

```
$to_email = 'luke@localhost';

// Tell gpg where to find the key ring
// On this system, user nobody's home directory is /tmp/
putenv('GNUPGHOME=/tmp/.gnupg');

//create a unique file name
$infile = tempnam('', 'pgp');
$outfile = $infile.'.asc';

//write the user's text to the file
$fp = fopen($infile, 'w');
fwrite($fp, $body);
fclose($fp);

//set up our command
$command = "/usr/local/bin/gpg -a \\
            --recipient 'Luke Welling <luke@tangledweb.com.au>' \\
            --encrypt -o $outfile $infile";

// execute our gpg command
system($command, $result);

//delete the unencrypted temp file
unlink($infile);

if($result==0)
{
  $fp = fopen($outfile, 'r');
  if(!$fp||filesize ($outfile)==0)
  {
    $result = -1;
  }
  else
  {
    //read the encrypted file
    $contents = fread ($fp, filesize ($outfile));
    //delete the encrypted temp file
    unlink($outfile);

    mail($to_email, $title, $contents, "From: $from\n");
    echo '<h1>Message Sent</h1>
          <p>Your message was encrypted and sent.</p>
          <p>Thank you.'</p>';
```

Listing 15.2   **Continued**

```
    }
  }

  if($result!=0)
  {
    echo '<h1>Error:</h1>
          <p>Your message could not be encrypted, so has not been sent.</p>
          <p>Sorry.</p>';
  }
?>
```

In order to make this code work for you, you will need to change a few things. Email will be sent to the address in $to_email.

The line

```
putenv('GNUPGHOME=/tmp/.gnupg');
```

will need to be changed to reflect the location of your GPG keyring. On our system, the Web server runs as the user nobody, and has the home directory /tmp/.

We are using the function tempnam() to create a unique temporary filename. You can specify both the directory and a filename prefix. We are going to create and delete these files in around one second, so it is not very important what we call them. We are specifying a prefix of 'pgp', but letting PHP use the system temporary directory.

The statement

```
$command =   '/usr/local/bin/gpg -a '.
             '--recipient 'Luke Welling <luke@tangledweb.com.au>' '.
             '--encrypt -o $outfile $infile';
```

sets up the command and parameters that will be used to call gpg. It will need to be modified to suit you. As with when we used it on the command line, you need to tell GPG which key to use to encrypt the message.

The statement

```
system($command, $result);
```

executes the instructions stored in $command and stores the return value in $result. We could ignore the return value, but it lets us have an if statement and tell the user that something went wrong.

When we have finished with the temporary files that we use, we delete them using the unlink() function. This means that our user's unencrypted email is being stored on the server for a short time. It is even possible that if the server failed during execution, the file could be left on the server.

While we are thinking about the security of our script, it is important to consider all flows of information within our system. GPG will encrypt our email and allow our recipient to decrypt it, but how does the information originally come from the sender?

If we are providing a Web interface to send GPG encrypted mail, the flow of information will look something like Figure 15.5.

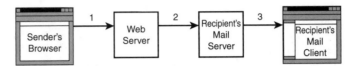

Figure 15.5   In our encrypted email application, the message is sent via the Internet three times.

In this figure, each arrow represents our message being sent from one machine to another. Each time the message is sent, it travels through the Internet and might pass through a number of intermediary networks and machines.

The script we are looking at here exists on the machine labeled Web Server in the diagram. At the Web server, the message will be encrypted using the recipient's public key. It will then be sent via SMTP to the recipient's mail server. The recipient will connect to his mail server, probably using POP or IMAP, and download the message using a mail reader. Here he will decrypt the message using his private key.

The data transfers in Figure 15.5 are labeled 1, 2, and 3. For stages 2 and 3, the information being transmitted is a GPG encrypted message and is of little value to anybody who does not have the private key. For transfer 1, the message being transmitted is the text that the sender entered in the form.

If our information is important enough that we need to encrypt it for the second and third leg of its journey, it is a bit silly to send it unencrypted for the first leg. Therefore, this script belongs on a server that uses SSL.

If we connect to our script using a port other than 443, it will provide a warning. This is the default port for SSL. If your server uses a non-default port for SSL, you might need to modify this code.

Rather than providing an error message, we could deal with this situation in other ways. We could redirect the user to the same URL via an SSL connection. We could also choose to ignore it because it is not usually important if the form was delivered using a secure connection. What is usually important is the details that the user has typed into the form are sent to us securely. We could simply have given a complete URL as the action of our form.

Currently, our open form tag looks like this:

```
<form method="post" action="send_private_mail.php">
```

We could alter it to send data via SSL even if the user connected without SSL, like this:

```
<form method="post" action="https://webserver/send_private_mail.php">
```

If we hard code the complete URL like this, we can be assured that visitors' data will be sent using SSL, but we will need to modify the code every time we use it on another server or even in another directory.

Although in this case, and many others, it is not important that the empty form is sent to the user via SSL, it is usually a good idea to do so. Seeing the little padlock symbol in the status bar of their browsers reassures people that their information is going to be sent securely. They should not need to look at your HTML source and see what the action attribute of the form is.

Further Reading

The specification for SSL version 3.0 is available from Netscape:

```
http://home.netscape.com/eng/ssl3/
```

If you would like to know more about how networks and networking protocols work, a classic introductory text is Andrew S. Tanenbaum's *Computer Networks*.

Next

That wraps up our discussion of e-commerce and security issues. In the next section, we'll look at some more advanced PHP techniques including interacting with other machines on the Internet, generating images on-the-fly, and using session control.

IV

Advanced PHP Techniques

## 16

Interacting with the File System and the Server

IN CHAPTER 2, "STORING AND RETRIEVING DATA," we saw how to read data from and write data to files on the Web server. In this chapter, we will cover other PHP functions that enable us to interact with the file system on the Web server.

We will discuss

- Uploading files with PHP
- Using directory functions
- Interacting with files on the server
- Executing programs on the server
- Using server environment variables

In order to discuss the uses of these functions, we will look at an example.

Consider a situation in which you would like your client to be able to update some of a Web site's content—for instance, the current news about their company. (Or maybe you want a friendlier interface than FTP for yourself.) One approach to this is to let the client upload the content files as plain text. These files will then be available on the site, through a template you have designed with PHP, as we did in Chapter 6, "Object-Oriented PHP."

Before we dive into the file system functions, let's briefly look at how file upload works.

Introduction to File Upload

One very useful piece of PHP functionality is support for HTTP upload. Instead of files coming from the server to the browser using HTTP, they go in the opposite direction, that is, from the browser to the server. Usually you implement this with an HTML form interface. The one we'll use in our example is shown in Figure 16.1.

Figure 16.1   The HTML form we use for file upload has different
fields and field types from those of a normal HTML form.

As you can see, the form has a box where the user can enter a filename, or click the
Browse button to browse files available to him locally. You might not have seen a file
upload form before. We'll look at how to implement this in a moment.

After a filename has been entered, the user can click Send File, and the file will be
uploaded to the server, where a PHP script is waiting for it.

HTML for File Upload

In order to implement file upload, we need to use some HTML syntax that exists specially for this purpose. The HTML for this form is shown in Listing 16.1.

Listing 16.1   **upload.html—HTML Form for File Upload**

```
<html>
<head>
  <title>Administration - upload new files</title>
</head>
<body>
<h1>Upload new news files</h1>
<form enctype="multipart/form-data" action="upload.php" method="post">
  <input type="hidden" name="MAX_FILE_SIZE" value="1000000">
  Upload this file: <input name="userfile" type="file">
  <input type="submit" value="Send File">
</form>
</body>
</html>
```

Note that this form uses POST. File uploads will also work with the PUT method supported by Netscape Composer and Amaya. They will not work with GET.

The extra features in this form are

- In the <form> tag, you must set the attribute enctype="multipart/
  form-data" to let the server know that a file is coming along with the regular
  form information.

- You must have a form field that sets the maximum size file that can be uploaded. This is a hidden field, and is shown here as

```
<input type="hidden" name="MAX_FILE_SIZE" value="1000000">
```

  The name of this form field must be MAX_FILE_SIZE. The value is the maximum size (in bytes) of files you will allow people to upload. At the moment we have set this to 1000000 bytes (roughly one megabyte). You may like to make it bigger or smaller for your application.

- You need an input of type file, shown here as

```
<input name="userfile" type="file">
```

  You can choose whatever name you like for the file, but keep it in mind as you will use this name to access your file from the receiving PHP script.

A Note on Security

Before we go any further, it's worth noting that some versions of PHP have had security vulnerabilities in the file upload code. If you decide to use file upload on your production server, you should make sure you are using the most up to date version of PHP and keep your eyes open for patches.

This shouldn't deter you from using such a useful technology, but you should be careful about how you write your code, and consider restricting access to file upload to, for example, site administrators and content managers.

Writing the PHP to Deal with the File

Writing the PHP to catch the file is pretty straightforward.

When the file is uploaded, it will go into a temporary location on the Web server. This is the Web server's default temporary directory. If you do not move or rename the file before your script finishes execution, it will be deleted.

Given that your HTML form has a field in it called userfile, you will end up with five variables being passed to PHP. There are several ways you can access these variables. You can use the superglobal array $_FILES, available from PHP 4.1.0. This is the recommended method. You can also access the variables through the $HTTP_POST_FILES array, or, if you have register_globals turned on you can access them directly. However, this is probably the area in which is most important to have register_globals turned off, so we recommend accessing the variables as follows:

- The value stored in $_FILE['userfile']['tmp_name'] or $HTTP_POST_FILES['userfile']['tmp_name'] is where the file has been temporarily stored on the Web server.

- The value stored in $_FILE['userfile']['name'] or $HTTP_POST_FILES['userfile']['name'] is the file's name on the user's system.

- The value stored in $_FILE['userfile']['size'] or $HTTP_POST_FILES['userfile']['size'] is the size of the file in bytes.
- The value stored in $_FILE['userfile']['type'] or $HTTP_POST_FILES['userfile'] ['type'] is the MIME type of the file, for example, text/plain or image/gif.
- The value stored in $_FILE['userfile']['error'] or $HTTP_POST_FILES['userfile'] ['error'] will give you any error codes associated with the file upload. This was added at PHP 4.2.0.

In the examples in this chapter we will use $HTTP_POST_FILES for backward compatibility but please be aware that if you plan to use file upload on your Web server you should use the most up to date version of PHP. (See "A Note On Security," above, for more information.)

Given that you know where the file is and what it's called, you can now copy it to somewhere useful. At the end of your script's execution, the temporary file will be deleted. Hence, you must move or rename the file if you want to keep it.

In our example, we're going to use the uploaded files as recent news articles, so we'll strip out any tags that might be in them, and move them to a more useful directory. A script that does this is shown in Listing 16.2.

Listing 16.2 **upload.php—PHP to Catch the Files from the HTML Form**

```
<html>
<head>
  <title>Uploading...</title>
</head>
<body>
<h1>Uploading file...</h1>
<?php

  // $userfile is where file went on webserver
  $userfile = $HTTP_POST_FILES['userfile']['tmp_name'];

  // $userfile_name is original file name
  $userfile_name = $HTTP_POST_FILES['userfile']['name'];

  // $userfile_size is size in bytes
  $userfile_size = $HTTP_POST_FILES['userfile']['size'];

  // $userfile_type is mime type e.g. image/gif
  $userfile_type = $HTTP_POST_FILES['userfile']['type'];

  // $userfile_error is any error encountered
  $userfile_error = $HTTP_POST_FILES['userfile']['error'];
```

Listing 16.2   **Continued**

```
// userfile_error was introduced at PHP 4.2.0
// use this code with newer versions
  if ($userfile_error > 0)
  {
    echo 'Problem: ';
    switch ($userfile_error)
    {
      case 1:  echo 'File exceeded upload_max_filesize';  break;
      case 2:  echo 'File exceeded max_file_size';  break;
      case 3:  echo 'File only partially uploaded';  break;
      case 4:  echo 'No file uploaded';  break;
    }
    exit;
  }
// end of code for 4.2.0

// prior to 4.2.0 use manual error checking as below
/*
  if ($userfile=='none')
  {
    echo 'Problem: no file uploaded';
    exit;
  }

  if ($userfile_size==0)
  {
    echo 'Problem: uploaded file is zero length';
    exit;
  }
*/
// end older version error checking

// one more check: does the file have the right MIME type?

  if ($userfile_type != 'text/plain')
  {
    echo 'Problem: file is not plain text';
    exit;
  }

// put the file where we'd like it
  $upfile = '/uploads/'.$userfile_name;

// is_uploaded_file and move_uploaded_file added at version 4.0.3
  if (is_uploaded_file($userfile))
  {
```

Listing 16.2 **Continued**

```
    if (!move_uploaded_file($userfile, $upfile))
    {
        echo 'Problem: Could not move file to destination directory';
        exit;
    }
}
else
{
    echo 'Problem: Possible file upload attack. Filename: '.$userfile_name;
    exit;
}

// older versions code as recommended in PHP manual
/*
  function is_uploaded_file($filename) {
    if (!$tmp_file = get_cfg_var('upload_tmp_dir')) {
        $tmp_file = dirname(tempnam('', ''));
    }
    $tmp_file .= '/' . basename($filename);
    // User might have trailing slash in php.ini...
    return (ereg_replace('/+', '/', $tmp_file) == $filename);
  }

  if (is_uploaded_file($userfile))
  {
    copy($userfile, $upfile);
  } else
  {
    echo 'Problem: Possible file upload attack. Filename: '.$userfile_name';
  }
*/
// end older version

  echo 'File uploaded successfully<br /><br />';

// reformat the file contents
  $fp = fopen($upfile, 'r');
  $contents = fread ($fp, filesize ($upfile));
  fclose ($fp);

  $contents = strip_tags($contents);
  $fp = fopen($upfile, 'w');
  fwrite($fp, $contents);
  fclose($fp);
```

Listing 16.2 **Continued**

```
// show what was uploaded
  echo 'Preview of uploaded file contents:<br /><hr />';
  echo $contents;
  echo '<br /><hr />';

?>
</body>
</html>
```

Interestingly enough, most of this script is error checking. File upload involves potential security risks, and we need to mitigate these where possible. We need to validate the uploaded file as carefully as possible to make sure it is safe to echo to our visitors.

Let's go through the main parts of the script.

We begin by checking the error code returned in $HTTP_POST_FILES ['userfile']['error']. This error code was introduced at PHP 4.2.0. From PHP 4.3 there is also a constant associated with each of the codes. The possible constants and values are as follows:

- UPLOAD_ERROR_OK, value 0, means no error occurred.

- UPLOAD_ERR_INI_SIZE, value 1, means that the size of the uploaded file exceeds the maximum value specified in your php.ini file with the upload_max_filesize directive.

- UPLOAD_ERR_FORM_SIZE, value 2, means that the size of the uploaded file exceeds the maximum value specified in the HTML form in the MAX_FILE_SIZE element.

- UPLOAD_ERR_PARTIAL, value 3, means that the file was only partially uploaded.

- UPLOAD_ERR_NO_FILE, value 4, means that no file was uploaded.

If you are using an older version of PHP, you can perform a manual version of some of these checks as follows. You can check whether $userfile is "none". This is the value set by PHP if no file was uploaded. We also test that the file has some content (by testing that $userfile_size is greater than 0).

Finally, regardless of version, in this case we have decided that we only want text files to be uploaded so we test the MIME type by testing $userfile_type).

We then check that the file we are trying to open has actually been uploaded and is not a local file such as /etc/passwd. We'll come back to this in a moment.

If that all works out okay, we then copy the file into our include directory. We use /uploads/ in this example—it's outside the Web document tree, and therefore a good place to put files that are to be included elsewhere.

We then open up the file, clean out any stray HTML or PHP tags that might be in the file using the strip_tags() function, and write the file back.

Finally we display the contents of the file so the user can see that their file uploaded successfully.

The results of one (successful) run of this script are shown in Figure 16.2.

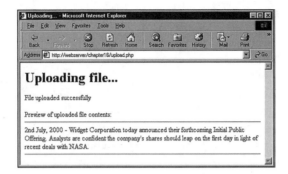

Figure 16.2   After the file is copied and reformatted, the uploaded file is displayed as confirmation to the user that the upload was successful.

In September 2000, an exploit was announced that could allow a cracker to fool your
file upload script into processing a local file as if it had been uploaded. This exploit was
documented on the BUGTRAQ mailing list. You can read the official security advisory
at one of the many BUGTRAQ archives, such as `http://lists.insecure.org/
bugtraq/2000/Sep/0237.html`.

We have used the `is_uploaded_file()` and `move_uploaded_file()` functions to
make sure that the file we are processing has actually been uploaded and is not a local
file such as `/etc/passwd`. This function is available from PHP version 4.0.3 onward. If
you are using an older version of PHP, we have again provided some sample code with
equivalent functionality (commented out).

Unless you write your upload handling script carefully, a malicious visitor could provide his own temporary filename and convince your script to handle that file as though
it were the uploaded file. As many file upload scripts echo the uploaded data back to the
user, or store it somewhere that it can be loaded, this could lead to people being able to
access any file that the Web server can read. This could include sensitive files such as
`/etc/passwd` and PHP source code including your database passwords.

Common Problems

There are a few things to keep in mind when performing file uploads.

- The previous example assumes that users have been authenticated elsewhere. You
  shouldn't allow just anybody to upload files on to your site.
- If you are allowing untrusted or unauthenticated users to upload files, it's a good
  idea to be pretty paranoid about the contents of them. The last thing you want is a
  malicious script being uploaded and run. You should be careful, not just of the type
  and contents of the file as we are here, but of the filename itself. It's a pretty good
  idea to rename uploaded files to something you know to be "safe".

- If you are using a Windows-based machine, be sure to use \\ or / instead of \ in file paths as per usual.

- If you are having problems getting this to work, check out your php.ini file. You will need to have set the upload_tmp_dir directive to point to some directory that you have access to. You might also need to adjust the memory_limit directive if you want to upload large files—this will determine the maximum file size in bytes that you can upload.

- If PHP is running in safe mode, you will get an error message about being unable to access the temporary file. This can only be fixed either by not running in safe mode or by writing a non-PHP script that copies the file to an accessible location. You can then execute this script from your PHP script. We'll look at how to execute programs on the server from PHP toward the end of this chapter.

Using Directory Functions

After the users have uploaded some files, it will be useful for them to be able to see what's been uploaded and manipulate the content files.

PHP has a set of directory and file system functions that are useful for this purpose.

Reading from Directories

First, we'll implement a script to allow directory browsing of the uploaded content. Browsing directories is actually very straightforward in PHP. In Listing 16.3, we show a simple script that can be used for this purpose.

Listing 16.3   **browsedir.php—A Directory Listing of the Uploaded Files**

```
<html>
<head>
  <title>Browse Directories</title>
</head>
<body>
<h1>Browsing</h1>
<?php
  $current_dir = '/uploads/';
  $dir = opendir($current_dir);

  echo "Upload directory is $current_dir<br />";
  echo 'Directory Listing:<br /><hr /><br />';
  while ($file = readdir($dir))
  {
      echo "$file<br />";
  }
  echo '<hr /><br />';
```

Listing 16.3 **Continued**

```
  closedir($dir);
?>
</body>
</html>
```

This script makes use of the `opendir()`, `closedir()`, and `readdir()` functions.

The function `opendir()` is used to open a directory for reading. Its use is very similar to the use of `fopen()` for reading from files. Instead of passing it a filename, you should pass it a directory name:

```
$dir = opendir($current_dir);
```

The function returns a directory handle, again in much the same way as `fopen()` returns a file handle.

When the directory is open, you can read a filename from it by calling `readdir($dir)` , as shown in the example. This returns false when there are no more files to be read. (Note that it will also return false if it reads a file called `"0"`—you could, of course, test for this if it is likely to occur.) Files aren't sorted in any particular order, so if you require a sorted list, you should read them into an array and sort that.

When you are finished reading from a directory, you call `closedir($dir)` to finish. This is again similar to calling `fclose()` for a file.

Sample output of the directory browsing script is shown in Figure 16.3.

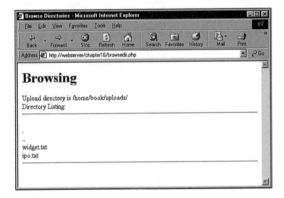

Figure 16.3   The directory listing shows all the files in the chosen directory, including the . (the current directory) and .. (one level up) directories. You can choose to filter these out.

If you are making directory browsing available via this mechanism, it is sensible to limit the directories that can be browsed so that a user cannot browse directory listings in areas not normally available to him.

An associated and sometimes useful function is rewinddir($dir), which resets the reading of filenames to the beginning of the directory.

As an alternative to these functions, you can use the dir class provided by PHP. This has the properties handle and path, and the methods read(), close(), and rewind(), which perform identically to the non-class alternatives.

Getting Info About the Current Directory

We can obtain some additional information given a path to a file.

The dirname($path) and basename($path) functions return the directory part of the path and the filename part of the path, respectively. This could be useful for our directory browser, particularly if we began to build up a complex directory structure of content based on meaningful directory names and filenames.

We could also add to our directory listing an indication of how much space is left for uploads by using the disk_free_space($path) function. If you pass this function a path to a directory, it will return the number of bytes free on the disk (Windows) or the file system (UNIX) that the directory is on.

Creating and Deleting Directories

In addition to passively reading information about directories, you can use the PHP functions mkdir() and rmdir() to create and delete directories. You will only be able to create or delete directories in paths that the user the script runs as has access to.

Using mkdir() is more complicated than you might think. It takes two parameters, the path to the desired directory (including the new directory name), and the permissions you would like that directory to have, for example,

```
mkdir("/tmp/testing", 0777);
```

However, the permissions you list are not necessarily the permissions you are going to get. The current umask will be ANDed (like subtraction) with this value to get the actual permissions. For example, if the umask is 022, you will get permissions of 0755.

You might like to reset the umask before creating a directory to counter this effect, by entering

```
$oldumask = umask(0);
mkdir("/tmp/testing", 0777);
umask($oldumask);
```

This code uses the umask() function, which can be used to check and change the current umask. It will change the current umask to whatever it is passed and return the old umask, or if called without parameters, it will just return the current umask.

Note that the umask() function has no effect on Windows systems.

The rmdir() function deletes a directory, as follows:

```
rmdir("/tmp/testing");
```

or

```
rmdir("c:\\tmp\\testing");
```

The directory you are trying to delete must be empty.

Interacting with the File System

In addition to viewing and getting information about directories, we can interact with and get information about files on the Web server. We've previously looked at writing to and reading from files. A large number of other file functions are available.

Get File Info

We can alter the part of our directory browsing script that reads files as follows:

```
while ($file = $dir->read())
{
  echo '<a href="filedetails.php?file='.$file.'">'.$file.'</a><br />';
}
```

We can then create the script `filedetails.php` to provide further information about a file. The contents of this file are shown in Listing 16.4.

One warning about this script: Some of the functions used here are not supported under Windows, including `posix_getpwuid()`, `fileowner()`, and `filegroup()`, or are not supported reliably.

Listing 16.4   **filedetails.php—File Status Functions and Their Results**

```
<html>
<head>
  <title>File Details</title>
</head>
<body>
<?php
  $current_dir = '/uploads/';
  $file = basename($file);  // strip off directory information for security

  echo '<h1>Details of file: '.$file.'</h1>';
  $file = $current_dir.$file;

  echo '<h2>File data</h2>';
  echo 'File last accessed: '.date('j F Y H:i', fileatime($file)).'<br />';
  echo 'File last modified: '.date('j F Y H:i', filemtime($file)).'<br />';

  $user = posix_getpwuid(fileowner($file));
  echo 'File owner: '.$user['name'].'<br />';
```

Listing 16.4 **Continued**

```
$group = posix_getgrgid(filegroup($file));
echo 'File group: '.$group['name'].'<br />';

echo 'File permissions: '.decoct(fileperms($file)).'<br />';

echo 'File type: '.filetype($file).'<br />';

echo 'File size: '.filesize($file).' bytes<br />';


echo '<h2>File tests</h2>';

echo 'is_dir: '.(is_dir($file)? 'true' : 'false').'<br />';
echo 'is_executable: '.(is_executable($file)? 'true' : 'false').'<br />';
echo 'is_file: '.(is_file($file)? 'true' : 'false').'<br />';
echo 'is_link: '.(is_link($file)? 'true' : 'false').'<br />';
echo 'is_readable: '.(is_readable($file)? 'true' : 'false').'<br />';
echo 'is_writable: '.(is_writable($file)? 'true' : 'false').'<br />';

?>
</body>
</html>
```

The results of one sample run of Listing 16.4 are shown in Figure 16.4.

Figure 16.4   The File Details view shows file system information about a file.
Note that permissions are shown in an octal format.

Let's talk about what each of the functions used in Listing 16.4 does.

As mentioned previously, the basename() function gets the name of the file without the directory. (You can also use the dirname() function to get the directory name without the filename.)

The fileatime() and filemtime() functions return the time stamp of the time the file was last accessed and last modified, respectively. We've reformatted the time stamp using the date() function to make it more human-readable. These functions will return the same value on some operating systems (as in the example) depending on what information the system stores.

The fileowner() and filegroup() functions return the user ID (uid) and group ID (gid) of the file. These can be converted to names using the functions posix_getpwuid() and posix_getgrgid(), respectively, which makes them a bit easier to read. These functions take the uid or gid as a parameter and return an associative array of information about the user or group, including the name of the user or group, as we have used in this script.

The fileperms() function returns the permissions on the file. We have reformatted them as an octal number using the decoct() function to put them into a format more familiar to UNIX users.

The filetype() function returns some information about the type of file being examined. The possible results are fifo, char, dir, block, link, file, and unknown.

The filesize() function returns the size of the file in bytes.

The second set of functions—is_dir(), is_executable(), is_file(), is_link(), is_readable(), and is_writable()—all test the named attribute of a file and return true or false.

We could alternatively have used the function stat() to gather a lot of the same information. When passed a file, this returns an array containing similar data to these functions. The lstat() function is similar, but for use with symbolic links.

All the file status functions are quite expensive to run in terms of time. Their results are therefore cached. If you want to check some file information before and after a change, you need to call

```
clearstatcache();
```

in order to clear the previous results. If you wanted to use the previous script before and after changing some of the file data, you should begin by calling this function to make sure the data produced is up-to-date.

Changing File Properties

In addition to viewing file properties, we can alter them.

Each of the chgrp(file, group), chmod(file, permissions), and chown(file, user) functions behaves similarly to its UNIX equivalent. None of these will work in Windows-based systems, although chown() will execute and always return true.

The chgrp() function is used to change the group of a file. It can only be used to change the group to groups of which the user is a member unless the user is root.

The chmod() function is used to change the permissions on a file. The permissions you pass to it are in the usual UNIX chmod form—you should prefix them with a "0" to show that they are in octal, for example,

```
chmod('somefile.txt', 0777);
```

The chown() function is used to change the owner of a file. It can only be used if the script is running as root, which should never happen.

Creating, Deleting, and Moving Files

You can use the file system functions to create, move, and delete files.

First, and most simply, you can create a file, or change the time it was last modified, using the touch() function. This works similarly to the UNIX command touch. The function has the following prototype:

```
int touch (string file, [int time [, int atime]])
```

If the file already exists, its modification time will be changed either to the current time, or the time given in the second parameter if it is specified. If you want to specify this, it should be given in time stamp format. If the file doesn't exist, it will be created. The access time of the file will also change: by default to the current system time or alternatively to the time stamp you specify in the optional *atime* parameter.

You can delete files using the unlink() function. (Note that this function is not called delete—there is no delete.) You use it like this:

```
unlink($filename);
```

This is one of the functions that doesn't work with some older Windows versions. However, if it doesn't work on your setup, you can delete a file in Windows with

```
system("del filename.ext");
```

You can copy and move files with the copy() and rename() functions, as follows:

```
copy($source_path, $destination_path);
```

```
rename($oldfile, $newfile);
```

You might have noticed that we used copy() in Listing 16.2.

The rename() function does double duty as a function to move files from place to place because PHP doesn't have a move function. Whether you can move files from file system to file system, and whether files are overwritten when rename() is used is operating system dependent, so check the effects on your server. Also, be careful about the path you use to the filename. If relative, this will be relative to the location of the script, not the original file.

Using Program Execution Functions

We'll move away from the file system functions now, and look at the functions that are available for running commands on the server.

This is useful when you want to provide a Web-based front end to an existing command line-based system. For example, we have used these commands to set up a front end for the mailing list manager `ezmlm`. We will use these again when we come to the case studies later in this book.

There are four main techniques you can use to execute a command on the Web server. They are all pretty similar, but there are some minor differences.

1. `exec()`

   The `exec()` function has the following prototype:

   ```
   string exec (string command [, array result [, int return_value]])
   ```

   You pass in the command that you would like executed, for example,

   ```
   exec("ls -la");
   ```

   The `exec()` function has no direct output.

   It returns the last line of the result of the command.

   If you pass in a variable as *result*, you will get back an array of strings representing each line of the output. If you pass in a variable as *return_value*, you will get the return code.

2. `passthru()`

   The `passthru()` function has the following prototype:

   ```
   void passthru (string command [, int return_value])
   ```

   The `passthru()` function directly echoes its output through to the browser. (This is useful if the output is binary, for example, some kind of image data.)

   It returns nothing.

   The parameters work the same way as `exec()`'s parameters do.

3. `system()`

   The `system()` function has the following prototype:

   ```
   string system (string command [, int return_value])
   ```

   The function echoes the output of the command to the browser. It tries to flush the output after each line (assuming you are running PHP as a server module), which distinguishes it from `passthru()`.

   It returns the last line of the output (upon success) or `false` (upon failure).

   The parameters work the same way as in the other functions.

4. Backticks

We mentioned these briefly in Chapter 1, "PHP Crash Course." These are actually an execution operator.

They have no direct output. The result of executing the command is returned as a string, which can then be echoed or whatever you like.

If you have more complicated needs, you can also use `popen()`, `proc_open()`, and `proc_close()`, which are used to fork external processes and pipe data to and from them. The last two of these functions were added at PHP 4.3.

The script shown in Listing 16.5 illustrates how to use each of the four techniques in an equivalent fashion.

Listing 16.5   **progex.php—File Status Functions and Their Results**

```php
<?php

    chdir('/uploads/');

///// exec version
    echo '<pre>';

    // unix
    exec('ls -la', $result);
    // windows
    // exec('dir', $result);
    foreach ($result as $line)
      echo "$line\n";

    echo '</pre>';
    echo '<br /><hr /><br />';

///// passthru version
    echo '<pre>';

    // unix
    passthru('ls -la');
    // windows
    // passthru('dir');

    echo '</pre>';
    echo '<br /><hr /><br />';

///// system version

    echo '<pre>';
```

Listing 16.5   **Continued**

```
// unix
$result = system('ls -la');
// windows
// $result = system('dir');
echo '</pre>';
echo '<br /><hr /><br />';
```

/////backticks version

```
echo '<pre>';
// unix
$result = `ls -al`;
// windows
// $result = `dir`;
echo $result;
echo '</pre>';
```

?>

We could have used one of these approaches as an alternative to the directory-browsing script we wrote earlier. Note that one of the side effects of using external functions is amply demonstrated by this code—your code is no longer portable. We have used Unix commands here and the code will clearly not run on Windows.

If you plan to include user-submitted data as part of the command you're going to execute, you should always run it through the escapeshellcmd() function first. This stops users from maliciously (or otherwise) executing commands on your system. You can call it like this, for example,

```
system(escapeshellcmd($command));
```

You should also use the escapeshellarg() function to escape any arguments you plan to pass to your shell command.

Interacting with the Environment: getenv() and putenv()

Before we leave this section, we'll look at how you can use environment variables from within PHP. There are two functions for this purpose: getenv(), which enables you to retrieve environment variables, and putenv(), which enables you to set environment variables.

Note that the environment we are talking about here is the environment in which PHP runs on the server.

You can get a list of all PHP's environment variables by running `phpinfo()`. Some are more useful than others, for example,

```
getenv("HTTP_REFERER");
```

will return the URL of the page from which the user came to the current page.

You can also set environment variables as required with `putenv()`, for example,

```
$home = "/home/nobody";
putenv (" HOME=$home ");
```

If you are a system administrator and would like to limit which environment variables programmers can set, you can use the `safe_mode_allowed_env_vars` directive in php.ini. When PHP runs in safe mode, users will only be able to set environment variables whose prefixes are listed in this directive.

If you would like more information about what some of the environment variables represent, you can look at the CGI specification:

```
http://hoohoo.ncsa.uiuc.edu/cgi/env.html
```

Further Reading

Most of the file system functions in PHP map to underlying operating system functions—try reading the man pages if you're using UNIX for more information.

Next

In Chapter 17, "Using Network and Protocol Functions," we'll use PHP's network and protocol functions to interact with systems other than our own Web server. This again expands the horizons of what we can do with our scripts.

17

Using Network and Protocol Functions

I N THIS CHAPTER, WE'LL LOOK AT the network-oriented functions in PHP that enable your scripts to interact with the rest of the Internet. There's a world of resources out there, and a wide variety of protocols available for using them. In this section we'll consider

- An overview of available protocols
- Sending and reading email
- Using other Web sites via HTTP
- Using network lookup functions
- Using FTP
- Using generic network communications with cURL

Overview of Protocols

Protocols are the rules of communication for a given situation. For example, you know the protocol when meeting another person: You say hello, shake hands, communicate for a while, and then say goodbye. Computer networking protocols are similar.

Like human protocols, different computer protocols are used for different situations and applications. We use HTTP, the Hypertext Transfer Protocol, for sending and receiving Web pages. You will probably also have used FTP, File Transfer Protocol, for transferring files between machines on a network. There are many others.

Protocols, and other Internet Standards, are described in documents called *RFCs*, or *Requests for Comments*. These protocols are defined by the Internet Engineering Task Force (IETF). The RFCs are widely available on the Internet. The base source is the RFC Editor at

```
http://www.rfc-editor.org/
```

If you have problems when working with a given protocol, the RFCs are the authoritative source and are often useful for troubleshooting your code. They are, however, very detailed, and often run to hundreds of pages.

Some examples of well-known RFCs are RFC2616, which describes the HTTP/1.1 protocol, and RFC822, which describes the format of Internet email messages.

In this chapter, we will look at aspects of PHP that use some of these protocols. Specifically, we will talk about sending mail with SMTP, reading mail with POP and IMAP, connecting to other Web servers via HTTP and HTTPS, and transferring files with FTP.

Sending and Reading Email

The main way to send mail in PHP is to use the simple mail() function. We discussed the use of this function in Chapter 4, "String Manipulation and Regular Expressions," so we won't visit it again here. This function uses SMTP (Simple Mail Transfer Protocol) to send mail.

You can use a variety of freely available classes to add to the functionality of mail(). In Chapter 28, "Building a Mailing List Manager," we will use an add-on class to send HTML attachments with a piece of mail. SMTP is only for sending mail. The IMAP (Internet Message Access Protocol, described in RFC2060) and POP (Post Office Protocol, described in RFC1939 or STD0053) protocols are used to read mail from a mail server. These protocols cannot send mail.

IMAP is used to read and manipulate mail messages stored on a server, and is more sophisticated than POP, which is generally used simply to download mail messages to a client and delete them from the server.

PHP comes with an IMAP library. This can also be used to make POP and NNTP (Network News Transfer Protocol) as well as IMAP connections.

We will look extensively at the use of the IMAP library in the project described in Chapter 27, "Building a Web-Based Email Service."

Using Other Web Sites

One of the great things you can do with the Web is use, modify, and embed existing services and information into your own pages. PHP makes this very easy. Let's look at an example to illustrate this.

Imagine that the company you work for would like a stock quote for your company displayed on its homepage. This information is available out there on some stock exchange site somewhere—but how do we get at it?

Start by finding an original source URL for the information. When you know this, every time someone goes to your home page, you can open a connection to that URL, retrieve the page, and pull out the information you require.

As an example, we've put together a script that retrieves and reformats a stock quote from the AMEX Web site. For the purpose of the example, we've retrieved the current stock price of Amazon.com. (The information you want to include on your page might differ, but the principles are the same.) This script is shown in Listing 17.1.

Listing 17.1   **lookup.php—Script Retrieves a Stock Quote from the NASDAQ for the Stock with the Ticker Symbol Listed in** $symbol

```php
<html>
<head>
  <title>Stock Quote from NASDAQ</title>
</head>
<body>
<?php
  // choose stock to look at
  $symbol='AMZN';
  echo "<h1>Stock Quote for $symbol</h1>";


$theurl='http://www.amex.com/equities/listCmp/EqLCDetQuote.jsp?Product_Symbol=AMZN
';


  if (!($fp = fopen($theurl, 'r')))
  {
    echo 'Could not open URL';
    exit;
  }
  $contents = fread($fp, 1000000);
  fclose($fp);

  //echo $contents;

  // find the part of the page we want and output it
  $pattern = "(\\\$[0-9 ]+\\.[0-9]+)";
  if (eregi($pattern, $contents, $quote))
  {
    echo "$symbol was last sold at: ";
    echo $quote[1];
  } else
  {
    echo 'No quote available';
  };

  // acknowledge source
  echo '<br />'
       .'This information retrieved from <br />'
```

Listing 17.1 **Continued**

```
          ."<a href=\"$theurl\">$theurl</a><br />"
          .'on '.(date('l jS F Y g:i a T'));
?>
</body>
</html>
```

The output from one sample run of Listing 17.1 is shown in Figure 17.1.

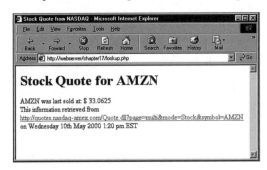

Figure 17.1 The script uses a regular expression to pull out the stock quote from information retrieved from the stock exchange.

The script itself is pretty straightforward—in fact, it doesn't use any functions we haven't seen before, just new applications of those functions.

You might recall that when we discussed reading from files in Chapter 2, "Storing and Retrieving Data," we mentioned that you could use the file functions to read from an URL. That's what we have done in this case. The call to fopen()

```
$fp = fopen($theurl, 'r')
```

returns a pointer to the start of the page at the URL we supply. Then it's just a question of reading from the page at that URL and closing it again:

```
$contents = fread($fp, 1000000);
fclose($fp);
```

You'll notice that we used a really large number to tell PHP how much to read from the file. With a file on the server, you'd normally use filesize(*$file*), but this doesn't work with a URL.

When we've done this, we have the entire text of the Web page at that URL stored in $contents. We can then use a regular expression and the eregi() function to find the part of the page that we want:

```
$pattern = "(\\\$[0-9 ]+\\.[0-9]+)";
if (eregi($pattern, $contents, $quote))
{
```

```
  echo "$symbol was last sold at: ";
  echo $quote[1];
}
```

That's it!

You can use this approach for a variety of purposes. Another good example is retrieving local weather information and embedding it in your page.

The best use of this approach is to combine information from different sources to add some value. One good example of this approach can be seen in Philip Greenspun's infamous script that produces the Bill Gates Wealth Clock:

```
http://www.webho.com/WealthClock
```

This page takes information from two sources. It obtains the current U.S. population from the U.S. Census Bureau's site. It looks up the current value of a Microsoft share and combines these two pieces of information, adds a healthy dose of the author's opinion, and produces new information—an estimate of Bill Gates's current worth.

One side note: If you're using an outside information source such as this for a commercial purpose, it's a good idea to check with the source first. There are intellectual property issues to consider in some cases.

If you're building a script like this, you might want to pass through some data. For example, if you're connecting to an outside URL, you might like to pass some parameters typed in by the user. If you're doing this, it's a good idea to use the `urlencode()` function. This will take a string and convert it to the proper format for a URL, for example, transforming spaces into plus signs. You can call it like this:

```
$encodedparameter = urlencode($parameter);
```

One problem with this overall approach is that the site you're getting the information from may change their data format which will stop your script from working.

A better way of doing the same thing has recently begun being used—Web Services. These are like remote objects that you can connect to in order to retrieve data such as stock quotes. PHP's unofficial support for Web Services is growing, and an official SOAP extension is in the works. You can find more information about Web Services in Chapter 31, "Connecting to Web Services with XML and SOAP."

Using Network Lookup Functions

PHP offers a set of "lookup" functions that can be used to check information about hostnames, IP addresses, and mail exchanges. For example, if you were setting up a directory site such as Yahoo! when new URLs were submitted, you might like to automatically check that the host of a URL and the contact information for that site are valid. This way, you can save some overhead further down the track when a reviewer comes to look at a site and finds that it doesn't exist, or that the email address isn't valid.

Listing 17.2 shows the HTML for a submission form for a directory like this.

Listing 17.2   directory_submit.html—HTML for the Submission Form

```
<head>
  <title>Submit your site</title>
</head>
<body>
<h1>Submit site</h1>
<form method="post" action="directory_submit.php">
URL: <input type="text" name="url" size="30" value="http://"><br />
Email contact: <input type="text" name="email" size="23"><br />
<input type="submit" name="Submit site">
</form>
</body>
</html>
```

This is a very simple form—the rendered version, with some sample data entered, is shown in Figure 17.2.

Figure 17.2   Directory submissions typically require your URL and some contact details so directory administrators can notify you when your site is added to the directory.

When the submit button is pressed, we want to check, first, that the URL is hosted on a real machine, and, second, that the host part of the email address is also on a real machine. We have written a script to check these things, and the output is shown in Figure 17.3.

The script that performs these checks uses two functions from the PHP network functions suite—gethostbyname() and getmxrr(). The full script is shown in Listing 17.3.

Figure 17.3   This version of the script displays the results of checking the
hostnames for the URL and email address—a production version
might not display these results, but it is interesting to see the
information returned from our checks.

Listing 17.3   directory_submit.php—Script to Verify URL and Email Address

```
<html>
<head>
  <title>Site submission results</title>
</head>
<body>
<h1>Site submission results</h1>
<?php

  // Extract form fields

  $url = $HTTP_POST_VARS['url'];
  $email = $HTTP_POST_VARS['email'];

  // Check the URL

  $url = parse_url($url);
  $host = $url['host'];
  if(!($ip = gethostbyname($host)))
  {
    echo 'Host for URL does not have valid IP';
    exit;
  }

echo "Host is at IP $ip <br />";

  // Check the email address

  $email = explode('@', $email);
```

Listing 17.3   **Continued**

```
$emailhost = $email[1];

// note that the getmxrr() function is *not implemented* in
// Windows versions of PHP
if (!getmxrr($emailhost, $mxhostsarr))
{
  echo 'Email address is not at valid host';
  exit;
}

echo 'Email is delivered via: ';
foreach ($mxhostsarr as $mx)
  echo "$mx ";

// If reached here, all ok

echo '<br />All submitted details are ok.<br />';
echo 'Thank you for submitting your site.<br />'
     .'It will be visited by one of our staff members soon.'

// In real case, add to db of waiting sites...
?>
</body>
</html>
```

Let's go through the interesting parts of this script.

First, we take the URL and apply the parse_url() function to it. This function returns an associative array of the different parts of a URL. The available pieces of information are the scheme, user, pass, host, port, path, query, and fragment. Typically, you aren't going to need all of these, but here's an example of how they make up a URL.

Given a URL such as

http://nobody:secret@bigcompany.com:80/script.php?variable=value#anchor

the values of each of the parts of the array would be

- scheme: http://
- user: nobody
- pass: secret
- host: bigcompany.com
- port: 80
- path: script.php
- query: variable=value
- fragment: anchor

In our script, we only want the `host` information, so we pull it out of the array as follows:

```
$url = parse_url($url);
$host = $url['host'];
```

After we've done this, we can get the IP address of that host, if it is in the DNS. We can do this using the `gethostbyname()` function, which will return the IP if there is one, or `false` if not:

```
$ip = gethostbyname($host);
```

You can also go the other way using the `gethostbyaddr()` function, which takes an IP as parameter and returns the hostname. If you call these functions in succession, you might well end up with a different hostname from the one you began with. This can mean that a site is using a virtual hosting service.

If the URL is valid, we then go on to check the email address. First, we split it into username and hostname with a call to `explode()`:

```
$email = explode('@', $email);
$emailhost = $email[1];
```

When we have the host part of the address, we can check to see if there is a place for that mail to go using the `getmxrr()` function:

```
getmxrr($emailhost, $mxhostsarr);
```

This function returns the set of MX (Mail Exchange) records for an address in the array you supply at `$mxhostarr`.

An MX record is stored at the DNS and is looked up like a hostname. The machine listed in the MX record isn't necessarily the machine where the email will eventually end up. Instead it's a machine that knows where to route that email. (There can be more than one, hence this function returns an array rather than a hostname string.) If we don't have an MX record in the DNS, there's nowhere for the mail to go.

Note that the `getmxrr()` function is not implemented in Windows versions of PHP.

If all these checks are okay, we can put this form data in a database for later review by a staff member.

In addition to the functions we've just used, you can use the more generic function `checkdnsrr()`, which takes a hostname and returns `true` if there is any record of it in the DNS.

Using FTP

File Transfer Protocol, or FTP, is used to transfer files between hosts on a network. Using PHP, you can use `fopen()` and the various file functions with FTP as you can with HTTP connections, to connect to and transfer files to and from an FTP server. However, there is also a set of FTP-specific functions that comes with the standard PHP install.

These functions are not built in to the standard install by default. In order to use them under UNIX, you will need to run the PHP `configure` program with the `--enable-ftp` option and then rerun `make`.

If you are using the standard Windows install, FTP functions are enabled automatically.

(For more details on configuring PHP, see Appendix A, "Installing PHP 4 and MySQL.")

Using FTP to Back Up or Mirror a File

The FTP functions are useful for moving and copying files from and to other hosts. One common use you might make of this is to back up your Web site or mirror files at another location. We will look at a simple example using the FTP functions to mirror a file. This script is shown in Listing 17.4.

Listing 17.4   **ftpmirror.php—Script to Download New Versions of a File from an FTP Server**

```
<html>
<head>
  <title>Mirror update</title>
</head>
<body>
<h1>Mirror update</h1>
<?php
// set up variables - change these to suit application
$host = 'ftp.cs.rmit.edu.au';
$user = 'anonymous';
$password = 'laura@tangledweb.com.au';
$remotefile = '/pub/tsg/teraterm/ttssh14.zip';
$localfile = '/tmp/writable/ttssh14.zip';

// connect to host
$conn = ftp_connect("$host");
if (!$conn)
{
  echo 'Error: Could not connect to ftp server<br />';
  exit;
}
echo "Connected to $host.<br />";

// log in to host
@ $result = ftp_login($conn, $user, $pass);
if (!$result)
{
  echo "Error: Could not log on as $user<br />";
```

Listing 17.4 **Continued**

```php
  ftp_quit($conn);
  exit;
}
echo "Logged in as $user<br />";

// check file times to see if an update is required
echo 'Checking file time...<br />';
if (file_exists($localfile))
{
  $localtime = filemtime($localfile);
  echo 'Local file last updated ';
  echo date('G:i j-M-Y', $localtime);
  echo '<br />';
}
else
  $localtime=0;
$remotetime = ftp_mdtm($conn, $remotefile);
if (!($remotetime >= 0))
{
   // This doesn't mean the file's not there, server may not support mod time
   echo 'Can\'t access remote file time.<br />';
   $remotetime=$localtime+1;  // make sure of an update
}
else
{
  echo 'Remote file last updated ';
  echo date('G:i j-M-Y', $remotetime);
  echo '<br />';
}
if (!($remotetime > $localtime))
{
   echo 'Local copy is up to date.<br />';
   exit;
}

// download file
echo 'Getting file from server...<br />';
$fp = fopen ($localfile, 'w');
if (!$success = ftp_fget($conn, $fp, $remotefile, FTP_BINARY))
{
  echo 'Error: Could not download file';
  ftp_quit($conn);
  exit;
}
```

Listing 17.4 **Continued**

```
fclose($fp);
echo 'File downloaded successfully';

// close connection to host
ftp_quit($conn);

?>
</body>
</html>
```

The output from running this script on one occasion is shown in Figure 17.4.

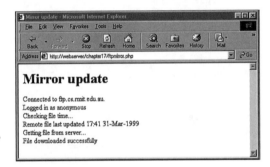

Figure 17.4   The FTP mirroring script checks whether the local version of a
file is up-to-date, and downloads a new version if not.

This is quite a generic script. You'll see that it begins by setting up some variables:

```
$host = 'ftp.cs.rmit.edu.au';
$user = 'anonymous';
$password = 'laura@tangledweb.com.au';
$remotefile = '/pub/tsg/teraterm/ttssh14.zip';
$localfile = "/tmp/writable/ttssh14.zip";
```

The $host variable should contain the name of the FTP server you want to connect to,
and the $user and $password correspond to the username and password you would like
to log in with.

Many FTP sites support what is called *anonymous login*, that is, a freely available username that anybody can use to connect. No password is required, but it is a common
courtesy to supply your email address as a password so that the system's administrators
can see where their users are coming from. We have followed this convention here.

The $remotefile variable contains the path to the file we would like to download.
In this case we are downloading and mirroring a local copy of Tera Term SSH, an SSH
client for Windows. (SSH stands for secure shell. This is an encrypted form of telnet.)

The $localfile variable contains the path to the location where we are going to store the downloaded file on our machine. In this case we have created a directory called /tmp/writable with permissions set up so that PHP can write a file there.

You should be able to change these variables to adapt this script for your purposes.

The basic steps we follow in this script are the same as if you wanted to manually FTP the file from a command line interface:

1. Connect to the remote FTP server.

2. Log in (either as a user or anonymous).

3. Check whether the remote file has been updated.

4. If it has, download it.

5. Close the FTP connection.

Let's take each of these in turn.

Connecting to the Remote FTP Server

This step is equivalent to typing

```
ftp hostname
```

at a command prompt on either a Windows or UNIX platform. We accomplish this step in PHP with the following code:

```
$conn = ftp_connect("$host");
if (!$conn)
{
  echo 'Error: Could not connect to ftp server<br />';
  exit;
}
echo "Connected to $host.<br />";
```

The function call here is to ftp_connect(). This function takes a hostname as parameter, and returns either a handle to a connection, or false if a connection could not be established. The function can also take the port number on the host to connect to as an optional second parameter. (We have not used this here.) If you don't specify a port number, it will default to port 21, the default for FTP.

Logging In to the FTP Server

The next step is to log in as a particular user with a particular password. You can achieve this using the ftp_login() function:

```
@ $result = ftp_login($conn, $user, $pass);
if (!$result)
{
  echo "Error: Could not log on as $user<br />";
  ftp_quit($conn);
```

```
    exit;
}
echo "Logged in as $user<br />";
```

The function takes three parameters: an FTP connection (obtained from `ftp_connect()`), a username, and a password. It will return `true` if the user can be logged in, and `false` if he can't. You will notice that we put an `@` symbol at the start of the line to suppress errors. We do this because, if the user cannot be logged in, you will get a PHP warning in your browser window. You can catch the error as we have done here by testing `$result`, and supplying your own, more user-friendly error message.

Notice that if the login attempt fails, we actually close the FTP connection using `ftp_quit()`—more on this in a minute.

Checking File Update Times

Given that we are updating a local copy of a file, it is sensible to check whether the file needs updating first because you don't want to have to re-download a file, particularly a large one, if it's up-to-date. This will avoid unnecessary network traffic. Let's look at the code that does this.

First, we check that we have a local copy of the file, using the `file_exists()` function. If we don't then obviously we need to download the file. If it does exist, we get the last modified time of the file using the `filemtime()` function, and store it in the `$localtime` variable. If it doesn't exist, we set the `$localtime` variable to 0 so that it will be "older" than any possible remote file modification time:

```
echo 'Checking file time...<br />';
if (file_exists($localfile))
{
    $localtime = filemtime($localfile);
    echo 'Local file last updated ';
    echo date('G:i j-M-Y', $localtime);
    echo '<br />';
}
else
    $localtime=0;
```

(You can read more about the `file_exists()` and `filemtime()` functions in Chapter 2 and Chapter 16, "Interacting with the File System and the Server," respectively.)

After we have sorted out the local time, we need to get the modification time of the remote file. You can get this using the `ftp_mdtm()` function:

```
$remotetime = ftp_mdtm($conn, $remotefile);
```

This function takes two parameters—the FTP connection handle, and the path to the remote file—and returns either the UNIX time stamp of the time the file was last modified, or –1 if there is an error of some kind. Not all FTP servers support this feature, so we might not get a useful result from the function. In this case, we choose to artificially set the `$remotetime` variable to be "newer" than the `$localtime` variable by adding 1 to it. This will ensure that an attempt is made to download the file:

```
if (!($remotetime >= 0))
{
  // This doesn't mean the file's not there, server may not support mod time
  echo 'Can't access remote file time.<br />';
  $remotetime=$localtime+1;  // make sure of an update
}
else
{
  echo 'Remote file last updated ';
  echo date('G:i j-M-Y', $remotetime);
  echo '<br />';
}
```

When we have both times, we can compare them to see whether we need to download the file or not:

```
if (!($remotetime > $localtime))
{
  echo 'Local copy is up to date.<br />';
  exit;
}
```

Downloading the File

At this stage we will try to download the file from the server:

```
echo 'Getting file from server...<br />';
$fp = fopen ($localfile, 'w');
if (!$success = ftp_fget($conn, $fp, $remotefile, FTP_BINARY))
{
  echo 'Error: Could not download file';
  fclose($fp);
  ftp_quit($conn);
  exit;
}
fclose($fp);
echo 'File downloaded successfully';
```

We open a local file using `fopen()` as we have seen previously. After we have done this, we call the function `ftp_fget()`, which attempts to download the file and store in a local file. This function takes four parameters. The first three are straightforward—the FTP connection, the local file handle, and the path to the remote file. The fourth parameter is the FTP mode.

There are two modes for an FTP transfer, ASCII and binary. The ASCII mode is used for transferring text files (that is, files that consist solely of ASCII characters), and the binary mode, used for transferring everything else. PHP's FTP library comes with two predefined constants, FTP_ASCII and FTP_BINARY, that represent these two modes. You need to decide which mode fits your file type, and pass the corresponding constant to ftp_fget() as the fourth parameter. In this case we are transferring a zip file, and so we have used the FTP_BINARY mode.

The ftp_fget() function returns true if all goes well, or false if an error is encountered. We store the result in $success, and let the user know how it went.

After the download has been attempted, we close the local file using the fclose() function.

As an alternative to ftp_fget(), we could have used ftp_get(), which has the following prototype:

```
int ftp_get (int ftp_connection, string localfile_path,
        string remotefile_path, int mode)
```

This function works in much the same way as ftp_fget(), but does not require the local file to be open. You pass it the system filename of the local file you would like to write to rather than a file handle.

Note that there is no equivalent to the FTP command mget, which can be used to download multiple files at a time. You must instead make multiple calls to ftp_fget() or ftp_get().

Closing the Connection

After we have finished with the FTP connection, you should close it using the ftp_quit() function:

```
ftp_quit($conn);
```

You should pass this function the handle for the FTP connection.

Uploading Files

If you want to go the other way, that is, copy files from your server to a remote machine, you can use two functions that are basically the opposite of ftp_fget() and ftp_get(). These functions are called ftp_fput() and ftp_put(). They have the following prototypes:

```
int ftp_fput (int ftp_connection, string remotefile_path, int fp, int mode)
int ftp_put (int ftp_connection, string remotefile_path,
            string localfile_path, int mode)
```

The parameters are the same as for the _get equivalents.

Avoiding Timeouts

One problem you might face when FTPing files is exceeding the maximum execution time. You will know whether this happens because PHP will give you an error message. This is especially likely to occur if your server is running over a slow or congested network, or if you are downloading a large file, such as a movie clip.

The default value of the maximum execution time for all PHP scripts is defined in the php.ini file. By default, it's set to 30 seconds. This is designed to catch scripts that are running out of control. However, when you are FTPing files, if your link to the rest of the world is slow, or if the file is large, the file transfer could well take longer than this.

Fortunately, we can modify the maximum execution time for a particular script using the set_time_limit() function. Calling this function resets the maximum number of seconds the script is allowed to run, starting from the time the function is called. For example, if you call

```
set_time_limit(90);
```

then the script will be able to run for another 90 seconds from the time the function is called.

Using Other FTP Functions

There are a number of other useful FTP functions in PHP.

The function ftp_size() can tell you the size of a file on a remote server. It has the following prototype:

```
int ftp_size(int ftp_connection, string remotefile_path)
```

This function returns the size of the remote file in bytes, or –1 if there is an error. This is not supported by all FTP servers.

One handy use of ftp_size() is to work out the maximum execution time to set for a particular transfer. Given the file size and the speed of your connection, you can take a guess as to how long the transfer ought to take, and use the set_time_limit() function accordingly.

You can get and display a list of files in a directory on a remote FTP server with the following code:

```
$listing = ftp_nlist($conn, "$directory_path");
foreach ($listing as $filename)
  echo "$filename <br />";
```

This code uses the ftp_nlist() function to get a list of names of files in a particular directory.

In terms of other FTP functions, almost anything that you can do from an FTP command line, you can do with the FTP functions. You can find the specific functions corresponding to each FTP command in the PHP online manual at http://php.net/manual/en/ref.ftp.php.

The exception is mget (multiple get), but you can use `ftp_nlist()` to get a list of files and then fetch them as required.

Generic Network Communications with cURL

PHP (from version 4.0.2 onward) has a set of functions that acts as an interface to cURL, the Client URL library functions from libcurl, written by Daniel Stenberg. Previously in this chapter, we looked at using the `fopen()` function and the file-reading functions to read from a remote file using HTTP. This is pretty much the limit of what you can do with `fopen()`. We've also seen how to make FTP connections using the FTP functions.

The cURL functions enable you to make connections using FTP, HTTP, HTTPS, Gopher, Telnet, DICT, FILE, and LDAP. You can also use certificates for HTTPS, send HTTP POST and HTTP GET parameters, upload files via FTP upload or HTTP upload, work through proxies, set cookies, and perform simple HTTP user authentication.

In other words, just about any kind of network connection that you'd like to make can be done using cURL.

To use cURL with PHP, you will need to download libcurl, compile it, and run PHP's `configure` script with the `--with-curl=[path]` option. The directory in `path` should be the one that contains the lib and include directories on your system. You can download the library from

```
http://curl.haxx.se/
```

Be aware that you will need a version of cURL from 7.0.2-beta onward to work with PHP.

There are only a few simple functions to master in order to use the power of cURL. The typical procedure for using it is

1. Set up a cURL session with a call to the `curl_init()` function.
2. Set any parameters for transfer with calls to the `curl_setopt()` function. This is where you set options such as the URL to connect to, any parameters to send to that URL, or the destination of the output from the URL.
3. When everything is set up, call `curl_exec()` to actually make the connection.
4. Close the cURL session by calling `curl_close()`.

The only things that change with the application are the URL that you connect to and the parameters you set with `curl_opt()`. There are a large number of these that can be set.

Some typical applications of cURL are

- Downloading pages from a server that uses HTTPS (because `fopen()` can't be used for this purpose prior to PHP 4.3)

- Connecting to a script that normally expects data from an HTML form using
  POST
- Writing a script to send multiple sets of test data to your scripts and checking the
  output

We will consider the first example—it's a simple application that can't be done
another way.

This example, shown in Listing 17.5, will connect to the Equifax Secure Server via
HTTPS, and write the file it finds there to a file on our Web server.

Listing 17.5 **https-curl.php—Script to Make HTTPS Connections**

```php
<?php
echo '<h1>HTTPS transfer with cURL</h1>';

$outputfile = '/tmp/writable/ssl-download.html';
$fp = fopen($outputfile, 'w+');

echo 'Initializing cURL session...<br />';
$ch = curl_init();

echo 'Setting cURL options...<br />';
curl_setopt ($ch, CURLOPT_URL, 'https://www.verisign.com/');
curl_setopt ($ch, CURLOPT_FILE, $fp);

echo 'Executing cURL session...<br />';
curl_exec ($ch);

echo 'Ending cURL session...<br />';
curl_close ($ch);

fclose($fp);

echo 'Here is the content of the file:<hr />';
readfile($outputfile);
?>
```

Let's go through this script. We begin by opening a local file using fopen(). This is
where we are going to store the page we transfer from the secure connection.
When this is done, we need to create a cURL session using the curl_init() function:

```php
$ch = curl_init();
```

This function returns a handle for the cURL session. You can call it like this, with no
parameters, or optionally you can pass it a string containing the URL to connect to. You
can also set the URL using the curl_setopt() function, which is what we have done
in this case:

```
curl_setopt ($ch, CURLOPT_URL, 'https://www.equifaxsecure.com');
curl_setopt ($ch, CURLOPT_FILE, $fp);
```

The `curl_setopt()` function takes three parameters. The first is the session handle, the second is the name of the parameter to set, and the third is the value to which you would like the parameter set.

In this case we are setting two options. The first is the URL that we want to connect to. This is the `CURLOPT_URL` parameter. The second one is the file where we want the data from the connection to go. If you don't specify a file, the data from the connection will go to standard output—usually the browser. In this case we have specified the file handle of the output file we just opened.

When the options are set, we tell cURL to actually make the connection:

```
curl_exec ($ch);
```

Here, this will open a connection to the URL we have specified, download the page, and store it in the file pointed to by `$fp`.

After the connection has been made, we need to close the cURL session, and close the file we wrote to:

```
curl_close ($ch);
fclose($fp);
```

That's it for this simple example.

You might find it worthwhile to look at the Snoopy class, available from `http://snoopy.sourceforge.net/`.

This class provides Web client functionality through cURL.

Further Reading

We've covered a lot of ground in this chapter, and as you might expect, there's a lot of material out there on these topics.

For information on the individual protocols and how they work, you can consult the RFCs at `http://www.rfc-editor.org/`.

You might also find some of the protocol information at the World Wide Web Consortium interesting:

```
http://www.w3.org/Protocols/
```

You can also try consulting a book on TCP/IP such as *Computer Networks* by Andrew Tanenbaum.

The cURL Web site has some tips on how to use the command line versions of the cURL functions, and these are fairly easily translated into the PHP versions:

```
http://curl.haxx.se/docs/httpscripting.shtml
```

Next

We'll move on to Chapter 18, "Managing the Date and Time," and look at PHP's libraries of date and calendar functions. You'll see how to convert from user-entered formats to PHP formats to MySQL formats, and back again.

18

Managing the Date and Time

IN THIS CHAPTER, WE'LL DISCUSS CHECKING and formatting the date and time and converting between date formats. This is especially important when converting between MySQL and PHP date formats, Unix and PHP date formats, and dates entered by the user in an HTML form.

We'll cover

- Getting the date and time in PHP
- Converting between PHP and MySQL date formats
- Calculating dates
- Using the calendar functions

Getting the Date and Time from PHP

Way back in Chapter 1, "PHP Crash Course," we talked about using the date() function to get and format the date and time from PHP. We'll talk about it and some of PHP's other date and time functions in a little more detail now.

Using the date() Function

As you might recall, the date() function takes two parameters, one of them optional. The first one is a format string, and the second, optional one is a UNIX time stamp. If you don't specify a time stamp, then date() will default to the current date and time. It returns a formatted string representing the appropriate date.

A typical call to the date function could be

```
echo date('jS F Y');
```

This will produce a date of the format "27ᵗʰ August 2000".

The format codes accepted by date are listed in Table 18.1.

Table 18.1 **Format Codes for PHP's date() Function**

Code	Description
a	Morning or afternoon, represented as two lowercase characters, either "am" or "pm".
A	Morning or afternoon, represented as two uppercase characters, either "AM" or "PM".
B	Swatch Internet time, a universal time scheme. More information is available at http://www.swatch.com/.
d	Day of the month as a 2-digit number with a leading zero. Range is from "01" to "31".
D	Day of the week in 3-character abbreviated text format. Range is from "Mon" to "Sun".
F	Month of the year in full text format. Range is from "January" to "December".
g	Hour of the day in 12-hour format without leading zeroes. Range is from "1" to "12".
G	Hour of the day in 24-hour format without leading zeroes. Range is from "0" to "23".
h	Hour of the day in 12-hour format with leading zeroes. Range is from "01" to "12".
H	Hour of the day in 24-hour format with leading zeroes. Range is from "00" to "23".
i	Minutes past the hour with leading zeroes. Range is from "00" to "59".
I	Daylight savings time, represented as a Boolean value. This will return "1" if the date is in daylight savings and "0" if it is not.
j	Day of the month as a number without leading zeroes. Range is from "1" to "31".
l	Day of the week in full text format. Range is from "Monday" to "Sunday".
L	Leap year, represented as a Boolean value. This will return "1" if the date is in a leap year and "0" if it is not.
m	Month of the year as a 2-digit number with leading zeroes. Range is from "01" to "12".
M	Month of the year in 3-character abbreviated text format. Range is from "Jan" to "Dec".
n	Month of the year as a number without leading zeroes. Range is from "1" to "12".
O	Difference between the current timezone and Greenwich Mean Time in hours e.g. +1600.
r	RFC822 formatted date and time, for example Wed, 9 Oct 2002 18:45:30 +1600. (Added in PHP 4.0.4.)
s	Seconds past the minute with leading zeroes. Range is from "00" to "59".
S	Ordinal suffix for dates in 2-character format. This can be "st", "nd", "rd", or "th", depending on the number it is after.
t	Total number of days in the date's month. Range is from "28" to "31".
T	Timezone setting of the server in 3-character format, for example, "EST".
U	Total number of seconds from 1 January 1970 to this time; a.k.a., a UNIX time stamp for this date.
w	Day of the week as a single digit. Range is from "0" (Sunday) to "6" (Saturday).
W	Week number in the year, ISO-8601 compliant. (Added at PHP 4.1.0.)

Table 18.1   **Continued**

Code	Description
y	Year in 2-digit format, for example, "00".
Y	Year in 4-digit format, for example, "2000".
z	Day of the year as a number. Range is "0" to "365".
Z	Offset for the current timezone in seconds. Range is "-43200" to "43200".

Dealing with Unix Timestamps

The second parameter to the date() function is a Unix time stamp.

In case you are wondering exactly what this means, most Unix systems store the current time and date as a 32-bit integer containing the number of seconds since midnight, January 1, 1970, GMT, also known as the Unix Epoch. This can seem a bit esoteric if you are not familiar with it, but it's a standard.

Unix timestamps are a compact way of storing a date and time, but it is worth noting that they do not suffer from the year 2000 (Y2K) problem that affects some other compact or abbreviated date formats. If your software is still in use in 2038, there will be similar problems though. As timestamps do not have a fixed size, but are tied to the size of a C long, which is at least 32 bits, the most likely solution is that by 2038, your compiler will use a larger type.

Even if you are running PHP on a Windows server, this is still the format that is used by date() and a number of other PHP functions.

If you want to convert a date and time *to* a Unix time stamp, you can use the mktime() function. This has the following prototype:

```
int mktime (int hour, int minute, int second, int month,
           int day, int year [, int is_dst])
```

The parameters are fairly self-explanatory, with the exception of the last one, *is_dst*, which represents whether the date was in daylight savings time or not. You can set this to 1 if it was, 0 if it wasn't, or -1 (the default value) if you don't know. This is optional so you will rarely use it anyway.

The main trap to avoid with this function is that the parameters are in a fairly unintuitive order. The ordering doesn't lend itself to leaving out the time. If you are not worried about the time, you can pass in 0s to the *hour*, *minute*, and *second* parameters. You can, however, leave out values from the right side of the parameter list. If you leave the parameters blank, they will be set to the current values. Hence a call such as

```
$timestamp = mktime();
```

will return the Unix timestamp for the current date and time. You could, of course, also get this by calling

```
$timestamp = date("U");
```

You can pass in a 2- or 4-digit year to `mktime()`. Two-digit values from 0 to 69 will be interpreted as the years 2000 to 2069, and values from 70 to 99 will be interpreted as 1970 to 1999.

Using the getdate() Function

Another date-determining function you might find useful is the `getdate()` function. This function has the following prototype:

```
array getdate (int timestamp)
```

It takes a time stamp as parameter and returns an associative array representing the parts of that date and time as shown in Table 18.2.

Table 18.2 **Associative Array Key-Value Pairs from getdate() Function**

Key	Value
seconds	Seconds, numeric
minutes	Minutes, numeric
hours	Hours, numeric
mday	Day of the month, numeric
wday	Day of the week, numeric
mon	Month, numeric
year	Year, numeric
yday	Day of the year, numeric
weekday	Day of the week, full text format
month	Month, full text format

Validating Dates

You can use the `checkdate()` function to check whether a date is valid. This is especially useful for checking user input dates. The `checkdate()` function has the following prototype:

```
int checkdate (int month, int day, int year)
```

It will check whether the year is a valid integer between 0 and 32767, whether the month is an integer between 1 and 12, and whether the day given exists in that particular month. The function takes leap years into consideration.

For example,

```
checkdate(9, 18, 1972);
```

will return `true` while

```
checkdate(9, 31, 2000)
```

will not.

Converting Between PHP and MySQL Date Formats

Dates and times in MySQL are retrieved in a slightly different way than you might expect. Times work relatively normally, but MySQL expects dates to be entered year first. For example, the 29th of August 2000 could be entered as either 2000-08-29 or as 00-08-29. Dates retrieved from MySQL will also be in this order by default.

To communicate between PHP and MySQL then, we usually need to perform some date conversion. This can be done at either end.

When putting dates into MySQL from PHP, you can easily put them into the correct format using the `date()` function as shown previously. One minor caution is that you should use the versions of the day and month with leading zeroes to avoid confusing MySQL.

If you choose to do the conversion in MySQL, two useful functions are `DATE_FORMAT()` and `UNIX_TIMESTAMP()`.

The `DATE_FORMAT()` function works similarly to the PHP one but uses different format codes. The most common thing we want to do is format a date in MM-DD-YYYY format rather than in the YYYY-MM-DD format native to MySQL. You can do this by writing your query as follows:

```
SELECT DATE_FORMAT(date_column, '%m %d %Y')
FROM tablename;
```

The format code `%m` represents the month as a 2-digit number; `%d`, the day as a 2-digit number; and `%Y`, the year as a 4-digit number. A summary of the more useful MySQL format codes for this purpose is shown in Table 18.3.

Table 18.3   **Format Codes for MySQL's DATE_FORMAT() Function**

Code	Description
%M	Month, full text
%W	Weekday name, full text
%D	Day of month, numeric, with text suffix (for example, 1st)
%Y	Year, numeric, 4-digits
%y	Year, numeric, 2-digits
%a	Weekday name, 3-characters
%d	Day of month, numeric, leading zeroes
%e	Day of month, numeric, no leading zeroes
%m	Month, numeric, leading zeroes
%c	Month, numeric, no leading zeroes
%b	Month, text, 3-characters
%j	Day of year, numeric
%H	Hour, 24-hour clock, leading zeroes
%k	Hour, 24-hour clock, no leading zeroes
%h or %I	Hour, 12-hour clock, leading zeroes

Table 18.3 **Continued**

Code	Description
%l	Hour, 12-hour clock, no leading zeroes
%i	Minutes, numeric, leading zeroes
%r	Time, 12-hour (hh:mm:ss [AM|PM])
%T	Time, 24-hour (hh:mm:ss)
%S or %s	Seconds, numeric, leading zeroes
%p	AM or PM
%w	Day of the week, numeric, from 0 (Sunday) to 6 (Saturday)

The `UNIX_TIMESTAMP` function works similarly, but converts a column into a Unix time-stamp. For example,

```
SELECT UNIX_TIMESTAMP(date_column)
FROM tablename;
```

will return the date formatted as a Unix timestamp. You can then do as you will with it in PHP.

As a rule of thumb, use a Unix timestamp for date calculations and the standard date format when you are just storing or showing dates. It is simpler to do date calculations and comparisons with the Unix timestamp.

Date Calculations

The simplest way to work out the length of time between two dates in PHP is to use the difference between UNIX time stamps. We have used this approach in the script shown in Listing 18.1.

Listing 18.1   **calc_age.php—Script Works Out a Person's Age Based on His Birthdate**

```php
<?php
// set date for calculation
$day = 18;
$month = 9;
$year = 1972;

// remember you need bday as day month and year
$bdayunix = mktime ('', '', '', $month, $day, $year);
// get unix ts for bday
$nowunix = time(); // get unix ts for today
$ageunix = $nowunix - $bdayunix; // work out the difference
$age = floor($ageunix / (365 * 24 * 60 * 60)); // convert from seconds to years

echo "Age is $age";
?>
```

In this script, we have set the date for calculating the age. In a real application it is likely that this information might come from an HTML form. We begin by calling `mktime()` to work out the time stamp for the birthday and for the current time:

```
$bdayunix = mktime ('', '', '', $month, $day, $year);
$nowunix = mktime(); // get unix ts for today
```

Now that these dates are in the same format, we can simply subtract them:

```
$ageunix = $nowunix - $bdayunix;
```

Now, the slightly tricky part—to convert this time period back to a more human-friendly unit of measure. This is not a time stamp but instead the age of the person measured in seconds. We can convert it back to years by dividing by the number of seconds in a year. We then round it down using the `floor()` function as a person is not said to be, for example 20, until the end of his twentieth year:

```
$age = floor($ageunix / (365 * 24 * 60 * 60)); // convert from seconds to years
```

Note, however, that this approach is somewhat flawed as it is limited by the range of UNIX time stamps (generally 32-bit integers). This example may not be an ideal application for timestamps as it will only work for people born from 1970 onward.

Using the Calendar Functions

PHP has a set of functions that enables you to convert between different calendar systems. The main calendars you will work with are the Gregorian, Julian, and the Julian Day Count.

The Gregorian calendar is the one most Western countries currently use. The Gregorian date October 15, 1582, is equivalent to October 5, 1582, in the Julian calendar. Prior to that date, the Julian calendar was commonly used. Different countries converted to the Gregorian calendar at different times, and some not until early in the 20th century.

Although you might have heard of these two calendars, you might not have heard of the Julian Day Count. This is similar in many ways to a Unix timestamp. It is a count of the number of days since a date around 4000 BC. In itself, it is not particularly useful, but it is useful for converting between formats. To convert from one format to another, you first convert to a Julian Day Count (JD) and then to the desired output calendar.

To use these functions under Unix, you will need to have compiled the calendar extension into PHP. They are built into the standard Windows install.

To give you a taste for these functions, consider the prototypes for the functions you would use to convert from the Gregorian calendar to the Julian calendar:

```
int gregoriantojd (int month, int day, int year)
string jdtojulian(int julianday)
```

To convert a date, we would need to call both these functions:

```
$jd = gregoriantojd (9, 18, 1582);
echo jdtojulian($jd);
```

This echoes the Julian date in a mm/dd/yyyy format.

Variations of these functions exist for converting between the Gregorian, Julian, French, and Jewish calendars and UNIX time stamps.

Further Reading

If you'd like to read more about date and time functions in PHP and MySQL, you can consult the relevant sections of the manuals at

```
http://php.net/manual/en/ref.datetime.php
```

```
http://www.mysql.com/doc/en/Date_and_time_functions.html
```

If you are converting between calendars, try the manual page for PHP's calendar functions:

```
http://php.net/manual/en/ref.calendar.php
```

Or try consulting this reference:

```
http://genealogy.org/~scottlee/cal-overview.html
```

Next

One of the unique and useful things you can do with PHP is create images on-the-fly. Chapter 19, "Generating Images," discusses how to use the image library functions to achieve some interesting and useful effects.

19

Generating Images

ONE OF THE USEFUL THINGS YOU CAN do with PHP is create images on-the-fly. PHP has some built-in image information functions, and you can also use the gd library to create new images or manipulate existing ones. This chapter discusses how to use the image functions to achieve some interesting and useful effects.

We will look at

- Setting up image support in PHP
- Understanding image formats
- Creating images
- Using text and fonts to create images
- Drawing figures and graphing data

Specifically, we'll look at two examples: generating Web site buttons on-the-fly, and drawing a bar chart using figures from a MySQL database.

Setting Up Image Support in PHP

Image support in PHP is available via the gd library, available from

```
http://www.boutell.com/gd/
```

From PHP 4.3, PHP comes with its own version of the gd library, supported by the PHP team. This version has extra features and is usually more up-to-date, so it's advisable to use this version.

With some earlier versions of PHP you have a choice of using the gd or gd2 library: We recommend you use gd2 as it is more stable.

Under Windows, PNGs and JPEGs are automatically supported.

If you have Unix and want to work with PNGs, you will need to install libpng and zlib from the following places (respectively):

```
http://www.libpng.org/pub/png/
http://www.gzip.org/zlib/
```

You will then need to configure PHP with the following options:

```
--with-png-dir=/path/to/libpng
--with-zlib-dir=/path/to/zlib
```

If you have UNIX and want to work with JPEGs, you will need to download jpeg-6b, and recompile gd with jpeg support included. You can download this from

```
ftp://ftp.uu.net/graphics/jpeg/
```

You will then need to reconfigure PHP with the

```
--with-jpeg-dir=/path/to/jpeg-6b
```

option, and recompile it.

If you want to use True Type fonts in your images, you will also need the FreeType library. This also comes with PHP 4. Alternatively, you can download this from

```
http://www.freetype.org/
```

If you want to use PostScript Type 1 fonts instead, you will need to download t1lib, available from

```
ftp://sunsite.unc.edu/pub/Linux/libs/graphics/
```

You will then need to run PHP's configure program with

```
--with-t1lib[=path/to/t1lib]
```

Image Formats

The gd library supports JPEG, PNG, and WBMP formats. It no longer supports the GIF format. Let's briefly look at each of these formats.

JPEG

JPEG (pronounced "jay-peg") actually stands for *Joint Photographic Experts Group* and is the name of a standards body. The file format we mean when we refer to JPEGs is actually called JFIF, which corresponds to one of the standards issued by JPEG.

In case you are not familiar with them, JPEGs are usually used to store photographic or other images with many colors or gradations of color. This format uses lossy compression—that is, in order to squeeze a photograph into a smaller file, some image quality is lost. Because JPEGs should contain what are essentially analog images, with gradations of color, the human eye can tolerate some loss of quality. This format is not suitable for line drawings, text, or solid blocks of color.

You can read more about JPEG/JFIF at the official JPEG site:

```
http://www.jpeg.org/
```

PNG

PNG (pronounced "ping") stands for *Portable Network Graphics*. This file format is the replacement for *GIF (Graphics Interchange Format)* for reasons we'll discuss in a minute. The PNG Web site describes it as "a turbo-studly image format with lossless compression." Because it is lossless, this image format is suitable for images that contain text, straight lines, and simple blocks of color such as headings and Web site buttons—all the same purposes for which you previously might have used GIFs.

It offers better compression than GIF as well as variable transparency, gamma correction, and two-dimensional interlacing. It does not, however, support animations—for this you must use the extension format MNG, which is still in development.

You can read more about PNG at the official PNG site:

```
http://www.libpng.org/pub/png/
```

WBMP

WBMP stands for *Wireless Bitmap*. It is a file format designed specifically for wireless devices.

GIF

GIF stands for Graphics Interchange Format. It is a compressed lossless format widely used on the Web for storing images containing text, straight lines, and blocks of single color.

The question you are likely asking is, why doesn't gd support GIFs?

The answer is that it used to, up to version 1.3. If you want to install and use the GIF functions instead of the PNG functions, you can download gd version 1.3 from

```
http://www.linuxguruz.org/downloads/gd1.3.tar.gz
```

Note, however, that the makers of gd discourage you from using this version and no longer support it. This copy of the GIF version might not be available forever.

There is a good reason that gd no longer supports GIFs. Standard GIFs use a form of compression known as *LZW (Lempel Ziv Welch)*, which is subject to a patent owned by UNISYS. Providers of programs that read and write GIFs must pay licensing fees to UNISYS. For example, Adobe has paid a licensing fee for products such as Photoshop that are used to create GIFs. Code libraries appear to be in the situation in which the writers of the code library must pay a fee, and, in addition, the users of the library must also pay a fee. Thus, if you use a GIF version of the gd library on your Web site, you might owe UNISYS some fairly hefty licensing fees.

This situation is unfortunate because GIFs were in use for many years before UNISYS chose to enforce licensing. Thus, the format became one of the standards for the Web. A lot of ill feeling exists about the patent in the Web development community. You can read about this (and form your own opinion) at UNISYS's site

```
http://www.unisys.com/about__unisys/lzw/
```

and at Burn All Gifs, the opposition,

`http://burnallgifs.org/`

We are not lawyers, and none of this should be interpreted as legal advice, but we think it is easier to use PNGs, regardless of the politics.

Browser support for PNGs is improving; however, the LZW patent expires on June 19, 2003, so the final outcome is yet to be seen.

Creating Images

The four basic steps to creating an image in PHP are as follows:

1. Creating a canvas image on which to work.

2. Drawing shapes or printing text on that canvas.

3. Outputting the final graphic.

4. Cleaning up resources.

We'll begin by looking at a very simple image creation script. This script is shown in Listing 19.1.

Listing 19.1 **simplegraph.php—Outputs a Simple Line Graph with the Label Sales**

```php
<?php
// set up image
  $height = 200;
  $width = 200;
  $im = ImageCreate($width, $height);
  $white = ImageColorAllocate ($im, 255, 255, 255);
  $black = ImageColorAllocate ($im, 0, 0, 0);

// draw on image
  ImageFill($im, 0, 0, $black);
  ImageLine($im, 0, 0, $width, $height, $white);
  ImageString($im, 4, 50, 150, 'Sales', $white);

// output image
  Header ('Content-type: image/png');
  ImagePng ($im);

// clean up
  ImageDestroy($im);
?>
```

The output from running this script is shown in Figure 19.1.

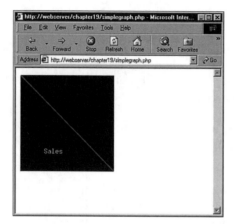

Figure 19.1   The script draws a black background and
then adds a line and a text label for the image.

We'll walk through the steps of creating this image one by one.

Creating a Canvas Image

To begin building or changing an image in PHP, you will need to create an image identifier. There are two basic ways to do this. One is to create a blank canvas, which you can
do with a call to the ImageCreate() function, as we have done in this script with the
following:

```
$im = ImageCreate($width, $height);
```

You need to pass two parameters to ImageCreate(). The first is the width of the new
image, and the second is the height of the new image. The function will return an identifier for the new image. (These work a lot like file handles.)

An alternative way is to read in an existing image file that you can then filter, resize,
or add to. You can do this with one of the functions ImageCreateFromPNG(),
ImageCreateFromJPEG(), or ImageCreateFromGIF(), depending on the file format you
are reading in. Each of these takes the filename as a parameter, as in, for
example,

```
$im = ImageCreateFromPNG('baseimage.png');
```

An example is shown later in this chapter using existing images to create buttons on-
the-fly.

Drawing or Printing Text on to the Image

There are really two stages to drawing or printing text on the image.

First, you must select the colors in which you want to draw. As you probably already
know, colors to be displayed on a computer monitor are made up of different amounts

of red, green, and blue light. Image formats use a color palette that consists of a specified subset of all the possible combinations of the three colors. To use a color to draw in an image, you need to add this color to the image's palette. You must do this for every color you want to use, even black and white.

You can select colors for your image by calling the ImageColorAllocate() function. You need to pass your image identifier and the red, green, and blue (RGB) values of the color you want to draw into the function.

In Listing 19.1, we are using two colors: black and white. We allocate these by calling

```
$white = ImageColorAllocate ($im, 255, 255, 255);
$black = ImageColorAllocate ($im, 0, 0, 0);
```

The function returns a color identifier that we can use to access the color later on.

Second, to actually draw into the image, a number of different functions are available, depending on what you want to draw—lines, arcs, polygons, or text.

The drawing functions generally require the following as parameters:

- The image identifier
- The start and sometimes the end coordinates of what you want to draw
- The color you want to draw in
- For text, the font information

In this case, we used three of the drawing functions. Let's look at each one in turn.

First, we painted a black background on which to draw using the ImageFill() function:

```
ImageFill($im, 0, 0, $black);
```

This function takes the image identifier, the start coordinates of the area to paint (x and y), and the color to fill in as parameters.

> **Note**
>
> One thing to note is that the coordinates of the image start from the top-left corner, which is x=0, y=0. The bottom-right corner of the image is x=$width, y=$height. This is the opposite of typical graphing conventions, so beware!

Next, we've drawn a line from the top-left corner (0, 0) to the bottom-right corner ($width, $height) of the image:

```
ImageLine($im, 0, 0, $width, $height, $white);
```

This function takes the image identifier, the start point x and y for the line, the end point, and then the color, as parameters.

Finally, we add a label to the graph:

```
ImageString($im, 4, 50, 150, 'Sales', $white);
```

The `ImageString()` function takes some slightly different parameters. The prototype for this function is

```
int imagestring (resource im, int font, int x, int y, string s, int col)
```

It takes as parameters the image identifier, the font, the x and y coordinates to start writing the text, the text to write, and the color.

The font is a number between 1 and 5. These represent a set of built-in fonts. As an alternative to these, you can use TrueType fonts, or PostScript Type 1 fonts. Each of these font sets has a corresponding function set. We will use the TrueType functions in the next example.

A good reason for using one of the alternative font function sets is that the text written by `ImageString()` and associated functions, such as `ImageChar()` (write a character to the image) is aliased. The TrueType and PostScript functions produce anti-aliased text.

If you're not sure what the difference is, look at Figure 19.2. Where curves or angled lines appear in the letters, the aliased text appears jagged. The curve or angle is achieved by using a "staircase" effect. In the anti-aliased image, when there are curves or angles in the text, pixels in colors between the background and the text color are used to smooth the text's appearance.

Figure 19.2   Normal text appears jagged, especially in a large font size.

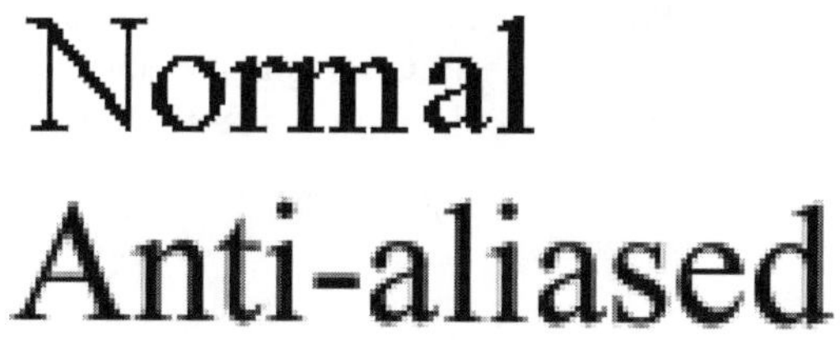

Normal
Anti-aliased

Anti-aliasing smooths the curves and corners of the letters.

Outputting the Final Graphic

You can output an image either directly to the browser, or to a file.

In this example, we've output the image to the browser. This is a two-stage process. First, we need to tell the Web browser that we are outputting an image rather than text or HTML. We do this by using the `Header()` function to specify the MIME type of the image:

```
Header ('Content-type: image/png');
```

Normally when you retrieve a file in your browser, the MIME type is the first thing the Web server sends. For an HTML or PHP page (post execution), the first thing sent will be

```
Content-type: text/html
```

This tells the browser how to interpret the data that follows.

In this case, we want to tell the browser that we are sending an image instead of the usual HTML output. We can do this using the Header() function, which we have not yet discussed.

This function sends raw HTTP header strings. Another typical application of this is to do HTTP redirects. These tell the browser to load a different page instead of the one requested. They are typically used when a page has been moved. For example,

```
Header ('Location: http://www.domain.com/new_home_page.html');
```

An important point to note when using the Header() function is that it cannot be executed if an HTTP header has already been sent for the page. PHP will send an HTTP header automatically for you as soon as you output anything to the browser. Hence, if you have any echo statements, or even any whitespace before your opening PHP tag, the headers will be sent, and you will get a warning message from PHP when you try to call Header(). However, you can send multiple HTTP headers with multiple calls to the Header() function in the same script, although they must all appear before any output is sent to the browser.

After we have sent the header data, we output the image data with a call to

```
ImagePng ($im);
```

This sends the output to the browser in PNG format. If you wanted it sent in a different format, you could call ImageJPEG()—if JPEG support is enabled—or ImageGIF() —if you have an older version of gd. You would also need to send the corresponding header first; that is, either

```
Header ('Content-type: image/jpeg');
```

or

```
Header ('Content-type: image/gif');
```

The second option you can use, as an alternative to all the previous ones, is to write the image to a file instead of to the browser. You can do this by adding the optional second parameter to ImagePNG() (or a similar function for the other supported formats):

```
ImagePNG($im, $filename);
```

Remember that all the usual rules about writing to a file from PHP apply (for example, having permissions set up correctly).

Cleaning Up

When you're done with an image, you should return the resources you have been using to the server by destroying the image identifier. You can do this with a call to ImageDestroy():

```
ImageDestroy($im);
```

Using Automatically Generated Images in Other Pages

Because a header can only be sent once, and this is the only way to tell the browser that we are sending image data, it is slightly tricky to embed any images we create on-the-fly in a regular page. Three ways you can do it are as follows:

1. You can have an entire page consist of the image output, as we did in the previous example.

2. You can write the image out to a file as previously mentioned, and then refer to it with a normal `<img>` tag.

3. You can put the image production script in an image tag.

We have covered methods 1 and 2 already. Let's briefly look at method 3.

To use this method, you include the image inline in HTML by having an image tag along the lines of the following:

```
<img src="simplegraph.php" height="200" width="200" alt="Sales going down" />
```

Instead of putting in a PNG, JPEG, or GIF directly, put in the PHP script that generates the image in the SRC tag. This will be retrieved and the output added inline, as shown in Figure 19.3.

Figure 19.3   The dynamically produced inline image appears the same as a regular image to the end user.

Using Text and Fonts to Create Images

We'll look at a more complicated example. It is useful to be able to create buttons or other images for your Web site automatically. You can build simple buttons based on a rectangle of background color using the techniques we've already discussed.

In this example, however, we'll generate buttons using a blank button template that allows us to have features like beveled edges and so on, which are a good deal easier to generate using Photoshop, the GIMP, or some other graphics tool. With the image library in PHP, we can begin with a base image and draw on top of that.

We will also use TrueType fonts so that we can use anti-aliased text. The TrueType font functions have their own quirks, which we'll discuss.

The basic process is to take some text and generate a button with that text on it. The text will be centered both horizontally and vertically on the button, and will be rendered in the largest font size that will fit on the button.

We've built a front end to the button generator for testing and experimenting. This interface is shown in Figure 19.4. (We have not included the HTML for this form here as it is very simple, but you can find it on the CD in `design_button.html`.)

Figure 19.4   The front end lets a user choose the button color and type in the required text.

You could use this type of interface for a program to automatically generate Web sites. You could also call the script we write in an inline fashion, to generate all a Web site's buttons on-the-fly!

Typical output from the script is shown in Figure 19.5.

The button is generated by a script called `make_button.php`. This script is shown in Listing 19.2.

Figure 19.5   A button generated by the make_button.php script.

Listing 19.2   **make_button.php—This Script Can Be Called from the Form in design_button.html or from Within an HTML Image Tag**

```php
<?php
// check we have the appropriate variable data
// variables are button-text and color

$button_text = $HTTP_POST_VARS['button_text'];
$color = $HTTP_POST_VARS['color'];

if (empty($button_text) || empty($color))
{
  echo 'Could not create image - form not filled out correctly';
  exit;
}

// create an image of the right background and check size
$im = imagecreatefrompng ($color.'-button.png');

$width_image = ImageSX($im);
$height_image = ImageSY($im);

// Our images need an 18 pixel margin in from the edge image
$width_image_wo_margins = $width_image - (2 * 18);
$height_image_wo_margins = $height_image - (2 * 18);

// Work out if the font size will fit and make it smaller until it does
// Start out with the biggest size that will reasonably fit on our buttons
$font_size = 33;
```

Listing 19.2   **Continued**

```php
// you need to tell GD2 where your fonts reside
putenv('GDFONTPATH=C:\WINNT\Fonts');
$fontname = 'arial';

do
{
  $font_size--;

  // find out the size of the text at that font size
  $bbox=imagettfbbox ($font_size, 0, $fontname, $button_text);

  $right_text = $bbox[2];    // right co-ordinate
  $left_text = $bbox[0];     // left co-ordinate
  $width_text = $right_text - $left_text;  // how wide is it?
  $height_text = abs($bbox[7] - $bbox[1]);  // how tall is it?


}
while ( $font_size>8 &&
        ( $height_text>$height_image_wo_margins ||
          $width_text>$width_image_wo_margins )
      );

if ( $height_text>$height_image_wo_margins ||
     $width_text>$width_image_wo_margins )
{
  // no readable font size will fit on button
  echo 'Text given will not fit on button.<br />';
}
else
{
  // We have found a font size that will fit
  // Now work out where to put it

  $text_x = $width_image/2.0 - $width_text/2.0;
  $text_y = $height_image/2.0 - $height_text/2.0 ;

  if ($left_text < 0)
      $text_x += abs($left_text);     // add factor for left overhang

  $above_line_text = abs($bbox[7]);   // how far above the baseline?
  $text_y += $above_line_text;        // add baseline factor

  $text_y -= 2;  // adjustment factor for shape of our template

  $white = ImageColorAllocate ($im, 255, 255, 255);
```

Listing 19.2   **Continued**

```
    ImageTTFText ($im, $font_size, 0, $text_x, $text_y, $white, $fontname,
                 $button_text);

    Header ('Content-type: image/png');
    ImagePng ($im);
}

ImageDestroy ($im);
?>
```

This is one of the longest scripts we've looked at so far. Let's step through it section by section. We begin with some basic error checking, and then set up the canvas on which we're going to work.

Setting Up the Base Canvas

In Listing 19.2, rather than starting from scratch, we will start with an existing image for the button. We have a choice of three colors in the basic button: red (red-button.png), green (green-button.png), and blue (blue-button.png).

The user's chosen color is stored in the $color variable from the form.

We begin by setting up a new image identifier based on the appropriate button:

```
$im = imagecreatefrompng ($color.'-button.png');
```

The function ImageCreateFromPNG() takes the filename of a PNG as a parameter, and returns a new image identifier for an image containing a copy of that PNG. Note that this does not modify the base PNG in any way. We can use the ImageCreateFromJPEG() and ImageCreateFromGIF() functions in the same way if the appropriate support is installed.

> **Note**
>
> The call to ImageCreateFromPNG() only creates the image in memory. To save the image to a file or
> output it to the browser, we must call the ImagePNG() function. We'll come to that in a minute, but we
> have other work to do with our image first.

Fitting the Text onto the Button

We have some text typed in by the user stored in the $button_text variable. What we want to do is print that text on the button in the largest font size that will fit. We do this by iteration, or strictly speaking, by iterative trial and error.

We start by setting up some relevant variables. The first two are the height and width of the button image:

```
$width_image = ImageSX($im);
$height_image = ImageSY($im);
```

The second two represent a margin in from the edge of the button. Our button images are beveled, so we'll need to leave room for that around the edges of the text. If you are using different images, this number will be different! In our case, the margin on each side is around 18 pixels.

```
$width_image_wo_margins = $width_image - (2 * 18);
$height_image_wo_margins = $height_image - (2 * 18);
```

We also need to set up the initial font size. We start with 32 (actually 33, but we'll decrement that in a minute) because this is about the biggest font that will fit on the button at all:

```
$font_size = 33;
```

With gd2, you need to tell it where your fonts live by setting the environment variable GDFONTPATH as follows:

```
putenv('GDFONTPATH=C:\WINNT\Fonts');
```

We also set up the name of the font we want to use. We're going to use this font with the TrueType functions, which will look for the font file in the above location and will append the file name with .ttf (TrueType Font).

```
$fontname = 'arial';
```

Note that depending on your operating system you may have to add '.ttf' to the end of the font name.

If you don't have Arial (the font we use here) on your system, you can easily change this to another TrueType font.

Now we loop, decrementing the font size at each iteration, until the submitted text will fit on the button reasonably:

```
do
{
  $font_size--;

  // find out the size of the text at that font size
  $bbox=imagettfbbox ($font_size, 0, $fontname, $button_text);

  $right_text = $bbox[2];    // right co-ordinate
  $left_text = $bbox[0];     // left co-ordinate
  $width_text = $right_text - $left_text;  // how wide is it?
  $height_text = abs($bbox[7] - $bbox[1]);  // how tall is it?

}
while ( $font_size>8 &&
        ( $height_text>$height_image_wo_margins ||
          $width_text>$width_image_wo_margins )
      );
```

This code tests the size of the text by looking at what is called the *bounding box* of the text. We do this using the ImageGetTTFBBox() function, which is one of the TrueType font functions. We will, after we have figured out the size, print on the button using a TrueType font (in this case Arial, but you can use whatever you like) and the ImageTTFText() function.

The bounding box of a piece of text is the smallest box you could draw around the text. An example of a bounding box is shown in Figure 19.6.

Figure 19.6   Coordinates of the bounding box are given relative to the baseline. The origin of the coordinates is shown here as (0,0).

To get the dimensions of the box, we call

```
$bbox=imagettfbbox ($font_size, 0, $fontname, $button_text);
```

This call says, "For given font size $font_size, with text slanted on an angle of zero degrees, using the TrueType font Arial, tell me the dimensions of the text in $button_text."

Note that you actually need to pass the path to the file containing the font into the function. In this case, it's in the same directory as the script (the default), so we haven't specified a longer path.

The function returns an array containing the coordinates of the corners of the bounding box. The contents of the array are shown in Table 19.1.

Table 19.1   **Contents of the Bounding Box Array**

Array Index	Contents
0	X coordinate, lower-left corner
1	Y coordinate, lower-left corner
2	X coordinate, lower-right corner
3	Y coordinate, lower-right corner
4	X coordinate, upper-right corner
5	Y coordinate, upper-right corner
6	X coordinate, upper-left corner
7	Y coordinate, upper-left corner

To remember what the contents of the array are, just remember that the numbering starts at the bottom-left corner of the bounding box and works its way around counter clockwise.

There is one tricky thing about the values returned from the ImageTTFBBox() function. They are coordinate values, specified from an origin. However, unlike coordinates for images, which are specified relative to the top-left corner, they are specified relative to a baseline.

Look at Figure 19.6 again. You will see that we have drawn a line along the bottom of most of the text. This is known as the *baseline*. Some letters hang below the baseline, such as y in this example. These are called *descenders*.

The left side of the baseline is specified as the origin of measurements—that is, X coordinate 0 and Y coordinate 0. Coordinates above the baseline have a positive X coordinate and coordinates below the baseline have a negative X coordinate.

In addition to this, text might actually have coordinate values that sit outside the bounding box. For example, the text might actually start at an X coordinate of −1.

What this all adds up to is the fact that care is required when performing calculations with these numbers.

We work out the width and height of the text as follows:

```
$right_text = $bbox[2];    // right co-ordinate
$left_text = $bbox[0];     // left co-ordinate
$width_text = $right_text - $left_text;  // how wide is it?
$height_text = abs($bbox[7] - $bbox[1]);  // how tall is it?
```

After we have this, we test the loop condition:

```
} while ( $font_size>8 &&
          ( $height_text>$height_image_wo_margins ||
            $width_text>$width_image_wo_margins )
        );
```

We are testing two sets of conditions here. The first is that the font is still readable—there's no point in making it much smaller than 8 point because the button becomes too difficult to read.

The second set of conditions tests whether the text will fit inside the drawing space we have for it.

Next, we check to see whether our iterative calculations found an acceptable font size or not, and report an error if not:

```
if ( $height_text>$height_image_wo_margins ||
     $width_text>$width_image_wo_margins )
{
  // no readable font size will fit on button
  echo 'Text given will not fit on button.<br />';
}
```

Positioning the Text

If all was okay, we next work out a base position for the start of the text. This is the midpoint of the available space.

```
$text_x = $width_image/2.0 - $width_text/2.0;
$text_y = $height_image/2.0 - $height_text/2.0 ;
```

Because of the complications with the baseline relative co-ordinate system, we need to add some correction factors:

```
if ($left_text < 0)
    $text_x += abs($left_text);     // add factor for left overhang

$above_line_text = abs($bbox[7]);   // how far above the baseline?
$text_y += $above_line_text;        // add baseline factor

$text_y -= 2;  // adjustment factor for shape of our template
```

These correction factors allow for the baseline and a little adjustment because our image is a bit "top heavy."

Writing the Text onto the Button

After that, it's all smooth sailing. We set up the text color, which will be white:

```
$white = ImageColorAllocate ($im, 255, 255, 255);
```

We can then use the `ImageTTFText()` function to actually draw the text onto the button:

```
ImageTTFText ($im, $font_size, 0, $text_x, $text_y, $white, $fontname,
              $button_text);
```

This function takes quite a lot of parameters. In order, they are the image identifier, the font size in points, the angle we want to draw the text at, the starting X and Y coordinates of the text, the text color, the font file, and, finally, the actual text to go on the button.

> **Note**
>
> The font file needs to be available on the server, and is not required on the client's machine because she will see it as an image.

Finishing Up

Finally, we can output the button to the browser:

```
Header ('Content-type: image/png');
ImagePng ($im);
```

Then it's time to clean up resources and end the script:

```
ImageDestroy ($im);
```

That's it! If all went well, we should now have a button in the browser window that looks similar to the one you saw in Figure 19.5.

Drawing Figures and Graphing Data

In that last application, we looked at existing images and text. We haven't yet looked at an example with drawing, so we'll do that now.

In this example, we'll run a poll on our Web site to test whom users will vote for in a fictitious election. We'll store the results of the poll in a MySQL database, and draw a bar chart of the results using the image functions.

Graphing is the other thing these functions are primarily used for. You can chart any data you want—sales, Web hits, or whatever takes your fancy.

For this example, we have spent a few minutes setting up a MySQL database called poll. It contains one table called poll_results, which holds the candidates' names in the candidate column, and the number of votes they have received in the num_votes column. We have also created a user for this database called poll, with password poll. This takes about five minutes to set up, and you can do this by running the SQL script shown in Listing 19.3. You can do this piping the script through a root login using

```
mysql -u root -p < pollsetup.sql
```

Of course, you could also use the login of any user with the appropriate MySQL privileges.

Listing 19.3 **pollsetup.sql—Setting Up the Poll Database**

```
create database poll;
use poll;
create table poll_results (
  candidate varchar(30),
  num_votes int
);
insert into poll_results values
  ('John Smith', 0),
  ('Mary Jones', 0),
  ('Fred Bloggs', 0)
;
grant all privileges
on poll.*
to poll@localhost
identified by 'poll';
```

This database contains three candidates. We provide a voting interface via a page called vote.html. The code for this page is shown in Listing 19.4.

Listing 19.4   **vote.html—Users Can Cast Their Votes Here**

```html
<html>
<head>
  <title>Polling</title>
<head>
<body>
<h1>Pop Poll</h1>
<p>Who will you vote for in the election?</p>
<form method="post" action="show_poll.php">
<input type="radio" name="vote" value="John Smith">John Smith<br />
<input type="radio" name="vote" value="Mary Jones">Mary Jones<br />
<input type="radio" name="vote" value="Fred Bloggs">Fred Bloggs<br /><br />
<input type="submit"  value="Show results">
</form>
</body>
```

The output from this page is shown in Figure 19.7.

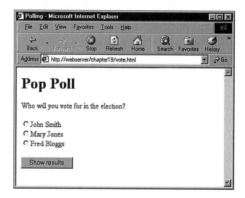

Figure 19.7   Users can cast their votes here, and clicking the
submit button will show them the current poll results.

The general idea is that, when users click the button, we will add their vote to the
database, get all the votes out of the database, and draw the bar chart of the current
results.

Typical output after some votes have cast is shown in Figure 19.8.

The script that generates this image is quite long. We have split it into four parts, and
we'll discuss each part separately.

Most of the script is familiar; we have looked at many MySQL examples similar to
this. We have looked at how to paint a background canvas in a solid color, and how to
print text labels on it.

The new parts of this script relate to drawing lines and rectangles. We will focus our
attention on these sections. Part 1 (of this four-part script) is shown in Listing 19.5.1.

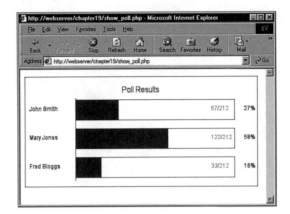

Figure 19.8   Vote results are created by drawing a series of
lines, rectangles, and text items onto a canvas.

Listing 19.5.1   **show_poll.php—Part 1 Updates the Vote Database and Retrieves the
New Results**

```php
<?php
/********************************************
  Database query to get poll info
********************************************/

// get vote from form
$vote=$HTTP_POST_VARS['vote'];

// log in to database
if (!$db_conn = @mysql_connect('localhost', 'poll', 'poll'))
{
  echo 'Could not connect to db<br />';
  exit;
};
@mysql_select_db('poll');

if (!empty($vote))  // if they filled the form out, add their vote
{
  $vote = addslashes($vote);
  $query = "update poll_results
            set num_votes = num_votes + 1
            where candidate = '$vote'";
  if(!($result = @mysql_query($query, $db_conn)))
  {
    echo 'Could not connect to db<br />';
```

Listing 19.5.1   **Continued**

```
    exit;
  }
};

// get current results of poll, regardless of whether they voted
$query = 'select * from poll_results';
if(!($result = @mysql_query($query, $db_conn)))
{
  echo 'Could not connect to db<br />';
  exit;
}
$num_candidates = mysql_num_rows($result);

// calculate total number of votes so far
$total_votes=0;
while ($row = mysql_fetch_object ($result))
{
    $total_votes += $row->num_votes;
}
mysql_data_seek($result, 0);  // reset result pointer
```

Part 1, shown in Listing 19.5.1, connects to the MySQL database, updates the votes according to what the user typed, and gets the new votes. After we have that information, we can begin making calculations in order to draw the graph. Part 2 is shown in Listing 19.5.2.

Listing 19.5.2   **showpoll.php—Part 2 Sets Up All the Variables for Drawing**

```
/*********************************************
  Initial calculations for graph
*********************************************/
// set up constants
putenv('GDFONTPATH=C:\WINNT\Fonts');
$width=500;        // width of image in pixels - this will fit in 640x480
$left_margin = 50; // space to leave on left of image
$right_margin= 50; // ditto right
$bar_height = 40;
$bar_spacing = $bar_height/2;
$font = 'arial';
$title_size= 16; // point
$main_size= 12; // point
$small_size= 12; // point
$text_indent = 10; // position for text labels on left

// set up initial point to draw from
$x = $left_margin + 60;  // place to draw baseline of the graph
```

Listing 19.5.2   **Continued**

```
$y = 50;                    // ditto
$bar_unit = ($width-($x+$right_margin)) / 100;    // one "point" on the graph

// calculate height of graph - bars plus gaps plus some margin
$height = $num_candidates * ($bar_height + $bar_spacing) + 50;
```

Part 2 sets up some variables that we will use to actually draw the graph.

Working out the values for these sorts of variables can be tedious, but a bit of fore-thought about what you want the finished image to look like will make the drawing process much easier. The values we use here were arrived at by sketching the desired effect on a piece of paper and estimating the required proportions.

The $width variable is the total width of the canvas we will use. We also set up the left and right margins (with $left_margin and $right_margin, respectively); the "fat-ness" and spacing between the bars ($bar_height and $bar_spacing); and the font, font sizes, and label position ($font, $title_size, $main_size, $small_size, and $text_indent).

Given these base values, we can then make a few calculations. We want to draw a baseline that all the bars stretch out from. We can work out the position for this baseline by using the left margin plus an allowance for the text labels for the X coordinate, and again an estimate from our sketch for the Y coordinate.

We also work out two important values: first, the distance on the graph that repre-sents one unit:

```
$bar_unit = ($width-($x+$right_margin)) / 100;    // one "point" on the graph
```

This is the maximum length of the bars—from the baseline to the right margin—divid-ed by 100 because our graph is going to show percentage values.

The second value is the total height that we need for the canvas:

```
$height = $num_candidates * ($bar_height + $bar_spacing) + 50;
```

This is basically the height per bar times the number of bars, plus an extra amount for the title. Part 3 is shown in Listing 19.5.3.

Listing 19.5.3   **showpoll.php—Part 3 Sets Up the Graph, Ready for the Data to Be Added**

```
/*********************************************
  Set up base image
*********************************************/
// create a blank canvas
$im = imagecreate($width,$height);

// Allocate colors
$white=ImageColorAllocate($im,255,255,255);
$blue=ImageColorAllocate($im,0,64,128);
```

Listing 19.5.3 **Continued**

```
$black=ImageColorAllocate($im,0,0,0);
$pink = ImageColorAllocate($im,255,78,243);

$text_color = $black;
$percent_color = $black;
$bg_color = $white;
$line_color = $black;
$bar_color = $blue;
$number_color = $pink;

// Create "canvas" to draw on
ImageFilledRectangle($im,0,0,$width,$height,$bg_color);

// Draw outline around canvas
ImageRectangle($im,0,0,$width-1,$height-1,$line_color);

// Add title
$title = 'Poll Results';
$title_dimensions = ImageTTFBBox($title_size, 0, $font, $title);
$title_length = $title_dimensions[2] - $title_dimensions[0];
$title_height = abs($title_dimensions[7] - $title_dimensions[1]);
$title_above_line = abs($title_dimensions[7]);
$title_x = ($width-$title_length)/2;  // center it in x
$title_y = ($y - $title_height)/2 + $title_above_line; // center in y gap
ImageTTFText($im, $title_size, 0, $title_x, $title_y,
              $text_color, $font, $title);

// Draw a base line from a little above first bar location
// to a little below last
ImageLine($im, $x, $y-5, $x, $height-15, $line_color);
```

In Part 3, we set up the basic image, allocate the colors, and then begin to draw the graph.

We fill in the background for the graph this time using

```
ImageFilledRectangle($im,0,0,$width,$height,$bg_color);
```

The `ImageFilledRectangle()` function, as you might imagine, draws a filled-in rectangle. The first parameter is, as usual, the image identifier. Then we must pass it the X and Y coordinates of the start point and the end point of the rectangle. These correspond to the upper-left corner and the lower-right corner, respectively. In this case, we are filling the entire canvas with the background color, which is the last parameter, and it's white.

We then call

```
ImageRectangle($im,0,0,$width-1,$height-1,$line_color);
```

to draw a black outline around the edge of the canvas. This function draws an outlined rectangle instead of a filled one. The parameters are the same. Notice that we have drawn the rectangle to $width-1 and $height-1—a canvas of width by height goes from (0, 0) to these values. If we drew it to $width and $height, the rectangle would be outside the canvas area.

We use the same logic and functions as we did in our last script to center and write the title on the graph.

Finally, we draw the baseline for the bars with

```
ImageLine ($im, $x, $y-5, $x, $height-15, $line_color);
```

The ImageLine() function draws a line on the image we specify ($im) from one set of coordinates ($x, $y-5) to another ($x, $height-15), in the color specified by $line_color.

In this case, we draw the baseline from a little above where we want to draw the first bar, to a little above the bottom of the canvas.

We are now ready to fill in the data on the graph. Part 4 is shown in Listing 19.5.4.

Listing 19.5.4   **showpoll.php—Part 4 Draws the Actual Data onto the Graph and Finishes Up**

```
/*******************************************
   Draw data into graph
*******************************************/
// Get each line of db data and draw corresponding bars
while ($row = mysql_fetch_object ($result))
{
  if ($total_votes > 0)
    $percent = intval(round(($row->num_votes/$total_votes)*100));
  else
    $percent = 0;

  // display percent for this value
  ImageTTFText ($im, $main_size, 0, $width-30, $y+($bar_height/2),
               $percent_color, $font, $percent.'%');
  if ($total_votes > 0)
    $right_value = intval(round(($row->num_votes/$total_votes)*100));
  else
    $right_value = 0;

  // length of bar for this value
  $bar_length = $x + ($right_value * $bar_unit);

  // draw bar for this value
  ImageFilledRectangle ($im, $x, $y-2, $bar_length, $y+$bar_height, $bar_color);
```

Listing 19.5.4 **Continued**

```
// draw title for this value
ImageTTFText($im, $main_size, 0, $text_indent, $y+($bar_height/2),
             $text_color, $font, $row->candidate);

// draw outline showing 100%
ImageRectangle($im, $bar_length+1, $y-2,
               ($x+(100*$bar_unit)), $y+$bar_height, $line_color);

// display numbers
ImageTTFText($im, $small_size, 0, $x+(100*$bar_unit)-50, $y+($bar_height/2),
             $number_color, $font, $row->num_votes.'/'.$total_votes);

// move down to next bar
$y=$y+($bar_height+$bar_spacing);
}


/*********************************************
  Display image
*********************************************/
Header('Content-type:  image/png');
ImagePng($im);


/*********************************************
  Clean up
*********************************************/
ImageDestroy($im);
?>
```

Part 4 goes through the candidates from the database one by one, works out the percentage of votes, and draws the bars and labels for each candidate.

Again we add labels using ImageTTFText(). We draw the bars as filled rectangles using ImageFilledRectangle():

```
ImageFilledRectangle($im, $x, $y-2, $bar_length, $y+$bar_height, $bar_color);
```

We add outlines for the 100% mark using ImageRectangle():

```
ImageRectangle($im, $bar_length+1, $y-2,
               ($x+(100*$bar_unit)), $y+$bar_height, $line_color);
```

After we have drawn all the bars, we again output the image using ImagePNG() and clean up after ourselves using ImageDestroy().

This is a long-ish script, but can be easily adapted to suit your needs, or to auto-generate polls via an interface. One important feature that this script is missing is any sort of anti-cheating mechanism. Users would quickly discover that they can vote repeatedly and make the result meaningless.

You can use a similar approach to draw line graphs, and even pie charts, if you are good at mathematics.

Other Image Functions

In addition to the image functions we have used in this chapter, there are functions to let you draw curved lines (ImageArc()) and polygons (ImagePolygon()), as well as variations on the ones we have used here. Always begin by sketching what you want to draw, and then you can hit the manual for any extra functions you might need.

Further Reading

A lot of reading material is available online. If you're having trouble with the image functions, it sometimes helps to look at the source documentation for gd because the PHP functions are wrappers for this library. The gd documentation is available at

http://www.boutell.com/gd/

There are also some excellent tutorials on particular types of graph applications, particularly at Zend and Devshed:

http://www.zend.com
http://devshed.com

The bar chart application in this chapter was inspired by the dynamic bar graph script written by Steve Maranda, available from Devshed.

Next

In the next chapter, we'll tackle PHP's handy session control functionality, new in PHP 4.

20

Using Session Control in PHP

THIS CHAPTER WILL DISCUSS THE SESSION control functionality in PHP 4. We will cover

- What session control is
- Cookies
- Setting up a session
- Session variables
- Sessions and authentication

What Session Control Is

You might have heard it said that "HTTP is a stateless protocol." What this means is that the protocol has no built-in way of maintaining state between two transactions. When a user requests one page, followed by another, HTTP does not provide a way for us to tell that both requests came from the same user.

The idea of session control is to be able to track a user during a single session on a Web site.

If we can do this, we can easily support logging in a user and showing content according to her authorization level or personal preferences. We can track the user's behavior. We can implement shopping carts.

In earlier versions of PHP, session control was supported via PHPLib, the PHP Base Library, which is still a useful toolkit. You can read about it at

http://phplib.sourceforge.net/

As of version 4, PHP includes native session control functions. They are conceptually similar to PHPLib, but PHPLib offers some extra functionality. If you find that the native functions do not quite meet your needs, you might want to take a look at it.

Basic Session Functionality

Sessions in PHP are driven by a unique session ID, a cryptographically random number. This session ID is generated by PHP and stored on the client side for the lifetime of a session. It can be either stored on a user's computer in a cookie, or passed along through URLs.

The session ID acts as a key that allows you to register particular variables as so-called session variables. The contents of these variables are stored at the server. The session ID is the only information visible at the client side. If, at the time of a particular connection to your site, the session ID is visible either through a cookie or the URL, you can access the session variables stored on the server for that session. By default, the session variables are stored in flat files on the server. (You can change this to use a database if you are willing to write your own function—more on this in the section "Configuring Session Control.")

You have probably used Web sites that store a session ID in the URL. If there's a string of random looking data in your URL, it is likely to be some form of session control.

Cookies are a different solution to the problem of preserving state across a number of transactions while still having a clean looking URL.

What Is a Cookie?

A *cookie* is a small piece of information that scripts can store on a client-side machine. You can set a cookie on a user's machine by sending an HTTP header containing data in the following format:

```
Set-Cookie: NAME=VALUE; [expires=DATE;] [path=PATH;]
 [domain=DOMAIN_NAME;] [secure]
```

This will create a cookie called NAME with the value VALUE. The other parameters are all optional. The expires field sets a date beyond which the cookie is no longer relevant. (Note that if no expiry date is set, the cookie is effectively permanent unless manually deleted by you or the user.) Together, the path and domain can be used to specify the URL or URLs for which the cookie is relevant. The secure keyword means that the cookie will not be sent over a plain HTTP connection.

When a browser connects to an URL, it first searches the cookies stored locally. If any of them are relevant to the URL being connected to, they will be transmitted back to the server.

Setting Cookies from PHP

You can manually set cookies in PHP using the setcookie() function. It has the following prototype:

```
int setcookie (string name [, string value [, int expire [, string path
[, string domain [, int secure]]]]])
```

The parameters correspond exactly to the ones in the Set-Cookie header mentioned previously.

If you set a cookie as

```
setcookie ('mycookie', 'value');
```

when the user visits the next page in your site (or reloads the current page), you will have access to the cookie via either $_COOKIE['mycookie'] or $HTTP_COOKIE_VARS["mycookie"]. (Or, if you have register_globals turned on, directly as $mycookie.)

You can delete a cookie by calling setcookie() again with the same cookie name and an expiry time in the past. You can also set a cookie manually via the Header() function and the cookie syntax given previously. One tip is that cookie headers must be sent *before any other headers*, or they will not work. (This is a cookie limitation rather than a PHP limitation.)

Using Cookies with Sessions

Cookies have some associated problems: Some browsers do not accept cookies, and some users might have disabled cookies in their browsers. This is one of the reasons PHP sessions use a dual cookie/URL method. (We'll discuss more about this in a minute.) When you are using PHP sessions, you will not have to manually set cookies. The session functions will take care of this for you.

You can use the function session_get_cookie_params() to see the contents of the cookie set by session control. It returns an associative array containing the elements lifetime, path, and domain.

You can also use

```
session_set_cookie_params($lifetime, $path, $domain [, $secure]);
```

to set the session cookie parameters.

If you want to read more about cookies, you can consult the cookie specification on Netscape's site:

```
http://home.netscape.com/newsref/std/cookie_spec.html
```

(You can probably ignore the fact that this document calls itself a "preliminary specification"—it's been that way since 1995.)

Storing the Session ID

PHP will use cookies by default with sessions. If possible, a cookie will be set to store the session ID.

The other method it can use is adding the session ID to the URL. You can set this to happen automatically if you compile PHP with the --enable-trans-sid option. This is the default from PHP 4.2 onward.

Alternatively, you can manually embed the session ID in links so that it is passed along. The session ID is stored in the constant SID. To pass it along manually, you add it to the end of a link similar to a GET parameter:

```
<a href="link.php?<?=SID?>">
```

It is generally easier to compile with --enable-trans-sid, where possible.

Implementing Simple Sessions

The basic steps of using sessions are

- Starting a session
- Registering session variables
- Using session variables
- Deregistering variables and destroying the session

Note that these steps don't necessarily all happen in the same script, and some of them will happen in multiple scripts. Let's talk about each of these steps in turn.

Starting a Session

Before you can use session functionality, you need to actually begin a session. There are three ways you can do this.

The first, and simplest, is to begin a script with a call to the session_start() function:

```
session_start();
```

This function checks to see whether there is already a current session ID. If not, it will create one. If one already exists, it essentially loads the registered session variables so that you can use them.

It's a good idea to call session_start() at the start of all your scripts that use sessions.

Second, a session will be started when you try to register a session variable using session_register() (see the next section).

The third way you can begin a session is to set PHP to start one automatically when someone comes to your site. You can do this with the session.auto_start option in your php.ini file—we'll look at this when we discuss configuration.

Registering Session Variables

Registering session variables has recently changed in PHP.

Session variables are stored in the superglobal array $_SESSION as of PHP 4.1, and also in the older $HTTP_SESSION_VARS. In order to create a session variable you simply set an element in one of these arrays, as follows:

```
$_SESSION['myvar'] = 5;
```

or

```
$HTTP_SESSION_VARS['myvar'] = 5;
```

If you are using an older version of PHP, or if you have `register_globals` turned on, in order for a variable to be tracked from one script to another, you can to register it with a call to `session_register()`. For example, to register the variable $myvar, you could use the following code

```
$myvar = 5;
session_register('myvar');
```

Note that you need to pass a string containing the name of the variable to `session_register()`. This string should not include the $ symbol.

This will record the variable name and track its value. The variable will be tracked until the session ends, or until you manually deregister it.

You can register more than one variable at once by providing a comma-separated list of variable names; for example

```
session_register('myvar1', 'myvar2');
```

If you are using the `$_SESSION` or `$HTTP_SESSION_VARS` arrays, do *not* try and use the `session_register()` function.

Using Session Variables

To bring a session variable into scope so that it can be used, you must first start a session. You can then access the variable via the arrays `$_SESSION` or `$HTTP_SESSION_VARS` as, for example, `$HTTP_SESSION_VARS['myvar']`. If you have `register_globals` turned on you can access it via its short form name, for example $myvar.

If you have `register_globals` on, bear in mind that a session variable cannot be overridden by GET or POST data, which is a good security feature, but something to bear in mind when coding.

On the other hand, you need to be careful when checking if session variables have been set (via, say, `isset()` or `empty()`). Remember that variables can be set by the user via GET or POST. You can check a variable to see if it is a registered session variable by calling the `session_is_registered()` function. You call this function like this:

```
$result = session_is_registered('myvar');
```

This will check whether $myvar is a registered session variable and return `true` or `false`.

If using `$_SESSION` or `$HTTP_POST_VARS` you should NOT use the `session_is_registered()` function. You can just check whether the array elements are set directly using, for example:

```
if (isset($HTTP_SESSION_VARS['myvar'])) ...
```

Deregistering Variables and Destroying the Session

When you are finished with a session variable, you can deregister it.

If you are using the $_SESSION or $HTTP_SESSION_VARS arrays, you can do this directly, for example:

```
unset($HTTP_SESSION_VARS['myvar']);
```

If you have register_globals on, you need to clear session variables using the session_unregister() function, as follows:

```
session_unregister("myvar");
```

Again, this function requires the name of the variable you want to deregister as a string, without the $ symbol. This function can only deregister a single session variable at a time (unlike session_register()). You can, however, use session_unset() to deregister all the current session variables.

Do *not* try to use the session_unregister() function if you are using $_SESSION or $HTTP_SESSION_VARS directly.

When you are finished with a session, you should first deregister all the variables and then call

```
session_destroy();
```

to clean up the session ID.

Simple Session Example

Some of this might seem a little abstract, so let's look at an example. We'll implement a set of three pages.

On the first page, we'll start a session and register the variable $HTTP_SESSION_VARS['sess_var']. The code to do this is shown in Listing 20.1.

Listing 20.1   **page1.php—Starting a Session and Registering a Variable**

```php
<?php
  session_start();

  $HTTP_SESSION_VARS['sess_var'] = "Hello world!";

  echo 'The content of $HTTP_SESSION_VARS[\'sess_var\'] is '
       .$HTTP_SESSION_VARS['sess_var'].'<br />';
?>
<a href="page2.php">Next page</a>
```

We have registered the variable and set its value. The output of this script is shown in Figure 20.1.

Figure 20.1   Initial value of the session variable shown by page1.php.

The *final* value of the variable on the page is the one that will be available on subsequent pages. At the end of the script, the session variable is *serialized*, or frozen, until it is reloaded via the next call to session_start().

We therefore begin the next script by calling session_start(). This script is shown in Listing 20.2.

Listing 20.2   page2.php—Accessing a Session Variable and Deregistering It

```
<?php
  session_start();

  echo 'The content of $HTTP_SESSION_VARS[\'sess_var\'] is '
       .$HTTP_SESSION_VARS['sess_var'].'<br />';

  unset($HTTP_SESSION_VARS['sess_var']);
?>
<a href="page3.php">Next page</a>
```

After calling session_start(), the variable $HTTP_SESSION_VARS['sess_var'] is available with its previously stored value, as you can see in Figure 20.2.

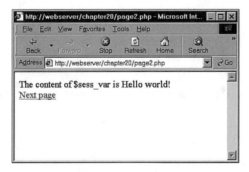

Figure 20.2   The value of the session variable has been passed along via the session ID to page2.php.

After we have used the variable, we unset it. The session still exists, but the variable
$HTTP_SESSION_VARS['sess_var'] is no longer a registered variable.

Finally we pass along to page3.php, the final script in our example. The code for this
script is shown in Listing 20.3.

Listing 20.3   **page3.php—Ending the Session**

```php
<?php

  session_start();

  echo 'The content of $HTTP_SESSION_VARS[\'sess_var\'] is '
       .$HTTP_SESSION_VARS['sess_var'].'<br />';

  session_destroy();
?>
```

As you can see in Figure 20.3, we no longer have access to the persistent value of
$HTTP_SESSION_VARS['sess_var'].

With some PHP versions prior to 4.3 you might encounter a bug when trying to
unset elements of $HTTP_SESSION_VARS or $_SESSION. If you find that you are
unable to unset elements (that is, they stay set) you can revert to using session_unreg-
ister() to clear these variables.

Using session_unregister() is no longer recommended, but if you want your code
to work reliably on all versions of PHP4 it is your only option.

Figure 20.3   The deregistered variable is no longer available.

We finish by calling session_destroy() to dispose of the session ID.

Configuring Session Control

There is a set of configuration options for sessions that you can set in your `php.ini` file. Some of the more useful options, and a description of each, are shown in Table 20.1.

Table 20.1   **Session Configuration Options**

Option Name	Default	Effect
session.auto_start	0 (disabled)	Automatically starts sessions.
session.cache_expire	180	Sets time-to-live for cached session pages, in minutes.
session.cookie_domain	none	Domain to set in session cookie.
session.cookie_lifetime	0	How long the session ID cookie will last on the user's machine. The default, 0, will last until the browser is closed.
session.cookie_path	/	Path to set in session cookie.
session.name	PHPSESSID	The name of the session that is used as the cookie name on a user's system.
session.save_handler	files	Defines where session data is stored. You can set this to point to a database, but you have to write your own functions.
session.save_path	/tmp	The path where session data is stored. More generally, the argument passed to the save handled and defined by `session.save_handler`.
session.use_cookies	1 (enabled)	Configures sessions to use cookies on the client side.

Implementing Authentication with Session Control

Finally, we will look at a more substantial example using session control.

Possibly the most common use of session control is to keep track of users after they have been authenticated via a login mechanism. In this example, we will combine authentication from a MySQL database with use of sessions to provide this functionality.

This functionality will form the basis of the project in Chapter 24, "Building User Authentication and Personalization," and will be reused in the other projects.

We will reuse the authentication database we set up in Chapter 14, "Implementing Authentication with PHP and MySQL," for using mod_auth_mysql. You can check Listing 14.3 in that chapter for details of the database.

The example consists of three simple scripts. The first, `authmain.php`, provides a login form and authentication for members of our Web site. The second, `members_only.php`, displays information only to members who have logged in successfully. The third, `logout.php`, logs out a member.

To understand how this works, look at Figure 20.4. This is the initial page displayed by `authmain.php`.

Figure 20.4   Because the user has not yet logged in, show her a login page.

This page gives the user a place to log in. If she attempts to access the Members section without logging in first, she will get the message shown in Figure 20.5.

Figure 20.5   Users who haven't logged in can't see the site content; they will be shown this message instead.

However, if the user logs in first (with username: testuser and password: test123 as set up in Chapter 14) and then attempts to see the Members page, she will get the output shown in Figure 20.6.

Figure 20.6   After the user has logged in, she can access the Members' areas.

Let's look at the code for this application. Most of the code is in `authmain.php`. This script can be seen in Listing 20.4. We will go through it bit by bit.

Listing 20.4   **authmain.php—The Main Part of the Authentication Application**

```php
<?php
session_start();

if (isset($HTTP_POST_VARS['userid']) && isset($HTTP_POST_VARS['password']))
{
  // if the user has just tried to log in
  $userid = $HTTP_POST_VARS['userid'];
  $password = $HTTP_POST_VARS['password'];

  $db_conn = mysql_connect('localhost', 'webauth', 'webauth');
  mysql_select_db('auth', $db_conn);
  $query = 'select * from auth '
         ."where name='$userid' "
         ." and pass=password('$password')";
  $result = mysql_query($query, $db_conn);
  if (mysql_num_rows($result) >0 )
  {
    // if they are in the database register the user id
    $HTTP_SESSION_VARS['valid_user'] = $userid;
```

Listing 20.4 **Continued**

```
    }
}
?>
<html>
<body>
<h1>Home page</h1>
<?
  if (isset($HTTP_SESSION_VARS['valid_user']))
  {
    echo 'You are logged in as: '.$HTTP_SESSION_VARS['valid_user'].' <br />';
    echo '<a href="logout.php">Log out</a><br />';
  }
  else
  {
    if (isset($userid))
    {
      // if they've tried and failed to log in
      echo 'Could not log you in';
    }
    else
    {
      // they have not tried to log in yet or have logged out
      echo 'You are not logged in.<br />';
    }

    // provide form to log in
    echo '<form method="post" action="authmain.php">';
    echo '<table>';
    echo '<tr><td>Userid:</td>';
    echo '<td><input type="text" name="userid"></td></tr>';
    echo '<tr><td>Password:</td>';
    echo '<td><input type="password" name="password"></td></tr>';
    echo '<tr><td colspan="2" align="center">';
    echo '<input type="submit" value="Log in"></td></tr>';
    echo '</table></form>';
  }
?>
<br>
<a href="members_only.php">Members section</a>
</body>
</html>
```

Some reasonably complicated logic is in this script because it displays the login form, is also the action of the form and contains HTML for a successful and failed login attempt. The script's activities revolve around the valid_user session variable. The basic idea is

that if someone logs in successfully, we will register a session variable called $HTTP_SES-
SION_VARS['valid_user'] that contains her userid.

The first thing we do in the script is call session_start(). This will load in the session variable valid_user if it has been registered.

In the first pass through the script, none of the if conditions will apply and the user
will fall through to the end of the script, where we tell her that she is not logged in and
provide her with a form to do so:

```
echo '<form method="post" action="authmain.php">';
echo '<table>';
echo '<tr><td>Userid:</td>';
echo '<td><input type="text" name="userid"></td></tr>';
echo '<tr><td>Password:</td>';
echo '<td><input type="password" name="password"></td></tr>';
echo '<tr><td colspan="2" align="center">';
echo '<input type="submit" value="Log in"></td></tr>';
echo '</table></form>';
```

When she presses the submit button on the form, this script is reinvoked and we start
again from the top. This time, we will have a userid and password to authenticate, stored
as $HTTP_POST_VARS['userid'] and $HTTP_POST_VARS['password']. If these variables
are set, we go into the authentication block:

```
if (isset($HTTP_POST_VARS['userid']) && isset($HTTP_POST_VARS['password']))
{
  // if the user has just tried to log in
  $userid = $HTTP_POST_VARS['userid'];
  $password = $HTTP_POST_VARS['password'];

  $db_conn = mysql_connect('localhost', 'webauth', 'webauth');
  mysql_select_db('auth', $db_conn);
  $query = 'select * from auth '
          ."where name='$userid' "
          ." and pass=password('$password')";
  $result = mysql_query($query, $db_conn);
```

We connect to a MySQL database and check the userid and password. If these are a
matching pair in the database, we create the variable
$HTTP_SESSION_VARS['valid_user'] that contains the userid for this particular user, so
we know who is logged in further down the track.

```
  if (mysql_num_rows($result) >0 )
  {
    // if they are in the database register the user id
    $HTTP_SESSION_VARS['valid_user'] = $userid;
  }
}
```

Because we now know who she is, we don't need to show her the login form again. Instead, we'll tell her we know who she is, and give her the option to log out:

```
if (isset($HTTP_SESSION_VARS['valid_user']))
{
  echo 'You are logged in as: '.$HTTP_SESSION_VARS['valid_user'].' <br />';
  echo '<a href="logout.php">Log out</a><br />';
}
```

If we tried to log her in and failed for some reason, we'll have a userid but not an `$HTTP_SESSION_VARS['valid_user']` variable, so we can give her an error message:

```
if (isset($userid))
{
  // if they've tried and failed to log in
  echo 'Could not log you in';
}
```

That's it for the main script. Now, let's look at the Members page. The code for this script is shown in Listing 20.5.

Listing 20.5   members_only.php—The Code for the Members' Section of Our Web Site Checks for Valid Users

```
<?php
  session_start();

  echo '<h1>Members only</h1>';

  // check session variable

  if (isset($HTTP_SESSION_VARS['valid_user']))
  {
    echo '<p>You are logged in as '.$HTTP_SESSION_VARS['valid_user'].'.</p>';
    echo '<p>Members only content goes here</p>';
  }
  else
  {
    echo '<p>You are not logged in.</p>';
    echo '<p>Only logged in members may see this page.</p>';
  }

  echo '<a href="authmain.php">Back to main page</a>';
?>
```

This code is very simple. All it does is start a session, and check if the current session contains a registered user by checking if the value of `$HTTP_SESSION_VARS` ['valid_user'] is set. If the user is logged in, we show her the members' content; otherwise, we tell her that she is not authorized.

Finally we have the logout.php script that signs a user out of the system. The code for this script is shown in Listing 20.6.

Listing 20.6   **logout.php—This Script Deregisters the Session Variable and Destroys the Session**

```php
<?php
  session_start();

  $old_user = $HTTP_SESSION_VARS['valid_user'];  // store  to test if they *were*
  logged in
  unset($HTTP_SESSION_VARS['valid_user']);
  session_destroy();
?>
<html>
<body>
<h1>Log out</h1>
<?php
  if (!empty($old_user))
  {
    echo 'Logged out.<br />';
  }
  else
  {
    // if they weren't logged in but came to this page somehow
    echo 'You were not logged in, and so have not been logged out.<br />';
  }
?>
<a href="authmain.php">Back to main page</a>
</body>
</html>
```

The code's very simple, but we do a little fancy footwork. We start a session, store the user's old username, unset the valid_user variable, and destroy the session. We then give the user a message that will be different if she was logged out, or was not logged in to begin with.

This simple set of scripts will form the basis for a lot of the work we'll do in later chapters.

Further Reading

Native sessions are new to PHP 4, but sessions have been provided by PHPLib for a while. The best things to read for more information are the PHPLib homepage and the cookies specification. We've listed both these URLs earlier in the chapter, but we'll reprint them here for reference:

```
http://phplib.sourceforge.net/
http://home.netscape.com/newsref/std/cookie_spec.html
```

Next

We're almost finished with this section of the book.

Before we move on to the projects, we'll briefly discuss some of the useful odds and ends of PHP that we haven't covered elsewhere.

21

Other Useful Features

Some useful PHP functions and features do not fit into any particular category. This chapter will explain these features.

We'll look at

- Using magic quotes
- Evaluating strings with `eval()`
- Terminating execution: `die` and `exit`
- Serialization
- Getting information about the PHP environment
- Temporarily altering the runtime environment
- Loading PHP extensions
- Source highlighting

Using Magic Quotes

You have probably noticed that you need to be careful when using quote symbols (' and ") and back slashes (\\) within strings. PHP will get confused by an attempted string statement like

```
echo "color = "#FFFFFF"";
```

and give a parse error. To include quotes inside a string, use the quote type that is different from the quotes enclosing the string. For example

```
echo "color = '#FFFFFF'";
```

or

```
echo 'color = "#FFFFFF"';
```

will both be valid.

The same problem occurs with user input, as well as input and output to, or from, other programs.

Trying to run a `mysql` query like

```
insert into company values ('Bob's Auto Parts');
```

will produce similar confusion in MySQL's parser.

We have already looked at the use of `addslashes()` and `stripslashes()` that will escape out any single quote, double quote, backslash, and NUL characters.

PHP has a useful capability to automatically or magically add and strip slashes for you. With two settings in your `php.ini` file, you can turn on or off magic quoting for GET, POST, cookie data, and for other sources.

The value of the `magic_quotes_gpc` directive controls whether magic quoting is used for GET, POST, and cookie operations.

With `magic_quotes_gpc` on, if somebody typed `"Bob's Auto Parts"` into a form on your site, your script would receive `"Bob\'s Auto Parts"` because the quote will be escaped for you.

The function `get_magic_quotes_gpc()` returns either 1 or 0, telling you the current value of `magic_quotes_gpc`. This is most useful for testing if you need to `stripslashes()` from data received from the user.

The value of `magic_quotes_runtime`, controls whether magic quoting is used by functions that get data from databases and files.

To get the value of `magic_quotes_runtime`, use the function `get_magic_quotes_runtime()`. This function returns either 1 or 0. Magic quoting can be turned on for a particular script using the function `set_magic_quotes_runtime()`.

Evaluating Strings: eval()

The function `eval()` will evaluate a string as PHP code.

For example,

```
eval ( "echo 'Hello World';" );
```

will take the contents of the string and execute it. This line will produce the same output as

```
echo 'Hello World';
```

There are a variety of cases in which `eval()` can be useful. You might want to store blocks of code in a database, and retrieve and `eval()` them at a later point. You might want to generate code in a loop, and then use `eval()` to execute it.

You can usefully use `eval()` to update or correct existing code. If you had a large collection of scripts that needed a predictable change, it would be possible (but inefficient) to write a script that loads an old script into a string, runs a `regexp` to make changes, and then uses `eval()` to execute the modified script.

It is even conceivable that a very trusting person somewhere might want to allow PHP code to be entered in a browser and executed on her server.

Terminating Execution: die and exit

So far in this book we have used the language construct `exit` to stop execution of a script. As you probably recall, it appears on a line by itself, like this:

```
exit;
```

It does not return anything. You can alternatively use its alias `die()`.

For a slightly more useful termination, we can pass a parameter to `exit()`. This can be used to output an error message or execute a function before terminating a script. This will be familiar to Perl programmers.

For example:

```
exit('Script ending now');
```

More commonly it is `ored` with a statement that might fail, such as opening a file or connecting to a database:

```
mysql_query($query) or die('Could not execute query');
```

Instead of just printing an error message, you can call one last function before the script terminates:

```
function err_msg()
{
    echo 'MySQL error was: ';
    echo mysql_error();
}

mysql_query($query) or die(err_msg());
```

This can be useful as a way of giving the user some reason why the script failed. Alternatively, you could email yourself so that you know if a major error has occurred, or add errors to a log file.

Serialization

Serialization is the process of turning anything you can store in a PHP variable or object into a bytestream that can be stored in a database or passed along via a URL from page to page. Without this, it is difficult to store or pass the entire contents of an array or object.

It has decreased in usefulness since the introduction of session control. Serializing data is principally used for the types of things you would now use session control for. In fact, the session control functions serialize session variables in order to store them between HTTP requests.

However, you might still want to store a PHP array or object in a file or database. If you do, there are two functions you need to know how to use: `serialize()` and `unserialize()`.

You can call the `serialize()` function as follows:

```
$serial_object = serialize($my_object);
```

If you want to know what the serialization actually does, take a look at what is returned from serialize. It turns the contents of an object or array into a string.

For example, we can look at the output of running serialize on a simple employee object, defined and instantiated thus:

```
class employee
{
  var $name;
  var $employee_id;
};

$this_emp = new employee;
$this_emp->name = 'Fred';
$this_emp->employee_id = 5324;
```

If we serialize this and echo it to the browser, the output is

```
O:8:"employee":2:{s:4:"name";s:4:"Fred";s:11:"employee_id";i:5324;}
```

It is fairly easy to see the relationship between the original object data and the serialized data.

As the serialized data is just text, you can write it to a database or whatever you like. Be aware that you should `addslashes()` to any data before writing it to a database, as per usual. You can see the need for this by noting the quotes in the previous serialized string.

To get the object back, call `unserialize()`:

```
$new_object = unserialize($serial_object);
```

Obviously, if you called `addslashes()` before putting the object into a database, you will need to call `stripslashes()` before unserializing the string.

Another point to note when serializing classes or using them as session variables: PHP needs to know the structure of a class before it can reinstantiate the class. Therefore, you will need to include the class definition file before calling `session_start()` or `unserialize()`.

Getting Information About the PHP Environment

A number of functions can be used to find out information about how PHP is configured.

Finding Out What Extensions Are Loaded

You can easily see what function sets are available, and what functions are available in each of those sets using the get_loaded_extensions() and get_extension_funcs() functions.

The get_loaded_extensions() function returns an array of all the function sets currently available to PHP. Given the name of a particular function set or extension, get_extension_funcs() returns an array of the functions in that set.

The script in Listing 21.1 lists all the functions available to your PHP installation by using these two functions.

Listing 21.1   **list_functions.php—This Script Lists All the Extensions Available to PHP, and with Each Extension, Provides a Bulleted List of Functions in That Extension**

```php
<?php
  echo 'Function sets supported in this install are:<br />';
  $extensions = get_loaded_extensions();
  foreach ($extensions as $each_ext)
  {
    echo "$each_ext <br />";
    echo '<ul>';
    $ext_funcs = get_extension_funcs($each_ext);
    foreach($ext_funcs as $func)
    {
        echo "<li> $func </li>";
    }
    echo '</ul>';
  }
?>
```

Note that the get_loaded_extensions() function doesn't take any parameters, and the get_extension_funcs() function takes the name of the extension as its only parameter.

This information can be helpful if you are trying to tell whether you have successfully installed an extension.

Identifying the Script Owner

You can find out the user who owns the script being run with a call to the get_current_user() function, as follows:

```
echo get_current_user();
```

This can sometimes be useful for solving permissions issues.

Finding Out When the Script Was Modified

Adding a last modification date to each page in a site is a fairly popular thing to do.

You can check the last modification date of a script with the `getlastmod()` (note the lack of underscores in the function name) function, as follows:

```
echo date('g:i a, j M Y',getlastmod());
```

The function returns a Unix timestamp, which we can feed to `date()` as we have done here, to produce a human readable date.

Loading Extensions Dynamically

You can actually load extension libraries at runtime, if they are not compiled in, using the `dl()` function.

This function expects as a parameter the name of the file containing the library. Under Unix, these will be filenames ending in `.so`; under Windows, they will end in `.dll`.

An example of a call to `dl()` is

```
dl('php_ftp.dll');
```

This will dynamically load the FTP extension (on a Windows machine).

You shouldn't specify the directory where the file lives: Instead, you should configure this in the `php.ini` file. A directive called `extension_dir` will specify the directory where PHP will look for libraries to dynamically load.

If you find you are having trouble dynamically loading extensions, also check your `php.ini` file for the `enable_dl` directive. If it's off, you won't be able to dynamically load extensions. Particularly if the machine you work on is not your own, this might be disabled for security reasons. You also won't be able to use `dl()` if PHP is running in safe mode.

Temporarily Altering the Runtime Environment

You can view the directives set in the php.ini file, or change them for the life of a single script. This can be particularly useful, for example, in conjunction with the `max_execution_time` directive if you know your script will take some time to run.

You can access and change the directives using the twin functions `ini_get()` and `ini_set()`. Listing 21.2 shows a simple script that uses these functions.

Listing 21.2   **iniset.php—This Script Resets Variables from the php.ini File**

```php
<?php
    $old_max_execution_time = ini_set('max_execution_time', 120);
    echo "old timeout is $old_max_execution_time <br />";

    $max_execution_time = ini_get('max_execution_time');
    echo "new timeout is $max_execution_time <br />";
?>
```

The `ini_set()` function takes two parameters. The first is the name of the configuration directive from php.ini that we would like to change, and the second is the value we would like to change it to. It returns the previous value of the directive.

In this case, we are resetting the value from the default 30 second maximum time for a script to run to 120 seconds.

The `ini_get()` function simply checks the value of a particular configuration directive. The directive name should be passed to it as a string. Here we are just using it to check that the value really did change.

Source Highlighting

PHP comes with a built-in syntax highlighter, similar to many IDEs. In particular, it is useful for sharing code with others, or presenting it for discussion on a Web page.

The functions `show_source()` and `highlight_file()` are the same. (The `show_source()` function is actually an alias for `highlight_file()`.)

Both of these functions accept a filename as parameter. (This file should be a PHP file, otherwise you won't get a very meaningful result.) For example,

```php
show_source('list_functions.php');
```

The file will be echoed to the browser with the text highlighted in various colors depending on whether it is a string, a comment, a keyword, or HTML. The output is printed on a background color. Content that doesn't fit into any of these categories is printed in a default color.

The `highlight_string()` function works similarly, but it takes a string as parameter, and prints it to the browser in a syntax-highlighted format.

You can set the colors for syntax highlighting in your `php.ini` file. The section you are looking for looks like this:

```ini
; Colors for Syntax Highlighting mode
highlight.string    =    #DD0000
highlight.comment   =    #FF8000
highlight.keyword   =    #007700
highlight.bg        =    #FFFFFF
highlight.default   =    #0000BB
highlight.html      =    #000000
```

The colors are in standard HTML RGB format.

Next

Part V, "Building Practical PHP and MySQL Projects," covers a number of relatively complicated practical projects using PHP and MySQL. These projects provide useful examples for similar tasks you might have, and demonstrate the use of PHP and MySQL on larger projects.

Chapter 22, "Using PHP and MySQL for Large Projects," addresses some of the issues you face when coding larger projects using PHP. These include software engineering principles such as design, documentation, and change management.

V

Building Practical PHP and MySQL Projects

22

Using PHP and MySQL for Large Projects

In the earlier parts of this book, we've discussed various components of and uses for PHP and MySQL. Although we've tried to make all our examples interesting and relevant, they have been pretty simple, consisting of one or two scripts of up to 100 or so lines of code.

When you are building real world Web applications, things are rarely this simple. There was a time a few years ago when an "interactive" Web site had form mail and that was it. However, these days, Web sites have become Web applications—that is, a regular piece of software delivered over the Web. This change in focus means a change in scale. Web sites grow from a handful of scripts to thousands and thousands of lines of code. Projects of this size require planning and management like any other software development.

Before we move on to look at the projects in this section of the book, we'll look at some of the techniques you can use to manage sizable Web projects. This is an emerging art and it's obviously difficult to get it right: You can see this by observation in the marketplace.

In this chapter, we'll look at

- Applying software engineering to Web development
- Planning and running a Web application project
- Re-using code
- Writing maintainable code
- Implementing version control
- Choosing a development environment
- Documenting your project

- Prototyping
- Separating logic, content, and presentation: PHP, HTML, and CSS
- Optimizing code

Applying Software Engineering to Web Development

As you probably already know, software engineering is the application of a systematic, quantifiable approach to software development. That is, it is the application of engineering principles to software development.

It is also an approach that is noticeably lacking in many Web projects. This is for two main reasons.

The first reason is that Web development is often managed in the same way as the development of written reports. It is an exercise in document structure, graphic design, and production. This is a document-oriented paradigm. This is all well and good for static sites of small to medium size, but as we increase the amount of dynamic content in Web sites to the level in which Web sites offer services rather than documents, this paradigm no longer fits. Many people do not think to use software engineering practices for a web project at all.

The second reason software engineering practices are not used is that Web application development is different from normal application development in many ways. We deal with much shorter lead times, a constant pressure to have the site built **now**. Software engineering is all about doing things in an orderly, planned manner, and spending time on planning. With Web projects, often the perception is that we don't have the time to plan.

When we fail to plan Web projects, we end up with the same problems as if we fail to plan any software project: buggy applications, missed deadlines, and unreadable code.

The trick, then, is in finding the parts of software engineering that work in this new discipline of Web application development, and discarding the parts that don't.

Planning and Running a Web Application Project

There is no best methodology or project lifecycle for Web projects. There are, however, a number of things you should consider doing for your project. We'll list them here, and talk about some of them in more detail in the following sections. These considerations are in a specific order, but you don't have to follow this order if it doesn't suit your project. The emphasis here is on being aware of the issues and choosing techniques that will work for you.

- Before you begin, think about what you are trying to build. Think about the end goal. Think about who is going to use your Web application; that is, your targeted audience. Many Web projects that are technically perfect fail because nobody checked that there were interested users for such an application.

- Try and break your application down in to components. What parts or process steps does your application have? How will each of those components work? How will they fit together? Drawing up scenarios, storyboards, or even use cases can be useful for figuring this out.

- After you have a list of components, see which of these already exist. If a prewritten module has that functionality, look at using it. Don't forget to look inside and outside your organization for existing code. Particularly in the Open Source community, many preexisting code components are freely available for use. Decide what code you have to write from scratch and roughly how big of a job that is.

- Make decisions about process issues. This is ignored too often in Web projects. By process issues, I mean things such as coding standards, directory structures, management of version control, development environment, documentation level and standards, and task allocations to team members.

- Build a prototype, based on all the previous information. Show it to users. Iterate.

- Remember that, in all of this, it is important and useful to separate content and logic in your application. We'll explain this idea in more detail in a minute.

- Make any optimizations you think are necessary.

- As you go, test, as thoroughly as you would with any software development project.

Reusing Code

Programmers often make the mistake of rewriting code that already exists. When you know what application components you need, or on a smaller scale, what functions you need, check what's available before beginning development.

One of the strengths of PHP as a language is its large built-in function library. Always check to see if a function exists that does what you are trying to do. It usually isn't too hard to find the one you want. A good way to do this is to browse the manual by function group.

Sometimes programmers rewrite functions accidentally because they haven't looked in the manual to see if an existing function supplies the functionality they need. Always keep the manual bookmarked if you are online, or download the current version and browse it locally. Take note, however, that the online manual gets updated quite frequently, and you also have the advantage of being able to browse the annotated manual. The annotated manual is a fantastic resource as it contains comments, suggestions, and sample code from other users that often answers the same questions you might have after reading the basic manual page. You can reach the English language version at

`http://www.php.net/manual/en/`

Some programmers who come from a different language background might be tempted to write wrapper functions to essentially rename PHP's functions to match the language with which they are familiar. This practice is sometimes called "syntactic sugar." It's a bad idea—it will make your code harder for others to read and maintain. If you're learning a new language, you should learn how to use it properly. In addition, adding a level of function call in this manner will slow down your code. All things considered, this is an approach that should be avoided.

If you find that the functionality you require is not in the main PHP library, you have two choices. If you need something pretty simple, you can choose to write your own function or object. However, if you're looking at building a fairly complex piece of functionality—such as a shopping cart, Web email system, or Web forums—you won't be surprised to find that these probably have already been built by somebody else. One of the strengths of working in the Open Source community is that code for application components such as these is often freely available. If you find a component similar to the one you want to build, even if it isn't exactly right, you can look at the source code as a starting point for modification or for building your own.

If you end up developing your own functions or components, you should seriously consider making them available to the PHP community when you have finished. This is the principle that keeps the PHP developer community such a helpful, active, and knowledgeable group.

Writing Maintainable Code

The issue of maintainability is often overlooked in Web applications, particularly because we often write them in a hurry. Getting started on the code, and getting it finished quickly sometimes seems more important than planning it first. However, a little time invested up front can save you a lot of time further down the road when you're ready to build the next iteration of an application.

Coding Standards

Most large IT organizations have coding standards—guidelines to the house style for choosing file and variable names, guidelines for commenting code, guidelines for indenting code, and so on.

Because of the document paradigm often previously applied to Web development, coding standards have sometimes been overlooked in this area. If you are coding on your own or in a small team, it's easy to underestimate the importance of coding standards. Don't do it because your team and project might grow. Then you will not only end up with a mess on your hands, but also a bunch of programmers who can't make heads or tails of any of the existing code.

Naming Conventions

The goals of defining a naming convention are

- To make the code easy to read. If you define variables and function names sensibly, you should be able to virtually read code as you would an English sentence, or at least pseudocode.

- To make identifier names easy to remember. If your identifiers are consistently formatted, it will be easier to remember what you called a particular variable or function.

Variable names should describe the data they contain. If you are storing somebody's surname, call it $surname. You need to find a balance between length and readability. For example, storing the name in $n will make it easy to type, but the code will be difficult to understand. Storing the name in $surname_of_the_current_user is more informative, but it's a lot to type (easier to make a typing error) and doesn't really add that much.

You need to make a decision on capitalization. Variable names are case sensitive in PHP, as we've mentioned before. You need to decide whether your variable names will be all lowercase, all uppercase, or a mix, for example, capitalizing the first letters of words. We tend to use all lowercase, as it's the easiest thing to remember.

It's also a good idea to distinguish between variables and constants with case—a common scheme is to use all lowercase for variables (for example, $result) and all uppercase for constants (for example, PI).

One bad practice some programmers use is to have two variables with the same name but different capitalization, just because they can, such as $name and $Name for instance. I hope it is obvious why this is a terrible idea.

It is also best to avoid amusing capitalization schemes such as $WaReZ because no one will be able to remember how it works.

You should also think about what scheme to use for multiword variable names. For example:

```
$username
$user_name
$UserName
```

are all schemes I have seen used. It doesn't matter which you opt for, but you should try to be consistent about this. You might also want to set a sensible maximum limit of two to three words in a variable name.

Function names have many of the same considerations, with a couple of extras. Function names should generally be verb oriented. Consider built-in PHP functions such as addslashes() or mysql_connect(), which describe what they are going to do to or with the parameters they are passed. This greatly enhances code readability. Notice that these two functions have a different naming scheme for dealing with multiword function names. PHP's functions are inconsistent in this regard, presumably partly as a result of having been written by a large group of people, but mostly because many function names have been adopted unchanged from various different languages and APIs.

Also remember that function names are not case sensitive in PHP. You should probably stick to a particular format anyway, just to avoid confusion.

You might want to consider using the module naming scheme used in many PHP modules, that is, prefixing the name of functions with the module name. For example, all the MySQL functions begin with `mysql_`, and all the IMAP functions begin with `imap_`. If, for example, you have a shopping cart module in your code, you could prefix the function in that module with `cart_`.

In the end, it doesn't really matter what conventions and standards you use when writing code, as long as some consistent guidelines are applied.

Commenting Your Code

All programs should be commented to a sensible level. You might ask what level of commenting is sensible. Generally you should consider adding a comment to each of the following items:

- Files, whether complete scripts or include files. Each file should have a comment stating what this file is, what it's for, who wrote it, and when it was updated.

- Functions. Function comments should specify what the function does, what input it expects, and what it returns.

- Classes. Comments should describe the purpose of the class. Class methods should have the same type and level of comments as any other function.

- Chunks of code within a script or function. I often find it useful to write a script by beginning with a set of pseudocode style comments and then filling in the code for each section. So an initial script might resemble this:

```
<?
// validate input data
// send to database
// report results
?>
```

  This is quite handy because after you've filled in all the sections with function calls or whatever, your code is already commented.

- Complex code or hacks. When it takes you all day to do something, or you have to do it in a weird way, write a comment explaining why you did it that way. This way, when you next look at the code, you won't be scratching your head and thinking, "What on earth was *that* supposed to do?"

Another general guideline to follow is that you should comment as you go. You might think you will come back and comment your code when you are finished with a project. I guarantee you this will not happen, unless you have far less punishing development timetables and more self-discipline than we do.

Indenting

As in any programming language, you should indent your code in a sensible and consistent fashion. It's like laying out a resumé or business letter. Indenting makes your code easier to read and faster to understand.

In general, any program block that belongs inside a control structure should be indented from the surrounding code. The degree of indenting should be noticeable (that is, more than one space) but not excessive. I generally think the use of tabs should be avoided. Although easy to type, they consume a lot of screen space on many people's monitors. We use an indent level of two to three spaces for all projects.

The way you lay out your curly braces is also an issue. The two most common schemes are as follows:

Scheme 1:

```
if (condition) {
  // do something
}
```

Scheme 2:

```
if (condition)
{
  // do something else
}
```

Which one you use is up to you. The scheme you choose should (again) be used consistently throughout a project to avoid confusion.

Breaking Up Code

Giant monolithic code is awful. Some people will have one huge script that does everything in one main line of code. It is far better to break up the code into functions and/or classes and put related items into include files. You can, for example, put all your database-related functions in a file called `dbfunctions.php`.

Reasons for breaking up your code into sensible chunks include the following:

- It makes your code easier to read and understand.
- It makes your code more reusable and minimizes redundancy. For example, with the previous `dbfunctions.php` file, you could reuse it in every script in which you need to connect to your database. If you need to change the way this works, you have to change it in only one place.

- It facilitates teamwork. If the code is broken into components, you can then assign responsibility for the components to team members. It also means that you can avoid the situation in which one programmer is waiting for another to finish working on `GiantScript.php` so that she can go ahead with her own work.

At the start of a project, you should spend some time thinking about how you are going to break up a project into planned components. This requires drawing lines between areas of functionality, but don't get bogged down in this as it might change after you get going on a project. You will also need to decide which components need to be built first, which components depend on other components, and the time line for developing all of them.

Even if all team members will be working on all pieces of the code, it's generally a good idea to assign primary responsibility for each component to a specific person. Ultimately this would be the person who is responsible if something goes wrong with her component. Someone should also take on the job of build manager—that is, the person who makes sure that all the components are on track and working with the rest of the components. This person usually also manages version control—we'll talk about this more later in the chapter. This person can be the project manager, or it can be allocated as a separate responsibility.

Using a Standard Directory Structure

When starting a project, you need to think about how your component structure will be reflected in your Web site's directory structure. Just as it is a bad idea to have one giant script containing all functionality, it's usually a bad idea to have one giant directory containing everything. Decide how you are going to split it up between components, logic, content, and shared code libraries. Document your structure and make sure that everybody working on the project has a copy so that they can find things. This leads in to the next point.

Documenting and Sharing In-House Functions

As you develop function libraries, make them available to other programmers in your team. Commonly, every programmer in a team writes her own set of database, date, or debugging functions. This is a time waster. Make functions and classes available to others. Remember that even if code is stored in an area or directory commonly available to your team, they won't know it's there unless you tell them. Develop a system for documenting in-house function libraries, and make it available to programmers on your team.

Implementing Version Control

Version control is the art of concurrent change management as applied to software development. Version control systems generally act as a central *repository* or archive and supply a controlled interface for accessing and sharing your code (and possibly documentation).

Imagine a situation in which you try to improve some code, but instead accidentally break it and can't roll it back to the way it was, no matter how hard you try. Or, you or a client decides that an earlier version of the site was better. Or, you need to go back to a previous version for legal reasons.

Imagine another situation in which two members of your programming team want to work on the same file. They might both open and edit the file at the same time, overwriting each other's changes. They might both have a copy that they work on locally and change in different ways. If you have thought about these things happening, one programmer might be sitting around doing nothing while she waits for another to finish editing a file.

You can solve all these problems with a version control system.

These systems can track changes to each file in the repository so that you can see not only the current state of a file, but also how it looked at any given time in the past. This feature allows you to roll back broken code to a known working version. You can tag a particular set of file instances as a release version, meaning that you can continue development on the code but get access to a copy of the currently released version at any time.

Version control systems also assist multiple programmers in working on code together. Each programmer can get a copy of the code in the repository (called *checking it out*) and when they make changes, these changes can be merged back into the repository (*checked in* or *committed*). Version control systems can therefore track who made each change to a system.

These systems usually have a facility for managing concurrent updates. What this means is that two programmers can actually modify the same file at the same time. For example, imagine that John and Mary have both checked out a copy of the most recent release of their project. John finishes his changes to a particular file and checks it in. Mary also changes that file, and tries to check it in as well. If the changes they have made are not in the same part of the file, the version control system will merge the two versions of the file. If the changes conflict with each other, Mary will be notified and shown the two different versions. She can then adjust her version of the code to avoid the conflicts.

The version control system used by the majority of Unix and/or Open Source developers is CVS, which stands for Concurrent Versions System. CVS is Open Source, comes bundled with virtually every Unix, and you can also get it for PCs running DOS or Windows and Macs. It supports a client-server model so that you can check code in or out from any machine with an Internet connection, assuming that the CVS server is visible on the net. It is used for the development of PHP, Apache, and Mozilla, among other high profile projects, at least in part for this reason.

You can download CVS for your system from the CVS homepage at
`http://www.cvshome.org/`

Although the base CVS system is a command-line tool, various add-ons give it a prettier front end, including Java-based and Windows front ends. These can also be accessed from the CVS home page.

There are commercial alternatives to CVS. One of these is perforce, which runs on most common platforms and has PHP support. Note that although it is commercial, free licenses are offered for Open Source projects at:

```
http://www.perforce.com/
```

Choosing a Development Environment

Talking about version control brings up the more general topic of development environments. All you really need are a text editor and a browser for testing, but programmers are often more productive in an integrated environment, or IDE.

There are a number of emerging free projects to build a dedicated PHP IDE, including KPHPDevelop, for the KDE desktop environment under Linux, available from:

```
http://kphpdev.sourceforge.net/
```

Currently, though, the best PHP IDEs are all commercial. Zend Studio from zend.com, Komodo from activestate.com, and PHPEd from nusphere.com all provide feature-rich IDEs. All have a trial download, but require payment for ongoing use. Komodo has a very cheap noncommercial use license.

Documenting Your Projects

You can produce many different kinds of documentation for your programming projects, including, but not limited to the following:

- Design documentation
- Technical documentation/developer's guide
- Data dictionary (including class documentation)
- User's guide (although most Web applications have to be self-explanatory)

Our goal here is not to teach you how to write technical documentation, but to suggest that you make your life easier by automating part of the process.

In some languages, there are ways of automatically generating some of these documents—particularly technical documentation and data dictionaries. For example, javadoc generates a tree of HTML files containing prototypes and descriptions of class members for Java programs.

Quite a few utilities of this type are available for PHP. Some of these are

- phpdoc, available from

  ```
  http://www.phpdoc.de/
  ```

This is the system used by PEAR for documenting code. Take note that the term phpDoc is used to describe several projects of this type, of which this is one.

- `PHPDocumentor`, available from

  `http://phpdocu.sourceforge.net`

  `PHPDocumentor` gives very similar output to `javadoc` and seems to work quite robustly. It seems to have a more active developer team than the two we have listed here.

- `phpautodoc`, available from

  `http://sourceforge.net/projects/phpautodoc/`

  Again, `phpautodoc` produces output similar to `javadoc`.

A good place to look for more applications of this type (and PHP components in general) is at SourceForge:

`http://sourceforge.net`

SourceForge is primarily used by the UNIX/Linux community, but there are also many projects for other platforms.

Prototyping

Prototyping is a development lifecycle commonly used for developing Web applications. A prototype is a useful tool for working out customer requirements. Usually it is a simplified, partially working version of an application that can be used in discussion with a client and as the basis of the final system. Often multiple iterations over a prototype produce the final application. The advantage of this approach is that it lets you work closely with a client or end user to produce a system that they will be pleased with and have some ownership of.

In order to be able to "knock together" a prototype quickly, you will need some particular skills and tools. This is where a component based approach works well. If you have access to a set of preexisting components, both in-house and publicly available, you will be able to do this much more quickly. Another useful tool for rapid development of prototypes is templates. We will look at these in the next section.

There are two main problems with using a prototyping approach. You need to be aware of what these problems are so that you can avoid them and use this approach to its maximum potential.

The first problem is that programmers often find it difficult to throw away the code that they have written for one reason or another. Prototypes are often written quickly, and with the benefit of hindsight, you can see that you have not built a prototype in the optimal, or even in a near optimal, way. Clunky sections of code can be fixed, but if the overall structure is wrong, you are in trouble. The problem is that Web applications are often built under enormous time pressure and there might not be time to fix it. You are then stuck with a poorly designed system that is difficult to maintain.

You can avoid this by doing a little planning as we have discussed earlier in this chapter. Remember, too, that sometimes it is easier to scrap something and start again than fix it. Although this might seem like something you don't have time for, it will often save you a lot of pain later on.

The second problem with prototyping is that a system can end up being an eternal prototype. Every time you think you're finished, your client will suggest some more improvements or additional functionality or updates to the site. This feature creep can stop you from ever signing off on a project.

To avoid this problem, draw up a project plan with a fixed number of iterations, and a date after which no new functionality can be added without replanning, budgeting, and scheduling.

Separating Logic and Content

You are probably familiar with the idea of using HTML to describe a Web document's structure, and *cascading style sheets (CSS)* to describe its appearance. This idea of separating presentation from content can be extended to scripting. In general, sites will be easier to use and maintain in the long run if you can separate logic from content from presentation. This boils down to separating your PHP and HTML.

For simple projects with a small number of lines of code or scripts, this can be more trouble than it's worth. As your projects become bigger, it is essential to find a way to separate logic and content. If you don't do this, your code will become increasingly difficult to maintain. If you or the powers that be decide to apply a new design to your Web site and a lot of HTML is embedded in your code, changing the design will be a nightmare.

Three basic approaches to separating logic and content are as follows:

- Use include files to store different parts of the content. This is a simplistic approach, but if your site is mostly static, it can work quite well. This type of approach was explained in the TLA Consulting example in Chapter 5, "Reusing Code and Writing Functions."

- Use a function or class API with a set of member functions to plug dynamic content into static page templates. We looked at this approach in Chapter 6, "Object-Oriented PHP."

- Use a template system. These parse static templates and use regular expressions to replace placeholder tags with dynamic data. The main advantage of this is that if somebody else designs your templates, such as a graphics designer, she doesn't have to know anything about PHP code at all. You should be able to use supplied templates with minimum modification.

A number of template systems are available. Probably the most popular one is Smarty, available from

```
http://smarty.php.net/
```

Optimizing Code

If you come from a non-Web programming background, optimization can seem really important. When using PHP, most of the time that a user waits for a Web application comes from connection and download times. Optimization of your code will have little effect on these times.

Using Simple Optimizations

There are, however, a few simple optimizations that you can do that will make a difference. Many of these relate to applications that integrate a database such as MySQL with your PHP code, and some are listed as follows:

- Reduce database connections. Connecting to a database is often the slowest part of any script. You can get around this by using persistent connections.

- Speed up database queries. Reduce the number of queries that you make, and make sure that they are optimized. With a complex (and therefore slow) query, there is usually more than one way to skin a cat. Run your queries from the database's command-line interface and experiment with different approaches to speed things up. In MySQL, you can use the EXPLAIN statement to see where a query might be going astray. (Use of this statement is discussed in Chapter 11, "Advanced MySQL.") In general, the principle is to minimize joins and maximize use of indexes.

- Minimize generation of static content from PHP. If every piece of HTML you produce comes from echo or print(), it will take a good deal longer. (This is one of the arguments for shifting toward separate logic and content as described previously.) This also applies to generating image buttons dynamically—you might want to use PHP to generate the buttons once and then re-use them as required. If you are generating purely static pages from functions or templates every time a page loads, consider running the functions or using the templates once and saving the result.

- Use string functions instead of regular expressions where possible. They are faster.

- Use single-quoted strings instead of double-quoted strings where possible. PHP evaluates double-quoted strings, looking for variables to replace. Single-quoted strings are not evaluated. On the other hand, if it's in single quotes, it's probably static content. Review what you are doing and see if you can get rid of the string altogether by turning it into static HTML.

Using Zend Products

Zend Technologies owns the (Open Source) PHP scripting engine for used in PHP 4 onward. In addition to the basic engine, you can also download the Zend Optimizer. This is a multi-pass optimizer that will optimize your code for you, and can increase the speed at which your scripts run from 40% to 100%. You will need PHP 4.0.2 or upward to run the optimizer. Although closed source, it is free for download from Zend's site:

```
http://www.zend.com
```

This add-on works by optimizing the code produced by the runtime compilation of your script. Other Zend products include the Zend Studio, Zend Accelerator, Zend Encoder, and commercial support agreements.

Testing

Reviewing and testing code is another basic point of software engineering that is often overlooked in Web development. It's easy enough to try running the system with two or three test cases, and then say, "yup, it works fine." This is a commonly made mistake. Ensure that you have extensively tested and reviewed several scenarios before making the project production ready.

We suggest two approaches you can use to reduce the bug level of your code. (You can never eliminate bugs altogether; but you can certainly eliminate or minimize most of them.)

First, adopt a practice of code review. This is the process in which another programmer or team of programmers look at your code and suggest improvements. This type of analysis will often suggest:

- Errors you have missed
- Test cases you have not thought of
- Optimization
- Improvements in security
- Existing components you could use to improve a piece of code
- Additional functionality

Even if you work alone, it can be a good thing to find a "code buddy" who is in the same situation and review code for each other.

The second suggestion that we have is that you find testers for your Web applications who represent the end users of the product. The primary difference between Web applications and desktop applications is that anyone and everyone will use Web applications. You shouldn't make assumptions that users will be familiar with computers. You can't supply them with a thick manual or quick reference card. You have to instead make Web applications self-documenting and self-evident. You must think about the ways in which users will want to use your application. Usability is absolutely paramount.

It can be really difficult to understand the problems that naive end users will encounter if you are an experienced programmer or Web surfer. One way to address this is to get testers who represent the typical user.

One way we have done this in the past is to release Web applications on a beta-only basis. When you think you have the majority of the bugs out, publicize the application to a small group of test users and get a low volume of traffic through the site. Offer free services to the first 100 users in return for feedback about the site. I guarantee you that they will come up with some combination of data or usage you have not thought of. If you are building a Web site for a client company, they can often supply a good set of naive users by getting staff at their company to work through the site. (This has the intrinsic benefit of increasing a client's sense of ownership in a site.)

Further Reading

There is so much material to cover in this area—basically we are talking about the science of software engineering, about which many, many books have been written.

A great book that explains the Web-site-as-document versus Web-site-as-application dichotomy is *Web Site Engineering: Beyond Web Page Design* by Thomas A. Powell. Any software engineering book you like will do as a backup.

For information on version control, visit the CVS Web site:

`http://www.cvshome.org`

There aren't many books on version control (this is surprising given how important it is!), but you can try either *Open Source Development with CVS* by Karl Franz Fogel, or the *CVS Pocket Reference* by Gregor N. Purdy.

If you are looking for PHP components, IDEs, or documentation systems, try SourceForge:

`http://sourceforge.net`

Many of the topics we have covered in this chapter are discussed in articles on Zend's site. You might consider going there for more information on the subject. You might also consider downloading the optimizer from the site when you are there.

`http://www.zend.com`

If you have found this chapter interesting, you might want to look at Extreme Programming, which is a software development methodology aimed at domains where requirements change frequently, such as Web development. The Web site for Extreme Programming is at

`http://www.extremeprogramming.org`

Next

In Chapter 23, "Debugging," we will look at different types of programming errors, PHP error messages, and techniques for finding and gracefully handling errors.

23

Debugging

THIS CHAPTER WILL DEAL WITH DEBUGGING PHP scripts. If you have been through some of the examples in the book or used PHP before, you will probably have developed some debugging skills and techniques of your own. As your projects get more complex, debugging can become more difficult. Although your skills improve, the errors are more likely to involve multiple files, or interactions between the code of multiple people.

Topics in this chapter include:

- Programming error types
    - Syntax errors
    - Runtime errors
    - Logic errors
- Error messages
- Error levels
- Triggering your own errors
- Handling errors gracefully
- Remote debugging

Programming Errors

Regardless of which language you are using, there are three general types of types of program errors:

- Syntax errors
- Runtime errors
- Logic errors

We will look briefly at each before discussing some tactics for detecting, handling, avoiding, and solving errors.

Syntax Errors

Languages have a set of rules called the *syntax* of a language, which statements must follow in order to be valid. This applies to both natural languages, such as English, and programming languages, such as PHP. If a statement does not follow the rules of a language, it is said to have a syntax error. Syntax errors are often also called parser errors when discussing interpreted languages, such as PHP, or compiler errors when discussing compiled languages, such as C or Java.

If we break the English language's syntax rules, there is a pretty good chance that people will still know what we intended to say. This usually is not the case with programming languages. If a script does not follow the rules of PHP's syntax—if it contains syntax errors—the PHP parser will not be able to process some or all of it. People are good at inferring information from partial or conflicting data. Computers are not.

Among many other rules, the syntax of PHP requires that statements end with semicolons, that strings be enclosed in quotes, and that parameters passed to functions be separated with commas and enclosed in parentheses. If we break these rules, our PHP script is unlikely to work, and likely to generate an error message the first time we try to execute it.

One of PHP's great strengths is the useful error messages that it provides when things go wrong. A PHP error message will usually tell you what went wrong, which file the error occurred in, and which line the error was found at.

An error message resembles the following:

Parse error: parse error in
/home/book/public_html/chapter23/error.php on line 2

This error was produced by the following script:

```php
<?php
    $date = date(m.d.y');
?>
```

You can see that we are attempting to pass a string to the `date()` function but have accidentally missed the opening quote that would mark the beginning of the string. Simple syntax errors such as this one are usually the easiest to find. We can make a similar, but harder to find error by forgetting to terminate the string, as shown in this example:

```php
<?php
    $date = date('m.d.y);
?>
```

This script will generate the following error message:

```
Parse error: parse error in
/home/book/public_html/chapter23/error.php on line 4
```

Obviously, as our script only has three lines, our error is not really on line four. Errors in which open something, but fail to close it will often show up like this. You can run into this problem with single and double quotes and also with the various forms of parentheses.

The following script will generate a similar syntax error:

```php
<?php
  if (true)
  {
    echo 'error here';
?>
```

These errors can be hard to find if they result from a combination of multiple files. They can also be difficult to find if they occur in a large file. Seeing "parse error on line 1001" of a 1000 line file can be enough to spoil your day and act as a subtle hint that you should try to write more modular code.

In general though, syntax errors are the easiest type of error to find. If you make a syntax error, PHP will give you a message telling you where to find your mistake.

Runtime Errors

Runtime errors can be harder to detect and fix. A script either contains a syntax error or it does not. If the script contains a syntax error, the parser will detect it. Runtime errors are not caused solely by the contents of your script. They can rely on interactions between your scripts and other events or conditions.

The following statement:

```
include ('filename.php');
```

is a perfectly valid PHP statement. It contains no syntax errors.

This statement might, however, generate a runtime error. If you execute this statement and filename.php does not exist or the user who the script runs as is denied read permission, you will get an error resembling this one:

```
Fatal error: Failed opening required 'filename.php'
(include_path='.:/usr/local/lib/php') in
/home/book/public_html/chapter23/error.php on line 1
```

Although nothing was wrong with our code, because it relies on a file that might or might not exist at different times when the code is run, it can generate a runtime error.

The following three statements are all valid PHP. Unfortunately, in combination, they are attempting to do the impossible—divide by zero.

```
$i = 10;
$j = 0;
$k = $i/$k;
```

This code snippet will generate the following warning:

Warning: Division by zero in
/home/book/public_html/chapter23/div0.php on line **3**

This will make it very easy to correct. Few people would try to write code that attempted to divide by zero on purpose, but neglecting to check user input often results in this type of error.

This is one of many different runtime errors that you might see while testing your code.

Common causes of runtime errors include the following:

- calls to functions that do not exist
- reading or writing files
- interaction with MySQL or other databases
- connections to network services
- failure to check input data

We will briefly discuss each.

Calls to Functions That Do Not Exist

It is easy to accidentally call functions that do not exist. The built-in functions are often inconsistently named. Why does `strip_tags()` have an underscore, whereas `stripslashes()` does not?

It is also easy to call one of your own functions that does not exist in the current script, but might exist elsewhere. If your code contains a call to a nonexistent function, such as

```
nonexistent_function();
```

you will see an error message similar to this:

Fatal error: Call to undefined function: nonexistent_function()
in **/home/book/public_html/chapter23/error.php** on line **1**

Similarly, if you call a function that exists, but call it with an incorrect number of parameters, you will receive a warning.

The function `strstr()` requires two strings: a haystack to search and a needle to find. If instead we call it like this:

```
strstr();
```

We will get the following warning:

Warning: Wrong parameter count for strstr() in
/home/book/public_html/chapter23/error.php on line **1**

As PHP does not allow function overloading, this line will always be wrong, but we might not necessarily always see this warning.

That same statement within the following script is equally wrong:

```php
<?php
  if($var == 4)
  {
    strstr();
  }
?>
```

but except in the, possibly rare, case in which the variable $var has the value 4, the call to strstr() will not occur, and no warning will be issued.

Calling functions incorrectly is easy to do, but as the resulting error messages identify the exact line and function call that are causing the problem, they are equally easy to fix. They are only difficult to find if your testing process is poor and does not test all conditionally executed code. When you test, one of the goals is to execute every line of code exactly once. Another goal is to test all the boundary conditions and classes of input.

Reading or Writing Files

Although anything can go wrong at some point during your program's useful life, some things are more likely than others. Errors accessing files are likely enough to occur that you need to handle them gracefully. Hard drives fail or fill up, and human error results in directory permissions changing.

Functions such as fopen() that are likely to fail occasionally generally have a return value to signal that an error occurred. For fopen(), a return value of false indicates failure.

For functions that provide failure notification, you need to carefully check the return value of every call and act on failures.

Interaction with MySQL or Other Databases

Connecting to and using MySQL can generate many errors. The function mysql_connect() alone can generate at least the following errors:

- MySQL Connection Failed: Can't connect to MySQL server on 'hostname' (111)

- MySQL Connection Failed: Can't connect to local MySQL server through socket '/tmp/mysql.sock' (111)

- MySQL Connection Failed: Unknown MySQL Server Host 'hostname' (2)

- MySQL Connection Failed: Access denied for user: 'username@local-host' (Using password: YES)

As you would probably expect, mysql_connect() provides a return value of false when an error occurs. This means that you can easily trap and handle these types of common errors.

If you do not stop the regular execution of your script and handle these errors, your script will attempt to continue interacting with the database. Trying to run queries and get results without a valid MySQL connection will result in your visitors seeing an unprofessional-looking screen full of error messages.

Many other commonly used MySQL related PHP functions such as mysql_pconnect(), mysql_select_db(), and mysql_query() also return false to indicate that an error occurred.

If an error occurs, you can access the text of the error message using the function mysql_error(),or an error code using the function mysql_errno(). If the last MySQL function did not generate an error, mysql_error() returns an empty string and mysql_errno() returns 0.

For example, assuming that we have connected to the server and selected a database for use, the following code snippet:

```
$result = mysql_query( 'select * from does_not_exist' );
echo mysql_errno();
echo '<br />';
echo mysql_error();
```

might output:

```
1146
Table 'dbname.does_not_exist' doesn't exist
```

Note that the output of these functions refers to the last MySQL function executed (other than mysql_error() or mysql_errno()). If you want to know the result of a command, make sure to check it before running others.

Like file interaction failures, database interaction failures will occur. Even after completing development and testing of a service, you will occasionally find that the MySQL daemon (mysqld) has crashed or run out of available connections. If your database runs on another physical machine, you are relying on another set of hardware and software components that could fail—another network connection, network card, routers, and so on between your Web server and the database machine.

You need to remember to check if your database requests succeed before attempting to use the result. There is no point in attempting to run a query after failing to connect to the database and no point in trying to extract and process the results after a running a query that failed.

It is important to note at this point that there is a difference between a query failing and a query that merely fails to return any data or affect any rows.

A SQL query that contains SQL syntax errors or refers to databases, tables, or columns that do exist might fail. The following query for example:

```
select * from does_not_exist;
```

will fail because the table name does not exist, and it generates an error number and message retrievable with `mysql_errno()` and `mysql_error()`.

A SQL query that is syntactically valid, and refers only to databases, tables, and columns that exist will not generally fail. The query might however return no results if it is querying an empty table or searching for data that does not exist. Assuming that you have connected to a database successfully, and have a table called `exists` and a column called `column name`, the following query, for example:

```
select * from exists where column_name = 'not in database';
```

will succeed but not return any results.

Before you use the result of the query, you will need to check for both failure and no results.

Connections to Network Services

Although devices and other programs on your system will occasionally fail, they should fail rarely unless they are of poor quality. When using a network to connect to other machines and the software on those machines, you will need to accept that some part of the system will fail often. To connect from one machine to another, you are relying on numerous devices and services that are not under your control.

At the risk of being repetitive, you really need to carefully check the return value of functions that attempt to interact with a network service.

A function call such as

```
$sp = fsockopen ( 'localhost', 5000 );
```

will not provide an error message if it fails in its attempt to connect to port 5000 on the machine `localhost`.

Rewriting the call as

```
$sp = fsockopen ( 'localhost', 5000, &$errorno, &$errorstr );
if(!$sp)
  echo "ERROR: $errorno: $errorstr";
```

will check the return value to see if an error occurred, and display an error message that might help you solve the problem. In this case, it would produce the output:

```
ERROR: 111: Connection refused
```

Runtime errors are harder to eliminate than syntax errors because the parser cannot signal the error the first time the code is executed. Because runtime errors occur in response to a combination of events, they can be hard to detect and solve. The parser cannot automatically tell you that a particular line will generate an error. Your testing needs to provide one of the situations that create the error.

Handling runtime errors requires a certain amount of forethought; to check for different types of failure that might occur, and then take appropriate action. It also takes careful testing to simulate each class of runtime error that might occur.

This does not mean that you need to attempt to simulate every different error that might occur. MySQL for example can provide one of around 200 different error numbers and messages. You do need to simulate an error in each function call that is likely to result in an error, and an error of each type that is handled by a different block of code.

Failure to Check Input Data

Often we make assumptions about the input data that will be entered by users. If this data does not fit our expectations, it might cause an error, either a runtime error or a logic error (detailed in the following section).

A classic example of a runtime error occurs when we are dealing with user input data and we forget to AddSlashes() to it. This means if we have a user with a name such as O'Grady that contains an apostrophe, we will get an error from the database function. We will talk more about errors because of assumptions about input data in the next section.

Logic Errors

Logic errors can be the hardest type of error to find and eliminate. This type of error is where perfectly valid code does exactly what it is instructed to do, but that was not what the writer intended.

Logic errors can be caused by a simple typing error, such as:

```
for ( $i = 0; $i < 10; $i++ );
{
  echo 'doing something<br />';
}
```

This snippet of code is perfectly valid. It follows valid PHP syntax. It does not rely on any external services, so it is unlikely to fail at runtime. Unless you looked at it very carefully, it probably will not do what you think it will or what the programmer intended it to do.

At a glance, it looks as if it will iterate through the for loop ten times, echoing "doing something" each time.

The addition of an extraneous semicolon at the end of the first line means that the loop has no effect on the following lines. The for loop will iterate ten times with no result, and then the echo statement will be executed once.

Because this code is a perfectly valid, but inefficient, way to write code to achieve this result, the parser will not complain. Computers are very good at some things, but they do not have any common sense or intelligence. A computer will do exactly as it is told. You need to make sure that what you tell it is exactly what you want.

Logic errors are not caused by any sort of failure of the code, but merely a failure of the programmer to write code that instructs the computer to do exactly what he wanted. As a result, errors cannot be detected automatically. You will not be told that an error has occurred, and you will not be given a line number to look for the problem at. Logic errors will be detected only by proper testing.

A logic error such as the previous trivial example is fairly easy to make, but also easy to correct as the first time your code runs you will see output other than what you expected. Most logic errors are a little more insidious.

Troublesome logic errors usually result from developers' assumptions being wrong. Chapter 22, "Using PHP and MySQL for Large Projects," recommended using other developers to review code to suggest additional test cases, and using people from the target audience rather than developers for testing. Assuming that people will enter only certain types of data is very easy to do and very easy to leave undetected if you do your own testing.

Let's say that you have an Order Quantity text box on a commerce site. Have you assumed that people will only enter positive numbers? If a visitor enters negative ten, will your software refund his credit card with ten times the price of the item?

Suppose that you have a box to enter a dollar amount. Do you allow people to enter the amount with or without a dollar sign? Do you allow people to enter numbers with thousands separated by commas? Some of these things can be checked at client-side (using, for example, JavaScript) to take a little load off your server.

If you are passing information to another page, has it occurred to you that there might be characters that have special significance in a URL such as spaces in the string you are passing?

An infinite number of logic errors is possible. There is no automated way to check for them. The only solution is, first, to try to eliminate assumptions that you have implicitly coded into the script and, second, test thoroughly with every type of valid and invalid input possible, ensuring that you get the anticipated result for all.

Variable Debugging Aid

As projects get more complex, it can be useful to have some utility code to help you identify the cause of errors. A piece of code that you might find useful is contained in Listing 23.1. This code will echo the contents of variables passed to your page.

Listing 23.1 **dump_variables.php—This Code Can Be Included in Pages to Dump the Contents of Variables for Debugging**

```php
<?php
  // these lines format the output as HTML comments
  // and call dump_array repeatedly

  echo '\n<!-- BEGIN VARIABLE DUMP -->\n\n';
```

Listing 23.1   **Continued**

```php
echo '<!-- BEGIN GET VARS -->\n';
echo '<!-- '.dump_array($HTTP_GET_VARS).' -->\n';

echo '<!-- BEGIN POST VARS -->\n';
echo '<!-- '.dump_array($HTTP_POST_VARS).' -->\n';

echo '<!-- BEGIN SESSION VARS -->\n';
echo '<!-- '.dump_array($HTTP_SESSION_VARS).' -->\n';

echo '<!-- BEGIN COOKIE VARS -->\n';
echo '<!-- '.dump_array($HTTP_COOKIE_VARS).' -->\n';

echo '\n<!-- END VARIABLE DUMP -->\n';

// dump_array() takes one array as a parameter
// It iterates through that array, creating a string
// to represent the array as a set

function dump_array($array)
{
  if(is_array($array))
  {
    $size = count($array);
    $string = '';
    if($size)
    {
      $count = 0;
      $string .= '{ ';
      // add each element's key and value to the string
      foreach($array as $var => $value)
      {
        $string .= "$var = $value";
        if($count++ < ($size-1))
        {
          $string .= ', ';
        }
      }
      $string .= ' }';
    }
    return $string;
  }
  else
  {
    // if it is not an array, just return it
```

Listing 23.1   **Continued**

```
    return $array;
  }
}
?>
```

This code will iterate through four arrays of variables that a page receives. If a page was called with GET variables, POST variables, cookies, or has session variables, these will be output.

A line of HTML will be generated for each type of variable.

The lines will resemble this:

```
<!-- { var1 = 'value1', var2 = 'value2', var3 = 'value3' } -->
```

We have put the output within an HTML comment so that it is viewable, but will not interfere with the way that the browser renders visible page elements. This is a good way to generate debugging information.

The exact output will depend on the variables passed to the page, but when added to Listing 20.4, one of the authentication examples from Chapter 20, "Using Session Control in PHP," it adds the following lines to the HTML generated by the script:

```
<!-- BEGIN VARIABLE DUMP -->

<!-- BEGIN GET VARS -->
<!--   -->
<!-- BEGIN POST VARS -->
<!-- { userid = testuser, password = test123 } -->
<!-- BEGIN SESSION VARS -->
<!-- { valid_user = testuser } -->
<!-- BEGIN COOKIE VARS -->
<!-- { PHPSESSID = 2552dc82bb465af56d65e9300f75fd68 } -->

<!-- END VARIABLE DUMP -->
```

You can see that it is displaying the POST variables sent from the login form on the previous page—userid and password. It is also showing the session variable that we are using to keep the user's name in—valid_user. As discussed in Chapter 20, PHP uses a cookie to link session variables to particular users. Our script is echoing the pseudo-random number, PHPSESSID, which is stored in that cookie to identify a particular user.

Error Reporting Levels

PHP allows you to set how fussy it should be with errors. You can modify what types of events will generate messages. By default, PHP will report all errors other than notices.

The error reporting level is set using a set of predefined constants, shown in Table 23.1.

Table 23.1 **Error Reporting Constants**

Value	Name	Meaning
1	E_ERROR	Report fatal errors at runtime
2	E_WARNING	Report nonfatal errors at runtime
4	E_PARSE	Report parse errors
8	E_NOTICE	Report notices, notifications that something you have done might be an error
16	E_CORE_ERROR	Report failures in the startup of the PHP engine
32	E_CORE_WARNING	Report nonfatal failures during the startup of the PHP engine
64	E_COMPILE_ERROR	Report errors in compilation
128	E_COMPILE_WARNING	Report nonfatal errors in compilation
256	E_USER_ERROR	Report user triggered errors
512	E_USER_WARNING	Report user triggered warnings
1024	E_USER_NOTICE	Report user triggered notices
2048	E_ALL	Report all errors and warnings

Each constant represents a type of error that can be reported or ignored. If for instance, you specify the error level as E_ERROR, only fatal errors will be reported. These constants can be combined using binary arithmetic, to produce different error levels.

The default error level, report all errors other than notices, is specified as

```
E_ALL & ~E_NOTICE
```

This expression consists of two of the predefined constants combined using bitwise arithmetic operators. The ampersand (&) is the bitwise AND operator and the tilde (~) is the bitwise NOT operator. This expression can be read as E_ALL AND NOT E_NOTICE.

E_ALL itself is effectively a combination of all the other error types. It could be replaced by the other levels ORed together using the bitwise OR operator (|).

```
E_ERROR | E_WARNING | E_PARSE | E_NOTICE | E_CORE_ERROR | E_CORE_WARNING |
E_COMPILE_ERROR |E_COMPILE_WARNING | E_USER_ERROR | E_USER_WARNING |
E_USER_NOTICE
```

Similarly, the default error reporting level could be specified by all error levels except notice ORed together.

```
E_ERROR | E_WARNING | E_PARSE | E_CORE_ERROR | E_CORE_WARNING | E_COMPILE_ERROR |
E_COMPILE_WARNING | E_USER_ERROR | E_USER_WARNING | E_USER_NOTICE
```

Altering the Error Reporting Settings

You can set the error reporting settings globally, in your `php.ini` file or on a per script basis.

To alter the error reporting for all scripts, you can modify these four lines in the default `php.ini` file:

```
error_reporting =       E_ALL & ~E_NOTICE
display_errors  =       On
log_errors      =       Off
track_errors    =       Off
```

The default global settings are to

- report all errors except notices
- output error messages as HTML to standard output
- not log error messages to disk
- not track errors, storing the error in the variable `$php_errormsg`

The most likely change you are to make is to turn the error reporting level up to `E_ALL`. This will result in many notices being reported, for incidents that might indicate an error, or might just result from the programmer taking advantage of PHP's weakly typed nature and the fact that it automatically initializes variables to `0`.

While debugging, you might find it useful to set the `error_reporting` level higher. In production code, if you are providing useful error messages of your own, it would be more professional looking to turn `display_errors` off and to turn `log_errors` on, while leaving the `error_reporting` level high. You will then be able to refer to detailed errors in the logs if problems are reported.

Turning `track_errors` on might help you to deal with errors in your own code, rather than letting PHP provide its default functionality. Although PHP provides useful error messages, its default behavior looks ugly when things go wrong.

By default, when a fatal error occurs, PHP will output the following:

```
<br>
<b>Error Type</b>:  error message in <b>path/file.php</b>
on line <b>lineNumber</b><br>
```

and stop executing the script. For nonfatal errors, the same text is output, but execution is allowed to continue.

This HTML output makes the error stand out, but looks poor. The style of the error message is unlikely to fit the rest of the site's look. It might also result in Netscape users seeing no output at all if the page's content is being displayed within a table. This is because HTML that opens but does not close table elements, such as

```
<table>
<tr><td>
```

```
<br>
<b>Error Type</b>:  error message in <b>path/file.php</b>
on line <b>lineNumber</b><br>
```

will be rendered as a blank screen by Netscape.

We do not have to keep PHP's default error handling behavior, or even use the same settings for all files. To change the error reporting level for the current script, you can call the function error_reporting().

Passing an error report constant, or a combination of them, sets the level in the same way that the similar directive in php.ini does. The function returns the previous error reporting level. A common way to use the function is like this:

```
// turn off error reporting
$old_level = error_reporting(0);
// here, put code that will generate warnings
// turn error reporting back on
error_reporting($old_level);
```

This code snippet will turn off error reporting, allowing us to execute some code that is likely to generate warnings that we do not want to see.

Turning off error reporting permanently is a bad idea as it makes it difficult to find your coding errors and fix them.

Triggering Your Own Errors

The function trigger_error() can be used to trigger your own errors. Errors created in this way will be handled in the same way as regular PHP errors.

The function requires an error message, and can optionally be given an error type. The error type needs to be one of E_USER_ERROR, E_USER_WARNING, or E_USER_NOTICE. If you do not specify a type, the default is E_USER_NOTICE.

You use trigger_error() as shown in the following:

```
trigger_error('This computer will self destruct in 15 seconds', E_USER_WARNING);
```

(Note that this function was added at PHP version 4.0.1.)

Handling Errors Gracefully

If you come from a C++ or Java background, you might miss exception handling when you use PHP. Exceptions allow functions to signal that an error has occurred and leave dealing with the error to an exception handler. Although PHP does not have exceptions, PHP 4.0.1 introduced a mechanism that can be used in a similar way.

You have already seen that you can trigger your own errors. You can also provide your own error handlers to catch errors.

The function set_error_handler() lets you provide a function to be called when user-level errors, warnings, and notices occur. You call set_error_handler() with the name of the function you want to use as your error handler.

Your error handling function must take two parameters: an error type and an error message. Based on these two variables, your function can decide how to handle the error. The error type must be one of the defined error type constants. The error message is a descriptive string.

A call to set_error_handler() will look like this:

```
set_error_handler('myErrorHandler');
```

Having told PHP to use a function called myErrorHandler(), we must then provide a function with that name. This function must have the following prototype:

```
myErrorHandler(int error_type, string error_msg)
```

but what it actually does is up to you.

Logical actions might include

- Displaying the error message provided

- Storing information in a log file

- Emailing the error to an address

- Terminating the script with a call to exit

Listing 23.2 contains a script that declares an error handler, sets the error handler using set_error_handler(), and then generates some errors.

Listing 23.2 **handle.php—This Script Declares a Custom Error Handler and Generates Different Errors**

```php
<?php
  // The error handler function
  function myErrorHandler ($errno, $errstr, $errfile, $errline)
  {
    echo "<br /><table bgcolor='#cccccc'><tr><td>
          <p><b>ERROR:</b> $errstr</p>
          <p>Please try again, or contact us and tell us that
          the error occurred in line $errline of file '$errfile'</p>";
    if ($errno == E_USER_ERROR||$errno == E_ERROR)
    {
      echo '<p>This error was fatal, program ending</p>';
      echo '</td></tr></table>';
      //close open resources, include page footer, etc
      exit;
    }
    echo '</td></tr></table>';
  }
  // Set the error handler
  set_error_handler('myErrorHandler');
```

Listing 23.2   **Continued**

```
//trigger different levels of error
trigger_error('Trigger function called', E_USER_NOTICE);
fopen('nofile', 'r');
trigger_error('This computer is beige', E_USER_WARNING);
include ('nofile');
trigger_error('This computer will self destruct in 15 seconds', E_USER_ERROR);
?>
```

The output from this script is shown in Figure 23.1.

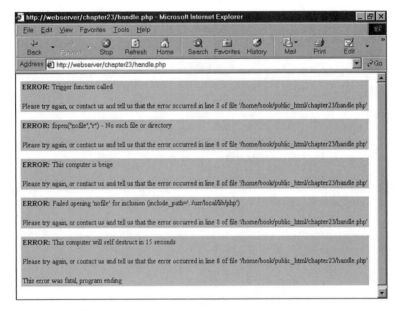

Figure 23.1   You can give friendlier error messages
than PHP if you use your own error handler.

This custom error handler does not do any more than the default behavior. Because this code is written by you, you can make it do anything. It gives you a choice about what to tell your visitors when something goes wrong and how to present that information so that it fits the rest of the site. More importantly, it gives you flexibility to decide what happens. Should the script continue? Should a message be logged or displayed? Should tech support be alerted automatically?

It is important to note that your error handler will not have the responsibility for dealing with all error types. Some errors, such as parse errors and fatal runtime errors will still trigger the default behavior. If this concerns you, make sure that you check parameters carefully before passing them to a function that can generate fatal errors and trigger your own E_USER_ERROR level error if your parameters are going to cause failure.

Next

In Chapter 24, "Building User Authentication and Personalization," we will begin our first project. In this project, we'll look at how you can recognize users who are coming back to your site and tailor your content appropriately.

24

Building User Authentication and Personalization

IN THIS PROJECT, WE'LL GET USERS to register at our Web site. When they've done that, we'll be able to keep track of what they're interested in and show them appropriate content. This is called user personalization.

This particular project will enable users to build a set of bookmarks on the Web and suggest other links they might find interesting based on their past behavior. More generally, user personalization can be used in almost any Web-based application to show users the content they want in the format in which they want it.

In this project, and the others to follow, we'll start by looking at a set of requirements similar to those you might get from a client. We'll develop those requirements into a set of solution components, build a design to connect those components together, and then implement each of the components.

In this project, we will implement the following functionality:

- Logging in and authenticating users
- Managing passwords
- Recording user preferences
- Personalizing content
- Recommending content based on existing knowledge about a user

The Problem

We want to build a prototype for an online bookmarking system, to be called PHPBookmark, similar (but more limited in functionality) to that available at Backflip:

```
http://backflip.com
```

Our system should enable users to log in and store their personal bookmarks and to get recommendations for other sites that they might like to visit based on their personal preferences.

These solution requirements fall into three main buckets.

First, we need to be able to identify individual users. We should also have some way of authenticating them.

Second, we need to be able to store bookmarks for an individual user. Users should be able to add and delete bookmarks.

Third, we need to be able to recommend to a user sites that might appeal to her, based on what we know about her already.

Solution Components

Now that we know the system requirements, we can begin designing the solution and its components. Let's look at possible solutions to each of the three main requirements we listed previously.

User Identification and Personalization

There are several alternatives for user authentication, as we have seen elsewhere in this book. Because we want to tie a user to some personalization information, we will store the users' login and password in a MySQL database and authenticate against that.

If we are going to let users log in with a username and password, we will need the following components:

- Users should be able to register a username and password. We will need some restrictions on the length and format of the username and password. We should store passwords in an encrypted format for security reasons.

- Users should be able to log in with the details they supplied in the registration process.

- Users should be able to log out when they have finished using a site. This is not particularly important if people use the site from their home PC, but is very important for security if they use the site from a shared PC.

- The site needs to be able to check whether a user is logged in or not, and access data for a logged-in user.

- Users should be able to change their password as an aid to security.

- Users will occasionally forget their passwords. They should be able to reset their password without needing personal assistance from us. A common way of doing this is to send the password to the user in an email address he has nominated at registration. This means we need to store his email address at registration. Because we store the passwords in an encrypted form and cannot decrypt the original password, we will actually need to generate a new password, set it, and mail it to the user.

We will write functions for all these pieces of functionality. Most of them will be reusable, or reusable with minor modifications, in other projects.

Storing Bookmarks

To store a user's bookmarks, we will need to set up some space in our MySQL database. We will need the following functionality:

- Users should be able to retrieve and view their bookmarks.
- Users should be able to add new bookmarks. We should check that these are valid URLs.
- Users should be able to delete bookmarks.

Again, we can write functions for each of these pieces of functionality.

Recommending Bookmarks

We could take a number of different approaches to recommending bookmarks to a user. We could recommend the most popular or the most popular within a topic. For this project, we are going to implement a "like minds" suggestion system that looks for users who have a bookmark the same as our logged-in user, and suggests their other bookmarks to our user. To avoid recommending any personal bookmarks, we will only recommend bookmarks stored by more than one other user.

We can again write a function to implement this functionality.

Solution Overview

After some doodling on napkins, we came up with the system flowchart shown in Figure 24.1.

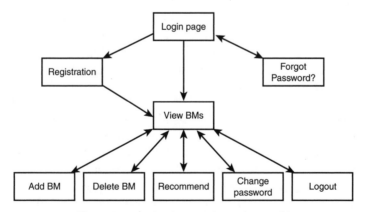

Figure 24.1   This diagram shows the possible
paths through the PHPBookmark system.

We'll build a module for each box on this diagram—some will need one script and others, two. We'll also set up function libraries for

- User authentication
- Bookmark storage and retrieval
- Data validation
- Database connections
- Output to the browser. We'll confine all the HTML production to this function library, ensuring that visual presentation is consistent throughout the site. (This is the function API approach to separating logic and content.)

We'll also need to build a back-end database for the system.

We'll go through the solution in some detail, but all of the code for this application can be found on the CD-ROM in the `chapter24` directory. A summary of included files is shown in Table 24.1.

Table 24.1 **Files in the PHPBookmark Application**

Filename	**Description**
`bookmarks.sql`	SQL statements to create the PHPBookmark database
`login.php`	Front page with login form for system
`register_form.php`	Form for users to register in the system
`register_new.php`	Script to process new registrations
`forgot_form.php`	Form for users to fill out if they've forgotten their passwords
`forgot_passwd.php`	Script to reset forgotten passwords
`member.php`	A user's main page, with a view of all his current bookmarks
`add_bm_form.php`	Form for adding new bookmarks
`add_bms.php`	Script to actually add new bookmarks to the database
`delete_bms.php`	Script to delete selected bookmarks from the user's list
`recommend.php`	Script to suggest recommendations to a user, based on users with similar interests
`change_passwd_form.php`	Form for members to fill out if they want to change their passwords
`change_passwd.php`	Script to change the user's password in the database
`logout.php`	Script to log a user out of the application
`bookmark_fns.php`	A collection of includes for the application
`data_valid_fns.php`	Functions to validate user-input data
`db_fns.php`	Functions to connect to the database
`user_auth_fns.php`	Functions for user authentication
`url_fns.php`	Functions for adding and deleting bookmarks and for making recommendations
`output_fns.php`	Functions that format output as HTML
`bookmark.gif`	Logo for PHPBookmark

We will begin by implementing the MySQL database for this application as it will be required for virtually all the other functionality to work.

Then we will work through the code in the order it was written, starting from the front page, going through the user authentication, to bookmark storage and retrieval, and finally to recommendations. This order is fairly logical—it's just a question of working out the dependencies and building first the things that will be required for later modules.

Note

For the code in this project to work as written, you will need to have switched on magic quotes. If you have not done this, then you will need to `addslashes()` to data being inserted to the MySQL database, and `stripslashes()` from data retrieved from the database. We have used this as a useful shortcut.

Implementing the Database

We only require a fairly simple schema for the PHPBookmark database. We need to store users and their email addresses and passwords. We also need to store the URL of a bookmark. One user can have many bookmarks, and many users can register the same bookmark. We therefore have two tables, user and bookmark, as shown in Figure 24.2.

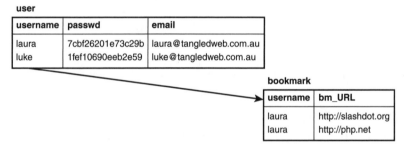

Figure 24.2   Database schema for the PHPBookmark system.

The user table will store the user's username (which is the primary key), password, and email address.

The bookmark table will store username and bookmark (bm_URL) pairs. The username in this table will refer back to a username from the user table.

The SQL to create this database, and to create a user for connecting to the database from the Web, is shown in Listing 24.1. You should edit it if you plan to use it on your system—change the user's password to something more secure!

Listing 24.1   **bookmarks.sql—SQL File to Set Up the Bookmark Database**

```
create database bookmarks;
use bookmarks;

create table user  (
  username varchar(16) primary key,
  passwd char(16) not null,
  email varchar(100) not null
);

create table bookmark (
  username varchar(16) not null,
  bm_URL varchar(255) not null,
  index (username),
  index (bm_URL)
);

grant select, insert, update, delete
on bookmarks.*
to bm_user@localhost identified by 'password';
```

You can set up this database on your system by running this set of commands as the root MySQL user. You can do this with the following command on your system's command line:

```
mysql -u root -p < bookmarks.sql
```

You will then be prompted to type in your password.

With the database set up, let's go on and implement the basic site.

Implementing the Basic Site

The first page we'll build will be called login.php because it provides users with the opportunity to log in to the system. The code for this first page is shown in Listing 24.2.

Listing 24.2   **login.php—Front Page of the PHPBookmark System**

```
<?php
require_once('bookmark_fns.php');
do_html_header('');

display_site_info();
display_login_form();

do_html_footer();
?>
```

This code looks very simple, as it is mostly calling functions from the function API that we will construct for this application. We'll look at the details of these functions in a minute. Just looking at this file, we can see that we are including a file (containing the functions) and then calling some functions to render an HTML header, display some content, and render an HTML footer.

The output from this script is shown in Figure 24.3.

Figure 24.3   The front page of the PHPBookmark system is produced by the HTML rendering functions in login.php.

The functions for the system are all included in the file `bookmark_fns.php`, shown in Listing 24.3.

Listing 24.3   bookmark_fns.php—Include File of Functions for the Bookmark Application

```php
<?php
  // We can include this file in all our files
  // this way, every file will contain all our functions
  require_once('data_valid_fns.php');
  require_once('db_fns.php');
  require_once('user_auth_fns.php');
  require_once('output_fns.php');
  require_once('url_fns.php');
?>
```

As you can see, this file is just a container for the five other include files we will use in this application. We have structured it like this because the functions fall into logical groups. Some of these groups might be useful for other projects, so we put each function group into a different file where we will know where to find them when we want them again. We constructed the `bookmark_fns.php` file because we will use most of the five function files in most of our scripts. It is easier to include this one file in each script rather than having five include statements.

Note that the `require_once()` construct only exists in PHP from version 4.0.1pl2. If you are using a prior version, you will need to use `require()` or `include()` and ensure that the files do not get loaded multiple times.

In this particular case, we are using functions from the file `output_fns.php`. These are all straightforward functions that output fairly plain HTML. This file includes the four functions we have used in login.php, that is, `do_html_header()`, `display_site_info()`, `display_login_form()`, and `do_html_footer()`, among others.

We will not go through all these functions in detail, but we will look at one as an example. The code for `do_html_header()` is shown in Listing 24.4.

Listing 24.4   **do_html_header() Function from output_fns.php—This Function Outputs the Standard Header That Will Appear on Each Page in the Application**

```php
function do_html_header($title)
{
  // print an HTML header
?>
  <html>
  <head>
    <title><?php echo $title;?></title>
    <style>
      body { font-family: Arial, Helvetica, sans-serif; font-size: 13px }
      li, td { font-family: Arial, Helvetica, sans-serif; font-size: 13px }
      hr { color: #3333cc; width=300; text-align=left}
      a { color: #000000 }
    </style>
  </head>
  <body>
  <img src="bookmark.gif" alt="PHPbookmark logo" border="0"
      align="left" valign="bottom" height="55" width="57" />
  <h1> PHPbookmark</h1>
  <hr />
<?php
  if($title)
    do_html_heading($title);
}
```

As you can see, the only logic in this function is to add the appropriate title and heading to the page. The other functions we have used in login.php are similar. The function `display_site_info()` adds some general text about the site; `display_login_form()` displays the grey form shown in Figure 24.3; and `do_html_footer()` adds a standard HTML footer to the page.

The advantages to isolating or removing HTML from your main logic stream are discussed in Chapter 22, "Using PHP and MySQL for Large Projects." We will use the function API approach here, and a template-based approach in the next chapter for contrast.

Looking at Figure 24.3, you can see that there are three options on this page—users can register, log in if they have already registered, or reset their password if they have forgotten it. To implement these modules we will move on to the next section, user authentication.

Implementing User Authentication

There are four main elements to the user authentication module: user registration, login and logout, changing passwords, and resetting passwords. We will look at each of these in turn.

Registering

To register a user, we need to get his details via a form and enter him in the database. When a user clicks on the "Not a member?" link on the login.php page, they will be taken to a registration form produced by `register_form.php`. This script is shown in Listing 24.5.

Listing 24.5   register_form.php—This Form Gives Users the Opportunity to Register with PHPBookmarks

```php
<?php
  require_once('bookmark_fns.php');
  do_html_header('User Registration');

  display_registration_form();

  do_html_footer();
?>
```

Again, you can see that this page is fairly simple and just calls functions from the output library in `output_fns.php`. The output of this script is shown in Figure 24.4.

The grey form on this page is output by the function `display_registration_form()`, contained in output_fns.php. When the user clicks on the Register button, he will be taken to the script `register_new.php`. This script is shown in Listing 24.6.

Figure 24.4 The registration form retrieves the details we need for the database. We get users to type their passwords twice, in case they make a mistake.

Listing 24.6 **register_new.php—This Script Validates the New User's Data and Puts It in the Database**

```php
<?php
  // include function files for this application
  require_once('bookmark_fns.php');

  //create short variable names
  $email=$HTTP_POST_VARS['email'];
  $username=$HTTP_POST_VARS['username'];
  $passwd=$HTTP_POST_VARS['passwd'];
  $passwd2=$HTTP_POST_VARS['passwd2'];
  // start session which may be needed later
  // start it now because it must go before headers
  session_start();


  // check forms filled in
  if (!filled_out($HTTP_POST_VARS))
  {
    do_html_header('Problem:');
    echo 'You have not filled the form out correctly - please go back'
       .' and try again.';
    do_html_footer();
```

Listing 24.6   **Continued**

```
      exit;
}


// email address not valid
if (!valid_email($email))
{
   do_html_header('Problem:');
   echo 'That is not a valid email address.   Please go back '
        .' and try again.';
   do_html_footer();
   exit;
}


// passwords not the same
if ($passwd != $passwd2)
{
   do_html_heading('Problem:');
   echo 'The passwords you entered do not match - please go back'
        .' and try again.';
   do_html_footer();
   exit;
}


// check password length is ok
// ok if username truncates, but passwords will get
// munged if they are too long.
if (strlen($passwd)<6 || strlen($passwd) >16)
{
   do_html_header('Problem:');
   echo 'Your password must be between 6 and 16 characters.'
        .'Please go back and try again.';
   do_html_footer();
   exit;
}
// attempt to register
$reg_result = register($username, $email, $passwd);
if ($reg_result === true)
{
  // register session variable
  $HTTP_SESSION_VARS['valid_user'] = $username;


  // provide link to members page
  do_html_header('Registration successful');
  echo 'Your registration was successful.  Go to the members page '
```

Listing 24.6 **Continued**

```
          .'to start setting up your bookmarks!';
    do_html_url('member.php', 'Go to members page');
  }
  else
  {
    // otherwise provide link back, tell them to try again
    do_html_header('Problem:');
    echo $reg_result;
    do_html_footer();
    exit;
  }

  // end page
  do_html_footer();

?>
```

This is the first script with any complexity to it that we have looked at in this application.

The script begins by including the application's function files and starting a session. (When the user is registered, we will create his username as a session variable as we did in Chapter 20, "Using Session Control in PHP.")

Next, we validate the input data from the user. There are a number of conditions we must test for. They are

- Check that the form is filled out. We test this with a call to the function `filled_out()` as follows:

  ```
  if (!filled_out($HTTP_POST_VARS))
  ```

  This function is one we have written ourselves. It is in the function library in the file `data_valid_fns.php`. We'll look at this function in a minute.

- Check that the email address supplied is valid. We test this as follows:

  ```
  if (valid_email($email))
  ```

  Again, this is a function that we've written, which is in the data_valid_fns.php library.

- Check that the two passwords the user has suggested are the same, as follows:

  ```
  if ($passwd != $passwd2)
  ```

- Check that the password is the appropriate length, as follows:

  ```
  if (strlen($passwd)<6 || strlen($passwd) >16)
  ```

  In our example, the password should be at least 6 characters long to make it harder to guess, and fewer than 16 characters, so it will fit in the database.

The data validation functions we have used here, filled_out() and valid_email(), are shown in Listing 24.7 and Listing 24.8, respectively.

Listing 24.7   **filled_out() Function from data_valid_fns.php—This Function Checks That the Form Has Been Filled Out**

```php
function filled_out($form_vars)
{
  // test that each variable has a value
  foreach ($form_vars as $key => $value)
  {
    if (!isset($key) || ($value == ''))
      return false;
  }
  return true;
}
```

Listing 24.8   **valid_email() Function from data_valid_fns.php—This Function Checks Whether an Email Address Is Valid**

```php
function valid_email($address)
{
  // check an email address is possibly valid
  if (ereg('^[a-zA-Z0-9_\.\-]+@[a-zA-Z0-9\-]+\.[a-zA-Z0-9\-\.]+$', $address))
    return true;
  else
    return false;
}
```

The function filled_out() expects to be passed an array of variables—in general, this will be the $HTTP_POST_VARS or $HTTP_GET_VARS arrays. It will check whether they are all filled out, and return true if they are and false if they are not.

The valid_email() function uses the regular expression we developed in Chapter 4, "String Manipulation and Regular Expressions," for validating email addresses. It returns true if an address appears valid, and false if it does not.

After we've validated the input data, we can actually try and register the user. If you look back at Listing 24.6, you'll see that we do this as follows:

```php
$reg_result = register($username, $email, $passwd);
if ($reg_result === true)
{
  // register session variable
  $HTTP_SESSION_VARS['valid_user'] = $username;

  // provide link to members page
  do_html_header('Registration successful');
```

```
    echo 'Your registration was successful.  Go to the members page '
        .'to start setting up your bookmarks!';
    do_html_url('member.php', 'Go to members page');
}
```

As you can see, we are calling the `register()` function with the username, email address, and password that were entered. If this succeeds, we register the username as a session variable and provide the user with a link to the main members' page. This is the output shown in Figure 24.5.

Figure 24.5   Registration was successful—the user can now go to the members page.

The `register()` function is in the included library called `user_auth_fns.php`. This function is shown in Listing 24.9.

Listing 24.9   **register() Function from user_auth_fns.php—This Function Attempts to Put the New User's Information in the Database**

```
function register($username, $email, $password)
// register new person with db
// return true or error message
{
  // connect to db
  $conn = db_connect();
  if (!$conn)
    return 'Could not connect to database server - please try later.';
```

Listing 24.9   **Continued**

```
// check if username is unique
$result = mysql_query("select * from user where username='$username'");
if (!$result)
    return 'Could not execute query';
if (mysql_num_rows($result)>0)
    return 'That username is taken - go back and choose another one.';

// if ok, put in db
$result = mysql_query("insert into user values
                        ('$username', password('$password'), '$email')");
if (!$result)
    return 'Could not register you  in database - please try again later.';

return true;
}
```

There is nothing particularly new in this function—it connects to the database we set up earlier. If the username selected is taken, or the database cannot be updated, it will return false. Otherwise, it will update the database and return true.

One thing to note is that we are performing the actual database connection with a function we have written, called db_connect(). This function simply provides a single location that contains the username and password to connect to the database. That way, if we change the database password, we only need to change one file in our application. The function is shown in Listing 24.10.

Listing 24.10   **db_connect() Function from db_fns.php—This Function Connects to the MySQL Database**

```
function db_connect()
{
   $result = mysql_pconnect('localhost', 'bm_user', 'password');
   if (!$result)
      return false;
   if (!mysql_select_db('bookmarks'))
      return false;

   return $result;
}
```

When users are registered, they can log in and out using the regular login and logout pages. We'll build these next.

Logging In

If users type their details into the form at login.php (see Figure 24.3) and submit it, they will be taken to the script called member.php. This script will log them in if they have come from this form. It will also display any relevant bookmarks to users who are logged in. It is the center of the rest of the application. This script is shown in Listing 24.11.

Listing 24.11   **member.php—This Script is the Main Hub of the Application**

```php
<?php

// include function files for this application
require_once('bookmark_fns.php');
session_start();

//create short variable names
$username = $HTTP_POST_VARS['username'];
$passwd = $HTTP_POST_VARS['passwd'];

if ($username && $passwd)
// they have just tried logging in
{
    if (login($username, $passwd))
    {
      // if they are in the database register the user id
      $HTTP_SESSION_VARS['valid_user'] = $username;
    }
    else
    {
      // unsuccessful login
      do_html_header('Problem:');
      echo 'You could not be logged in.
            You must be logged in to view this page.';
      do_html_url('login.php', 'Login');
      do_html_footer();
      exit;
    }
}

do_html_header('Home');
check_valid_user();
// get the bookmarks this user has saved
if ($url_array = get_user_urls($HTTP_SESSION_VARS['valid_user']));
  display_user_urls($url_array);

// give menu of options
display_user_menu();

do_html_footer();
?>
```

You might recognize the logic in this script: we are re-using some of the ideas from Chapter 20.

First, we check whether the user has come from the front page—that is, whether he has just filled in the login form—and try to log him in as follows:

```
if ($username && $passwd)
// they have just tried logging in
{
    if (login($username, $passwd))
    {
      // if they are in the database register the user id
      $HTTP_SESSION_VARS['valid_user'] = $username;
    }
```

You can see that we are trying to log him in using a function called login(). We have defined this in the user_auth_fns.php library, and we'll look at the code for it in a minute.

If he is logged in successfully, we register his session as we did before, storing the username in the session variable valid_user.

If all went well, we then show the user the members page:

```
do_html_header('Home');
check_valid_user();
// get the bookmarks this user has saved
if ($url_array = get_user_urls($HTTP_SESSION_VARS['valid_user']));
  display_user_urls($url_array);

// give menu of options
display_user_menu();

do_html_footer();
```

This page is again formed using the output functions. You will notice that we are using several other new functions. These are check_valid_user(), from user_auth_fns.php; get_user_urls(), from url_fns.php; and display_user_urls(), from output_fns.php. The check_valid_user() function checks that the current user has a registered session. This is aimed at users who have *not* just logged in, but are mid-session. The get_user_urls() function gets a user's bookmarks from the database, and display_user_urls() outputs the bookmarks to the browser in a table. We will look at check_valid_user() in a moment and at the other two in the section on bookmark storage and retrieval.

The member.php script ends the page by displaying a menu with the display_user_menu() function.

Some sample output as displayed by member.php is shown in Figure 24.6.

Figure 24.6   The member.php script checks that a user is logged in, retrieves and displays his bookmarks, and gives him a menu of options.

We will now look at the `login()` and `check_valid_user()` functions a little more closely. The `login()` function is shown in Listing 24.12.

Listing 24.12   The login() Function from user_auth_fns.php—This Function Checks a User's Details Against the Database

```
function login($username, $password)
// check username and password with db
// if yes, return true
// else return false
{
  // connect to db
  $conn = db_connect();
  if (!$conn)
    return false;

  // check if username is unique
  $result = mysql_query("select * from user
                    where username='$username'
                    and passwd = password('$password')");
  if (!$result)
    return false;
```

Listing 24.12   **Continued**

```
if (mysql_num_rows($result)>0)
    return true;
else
    return false;
}
```

As you can see, this function connects to the database and checks that there is a user with the username and password combination supplied. It will return true if there is, or false if there is not or if the user's credentials could not be checked.

The check_valid_user() function does not connect to the database again, but instead just checks that the user has a registered session, that is, that he has already logged in. This function is shown in Listing 24.13.

Listing 24.13   **The check_valid_user() Function from user_auth_fns.php—This Function Checks That the User Has a Valid Session**

```
function check_valid_user()
// see if somebody is logged in and notify them if not
{
  global $HTTP_SESSION_VARS;
  if (isset($HTTP_SESSION_VARS['valid_user']))
  {
      echo 'Logged in as '.$HTTP_SESSION_VARS['valid_user'].'.';
      echo '<br / >';
  }
  else
  {
      // they are not logged in
      do_html_heading('Problem:');
      echo 'You are not logged in.<br />';
      do_html_url('login.php', 'Login');
      do_html_footer();
      exit;
  }
}
```

If the user is not logged in, the function will tell him he has to be logged in to see this page, and give him a link to the login page.

Logging Out

You might have noticed that there is a link marked "Logout" on the menu in Figure 24.6. This is a link to the logout.php script. The code for this script is shown in Listing 24.14.

Listing 24.14 **logout.php—This Script Ends a User Session**

```php
<?php

// include function files for this application
require_once('bookmark_fns.php');
session_start();
$old_user = $HTTP_SESSION_VARS['valid_user'];
// store  to test if they *were* logged in
unset($HTTP_SESSION_VARS);
$result_dest = session_destroy();

// start output html
do_html_header('Logging Out');

if (!empty($old_user))
{
  if ($result_dest)
  {
    // if they were logged in and are now logged out
    echo 'Logged out.<br />';
    do_html_url('login.php', 'Login');
  }
  else
  {
   // they were logged in and could not be logged out
    echo 'Could not log you out.<br />';
  }
}
else
{
  // if they weren't logged in but came to this page somehow
  echo 'You were not logged in, and so have not been logged out.<br />';
  do_html_url('login.php', 'Login');
}

do_html_footer();

?>
```

Again, you might find that this code looks familiar. That's because it is based on the code
we wrote in Chapter 20.

Changing Passwords

If a user follows the "Change Password" menu option, he will be presented with the
form shown in Figure 24.7.

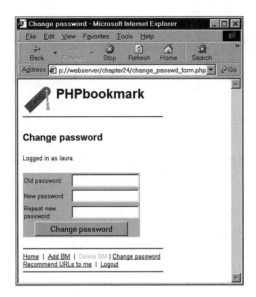

Figure 24.7   The change_passwd_form.php script supplies
a form where users can change their passwords.

This form is generated by the script change_passwd_form.php. This is a simple script
that just uses the functions from the output library, so we have not included the source
for it here.

  When this form is submitted, it triggers the change_passwd.php script, which is
shown in Listing 24.15.

Listing 24.15   change_passwd.php—This Script Attempts to Change a User Password

```php
<?php
  require_once('bookmark_fns.php');
  session_start();
  do_html_header('Changing password');

  // create short variable names
  $old_passwd = $HTTP_POST_VARS['old_passwd'];
  $new_passwd = $HTTP_POST_VARS['new_passwd'];
  $new_passwd2 = $HTTP_POST_VARS['new_passwd2'];


 check_valid_user();
 if (!filled_out($HTTP_POST_VARS))
 {
   echo 'You have not filled out the form completely.
        Please try again.';
```

Listing 24.15 **Continued**

```
  display_user_menu();
  do_html_footer();
  exit;
 }
 else
 {
   if ($new_passwd!=$new_passwd2)
      echo 'Passwords entered were not the same.  Not changed.';
   else if (strlen($new_passwd)>16 || strlen($new_passwd)<6)
      echo 'New password must be between 6 and 16 characters.  Try again.';
   else
   {
       // attempt update
       if (change_password($HTTP_SESSION_VARS['valid_user'], $old_passwd,
                           $new_passwd))
          echo 'Password changed.';
       else
          echo 'Password could not be changed.';
   }

 }
  display_user_menu();
  do_html_footer();
?>
```

This script checks that the user is logged in (using check_valid_user()), that she's filled out the password form (using filled_out()), and that the new passwords are the same and the right length. None of this is new. If all that goes well, it will call the change_password() function as follows:

```
if (change_password($HTTP_SESSION_VARS['valid_user'], $old_passwd, $new_passwd))
  echo 'Password changed.';
else
  echo 'Password could not be changed.';
```

This function is from our user_auth_fns.php library, and the code for it is shown in Listing 24.16.

Listing 24.16 **change_password() Function from user_auth_fns.php—This Function
         Attempts to Update a User Password in the Database**

```
function change_password($username, $old_password, $new_password)
// change password for username/old_password to new_password
// return true or false
{
  // if the old password is right
  // change their password to new_password and return true
  // else return false
```

Listing 24.16   **Continued**

```
if (login($username, $old_password))
{
  if (!($conn = db_connect()))
    return false;
  $result = mysql_query( "update user
                          set passwd = password('$new_password')
                          where username = '$username'");
  if (!$result)
    return false;  // not changed
  else
    return true;  // changed successfully
}
else
  return false; // old password was wrong
}
```

This function checks that the old password supplied was correct, using the login()
function that we have already looked at. If it's correct, then the function connects to the
database and updates the password to the new value.

Resetting Forgotten Passwords

In addition to changing passwords, we need to deal with the common situation in which
a user has forgotten her password. Notice that on the front page, login.php, we provide
a link for users in this situation, marked, "Forgotten your password?" This link will take
users to the script called forgot_form.php, which uses the output functions to display a
form as shown in Figure 24.8.

Figure 24.8   The forgot_form.php script supplies a form in which users can
ask to have their passwords reset and sent to them.

This script is very simple—just using the output functions—so we will not go through it here. When the form is submitted, it calls the forgot_passwd.php script, which is more interesting. This script is shown in Listing 24.17.

Listing 24.17   **forgot_passwd.php—This Script Resets a User's Password to a Random Value and Emails Her the New One**

```php
<?php
  require_once("bookmark_fns.php");
  do_html_header("Resetting password");

  //creating short variable name
  $username = $HTTP_POST_VARS['username'];

  if ($password=reset_password($username))
  {
    if (notify_password($username, $password))
      echo 'Your new password has been sent to your email address.';
    else
      echo 'Your password could not be mailed to you.'
          .' Try pressing refresh.';
  }
  else
    echo 'Your password could not be reset - please try again later.';

  do_html_url('login.php', 'Login');

  do_html_footer();
?>
```

As you can see, this script uses two main functions to do its job: reset_password() and notify_password(). Let's look at each of these in turn.

The reset_password() function generates a random password for the user and puts it into the database. The code for this function is shown in Listing 24.18.

Listing 24.18   **The reset_password() Function from user_auth_fns.php—This Script Resets a User's Password to a Random Value and Emails Them the New One**

```php
function reset_password($username)
// set password for username to a random value
// return the new password or false on failure
{
  // get a random dictionary word b/w 6 and 13 chars in length
  $new_password = get_random_word(6, 13);

  if($new_password==false)
    return false;
  // add a number  between 0 and 999 to it
```

Listing 24.18 **Continued**

```
  // to make it a slightly better password
  srand ((double) microtime() * 1000000);
  $rand_number = rand(0, 999);
  $new_password .= $rand_number;

  // set user's password to this in database or return false
  if (!($conn = db_connect()))
     return false;
  $result = mysql_query( "update user
                          set passwd = password('$new_password')
                          where username = '$username'");
  if (!$result)
    return false;  // not changed
  else
    return $new_password;  // changed successfully
}
```

This function generates its random password by getting a random word from a dictionary, using the get_random_word() function and suffixing it with a random number
between 0 and 999. The get_random_word() function is also in the user_auth_fns.php
library. This function is shown in Listing 24.19.

Listing 24.19 **The get_random_word() Function from user_auth_fns.php—This
Function Gets a Random Word from the Dictionary for Use in
Generating Passwords**

```
function get_random_word($min_length, $max_length)
// grab a random word from dictionary between the two lengths
// and return it
{
  // generate a random word
  $word = '';
  //remember to change this path to suit your system
  $dictionary = '/usr/dict/words';  // the ispell dictionary
  $fp = fopen($dictionary, 'r');
  if(!$fp)
    return false;
  $size = filesize($dictionary);

  // go to a random location in dictionary
  srand ((double) microtime() * 1000000);
  $rand_location = rand(0, $size);
  fseek($fp, $rand_location);

  // get the next whole word of the right length in the file
  while (strlen($word)< $min_length || strlen($word)>$max_length
                         || strstr($word, "'"))
```

Listing 24.19 **Continued**

```
{
    if (feof($fp))
        fseek($fp, 0);        // if at end, go to start
    $word = fgets($fp, 80);  // skip first word as it could be partial
    $word = fgets($fp, 80);  // the potential password
};
$word=trim($word); // trim the trailing \n from fgets
return $word;
}
```

To work, this function needs a dictionary. If you are using a UNIX system, the built-in spell checker ispell comes with a dictionary of words, typically located at /usr/dict/words, as it is here, or at /usr/share/dict/words. If you don't find it in one of these places, on most systems you will be able to find yours by typing

```
locate dict/words
```

If you are using some other system or do not want to install ispell, don't worry! You can download word lists as used by ispell from

```
http://wordlist.sourceforge.net/
```

This site also has dictionaries in many other languages, so if you would like a random, say, Norwegian or Esperanto word, you can download one of those dictionaries instead. These files are formatted with each word on a separate line, separated by newlines.

To get a random word from this file, we pick a random location between 0 and the filesize, and read from the file there. If we read from the random location to the next newline, we will most likely only get a partial word, so we skip the line we open the file to, and take the next word as our word by calling fgets() twice.

The function has two clever bits. The first is that, if we reach the end of the file while looking for a word, we go back to the beginning:

```
if (feof($fp))
    fseek($fp, 0);        // if at end, go to start
```

The second is that we can seek for a word of a particular length—we check each word that we pull from the dictionary, and, if it is not between $min_length and $max_length, we keep searching. At the same time, we also dump words with apostrophes (single quotes) in them. We could escape these out when using the word, but it is easier to just get the next word.

Back in reset_password(), after we have generated a new password, we update the database to reflect this, and return the new password back to the main script. This will then be passed on to notify_password(), which will email it to the user.

Let's have a look at the notify_password() function, shown in Listing 24.20.

Listing 24.20   **The notify_password() Function from user_auth_fns.php—This Function Emails a Reset Password to a User**

```
function notify_password($username, $password)
// notify the user that their password has been changed
{
    if (!($conn = db_connect()))
      return false;
    $result = mysql_query("select email from user
                           where username='$username'");
    if (!$result)
    {
      return false;  // not changed
    }
    else if (mysql_num_rows($result)==0)
    {
      return false; // username not in db
    }
    else
    {
      $email = mysql_result($result, 0, 'email');
      $from = "From: support@phpbookmark \r\n";
      $mesg = "Your PHPBookmark password has been changed to $password \r\n"
             ."Please change it next time you log in. \r\n";


      if (mail($email, 'PHPBookmark login information', $mesg, $from))
        return true;
      else
        return false;
    }
}
```

In this function, given a username and new password, we simply look up the email address for that user in the database, and use PHP's mail() function to send it to her.

It would be more secure to give users a truly random password—made from any combination of upper and lowercase letters, numbers, and punctuation—rather than our random word and number. However, a password like 'zigzag487' will be easier for our user to read and type than a truly random one. It is often confusing for users to work out whether a character in a random string is 0 or O (zero or capital O), or 1 or l (one or a lowercase L).

On our system, the dictionary file contains about 45,000 words. If a cracker knew how we were creating passwords, and knew a user's name, he would still have to try 22,500,000 passwords on average to guess one. This level of security seems adequate for this type of application even if our users disregard the emailed advice to change it.

Implementing Bookmark Storage and Retrieval

Now we'll move on and look at how a user's bookmarks are stored, retrieved, and deleted.

Adding Bookmarks

Users can add bookmarks by clicking on the Add BM link in the user menu. This will take them to the form shown in Figure 24.9.

Figure 24.9   The add_bm_form.php script supplies a form
where users can add bookmarks to their bookmark pages.

Again, this script is simple and uses just the output functions, so we will not go through it here. When the form is submitted, it calls the add_bms.php script, which is shown in Listing 24.21.

Listing 24.21   **add_bms.php—This Script Adds New Bookmarks to a User's Personal Page**

```php
<?php
 require_once('bookmark_fns.php');
 session_start();

 //create short variable name
 $new_url = $HTTP_POST_VARS['new_url'];

 do_html_header('Adding bookmarks');
 check_valid_user();
```

Listing 24.21   **Continued**

```php
if (!filled_out($HTTP_POST_VARS))
{
  echo 'You have not filled out the form completely.
        Please try again.';
  display_user_menu();
  do_html_footer();
  exit;
}
else
{
  // check URL format
  if (strstr($new_url, 'http://')===false)
    $new_url = 'http://'.$new_url;

  // check URL is valid
  if (@fopen($new_url, 'r'))
  {
    // try to add bm
    if (add_bm($new_url))
      echo 'Bookmark added.';
    else
      echo 'Could not add bookmark.';
  }
  else
    echo 'Not a valid URL.';
}

  // get the bookmarks this user has saved
  if ($url_array = get_user_urls($HTTP_SESSION_VARS['valid_user']));
    display_user_urls($url_array);

  display_user_menu();
  do_html_footer();
?>
```

Again this script follows the pattern of validation, database entry, and output.

To validate, we first check whether the user has filled out the form using
`filled_out()`.

We then perform two URL checks. First, using `strstr()`, we see whether the URL
begins with `http://`. If it doesn't, we add this to the start of the URL. After we've done
this, we can actually check that the URL really exists. As you might recall from Chapter
17, "Using Network and Protocol Functions," we can use `fopen()` to open an URL that
starts with `http://`. If we can open this file, we assume the URL is valid and call the
function `add_bm()` to add it to the database.

Note that fopen() will only be able to open files if your server has direct access to the Internet. If it needs to access other HTTP servers via a proxy server, fopen() will not work.

This function and the others relating to bookmarks are all in the function library url_fns.php. You can see the code for the add_bm() function in Listing 24.22.

Listing 24.22   **The add_bm() function from url_fns.php—This Function Adds New Bookmarks to the Database**

```
function add_bm($new_url)
{
  // Add new bookmark to the database

  echo "Attempting to add ".htmlspecialchars($new_url).'<br />';
  global $HTTP_SESSION_VARS;
  $valid_user = $HTTP_SESSION_VARS['valid_user'];

  if (!($conn = db_connect()))
    return false;

  // check not a repeat bookmark
  $result = mysql_query("select * from bookmark
                         where username='$valid_user'
                         and bm_URL='$new_url'");
  if ($result && (mysql_num_rows($result)>0))
    return false;

  // insert the new bookmark
  if (!mysql_query( "insert into bookmark values
                          ('$valid_user', '$new_url')"))
    return false;

  return true;
}
```

This function is fairly simple. It checks that a user does not already have this bookmark listed in the database. (Although it is unlikely that users would enter a bookmark twice, it is possible and even likely that they might refresh the page.) If the bookmark is new, then it is entered into the database.

Looking back at add_bm.php, you can see that the last thing it does is call get_user_urls() and display_user_urls(), the same as member.php. We'll move on and look at these functions next.

Displaying Bookmarks

In the member.php script and the add_bm() function, we used the functions get_user_urls() and display_user_urls(). These functions get the user's bookmarks from the database and display them, respectively. The `get_user_urls()` function is in the url_fns.php library, and the `display_user_urls()` function is in the output_fns.php library.

The `get_user_urls()` function is shown in Listing 24.23.

Listing 24.23   The get_user_urls() Function from url_fns.php—This Function Retrieves a User's Bookmarks from the Database

```
function get_user_urls($username)
{
  //extract from the database all the URLs this user has stored
  if (!($conn = db_connect()))
    return false;
  $result = mysql_query( "select bm_URL
                          from bookmark
                          where username = '$username'");
  if (!$result)
    return false;

  //create an array of the URLs
  $url_array = array();
  for ($count = 1; $row = mysql_fetch_row ($result); ++$count)
  {
    $url_array[$count] = addslashes($row[0]);
  }
  return $url_array;
}
```

Let's briefly step through this function. It takes a username as parameter, and retrieves the bookmarks for that user from the database. It will return an array of these URLs or false if the bookmarks could not be retrieved.

The array from `get_user_urls()` can be passed to `display_user_urls()`. This is again a simple HTML output function to print the user's URLs in a nice table format, so we won't go through it here. Refer back to Figure 24.6 to see what the output looks like. The function actually puts the URLs into a form. Next to each URL is a check box that enables bookmarks to be marked for deletion. We will look at this next.

Deleting Bookmarks

When a user marks some bookmarks for deletion and clicks on the Delete BM option in the menu, the form containing the URLs will be submitted. Each one of the check boxes is produced by the following code in the `display_user_urls()` function:

```
echo "<td><input type=\"checkbox\" name=\"del_me[]\"
            value=\"$url\"></td>";
```

The name of each input is `del_me[]`. This means that, in the PHP script activated by this form, we will have access to an array called `$del_me` that will contain all the bookmarks to be deleted.

Clicking on the Delete BM option activates the `delete_bms.php` script. This script is shown in Listing 24.24.

Listing 24.24   **delete_bms.php—This Script Deletes Bookmarks from the Database**

```php
<?php
  require_once('bookmark_fns.php');
  session_start();

  //create short variable names
  $del_me = $HTTP_POST_VARS['del_me'];
  $valid_user = $HTTP_SESSION_VARS['valid_user'];

  do_html_header('Deleting bookmarks');
  check_valid_user();
  if (!filled_out($HTTP_POST_VARS))
  {
    echo 'You have not chosen any bookmarks to delete.
         Please try again.';
    display_user_menu();
    do_html_footer();
    exit;
  }
  else
  {
    if (count($del_me) >0)
    {
      foreach($del_me as $url)
      {
        if (delete_bm($valid_user, $url))
          echo 'Deleted '.htmlspecialchars($url).'.<br />';
        else
          echo 'Could not delete '.htmlspecialchars($url).'.<br />';
      }
    }
    else
      echo 'No bookmarks selected for deletion';
  }
```

Listing 24.24 **Continued**

```
  // get the bookmarks this user has saved
  if ($url_array = get_user_urls($valid_user));
    display_user_urls($url_array);

  display_user_menu();
  do_html_footer();
?>
```

We begin this script by performing the usual validations. When we know that the user has selected some bookmarks for deletion, we delete them in the following loop:

```
foreach($del_me as $url)
{
  if (delete_bm($valid_user, $url))
    echo 'Deleted '.htmlspecialchars($url).'.<br />';
  else
    echo 'Could not delete '.htmlspecialchars($url).'.<br />';
}
```

As you can see, the `delete_bm()` function does the actual work of deleting the book-mark from the database. This function is shown in Listing 24.25.

Listing 24.25 **delete_bm()Function in url_fns.php—This Function Deletes a Single Bookmark from a User's List**

```
function delete_bm($user, $url)
{
  // delete one URL from the database
  if (!($conn = db_connect()))
    return false;

  // delete the bookmark
  if (!mysql_query( "delete from bookmark
                       where username='$user' and bm_url='$url'"))
    return false;
  return true;
}
```

As you can see, this is again a pretty simple function. It attempts to delete the bookmark for a particular user from the database. One thing to note is that we want to remove a particular username-bookmark pair. Other users might still have this URL bookmarked.

Some sample output from running the delete script on our system is shown in Figure 24.10.

As in the `add_bms.php` script, when the changes to the database have been made, we display the new bookmark list using `get_user_urls()` and `display_user_urls()`.

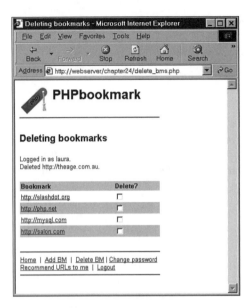

Figure 24.10   The deletion script notifies the user of deleted
bookmarks and then displays the remaining bookmarks.

Implementing Recommendations

Finally, we come to the link recommender script, `recommend.php`.

There are many different ways we could approach recommendations. We have decided to perform what we call a "like-minds" recommendation. That is, we will look for other users who have at least one bookmark the same as our given user. The other bookmarks of those other users might appeal to our given user as well.

The easiest way to implement this as an SQL query would be to use a subquery. First, we get the list of similar users in a subquery, and then we look at their bookmarks in an outer query.

However, as you might recall, MySQL does not support subqueries. We will have to perform two different queries and feed the output of the first into the next. We can do this either by setting up a temporary table with the results from the first query, or by processing the first query results through PHP.

We have chosen the second approach. Both approaches have merit. Using a temporary table is probably slightly faster, but processing in PHP makes it easier to test and modify the code.

We begin by running the following query:

```
select distinct(b2.username)
from bookmark b1, bookmark b2
```

```
where b1.username='$valid_user'
and b1.username != b2.username
and b1.bm_URL = b2.bm_URL
```

This query uses aliases to join the database table bookmark to itself—a strange but some-times useful concept. Imagine that there are actually two bookmark tables, one called b1 and one called b2. In b1, we look at the current user and his bookmarks. In the other table, we look at the bookmarks of all the other users. We are looking for other users (b2.username) who have an URL the same as the current user (b1.bm_URL = b2.bm_URL) and are not the current user (b1.username != b2.username).

This query will give us a list of like-minded people to our current user. Armed with this list, we can search for their other bookmarks with the following query:

```
select bm_URL
from bookmark
where username in $sim_users
and bm_URL not in $user_urls
group by bm_URL
having count(bm_URL)>$popularity
```

The variable $sim_users contains the list of like-minded users. The $user_urls variable contains the list of the current user's bookmarks—if b1 already has a bookmark, there's no point in recommending it to him. Finally, we add some filtering with the $popular-ity variable—we don't want to recommend any URLs that are too personal, so we only suggest URLs that a certain number of other users in the list of like-minded users have bookmarked.

If we were anticipating a lot of users using our system, we could adjust $popularity upwards to only suggest URLs have been bookmarked by a large number of users. URLs bookmarked by many people might be higher quality and certainly have more general appeal than an average Web page.

The full script for making recommendations is shown in Listing 24.26 and 24.27. The main script for making recommendations is called recommend.php (see Listing 24.26). It calls the recommender function recommend_urls() from url_fns.php (see Listing 24.27) .

Listing 24.26   recommend.php—This Script Suggests Some Bookmarks That a User Might Like

```php
<?php
  require_once('bookmark_fns.php');
  session_start();
  do_html_header('Recommending URLs');
  check_valid_user();
  $urls = recommend_urls($HTTP_SESSION_VARS['valid_user']);
  display_recommended_urls($urls);
```

Listing 24.26 **Continued**

```
  display_user_menu();
  do_html_footer();
?>
```

Listing 24.27 **recommend_urls() Function from url_fns.php—This Script Works Out
the Actual Recommendations**

```
function recommend_urls($valid_user, $popularity = 1)
{
  // We will provide semi intelligent recomendations to people
  // If they have an URL in common with other users, they may like
  // other URLs that these people like
  if (!($conn = db_connect()))
    return false;

  // find other matching users
  // with an url the same as you

  if (!($result = mysql_query("
                  select distinct(b2.username)
                  from bookmark b1, bookmark b2
                  where b1.username='$valid_user'
                  and b1.username != b2.username
                  and b1.bm_URL = b2.bm_URL
                  ")))
    return false;
  if (mysql_num_rows($result)==0)
    return false;

  // create set of users with urls in common
  // for use in IN clause
  $row = mysql_fetch_object($result);
  $sim_users = "('".($row->username)."'";
  while ($row = mysql_fetch_object($result))
  {
    $sim_users .= ", '".($row->username)."'";
  }
  $sim_users .= ')';

  // create list of user urls
  // to avoid replicating ones we already know about
  if (!($result = mysql_query("
                  select bm_URL
                  from bookmark
```

```
                       where username='$valid_user'")))
    return false;

// create set of user urls for use in IN clause
$row = mysql_fetch_object($result);
$user_urls = "('".($row->bm_URL)."'";
while ($row = mysql_fetch_object($result))
{
    $user_urls .= ", '".($row->bm_URL)."'";
}
$user_urls .= ')';

// as a simple way of excluding people's private pages, and
// increasing the chance of recommending appealing URLs, we
// specify a minimum popularity level
// if $popularity = 1, then more than one person must have
// an URL before we will recomend it

// find out max number of possible URLs
if (!($result = mysql_query("
                   select bm_URL
                   from bookmark
                   where username in $sim_users
                   and bm_URL not in $user_urls
                   group by bm_URL
                   having count(bm_URL)>$popularity
                 ")))
    return false;

if (!($num_urls=mysql_num_rows($result)))
    return false;

$urls = array();
// build an array of the relevant urls
for ($count=0; $row = mysql_fetch_object($result); $count++)
{
    $urls[$count] = $row->bm_URL;
}

return $urls;
}
```

Some sample output from recommend.php is shown in Figure 24.11.

Figure 24.11 The script has recommended that this user might like pets.com. Two other users in the database who both like slashdot.org have this bookmarked.

Wrapping Up and Possible Extensions

That's the basic functionality of the PHPBookmark application. There are many possible extensions. You might consider adding

- A grouping of bookmarks by topic
- An "Add this to my bookmarks" link for recommendations
- Recommendations based on the most popular URLs in the database, or on a particular topic
- An administrative interface to set up and administer users and topics
- Ways to make recommended bookmarks more intelligent or faster
- Additional error checking of user input

Experiment! It's the best way to learn.

Next

In the next project we'll build a shopping cart that will enable users to browse our site, adding purchases as they go, before finally checking out and making an electronic payment.

25

Building a Shopping Cart

In this chapter, you will learn how to build a basic shopping cart. We will add this on top of the Book-O-Rama database that we implemented in Part II, "Using MySQL." We will also explore another option—setting up and using an existing Open Source PHP shopping cart.

In case you have not heard it before, the term *shopping cart* (sometimes also called a *shopping basket*) is used to describe a specific online shopping mechanism. As you browse an online catalog, you can add items to your shopping cart. When you've finished browsing, you check out of the online store—that is, purchase the items in your cart.

In order to implement the shopping cart, we will implement the following functionality:

- A database of the products we want to sell online
- An online catalog of products, listed by category
- A shopping cart to track the items a user wants to buy
- A checkout script that processes payment and shipping details
- An administration interface

The Problem

You will probably remember the Book-O-Rama database we developed in Part II. In this project, we will get Book-O-Rama's online store up and going. The following are requirements for this system:

- We will need to find a way of connecting the database to a user's browser. Users should be able to browse items by category.
- Users should also be able to select items from the catalog for later purchase. We will need to be able to track which items they have selected.

- When they have finished shopping, we will need to be able to total up their order, take their delivery details, and process their payment.

- We should also build an administrator interface to Book-O-Rama's site so that the administrator can add and edit books and categories on the site.

Solution Components

Let's look at the solutions to meeting each of the requirements listed previously.

Building an Online Catalog

We already have a database for the Book-O-Rama catalog. However, it will probably need some alterations and additions for this application. One of these will be to add categories of books, as stated in the requirements.

We'll also need to add some information to our existing database about shipping addresses, payment details, and so on.

We already know how to build an interface to a MySQL database using PHP, so this part of the solution should be pretty easy.

Tracking a User's Purchases While She Shops

There are two basic ways we can track a user's purchases while she shops. One is to put her selections into our database, and the other is to use a session variable.

Using a session variable to track selections from page to page will be easier to write as it will not require us to constantly query the database for this information. It will also avoid the situation where we end up with a lot of junk data in the database from users who are just browsing and change their minds.

We need, therefore, to design a session variable or set of variables to store a user's selections. When a user finishes shopping and pays for her purchases, we will put this information in our database as a record of the transaction.

We can also use this data to give a summary of the current state of the cart in one corner of the page, so a user knows at any given time how much she is planning to spend.

Payment

In this project, we will add up the user's order and take the delivery details. We will not actually process payments. Many, many payment systems are available, and the implementation for each one is different. We will write a *dummy* function that can be replaced with an interface to your chosen system.

Payment systems are generally sold in more specific geographic areas than this book. The way the different real-time processing interfaces work is generally similar. You will need to organize a merchant account with a bank for the cards you want to accept. Your payment system provider will specify what parameters you will need to pass to their system.

The payment system will transmit your data to a bank and return a success code or one of many different types of error codes. In exchange for passing on your data, the payment gateway will charge you a setup or annual fee, as well as a fee based on the number or value of your transactions. Some providers even charge for declined transactions.

Your chosen payment system will need information from the customer (such as a credit card number), identifying information from you (to specify which merchant account is to be credited), and the total amount of the transaction.

We can work out the total of an order from a user's shopping cart session variable. We will record the final order details in the database, and get rid of the session variable at that time.

Administration Interface

In addition to all this, we will build an administrator interface that will let us add, delete, and edit books and categories from the database.

One common edit that we might make is to alter the price of an item (for example, for a special offer or sale). This means that when we store a customer's order, we should also store the price she paid for an item. It would make for an accounting nightmare if the only records we had were what items each customer ordered, and what the current price of each is. This also means that if the customer has to return or exchange the item, we will give her the right amount of credit.

We are not going to build a fulfillment and order tracking interface for this example. You can add one onto this base system to suit your needs.

Solution Overview

Let's put all the pieces together.

There are two basic views of the system: the user view and the administrator view. After considering the functionality required, we came up with two system flow designs, one for each view. These are shown in Figure 25.1 and Figure 25.2, respectively.

In Figure 25.1, we show the main links between scripts in the user part of the site. A customer will come first to the main page, which lists all the categories of books in the site. From there, she can go to a particular category of books, and from there to an individual book's details.

We will give the user a link to add a particular book to her cart. From the cart, she will be able to check out of the online store.

Figure 25.2 shows the administrator interface—this has more scripts, but not much new code. These scripts let an administrator log in and insert books and categories.

The easiest way to implement editing and deletion of books and categories is to show the administrator a slightly different version of the user interface to the site. The administrator will still be able to browse categories and books, but instead of having access to the shopping cart, the administrator will be able to go to a particular book or category and edit or delete that book or category. By making the same scripts suit both normal and administrator users, we can save ourselves time and effort.

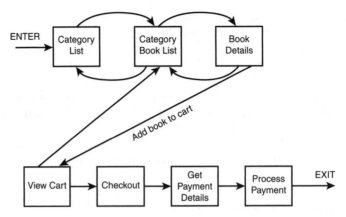

Figure 25.1   The user view of the Book-O-Rama system lets users browse books by category, view book details, add books to their cart, and purchase them.

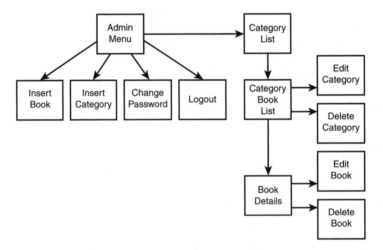

Figure 25.2   The administrator view of the Book-O-Rama system allows insertion, editing, and deletion of books and categories.

The three main code modules for this application are as follows:

- Catalog
- Shopping cart and order processing (We've bundled these together because they are strongly related.)
- Administration

As in the last project, we will also build and use a set of function libraries. For this project, we will use a function API similar to the one in the last project. We will try to confine the parts of our code that output HTML to a single library to support the principle of separating logic and content and, more importantly, to make our code easier to read and maintain.

We will also need to make some minor changes to the Book-O-Rama database for this project. We have renamed the database book_sc (Shopping Cart) to distinguish the shopping cart database from the one we built in Part II.

All the code for this project can be found on the CD-ROM. A summary of the files in the application is shown in Table 25.1.

Table 25.1   **Files in the Shopping Cart Application**

Name	Module	Description
index.php	Catalog	Main front page of site for users. Shows the user a list of categories in the system.
show_cat.php	Catalog	Shows the user all the books in a particular category.
show_book.php	Catalog	Shows the user details of a particular book.
show_cart.php	Shopping cart	Shows the user the contents of her shopping cart. Also used to add items to the cart.
checkout.php	Shopping cart	Presents the user with complete order details. Gets shipping details.
purchase.php	Shopping cart	Gets payment details from user.
process.php	Shopping cart	Processes payment details and adds order to database.
login.php	Administration	Allows administrator to log in to make changes.
logout.php	Administration	Logs out admin user.
admin.php	Administration	Main administration menu.
change_password_form.php	Administration	Form to let administrator change her log password.
change_password.php	Administration	Changes administrator password.
insert_category_form.php	Administration	Form to let administrator add a new category to database.
insert_category.php	Administration	Inserts new category into database.
insert_book_form.php	Administration	Form to let administrator add a new book to system.
insert_book.php	Administration	Inserts new book into database.
edit_category_form.php	Administration	Form to let administrator edit a category.
edit_category.php	Administration	Updates category in database.

Table 25.1   **Continued**

Name	Module	Description
edit_book_form.php	Administration	Form to let administrator edit a book's details.
edit_book.php	Administration	Updates book in database.
delete_category.php	Administration	Deletes a category from the database.
delete_book.php	Administration	Deletes a book from the database.
book_sc_fns.php	Functions	Collection of include files for this application.
admin_fns.php	Functions	Collection of functions used by administrative scripts.
book_fns.php	Functions	Collection of functions for storing and retrieving book data.
order_fns.php	Functions	Collection of functions for storing and retrieving order data.
output_fns.php	Functions	Collection of functions for outputting HTML.
data_valid_fns.php	Functions	Collection of functions for validating input data.
db_fns.php	Functions	Collection of functions for connecting to the book_sc database.
user_auth_fns.php	Functions	Collection of functions for authenticating administrative users.
book_sc.sql	SQL	SQL to set up the book_sc database
populate.sql	SQL	SQL to insert some sample data into the book_sc database.

Now, let's look at the implementation of each of the modules.

> **Note**
>
> There is a lot of code in this application. Much of it implements functionality we have looked at already (particularly in the last chapter), such as storing data to and retrieving it from the database, and authenticating the administrative user. We will look very briefly at this code, but spend most of our time on the shopping cart functions.
>
> For the code in this project to work as written, you will need to have magic quotes switched on. If you have not done this, you will need to addslashes() to data going to the MySQL database, and stripslashes() from data coming back from the database. We have used this as a useful shortcut.
>
> You can enable magic quotes on a per-directory basis in an .htaccess file with the directive
>
> php_value magic_quotes_gpc on (for PHP 4)
>
> or
>
> php3_magic_quotes_gpc on (for PHP 3)

Implementing the Database

As we mentioned earlier, we have made some minor modifications to the Book-O-Rama database presented in Part II.

The SQL to create the book_sc database is shown in Listing 25.1.

Listing 25.1 book_sc.sql—SQL to Create the book_sc Database

```
create database book_sc;

use book_sc;

create table customers
(
  customerid int unsigned not null auto_increment primary key,
  name char(40) not null,
  address char(40) not null,
  city char(20) not null,
  state char(20),
  zip char(10),
  country char(20) not null
);

create table orders
(
  orderid int unsigned not null auto_increment primary key,
  customerid int unsigned not null,
  amount float(6,2),
  date date not null,
  order_status char(10),
  ship_name char(40) not null,
  ship_address char(40) not null,
  ship_city char(20) not null,
  ship_state char(20),
  ship_zip char(10),
  ship_country char(20) not null
);

create table books
(
   isbn char(13) not null primary key,
   author char(30),
   title char(60),
   catid int unsigned,
   price float(4,2) not null,
   description varchar(255)
);
```

Listing 25.1 **Continued**

```
create table categories
(
  catid int unsigned not null auto_increment primary key,
  catname char(40) not null
);

create table order_items
(
  orderid int unsigned not null,
  isbn char(13) not null,
  item_price float(4,2) not null,
  quantity tinyint unsigned not null,
  primary key (orderid, isbn)
);

create table admin
(
  username char(16) not null primary key,
  password char(16) not null
);

grant select, insert, update, delete
on book_sc.*
to book_sc@localhost identified by 'password';
```

Although nothing was wrong with the original Book-O-Rama interface, we have a few other requirements now that we are going to make it available online.

The changes we have made to the original database are as follows:

- The addition of more address fields for customers—this is more important now that we are building a more realistic application.

- The addition of a shipping address to an order. A customer's contact address might not be the same as the shipping address, particularly if she is using the site to buy a gift.

- The addition of a categories table and a catid to books table. Sorting books into categories will make the site easier to browse.

- The addition of item_price to the order_items table to recognize the fact that an item's price might change. We want to know how much it cost when the customer ordered it.

- The addition of an admin table to store administrator login and password details.

- The removal of the reviews table—you could add reviews as an extension to this project. Instead, each book has a description field which will contain a brief blurb about the book.

To set this database up on your system, run the `book_sc.sql` script through MySQL as the root user, as follows:

```
mysql -u root -p < book_sc.sql
```

(You will need to supply your root password.)

Beforehand, you should change the password for the `book_sc` user to something better than `'password'`. Note that if you change the password in book_sc.sql you will also need to change it in db_fns.php. (You'll see where in a minute.)

We have also included a file of sample data. This is called `populate.sql`. You can put the sample data into the database by running it through MySQL in this same way.

Implementing the Online Catalog

Three catalog scripts are in this application: the main page, the category page, and the book details page.

The front page of the site is produced by the script called `index.php`. The output of this script is shown in Figure 25.3.

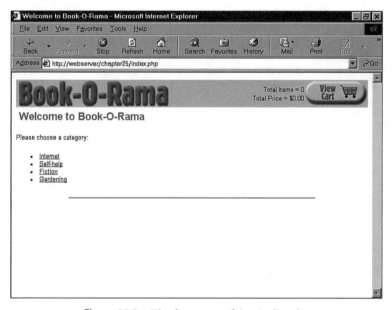

Figure 25.3 The front page of the site lists the categories of books available for purchase.

You'll notice that, in addition to the list of categories on the site, there is a link to the shopping cart in the top-right corner of the screen and some summary information about what's in the cart. This will appear on every page while a user browses and shops.

If a user clicks one of the categories, she'll be taken to the category page, produced by the script show_cat.php. The category page for the Internet books section is shown in Figure 25.4.

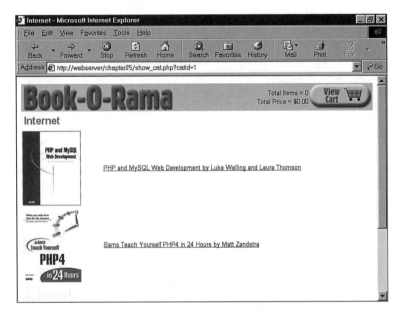

Figure 25.4   Each book in the category is listed with a photo.

All the books in the Internet category are listed as links. If a user clicks one of these links, she will be taken to the book details page. The book details page for one book is shown in Figure 25.5.

On this page, as well as the View Cart link, we have an Add to Cart link in which the user can select an item. We'll return to that when we look at how to build the shopping cart later.

Let's look at each of these three scripts.

Listing Categories

The first script, index.php, lists all the categories in the database. It is shown in Listing 25.2.

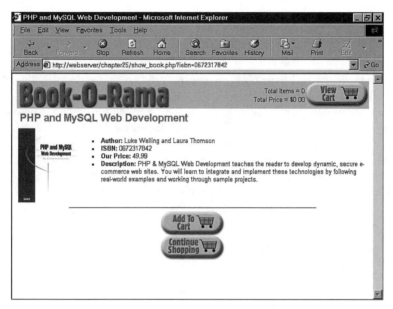

Figure 25.5   Each book has a details page that shows more
information including a long description.

Listing 25.2   **index.php—Script to Produce the Front Page of the Site**

```php
<?php
  include ('book_sc_fns.php');
  // The shopping cart needs sessions, so start one
  session_start();
  do_html_header('Welcome to Book-O-Rama');

  echo '<p>Please choose a category:</p>';

  // get categories out of database
  $cat_array = get_categories();

  // display as links to cat pages
  display_categories($cat_array);

  // if logged in as admin, show add, delete, edit cat links
  if(isset($HTTP_SESSION_VARS['admin_user']))
  {
    display_button('admin.php', 'admin-menu', 'Admin Menu');
  }
```

Listing 25.2 **Continued**

```
  do_html_footer();
?>
```

The script begins by including book_sc_fns.php, the file that includes all the function libraries for this application.

After that, we must begin a session. This will be required for the shopping cart functionality to work. Every page in the site will use the session.

There are some calls to HTML output functions such as do_html_header() and do_html_footer() (both contained in output_fns.php).

We also have some code that checks if the user is logged in as an administrator and gives her some different navigation options if she is—we'll return to this in the section on the administration functions.

The most important part of this script is

```
// get categories out of database
$cat_array = get_categories();

// display as links to cat pages
display_categories($cat_array);
```

The functions get_categories() and display_categories() are in the function libraries book_fns.php and output_fns.php, respectively. The function get_categories() returns an array of the categories in the system, which we then pass to display_categories(). Let's look at the code for get_categories(). It is shown in Listing 25.3.

Listing 25.3 **get_categories() Function from book_fns.php—Function That Retrieves a Category List from the Database**

```
function get_categories()
{
    // query database for a list of categories
    $conn = db_connect();
    $query = 'select catid, catname
                from categories';
    $result = @mysql_query($query);
    if (!$result)
      return false;
    $num_cats = @mysql_num_rows($result);
    if ($num_cats ==0)
        return false;
    $result = db_result_to_array($result);
    return $result;
}
```

As you can see, this function connects to the database and retrieves a list of all the category IDs and names. We have written and used a function called `db_result_to_array()`, located in `db_fns.php`. This function is shown in Listing 25.4. It takes a MySQL result identifier and returns a numerically indexed array of rows, where each row is an associative array.

Listing 25.4   db_result_to_array() Function from db_fns.php—Function That Converts a MySQL Result Identifier into an Array of Results

```php
function db_result_to_array($result)
{
    $res_array = array();

    for ($count=0; $row = @mysql_fetch_array($result); $count++)
        $res_array[$count] = $row;

    return $res_array;
}
```

In our case, we will return this array back all the way to `index.php`, where we pass it to the `display_categories()` function from `output_fns.php`. This function displays each category as a link to the page containing the books in that category. The code for this function is shown in Listing 25.5.

Listing 25.5   display_categories() Function from output_fns.php—Function That Displays an Array of Categories as a List of Links to Those Categories

```php
function display_categories($cat_array)
{
    if (!is_array($cat_array))
    {
        echo 'No categories currently available<br />';
        return;
    }
    echo '<ul>';
    foreach ($cat_array as $row)
    {
        $url = 'show_cat.php?catid='.($row['catid']);
        $title = $row['catname'];
        echo '<li>';
        do_html_url($url, $title);
        echo '</li>';
    }
    echo '</ul>';
    echo '<hr />';
}
```

This function converts each category from the database into a link. Each link goes to the next script—show_cat.php—but each has a different parameter, the category ID or catid. (This is a unique number, generated by MySQL, and used to identify the category.)

This parameter to the next script will determine which category we end up looking at.

Listing Books in a Category

The process for listing books in a category is similar. The script that does this is called show_cat.php. It is shown in Listing 25.6.

Listing 25.6 **show_cat.php—This Script Shows the Books in a Particular Category**

```php
<?php
  include ('book_sc_fns.php');
  // The shopping cart needs sessions, so start one
  session_start();

  $catid = $HTTP_GET_VARS['catid'];
  $name = get_category_name($catid);

  do_html_header($name);

  // get the book info out from db
  $book_array = get_books($catid);

  display_books($book_array);


  // if logged in as admin, show add, delete book links
  if(isset($HTTP_SESSION_VARS['admin_user']))
  {
    display_button('index.php', 'continue', 'Continue Shopping');
    display_button('admin.php', 'admin-menu', 'Admin Menu');
    display_button("edit_category_form.php?catid=$catid",
      'edit-category', 'Edit Category');
  }
  else
    display_button('index.php', 'continue-shopping', 'Continue Shopping');

  do_html_footer();
?>
```

This script is very similar in structure to the index page, with the difference being that we are retrieving books instead of categories.

We start with `session_start()` as usual, and then convert the category ID we have been passed into a category name using the `get_category_name()` function as follows:

```
$name = get_category_name($catid);
```

This function looks up the category name in the database. It is shown in Listing 25.7.

Listing 25.7   **get_category_name() Function from book_fns.php—This Function Converts a Category ID to a Category Name**

```
function get_category_name($catid)
{
  // query database for the name for a category id
  $conn = db_connect();
  $query = "select catname
            from categories
            where catid = $catid";
  $result = @mysql_query($query);
  if (!$result)
    return false;
  $num_cats = @mysql_num_rows($result);
  if ($num_cats ==0)
     return false;
  $result = mysql_result($result, 0, 'catname');
  return $result;
}
```

After we have retrieved the category name, we can render an HTML header and proceed to retrieve and list the books from the database that fall into our chosen category, as follows:

```
$book_array = get_books($catid);
display_books($book_array);
```

The functions `get_books()` and `display_books()` are extremely similar to the `get_categories()` and `display_categories()` functions, so we will not go into them here. The only difference is that we are retrieving information from the books table rather than the categories table.

The `display_books()` function provides a link to each book in the category via the `show_book.php` script. Again, each link is suffixed with a parameter. This time around, it's the ISBN for the book in question.

At the bottom of the `show_cat.php` script, you will see that there is some code to display some additional functions if an administrator is logged in. We will look at these in the section on administrative functions.

Showing Book Details

The show_book.php script takes an ISBN as a parameter and retrieves and displays the details of that book. The code for this script is shown in Listing 25.8.

Listing 25.8 **show_book.php—This Script Shows the Details of a Particular Book**

```php
<?php
  include ('book_sc_fns.php');
  // The shopping cart needs sessions, so start one
  session_start();

  $isbn = $HTTP_GET_VARS['isbn'];

  // get this book out of database
  $book = get_book_details($isbn);
  do_html_header($book['title']);
  display_book_details($book);

  // set url for "continue button"
  $target = 'index.php';
  if($book['catid'])
  {
    $target = 'show_cat.php?catid='.$book['catid'];
  }
  // if logged in as admin, show edit book links
  if( check_admin_user() )
  {
    display_button("edit_book_form.php?isbn=$isbn", 'edit-item', 'Edit Item');
    display_button('admin.php', 'admin-menu', 'Admin Menu');
    display_button($target, 'continue', 'Continue');
  }
  else
  {
    display_button("show_cart.php?new=$isbn", 'add-to-cart', 'Add '
                    .$book['title'].' To My Shopping Cart');
    display_button($target, 'continue-shopping', 'Continue Shopping');
  }

  do_html_footer();
?>
```

Again with this script, we are doing very similar things as in the previous two pages. We begin by starting the session, and then use

```php
$book = get_book_details($isbn);
```

to get the book information out of the database, and

```
display_book_details($book);
```

to output the data in HTML.

One thing to note here is that `display_book_details()` looks for an image file for the book as `images/$isbn.jpg`. If this file does not exist, no image will be displayed.

The remainder of the script sets up navigation. A normal user will have the choices Continue Shopping, which will take her back to the category page, and Add to Cart, which will add the book to her shopping cart. If a user is logged in as an administrator, she will get some different options, which we'll look at in the section on administration.

That completes the basics of the catalog system. Let's go ahead and look at the code for the shopping cart functionality.

Implementing the Shopping Cart

The shopping cart functionality all revolves around a session variable called `cart`. This is an associative array that has ISBNs as keys and quantities as values. For example, if I add a single copy of this book to my shopping cart, the array would contain

```
0672317842 => 1
```

That is, one copy of the book with the ISBN 0672317842. When we add items to the cart, they will be added to the array. When we view the cart, we will use the `cart` array to look up the full details of the items in the database.

We also use two other session variables to control the display in the header that shows Total Items and Total Price. These variables are called `items` and `total_price`, respectively.

Using the show_cart.php Script

Let's begin looking at how the shopping cart code is implemented by looking at the `show_cart.php` script. This is the script that displays the page we will visit if we click on any View Cart or Add to Cart links. If we call `show_cart.php` without any parameters, we will get to see the contents of it. If we call it with an ISBN as parameter, the item with that ISBN will be added to the cart.

To understand this fully, look first at Figure 25.6.

In this case, we have clicked the View Cart link when our cart is empty; that is, we have not yet selected any items to purchase.

Figure 25.7 shows our cart a bit further down the track when we have selected two books to buy. In this case, we have gotten to this page by clicking the Add to Cart link on the `show_book.php` page for this book, *PHP and MySQL Web Development*. If you look closely at the URL bar, you will see that we have called the script with a parameter this time. The parameter is called `new` and has the value `0672317842`—that is, the ISBN for the book we have just added to the cart.

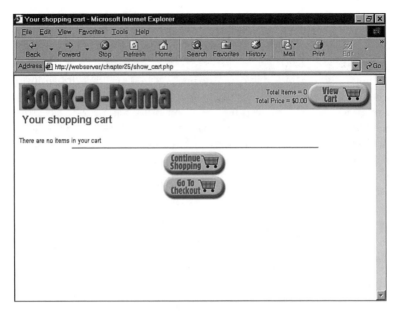

Figure 25.6   The show_cart.php script with no parameters just shows us the contents of our cart.

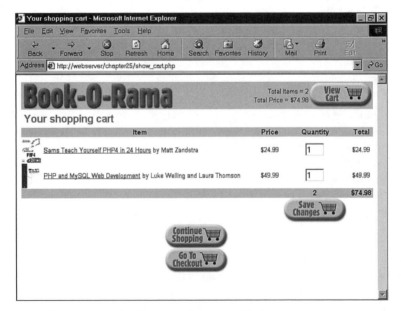

Figure 25.7   The show_cart.php script with the new parameter adds a new item to the cart.

From this page, you can see that we have two other options. There is a Save Changes button that we can use to change the quantity of items in the cart. To do this, you can alter the quantities directly and click Save Changes. This is actually a submit button that takes us back to the show_cart.php script again to update the cart.

In addition, there's a Go to Checkout button that a user can click when she is ready to leave. We'll come back to that in a minute.

For now, let's look at the code for the show_cart.php script. This code is shown in Listing 25.9.

Listing 25.9   **show_cart.php—This Script Controls the Shopping Cart**

```php
<?php
  include ('book_sc_fns.php');
  // The shopping cart needs sessions, so start one
  session_start();

  @ $new = $HTTP_GET_VARS['new'];

  if($new)
  {
    //new item selected
    if(!isset($HTTP_SESSION_VARS['cart']))
    {
      $HTTP_SESSION_VARS['cart'] = array();
      $HTTP_SESSION_VARS['items'] = 0;
      $HTTP_SESSION_VARS['total_price'] ='0.00';
    }
    if(isset($HTTP_SESSION_VARS['cart'][$new]))
      $HTTP_SESSION_VARS['cart'][$new]++;
    else
      $HTTP_SESSION_VARS['cart'][$new] = 1;
    $HTTP_SESSION_VARS['total_price'] =
                              calculate_price($HTTP_SESSION_VARS['cart']);
    $HTTP_SESSION_VARS['items'] = calculate_items($HTTP_SESSION_VARS['cart']);

  }
  if(isset($HTTP_POST_VARS['save']))
  {
    foreach ($HTTP_SESSION_VARS['cart'] as $isbn => $qty)
    {
      if($HTTP_POST_VARS[$isbn]=='0')
        unset($HTTP_SESSION_VARS['cart'][$isbn]);
      else
        $HTTP_SESSION_VARS['cart'][$isbn] = $HTTP_POST_VARS[$isbn];
    }
    $HTTP_SESSION_VARS['total_price'] =
```

Listing 25.9   **Continued**

```
calculate_price($HTTP_SESSION_VARS['cart']);
    $HTTP_SESSION_VARS['items'] = calculate_items($HTTP_SESSION_VARS['cart']);
  }

  do_html_header('Your shopping cart');

  if($HTTP_SESSION_VARS['cart']&&array_count_values($HTTP_SESSION_VARS['cart']))
    display_cart($HTTP_SESSION_VARS['cart']);
  else
  {
    echo '<p>There are no items in your cart</p>';
    echo '<hr />';
  }
  $target = 'index.php';

  // if we have just added an item to the cart, continue shopping in that category
  if($new)
  {
    $details =  get_book_details($new);
    if($details['catid'])
      $target = 'show_cat.php?catid='.$details['catid'];
  }
  display_button($target, 'continue-shopping', 'Continue Shopping');

  // use this if SSL is set up
  // $path = $HTTP_SERVER_VARS['PHP_SELF'];
  // $server = $HTTP_SERVER_VARS['SERVER_NAME'];
  // $path = str_replace('show_cart.php', '', $path);
  // display_button('https://'.$server.$path.'checkout.php',
                    'go-to-checkout', 'Go To Checkout');

  // if no SSL use below code
  display_button('checkout.php', 'go-to-checkout', 'Go To Checkout');


  do_html_footer();
?>
```

There are three main parts to this script: displaying the cart, adding items to the cart, and saving changes to the cart. We'll cover these in the next three sections.

Viewing the Cart

No matter which page we have come from, we will display the contents of the cart. In the base case, when a user has just clicked View Cart, this is the only part of the code that will be executed, as follows:

```
if($HTTP_SESSION_VARS['cart']&&array_count_values($HTTP_SESSION_VARS['cart']))
   display_cart($HTTP_SESSION_VARS['cart']);
else
{
   echo '<p>There are no items in your cart</p>';
   echo '<hr />';
}
```

As you can see from this code, if we have a cart with some contents, we will call the display_cart() function. If the cart is empty, we'll give the user a message to that effect.

The display_cart() function just prints the contents of the cart as a readable HTML format, as you can see in Figures 25.6 and 25.7. The code for this function can be found in output_fns.php, which is included here as Listing 25.10. Although it is a display function, it is reasonably complex, so we include it here.

Listing 25.10   **display_cart() Function from output_fns.php—This Function Formats and Prints the Contents of the Shopping Cart**

```
function display_cart($cart, $change = true, $images = 1)
{
  // display items in shopping cart
  // optionally allow changes (true or false)
  // optionally include images (1 - yes, 0 - no)

  global $HTTP_SESSION_VARS;

  echo '<table border="0" width="100%" cellspacing="0">
       <form action="show_cart.php" method="post">
       <tr><th colspan="'. (1+$images) .'" bgcolor="#cccccc">Item</th>
       <th bgcolor="#cccccc">Price</th><th bgcolor="#cccccc">Quantity</th>
       <th bgcolor="#cccccc">Total</th></tr>';

  //display each item as a table row
  foreach ($cart as $isbn => $qty)
  {
    $book = get_book_details($isbn);
    echo '<tr>';
    if($images ==true)
    {
      echo '<td align="left">';
      if (file_exists("images/$isbn.jpg"))
      {
        $size = GetImageSize('images/'.$isbn.'.jpg');
        if($size[0]>0 && $size[1]>0)
        {
          echo '<img src="images/'.$isbn.'.jpg" border=0 ';
```

Listing 25.10 **Continued**

```php
            echo 'width = '. $size[0]/3 .' height = ' .$size[1]/3 . '>';
        }
    }
    else
        echo ' ';
    echo '</td>';
}
echo '<td align="left">';
echo '<a href="show_book.php?isbn='.$isbn.'">'.$book['title'].
    '</a> by '.$book['author'];
echo '</td><td align="center">$'.number_format($book['price'], 2);
echo '</td><td align="center">';
// if we allow changes, quantities are in text boxes
if ($change == true)
    echo '<input type="text" name="$isbn" value="$qty" size="3">';
else
    echo $qty;
echo '</td><td align="center">$'.number_format($book['price']*$qty,2).
    '</td></tr>\n';
}
// display total row
echo '<tr>
        <th colspan="'. (2+$images) .'" bgcolor="#cccccc"> </td>
        <th align = center bgcolor="#cccccc">
            '.$HTTP_SESSION_VARS['items'].'
        </th>
        <th align = center bgcolor="#cccccc">
            $'..number_format($HTTP_SESSION_VARS['total_price'], 2).
        '</th>
    </tr>';
// display save change button
if($change == true)
{
    echo '<tr>
            <td colspan="'. (2+$images) .'"> </td>
            <td align="center">
                <input type="hidden" name="save" value="true">
                <input type="image" src="images/save-changes.gif"
                        border="0" alt="Save Changes">
            </td>
            <td> </td>
        </tr>';
}
echo '</form></table>';
}
```

The basic flow of this function is as follows:

1. Loop through each item in the cart and pass the ISBN of each item to
   `get_book_details()` so that we can summarize the details of each book.

2. Provide an image for each book, if one exists. We use the HTML image height
   and width tags to resize the image a little smaller here. This means that the images
   will be a little distorted, but they are small enough that this isn't much of a problem. (If it bothers you, you can always resize the images using the gd library discussed in Chapter 19, "Generating Images," or manually generate different size
   images for each product)

3. Make each cart entry a link to the appropriate book, that is, to `show_book.php`
   with the ISBN as a parameter.

4. If we are calling the function with the `change` parameter set to `true` (or not
   set—it defaults to `true`), show the boxes with the quantities in them as a form
   with the Save Changes button at the end. (When we reuse this function after
   checking out, we won't want the user to be able to change her order.)

Nothing is terribly complicated in this function, but it does quite a lot of work, so you
might find it useful to read it through carefully.

Adding Items to the Cart

If a user has come to the `show_cart.php` page by clicking an Add to Cart button, we
have to do some work before we can show her the contents of her cart. Specifically, we
need to add the appropriate item to the cart, as follows.

First, if the user has not put any items in her cart before, she will not have a cart, so
we need to create one:

```
if(!isset($HTTP_SESSION_VARS['cart']))
{
  $HTTP_SESSION_VARS['cart'] = array();
  $HTTP_SESSION_VARS['items'] = 0;
  $HTTP_SESSION_VARS['total_price'] ='0.00';
}
```

To begin with, the cart is empty.

Second, after we know that a cart is set up, we can add the item to it:

```
if(isset($HTTP_SESSION_VARS['cart'][$new]))
  $HTTP_SESSION_VARS['cart'][$new]++;
else
  $HTTP_SESSION_VARS['cart'][$new] = 1;
```

Here, we are checking whether the item's already in the cart. If it is, we increment the
quantity of that item in the cart by one. If not, we add the new item to the cart.

Third, we need to work out the total price and number of items in the cart. For this,
we use the `calculate_price()` and `calculate_items()` functions, as follows:

```
$HTTP_SESSION_VARS['total_price'] = calculate_price($HTTP_SESSION_VARS['cart']);
$HTTP_SESSION_VARS['items'] = calculate_items($HTTP_SESSION_VARS['cart']);
```

These functions are located in the book_fns.php function library. The code for them is shown in Listings 25.11 and 25.12, respectively.

Listing 25.11 **calculate_price() Function from book_fns.php—This Function Calculates and Returns the Total Price of the Contents of the Shopping Cart**

```
function calculate_price($cart)
{
  // sum total price for all items in shopping cart
  $price = 0.0;
  if(is_array($cart))
  {
    $conn = db_connect();
    foreach($cart as $isbn => $qty)
    {
      $query = "select price from books where isbn='$isbn'";
      $result = mysql_query($query);
      if ($result)
      {
        $item_price = mysql_result($result, 0, 'price');
        $price +=$item_price*$qty;
      }
    }
  }
  return $price;
}
```

As you can see, the calculate_price() function works by looking up the price of each item in the cart in the database. This is somewhat slow, so to avoid doing this more often than we need to, we'll store the price (and the total number of items, as well) as session variables and only recalculate when the cart changes.

Listing 25.12 **calculate_items() Function from book_fns.php—This Function Calculates and Returns the Total Number of Items in the Shopping Cart**

```
function calculate_items($cart)
{
  // sum total items in shopping cart
  $items = 0;
  if(is_array($cart))
  {
    foreach($cart as $isbn => $qty)
    {
      $items += $qty;
    }
```

Listing 25.12   **Continued**

```
  }
  return $items;
}
```

The `calculate_items()` function is simpler—it just goes through the cart and adds up the quantities of each item to get the total number of items.

Saving the Updated Cart

If we have come to the `show_cart.php` script from clicking the Save Changes button, the process is a little different. In this case, we have come via a form submission. If you look closely at the code, you will see that the Save Changes button is the submit button for a form. This form contains the hidden variable `save`. If this variable is set, we know that we have come to this script from the Save Changes button. This means that the user has presumably edited the quantity values in the cart, and we need to update them.

If you look back at the text boxes in the Save Changes form part of the script, you will see that they are named after the ISBN of the item that they represent, as follows:

```
echo '<input type="text" name="$isbn" value="$qty" size="3">';
```

Now look at the part of the script that saves the changes:

```
if(isset($HTTP_POST_VARS['save']))
{
  foreach ($HTTP_SESSION_VARS['cart'] as $isbn => $qty)
  {
    if($HTTP_POST_VARS[$isbn]=='0')
      unset($HTTP_SESSION_VARS['cart'][$isbn]);
    else
      $HTTP_SESSION_VARS['cart'][$isbn] = $HTTP_POST_VARS[$isbn];
  }
  $HTTP_SESSION_VARS['total_price'] = calculate_price($HTTP_SESSION_VARS['cart']);
  $HTTP_SESSION_VARS['items'] = calculate_items($HTTP_SESSION_VARS['cart']);
}
```

You can see that we are working our way through the shopping cart, and for each `isbn` in the cart, we are checking the POST variable with that name. These are the form fields from the Save Changes form.

If any of the fields were set to zero, we remove that item from the shopping cart altogether, using `unset()`. Otherwise, we update the cart to match the form fields, as follows:

```
if($HTTP_POST_VARS[$isbn]=='0')
  unset($HTTP_SESSION_VARS['cart'][$isbn]);
else
  $HTTP_SESSION_VARS['cart'][$isbn] = $HTTP_POST_VARS[$isbn];
```

After these updates, we again use `calculate_price()` and `calculate_items()` to work out the new values of the `total_price` and `items` session variables.

Printing a Header Bar Summary

You will have noticed that in the header bar of each of the pages in the site, a summary of what's in the shopping cart is presented. This is obtained by printing out the values of the session variables `total_price` and `items`. This is done in the `do_html_header()` function.

These variables are registered when the user first visits the `show_cart.php` page. We also need some logic to deal with the cases where a user has not yet visited that page. This logic is also in the `do_html_header()` function:

```
if(!$HTTP_SESSION_VARS['items']) $HTTP_SESSION_VARS['items'] = '0';
if(!$HTTP_SESSION_VARS['total_price']) $HTTP_SESSION_VARS['total_price'] = '0.00';
```

Checking Out

When the user clicks the Go to Checkout button from the shopping cart, this will activate the `checkout.php` script. The checkout page and the pages behind it should be accessed via SSL, but the sample application does not force you to do this. (To read more about SSL, review Chapter 15, "Implementing Secure Transactions with PHP and MySQL.")

The checkout page is shown in Figure 25.8.

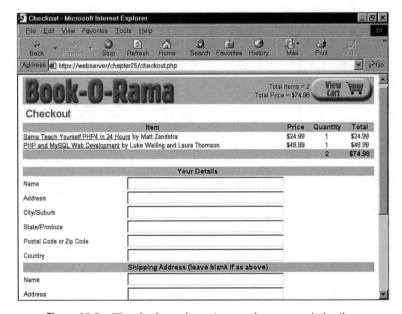

Figure 25.8 The checkout.php script gets the customer's details.

This script requires the customer to enter her address (and shipping address if it is different). It is quite a simple script, which you can see by looking at the code in Listing 25.13.

Listing 25.13   checkout.php—This Script Gets the Customer Details

```php
<?php
  //include our function set
  include ('book_sc_fns.php');

  // The shopping cart needs sessions, so start one
  session_start();

  do_html_header('Checkout');

  if($HTTP_SESSION_VARS['cart']&&array_count_values($HTTP_SESSION_VARS['cart']))
  {
    display_cart($HTTP_SESSION_VARS['cart'], false, 0);
    display_checkout_form();
  }
  else
    echo '<p>There are no items in your cart</p>';

  display_button('show_cart.php', 'continue-shopping', 'Continue Shopping');

  do_html_footer();
?>
```

There are no great surprises in this script. If the cart is empty, the script will notify the customer; otherwise, it will display the form you can see in Figure 25.8.

If a user continues by clicking the Purchase button at the bottom for the form, she will be taken to the purchase.php script. You can see the output of this script in Figure 25.9.

The code for this script is slightly more complicated than the code for checkout.php. It is shown in Listing 25.14.

Listing 25.14   purchase.php—This Script Stores the Order Details in the Database and Gets the Payment Details

```php
<?php

  include ('book_sc_fns.php');
  // The shopping cart needs sessions, so start one
  session_start();

  do_html_header("Checkout");
```

Listing 25.14 **Continued**

```
//create short variable names
$name = $HTTP_POST_VARS['name'];
$address = $HTTP_POST_VARS['address'];
$city = $HTTP_POST_VARS['city'];
$zip = $HTTP_POST_VARS['zip'];
$country = $HTTP_POST_VARS['country'];

// if filled out
if($HTTP_SESSION_VARS['cart']&&$name&&$address&&$city&&$zip&&$country)
{
  // able to insert into database
  if( insert_order($HTTP_POST_VARS)!=false )
  {
    //display cart, not allowing changes and without pictures
    display_cart($HTTP_SESSION_VARS['cart'], false, 0);

    display_shipping(calculate_shipping_cost());

    //get credit card details
    display_card_form($name);

    display_button('show_cart.php', 'continue-shopping', 'Continue Shopping');
  }
  else
  {
    echo 'Could not store data, please try again.';
    display_button('checkout.php', 'back', 'Back');
  }
}
else
{
  echo 'You did not fill in all the fields, please try again.<hr />';
  display_button('checkout.php', 'back', 'Back');
}

do_html_footer();
?>
```

The logic here is straightforward: We check that the user filled out the form and inserted details into the database using a function called insert_order(). This is a simple function that pops the customer details into the database. The code for it is shown in Listing 25.15.

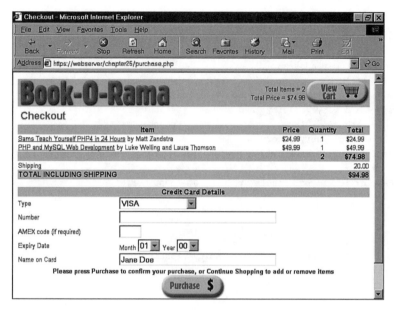

Figure 25.9   The purchase.php script calculates shipping and the final order
total, and gets the customer's payment details.

Listing 25.15   **insert_order() Function from order_fns.php—This Function Inserts All
the Details of the Customer's Order into the Database**

```
function insert_order($order_details)
{
  global $HTTP_SESSION_VARS;

  //extract order_details out as variables
  extract($order_details);


  //set shipping address same as address
  if(!$ship_name&&!$ship_address&&!$ship_city&&
    !$ship_state&&!$ship_zip&&!$ship_country)
  {
    $ship_name = $name;
    $ship_address = $address;
    $ship_city = $city;
    $ship_state = $state;
    $ship_zip = $zip;
    $ship_country = $country;
  }
```

Listing 25.15 **Continued**

```
$conn = db_connect();

//insert customer address
$query = "select customerid from customers where
          name = '$name' and address = '$address'
          and city = '$city' and state = '$state'
          and zip = '$zip' and country = '$country'";
$result = mysql_query($query);
if(mysql_numrows($result)>0)
{
  $customer_id = mysql_result($result, 0, 'customerid');
}
else
{
  $query = "insert into customers values
          ('', '$name','$address','$city','$state','$zip','$country')";
  $result = mysql_query($query);
  if (!$result)
    return false;
}
$query = "select customerid from customers where
          name = '$name' and address = '$address'
          and city = '$city' and state = '$state'
          and zip = '$zip' and country = '$country'";
$result = mysql_query($query);
if(mysql_numrows($result)>0)
  $customerid = mysql_result($result, 0, 'customerid');
else
  return false;
$date = date('Y-m-d');
$query = "insert into orders values
          ('', $customerid, ".$HTTP_SESSION_VARS['total_price'].
          ", '$date', 'PARTIAL', '$ship_name',
          '$ship_address','$ship_city','$ship_state','$ship_zip',
          '$ship_country')";
$result = mysql_query($query);
if (!$result)
  return false;

$query = "select orderid from orders where
            customerid = $customerid and
            amount > ".$HTTP_SESSION_VARS['total_price']."-.001 and
            amount < ".$HTTP_SESSION_VARS['total_price']."+.001 and
            date = '$date' and
```

Listing 25.15   **Continued**

```
                 order_status = 'PARTIAL' and
                 ship_name = '$ship_name' and
                 ship_address = '$ship_address' and
                 ship_city = '$ship_city' and
                 ship_state = '$ship_state' and
                 ship_zip = '$ship_zip' and
                 ship_country = '$ship_country'";
  $result = mysql_query($query);
  if(mysql_numrows($result)>0)
    $orderid = mysql_result($result, 0, 'orderid');
  else
    return false;


  // insert each book
  foreach($HTTP_SESSION_VARS['cart'] as $isbn => $quantity)
  {
    $detail = get_book_details($isbn);
    $query = "delete from order_items where
                 orderid = '$orderid' and isbn =  '$isbn'";
    $result = mysql_query($query);
    $query = "insert into order_items values
                 ('$orderid', '$isbn', ".$detail['price'].", $quantity)";
    $result = mysql_query($query);
    if(!$result)
      return false;
  }

  return $orderid;
}
```

This function is rather long because we need to insert the customer's details, the order details, and the details of each book they want to buy.

We then work out the shipping costs to the customer's address and tell them how much it will be with the following line of code:

```
display_shipping(calculate_shipping_cost());
```

The code we are using here for `calculate_shipping_cost()` always returns $20. When you actually set up a shopping site, you will have to choose a delivery method, find out how much it costs for different destinations, and calculate costs accordingly.

We then display a form for the user to fill in her credit card details using the `display_card_form()` function from the `output_fns.php` library.

Implementing Payment

When the user clicks the Purchase button, we will process her payment details using the process.php script. You can see the results of a successful payment in Figure 25.10.

The code for process.php can be found in Listing 25.16.

Listing 25.16   **process.php—The process.php Script Processes the Customer's Payment and Tells Her the Result**

```php
<?php
  include ('book_sc_fns.php');
  // The shopping cart needs sessions, so start one
  session_start();

  do_html_header('Checkout');

  $card_type = $HTTP_POST_VARS['card_type'];
  $card_number = $HTTP_POST_VARS['card_number'];
  $card_month = $HTTP_POST_VARS['card_month'];
  $card_year = $HTTP_POST_VARS['card_year'];
  $card_name = $HTTP_POST_VARS['card_name'];

  if($HTTP_SESSION_VARS['cart']&&$card_type&&$card_number&&
     $card_month&&$card_year&&$card_name )
  {
    //display cart, not allowing changes and without pictures
    display_cart($HTTP_SESSION_VARS['cart'], false, 0);

    display_shipping(calculate_shipping_cost());

    if(process_card($HTTP_POST_VARS))
    {
      //empty shopping cart
      session_destroy();
      echo 'Thankyou for shopping with us.  Your order has been placed.';
      display_button('index.php', 'continue-shopping', 'Continue Shopping');
    }
    else
    {
    echo 'Could not process your card. ';
    echo 'Please contact the card issuer or try again.';
      display_button('purchase.php', 'back', 'Back');
    }
  }
  else
  {
    echo 'You did not fill in all the fields, please try again.<hr />';
    display_button('purchase.php', 'back', 'Back');
```

Listing 25.16   **Continued**

```
    }

    do_html_footer();
?>
```

The crux of this script is these lines:

```
if(process_card($HTTP_POST_VARS))
{
    //empty shopping cart
    session_destroy();
    echo 'Thankyou for shopping with us.  Your order has been placed.';
    display_button('index.php', 'continue-shopping', 'Continue Shopping');
}
```

We process the user's card, and, if all is successful, destroy her session.

The card processing function as we have written it simply returns true. If you were actually implementing it, you would need to perform some validation (checking that the expiry date was valid and the card number well-formed) and then process the actual payment.

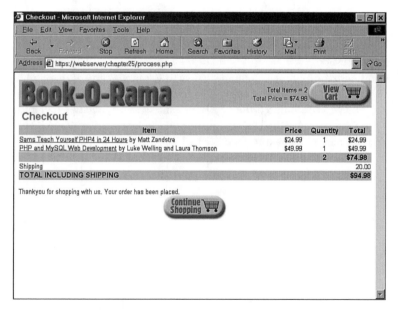

Figure 25.10   This transaction was successful, and the items will now be shipped.

When you set up a live site, you will need to make a decision about what transaction clearing mechanism you want to use. You can

- Sign up with a transaction clearing provider. There are many, many alternatives here depending on the area you live in. Some of these will offer real-time clearing, and others won't. Whether you need live clearing depends on the service you are offering. If you are providing a service online, you will most likely want it; if you are shipping goods, it's less crucial. Either way, these providers relieve you of the responsibility of storing credit card numbers.

- Send a credit card number to yourself via encrypted email, for example, by using PGP or GPG as covered in Chapter 15. When you receive and decrypt the email, you can process these transactions manually.

- Store the credit card numbers in your database. We do not recommend this option unless you really, seriously know what you're doing with system security. You can read Chapter 15 for more details about why this is a bad idea.

That's it for the shopping cart and payment modules.

Implementing an Administration Interface

The administration interface we have implemented is very simple. All we have done is build a Web interface to the database with some front end authentication. This is much of the same code as used in Chapter 24. We have included it here for completeness, but with little discussion.

The administration interface requires a user to log in via the `login.php` file, which then takes her to the administration menu, `admin.php`. The login page is shown in Figure 25.11. (We have omitted the `login.php` file here for brevity—it's almost exactly the same as the one in Chapter 24. If you want to look at it, it's on the CD-ROM.) The administration menu is shown in Figure 25.12.

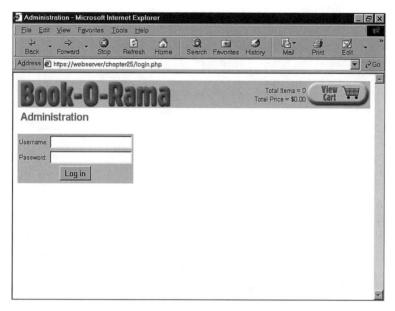

Figure 25.11   Users must pass through the login page to access the admin functions.

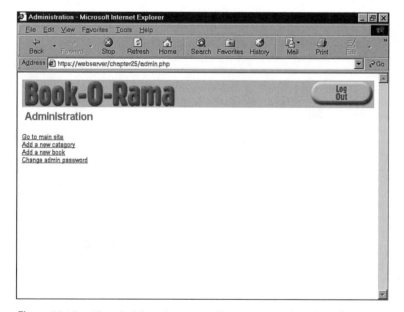

Figure 25.12   The administration menu allows access to the admin functions.

The code for the admin menu is shown in Listing 25.17.

Listing 25.17   **admin.php—This Script Authenticates the Administrator and Lets Her Access the admin Functions**

```php
<?php

// include function files for this application
require_once('book_sc_fns.php');
session_start();


if ($HTTP_POST_VARS['username'] && $HTTP_POST_VARS['passwd'])
// they have just tried logging in
{

    $username = $HTTP_POST_VARS['username'];
    $passwd = $HTTP_POST_VARS['passwd'];

    if (login($username, $passwd))
    {
      // if they are in the database register the user id
      $HTTP_SESSION_VARS['admin_user'] = $username;
    }
    else
    {
      // unsuccessful login
      do_html_header('Problem:');
      echo 'You could not be logged in.
            You must be logged in to view this page.<br />';
      do_html_url('login.php', 'Login');
      do_html_footer();
      exit;
    }
}

do_html_header('Administration');
if (check_admin_user())
  display_admin_menu();
else
  echo 'You are not authorized to enter the administration area.';

do_html_footer();

?>
```

This code probably looks familiar; it is similar to a script from Chapter 24. After the administrator reaches this point, she can change her password or log out—this code is identical to the code in Chapter 24, so we will not cover it here.

We identify the administration user after login by means of the `admin_user` session variable and the `check_admin_user()` function. This function and the others used by the administrative scripts can be found in the function library `admin_fns.php`.

If the administrator chooses to add a new category or book, she will go to either `insert_category_form.php` or `insert_book_form.php`, as appropriate. Each of these scripts presents the administrator with a form to fill in. Each is processed by a corresponding script (`insert_category.php` and `insert_book.php`), which verifies that the form is filled out and inserts the new data into the database. We will look at the book versions of the scripts only, as they are very similar to one another.

The output of `insert_book_form.php` is shown in Figure 25.13.

You will notice that the Category field for books is an HTML SELECT element. The options for this SELECT come from a call to the `get_categories()` function we have looked at previously.

When the Add Book button is clicked, the `insert_book.php` script will be activated. The code for this script is shown in Listing 25.18.

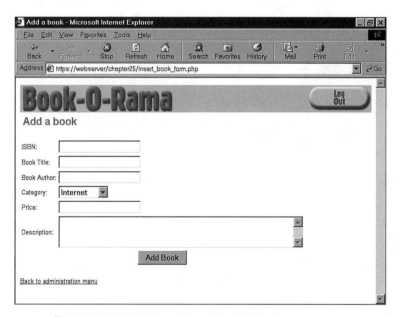

Figure 25.13   This form allows the administrator to enter new books into the online catalog.

Listing 25.18   **insert_book.php—This Script Validates the New Book Data and Puts It into the Database**

```php
<?php

// include function files for this application
require_once('book_sc_fns.php');
session_start();

do_html_header('Adding a book');
if (check_admin_user())
{
  if (filled_out($HTTP_POST_VARS))
  {
    $isbn = $HTTP_POST_VARS['isbn'];
    $title = $HTTP_POST_VARS['title'];
    $author = $HTTP_POST_VARS['author'];
    $catid = $HTTP_POST_VARS['catid'];
    $price = $HTTP_POST_VARS['price'];
    $description = $HTTP_POST_VARS['description'];

    if(insert_book($isbn, $title, $author, $catid, $price, $description))
      echo "Book '".stripslashes($title)."' was added to the database.<br />";
    else
      echo "Book '".stripslashes($title).
          "' could not be added to the database.<br />";
  }
  else
    echo 'You have not filled out the form.  Please try again.';
  do_html_url('admin.php', 'Back to administration menu');
}
else
  echo 'You are not authorised to view this page.';

do_html_footer();

?>
```

You can see that this script calls the function `insert_book()`. This function and the others used by the administrative scripts can be found in the function library `admin_fns.php`.

In addition to adding new categories and books, the administrative user can edit and delete these items. We have implemented this by reusing as much code as possible. When the administrator clicks the Go to Main site link in the administration menu, she will go to the category index at `index.php` and can navigate the site in the same way as a regular user, using the same scripts.

There is a difference in the administrative navigation, however: Administrators will see different options based on the fact that they have the registered session variable admin_user. For example, if we look at the show_book.php page that we were looking at previously in the chapter, we will see some different menu options. Look at Figure 25.14.

The administrator has access to two new options on this page: Edit Item and Admin Menu. You will also notice that we don't see the shopping cart in the upper-right corner—instead, we have a Log Out button.

The code for this is all there, back in Listing 25.8, as follows:

```
if( check_admin_user() )
{
  display_button("edit_book_form.php?isbn=$isbn", 'edit-item', 'Edit Item');
  display_button('admin.php', 'admin-menu', 'Admin Menu');
  display_button($target, 'continue', 'Continue');
}
```

If you look back at the show_cat.php script, you will see that it also has these options built in to it.

If the administrator clicks the Edit Item button, she will go to the edit_book_form.php script. The output of this script is shown in Figure 25.15.

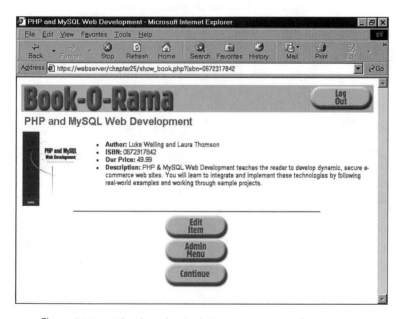

Figure 25.14   The show_book.php script produces different output for an administrative user.

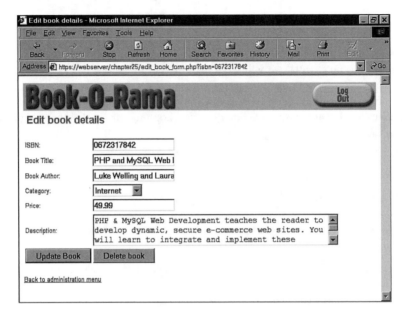

Figure 25.15   The edit_book_form.php script gives the administrator access
to edit book details or delete a book.

This is, in fact, the same form we used to get the book's details in the first place. We built
an option into that form to pass in and display existing book data. We did the same thing
with the category form. To see what we mean, look at Listing 25.19.

**Listing 25.19   display_book_form() Function from admin_fns.php—This Form Does
Double Duty as an Insertion and Editing Form**

```
function display_book_form($book = '')
// This displays the book form.
// It is very similar to the category form.
// This form can be used for inserting or editing books.
// To insert, don't pass any parameters.  This will set $edit
// to false, and the form will go to insert_book.php.
// To update, pass an array containing a book.  The
// form will be displayed with the old data and point to update_book.php.
// It will also add a "Delete book" button.
{

  // if passed an existing book, proceed in "edit mode"
  $edit = is_array($book);

  // most of the form is in plain HTML with some
  // optional PHP bits throughout
```

Listing 25.19   **Continued**

```php
?>
  <form method="post"
        action="<?php echo $edit?'edit_book.php':'insert_book.php';?>">
  <table border="0">
  <tr>
    <td>ISBN:</td>
    <td><input type="text" name="isbn"
        value="<?php echo $edit?$book['isbn']:''; ?>"></td>
  </tr>
  <tr>
    <td>Book Title:</td>
    <td><input type="text" name="title"
        value="<?php echo $edit?$book['title']:''; ?>"></td>
  </tr>
  <tr>
    <td>Book Author:</td>
    <td><input type="text" name="author"
        value="<?php echo $edit?$book['author']:''; ?>"></td>
  </tr>
  <tr>
    <td>Category:</td>
    <td><select name="catid">
    <?php
        // list of possible categories comes from database
        $cat_array=get_categories();
        foreach ($cat_array as $thiscat)
        {
            echo '<option value="';
            echo $thiscat['catid'];
            echo '"';
            // if existing book, put in current catgory
            if ($edit && $thiscat['catid'] == $book['catid'])
                echo ' selected';
            echo '>';
            echo $thiscat['catname'];
            echo "\n";
        }
        ?>
        </select>
      </td>
  </tr>
  <tr>
    <td>Price:</td>
    <td><input type="text" name="price"
            value="<?php echo $edit?$book['price']:''; ?>"></td>
  </tr>
```

Listing 25.19 **Continued**

```
      <tr>
        <td>Description:</td>
        <td><textarea rows="3" cols="50"
            name="description">
            <?php echo $edit?$book['description']:''; ?>
            </textarea></td>
      </tr>
      <tr>
        <td <?php if (!$edit) echo 'colspan="2"'; ?> align="center">
          <?php
            if ($edit)
              // we need the old isbn to find book in database
              // if the isbn is being updated
              echo '<input type="hidden" name="oldisbn"
                    value="'.$book['isbn'].'">';
          ?>
          <input type="submit"
                value="<?php echo $edit?'Update':'Add'; ?> Book">
        </form></td>
        <?php
          if ($edit)
          {
            echo '<td>';
            echo '<form method="post" action="delete_book.php">';
            echo '<input type="hidden" name="isbn"
                  value="'.$book['isbn'].'">';
            echo '<input type="submit"
                  value="Delete book">';
            echo '</form></td>';
          }
        ?>
        </td>
      </tr>
    </table>
  </form>
<?php
}
```

If we pass in an array containing the book data, the form will be rendered in edit mode and will fill in the fields with the existing data:

```
<input type="text" name="price"
                value="<?php echo $edit?$book['price']:''; ?>">
```

We even get a different submit button. In fact, for the edit form we get two—one to update the book, and one to delete it. These call the scripts edit_book.php and delete_book.php, which update the database accordingly.

The category versions of these scripts work in much the same way except for one thing. When an administrator tries to delete a category, it will not be deleted if any books are still in it. (This is checked with a database query.) This avoids any problems we might get with deletion anomalies. We discussed these in Chapter 7, "Designing Your Web Database." In this case, if a category was deleted that still had books in it, these books would become orphans. We wouldn't know what category they were in, and we would have no way of navigating to them!

That's the overview of the administration interface. For more details, refer to the code—it's all on the CD-ROM.

Extending the Project

We have built a fairly simple shopping cart system. There are many additions and enhancements we could make:

- In a real online store, you would need to build some kind of order tracking and fulfillment system—at the moment, there's no way to see the orders that have been placed.

- Customers want to be able to check the progress of their orders without having to contact you. We feel that it is important that a customer does not have to log in to browse. However, providing existing customers a way to authenticate themselves gives them the ability to see past orders, and gives you the ability to tie behaviors together into a profile.

- At present, the images for books have to be FTPed to the image directory and given the correct name. You could add file upload to the book insertion page to make this easier.

- You could add user login, personalization, and book recommendations; online reviews; affiliate programs; stock level checking; and so on. The possibilities are endless.

Using an Existing System

If you want to get a highly featured shopping cart up and running quickly, you might want to try using an existing shopping cart system. One well known Open Source cart implemented in PHP is FishCartSQL, available from

```
http://www.fishcart.org/
```

This has a lot of advanced features such as customer tracking, timed sales, multiple languages, credit card processing, and support for multiple online shops on one server. Of course, when you use an existing system, you always find there are things that it does not have that you want, and vice versa. The advantage of an Open Source product is that you can go in and change the things you don't like.

Next

In the next chapter, we'll look at how to build an online content management system suitable for managing digital assets—this can be useful if you are running a content-based site.

26

Building a Content Management System

IN THIS CHAPTER, WE'LL LOOK AT A content management system for storing, indexing, and searching text and multimedia content.

Content management systems are extremely useful on Web sites where the site content is maintained by more than one author, where maintenance is performed by non-technical staff, or where the content and graphic design are developed by different people or departments.

We will build an application that helps authorized users to manage an organization's digital assets.

We will cover the following:

- Presenting Web pages using a series of templates
- Building a search engine that indexes documents according to metadata

The Problem

Let's imagine that the busy Web development team for SuperFastOnlineNews consists of an excellent graphic designer and some award-winning writers. The site contains regularly updated news, sports, and weather pages. The main page shows the latest headline from each of the three category pages.

At SuperFastOnlineNews, the designers ensure that the Web site content looks great. This is what they do best. Writers, on the other hand, write excellent articles, but can't draw well or build Web sites.

We need to allow everyone to concentrate on what they are best at and bring their output together to provide the super fast news service that the name implies.

Solution Requirements

We need to produce a system that

- Increases productivity by having the writers concentrate on writing and the designers on designing
- Allows the editor to review stories and decide which ones should be published
- Presents a consistent look and feel throughout the site using page templates
- Allows writers access only to their designated areas of the site
- Enables the look and feel to be easily changed for a section or throughout the site
- Prevents live content from being changed

Editing Content

First, we need to think about how we will get content into the system, and how we will store and edit that content.

Getting Content into the System

We need to decide on a way that stories and design components will be submitted. Three possible methods can be used.

FTP

The writers and designers could be given FTP access to areas on the Web server, and they could then upload files from their local machine to the server. There would need to be a rigid naming standard for the uploaded files (to identify which pictures belonged to which stories) or a Web-based system to deal with this separately from the FTP upload.

Using FTP also creates issues with permissions in this situation. Because of the flexibility required by this example, we will not be using FTP to allow users to upload files.

File Upload Method

As we discussed in Chapter 16, "Interacting with the File System and the Server," the HTTP protocol provides a method for files to be uploaded via the Web browser. PHP is able to deal with this very easily.

The file upload method also gives us the opportunity to store text in a database rather than as a file. To do this, we would read in the temporary file and store its contents in the database, rather than copying it to another place in the file system. We will not use file upload for stories in this project.

We will discuss the superiority of a database over the file system later.

Editing Online

We can let users create and edit documents without using either FTP or file upload. Instead you can give the contributors a large text area input box onscreen in which their story content can be edited.

This method is simple, but often effective. The Web browser does not provide any text editing facilities beyond the cut-and-paste functionality of the operating system. However, when you just need to make a small change—for instance, to correct a spelling mistake—it's very fast to bring up the content and amend it.

Similar to file upload, the form data could either be written to a file or stored in a database.

Databases Versus File Storage

An important decision to make at an early stage is how the content will be stored after it has been uploaded into the system.

Because we will be storing metadata alongside the story text, we have chosen to put the text parts of the content into the database. Although MySQL is capable of storing multimedia data, we choose to store uploaded images on the file system. As discussed in Part II, "Using MySQL," using BLOB data in your MySQL database can reduce performance.

We will just store the image filename in the database. Using the file system, the <IMG SRC> tag can reference the image file directly as usual.

When a large amount of data is being stored, it is important to optimize your data store. Just as the database would require proper indexes to be efficient, the file system will benefit greatly from a well thought out directory structure.

An example of this can be seen in Figure 26.1.

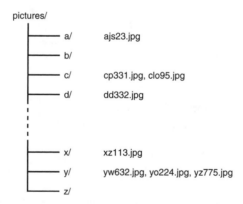

Figure 26.1   This directory structure has been structured for file uploads.

The file system in this case is split into directories representing the first character of each filename. 10,000 files would therefore be spread across 26 directories with around 400 files in each directory. This would be much quicker to access than 10,000 files all in one directory. It is worth pointing out that the filename used should be generated by the upload processing script to ensure that it is unique.

The example in Figure 26.1 assumes that all filenames will start with a lowercase letter.

Document Structure

The example stories we will be using are short one- or two-paragraph news stories with a single image, designed for people in a hurry. They are structured documents in as much as they contain a headline and one or two paragraphs of text with an image.

The more structured a document is, the more easily it can be split up for storage in a database. The advantage of this is that all the documents can be presented in a very consistent, structured manner.

Take our news story example. We will store the headline in a field separate from the story text, and by its nature the image is a separate component of the document.

With the headline as a separate item, we can define a standard typeface and style for that to be displayed in, and can easily separate it from the rest of the story to form our main headlines page.

Another approach for large documents would be to have a one-to-many relationship with the individual paragraphs; that is, to store each paragraph as a separate row in the database, each linked to a master document ID. That kind of dynamic document structure would allow you to present a contents page for each document and display each section independently, or display the whole document at once.

Using Metadata

We have already decided that each story record comprises a headline, story text, and an image. However there's no reason we can't store other data in the same record.

Our system will automatically insert values for who created the story and when it was last modified. These can be automatically displayed at the bottom of a story to sign and timestamp it without the author needing to worry about adding the information.

It might also be useful to add data that is not displayed, known as *metadata*. A good example of this is to store keywords that would be used for the search engine index.

Rather than scan the entire text of every story, the search engine will look at the keyword metadata for each story and determine relevance solely from that. This allows the site administrator to have total control over which search words and phrases match which documents.

In our example, we will allow any number of keywords to be associated with a story, and assign each keyword a weight value to indicate how relevant that keyword is on a scale from 1 to 10.

We can then develop a search engine algorithm that ranks matches according to this human-specified relevance for stories, rather than a complex algorithm that has to interpret English prose and make decisions based on its limited understanding and governed by fixed rules.

This isn't to say that you have to store metadata in the database. There's nothing to stop you from using the <META> tag in HTML, or even using XML to build your documents. However it's worth taking advantage of the database that is already looking after your documents whenever you can.

Formatting the Output

Our news site example follows a simple but structured format when displaying a page. Each page contains a number of stories that are all formatted the same way. First of all, the headline is displayed in a large type, followed by the photograph underneath on the left and then the story text on the right. The whole page is contained in a standard page template to preserve the site branding and consistency throughout.

Figure 26.2 shows the logical page structure that we will be using.

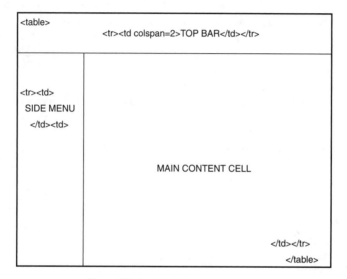

Figure 26.2   Logical page structure.

This kind of layout is extremely popular—how many sites do you visit regularly that have a menu bar at the left hand side or quick links at the top, with that outside navigation remaining in place no matter which page you are viewing?

Implementing a templated structure such as this from a page design is very simple. In the HTML source, you will find the <TD> where the main content cell begins. At this point, split the HTML into two files; the first half becoming the header file and the second, the footer. Whenever you display a page, show the header first, the page, and finally the footer.

Implementing the site with a header and footer template allows these template files to be easily changed if the site design is updated.

PHP provides two configuration options that appear useful in this situation. The directives auto_prepend_file and auto_append_file can be set on a per-directory basis to specify files that are included before or after any script is processed.

However this has some limitations. If you had any scripts that produce no output and send a redirect header such as

```
<? header('Location: destination.php'); ?>
```

the header and footer files would still be displayed and the redirect would fail because output has already been sent to the Web browser. This also causes problems with cookies and the built-in PHP 4 session management functions because a cookie header will not function correctly after any output has been sent to the Web browser.

Image Manipulation

The writers who contribute stories will probably supply their own photographs to complement the story. We want consistency, but what happens when one writer uploads a large, high quality image and another writer uploads a small thumbnail?

Assuming that the pictures in question are primarily photographs, we can insist on JPEG images only, and take advantage of functions in PHP to manipulate the images. This topic is covered in detail in Chapter 19, "Generating Images."

We have created a simple script called `resize_image.php` that will resize an image on-the-fly so that it can be displayed with an `<img src>` tag. This script is shown in Listing 26.1.

Listing 26.1   **resize_image.php—Resizes a JPEG Image On-the-Fly**

```php
<?php

$image = $HTTP_GET_VARS['image'];

if (!$max_width)
  $max_width = 80;
if (!$max_height)
  $max_height = 60;

$size = GetImageSize($image);
$width = $size[0];
$height = $size[1];

$x_ratio = $max_width / $width;
$y_ratio = $max_height / $height;

if ( ($width <= $max_width) && ($height <= $max_height) ) {
  $tn_width = $width;
  $tn_height = $height;
}
else if (($x_ratio * $height) < $max_height) {
  $tn_height = ceil($x_ratio * $height);
  $tn_width = $max_width;
}
else {
  $tn_width = ceil($y_ratio * $width);
  $tn_height = $max_height;
```

Listing 26.1 **Continued**

```
}

$src = ImageCreateFromJpeg($image);
$dst = ImageCreate($tn_width,$tn_height);
ImageCopyResized($dst, $src, 0, 0, 0, 0,
    $tn_width,$tn_height,$width,$height);
header('Content-type: image/jpeg');
ImageJpeg($dst, null, -1);
ImageDestroy($src);
ImageDestroy($dst);

?>
```

The script takes three parameters—the filename of the image to display, the maximum width, and the maximum height in pixels. It is not to say that if the maximum size specified is 200×200, the image will be scaled to 200×200. Rather, it will be scaled down in proportion so that the larger of the width or height is 200 pixels and the other dimension is 200 pixels or smaller. For instance, a 400×300 image would be reduced to 200×150. This way the proportions of the image will be maintained.

Resizing on-the-fly on the server is a better option than just specifying HEIGHT and WIDTH attributes to the <img> tag. The large, high-resolution image that a writer submitted might be several megabytes in size; but when scaled to a reasonable size, it could be under 100k. There is then no need to download the huge file and ask the browser to resize it.

The image manipulation functions are covered in detail in Chapter 19. Here we are using the ImageCopyResized() function to scale the image on-the-fly to the required size.

The key to the resize operation is the calculation of the new width and height parameters. We find the ratio between the actual and maximum dimensions. $max_width and $max_height can be passed in on the query string; otherwise, the default values specified at the top of the listing will be used.

```
$x_ratio = $max_width / $width;
$y_ratio = $max_height / $height;
```

If the image is already smaller than the specified maximum dimensions, the width and height are left unchanged. Otherwise, either the X or Y ratio is then used to scale both dimensions equally so that the reduced size image is not stretched or squashed, as follows:

```
if ( ($width <= $max_width) && ($height <= $max_height) ) {
  $tn_width = $width;
  $tn_height = $height;
}
else if (($x_ratio * $height) < $max_height) {
  $tn_height = ceil($x_ratio * $height);
```

```
    $tn_width = $max_width;
}
else {
    $tn_width = ceil($y_ratio * $width);
    $tn_height = $max_height;
}
```

Solution Design/Overview

A summary of the files in this application is shown in Table 26.1.

Table 26.1   **Files in the Content Management Application**

Name	Type	Description
create_database.sql	SQL	SQL to set up the content database and some sample data
include_fns.php	Functions	Collection of include files for this application
db_fns.php	Functions	Collection of functions for connecting to content database
select_fns.php	Functions	Collection of functions to aid creation of SELECT lists
user_auth_fns.php	Functions	Collection of functions for authenticating users
header.php	Template	Shown at the top of every content page
footer.php	Template	Shown at the bottom of every content page
logo.gif	Image	The logo file displayed in header.php
headlines.php	Application	Shows the most recent headline from each page of the site
page.php	Application	Lists the headlines and story text for a particular page
resize_image.php	Application	Resizes an image on-the-fly for headlines.php
search_form.php	Application	Form to enter keywords for searching the site content
search.php	Application	Displays headlines of content matching keyword criteria
login.php	Application	Authenticates a user's password and logs her in to the system
logout.php	Application	Logs a user out of the system
stories.php	Application	Lists stories that the logged-in user has written with an option to add, modify, or delete stories
story.php	Application	The story detail screen for editing or adding a new story

Table 26.1   **Continued**

Name	Type	Description
story_submit.php	Application	Adds new story or commits changes from data entered in story.php
delete_story.php	Application	Processes story delete request from stories.php
keywords.php	Application	Lists keywords for a story with option to add or delete keywords
keyword_add.php	Application	Processes keyword add request from keywords.php
keyword_delete.php	Application	Processes keyword delete request from keywords.php
publish.php	Application	Editor's list of stories showing which ones are published with an option to toggle each one's status
publish_story.php	Application	Processes a publish request from publish.php
unpublish_story.php	Application	Processes an unpublish request from publish.php

Designing the Database

Listing 26.2 shows the SQL queries used to create the database for the content system. This listing is part of the file create_database.sql. The file on the CD also contains queries to populate the database with some sample users and stories.

Listing 26.2   **Excerpt from create_database.sql—SQL File to Set Up the Content Database**

```
drop database if exists content;

create database content;

use content;

drop table if exists writers;

create table writers (
  username    varchar(16) primary key,
  password    varchar(16) not null,
  full_name   text
);

drop table if exists stories;
```

Listing 26.2   **Continued**

```
create table stories (
    id          int primary key auto_increment,
    writer      varchar(16) not null,           # foreign key writers.username
    page        varchar(16) not null,           # foreign key pages.code
    headline    text,
    story_text  text,
    picture     text,
    created     int,
    modified    int,
    published   int
);

drop table if exists pages;

create table pages (
    code        varchar(16) primary key,
    description text
);

drop table if exists writer_permissions;

create table writer_permissions (
    writer      varchar(16) not null,           # foreign key writers.username
    page        varchar(16) not null            # foreign key pages.code
);

drop table if exists keywords;

create table keywords (
    story       int not null,                   # foreign key stories.id
    keyword     varchar(32) not null,
    weight      int not null
);

grant select, insert, update, delete
on content.*
to content@localhost identified by 'password';
```

We need to store a little information about each writer, including a login name and password, in the `writers` table. We'll store their full names for displaying after each article and for greeting them when they log in.

The `pages` table contains the page heading for each page on which stories can be displayed. The `writer_permissions` table implements a many-to-many relationship indicating for which pages a writer can submit stories.

The `stories` table contains separate fields for `headline`, `story_text`, and `picture` as discussed previously. The created, modified, and published fields are integer fields and will store the Unix timestamp value of the relevant times.

To create the database, run the following command:

```
mysql -u root < create_database.sql
```

Implementation

Now that we have a database and image resize function to draw on, let's go about building the main part of the system.

Front End

Let's start by looking at headlines.php, shown in Listing 26.3, which would be the first page that a visitor to the site would see. We want to show her the headlines of the latest story from each page.

Listing 26.3   **headlines.php—Shows the Most Recent Headline from Each Page**

```php
<?php

include('include_fns.php');
include('header.php');


$conn = db_connect();


$pages_sql = 'select * from pages order by code';
$pages_result = mysql_query($pages_sql, $conn);

while ($pages = mysql_fetch_array($pages_result)) {

  $story_sql = "select * from stories
                where page = '".$pages['code']."'
                and published is not null
                order by published desc";
  $story_result = mysql_query($story_sql, $conn);
  if (mysql_num_rows($story_result)) {
    $story = mysql_fetch_array($story_result);
    print '<table border="0" width="400">';
    print '<tr>';
    print '<td rowspan="2" width="100">';
    if ($story[picture])
      print "<img src=\"resize_image.php?image=$story[picture]\" />";
    print '</td>';
    print '<td>';
    print '<h3>'.$pages['description'].'</h3>';
    print $story['headline'];
    print '</td>';
    print '</tr>';
```

Listing 26.3   **Continued**

```
    print '<tr><td align="right">';
    print '<a href="page.php?page='.$pages['code'].'">';
    print '<font size="1">Read more '.$pages['code'].' ...</font>';
    print '</a>';
    print '</table>';
  }
}

include('footer.php');
?>
```

This script, as with all the public scripts, includes header.php at the start and
footer.php at the end. Any output generated by the script is therefore displayed within
the main content cell in the page.

The hard work is done by two database queries. First,

```
select * from pages order by code
```

will retrieve the list of pages that are in the database. Next the contents of the loop

```
"select * from stories
where page = '".$pages['code']."'
and published is not null
order by published desc"
```

is executed to find the stories on that page in reverse order of the date published.
Figure 26.3 shows the output from headline.php using the sample application data.

Figure 26.3   Showing the headlines from each page within the site.

Next to each headline, a link is generated in the following form:

```
<a href="page.php?page=1"><font size="1">Read more news...</font></a>
```

This is done within the previous loop so that the query string value of `page` and the page name are printed next to the relevant headline. Clicking this link takes the visitor to `page.php`—the full list of stories for the particular page. The source for `page.php` can be found in Listing 26.4.

Listing 26.4   **page.php—Displays All the Published Stories on a Page**

```php
<?php

if (!isset($HTTP_GET_VARS['page']))
{
  header('Location: headlines.php');
  exit;
}

$page = $HTTP_GET_VARS['page'];

include('include_fns.php');
include('header.php');

$conn = db_connect();


$sql = "select * from stories
        where page = '$page'
        and published is not null
        order by published desc";
$result = mysql_query($sql, $conn);

while ($story = mysql_fetch_array($result))
{
  print '<h2>'.$story['headline'].'</h2>';
  if ($story['picture']) {
    $size = getImageSize($story['picture']);
    $width  = $size[0];
    $height = $size[1];
    print "<img src=\"".$story['picture']."\" height=\"$height\" width=\"$width\"
align=\"left\" />";

  }
  print $story['story_text'];
  $w = get_writer_record($story['writer']);
  print '<br /><font size="1">';
  print $w[full_name].', ';
  print date('M d, H:i', $story['modified']);
```

Listing 26.4 **Continued**

```
  print '</font>';
}


include('footer.php');
?>
```

Note that page.php requires a value for page to formulate the first query correctly. In case page.php is ever called directly without the query string, the first condition

```
if (!isset($HTTP_GET_VARS['page']))
{
  header('Location: headlines.php');
  exit;
}
```

will send the visitor back to the headline page so that the omission of page will not cause an error.

The first query

```
select * from stories
where page = '$page'
and published is not null
order by published desc
```

finds all stories published on the specified page, with the most recently published first. Within each loop, the uploaded image and story text are printed to the screen, followed by the writer's name and date of last change.

Figure 26.4 shows page.php in action, displaying all the news page items for our sample application.

Back End

Let's look next at how stories can be added to the system. Writers begin at stories.php. This script, after a writer is authenticated, displays a list of the stories the author has written and either displays the published date, or offers options of adding a new story, editing or deleting an existing one, or setting the search keywords. An example is shown in Figure 26.5.

These screens are not formatted inside the header and footer files, although they could be if desired. Because only the writers and editor will use these scripts, in our example we have chosen only to format as much as needed to create a usable system. The code for stories.php is shown in Listing 26.5.

Figure 26.4   Showing all published stories on the news page.

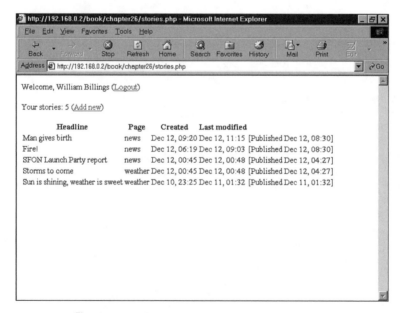

Figure 26.5   The story management page for writers.

Listing 26.5 **stories.php—Is the Interface for Writers to Manage Their Stories**

```php
<?php

include('include_fns.php');
session_start();

if (!check_auth_user()) {
?>
<form action="login.php" method="post">
<table border="0">
<tr>
  <td>Username</td>
  <td><input size="16" name="username"></td>
</tr>
<tr>
  <td>Password</td>
  <td><input size="16" type="password" name="password"></td>
</tr>
</table>
<input type="submit" value="Log in">
</form>
<?php
}
else {
  $conn = db_connect();

  $w = get_writer_record($HTTP_SESSION_VARS['auth_user']);

  print 'Welcome, '.$w['full_name'];
  print ' (<a href="logout.php">Logout</a>)';
  print '<p>';

  $sql = 'select * from stories where writer = \''.
         '$HTTP_SESSION_VARS['auth_user'].'\''.'order by created desc';
  $result = mysql_query($sql, $conn);

  print 'Your stories: ';
  print mysql_num_rows($result);
  print ' (<a href="story.php">Add new</a>)';
  print '</p><br /><br />';

  if (mysql_num_rows($result)) {
    print '<table>';
    print '<tr><th>Headline</th><th>Page</th>';
    print '<th>Created</th><th>Last modified</th></tr>';
    while ($qry = mysql_fetch_array($result)) {
```

Listing 26.5 **Continued**

```php
    print '<tr>';
    print '<td>';
    print $qry['headline'];
    print '</td>';
    print '<td>';
    print $qry['page'];
    print '</td>';
    print '<td>';
    print date('M d, H:i', $qry['created']);
    print '</td>';
    print '<td>';
    print date('M d, H:i', $qry['modified']);
    print '</td>';
    print '<td>';
    if ($qry['published'])
      print '[Published '.date('M d, H:i', $qry['published']).']';
    else {
      print '[<a href="story.php?story='.$qry['id'].'">edit</a>] ';
      print '[<a href="delete_story.php?story='.$qry['id'].'">delete</a>] ';
      print '[<a href="keywords.php?story='.$qry['id'].'">keywords</a>]';
    }
    print '</td>';
    print '</tr>';
  }
  print '</table>';
}


}
?>
```

The first step is to check whether a user has been authenticated, and if not, to display only a login form.

The session variable auth_user will be set after a writer has logged in. The authentication here isn't particularly secure, and in reality you would take more care to ensure that the writers are properly authenticated. This is dealt with in detail in Chapter 14, "Implementing Authentication with PHP and MySQL."

The login form submits to login.php, which checks the username and password against database values. If the login is successful, the user is returned to the page she came from, using the HTTP_REFERER value. This means that the login script can be invoked from any calling page within the system.

Next, we welcome the writer by name and give her the opportunity to log out. This link will always appear at the top of stories.php so she can easily log out when she is done.

```
$w = get_writer_record($HTTP_SESSION_VARS['auth_user']);

print 'Welcome, '.$w['full_name'];
print ' (<a href="logout.php">Logout</a>)';
```

The function `get_writer_record()` is defined in `db_fns.php` and returns an array of all the fields in the writer table for the passed in username. The script `logout.php` simply unsets the value of `auth_user`.

The following SQL finds all a writer's stories, starting with the most recently added:

```
$sql = 'select * from stories where writer = \''
       '.$HTTP_SESSION_VARS['auth_user'].'\'' .order by created desc';
```

We are storing a created, modified, and published timestamp against each story record. When a new story is added, both the created and modified timestamps are set to the system time. Each subsequent change updates only the modified field.

All this information is shown on the stories screen, first with

```
print date('M d, H:i', $qry['created']);
```

and then

```
print date('M d, H:i', $qry['modified']);
```

and finally

```
if ($qry['published'])
  print '[Published '.date('M d, H:i', $qry['published']).']';
else {
  print '[<a href="story.php?story='.$qry['id'].'">edit</a>] ';
  print '[<a href="delete_story.php?story='.$qry['id'].'">delete</a>] ';
  print '[<a href="keywords.php?story='.$qry['id'].'">keywords</a>]';
}
```

This will show the published date if appropriate; otherwise, it will show links to edit or delete that story and to set search keywords.

The script for entering a new story or editing an existing one is `story.php`, and is shown in Figure 26.6 editing one of the stories in the sample application database.

The complete listing of `story.php` can be seen in listing 26.6.

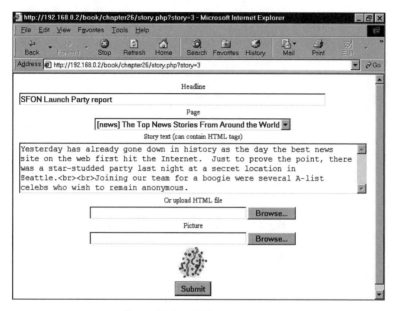

Figure 26.6   Editing a story.

Listing 26.6   **story.php—Is Used to Create or Edit a Story**

```php
<?php

include ('include_fns.php');

if (isset($HTTP_GET_VARS['story']))
  $s = get_story_record($HTTP_GET_VARS['story']);

?>

<form action="story_submit.php" method="post" enctype="multipart/form-data">
<input type="hidden" name="story" value="<?php print $HTTP_GET_VARS['story'];?>">
<input type="hidden" name="destination"
value="<?php print $HTTP_SERVER_VARS['HTTP_REFERER'];?>">
<table>

<tr>
  <td align="center">Headline<td>
</tr>
<tr>
```

Listing 26.6   **Continued**

```
  <td><input size="80" name="headline"
            value="<?php print $s['headline'];?>"></td>
</tr>

<tr>
  <td align="center">Page</td>
</tr>
<tr>
  <td align="center"><?php print query_select('page',
            "select p.code, p.description
            from pages p, writer_permissions wp, stories s
            where p.code = wp.page
            and wp.writer = s.writer
            and s.id =".$HTTP_GET_VARS['story'], $s['page']);?></td>
</tr>

<tr>
  <td align="center">Story text (can contain HTML tags)</td>
</tr>
<tr>
  <td><textarea cols="80" rows="7" name="story_text"
            wrap="virtual"><?php print $s['story_text'];?></textarea>
  </td>
</tr>

<tr>
  <td align="center">Or upload HTML file</td>
</tr>
<tr>
  <td align="center"><input type="file" name="html" size="40"></td>
</tr>

<tr>
  <td align="center">Picture</td>
</tr>
<tr>
  <td align="center"><input type="file" name="picture" size="40"></td>
</tr>

<?php
if ($s[picture]) {
  $size   = getImageSize($s['picture']);
  $width  = $size[0];
  $height = $size[1];
?>
<tr>
```

Listing 26.6   **Continued**

```
  <td align="center">
    <img src="<?php print $s['picture'];?>"
         width="<?php print $width;?>" height="<?php print $height;?>">
  </td>
</tr>
<?php } ?>


<tr>
  <td align="center"><input type="submit" value="Submit"></td>
</tr>

</table>
</form>
```

The same script can be used whether adding or editing, and the action depends on whether story is set when the script is called.

```
if (isset($HTTP_GET_VARS['story']))
  $s = get_story_record($HTTP_GET_VARS['story']);
```

The function get_story_record() is defined in db_fns.php and returns an array of all the fields in the stories table for the specified story ID. If no story ID is passed in, $story will be null and $s will not contain the array elements.

```
<input size="80" name="headline"
             value="<?php print $s['headline'];?>">
```

If story is not set, the preceding code will produce no value from the PHP statement, so the headline input box will be blank. If story is set, it will contain the headline text for the story being edited.

```
print query_select('page',
             "select p.code, p.description
              from pages p, writer_permissions wp
              where p.code = wp.page
              and wp.writer = '".$HTTP_SESSION_VARS['auth_user']."'", $s['page']);
```

The function query_select() is defined in select_fns.php and returns the HTML code to produce a SELECT list from a given SQL query. The first parameter is the NAME attribute for the SELECT. The SQL query in the second parameter selects two columns, where the first is the VALUE part of each option, and the second appears after the OPTION tag and is the text actually displayed in the list. The third parameter is optional. It adds a SELECTED attribute to the option whose value matches the specified value.

```
<input type="hidden" name="story" value="<?php print $HTTP_GET_VARS['story'];?>">
```

This sets up a placeholder variable, setting the new value for story from the passed in story. When the form is submitted, story_submit.php checks whether there is a value for story and generates an SQL UPDATE or INSERT statement accordingly.

The code for story_submit.php is shown in Listing 26.7.

Listing 26.7 **story_submit.php—Is Used to Insert or Update a Story in the Database**

```php
<?php

// story_submit.php
// add / modify story record

include('include_fns.php');

$conn = db_connect();

$headline = $HTTP_POST_VARS['headline'];
$page = $HTTP_POST_VARS['page'];
$time = time();

if ( (isset($HTTP_POST_FILES['html']['name']) &&
  (dirname($HTTP_POST_FILES['html']['type']) == 'text')
      && is_uploaded_file($HTTP_POST_FILES['html']['tmp_name'])))
{
  $fp = fopen($HTTP_POST_FILES['html']['tmp_name'], 'r');
  $story_text = addslashes(fread($fp,
filesize($HTTP_POST_FILES['html']['tmp_name'])));
  fclose($fp);
}
else
  $story_text = $HTTP_POST_VARS['story_text'];



if (isset($HTTP_POST_VARS['story']) && $HTTP_POST_VARS['story']!='')
{   // It's an update
  $story = $HTTP_POST_VARS['story'];

  $sql = "update stories
        set headline = '$headline',
            story_text = '$story_text',
            page = '$page',
            modified = $time
        where id = $story";
}
else {          // It's a new story
  $sql = "insert into stories
```

Listing 26.7   **Continued**

```
            (headline, story_text, page, writer, created, modified)
        values
            ('$headline', '$story_text', '$page', '"
            .$HTTP_SESSION_VARS['auth_user']."', $time, $time)";
}

$result = mysql_query($sql, $conn);

if (!$result) {
  print "There was a database error when executing <pre>$sql</pre>";
  print mysql_error();
  exit;
}


if ( (isset($HTTP_POST_FILES['picture']['name']) &&
     is_uploaded_file($HTTP_POST_FILES['picture']['tmp_name']))))
{

  if (!isset($story))
    $story = mysql_insert_id();

  $type = basename($HTTP_POST_FILES['picture']['type']);

  switch ($type) {
    case 'jpeg':
    case 'pjpeg':  $filename = "pictures/$story.jpg";
                   move_uploaded_file($HTTP_POST_FILES['picture']['tmp_name'],
                    $filename);
                   $sql = "update stories
                           set picture = '$filename'
                           where id = $story";
                   $result = mysql_query($sql, $conn);
                   break;
    default:       print 'Invalid picture format: '.
                         $HTTP_POST_FILES['picture']['type'];
  }
}

header('Location: '.$HTTP_POST_VARS['destination']);

?>
```

The delete story link calls delete_story.php, which actions a simple DELETE statement and returns the writer to the calling page. The code for delete_story.php is shown in Listing 26.8.

Listing 26.8   **delete_story.php—Is Used to Delete a Story from the Database**

```php
<?php

// delete_story.php

include('include_fns.php');

$conn = db_connect();


$story = $HTTP_GET_VARS['story'];
$sql = "delete from stories where id = $story";
$result = mysql_query($sql, $conn);

header('Location: '.$HTTP_SERVER_VARS['HTTP_REFERER']);
?>
```

Searching

Clicking the keywords link on the stories list brings up a new form for entering keywords against the story. There is no limit to the number of keywords that can be entered, and each keyword is given a weight value, with a higher value indicating that it is more relevant.

Figure 26.7 shows the screen used to set keywords against a particular story.

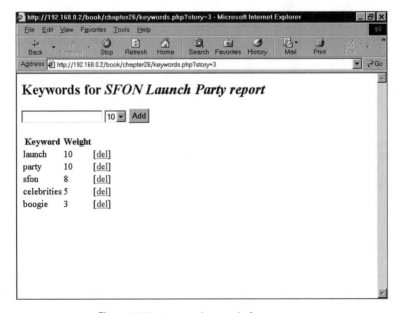

Figure 26.7   Setting keywords for a story.

The script `keywords.php` is fairly straightforward, so we won't look at it in any detail. It is included on the CD-ROM.

This script triggers the `keyword_add.php` and `keyword_delete.php` scripts. These scripts are also straightforward, and are therefore not included here.

The script `keyword_add.php` uses the following query to add new keywords to the database:

```
insert into keywords (story, keyword, weight)
values ($story, '$keyword', $weight)
```

In a similar vein, `keyword_delete.php` uses the following query to remove a keyword:

```
delete from keywords where story = $story and keyword = '$keyword'
```

What is interesting is the way in which the weight values are used to calculate a percentage relevance figure when searching.

The search form in `search_form.php` contains a single field for keywords, and submits to `search.php`, which queries the database of live stories to find matching content. The source for *search.php* is shown in Listing 26.9.

Listing 26.9   **search.php—Finds Matching Stories and Calculates a Percentage Match Score**

```php
<?php

include('include_fns.php');
include('header.php');

$conn = db_connect();

if ($HTTP_POST_VARS['keyword']) {
  $k = split(' ', $HTTP_POST_VARS['keyword']);
  $num_keywords = count($k);
  for ($i=0; $i<$num_keywords; $i++) {
    if ($i)
      $k_string .= "or k.keyword = '".$k[$i]."' ";
    else
      $k_string .= "k.keyword = '".$k[$i]."' ";
  }
  $and .= "and ($k_string) ";
}


$sql = "select s.id,
              s.headline,
              10 * sum(k.weight) / $num_keywords as score
        from stories s, keywords k
        where s.id = k.story
```

Listing 26.9   **Continued**

```
              $and
              group by s.id, s.headline
              order by score desc, s.id desc";


$result = mysql_query($sql, $conn);
}
print '<h2>Search results</h2>';

if ($result  && mysql_num_rows($result)) {
  print '<table>';
  while ($qry = mysql_fetch_array($result)) {
    print '<tr><td>';
    print $qry['headline'];
    print '</td><td>';
    print floor($qry['score']).'%';
    print '</td></tr>';
  }
  print '</table>';
}
else {
  print 'No matching stories found';
}
include('footer.php');
?>
```

First, the keyword string passed into the script is split up into individual search words. We are not using any advanced search techniques in this example, such as allowing the searcher to use AND or OR keywords or group words together into a phrase.

```
if ($HTTP_POST_VARS['keyword']) {
  $k = split(' ', $HTTP_POST_VARS['keyword']);
  $num_keywords = count($k);
  for ($i=0; $i<$num_keywords; $i++) {
    if ($i)
      $k_string .= "or k.keyword = '".$k[$i]."' ";
    else
      $k_string .= "k.keyword = '".$k[$i]."' ";
  }
  $and .= "and ($k_string) ";
```

This code uses the PHP function split() to create an array containing each word in the keyword string separated by a space character. If only one word is specified, it still returns a single element array and the subsequent loop is executed once. Ultimately the condition stored in $and will look something similar to

```
and (k.keyword = 'keyword1' or k.keyword = 'keyword2' or k.keyword = 'keyword3')
```

The search query built based on the previous code would be

```
select s.id,
       s.headline,
       10 * sum(k.weight) / $num_keywords as score
from stories s, keywords k
where s.id = k.story
and (k.keyword = 'keyword1'
  or k.keyword = 'keyword2'
  or k.keyword = 'keyword3')
group by s.id, s.headline
order by score desc, s.id desc
```

The calculation for the score is the sum of the weights from all matching keywords divided by the number of keywords searched for and then multiplied by ten. This favors searches in which all the keywords entered match the keywords in the database.

Because the weights range from 1 to 10, the maximum value for the score is 100. A search for three keywords would only be a 100% match with a story if all three were found for that story and each had a weight of 10.

Editor Screen

The only part of the system we haven't covered is how a story actually gets published after it has been written. The script `publish.php` makes a story live. It is shown in Listing 26.10.

Listing 26.10   **publish.php—Lists All Documents So the Editor Can Choose Which Ones Are Shown on the Live Site**

```php
<?php

include('include_fns.php');

$conn = db_connect();

$sql = 'select * from stories order by modified desc';
$result = mysql_query($sql, $conn);

print '<h2>Editor admin</h2>';
print '<table>';
print '<tr><th>Headline</th><th>Last modified</th></tr>';
while ($story = mysql_fetch_array($result)) {
  print '<tr><td>';
  print $story['headline'];
  print '</td><td>';
  print date('M d, H:i', $story['modified']);
  print '</td><td>';
```

Listing 26.10   **Continued**

```
  if ($story[published]) {
    print '[<a href="unpublish_story.php?story='.$story['id'].'">unpublish</a>] ';
  }
  else {
    print '[<a href="publish_story.php?story='.$story['id'].'">publish</a>] ';
    print '[<a href="delete_story.php?story='.$story['id'].'">delete</a>] ';
  }
  print '[<a href="story.php?story='.$story['id'].'">edit</a>] ';

  print '</td></tr>';
}
print '</table>';
?>
```

This script should be made available only to the people who are authorized to publish stories to the live site. In our sample application, this would be the site editor, but there is no access control on this script for simplicity. It should, however, be protected in a live situation.

This is very similar to stories.php except that the editor is given a screen showing the stories for every writer, not just her own. The if statement ensures that appropriate options are presented for each story. Published stories can be unpublished, and unpublished stories can be published or deleted.

These three links submit to unpublish_story.php, publish_story.php, and delete_story.php, respectively.

The script publish_story.php uses the following SQL query:

```
update stories set published = $now
        where id = $story
```

This will mark a story as published and authorize it for public viewing.

Similarly, unpublish_story.php uses the following query to mark a story as unpublished and stop it from being displayed to the public:

```
update stories set published = null
        where id = $story
```

The edit link appears regardless of whether a story is published, so the editor can always make changes. This is different to the writers' level of access, where they can only modify a story before it has been published.

Extending the Project

There are several ways this project could be extended to make a more comprehensive content management system:

- You could allow groups of users to work on stories together (collaboration).
- You could implement a more flexible page layout so that editors can position text and images on the page.
- An image library could be built so that frequently used pictures are not duplicated, and search keywords are assigned to images as well as story text.
- You could also add spell-checking functionality to the content editor. A check could be implemented using, for example, the aspell library.

Next

In the next project, we will build a Web-based interface that will allow you to check and send email from the Web using IMAP.

27

Building a Web-Based Email
Service

M ORE AND MORE OFTEN THESE DAYS, sites want to offer Web-based email to their users. This chapter explains how to implement a Web interface to an existing mail server using the PHP IMAP library. You can use it to check your own existing mailbox through a Web page, or perhaps extend it to support many users for mass Web-based email like Hotmail.

In this project, we will build an email client, Warm Mail, that will enable users to

- Connect to their accounts on POP3 or IMAP mail servers
- Read mail
- Send mail
- Reply to mail messages
- Forward mail messages
- Delete mail from their accounts

The Problem

In order for a user to be able to read his mail, we will need to find a way to connect to his mail server. This generally won't be the same machine as the Web server.

We will need a way to interact with his mailbox, to see what messages have been received and to deal with each message individually.

Two main protocols are supported by mail servers for reading user mailboxes: POP3 and IMAP. If possible, we should support both of these. POP3 stands for Post Office Protocol version 3, and IMAP stands for Internet Message Access Protocol.

The main difference between these two is that POP3 is intended for, and usually used by, people who connect to a network for a short time to download and delete their mail from a server. IMAP is intended for online use, to interact with mail permanently kept on the remote server. IMAP has some more advanced features that we won't use here.

If you are interested in the differences between these protocols, you can consult the RFCs for them (RFC 1939 for POP version 3 and RFC 2060 for IMAP version 4 rev1). An excellent article comparing the two can be found at

```
http://www.imap.org/papers/imap.vs.pop.brief.html
```

Neither of these protocols is designed for sending mail—for that we must use the *SMTP (Simple Mail Transfer Protocol)*, which we have used before from PHP via the `mail()` function. This protocol is described in RFC 821.

Solution Components

PHP has excellent IMAP and POP3 support, but it is provided via the IMAP function library. In order to use the code presented in this chapter, you will need to have installed the IMAP library. You can tell if you already have this installed by looking at the output of the `phpinfo()` function.

If not, you will need to download the extension. You can get the latest version via FTP from

```
ftp://ftp.cac.washington.edu/imap/c-client.tar.Z
```

Under UNIX, download the source and compile it for your operating system. When you have done this, copy `rfc822.h`, `mail.h`, and `linkage.h` to `/usr/local/include` or another directory in your include path, run PHP's configure script, adding the `--with-imap` directive to any other parameters you use, and recompile PHP. Documentation exists on compiling the Windows version yourself, but it is much more complex than compiling for UNIX. To use the IMAP extension with Windows, download the Zip file version of PHP rather than the Install Wizard. The Zip file contains many extensions including IMAP. Open your `php.ini` file and uncomment out the line:

```
extension=php_imap.dll
```

One interesting thing to note is that although these are called IMAP functions they also work equally well with POP3 and NNTP (Network News Transfer Protocol). We will use them for IMAP and POP3, but the Warm Mail application could be easily extended to use NNTP and be a newsreader as well as mail client.

There are a very large number of functions in this library, but in order to implement the functionality in this application, we will use only a few. We'll explain these functions as we use them, but be aware that there are many more. See the documentation if your needs are different from ours, or if you want to add extra features to the application.

You can build a fairly useful mail application with only a fraction of the built-in functions. This means that you need only plow through a fraction of the documentation. The IMAP functions we use in this chapter are

- `imap_open()`
- `imap_close()`
- `imap_headers()`
- `imap_header()`
- `imap_fetchheader()`
- `imap_body()`
- `imap_delete()`
- `imap_expunge()`

For a user to read his mail, we will need to get his server and account details. Rather than getting these details from the user every time, we'll set up a username and password database for a user so that we can store his details.

Often people have more than one email account (one for home and another for work, for example), and we should allow them to connect to any of their accounts. We should therefore allow them to have multiple sets of account information in the database.

We should enable users to read, reply to, forward, and delete existing emails, as well as send new ones. We can do all the reading parts using IMAP or POP3, and all the sending parts using SMTP with `mail()`.

Let's look at how we'll put it all together.

Solution Overview

The general flow through this Web-based system won't be much different from other email clients. A diagram showing the system flow and modules is shown in Figure 27.1.

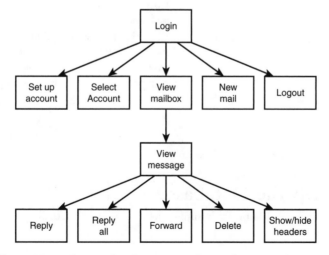

Figure 27.1   The interface for Warm Mail gives the user mailbox-level functionality and message-level functionality.

As you can see, we will first require a user to log in, and then give him a choice of options. He will be able to set up a new mail account or select one of his existing accounts for use. He will also be able to view his incoming mail—responding to, for-warding, or deleting it—and send new mail.

We will also give him the option of viewing detailed headers for a particular message. Viewing the complete headers can tell you a lot about a message. You can see which machine the mail came from—a useful tool for tracking down spam. You can see which machine forwarded it and at what time it reached each host—useful for assigning blame for delayed messages. You might also be able to see which email client the sender used if the application adds optional information to the headers.

We have used a slightly different application architecture for this project. Instead of having a set of scripts, one for each module, we have a slightly longer script, index.php, that works like the event loop of a GUI-driven program. Each action we take on the site by pressing a button will bring us back to `index.php`, but with a different parameter. Depending on the parameter, different functions will be called to show the appropriate output to the user. The functions are in function libraries, as usual.

This architecture is suitable for small applications such as this. It suits applications that are very event driven, where user actions trigger functionality. Using a single event handler is not very suitable for larger architectures or projects being worked on by a team.

A summary of the files in the Warm Mail project is shown in Table 27.1.

Table 27.1 **Files in the Warm Mail Application**

Name	Type	Description
index.php	Application	The main script that runs the entire application
include_fns.php	Functions	Collection of include files for this application
data_valid_fns.php	Functions	Collection of functions for validating input data
db_fns.php	Functions	Collection of functions for connecting to the mail database
mail_fns.php	Functions	Collection of email-related functions for opening mailboxes, reading mail, and so on
output_fns.php	Functions	Collection of functions for outputting HTML
user_auth_fns.php	Functions	Collection of functions for authenticating users
create_database.sql	SQL	SQL to set up the book_sc database and set up a user

Let's go ahead and look at the application.

Setting Up the Database

The database for Warm Mail is fairly simple because we aren't actually going to store any of the emails in it.

We will need to store users of the system. For each user, we will need to store the following fields:

- username—Their preferred username for Warm Mail
- password—Their preferred password for Warm Mail
- address—Their preferred email address, which will appear in the From field of emails they send from the system
- displayname—The "human-readable" name that they would like displayed in emails from them to others.

We will also need to store each account that users would like to check with the system. For each account, we will need to store the following information:

- username—The Warm Mail user who this account belongs to.
- server—The machine on which the account resides, for example, localhost or mail.tangledweb.com.au.
- port—The port to connect to when using this account. Usually this will be 110 for POP3 servers and 143 for IMAP servers.
- type—The protocol used to connect to this server, either 'POP3' or 'IMAP'.
- remoteuser—The username for connecting to the mail server.
- remotepassword—The password for connecting to the mail server.
- accountid—A unique key for identifying accounts.

You can set up the database for this application by running the SQL shown in Listing 27.1.

Listing 27.1 **create_database.sql—SQL to Create the Mail Database**

```
create database mail;

use mail;

create table users
(
  username char(16) not null primary key,
  password char(16) not null,
  address char(100) not null,
  displayname char(100) not null
);

create table accounts
(
  username char(16) not null,
  server char(100) not null,
```

Listing 27.1   **Continued**

```
  port int not null,
  type char(4) not null,
  remoteuser char(50) not null,
  remotepassword char(50) not null,
  accountid int unsigned not null auto_increment primary key
);

grant select, insert, update, delete
on mail.*
to mail@localhost identified by 'password';
```

Remember that you can execute this SQL by typing

```
mysql -u root -p < create_database.sql
```

You will need to supply your root password. You should change the password for the mail user in `create_database.sql` and in `db_fns.php` before running it.

On the CD-ROM, we have also provided an SQL file called `populate.sql`. In this application, we are not going to create a user registration or administration process. You can add one yourself if you want to use this software on a larger scale, but if you want it for personal use, you will just need to insert yourself into the database. The `populate.sql` script provides a proforma for doing this, so insert your details into it and run it to set yourself up as a user.

Script Architecture

As we mentioned before, this application uses one script to control everything. This script is called `index.php`. It is shown in Listing 27.2. This script is quite long, but we will go through it section by section.

Listing 27.2   **index.php—The Backbone of the Warm Mail System**

```php
<?php
// This file is the main body of the Warm Mail application.
// It works basically as a state machine and shows users the
// output for the action they have chosen.

//****************************************************************************
// Stage 1: pre-processing
// Do any required processing before page header is sent
// and decide what details to show on page headers
//****************************************************************************

  include ('include_fns.php');
  session_start();
```

Listing 27.2   **Continued**

```php
//create short variable names
$username = $HTTP_POST_VARS['username'];
$passwd = $HTTP_POST_VARS['passwd'];
if(isset($HTTP_POST_VARS['action']))
  $action = $HTTP_POST_VARS['action'];
else
  $action = $HTTP_GET_VARS['action'];
if(isset($HTTP_POST_VARS['account']))
  $account = $HTTP_POST_VARS['account'];
else
  $account = $HTTP_GET_VARS['account'];

$messageid = $HTTP_GET_VARS['messageid'];

$to =   $HTTP_POST_VARS['to'];
$cc =   $HTTP_POST_VARS['cc'];
$subject =   $HTTP_POST_VARS['subject'];
$message =   $HTTP_POST_VARS['message'];

$buttons = array();

//append to this string if anything processed before header has output
$status = '';

// need to process log in or out requests before anything else
if($username||$password)
{
  if(login($username, $passwd))
  {
    $status .= '<p>Logged in successfully.</p><br /><br /><br /><br />
     <br /><br />';
    $HTTP_SESSION_VARS['auth_user'] = $username;
    if(number_of_accounts($HTTP_SESSION_VARS['auth_user'])==1)
    {
      $accounts = get_account_list($HTTP_SESSION_VARS['auth_user']);
      $HTTP_SESSION_VARS['selected_account'] = $accounts[0];
    }
  }
  else
  {
    $status .= '<p>Sorry, we could not log you in with that
                username and password.</p><br /><br /><br /><br />
                <br /><br />';
  }
}
```

Listing 27.2 **Continued**

```
  if($action == 'log-out')
  {
    session_destroy();
    unset($action);
    unset($HTTP_SESSION_VARS);
  }

  //need to process choose, delete or store account before drawing header
  switch ( $action )
  {
    case 'delete-account' :
    {
      delete_account($HTTP_SESSION_VARS['auth_user'], $account);
      break;
    }
    case 'store-settings' :
    {
      store_account_settings($HTTP_SESSION_VARS['auth_user'], $HTTP_POST_VARS);
      break;
    }
    case 'select-account' :
    {
      // if have chosen a valid account, store it as a session variable
      if($account&&account_exists($HTTP_SESSION_VARS['auth_user'], $account))
      {
        $HTTP_SESSION_VARS['selected_account'] = $account;
      }
    }
  }
  // set the buttons that will be on the tool bar
  $buttons[0] = 'view-mailbox';
  $buttons[1] = 'new-message';
  $buttons[2] = 'account-setup';
  //only offer a log out button if logged in
  if(check_auth_user())
  {
    $buttons[4] = 'log-out';
  }

//******************************************************************************
// Stage 2: headers
// Send the HTML headers and menu bar appropriate to current action
//******************************************************************************
  if($action)
  {
```

Listing 27.2   **Continued**

```
    // display header with application name and description of page or action
    do_html_header($HTTP_SESSION_VARS['auth_user'], "Warm Mail - ".
                   format_action($action),
                   $HTTP_SESSION_VARS['selected_account']);
  }
  else
  {
    // display header with just application name
    do_html_header($HTTP_SESSION_VARS['auth_user'], "Warm Mail",
      $HTTP_SESSION_VARS['selected_account']);
  }

  display_toolbar($buttons);

//*****************************************************************************
// Stage 3: body
// Depending on action, show appropriate main body content
//*****************************************************************************
  //display any text generated by functions called before header
  echo $status;

  if(!check_auth_user())
  {
    echo '<p>You need to log in';
    if($action&&$action!='log-out')
      echo ' to go to '.format_action($action);
    echo '.</p><br /><br />';
    display_login_form($action);
  }
  else
  {
    switch ( $action )
    {
      // if we have chosen to setup a new account, or have just added or
      // deleted an account, show account setup page
      case 'store-settings' :
      case 'account-setup' :
      case 'delete-account' :
      {
        display_account_setup($HTTP_SESSION_VARS['auth_user']);
        break;
      }
      case 'send-message' :
      {
        if(send_message($to, $cc, $subject, $message))
          echo '<p>Message sent.</p><br /><br /><br /><br /><br /><br />';
```

Listing 27.2 **Continued**

```
    else
      echo '<p>Could not send message.</p><br /><br /><br /><br />
            <br /><br />';
    break;
  }
  case 'delete' :
  {
    delete_message($HTTP_SESSION_VARS['auth_user'],
                   $HTTP_SESSION_VARS['selected_account'], $messageid);
    //note deliberately no 'break' - we will continue to the next case
  }
  case 'select-account' :
  case 'view-mailbox' :
  {
    // if mailbox just chosen, or view mailbox chosen, show mailbox
    display_list($HTTP_SESSION_VARS['auth_user'],
      $HTTP_SESSION_VARS['selected_account']);
    break;
  }
  case 'show-headers' :
  case 'hide-headers' :
  case 'view-message' :
  {
    // if we have just picked a message from the list, or were looking at
    // a message and chose to hide or view headers, load a message
    $fullheaders = ($action=='show-headers');
    display_message($HTTP_SESSION_VARS['auth_user'],
                    $HTTP_SESSION_VARS['selected_account'],
                    $messageid, $fullheaders);
    break;
  }
  case 'reply-all' :
  {
    //set cc as old cc line
    if(!$imap)
      $imap = open_mailbox($HTTP_SESSION_VARS['auth_user'],
                           $HTTP_SESSION_VARS['selected_account']);
    if($imap)
    {
      $header = imap_header($imap, $messageid);
      if($header->reply_toaddress)
        $to = $header->reply_toaddress;
      else
        $to = $header->fromaddress;
      $cc = $header->ccaddress;
      $subject = 'Re: '.$header->subject;
```

Listing 27.2 **Continued**

```php
      $body = add_quoting(stripslashes(imap_body($imap, $messageid)));
      imap_close($imap);

      display_new_message_form($HTTP_SESSION_VARS['auth_user'],
      $to, $cc, $subject, $body);
    }
    break;
  }
  case 'reply' :
  {
    //set to address as reply-to or from of the current message
    if(!$imap)
      $imap = open_mailbox($HTTP_SESSION_VARS['auth_user'],
                           $HTTP_SESSION_VARS['selected_account']);
    if($imap)
    {
      $header = imap_header($imap, $messageid);
      if($header->reply_toaddress)
        $to = $header->reply_toaddress;
      else
        $to = $header->fromaddress;
      $subject = 'Re: '.$header->subject;
      $body = add_quoting(stripslashes(imap_body($imap, $messageid)));
      imap_close($imap);

      display_new_message_form($HTTP_SESSION_VARS['auth_user'],
                                   $to, $cc, $subject, $body);
    }

    break;
  }
  case 'forward' :
  {
    //set message as quoted body of current message
    if(!$imap)
      $imap = open_mailbox($HTTP_SESSION_VARS['auth_user'],
                           $HTTP_SESSION_VARS['selected_account']);
    if($imap)
    {
      $header = imap_header($imap, $messageid);
      $body = add_quoting(stripslashes(imap_body($imap, $messageid)));
      $subject = 'Fwd: '.$header->subject;
      imap_close($imap);

      display_new_message_form($HTTP_SESSION_VARS['auth_user'],
                                   $to, $cc, $subject, $body);
```

Listing 27.2   **Continued**

```
            }
         break;
      }
      case 'new-message' :
      {
         display_new_message_form($HTTP_SESSION_VARS['auth_user'],
                               $to, $cc, $subject, $body);

         break;
      }
   }
}
//*******************************************************************************
// Stage 4: footer
//*******************************************************************************
   do_html_footer();
?>
```

This script uses an event handling approach. It contains the knowledge or logic about which function needs to be called for each event. The events in this case are triggered by the user clicking the various buttons in the site, each of which selects an action. Most buttons are produced by the `display_button()` function, but the `display_form_button()` function is used if it's a submit button. These functions are both in `output_fns.php`. These all jump to URLs of the form

`index.php?action=log-out`

The value of the `action` variable when `index.php` is called determines which event handler to activate.

The four main sections to the script are as follows:

1. We do some processing that must take place before we send the page header to the browser, such as starting the session, executing any preprocessing for the action the user has selected, and deciding what the headers will look like.

2. We process and send the appropriate headers and menu bar for the action the user has selected.

3. We choose which body of the script to execute, depending on the selected action. The different actions trigger different function calls.

4. We send the page footers.

If you look briefly through the code for the script, you will see that these four sections are marked with comments.

To understand this script fully, let's walk through actually using the site action by action.

Logging In and Out

When a user loads the page index.php, he will see the output shown in Figure 27.2.

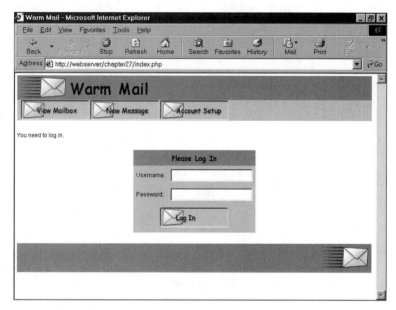

Figure 27.2   The login screen for Warm Mail asks for your
username and password.

This is the default behavior for the application. With no $action chosen yet, and no
login details supplied, we will execute the following parts of the code.

In the preprocessing stage we first execute the following code:

```
include ('include_fns.php');
session_start();
```

These lines start the session that will be used to keep track of the $auth_user and
$selected_account session variables, which we'll come to later on.

As in our other applications, we create short variable names. We have done this in
every form related script since chapter one, so it barely needs mention except for the
variable action. Depending on where in the application this comes from, it might be
either a GET or POST variable. We test for the existence of
$HTTP_POST_VARS['action'] and if it is not set we use the GET version. The relevant
code is these four lines:

```
if(isset($HTTP_POST_VARS['action']))
  $action = $HTTP_POST_VARS['action'];
else
  $action = $HTTP_GET_VARS['action'];
```

We have to do the same thing with the `account` variable, as it is usually accessed via GET, but is accessed via POST when deleting an account.

If you are using PHP 4.1 or newer you can avoid these issues by accessing the form variables via the `$_REQUEST` superglobal. (We have not used it here for backward compatibility.)

To save work when customizing the user interface, the buttons that appear on the toolbar are controlled by an array. We declare an empty array,

```
$buttons = array();
```

and set the buttons that we want on the page:

```
$buttons[0] = 'view-mailbox';
$buttons[1] = 'new-message';
$buttons[2] = 'account-setup';
```

For the header stage, we print a plain vanilla header:

```
do_html_header($HTTP_SESSION_VARS['auth_user'], 'Warm Mail',
                        $HTTP_SESSION_VARS['selected_account']);
...
display_toolbar($buttons);
```

This code prints the title and header bar and then the toolbar of buttons you can see in Figure 27.2. These functions can be found in the `output_fns.php` function library, but as you can easily see their effect in the figure, we won't go through them here.

Now we come to the body of the code:

```
if(!check_auth_user())
{
  echo '<p>You need to log in';
  if($action&&$action!='log-out')
  echo ' to go to '.format_action($action);
  echo '.</p><br /><br />';
  display_login_form($action);
}
```

The `check_auth_user()` function is from the `user_auth_fns.php` library. We have used very similar code in some of the previous projects—it checks if the user is logged in. If he is not, which is the case here, we will show him a login form, which you can see in Figure 27.2. We draw this form in the `display_login_form()` function from `output_fns.php`.

If the user fills in the form correctly and presses the Log In button, he will see the output shown in Figure 27.3.

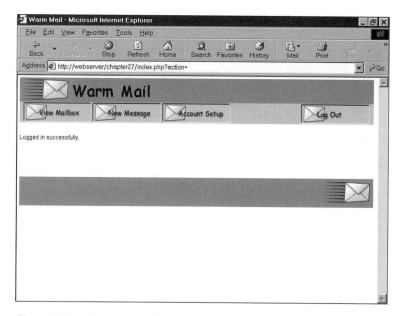

Figure 27.3   After successful login, the user can begin using the application.

On this execution of the script, we will activate different sections of code. The login form has two fields, $username and $password. If these have been filled in, the following segment of preprocessing code will be activated:

```
if($username||$password)
{
  if(login($username, $passwd))
  {
    $status .= '<p>Logged in successfully.</p><br /><br /><br /><br />
              <br /><br />';
    $HTTP_SESSION_VARS['auth_user'] = $username;
    if(number_of_accounts($HTTP_SESSION_VARS['auth_user'])==1)
    {
      $accounts = get_account_list($HTTP_SESSION_VARS['auth_user']);
      $HTTP_SESSION_VARS['selected_account'] = $accounts[0];
    }
  }
  else
  {
    $status .= '<p>Sorry, we could not log you in with that
              username and password.</p><br /><br /><br /><br /><br />';
  }
}
```

As you can see, the code calls the `login()` function, which is similar to the one used in Chapters 24 and 25. If all goes well, we register the username in the session variable `auth_user`.

In addition to setting up the buttons we saw while not logged in, we add another button to allow the user to log out again, as follows:

```
if(check_auth_user())
{
    $buttons[4] = 'log-out';
}
```

You can see this Log Out button in Figure 27.3.

In the header stage, we again display the header and the buttons. In the body, we display the status message we set up earlier:

```
echo $status;
```

After that, it's just a case of printing the footer and waiting to see what the user will do next.

Setting Up Accounts

When a user first starts using the Warm Mail system, he will need to set up some email accounts. If the user clicks on the Account Setup button, this will set the `action` variable to `account-setup` and recall the `index.php` script. The user will then see the output shown in Figure 27.4.

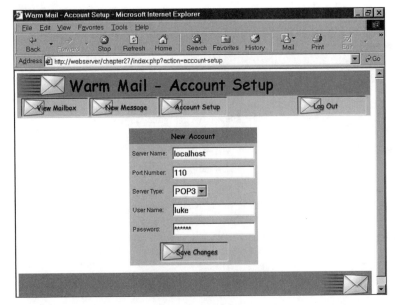

Figure 27.4 A user needs to set up his email account details before he can read his email.

Look back at the script in Listing 27.2. This time around because of the value of $action, we get different behavior.

We get a slightly different header, as follows:

```
do_html_header($HTTP_SESSION_VARS['auth_user'], 'Warm Mail - '.
                format_action($action), $HTTP_SESSION_VARS['selected_account']);
```

More importantly, we get a different body, as follows:

```
case 'store-settings' :
case 'account-setup' :
case 'delete-account' :
{
  display_account_setup($HTTP_SESSION_VARS['auth_user']);
  break;
}
```

This is the typical pattern: Each command calls a function. In this case, we call the display_account_setup() function. The code for this function is shown in Listing 27.3.

Listing 27.3   display_account_setup() Function from output_fns.php—Function to Get and Display Account Details

```
function display_account_setup($auth_user)
{
  //display empty 'new account' form

  display_account_form($auth_user);
  $list = get_accounts($auth_user);
  $accounts = sizeof($list);

  // display each stored account
  foreach($list as $key => $account)
  {
    // display form for each accounts details.
    // note that we are going to send the password for all accounts in the HTML
    // this is not really a very good idea
    display_account_form($auth_user, $account['accountid'], $account['server'],
                         $account['remoteuser'], $account['remotepassword'],
                         $account['type'], $account['port']);
  }
}
```

When we call this function, it displays a blank form to add a new account, followed by editable forms containing each of the user's current email accounts. The display_account_form() function will display the form that we can see in Figure 27.4. You can see that we use it in two different ways here: We use it with no parameters to display an empty form, and we use it with a full set of parameters to display an existing record. This function is in the output_fns.php library; it simply outputs HTML so we will not go through it here.

The function that retrieves any existing accounts is `get_accounts()`, from the `mail_fns.php` library. This function is shown in Listing 27.4.

Listing 27.4 get_accounts() Function from mail_fns.php—Function to Retrieve All the Account Details for a Particular User

```
function get_accounts($auth_user)
{
  $list = array();
  if(db_connect())
  {
    $query = "select * from accounts where username = '$auth_user'";
    $result = mysql_query($query);
        if($result)
    {
      while($settings = mysql_fetch_array($result))
        array_push( $list, $settings);
    }
    else
      return false;
  }
  return $list;
}
```

As you can see, this function connects to the database, retrieves all the accounts for a particular user, and returns them as an array.

Creating a New Account

If a user fills out the account form and clicks the Save Changes button, the `store-settings` action will be activated. Let's look at the event handling code for this from `index.php`. In the preprocessing stage, we execute the following code:

```
case 'store-settings' :
{
  store_account_settings($HTTP_SESSION_VARS['auth_user'], $HTTP_POST_VARS);
  break;
}
```

The `store_account_settings()` function writes the new account details into the database. The code for this function is shown in Listing 27.5.

Listing 27.5 store_account_settings() Function from mail_fns.php—Function to Save New Account Details for a User

```
function store_account_settings($auth_user, $settings)
{
  if(!filled_out($settings))
```

Listing 27.5   **Continued**

```
  {
    echo 'All fields must be filled in.  Try again.<br /><br />';
    return false;
  }
  else
  {
    if($settings['account']>0)
      $query = "update accounts  set server = '$settings[server]',
                    port = $settings[port], type = '$settings[type]',
                    remoteuser = '$settings[remoteuser]',
                    remotepassword = '$settings[remotepassword]'
                 where accountid = $settings[account]
                    and username = '$auth_user'";
    else
      $query = "insert into accounts values ('$auth_user',
                    '$settings[server]', $settings[port],
                    '$settings[type]', '$settings[remoteuser]',
                    '$settings[remotepassword]', NULL)";
    if(db_connect() && mysql_query($query))
    {
      return true;
    }
    else
    {
      echo 'could not store changes.<br /><br /><br /><br /><br /><br />';
      return false;
    }
  }
}
```

As you can see, two choices within this function correspond to inserting a new account or updating an existing account. The function executes the appropriate query to save the account details.

After storing the account details, we go back to index.php, to the main body stage:

```
case 'store-settings' :
case 'account-setup' :
case 'delete-account' :
{
  display_account_setup($HTTP_SESSION_VARS['auth_user']);
  break;
}
```

As you can see, we then execute the display_account_setup() function as before to list the user's account details. The newly added account will now be included.

Modifying an Existing Account

The process for modifying an existing account is very similar. The user can change the account details and click the Save Changes button. Again this will trigger the store-settings action, but this time it will update the account details instead of inserting them.

Deleting an Account

To delete an account, the user can click the Delete Account button that is shown under each account listing. This activates the delete-account action.

In the preprocessing section of the index.php script, we will execute the following code:

```
case 'delete-account' :
{
  delete_account($HTTP_SESSION_VARS['auth_user'], $account);
  break;
}
```

This code calls the delete_account() function. The code for this function is shown in Listing 27.6. Deleting accounts needs to be handled before the header because a choice of which account to use is inside the header. The account list needs to be updated before this can be correctly drawn.

Listing 27.6 **delete_account() Function from mail_fns.php—Function to Delete a Single Account's Details**

```
function delete_account($auth_user, $accountid)
{
  //delete one of this user's account from the DB

  $query = "delete from accounts where accountid='$accountid'
                          and username ='$auth_user'";
  if(db_connect())
  {
    $result = mysql_query($query);
  }
  return $result;
}
```

After execution returns to index.php, the body stage will run the following code:

```
case 'store-settings' :
case 'account-setup' :
case 'delete-account' :
{
  display_account_setup($HTTP_SESSION_VARS['auth_user']);
  break;
}
```

You will recognize this as the same code we ran before—it just displays the list of the user's accounts.

Reading Mail

After the user has set up some accounts, we can move on to the main game: connecting to these accounts and reading mail.

Selecting an Account

We need to select one of the user's accounts to read mail from. The currently selected account is stored in the $selected_account session variable.

If the user has a single account registered in the system, it will be automatically selected when he logs in, as follows:

```
if(number_of_accounts($HTTP_SESSION_VARS['auth_user'])==1)
{
  $accounts = get_account_list($HTTP_SESSION_VARS['auth_user']);
  $HTTP_SESSION_VARS['selected_account'] = $accounts[0];
}
```

The number_of_accounts() function, from mail_fns.php, is used to work out whether the user has more than one account. The get_account_list() function retrieves an array of the names of the user's accounts. In this case there is exactly one, so we can access it as the array's 0 value.

The number_of_accounts() function is shown in Listing 27.7.

Listing 27.7   number_of_accounts() Function from mail_fns.php—Function to Work Out How Many Accounts a User Has Registered

```
function number_of_accounts($auth_user)
{
  // get the number of accounts that belong to this user

  $query = "select count(*) from accounts where username = '$auth_user'";

  if(db_connect())
  {
    $result = mysql_query($query);
      if($result)
        return mysql_result($result, 0, 0);
  }
  return 0;
}
```

The get_account_list() function is similar to the get_accounts() function we looked at before except that it only retrieves the account names.

If a user has multiple accounts registered, he will need to select one to use. In this case, the headers will contain a SELECT that lists the available mailboxes. Choosing the appropriate one will automatically display the mailbox for that account. You can see this in Figure 27.5.

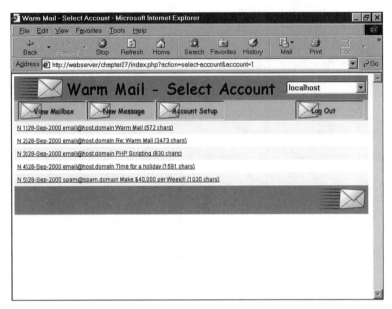

Figure 27.5   After the localhost account is selected from the SELECT box, the mail from that account is downloaded and displayed.

This SELECT option is generated in the do_html_header() function from output_fns.php, as shown in the following code fragment:

```
// include the account select box only if the user has more than one account
if(number_of_accounts($auth_user)>1)
{
  echo '<form target="index.php?action=open-mailbox" method="post">';
  echo '<td bgcolor="#ff6600" align="right" valign="middle">';
  display_account_select($auth_user, $selected_account);
  echo '</td>';
  echo '</form>';
}
```

We have generally avoided discussing the HTML used in the examples in this book, but the HTML generated by the function display_account_select() bears a visit.

Depending on the accounts the current user has, display_account_select() will generate HTML like this:

```
<select onchange="window.location=this.options[selectedIndex].value"
        name="account">
  <option value="0" selected>
    Choose Account</a>
  <option value="index.php?action=select-account&account=10">
    mail.domain.com
  </option>
  <option value="index.php?action=select-account&account=11">
    mail.server.com
  </option>
  <option value="index.php?action=select-account&account=9">
    localhost
  </option>
</select>
```

Most of this code is just an HTML select element, but it also includes a little JavaScript. In the same way that PHP can generate HTML, it can also be used to generate client-side scripts.

Whenever a change event happens to this element, JavaScript will set `window.location` to the value of the option. If your user selects the first option in the select, `window.location` will be set to `'index.php?action=select-account&account=10'`. This will result in this URL being loaded. Obviously, if the user has a browser that does not support JavaScript or has JavaScript disabled, this code will have no effect.

The `display_account_select()` function, from `output_fns.php`, is used to get the available account list and display the SELECT. It also uses the `get_account_list()` function we discussed previously.

Choosing one of the options in the SELECT activates the `select_account` event. If you look at the URL in Figure 27.5, you can see this appended to the end of the URL, along with the account ID of the chosen account.

This has two effects. First, in the preprocessing stage of index.php, the chosen account will be stored in the session variable `$selected_account`, as follows:

```
case 'select-account' :
{
  // if have chosen a valid account, store it as a session variable
  if($account&&account_exists($HTTP_SESSION_VARS['auth_user'], $account))
  {
    $HTTP_SESSION_VARS['selected_account'] = $account;
  }
}
```

Second, when the body stage of the script is executed, the following code will be executed:

```
case 'select-account' :
case 'view-mailbox' :
{
```

```
// if mailbox just chosen, or view mailbox chosen, show mailbox
display_list($HTTP_SESSION_VARS['auth_user'],
            $HTTP_SESSION_VARS['selected_account']);
break;
}
```

As you can see, we take the same action here as if the user had chosen the View Mailbox option. We'll look at that next.

Viewing Mailbox Contents

Mailbox contents can be viewed with the `display_list()` function. This displays a list of all the messages in the mailbox. The code for this function is shown in Listing 27.8.

Listing 27.8 **display_list() Function from output_fns.php—Function to Display All Mailbox Messages**

```
function display_list($auth_user, $accountid)
{
  // show the list of messages in this mailbox

  global $table_width;

  if(!$accountid)
  {
    echo 'No mailbox selected<br /><br /><br /><br /><br /><br />.';
  }
  else
  {

    $imap = open_mailbox($auth_user, $accountid);

    if($imap)
    {
      echo "<table width=$table_width' cellspacing='0'
                  cellpadding='6'  border='0'>";

      $headers = imap_headers($imap);
      // we could reformat this data, or get other details using
      // imap_fetchheaders, but this is not a bad summary so we just echo each

      $messages = sizeof($headers);
      for($i = 0; $i<$messages; $i++)
      {
        echo '<tr><td bgcolor = "';
        if($i%2)
          echo '#ffffff';
```

Listing 27.8   **Continued**

```
        else
          echo '#ffffcc';
        echo '"><a href="index.php?action=view-message&messageid='.($i+1).'">';
        echo $headers[$i];
        echo "</a></td></tr>\n";
      }
      echo '</table>';
    }
    else
    {
      $account = get_account_settings($auth_user, $accountid);
      echo 'could not open mail box '.$account['server'].
           '.<br /><br /><br /><br />';
    }
  }
}
```

In this function, we actually begin to use PHP's IMAP functions. The two key parts of this function are opening the mailbox and reading the message headers.

We open the mailbox for a user account with a call to the open_mailbox() function that we have written in mail_fns.php. This function is shown in Listing 27.9.

Listing 27.9   **open_mailbox() Function from mail_fns.php—This Function Connects to a User Mailbox**

```
function open_mailbox($auth_user, $accountid)
{
  global $HTTP_SESSION_VARS;

  // select mailbox if there is only one
  if(number_of_accounts($auth_user)==1)
  {
    $accounts = get_account_list($auth_user);
    $HTTP_SESSION_VARS['selected_account'] = $accounts[0];
    $accountid = $accounts[0];
  }

  // connect to the POP3 or IMAP server the user has selected
  $settings = get_account_settings($auth_user, $accountid);
  if(!sizeof($settings)) return 0;
  $mailbox = '{'.$settings[server];
  if($settings[type]=='POP3')
    $mailbox .= '/pop3';

  $mailbox .= ':'.$settings[port].'}INBOX';
```

Listing 27.9 **Continued**

```
  // suppress warning, remember to check return value
@ $imap = imap_open($mailbox, $settings['remoteuser'],
         $settings['remotepassword']);

  return $imap;
}
```

We actually open the mailbox with the imap_open() function. This function has the following prototype:

```
int imap_open (string mailbox, string username, string password [, int options])
```

The parameters you need to pass to it are as follows:

- mailbox—This string should contain the server name and mailbox name, and optionally a port number and protocol. The format of this string is

  {hostname/protocol:port}boxname

  If the protocol is not specified, it defaults to IMAP. In the code we have written, you can see that we specify POP3 if the user has specified that protocol for a particular account.

  For example, to read mail from the local machine using the default ports, we would use the following mailbox name for IMAP:

  {localhost:143}INBOX

  and this one for POP3

  {localhost/pop3:110}INBOX

- username—The username for the account
- password—The password for the account

You can also pass it optional flags to specify options such as "open mailbox in read-only mode".

One thing to note is that we have constructed the mailbox string piece by piece with the concatenation operator before passing it to imap_open(). You need to be careful how you construct this string because strings containing {$ cause problems in PHP 4.

This function call returns an IMAP stream if the mailbox can be opened, and false if it cannot.

When you are finished with an IMAP stream, you can close it using imap_close(*imap_stream*).

In our function, the IMAP stream is passed back to the main program. We then use the imap_headers() function to get the email headers for display:

```
$headers = imap_headers($imap);
```

This function returns header information for all mail messages in the mailbox we have connected to. The information is returned as an array, one line per message. We haven't formatted this. It just outputs one line per message, so you can see from looking at Figure 27.5 what the output looks like.

You can get more information about email headers using the confusing, similarly named `imap_header()`. In this case, the `imap_headers()` function gives us enough detail for our purpose.

Reading a Mail Message

We have set up each of the messages in the previous `display_list()` function to link to specific email messages.

Each link is of the form

```
index.php?action=view-message&messageid=6
```

The `messageid` is the sequence number used in the headers we retrieved earlier. Note that IMAP messages are numbered from 1, not 0.

If the user clicks one of these links, he will see output like that shown in Figure 27.6.

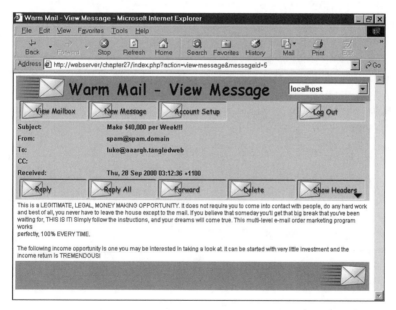

Figure 27.6   Using the `view-message` action shows us a particular message—in this case, it's a piece of spam.

When we enter these parameters into the `index.php` script, we execute the following code:

```
case 'show-headers' :
case 'hide-headers' :
case 'view-message' :
{
  // if we have just picked a message from the list, or were looking at
  // a message and chose to hide or view headers, load a message
  $fullheaders = ($action=='show-headers');
  display_message($HTTP_SESSION_VARS['auth_user'],
                  $HTTP_SESSION_VARS['selected_account'],
                  $messageid, $fullheaders);
  break;
}
```

You'll notice that we're checking the value of the $action being equal to 'show-headers'. In this case, it will be false, and $fullheaders will be set equal to false. We'll look at the 'show-headers' action in a moment.

The line

```
$fullheaders = ($action=='show-headers');
```

could have been more verbosely—but perhaps more clearly—written as

```
if($action=='show-headers')
  $fullheaders = true;
else
  $fullheaders = false;
```

Next, we call the display_message() function. Most of this function outputs plain HTML, so we will not go through it here. It calls the retrieve_message() function to get the appropriate message from the mailbox:

```
$message = retrieve_message($auth_user, $accountid, $messageid, $fullheaders);
```

The retrieve_message() function is in the mail_fns.php library. You can see the code for it in Listing 27.10.

Listing 27.10   **retrieve_message() Function from mail_fns.php—This Function Retrieves One Specific Message from a Mailbox**

```
function retrieve_message($auth_user, $accountid, $messageid, $fullheaders)
{
  $message = array();

  if(!($auth_user && $messageid && $accountid))
    return false;

  $imap = open_mailbox($auth_user, $accountid);
  if(!$imap)
    return false;
```

Listing 27.10   **Continued**

```
$header = imap_header($imap, $messageid);

if(!$header)
  return false;

$message['body'] = imap_body($imap, $messageid);
if(!$message['body'])
  $message['body'] = "[This message has no body]\n\n\n\n\n\n";

if($fullheaders)
  $message['fullheaders'] = imap_fetchheader($imap, $messageid);
else
  $message['fullheaders'] = '';

$message['subject'] = $header->subject;
$message['fromaddress'] =  $header->fromaddress;
$message['toaddress'] =  $header->toaddress;
$message['ccaddress'] =  $header->ccaddress;
$message['date'] =  $header->date;

// note we can get more detailed information by using from and to
// rather than fromaddress and toaddress, but these are easier

imap_close($imap);
return $message;
}
```

Again we have used open_mailbox() to open the user's mailbox.

This time, however, we are after a specific message. Using this function library, we download the message headers and message body separately.

The three IMAP functions we use here are imap_header(), imap_fetchheader(), and imap_body(). Note that the two header functions are distinct from imap_headers(), the one we used previously. They are somewhat confusingly named. In summary,

- imap_headers()—Returns a summary of the headers for all the messages in a mailbox. It returns them as an array with one element per message.

- imap_header()—Returns the headers for one specific message in the form of an object.

- imap_fetchheader()—Returns the headers for one specific message in the form of a string.

In this case we use imap_header() to fill out specific header fields and imap_fetchheader() to show the user the full headers if requested. (We'll come back to this.)

We use `imap_header()` and `imap_body()` to build an array containing all the elements of a message that we are interested in.

We call `imap_header()` as follows:

```
$header = imap_header($imap, $messageid);
```

We can then extract each of the fields we require from the object:

```
$message['subject'] = $header->subject;
```

We call `imap_body()` to add the message body to our array as follows:

```
$message['body'] = imap_body($imap, $messageid);
```

Finally we close the mailbox with `imap_close()` and return the array we have built. The `display_message()` function can then display the message's fields in the form you can see in Figure 27.6.

Viewing Message Headers

As you can see in Figure 27.6, there is a Show Headers button. This activates the show-headers option, which adds the full message headers to the message display. If the user clicks this button, he will see output similar to that shown in Figure 27.7.

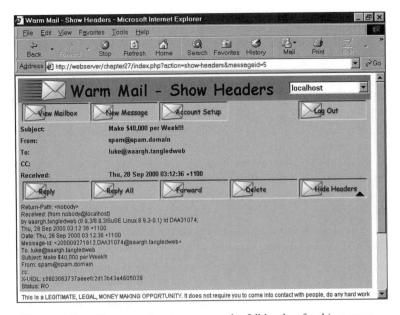

Figure 27.7 Using `show-headers` to see the full headers for this message will help a user track down the source of the spam.

As you probably noticed, the event handling for `view-message` covers `show-headers` (and its counterpart `hide-headers`) too. If this option is selected, we do the same things as before. But in `retrieve_message()`, we also grab the full text of the headers, as follows:

```
if($fullheaders)
    $message['fullheaders'] = imap_fetchheader($imap, $messageid);
```

We can then display these headers for the user.

Deleting Mail

If a user clicks the Delete button on a particular email, he will activate the `"delete"` action. This will execute the following code from `index.php`:

```
case 'delete' :
{
  delete_message($HTTP_SESSION_VARS['auth_user'],
                 $HTTP_SESSION_VARS['selected_account'], $messageid);
  //note deliberately no 'break' - we will continue to the next case
}
case 'select-account' :
case 'view-mailbox' :
{
  // if mailbox just chosen, or view mailbox chosen, show mailbox
  display_list($HTTP_SESSION_VARS['auth_user'],
               $HTTP_SESSION_VARS['selected_account']);
  break;
}
```

As you can see, the message is deleted using the `delete_message()` function, and then the resulting mailbox is displayed as discussed previously.

The code for the `delete_message()` function is shown in Listing 27.11.

Listing 27.11   delete_message() Function from mail_fns.php—This Function Deletes One Specific Message from a Mailbox

```
function delete_message($auth_user, $accountid, $message_id)
{
  // delete a single message from the server

  $imap = open_mailbox($auth_user, $accountid);
  if($imap)
  {
    imap_delete($imap, $message_id);
    imap_expunge($imap);
    imap_close($imap);
    return true;
```

Listing 27.11   **Continued**

```
  }
  return false;
}
```

As you can see, this function uses a number of the IMAP functions. The new ones are
`imap_delete()` and `imap_expunge()`. Note that `imap_delete()` only marks messages
for deletion. You can mark as many messages as you like. The call to `imap_expunge()`
actually deletes the messages.

Sending Mail

Finally we come to sending mail. There are a few ways to do this from this script: The
user can send a new message, reply to, or forward mail. Let's see how these work.

Sending a New Message

The user can choose this option by clicking the New Message button. This activates the
`"new-message"` action, which executes the following code in `index.php`:

```
case 'new-message' :
{
  display_new_message_form($HTTP_SESSION_VARS['auth_user'],
                           $to, $cc, $subject, $body);
  break;
}
```

The new message form is just a form for sending mail. You can see what it looks like in
Figure 27.8. This figure actually shows mail forwarding rather than new mail, but the
form is the same. We'll look at forwarding and replies next.

   Clicking the Send Message button invokes the `"send-message"` action, which executes the following code:

```
case 'send-message' :
{
  if(send_message($to, $cc, $subject, $message))
    echo "<p>Message sent.</p><br /><br /><br /><br /><br />";
  else
    echo "<p>Could not send message.</p><br /><br /><br /><br /><br />";
  break;
}
```

This code calls the `send_message()` function, which actually sends the mail. This function is shown in Listing 27.12.

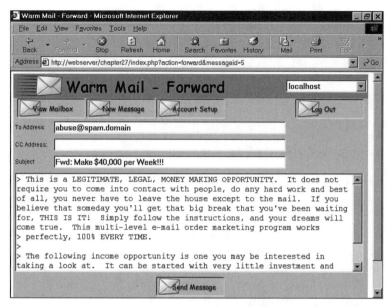

Figure 27.8   Using mail forwarding, we can report the spammer.

**Listing 27.12   send_message() Function from mail_fns.php—This Function Sends the
Message That the User Has Typed In**

```
function send_message($to, $cc, $subject, $message)
{
  //send one email via PHP
  global $HTTP_SESSION_VARS;

  if (!db_connect())
  {
    return false;
  }
  $query = 'select address from users where username=\''.
           $HTTP_SESSION_VARS['auth_user']."'";

  $result = mysql_query($query);
  if (!$result)
  {
    return false;
  }
  else if (mysql_num_rows($result)==0)
  {
    return false;
```

Listing 27.12   **Continued**

```
    }
  else
  {
    $other = 'From: '.mysql_result($result, 0, 'address')."\r\nCc: $cc";
    if (mail($to, $subject, $message, $other))
    {
      return true;
    }
    else
    {
      return false;
    }
  }
}
```

As you can see, this function uses `mail()` to send the email. First, however, it loads the user's email address out of the database to use in the From field of the email.

Replying to or Forwarding Mail

The Reply, Reply All, and Forward functions all send mail in the same way that New Message does. The difference in how they work is that they fill in parts of the new message form before showing it to the user. Look back at Figure 27.8. The message we are forwarding has been indented with the > symbol, and the Subject line prefaced with To. Similarly, the Reply and Reply All options will fill in the recipients, subject line, and indented message.

The code to do this is activated in the body section of `index.php`, as follows:

```
case 'reply-all' :
{
  //set cc as old cc line
  if(!$imap)
    $imap = open_mailbox($HTTP_SESSION_VARS['auth_user'],
                    $HTTP_SESSION_VARS['selected_account']);
  if($imap)
  {
    $header = imap_header($imap, $messageid);
    if($header->reply_toaddress)
      $to = $header->reply_toaddress;
    else
      $to = $header->fromaddress;
    $cc = $header->ccaddress;
    $subject = 'Re: '.$header->subject;
    $body = add_quoting(stripslashes(imap_body($imap, $messageid)));
    imap_close($imap);
```

```
       display_new_message_form($HTTP_SESSION_VARS['auth_user'],
                              $to, $cc, $subject, $body);
     }
     break;
   }
   case 'reply' :
   {
     //set to address as reply-to or from of the current message
     if(!$imap)
       $imap = open_mailbox($HTTP_SESSION_VARS['auth_user'],
                          $HTTP_SESSION_VARS['selected_account']);
     if($imap)
     {
       $header = imap_header($imap, $messageid);
       if($header->reply_toaddress)
         $to = $header->reply_toaddress;
       else
         $to = $header->fromaddress;
       $subject = 'Re: '.$header->subject;
       $body = add_quoting(stripslashes(imap_body($imap, $messageid)));
       imap_close($imap);

       display_new_message_form($HTTP_SESSION_VARS['auth_user'],
                              $to, $cc, $subject, $body);
     }

     break;
   }
   case 'forward' :
   {
     //set message as quoted body of current message
     if(!$imap)
       $imap = open_mailbox($HTTP_SESSION_VARS['auth_user'],
                          $HTTP_SESSION_VARS['selected_account']);
     if($imap)
     {
       $header = imap_header($imap, $messageid);
       $body = add_quoting(stripslashes(imap_body($imap, $messageid)));
       $subject = 'Fwd: '.$header->subject;
       imap_close($imap);

       display_new_message_form($HTTP_SESSION_VARS['auth_user'],
                              $to, $cc, $subject, $body);
     }
     break;
   }
```

You can see that each of these options sets up the appropriate headers, applies formatting as necessary, and calls the `display_new_message_form()` function to set up the form.

That's the full set of functionality for our Web mail reader.

Extending the Project

There are many extensions or improvements you could make to this project. You can look to the mail reader you normally use for inspiration, but some useful additions are the following:

- Add the ability for users to register with this site. (You could reuse some of the code from Chapter 24, "Building User Authentication and Personalization," for this purpose.)

- Many users have more than one email address; perhaps a personal address and a work address. By moving their stored email address from the users table to the accounts table, you could allow them to use many addresses. You would need to change a limited amount of other code too. The send mail form would need a drop-down box to select which address to use.

- Add the ability to send, receive, and view mail with attachments. If users are to be able to send attachments, you will need to build in file upload capabilities as discussed in Chapter 16, "Interacting with the File System and the Server." Sending mail with attachments is covered in Chapter 28, "Building a Mailing List Manager."

- Add address book capabilities.

- Add network news reading abilities. Reading from an NNTP server using the IMAP functions is almost identical to reading from a mailbox. You just need to specify a different port number and protocol in the `imap_open()` call. Instead of naming a mailbox like INBOX, you name a newsgroup to read from instead. You could combine this with the thread-building capabilities from the project in Chapter 29, "Building Web Forums," to build a threaded Web-based newsreader.

Next

In the next chapter, we'll build another email-related project—in this one, we'll build an application to support sending newsletters on multiple topics to people who subscribe through our site.

## 28

Building a Mailing List Manager

AFTER YOU'VE BUILT UP A BASE of subscribers to your Web site, it's nice to be able to keep in touch with them by sending out a newsletter. In this chapter, we will implement a front end for a mailing list manager (or MLM). Some MLMs allow each subscriber to send messages to other subscribers. Our program will be a newsletter system, in which only the list administrator can send messages. We will call our system Pyramid-MLM.

This system will be similar to others already in the marketplace. To get some idea of what we are aiming for, take a look at

```
http://www.topica.com
```

Our application will let an administrator create multiple mailing lists and send newsletters to each of those lists separately. This application will use file upload to enable an administrator to upload text and HTML versions of newsletters that they have created offline. This means administrators can use whatever software they prefer to create newsletters.

Users will be able to subscribe to any of the lists at our site and select whether to receive newsletters in text or HTML.

The Problem

We want to build an online newsletter composition and sending system. This system should allow various newsletters to be created and sent to users, and allow users to subscribe to one or many of the newsletters.

Specifically, the requirements for this system are

- Administrators should be able to set up and modify mailing lists.
- Administrators should be able to send text and HTML newsletters to all the subscribers of a single mailing list.
- Users should be able to register to use the site, and enter and modify their details.
- Users should be able to subscribe to any of the lists on a site.

- Users should be able to unsubscribe from lists they are subscribed to.
- Users should be able to store their preference for either HTML formatted or plain text newsletters.
- For security reasons, users should not be able to send mail to the lists or to see each other's email addresses
- Users and administrators should be able to view information about mailing lists.
- Users and administrators should be able to view past newsletters that have been sent to a list (the archive).

Solution Components

There are a number of components we will need to fulfil the requirements. The main ones are setting up a database of lists, subscribers, and archived newsletters; uploading newsletters that have been created offline; and sending mail with attachments.

Setting Up a Database of Lists and Subscribers

We will track the username and password of each system user, as well as a list of the lists they have subscribed to. We will also store each user's preference for receiving text or HTML email, so we can send a user the appropriate version of the newsletter.

An administrator will be a specialized user with the ability to create new mailing lists and send newsletters to those lists.

A nice piece of functionality to have for a system like this is an archive of previous newsletters. Subscribers might not keep previous postings, but might want to look something up. An archive can also act as a marketing tool for the newsletter as potential subscribers can see what the newsletters are like.

Setting up this database in MySQL and an interface to it in PHP will have nothing new or difficult in it.

File Upload

We need an interface to allow the administrator to send newsletters, as mentioned previously. What we haven't talked about is how administrators will create that newsletter. We could provide them with a form where they could type or paste the newsletter content. However, it will increase the user-friendliness of our system to let administrators create a newsletter in their favorite editor and then upload the file to the Web server. This will also make it easy for an administrator to add images to an HTML newsletter.

For this we can use the file upload capability discussed in Chapter 16, "Interacting with the File System and the Server."

We will need to use a slightly more complicated form than we have used in the past. We will require the administrator to upload both text and HTML versions of the newsletter, along with any inline images that go into the HTML.

When the newsletter has been uploaded, we need to create an interface so that the administrator can preview the newsletter before sending it. This way, he can confirm that all the files were uploaded correctly.

Note that we will store all these files in an archive directory so that users can read back issues of newsletters. This directory needs to be writable by the user your Web server runs as. The upload script will try to write the newsletters into ./archive/ so make sure you create that directory and set permissions on it appropriately.

Sending Mail with Attachments

For this project, we would like to be able to send users either a plain text newsletter or a "fancy" HTML version, according to their preference.

To send an HTML file with embedded images, we will need to find a way to send attachments. PHP's simple `mail()` function doesn't easily support sending attachments. Instead, we will use the excellent Mail_Mime package from PEAR, created by Richard Heyes. This can deal with HTML attachments, and can also be used to attach any images that are contained in the HTML file.

Installation instructions for this package are included in Appendix A, "Installing PHP and MySQL," under PEAR Installation.

Solution Overview

For this project, we will again use an event-driven approach to writing our code, as we did in Chapter 27, "Building a Web-Based Email Service."

We have again begun by drawing a set of system flow diagrams to show the paths users might take through the system. In this case, we have drawn three diagrams to represent the three different sets of interactions users can have with the system. Users have different allowable actions when they are not logged in, when they are logged in as regular users, and when they are logged in as administrators. These actions are shown in Figures 28.1, 28.2, and 28.3, respectively.

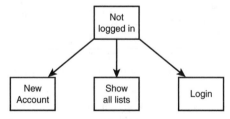

Figure 28.1   A user can only choose a limited number of actions
when he is not logged in.

In Figure 28.1 you can see the actions that can be taken by a user who is not logged in. As you can see, he can log in (if he already has an account), create an account (if he doesn't already have one), or view the mailing lists available for signup (as a marketing tactic).

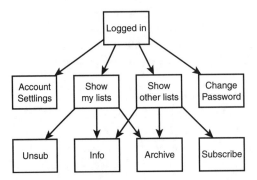

Figure 28.2   After logging in, users can change their preferences
through a variety of options.

Figure 28.2 shows the actions a user can take after logging in. He can change his account setup (email address and preferences), change his password, and change which lists he is subscribed to.

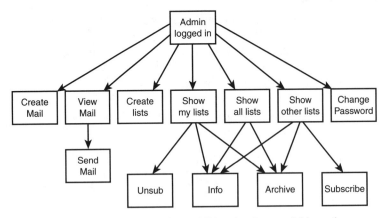

Figure 28.3   Administrators have additional actions available to them.

Figure 28.3 shows the actions available if an administrator has logged in. As you can see, an administrator has most of the functionality available to a user, and some additional options. She can also create new mailing lists, create new messages for a mailing list by uploading files, and preview messages before sending them.

Because we have used an event-driven approach again, the backbone of the application is contained in one file, index.php, which calls on a set of function libraries. An overview of the files in this application is shown in Table 28.1.

Table 28.1   **Files in the Mailing List Manager Application**

Filename	Type	Description
index.php	Application	The main script that runs the entire application.
include_fns.php	Functions	Collection of include files for this application.
data_valid_fns.php	Functions	Collection of functions for validating input data.
db_fns.php	Functions	Collection of functions for connecting to the mlm database.
mlm_fns.php	Functions	Collection of functions specific to this application.
output_fns.php	Functions	Collection of functions for outputting HTML.
upload.php	Component	Script that manages the file upload component of the administrator role. Separated out to make security easier.
user_auth_fns.php	Functions	Collection of functions for authenticating users.
create_database.sql	SQL	SQL to set up the mlm database and set up a Web user and an administrative user.

We will work our way through the project implementation, beginning with the database in which we will store subscriber and list information.

Setting Up the Database

For this application we will need to store details of

- Lists: Mailing lists available for subscription.
- Subscribers: Users of the system and their preferences.
- Sub_lists: A record of which users have subscribed to which lists (a many-to-many relationship)
- Mail: A record of email messages that have been sent.
- Images: Because we want to be able to send email messages that consist of multiple files (that is, text and HTML plus a number of images), we also need to track which images go with each email.

The SQL we have written to create this database is shown in Listing 28.1.

Listing 28.1   **create_database.sql—SQL to Create the mlm Database**

```
create database mlm;

use mlm;

create table lists
(
    listid int auto_increment not null primary key,
    listname char(20) not null,
```

Listing 28.1 **Continued**

```
    blurb varchar(255)
);

create table subscribers
(
  email char(100) not null primary key,
  realname char(100) not null,
  mimetype char(1) not null,
  password char(16) not null,
  admin tinyint not null
);

# stores a relationship between a subscriber and a list
create table sub_lists
(
  email char(100) not null,
  listid int not null
);

create table mail
(
  mailid int auto_increment not null primary key,
  email char(100) not null,
  subject char(100) not null,
  listid int not null,
  status char(10) not null,
  sent datetime,
  modified timestamp
);

#stores the images that go with a particular mail
create table images
(
  mailid int  not null,
  path char(100) not null,
  mimetype char(100) not null
);

grant select, insert, update, delete
on mlm.*
to mlm@localhost identified by 'password';

insert into subscribers values
('admin@localhost', 'Administrative User', 'H', password('admin'), 1);
```

Remember that you can execute this SQL by typing

```
mysql -u root -p < create_database.sql
```

You will need to supply your root password. (You could, of course, execute this script via any MySQL user with the appropriate privileges; we have just used root here for simplicity.) You should change the password for the `mlm` user and the administrator in your script before running it.

Some of the fields in this database require a little further explanation, so let's briefly run through them.

The `lists` table contains a `listid` and `listname`. It also contains a `blurb`, which is a description of what the list is about.

The `subscribers` table contains email addresses (`email`) and names (`realname`) of the subscribers. It also stores their `password` and a flag (`admin`) to indicate whether or not this user is an administrator. We will also store the type of mail they prefer to receive in `mimetype`. This can be either `H` for HTML or `T` for text.

The `sublists` table contains email addresses (`email`) from the `subscribers` table and `listid`s from the `lists` table.

The `mail` table contains information about each email message that is sent through the system. It stores a unique id (`mailid`), the address the mail is sent from (`email`), the subject line of the email (`subject`), and the `listid` of the list it has been sent to or will be sent to. The actual text or HTML of the message could be a large file, so we will store the archive of the actual messages outside the database. We will also track some general status information: whether the message has been sent (`status`), when it was sent (`sent`), and a timestamp to show when this record was last modified (`modified`).

Finally, we use the `images` table to track any images associated with HTML messages. Again, these images can be large, so we will store them outside the database for efficiency. Instead, we will track the `mailid` they are associated with, the `path` to the location where the image is actually stored, and the MIME type of the image (`mimetype`), for example, `image/gif`.

The SQL shown previously also sets up a user for PHP to connect as, and an administrative user for the system.

Script Architecture

As in the last project, we have used an event-driven approach to this project. The backbone of the application is in the file index.php. This script has four main segments, which are

1. Preprocessing: Do any processing that must be done before headers can be sent.

2. Set up and send headers: Create and send the start of the HTML page.

3. Perform action: Respond to the event that has been passed in. As in our last example, the event is contained in the $action variable.

4. Send footers.

Almost all of the application's processing is done in this file. The application also uses the function libraries listed in Table 28.1, as mentioned previously.

The full listing of the index.php script is shown in Listing 28.2.

Listing 28.2   **index.php—Main Application File for Pyramid–MLM**

```php
<?php

/**********************************************************************
* Section 1 : pre-processing
**********************************************************************/

  include ('include_fns.php');
  session_start();

  $action = $HTTP_GET_VARS['action'];
  $buttons = array();

  //append to this string if anything processed before header has output
  $status = '';

  // need to process log in or out requests before anything else
  if($HTTP_POST_VARS['email']&&$HTTP_POST_VARS['password'])
  {
    $login = login($HTTP_POST_VARS['email'], $HTTP_POST_VARS['password']);

    if($login == 'admin')
    {
      $status .= "<p><b>".get_real_name($HTTP_POST_VARS['email']).
                 "</b> logged in"." successfully as <b>Administrator</b></p>
                 <br /><br /><br /><br /><br />";
      $HTTP_SESSION_VARS['admin_user'] = $HTTP_POST_VARS['email'];
    }
    else if($login == 'normal')
    {
      $status .= "<p><b>".get_real_name($HTTP_POST_VARS['email'])."</b> logged in"
                 ." successfully.</p><br /><br />";
      $HTTP_SESSION_VARS['normal_user'] = $HTTP_POST_VARS['email'];
    }
    else
    {
      $status .= "<p>Sorry, we could not log you in with that
                 email address and password.</p><br />";

    }
  }

  if($action == 'log-out')
```

Listing 28.2   **Continued**

```
  {
    unset($action);
    unset($HTTP_SESSION_VARS);
    session_destroy();
  }


/***********************************************************************
 * Section 2: set up and display headers
 ***********************************************************************/

  // set the buttons that will be on the tool bar
  if(check_normal_user())
  {
    // if a normal user
    $buttons[0] = 'change-password';
    $buttons[1] = 'account-settings';
    $buttons[2] = 'show-my-lists';
    $buttons[3] = 'show-other-lists';
    $buttons[4] = 'log-out';
  }
  else if(check_admin_user())
  {
    // if an administrator
    $buttons[0] = 'change-password';
    $buttons[1] = 'create-list';
    $buttons[2] = 'create-mail';
    $buttons[3] = 'view-mail';
    $buttons[4] = 'log-out';
    $buttons[5] = 'show-all-lists';
    $buttons[6] = 'show-my-lists';
    $buttons[7] = 'show-other-lists';
  }
  else
  {
    // if not logged in at all
    $buttons[0] = 'new-account';
    $buttons[1] = 'show-all-lists';
    $buttons[4] = 'log-in';
  }

  if($action)
  {
    // display header with application name and description of page or action
    do_html_header('Pyramid-MLM - '.format_action($action));
  }
```

Listing 28.2 **Continued**

```
  else
  {
    // display header with just application name
    do_html_header('Pyramid-MLM');
  }

  display_toolbar($buttons);

  //display any text generated by functions called before header
  echo $status;

/***********************************************************************
 * Section 3: perform action
 ***********************************************************************/

  // only these actions can be done if not logged in
  switch ( $action )
  {
    case 'new-account' :
    {
      // get rid of session variables
      session_destroy();
      display_account_form();
      break;
    }
    case 'store-account' :
    {
      if (store_account($HTTP_SESSION_VARS['normal_user'],
              $HTTP_SESSION_VARS['admin_user'], $HTTP_POST_VARS))
        $action = '';
      if(!check_logged_in())
        display_login_form($action);
      break;
    }
    case 'log-in' :
    case '':
    {
      if(!check_logged_in())
        display_login_form($action);
      break;
    }
    case 'show-all-lists' :
    {
      display_items('All Lists', get_all_lists(), 'information',
                    'show-archive','');
      break;
```

Listing 28.2   **Continued**

```
    }
    case 'show-archive' :
    {
      display_items('Archive For '.get_list_name($HTTP_GET_VARS['id']),
                    get_archive($HTTP_GET_VARS['id']), 'view-html',
                    'view-text', '');
      break;
    }
    case 'information' :
    {
      display_information($HTTP_GET_VARS['id']);
      break;
    }

  }


  //all other actions require user to be logged in
  if(check_logged_in())
  {
    switch ( $action )
    {
      case 'account-settings' :
      {
        display_account_form(get_email(),
             get_real_name(get_email()), get_mimetype(get_email()));
        break;
      }
      case 'show-other-lists' :
      {
        display_items('Unsubscribed Lists',
                      get_unsubscribed_lists(get_email()), 'information',
                      'show-archive', 'subscribe');
        break;
      }
      case 'subscribe' :
      {
        subscribe(get_email(), $HTTP_GET_VARS['id']);
        display_items('Subscribed Lists', get_subscribed_lists(get_email()),
                      'information', 'show-archive', 'unsubscribe');
        break;
      }
      case 'unsubscribe' :
      {
        unsubscribe(get_email(), $HTTP_GET_VARS['id']);
        display_items('Subscribed Lists', get_subscribed_lists(get_email()),
                      'information', 'show-archive', 'unsubscribe');
```

Listing 28.2 **Continued**

```
        break;
    }
    case '':
    case 'show-my-lists' :
    {
      display_items('Subscribed Lists', get_subscribed_lists(get_email()),
                'information', 'show-archive', 'unsubscribe');
      break;
    }
    case 'change-password' :
    {
      display_password_form();
      break;
    }
    case 'store-change-password' :
    {
      if(change_password(get_email(), $HTTP_POST_VARS['old_passwd'],
         $HTTP_POST_VARS['new_passwd'], $HTTP_POST_VARS['new_passwd2']))
      {
        echo '<p>OK: Password changed.</p>
             <br /><br /><br /><br /><br /><br />';
      }
      else
      {
        echo '<p>Sorry, your password could not be changed.</p>';
        display_password_form();
      }
      break;
    }
  }
}
// The following actions may only be performed by an admin user
if(check_admin_user())
{
  switch ( $action )
  {
    case 'create-mail' :
    {
      display_mail_form(get_email());
      break;
    }
    case 'create-list' :
    {
      display_list_form(get_email());
      break;
```

Listing 28.2   **Continued**

```
    }
    case 'store-list' :
    {
      if(store_list($HTTP_SESSION_VARS['admin_user'], $HTTP_POST_VARS))
      {
        echo '<p>New list added</p><br />';
        display_items('All Lists', get_all_lists(), 'information',
                    'show-archive','');
      }
      else
        echo '<p>List could not be stored, please try '
              .'again.</p><br /><br /><br /><br /><br />';

      break;
    }
    case 'send' :
    {
      send($HTTP_GET_VARS['id'], $HTTP_SESSION_VARS['admin_user']);
      break;
    }
    case 'view-mail' :
    {
      display_items('Unsent Mail', get_unsent_mail(get_email()),
                    'preview-html', 'preview-text', 'send');
      break;
    }
  }
}

/************************************************************************
* Section 4: display footer
************************************************************************/

  do_html_footer();
?>
```

You can see the four segments of the code clearly marked in this listing.

In the preprocessing stage, we set up the session and process any actions that need to be done before headers can be sent. In this case, this includes logging in and out.

In the header stage, we set up the menu buttons that the user will see, and display the appropriate headers using the do_html_header() function from output_fns.php. This function just displays the header bar and menus, so we won't go into it here.

In the main section of the script, we respond to the action the user has chosen. These actions are divided into three subsets: actions that can be taken if not logged in, actions that can be taken by normal users, and actions that can be taken by administrative users. We check to see whether access to the latter two sets of actions is allowed using the `check_logged_in()` and `check_admin_user()` functions. These functions are located in the user_auth_fns.php function library. The code for the functions, and for the `check_normal_user()` function are shown in Listing 28.3.

Listing 28.3 **Functions from user_auth_fns.php—Checking Whether or Not a User Is Logged In, and at What Level**

```
function check_normal_user()
// see if somebody is logged in and notify them if not
{
  global $HTTP_SESSION_VARS;

  if (isset($HTTP_SESSION_VARS['normal_user']))
    return true;
  else
    return false;
}

function check_admin_user()
// see if somebody is logged in and notify them if not
{
  global $HTTP_SESSION_VARS;

  if (isset($HTTP_SESSION_VARS['admin_user']))
    return true;
  else
    return false;
}


function check_logged_in()
{
  return ( check_normal_user() || check_admin_user() );
}
```

As you can see, these functions use the session variables normal_user and admin_user to check whether a user has logged in. We'll talk about setting these session variables up in a minute.

In the final section of the script, we send an HTML footer using the `do_html_footer()` function from output_fns.php.

Let's look briefly at an overview of the possible actions in the system. These actions are shown in Table 28.2

Table 28.2   **Possible Actions in the Mailing List Manager Application**

Action	Usable By	Description
log-in	Anyone	Gives a user a login form
log-out	Anyone	Ends a session
new-account	Anyone	Creates a new account for a user
store-account	Anyone	Stores account details
show-all-lists	Anyone	Shows a list of available mailing lists
show-archive	Anyone	Displays archived newsletters for a particular list
information	Anyone	Shows basic information about a particular list
account-settings	Logged-in users	Displays user account settings
show-other-lists	Logged-in users	Displays mailing lists to which the user is not subscribed
show-my-lists	Logged-in users	Displays mailing lists to which the user is subscribed
subscribe	Logged-in users	Subscribes a user to a particular list
unsubscribe	Logged-in users	Unsubscribes a user from a particular list
change-password	Logged-in users	Displays the change of password form
store-change-password	Logged-in users	Updates user's password in the database
create-mail	Administrators	Displays form to allow upload of newsletters
create-list	Administrators	Displays form to allow new mailing lists to be created
store-list	Administrators	Stores mailing list details in the database
view-mail	Administrators	Display newsletters that have been uploaded but not yet sent
send	Administrators	Sends newsletters to subscribers

One noticeable omission from this table is an option along the lines of store-mail, that is, an action that actually uploads the newsletters entered via create-mail by administrators. This single piece of functionality is actually in a different file, upload.php. We put this in a separate file because it makes it a little easier on us, the programmers, to keep track of security issues.

We will discuss the implementation of these actions in the three groups listed in the Table 28.2, that is, actions for people who are not logged in, actions for logged-in users, and actions for administrators.

Implementing Login

When a brand new user comes to our site, there are three things we would like him to do. First, look at what we have to offer; second, sign up with us; and third, log in. We will look at each of these in turn.

In Figure 28.4, you can see the screen we present to users when they first come to our site.

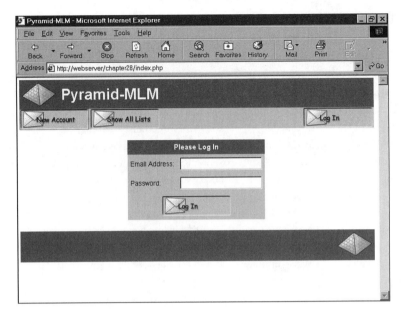

Figure 28.4   On arrival, users can create a new account, view
available lists, or just log in.

We'll look at creating a new account and logging in now, and return to viewing list
details in the "Implementing User Functions" and "Implementing Administrative
Functions" sections later on.

Creating a New Account

If a user selects the New Account menu option, this activates the `new-account` action.
This activates the following code in index.php:

```
case 'new-account' :
    {
        // get rid of session variables
        session_destroy();
        display_account_form();
        break;
    }
```

This code effectively logs out a user if she is currently logged in, and displays the
account details form as shown in Figure 28.5.

This form is generated by the `display_account_form()` function from the
output_fns.php library. This function is used both here and in the account-settings action
to display a form to enable the user to set up an account. If the function is invoked from
the account-settings action, the form will be filled with the user's existing account data.

Here the form is blank, ready for new account details. Because this function only outputs HTML, we will not go through it here.

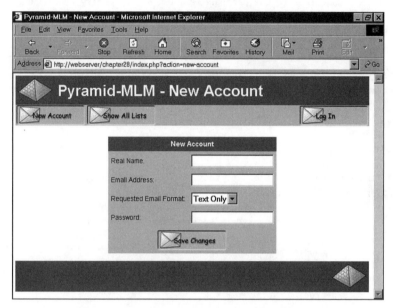

Figure 28.5   The new account creation form
enables users to enter their details.

The submit button on this form invokes the `store-account` action. The code for this action is as follows:

```
case 'store-account' :
   {
     if (store_account($HTTP_SESSION_VARS['normal_user'],
             $HTTP_SESSION_VARS['admin_user'], $HTTP_POST_VARS))
       $action = '';
     if(!check_logged_in())
       display_login_form($action);
     break;
   }
```

The `store_account()` function writes the account details to the database. The code for this function is shown in Listing 28.4.

Listing 28.4   **store_account() Function from mlm_fns.php—These Functions Add a New User or Modify an Existing User in the Database.**

```php
// add a new subscriber to the database, or let a user modify their data
function store_account($normal_user, $admin_user, $details)
{
  if(!filled_out($details))
  {
    echo 'All fields must be filled in.  Try again.<br /><br />';
    return false;
  }
  else
  {
    if(subscriber_exists($details['email']))
    {
      //check logged in as the user they are trying to change
      if(get_email()==$details['email'])
      {
        $query = "update subscribers set realname = '$details[realname]',
                                          mimetype = '$details[mimetype]'
                  where email = '" . $details[email] . "'";
        if(db_connect() && mysql_query($query))
        {
          return true;
        }
        else
        {
          echo 'could not store changes.<br /><br /><br /><br /><br />';
          return false;
        }
      }
      else
      {
        echo '<p>Sorry, that email address is already registered here.</p>';
        echo '<p>You will need to log in with that address to change '
             .' its settings.</p>';
        return false;
      }
    }
    else // new account
    {
      $query = "insert into subscribers
                        values ('$details[email]',
                        '$details[realname]',
                        '$details[mimetype]',
                         password('$details[new_password]'),
                                        0)";
```

Listing 28.4 **Continued**

```
    if(db_connect() && mysql_query($query))
    {
      return true;
    }
    else
    {
      echo 'Could not store new account.<br /><br /><br /><br /><br />';
      return false;
    }
  }
 }
}
```

This function first checks that the user has filled in the required details.
If this is okay, the function will then either create a new user, or update the account
details if the user already exists. A user can only update the account details of the user he
is logged in as.

This is checked using the `get_email()` function, which retrieves the email address of
the user who is currently logged in. We'll return to this later, as it uses session variables
that are set up when the user logs in.

Logging In

If a user fills in the login form we saw back in Figure 28.4 and clicks on the Log In button, she will enter the index.php script with the `email` and `password` variables set. This
will activate the login code, which is in the pre-processing stage of the script, as follows:

```
// need to process log in or out requests before anything else
if($HTTP_POST_VARS['email']&&$HTTP_POST_VARS['password'])
{
  $login = login($HTTP_POST_VARS['email'], $HTTP_POST_VARS['password']);

  if($login == 'admin')
  {
    $status .= '<p><b>'.get_real_name($HTTP_POST_VARS['email']).'</b> logged in'.
               ' successfully as <b>Administrator</b></p>'
               '<br /><br /><br /><br /><br />';
    $HTTP_SESSION_VARS['admin_user'] = $HTTP_POST_VARS['email'];
  }
  else if($login == 'normal')
  {
    $status .= "<p><b>".get_real_name($HTTP_POST_VARS['email'])."</b> logged in"
               ." successfully.</p><br /><br />";
    $HTTP_SESSION_VARS['normal_user'] = $HTTP_POST_VARS['email'];
```

```
  }
  else
  {
    $status .= "<p>Sorry, we could not log you in with that
                email address and password.</p><br />";
  }
}
```

As you can see, we first try to log them in using the `login()` function from the
user_auth_fns.php library. This is slightly different from the login functions we have used
elsewhere, so we'll take a look at it. The code for this function is shown in Listing 28.5.

Listing 28.5 **login() Function from user_auth_fns.php—Checking a User's Login
              Details**

```
function login($email, $password)
// check username and password with db
// if yes, return login type
// else return false
{
  // connect to db
  $conn = db_connect();
  if (!$conn)
    return 0;

  $query = "select admin from subscribers
                      where email='$email'
                      and password = password('$password')";
  //echo $query;
  $result = mysql_query($query);
  if (!$result)
    return false;

  if (mysql_num_rows($result)<1)
    return false;

  if(mysql_result($result, 0, 0) == 1)
    return 'admin';
  else
    return 'normal';
}
```

Previously with login functions, we have returned `true` if the login was successful and
`false` if it was not. In this case, we still return `false` if the login failed, but if it was successful we return the user type, either `'admin'` or `'normal'`. We check the user type by
retrieving the value stored in the admin column in the subscribers' table, for a particular
combination of email address and password. If no results are returned, we return `false`.
If a user is an administrator, this value will be 1 (`true`), and we return `'admin'`.
Otherwise, we return `'normal'`.

Returning to the main line of execution, we register a session variable to keep track of who our user is. This will either be `admin_user` if she is an administrator, or `normal_user` if she is a regular user. Whichever one of these variables we set will contain the email address of the user. To simplify checking for the email address of a user, we use the `get_email()` function mentioned earlier.

This function is shown in Listing 28.6.

Listing 28.6 get_email() function from user_auth_fns.php—Returns the Email Address of the Logged In User

```php
function get_email()
{
  global $HTTP_SESSION_VARS;

  if (isset($HTTP_SESSION_VARS['normal_user']))
    return $HTTP_SESSION_VARS['normal_user'];
  if (isset($HTTP_SESSION_VARS['admin_user']))
   return $HTTP_SESSION_VARS['admin_user'];

  return false;
}
```

Back in our main program, we report to the user whether she was logged in or not, and at what level.

The output from one login attempt is shown in Figure 28.6.

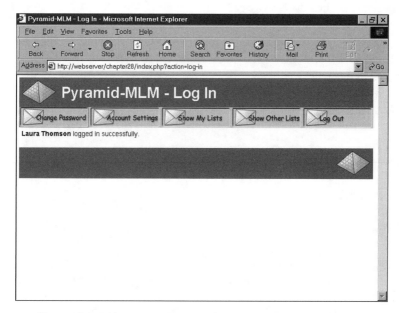

Figure 28.6 The system reports to the user that login was successful.

Now that we have logged in a user, we can proceed to the user functions.

Implementing User Functions

There are five things we want our users to be able to do after they have logged in:

- Look at the lists available for subscription
- Subscribe and unsubscribe from lists
- Change the way their accounts are set up
- Change their passwords
- Log out

You can see most of these options in Figure 28.6. We will now look at the implementation of each of these options.

Viewing Lists

We will implement a number of options for viewing available lists and list details. In Figure 28.6, you can see two of these options: Show My Lists, which will retrieve the lists this user is subscribed to, and Show Other Lists, which will retrieve the lists the user is not subscribed to.

If you look back at Figure 28.4, you will see that we have another option, Show All Lists, which will retrieve all the available mailing lists on the system. For the system to be truly scalable, we should add paging functionality (to display, say, 10 results per page). We have not done this here for brevity.

These three menu options activate the `show-my-lists`, `show-other-lists`, and `show-all-lists` actions, respectively. As you have probably realized, all these actions work quite similarly. The code for these three actions is as follows:

```
case 'show-all-lists' :
{
  display_items('All Lists', get_all_lists(), 'information',
                'show-archive','');
  break;
}


case 'show-other-lists' :
{
  display_items('Unsubscribed Lists',
                get_unsubscribed_lists(get_email()), 'information',
                'show-archive', 'subscribe');
  break;
}
```

```
case '':
case 'show-my-lists' :
{
  display_items('Subscribed Lists', get_subscribed_lists(get_email()),
              'information', 'show-archive', 'unsubscribe');
  break;
}
```

As you can see, all these actions call the `display_items()` function from the output_fns.php library, but they each call it with different parameters. They all also use the `get_email()` function we mentioned earlier to get the appropriate email address for this user.

To see what this function does, look at Figure 28.7.

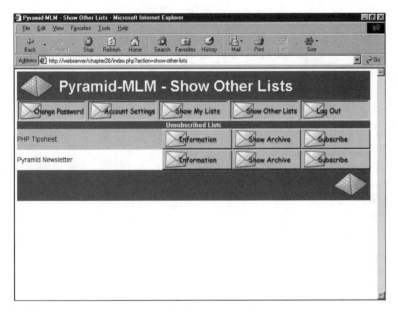

Figure 28.7   The display_items() function has been used to lay out a list of
the lists that the user is not subscribed to.

This is the Show Other Lists page.

Let's look at the code for the `display_items()` function. It is shown in Listing 28.7.

**Listing 28.7   display_items() Function from output_fns.php—This Function Is Used to
Display a List of Items with Associated Actions**

```
function display_items($title, $list, $action1='', $action2='', $action3='')
{
  global $table_width;
```

Listing 28.7   **Continued**

```
echo "<table width=\"$table_width\" cellspacing=\"0\" cellpadding=\"0\"
      border=\"0\">";

// count number of actions
$actions = (($action1!='') + ($action2!='') + ($action3!=''));

echo '<tr>
      <th colspan="'. (1+$actions) .'" bgcolor="#5B69A6">'. $title .'</th>
      </tr>';

// count number of items
$items = sizeof($list);

if($items == 0)
  echo '<tr>
        <td colspan="'.(1+$actions).'" align="center">No Items to Display</td>
        </tr>';
else
{
  // print each row
  for($i = 0; $items; $i++)
  {
    if($i%2) // background colors alternate
      $bgcolor = "'#ffffff'";
    else
      $bgcolor = "'#ccccff'";
    echo "<tr>
          <td bgcolor=$bgcolor
            width=\"".($table_width - ($actions*149)).'">';
    echo $list[$i][1];
    if($list[$i][2])
      echo ' - '.$list[$i][2];
    echo '</td>';

    // create buttons for up to three actions per line
    for($j = 1; $j<=3; $j++)
    {
      $var = 'action'.$j;
      if($$var)
      {
        echo "<td bgcolor=\"$bgcolor\" width=\"149\">";
        // view/preview buttons are a special case as they link to a file
        if($$var == 'preview-html'||$$var == 'view-html'||
           $$var == 'preview-text'||$$var == 'view-text')
          display_preview_button($list[$i][3], $list[$i][0], $$var);
```

Listing 28.7   **Continued**

```
         else
            display_button( $$var, '&id=' . $list[$i][0] );
            echo '</td>';
        }
      }
      echo "</tr>\n";
    }
    echo '</table>';
  }
}
```

This function will output a table of items, with each item having up to three associated action buttons. The function expects five parameters, which are, in order:

- `$title` is the title that appears at the top of the table—in the case shown in Figure 28.7, we are passing in the title Unsubscribed Lists, as shown in the previously discussed code snippet for the action "Show Other Lists".

- `$list` is an array of items to display in each row of the table. In this case, it is an array of the lists the user is not currently subscribed to. We are building this array (in this case) in the function `get_unsubscribed_lists()`, which we'll discuss in a minute. This is a multidimensional array, with each row in the array containing up to four pieces of data about each row. In order, again:

  - `$list[n][0]` should contain the item id, which will usually be a row number. This gives the action buttons the id of the row they are to operate upon. In our case, we will use ids from the database—more on this in a minute.

  - `$list[n][1]` should contain the item name. This will be the text displayed for a particular item. For example, in the case shown in Figure 28.7, the item name in the first row of the table is PHP Tipsheet.

  - `$list[n][2]` and `$list[n][3]` are optional. We use these to convey that there is more information. They correspond to the more information text and the more information id, respectively. We will look at an example using these two parameters when we come to the View Mail action in the "Implementing Administrative Functions" section.

We could, as an alternative, have used keywords as indices to the array.

The third, fourth, and fifth parameters to the function are used to pass in three actions that will be displayed on buttons corresponding to each item. In Figure 28.7, these are the three action buttons shown as Information, Show Archive, and Subscribe.

We got these three buttons for the Show All Lists page by passing in the action names, `information`, `show-archive`, and `subscribe`. By using the `display_button()` function, these actions have been turned into buttons with those words on them, and the appropriate action assigned to them.

Each of the Show actions calls the `display_items()` function in a different way, as you can see by looking back at their actions. As well as having different titles and action buttons, each of the three uses a different function to build the array of items to display. Show All Lists uses the function `get_all_lists()`, Show Other Lists uses the function `get_unsubscribed_lists()`, and Show My Lists uses the function `get_subscribed_lists()`. All these functions work in a similar fashion. They are all from the mlm_fns.php function library.

We'll look at `get_unsubscribed_lists()` because that's the example we've followed so far. The code for the `get_unsubscribed_lists()` function is shown in Listing 28.8.

Listing 28.8   get_unsubscribed_lists() Function from mlm_fns.php—Building an Array of Mailing Lists That a User Is Not Subscribed To

```
function get_unsubscribed_lists($email)
{
  $list = array();

  $query = "select lists.listid, listname, email from lists left join sub_lists
                on lists.listid = sub_lists.listid
                and email='$email' where email is NULL order by listname";
  if(db_connect())
  {
    $result = mysql_query($query);
    if(!$result)
      echo '<p>Unable to get list from database.</p>';
    $num = mysql_numrows($result);
    for($i = 0; $i<$num; $i++)
    {
      array_push($list, array(mysql_result($result, $i, 0),
              mysql_result($result, $i, 1)));
    }
  }
  return $list;
}
```

As you can see, this function requires an email address passed into it. This should be the email address of the subscriber that we are working with. The `get_subscribed_lists()` function also requires an email address as a parameter, but the `get_all_lists()` function does not for obvious reasons.

Given a subscriber's email address, we connect to the database and fetch all the lists the subscriber is not subscribed to. As usual for this kind of query in MySQL, we use a LEFT JOIN to find unmatched items.

We loop through the result and build the array row by row using the `array_push()` built-in function.

Now that we know how this list is produced, let's look at the action buttons associated with these displays.

Viewing List Information

The Information button shown in Figure 28.7 triggers the `'information'` action, which is as follows:

```
case 'information' :
{
  display_information($HTTP_GET_VARS['id']);
  break;
}
```

To see what the `display_information()` function does, look at Figure 28.8.

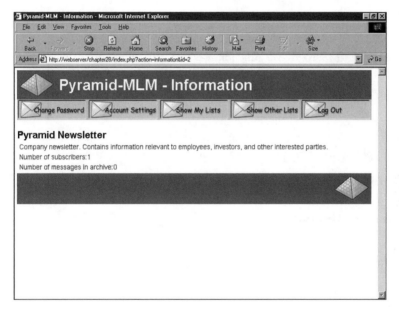

Figure 28.8   The display_information() function
shows a blurb about a mailing list.

The function displays some general information about a particular mailing list, as well as listing the number of subscribers and the number of newsletters that have been sent out to that list and are available in the archive (more on that in a minute).

The code for this function is shown in Listing 28.9.

Listing 28.9   **display_information() Function from output_fns.php—Displaying List Information**

```
function display_information($listid)
{
  if(!$listid)
    return false;

  $info = load_list_info($listid);

  if($info)
  {
    echo '<h2>'.pretty($info[listname]).'</h2>';
    echo '<p>'.pretty($info[blurb])'</p>';
    echo '<p>Number of subscribers:' . $info[subscribers]'</p>';
    echo '<p>Number of messages in archive:' . $info[archive]'</p>';
  }
}
```

The display_information() function uses two other functions to help it achieve its Web task: the load_list_info() function and the pretty() function. The load_list_info() function actually retrieves the data from the database. The pretty() function simply formats the data from the database by stripping out slashes, turning newlines into HTML line breaks, and so on.

Let's look briefly at the load_list_info() function. This function is in the mlm_fns.php function library. The code for it is shown in Listing 28.10.

Listing 28.10   **load_list_info() Function from mlm_fns.php—Building an Array of List Information**

```
function load_list_info($listid)
{
  if(!$listid)
    return false;

  if(!db_connect())
    return false;

  $query = "select listname, blurb from lists where listid = $listid";
  $result = mysql_query($query);
      if(!$result)
  {
    echo 'Cannot retrieve this list';
    return false;
  }
  $info =  mysql_fetch_array($result);
```

Listing 28.10 **Continued**

```
$query = "select count(*) from sub_lists where listid = $listid";
$result = mysql_query($query);
      if($result)
{
  $info['subscribers'] = mysql_result($result, 0, 0);
}
$query = "select count(*) from mail where listid = $listid
          and status = 'SENT'";
$result = mysql_query($query);
      if($result)
{
  $info['archive'] = mysql_result($result, 0, 0);
}
  return $info;
}
```

This function runs three database queries to collect the name and blurb for a list from the `lists` table, the number of subscribers from the `sub_lists` table, and the number of newsletters sent from the `mail` table.

Viewing List Archives

In addition to viewing the list blurb, users can look at all the mail that has been sent to a mailing list by clicking on the Show Archive button. This activates the show-archive action, which triggers the following code:

```
case 'show-archive' :
{
  display_items('Archive For '.get_list_name($HTTP_GET_VARS['id']),
                get_archive($HTTP_GET_VARS['id']), 'view-html', 'view-text', '');
  break;
}
```

Again, this function uses the `display_items()` function to list out the various items of mail that have been sent to the list. These items are retrieved using the `get_archive()` function from mlm_fns.php. This function is shown in Listing 28.11.

Listing 28.11 **get_archive() Function from mlm_fns.php—Building an Array of
                Archived Newsletters for a Given List**

```
function get_archive($listid)
{
  //returns an array of the archived mail for this list
  //array has rows like (mailid, subject)

  $list = array();
```

Listing 28.11 **Continued**

```
$listname = get_list_name($listid);

$query = "select mailid, subject, listid from mail
            where listid = $listid and status = 'SENT' order by sent";

if(db_connect())
{
  $result = mysql_query($query);
  if(!$result)
  {
    echo "<p>Unable to get list from database - $query.</p>";
    return false;
  }
  $num = mysql_numrows($result);
  for($i = 0; $i<$num; $i++)
  {
    $row = array(mysql_result($result, $i, 0),
                 mysql_result($result, $i, 1), $listname, $listid);
    array_push($list, $row);
  }
}
  return $list;
}
```

Again, this function gets the required information—in this case, the details of mail that has been sent—from the database and builds an array suitable for passing to the `display_items()` function.

Subscribing and Unsubscribing

On the list of mailing lists shown in Figure 28.7, each list has a button that enables users to subscribe to it. Similarly, if users use the Show My Lists option to see the lists to which they are already subscribed, they will see an Unsubscribe button next to each list.

These buttons activate the subscribe and unsubscribe actions, which trigger the following two pieces of code, respectively:

```
case 'subscribe' :
{
  subscribe(get_email(), $HTTP_GET_VARS['id']);
  display_items('Subscribed Lists', get_subscribed_lists(get_email()),
                'information', 'show-archive', 'unsubscribe');
  break;
}
case 'unsubscribe' :
{
```

```
    unsubscribe(get_email(), $HTTP_GET_VARS['id']);
    display_items('Subscribed Lists', get_subscribed_lists(get_email()),
                  'information', 'show-archive', 'unsubscribe');
    break;
}
```

In each case, we call a function (subscribe() or unsubscribe()) and then redisplay a list of mailing lists the user is now subscribed to using the display_items() function again.

The subscribe() and unsubscribe() functions are shown in Listing 28.12.

Listing 28.12   **subscribe() and unsubscribe() Functions from mlm_fns.php—These
                Functions Add and Remove Subscriptions for a User**

```
function subscribe($email, $listid)
{
  if(!$email||!$listid||!list_exists($listid)||!subscriber_exists($email))
    return false;

  //if already subscribed exit
  if(subscribed($email, $listid))
    return false;

  if(!db_connect())
    return false;

  $query = "insert into sub_lists values ('$email', $listid)";

  $result = mysql_query($query);
      return $result;
}

function unsubscribe($email, $listid)
{
  if(!$email||!$listid)
    return false;

  if(!db_connect())
    return false;

  $query = "delete from sub_lists where email = '$email' and listid = $listid";

  $result = mysql_query($query);
  return $result;
}
```

The `subscribe()` function adds a row to the `sub_lists` table corresponding to the subscription; the `unsubscribe()` function deletes this row.

Changing Account Settings

The Account Settings button, when clicked, activates the account-settings action. The code for this action is as follows:

```
case 'account-settings' :
{
  display_account_form(get_email(),
      get_real_name(get_email()), get_mimetype(get_email()));
  break;
}
```

As you can see, we are reusing the `display_account_form()` function that we used to create the account in the first place. However, this time we are passing in the user's current details, which will be displayed in the form for easy editing. When the user clicks on the submit button in this form, the `store-account` action is activated as discussed previously.

Changing Passwords

Clicking on the Change Password button activates the `change-password` action, which triggers the following code:

```
case 'change-password' :
{
  display_password_form();
  break;
}
```

The `display_password_form()` function (from the output_fns.php library) simply displays a form for the user to change his password. This form is shown in Figure 28.9.

When a user clicks on the Change Password button at the bottom of this form, the `store-change-password` action will be activated. The code for this is as follows:

```
case 'store-change-password' :
{
  if(change_password(get_email(), $HTTP_POST_VARS['old_passwd'],
    $HTTP_POST_VARS['new_passwd'], $HTTP_POST_VARS['new_passwd2']))
  {
    echo '<p>OK: Password changed.</p><br /><br /><br /><br /><br /><br />';
  }
  else
  {
    echo '<p>Sorry, your password could not be changed.</p>';
    display_password_form();
```

```
  }
  break;
}
```

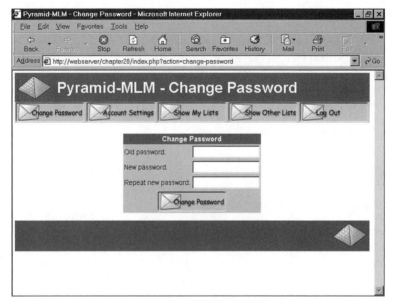

Figure 28.9   The display_password_form() function enables users
to change their passwords.

As you can see, this code tries to change the password using the change_password()
function and reports success or failure to the user. The change_password() function can
be found in the user_auth_fns.php function library. The code for this function is shown
in Listing 28.13.

Listing 28.13   **change_password() Function from user_auth_fns.php—This Function
Validates and Updates a User's Password**

```
function change_password($email, $old_password, $new_password,
                         $new_password_conf)
// change password for email/old_password to new_password
// return true or false
{

  // if the old password is right
  // change their password to new_password and return true
  // else return false
  if (login($email, $old_password))
  {
```

Listing 28.13 **Continued**

```
    if($new_password==$new_password_conf)
    {
      if (!($conn = db_connect()))
        return false;
      $query = "update subscribers
                set password = password('$new_password')
                where email = '$email'";
      $result = mysql_query($query);
      return $result;
    }
    else
      echo '<p> Your passwords do not match.</p>;
  }
  else
    echo '<p> Your old password is incorrect.</p>';

  return false; // old password was wrong
}
```

This function is similar to other password setting and changing functions we have looked at. It compares the two new passwords entered by the user to make sure they are the same, and if they are, tries to update the user's password in the database.

Logging Out

When a user clicks on the Log Out button, it triggers the log-out action. The code executed by this action in the main script is actually in the preprocessing section of the script, as follows:

```
if($action == 'log-out')
{
  unset($HTTP_SESSION_VARS);
  session_destroy();
}
```

This snippet of code disposes of the session variables and destroys the session. Notice that it also unsets the `action` variable—this means that we enter the main case statement without an action, triggering the following code:

```
case '':
{
  if(!check_logged_in())
    display_login_form($action);
  break;
}
```

This will allow another user to log in, or allow the user to log in as someone else.

Implementing Administrative Functions

If someone logs in as an administrator, she will get some additional menu options, which can be seen in Figure 28.10.

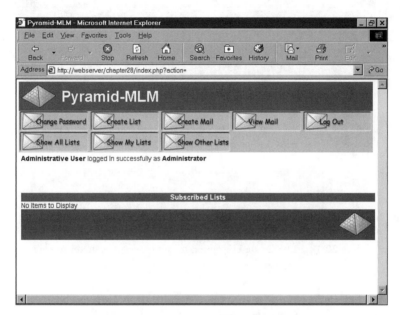

Figure 28.10   The administrator menu allows for mailing list creation and maintenance.

The extra options they have are Create List (create a new mailing list), Create Mail (create a new newsletter), and View Mail (view and send created newsletters that have not yet been sent). We will look at each of these in turn.

Creating a New List

If the administrator chooses to set up a new list by clicking on the Create List button, she will activate the `create-list` action, which is associated with the following code:

```
case 'create-list' :
{
  display_list_form(get_email());
  break;
}
```

The `display_list_form()` function displays a form that enables the administrator to enter the details of a new list. It can be found in the output_fns.php library. It just outputs HTML, so we will not go through it here. The output of this function is shown in Figure 28.11.

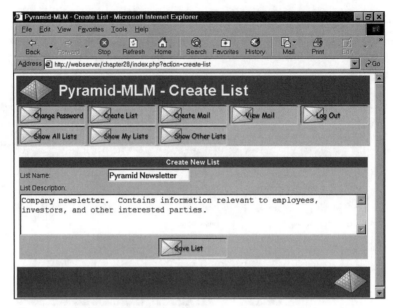

Figure 28.11   The Create List option requires the administrator to enter a
name and description (or blurb) for the new list.

When the administrator clicks on the Save List button, this activates the store-list
action, which triggers the following code in index.php:

```
case 'store-list' :
{
  if(store_list($HTTP_SESSION_VARS['admin_user'], $HTTP_POST_VARS))
  {
    echo '<p>New list added</p><br />';
    display_items('All Lists', get_all_lists(), 'information',
                  'show-archive','');
  }
  else
    echo '<p>List could not be stored, please try '
         .'again.</p><br /><br /><br /><br /><br />';

  break;
}
```

As you can see, the code tries to store the new list details and then displays the new list
of lists. The list details are stored with the store_list() function. The code for this
function is shown in Listing 28.14.

Listing 28.14   store_list() Function from mlm_fns.php—This Function Inserts a New Mailing List into the Database

```php
function store_list($admin_user, $details)
{
  if(!filled_out($details))
  {
    echo 'All fields must be filled in.  Try again.<br /><br />';
    return false;
  }
  else
  {
    if(!check_admin_user($admin_user))
      return false;
      // how did this function get called by somebody not logged in as admin?

    if(!db_connect())
    {
      return false;
    }

    $query = "select count(*) from lists where listname = '"
              .$details['name']."'";
    $result = mysql_query($query);
    if(mysql_result($result, 0, 0) > 0)
    {
      echo 'Sorry, there is already a list with this name.';
      return false;
    }

    $query = "insert into lists values (NULL,
                             '".$details['name']."',
                             '".$details['blurb']."')";

    $result = mysql_query($query);
    return $result;
  }
}
```

This function performs a few validation checks before writing to the database: It checks that all the details were supplied, that the current user is an administrator, and that the list name is unique. If all goes well the list is added to the `lists` table in the database.

Uploading a New Newsletter

Finally we come to the main thrust of this application: uploading and sending newsletters to mailing lists.

When an administrator clicks on the Create Mail button, it activates the `create-mail` action, as follows:

```
case 'create-mail' :
{
  display_mail_form(get_email());
  break;
}
```

The administrator will see the form shown in Figure 28.12.

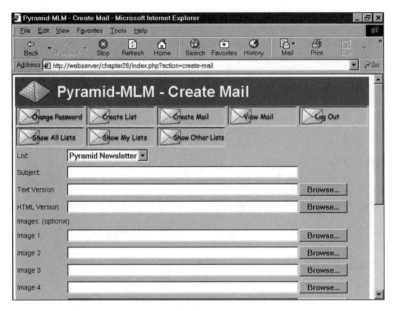

Figure 28.12   The Create Mail option gives the administrator an interface for uploading newsletter files.

Remember that for this application we are assuming that the administrator has created a newsletter offline in both HTML and text formats and will upload both versions before sending. We chose to implement it this way so that administrators can use their favorite software to create the newsletters. This makes the application more accessible.

You can see that this form has a number of fields for an administrator to fill out. At the top is a drop-down box of mailing lists to choose from. The administrator must also fill in a subject for the newsletter—this is the Subject line for the eventual email.

All the other form fields are file upload fields, which you can see from the Browse buttons next to them. In order to send a newsletter, an administrator must list both the text and HTML versions of this newsletter (although obviously you could change this to suit your needs). There are also a number of optional image fields where an administrator can upload any images that she has embedded in her HTML. Each of these files must be specified and uploaded separately.

The form you see is similar to a regular file upload form except that, in this case, we are using it to upload multiple files. This necessitates some minor differences in the form syntax, and in the way we deal with the uploaded files at the other end.

The code for the `display_mail_form()` function is shown in Listing 28.15.

Listing 28.15   **display_mail_form() Function from output_fns.php—This Function Displays the File Upload Form**

```php
function display_mail_form($email, $listid=0)
{
  // display html form for uploading a new message
  global $table_width;
  $list = get_all_lists();
  $lists = sizeof($list);
?>
  <table cellpadding="4" cellspacing="0" border="0"
        width="<?php echo $table_width?>">
  <form enctype='multipart/form-data' action='upload.php' method='post'>
  <tr>
    <td bgcolor="#cccccc">
      List:
    </td>
    <td bgcolor="#cccccc">
      <select name="list">
      <?php
      for($i = 0; $i<$lists; $i++)
      {
        echo '<option value = '.$list[$i][0];
        if ($listid== $list[$i][0]) echo ' selected';
        echo '>'.$list[$i][1]."</option>\n";
      }
      ?>
      </select>
    </td>
  </tr>
  <tr>
    <td bgcolor="#cccccc">
      Subject:
    </td>
    <td bgcolor="#cccccc">
      <input type="text" name="subject" value="<?php echo $subject?>"
        size = 60 ></td>
  </tr>
  <tr><td bgcolor="#cccccc">
```

Listing 28.15   **Continued**

```
   Text Version:
 </td><td bgcolor="#cccccc">
   <input type=file name='userfile[0]' size = 60>
 </td></tr>
 <tr><td bgcolor="#cccccc">
   HTML Version:
 </td><td bgcolor="#cccccc">
   <input type=file name='userfile[1]' size = 60>
 </td></tr>
 <tr><td bgcolor="#cccccc" colspan="2">Images: (optional)

<?php
 $max_images = 10;
 for($i = 0; $i<10; $i++)
 {
    echo "<tr><td bgcolor='#cccccc'>Image ". ($i+1) .' </td>';
    echo "<td bgcolor='#cccccc'>";
    echo "<input type='file' name='userfile[".($i+2)."]' size='60'></td></tr>";
 }
?>
 <tr><td colspan="2" bgcolor="#cccccc" align="center">
 <input type="hidden" name="max_images"  value="<?php echo $max_images?>">
 <input type="hidden" name="listid"  value="<?php echo $listid?>">
 <?php display_form_button('upload-files'); ?>
 </td>
 </form>
 </tr>
 </table>
<?php
}
```

The thing to note here is that the files we want to upload will have their names entered in a series of inputs, each of type `file`, and with names that range from `userfile[0]` to `userfile[n]`. In essence, we are treating these form fields in the same way that we would treat check boxes, and naming them using an array convention.

If you want to upload multiple files through a PHP script, you need to follow this convention.

In the script that processes this form, we will actually end up with *three arrays*. Let's look at that script.

Handling Multiple File Upload

You might remember that we put the file upload code in a separate file. The complete listing of that file, upload.php, is shown in Listing 28.16.

Listing 28.16 **upload.php—This Script Uploads All the Files Needed for a Newsletter**

```php
<?php
  // this functionality is in a separate file to allow us to be
  // more paranoid with it

  // if anything goes wrong, we will exit

  $max_size = 50000;

  include ('include_fns.php');
  session_start();

  // only admin users can upload files
  if(!check_admin_user())
  {
    echo 'You do not seem to be authorized to use this page.';
    exit;
  }

  // set up the admin toolbar buttons
  $buttons = array();
  $buttons[0] = 'change-password';
  $buttons[1] = 'create-list';
  $buttons[2] = 'create-mail';
  $buttons[3] = 'view-mail';
  $buttons[4] = 'log-out';
  $buttons[5] = 'show-all-lists';
  $buttons[6] = 'show-my-lists';
  $buttons[7] = 'show-other-lists';

  do_html_header('Pyramid-MLM - Upload Files');

  display_toolbar($buttons);

  // check that the page is being called with the required data
  if(!$HTTP_POST_FILES['userfile']['name'][0]
     ||!$HTTP_POST_FILES['userfile']['name'][1]
     ||!$HTTP_POST_VARS['subject']||!$HTTP_POST_VARS['list'])
  {
      echo 'Problem: You did not fill out the form fully. The images are the
            only optional fields.  Each message needs a subject, text version
            and an HTML version.';
      do_html_footer();
      exit;
  }
```

Listing 28.16 **Continued**

```
$list = $HTTP_POST_VARS['list'];
$subject = $HTTP_POST_VARS['subject'];

if (!db_connect())
{
   echo '<p>Could not connect to db</p>';
   do_html_footer();
   exit;
}

// add mail details to the DB
$query = "insert into mail values (NULL,
                        '".$HTTP_SESSION_VARS['admin_user']."',
                        '".$subject."',
                        '".$list."',
                        'STORED', NULL, NULL)";
$result = mysql_query($query);
if (!$result)
{
  do_html_footer();
  exit;
}

//get the id MySQL assigned to this mail
$mailid = mysql_insert_id();

if (!$mailid)
{
  do_html_footer();
  exit;
}


// creating directory will fail if this is not the first message archived
// that's ok
@ mkdir('archive/'.$list, 0700);

// it is a problem if creating the specific directory for this mail fails
if (!mkdir('archive/'.$list."/$mailid", 0700))
{
  do_html_footer();
  exit;
}

// iterate through the array of uploaded files
$i = 0;
```

Listing 28.16 **Continued**

```php
while ($HTTP_POST_FILES['userfile']['name'][$i]&&
       $$HTTP_POST_FILES['userfile']['name'][$i]!='none')
{
  echo '<p>Uploading '.$HTTP_POST_FILES['userfile']['name'][$i].' - ';
  echo $HTTP_POST_FILES['userfile']['size'][$i].' bytes.</p>';
  if ($HTTP_POST_FILES['userfile']['size'][$i]==0)
  {
    echo 'Problem: '.$HTTP_POST_FILES['userfile']['name'][$i].
        ' is zero length';
    $i++;
    continue;
  }

  if ($HTTP_POST_FILES['userfile']['size'][$i]>$max_size)
  {
    echo 'Problem: '.$HTTP_POST_FILES['userfile']['name'][$i].' is over '
        .$max_size.' bytes';
    $i++;
    continue;
  }

  // we would like to check that the uploaded image is an image
  // if getimagesize() can work out its size, it probably is.
  if($i>1&&!getimagesize($HTTP_POST_FILES['userfile']['tmp_name'][$i]))
  {
    echo 'Problem: '.$HTTP_POST_FILES['userfile']['name'][$i].
        ' is corrupt, or not a gif, jpeg or png';
    $i++;
    continue;
  }

  // file 0 (the text message) and file 1 (the html message) are special cases
  if($i==0)
    $destination = "archive/$list/$mailid/text.txt";
  else if($i == 1)
    $destination = "archive/$list/$mailid/index.html";
  else
  {
    $destination = "archive/$list/$mailid/"
                  .$HTTP_POST_FILES['userfile']['name'][$i];
    $query = "insert into images values ($mailid,
                      '".$HTTP_POST_FILES['userfile']['name'][$i]."',
                      '".$HTTP_POST_FILES['userfile']['type'][$i]."')";
    $result = mysql_query($query);
  }
```

Listing 28.16 **Continued**

```
    //if we are using PHP version >= 4.03

    if (!is_uploaded_file($HTTP_POST_FILES['userfile']['tmp_name'][$i]))
    {
      // possible file upload attack detected
      echo 'Something funny happening with '
          .$HTTP_POST_FILES['userfile']['name'].', not uploading.';
      do_html_footer();
      exit;
    }

    move_uploaded_file($HTTP_POST_FILES['userfile']['tmp_name'][$i],
                       $destination);
/*
    // if version <= 4.02
    copy ($userfile[$i], $destination);

    unlink($userfile[$i]);
*/

    $i++;
  }

  display_preview_button($list, $mailid, 'preview-html');
  display_preview_button($list, $mailid, 'preview-text');
  display_button('send', "&id=$mailid");

  echo '<br /><br /><br /><br /><br />';
  do_html_footer();
?>
```

Let's walk through the steps in Listing 28.16.

First, we start a session and check that the user is logged in as an administrator—we don't want to let anybody else upload files.

Strictly speaking, we should probably also check the list and mailid variables for unwanted characters, but we have ignored this for the sake of brevity.

Next, we set up and send the headers for the page, and validate that the form was filled in correctly. This is important here as it's quite a complex form for the user to fill out.

Then we create an entry for this mail in the database, and set up a directory in the archive for the mail to be stored in.

Next comes the main part of the script, which checks and moves each of the uploaded files. This is the part that is different when uploading multiple files. We now have four arrays to deal with. These arrays are called $HTTP_POST_FILES['userfile']['name'], $HTTP_POST_FILES['userfile']['tmp_name'],

`$HTTP_POST_FILES['userfile']['size']` and
`$HTTP_POST_FILES['userfile']['type']`. They correspond to their similarly named
equivalents in a single file upload, except that each of them is an array. The first file in
the form will be detailed in `$HTTP_POST_FILES['userfile']['tmp_name'][0]`,
`$HTTP_POST_FILES['userfile']['name'][0]`, `$HTTP_POST_FILES`
`['userfile']['size'][0]`, and `$HTTP_POST_FILES['userfile']['type'][0]`.

Given these three arrays, we perform the usual safety checks and move the files into
the archive.

Finally, we give the administrator some buttons that they can use to preview the
newsletter they have uploaded before they send it, and a button to send it. You can see
the output from upload.php in Figure 28.13.

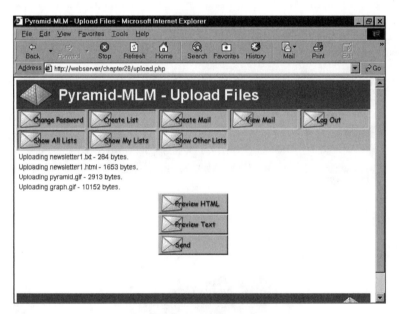

Figure 28.13   The upload script reports the files uploaded and their sizes.

Previewing the Newsletter

There are two ways the administrator can preview a newsletter before sending. She can
access the preview functions from the upload screen if she wants to preview immediately
after upload. She can also click on the View Mail button, which will show her all the
unsent newsletters in the system, if she wants to preview and send mail later. The View
Mail button activates the `view-mail` action, which triggers the following code:

```
case 'view-mail' :
{
```

```
display_items('Unsent Mail', get_unsent_mail(get_email()),
              'preview-html', 'preview-text', 'send');
    break;
}
```

As you can see, this again uses the `display_items()` function with buttons for the `pre-view-html`, `preview-text`, and `send` actions.

One interesting point to note is that the "Preview" buttons do not actually trigger an action, but instead link directly to the newsletter in the archive. If you look back at Listings 28.7 and 28.16, you will see that we use the `display_preview_button()` function to create these buttons, instead of the usual `display_button()` function.

The `display_button()` function creates an image link to a script with GET parameters where required; the `display_preview_button()` function gives a plain link into the archive. This link will pop up in a new window, achieved using the `target=new` attribute of the HTML anchor tag. You can see the result of previewing the HTML version of a newsletter in Figure 28.14.

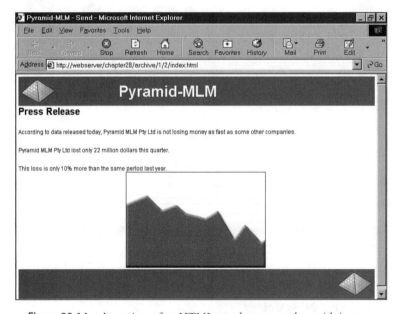

Figure 28.14   A preview of an HTML newsletter, complete with images.

Sending the Message

Clicking on the Send button for a newsletter activates the send action, which triggers the following code:

```
case 'send' :
{
  send($HTTP_GET_VARS['id'], $HTTP_SESSION_VARS['admin_user']);
  break;
}
```

This calls the `send()` function, which you can find in the mlm_fns.php library. This is quite a long function. It is also the point at which we use the `Mail_mime` class.

The code for our function is shown in Listing 28.17.

Listing 28.17   send() Function from mlm_fns.php—This Function Finally Sends Out a Newsletter

```
// create the message from the stored DB entries and files
// send test messages to the administrator, or real messages to the whole list
function send($mailid, $admin_user)
{
  if(!check_admin_user($admin_user))
    return false;

  if(!($info = load_mail_info($mailid)))
  {
    echo "Cannot load list information for message $mailid";
    return false;
  }
  $subject = $info[0];
  $listid = $info[1];
  $status = $info[2];
  $sent = $info[3];

  $from_name = 'Pyramid MLM';

  $from_address = 'return@address';

  $query = "select email from sub_lists where listid = $listid";

  $result = mysql_query($query);
  if (!$result)
  {
    echo $query;
    return false;
  }
  else if (mysql_num_rows($result)==0)
  {
    echo "There is nobody subscribed to list number $listid";
    return false;
  }
```

Listing 28.17 **Continued**

```
else
{
  // include PEAR mail classes
  include('Mail.php');
  include('Mail/mime.php');

  // instantiate MIME class and pass it the carriage return/line feed
  // character used on this system
  $message = new Mail_mime("\r\n");

  // read in the text version of the newsletter
  $textfilename = "archive/$listid/$mailid/text.txt";
  $tfp = fopen($textfilename, "r");
  $text = fread($tfp, filesize($textfilename));
  fclose($tfp);

  // read in the HTML version of the newsletter
  $htmlfilename = "archive/$listid/$mailid/index.html";
  $hfp = fopen($htmlfilename, "r");
  $html = fread($hfp, filesize($htmlfilename));
  fclose($hfp);

  // add HTML and text to the mimemail object
  $message->setTXTBody($text);
  $message->setHTMLBody($html);

  // get the list of images that relate to this message
  $query = "select path, mimetype from images where mailid = $mailid";
  if(db_connect())
  {
    $result = mysql_query($query);
    if(!$result)
    {
      echo '<p>Unable to get image list from database.</p>';
      return false;
    }
    $num = mysql_numrows($result);
    for($i = 0; $i<$num; $i++)
    {
      //load each image from disk
      $imgfilename = "archive/$listid/$mailid/".mysql_result($result, $i, 0);
      $imgtype = mysql_result($result, $i, 1);

      // add each image to the object
      $message->addHTMLImage($imgfilename, $imgtype, $imgfilename, true);
    }
```

Listing 28.17   **Continued**

```
  }

  // create message body
  $body = $message->get();

  // create message headers
  $from = '"'.get_real_name($admin_user).'" <'.$admin_user.'>';
  $hdrarray = array(
              'From'    => $from,
              'Subject' => $subject);

  $hdrs = $message->headers($hdrarray);

  // create the actual sending object
  $sender =& Mail::factory('mail');

  if($status == 'STORED')
  {

    // send the HTML message to the administrator
    $sender->send($admin_user, $hdrs, $body);

    // send the plain text version of the message to administrator
    mail($admin_user, $subject, $text, 'From: "'
        .get_real_name($admin_user).'" <'.$admin_user.">");

    echo "Mail sent to $admin_user";

    // mark newsletter as tested
    $query = "update mail set status = 'TESTED' where mailid = $mailid";
    if(db_connect())
    {
      $result = mysql_query($query);
    }

    echo '<p>Press send again to send mail to whole list.</p><center>';
    display_button('send', "&id=$mailid");
    echo '</center>';
  }
  else if($status == 'TESTED')
  {
    //send to whole list

    $query = "select subscribers.realname, sub_lists.email,
                    subscribers.mimetype
             from sub_lists, subscribers
```

Listing 28.17   **Continued**

```
                   where listid = $listid and
                       sub_lists.email = subscribers.email";

    if(!db_connect())
      return false;

    $result = mysql_query($query);
    if(!$result)
      echo '<p>Error getting subscriber list</p>';

    $count = 0;
    // for each subscriber
    while( $subscriber = mysql_fetch_row($result) )
    {
      if($subscriber[2]=='H')
      {
        //send HTML version to people who want it
        $sender->send($subscriber[1], $hdrs, $body);
      }
      else
      {
        //send text version to people who don't want HTML mail
        mail($subscriber[1], $subject, $text,
             'From: "'.get_real_name($admin_user).'" <'.$admin_user.">");
      }
      $count++;
    }

    $query = "update mail set status = 'SENT', sent = now()
             where mailid = $mailid";
    if(db_connect())
    {
      $result = mysql_query($query);
    }
    echo "<p>A total of $count messages were sent.</p>";
  }
  else if($status == 'SENT')
  {
    echo '<p>This mail has already been sent.</p>';
  }
 }
}
```

This function does several different things.

It test mails the newsletter to the administrator before sending it. It keeps track of this by tracking the status of a piece of mail in the database. When the upload script uploads a piece of mail, it sets the initial status of that mail to "STORED".

If the send() function finds that a mail has the status "STORED", it will update this to "TESTED" and send it to the administrator. The status "TESTED" means the newsletter has been test mailed to the administrator. If the status is "TESTED", it will be changed to "SENT" and sent to the whole list.

This means each piece of mail must essentially be sent twice: once in test mode and once in real mode.

The function also sends two different kinds of email: the text version, which it sends using PHP's mail() function; and the HTML kind, which it sends using the Mail_mime class. We've used mail() many times in this book, so let's look at how we use the Mail_mime class. We will not cover this class comprehensively, but instead explain how we have used it in this fairly typical application.

We begin by including the class files and creating an instance of the Mail_mime class:

```
// include PEAR mail classes
include('Mail.php');
include('Mail/mime.php');


// instantiate MIME class and pass it the carriage return/line feed
// character used on this system
$message = new Mail_mime("\r\n");
```

You will note that we are including two class files here. We will use the generic Mail class from PEAR later in this script to actually send the mail. This class comes with your PEAR installation.

The Mail_mime class is used to create the MIME format message which will be sent.

We next read in the text and HTML versions of the mail and add them to the Mail_mime class:

```
// read in the text version of the newsletter
$textfilename = "archive/$listid/$mailid/text.txt";
$tfp = fopen($textfilename, "r");
$text = fread($tfp, filesize($textfilename));
fclose($tfp);


// read in the HTML version of the newsletter
$htmlfilename = "archive/$listid/$mailid/index.html";
$hfp = fopen($htmlfilename, "r");
$html = fread($hfp, filesize($htmlfilename));
fclose($hfp);


// add HTML and text to the mimemail object
```

```
$message->setTXTBody($text);
$message->setHTMLBody($html);
```

We then load the image details from the database and loop through them, adding each image to the piece of mail we want to send:

```
// load each image from disk
$imgfilename = "archive/$listid/$mailid/".mysql_result($result, $i, 0);
$imgtype = mysql_result($result, $i, 1);

// add each image to the object
$message->addHTMLImage($imgfilename, $imgtype, $imgfilename, true);
```

The parameters we pass to addHTMLImage() are the name of the image file (or we could also pass the image data), the MIME type of the image, the filename again, and true to signify that the first parameter is a filename rather than file data. (If we wanted to pass raw image data we would pass the data, the MIME type, an empty parameter, and false.) These parameters are a little cumbersome.

At this stage we need to create the message body. We need to do this before we can set up the message headers. We create the body as follows:

```
// create message body
$body = $message->get();
```

We can then create the message headers with a call to Mail_mime's headers() function:

```
// create message headers
$from = '"'.get_real_name($admin_user).'" <'.$admin_user.'>';
$hdrarray = array(
                'From'    => $from,
                'Subject' => $subject);
$hdrs = $message->headers($hdrarray);
```

Finally, having set up the message, we can send it.

In order to do this we need to instantiate the PEAR Mail class and pass to it the message we have created. We begin by instantiating the class, as follows:

```
// create the actual sending object
$sender =& Mail::factory('mail');
```

(The parameter 'mail' here just tells the Mail class to use PHP's mail() function to send messages. We could also use 'sendmail' or 'smtp' as the value for this parameter for the obvious results.)

Next we send the mail to each of our subscribers.

We do this by retrieving and looping through each of the users subscribed to this list, and using either the Mail send() or regular mail() depending on the user's MIME type preference:

```
if($subscriber[2]=='H')
{
  //send HTML version to people who want it
  $sender->send($subscriber[1], $hdrs, $body);
}
else
{
  //send text version to people who don't want HTML mail
  mail($subscriber[1], $subject, $text,
                 'From: "'.get_real_name($admin_user).'" <'.$admin_user.">");
}
```

The first parameter of `$sender->send()` should be the user's email address, the second the headers, and the third the message body.

That's it! We have now completed building the mailing list application.

Extending the Project

As usual with these projects, there are many ways you could extend the functionality. You might like to

- Confirm membership with subscribers so that people can't be subscribed without their permission. This is typically done by sending email to their accounts and deleting those who do not reply. This approach will also clean out any incorrect email addresses from the database.

- Give the administrator powers to approve or reject users who want to subscribe to their lists.

- Add open list functionality that allows any member to send email to the list.

- Let only registered members see the archive for a particular mailing list.

- Allow users to search for lists that match specific criteria. For example, users might be interested in golf newsletters. Once the number of newsletters grows past a particular size, a search would be useful to find specific ones.

- If you expected to have a large mailing list a PHP application would not be the ideal way to send out the messages. A purpose built mailing list manager like exmlm would be much more efficient that calling `mail()` many times in PHP. Of course you could still build the front end in PHP, but have exmlm handle the grunt work.

Next

In the next chapter, we will implement a Web forum application that will enable users to have online discussions structured by topic and conversational threads.

## 29

Building Web Forums

O NE GOOD WAY TO GET USERS TO return to your site is to offer Web forums. These can be used for purposes as varied as philosophical discussion groups and product technical support. In this chapter, we implement a Web forum in PHP. An alternative is to use an existing package, such as Phorum, to set up your forums.

Web forums are sometimes also called *discussion boards* or *threaded discussion groups*. The idea of a forum is that people can post articles or questions to them, and others can read and reply to their questions. Each topic of discussion in a forum is called a *thread*.

We will implement a Web forum called blah-blah with the following functionality. Users will be able to

- Start new threads of discussion by posting articles
- Post articles in reply to existing articles
- View articles that have been posted
- View the threads of conversation in the forum
- View the relationship between articles, that is, see which articles are replies to other articles

The Problem

Setting up a forum is actually quite an interesting problem. We will need some way of storing the articles in a database with author, title, date, and content information. At first glance this might not seem much different from the Book-O-Rama database.

However, the way most threaded discussion software works is that, along with showing you the available articles, it will show you the relationship between articles. That is, you are able to see which articles are replies to other articles (and which article they're following up) and which articles are new topics of discussion.

You can see examples of discussion boards that implement this in many places, including Slashdot:

```
http://slashdot.org
```

Deciding how to display these relationships will require some careful thought. For this system, a user should be able to view an individual message, a thread of conversation with the relationships shown, or all the threads on the system.

Users must also be able to post new topics or replies. This is the easy part.

Solution Components

As we've said previously, storing and retrieving the author and text of a message is easy.

The most difficult part of this application is finding a database structure that will store the information we want, and a way of navigating that structure efficiently.

The structure of articles in a discussion might look like the one shown in Figure 29.1.

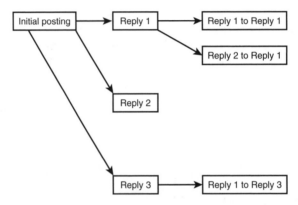

Figure 29.1   An article in a threaded discussion might be the first article in a new topic, but more commonly it is a response to another article.

In this diagram, you can see that we have an initial posting starting off a topic, with three replies. Some of the replies have replies. These replies could have replies, and so on.

Looking at the diagram gives us a clue as to how we can store and retrieve the article data and the links between articles. This diagram shows a *tree structure*. If you've done much programming, you'll know that this is one of the staple data structures used. In the diagram there are *nodes*—or articles—and *links*—or relationships between articles—just as in any tree structure. (If you are not familiar with trees as a data structure, don't worry—we will cover the basics as we go.)

The tricks to getting this all to work are

1. Finding a way to map this tree structure into storage—in our case, into a MySQL database

2. Finding a way to reconstruct the data as required

We will begin by implementing a MySQL database that will enable us to store articles between use.

We will build simple interfaces to enable saving of articles.

When we load the list of articles for viewing, we will load the headers of each article into a `tree_node` PHP class. Each `tree_node` will contain an article's headers and a set of the replies to that article.

The replies will be stored in an array. Each reply will itself be a `tree_node`, that can contain an array of replies to that article, which are themselves `tree_nodes`, and so on. This continues until we reach the so-called *leaf nodes* of the tree, the nodes that do not have any replies. We will then have a tree structure that looks like the one in Figure 29.1.

Some terminology: The message that we are replying to can be called the *parent* node of the current node. Any replies to the message can be called the *children* of the current node. If you imagine that this tree structure is like a family tree, this will be easy to remember.

The first article in this tree structure—the one with no parent—is sometimes called the *root* node.

> **Note**
>
> This can be unintuitive because we usually draw the root node at the top of diagrams, unlike the roots of real trees.

To build and display this tree structure, we will write recursive functions. (We discussed recursion in Chapter 5, "Reusing Code and Writing Functions.")

We decided to use a class for this structure because it's the easiest way to build a complex, dynamically expanding data structure for this application. It also means we have quite simple, elegant code to do something quite complex.

Solution Overview

To really understand what we have done with this project, it's probably a good idea to work through the code, which we'll do in a moment. There is less bulk in this application than in some of the others, but the code is a bit more complex.

There are only three real pages in the application.

We will have a main index page that shows all the articles in the forum as links to the articles. From here, you will be able to add a new article, view a listed article, or change the way the articles are viewed by expanding and collapsing branches of the tree. (More on this in a minute.)

From the article view, you will be able to post a reply to that article or view the existing replies to that article.

The new article page enables you to enter a new post, either a reply to an existing message, or a new unrelated message.

The system flow diagram is shown in Figure 29.2.

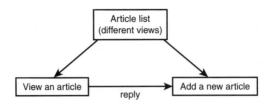

Figure 29.2   There are three main parts of the blah-blah forum system.

A summary of the files in this application is shown in Table 29.1.

Table 29.1   **Files in the Web Forum Application**

Name	Type	Description
index.php	Application	The main page users will see when they enter the site. Contains an expandable and collapsible list of all the articles on the site.
new_post.php	Application	Form used for posting new articles.
store_new_post.php	Application	Stores articles entered in the new_post.php form.
view_post.php	Application	Displays an individual post and a list of the replies to that post.
treenode_class.php	Library	Contains the treenode class, which we will use to display the hierarchy of posts.
include_fns.php	Library	Brings all the other function libraries for this application together (the other Library-type files listed here).
data_valid_fns.php	Library	Data validation functions.
db_fns.php	Library	Database connectivity functions.
discussion_fns.php	Library	Functions for dealing with storing and retrieving postings.
output_fns.php	Library	Functions for outputting HTML.
create_database.sql	SQL	SQL to set up the database required for this application.

Let's go ahead and look at the implementation.

Designing the Database

There are a few attributes we'll need to store about each article posted to the forum: the person who wrote it, called the *poster*; the title of the article; when it was posted; and the article body. We will therefore need a table of articles. We'll create a unique ID for each article, called the postid.

Each article needs to have some information about where it belongs in the hierarchy. We could store information about an article's children with the article. However, each article can have many replies, so this can lead to some problems in database construction. As each article can only be a reply to one other, it is easier to store a reference to the parent article, that is, the article that this article is replying to.

That gives us the following data to store for each article:

- `postid`: A unique ID for each article
- `parent`: The `postid` of the parent article
- `poster`: The author of this article
- `title`: The title of this article
- `posted`: The date and time that the article was posted
- `message`: The body of the article

We will add a couple of optimizations to this.

When we are trying to determine whether an article has any replies, we will have to run a query to see whether any other articles have this article as a parent. We will need this information for every post that we list. The fewer queries we have to run, the faster our code will run. We can remove the need for these queries by adding a field to show whether there are any replies. We will call this field `children` and make it effectively Boolean—the value will be 1 if the node has children, and 0 if it does not.

There is always a price to pay for optimizations. Here we are choosing to store redundant data. As we are storing the data in two ways, we must be careful to make sure that the two representations agree with each other. When we add children, we must update the parent. If we allow the deletion of children, we need to update the parent node to make sure the database is consistent. In this project we are not going to build a facility for deleting articles, so we will avoid half of this problem. If you decide to extend this code, bear this issue in mind.

It is worth noting that some databases would help us out a little more here. If we were using Oracle, it could maintain relational integrity for us. Using MySQL, which does not support triggers or foreign key constraints, we need to write our own checks and balances to make sure that data still makes sense each time we add or delete a record.

We will make one other optimization: We will separate the message bodies from the other data and store them in a separate table. The reason for this is that this attribute will have the MySQL type `text`. Having this type in a table can slow down queries on that table. Because we will do many small queries to build the tree structure, this would slow it down quite a lot. With the message bodies in a separate table, we can just retrieve them when a user wants to look at a particular message.

MySQL can search fixed size records faster than variable sized records. If we need to use variable sized data, we can help by creating indexes on the fields that will be used to search the database. For some projects, we would be best served by leaving the text field in the same record as everything else and specifying indexes on all the columns that we will search on. Indexes take time to generate though, and the data in our forums is likely to be changing all the time, so we would need to regenerate our indexes frequently.

We will also add an `area` attribute in case we later decide to implement multiple chats with the one application. We won't implement this here, but this way it is reserved for future use.

Given all these considerations, the SQL to create the database for the forum database is shown in Listing 29.1.

Listing 29.1   **create_database.sql—SQL to Create the Discussion Database**

```
create database discussion;

use discussion;

create table header
(
  parent int not null,
  poster char(20) not null,
  title char(20) not null,
  children int default 0 not null,
  area int default 1 not null,
  posted datetime not null,
  postid int unsigned not null auto_increment primary key
);

create table body
(
  postid int unsigned not null primary key,
  message text
);



grant select, insert, update, delete
on discussion.*
to discussion@localhost identified by 'password';
```

You can create this database structure by running this script through MySQL as follows:

```
mysql -u root -p < create_database.sql
```

You will need to supply your root password. You should probably also change the password we have set up for the discussion user to something better.

To understand how this structure will hold articles and their relationship to each other, look at Figure 29.3.

As you can see, the parent field for each article in the database holds the `postid` of the article above it in the tree. The parent article is the article that is being replied to.

You can also see that the root node, `postid` 1, has no parent. All new topics of discussion will be in this position. For articles of this type, we store their parent as a 0 (zero) in the database.

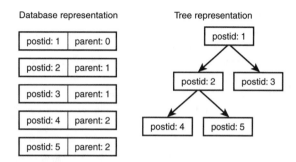

Figure 29.3   The database holds the tree structure in a flattened
relational form.

Viewing the Tree of Articles

Next, we need a way of getting information out of the database and representing it back
in the tree structure. We will do this with the main page, index.php. For the purposes of
this explanation, we have input some sample posts via the article posting scripts
new_post.php and store_new_post.php. We will look at these in the next section.

We will cover the article list first because it is the backbone of the site. After this,
everything else will be easy.

Figure 29.4 shows the initial view of the articles in the site that a user would see.

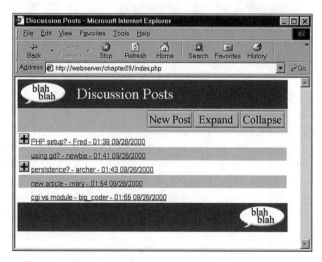

Figure 29.4   The initial view of the article list shows the
articles in "collapsed" form.

What we see here are all the initiating articles. None of these are replies; they are all the first article on a particular topic.

You will see that we have a number of options. There is a menu bar that will let us add a new post and expand or collapse the view that we have of the articles.

To understand what this means, look at the posts. Some of them have plus symbols next to them. This means that these articles have been replied to. To see the replies to a particular article, you can click the plus symbol. The result of clicking one of these symbols is shown in Figure 29.5.

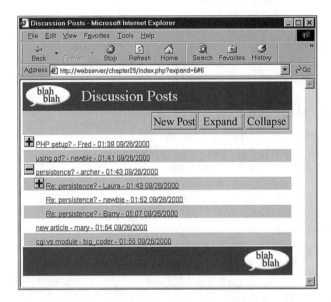

Figure 29.5   The thread of discussion about persistence has been expanded.

As you can see, clicking the plus symbol has displayed the replies to that first article. The plus symbol has now turned to a minus symbol. If we click this, all the articles in this thread will be collapsed, returning us to the initial view.

You might also notice that one of the replies has a plus symbol next to it. This means that there are replies to this reply. This can continue to an arbitrary depth, and you can view each reply set by clicking on the appropriate plus symbol.

The two menu bar options, Expand and Collapse, will expand all possible threads and collapse all possible threads, respectively. The result of clicking the Expand button is shown in Figure 29.6.

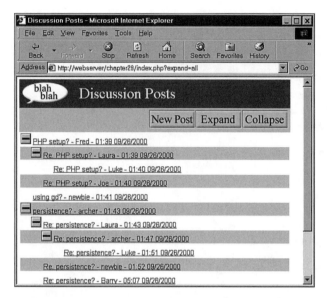

Figure 29.6   All the threads have now been expanded.

If you look closely at Figures 29.5 and 29.6, you can see that we are passing some parameters back to `index.php` in the command line. In Figure 29.5, the URL looks as follows:

```
http://webserver/chapter29/index.php?expand=6#6
```

The script reads this as "Expand the item with postid 6". The # is just an HTML anchor that will scroll the page down to the part that has just been expanded.

In Figure 29.6, the URL reads

```
http://webserver/chapter29/index.php?expand=all
```

Clicking the Expand button has passed the parameter `expand` with the value `all`.

Expanding and Collapsing

Let's see how it's done by looking at the `index.php` script, shown in Listing 29.2.

Listing 29.2   **index.php—Script to Create the Article View on the Main Page of the Application**

```php
<?php
  include ('include_fns.php');
  session_start();

  // check if we have created our session variable
  if(!isset($HTTP_SESSION_VARS['expanded']))
```

Listing 29.2   **Continued**

```
  {
    $HTTP_SESSION_VARS['expanded'] = array();
  }

  // check if an expand button was pressed
  // expand might equal 'all' or a postid or not be set
  if(isset($HTTP_GET_VARS['expand']))
  {
    if($HTTP_GET_VARS['expand'] == 'all')
      expand_all($HTTP_SESSION_VARS['expanded']);
    else
      $HTTP_SESSION_VARS['expanded'][$HTTP_GET_VARS['expand']] = true;
  }

  // check if a collapse button was pressed
  // collapse might equal all or a postid or not be set
  if(isset($HTTP_GET_VARS['collapse']))
  {
    if($HTTP_GET_VARS['collapse']=='all')
      $HTTP_SESSION_VARS['expanded'] = array();
    else
      unset($HTTP_SESSION_VARS['expanded'][$HTTP_GET_VARS['collapse']]);
  }

  do_html_header('Discussion Posts');

  display_index_toolbar();

  // display the tree view of conversations
  display_tree($HTTP_SESSION_VARS['expanded']);

  do_html_footer();
?>
```

This script uses three variables to do its job. They are

- The session variable expanded, which keeps track of which threads are expanded.
  This can be maintained from view to view, so we can have multiple threads
  expanded. This variable is an associative array that contains the postid of articles
  which will have their replies displayed expanded.
- The parameter expand, which tells the script which new threads to expand.
- The parameter collapse, which tells the script which threads to collapse.

When we click a plus or minus symbol or the Expand or Collapse button, they will recall the index.php script with new parameters for expand or collapse. We use

expanded from page to page to track which threads should be expanded in any given view.

The script begins by starting a session and adding the expanded variable as a session variable if this has not already been done.

After that, the script checks whether it has been passed an expand or collapse parameter and modifies the expanded array accordingly. Look at the code for the expand parameter:

```
if(isset($HTTP_GET_VARS['expand']))
{
  if($HTTP_GET_VARS['expand'] == 'all')
    expand_all($HTTP_SESSION_VARS['expanded']);
  else
    $HTTP_SESSION_VARS['expanded'][$HTTP_GET_VARS['expand']] = true;
}
```

If we have clicked on the Expand button, the function expand_all() is called to add all the threads that have replies into the expanded array. (We'll look at this in a moment.)

If we are trying to expand a particular thread, we will have been passed a postid via expand. We therefore add a new entry to the expanded array to reflect this.

The expand_all() function is shown in Listing 29.3.

Listing 29.3   **expand_all() Function from discussion_fns.php—Processes the $expanded Array to Expand All the Threads in the Forum**

```
function expand_all(&$expanded)
{
  // mark all threads with children as to be shown expanded
  $conn = db_connect();
  $query = 'select postid from header where children = 1';
  $result = mysql_query($query);
  $num = mysql_numrows($result);
  for($i = 0; $i<$num; $i++)
  {
    $expanded[mysql_result($result, $i, 0)]=true;
  }
}
```

This function runs a database query to work out which of the threads in the forum have replies, as follows:

```
select postid from header where children = 1
```

Each of the articles returned is then added to the expanded array. We run this query to save time later. We could simply add all articles to the expanded list, but it would be wasteful to try processing replies that do not exist.

Collapsing the articles works in a similar but opposite way, as follows:

```
if(isset($HTTP_GET_VARS['collapse']))
{
  if($HTTP_GET_VARS['collapse']=='all')
    $HTTP_SESSION_VARS['expanded'] = array();
  else
    unset($HTTP_SESSION_VARS['expanded'][$HTTP_GET_VARS['collapse']]);
}
```

You can remove items from the `expanded` array by unsetting them. We remove the thread that is to be collapsed, or unset the entire array if the entire page is to be collapsed.

All this is preprocessing, so we know which articles should be displayed and which should not. The key part of the script is the call to `display_tree($HTTP_SESSION_VARS['expanded'])`; which will actually generate the tree of displayed articles.

Displaying the Articles

Let's look at the `display_tree()` function, shown in Listing 29.4.

Listing 29.4 **display_tree() Function from output_fns.php—Creates the Root Node of the Tree Structure**

```
function display_tree($expanded, $row = 0, $start = 0)
{
  // display the tree view of conversations

  global $table_width;
  echo "<table width=\"$table_width\">";

  // see if we are displaying the whole list or a sublist
  if($start>0)
    $sublist = true;
  else
    $sublist = false;

  // construct tree structure to represent conversation summary
  $tree = new treenode($start, '', '', '', 1, true, -1, $expanded, $sublist);

  // tell tree to display itself
  $tree->display($row, $sublist);

  echo '</table>';
}
```

The main role of this function is to create the root node of the tree structure. We use it both to display the whole index and to create subtrees of replies on the view_post.php page. As you can see, it takes three parameters. The first, $expanded, is the list of article postids to display in an expanded fashion. The second, $row, is an indicator of the row number which will be used to work out the alternating colors of the rows in the list.

The third parameter, $start, tells the function where to start displaying articles. This is the postid of the root node for the tree to be created and displayed. If we are displaying the whole thing, as we are on the main page, this will be 0 (zero), meaning display all the articles with no parent. If this parameter is 0, we set $sublist to false and display the whole tree.

If the parameter is greater than 0, we use it as the root node of the tree to display, set $sublist to true and build and display only part of the tree. (We will use this in the view_post.php script.)

The most important thing this function does is instantiate an instance of the treenode class that represents the root of the tree. This is not actually an article but it acts as the parent of all the first level articles, which have no parent. After the tree has been constructed, we simply call its display function to actually display the list of articles.

Using the treenode Class

The code for the treenode class is shown in Listing 29.5. (You might find it useful at this stage to look over Chapter 6, "Object-Oriented PHP," to remind yourself how classes work.)

Listing 29.5   **treenode Class from treenode_class.php—The Backbone of the Application**

```php
<?php
// functions for loading, contructing and
// displaying the tree are in this file

class treenode
{
  // each node in the tree has member variables containing
  // all the data for a post except the body of the message
  var $m_postid;
  var $m_title;
  var $m_poster;
  var $m_posted;
  var $m_children;
  var $m_childlist;
  var $m_depth;

  function treenode($postid, $title, $poster, $posted, $children,
                    $expand, $depth, $expanded, $sublist)
```

Listing 29.5 **Continued**

```
{
  // the constructor sets up the member variables, but more
  // importantly recursively creates lower parts of the tree
  $this->m_postid = $postid;
  $this->m_title = $title;
  $this->m_poster = $poster;
  $this->m_posted = $posted;
  $this->m_children =$children;
  $this->m_childlist = array();
  $this->m_depth = $depth;

  // we only care what is below this node if it
  // has children and is marked to be expanded
  // sublists are always expanded
  if(($sublist||$expand) && $children)
  {
    $conn = db_connect();

    $query = "select * from header where parent = $postid order by posted";
    $result = mysql_query($query);

    for ($count=0; $row = @mysql_fetch_array($result); $count++)
    {
      if($sublist||$expanded[ $row['postid'] ] == true)
        $expand = true;
      else
        $expand = false;
      $this->m_childlist[$count]= new treenode($row['postid'],$row['title'],
                                  $row['poster'],$row['posted'],
                                  $row['children'], $expand,
                                  $depth+1, $expanded, $sublist);
    }
  }
}


function display($row, $sublist = false)
{
  // as this is an object, it is responsible for displaying itself

  // $row tells us what row of the display we are up to
  // so we know what color it should be

  // $sublist tells us whether we are on the main page
  // or the message page.  Message pages should have
  // $sublist = true.
```

Listing 29.5   **Continued**

```
// On a sublist, all messages are expanded and there are
// no "+" or "-" symbols.

// if this is the empty root node skip displaying
if($this->m_depth>-1)
{
  //color alternate rows
  echo '<tr><td bgcolor="';
  if ($row%2)
    echo '#cccccc">';
  else
    echo '#ffffff">';

  // indent replies to the depth of nesting
  for($i = 0; $i<$this->m_depth; $i++)
  {
    echo '<img src="images/spacer.gif" height="22"
                   width="22" alt="" valign="bottom">';
  }

  // display + or - or a spacer
  if ( !$sublist && $this->m_children && sizeof($this->m_childlist))
  // we're on the main page, have some children, and they're expanded
  {
    // we are expanded - offer button to collapse
    echo '<a href="index.php?collapse='.
                    $this->m_postid.'#'.$this->m_postid.'"
         ><img src="images/minus.gif" valign="bottom"
         height="22" width="22" alt="Collapse Thread" border="0"></a>';
  }
  else if(!$sublist && $this->m_children)
  {
    // we are collapsed - offer button to expand
    echo '<a href="index.php?expand='.
         $this->m_postid.'#'.$this->m_postid.'"><img src="images/plus.gif"
         height="22" width="22" alt="Expand Thread" border="0"></a>';
  }
  else
  {
    // we have no children, or are in a sublist, do not give button
    echo '<img src="images/spacer.gif" height="22" width="22"
            alt="" valign="bottom">';
  }


  echo " <a name = $this->m_postid ><a href =
```

Listing 29.5   **Continued**

```
                'view_post.php?postid=$this->m_postid'>$this->m_title -
                $this->m_poster - ".reformat_date($this->m_posted).'</a>';
        echo '</td></tr>';

        // increment row counter to alternate colors
        $row++;
    }
    // call display on each of this node's children
    // note a node will only have children in its list if expanded
    $num_children = sizeof($this->m_childlist);
    for($i = 0; $i<$num_children; $i++)
    {
        $row = $this->m_childlist[$i]->display($row, $sublist);
    }
    return $row;
  }

};

?>
```

This class contains the functionality that drives the tree view in this application.

One instance of the treenode class contains details about a single posting and links to all the reply postings of that class. This gives us the following member variables:

```
var $m_postid;
var $m_title;
var $m_poster;
var $m_posted;
var $m_children;
var $m_childlist;
var $m_depth;
```

Notice that the treenode does not contain the body of the article. There is no need to load this until a user goes to the view_post.php script. We need to try to make this relatively fast, as we are doing a lot of data manipulation to display the tree list, and need to recalculate when the page is refreshed, or a button is pressed.

The naming scheme for these variables follows a naming scheme commonly used in OO applications—starting variables with m_ to remind us that they are member variables of the class.

Most of these variables correspond directly to rows from the header table in our database.

The exceptions are $m_childlist and $m_depth. We will use the variable $m_childlist to hold the replies to this article. The variable $m_depth will hold the number of tree levels that we are down—this will be used for creating the display.

The constructor function sets up the values of all the variables, as follows:

```
function treenode($postid, $title, $poster, $posted, $children,
                  $expand, $depth, $expanded, $sublist)
{
  // the constructor sets up the member variables, but more
  // importantly recursively creates lower parts of the tree
  $this->m_postid = $postid;
  $this->m_title = $title;
  $this->m_poster = $poster;
  $this->m_posted = $posted;
  $this->m_children =$children;
  $this->m_childlist = array();
  $this->m_depth = $depth;
```

When we construct the root treenode from display_tree() from the main page, we are actually creating a –*dummy* node with no article associated with it. We pass in some initial values:

```
$tree = new treenode($start, '', '', '', 1, true, -1, $expanded, $sublist);
```

This creates a root node with a $postid of zero. This can be used to find all the first-level postings because they have a parent of zero. We set the depth to -1 because this node isn't actually part of the display. All the first-level postings will have a depth of zero, and be at the far left of the screen. Subsequent depths step toward the right.

The most important thing that happens in this constructor is that the children nodes of this node are instantiated. We begin this process by checking if we need to expand the children nodes. We only perform this process if a node has some children, and we have elected to display them:

```
    if(($sublist||$expand) && $children)
    {
      $conn = db_connect();
```

We then connect to the database, and retrieve all the child posts, as follows:

```
      $query = "select * from header where parent = $postid order by posted";
      $result = mysql_query($query);
```

We then fill the array $m_childlist with instances of the treenode class, containing the replies to the post stored in this treenode, as follows:

```
for ($count=0; $row = @mysql_fetch_array($result); $count++)
{
  if($sublist||$expanded[ $row['postid'] ] == true)
    $expand = true;
  else
    $expand = false;
  $this->m_childlist[$count]= new treenode($row['postid'],$row['title'],
                                 $row['poster'],$row['posted'],
```

```
                                $row['children'], $expand,
                                $depth+1, $expanded, $sublist);
    }
```

This last line will create the new `treenodes`, following exactly the same process we have just walked through, but for the next level down the tree. This is the recursive part. A parent tree node is calling the `treenode` constructor, passing its own `postid` as parent, and adding one to its own depth before passing it.

Each `treenode` in turn will be created and create its own children until we run out of replies or levels that we want to expand to.

After all that's done, we call the root `treenode`'s display function (this is back in `display_tree()`), as follows:

```
$tree->display($row, $sublist);
```

The `display()` function begins by checking whether this is the dummy root node:

```
if($this->m_depth>-1)
```

In this way, the dummy can be left out of the display. We don't want to completely skip the root node though. We do not want it to appear, but it needs to notify its children that they need to display themselves.

The function then starts drawing the table containing the articles. It uses the modulus operator (`%`) to decide what color background this row should have (hence they alternate):

```
//color alternate rows
echo '<tr><td bgcolor = ';
if ($row%2)
  echo "'#cccccc'>";
else
  echo "'#ffffff'>";
```

It then uses the `$m_depth` member variable to work out how much to indent the current item. You will see by looking back at the figures that the deeper level a reply is on, the further it is indented. This is done as follows:

```
// indent replies to the depth of nesting
for($i = 0; $i<$this->m_depth; $i++)
{
  echo '<img src="images/spacer.gif" height="22"
                width="22" alt="" valign="bottom">';
}
```

The next part of the function works out whether to supply a plus or minus button or nothing at all:

```
// display + or - or a spacer
if ( !$sublist && $this->m_children && sizeof($this->m_childlist))
```

```
// we're on the main page, have some children, and they're expanded
{
  // we are expanded - offer button to collapse
      echo '<a href="index.php?collapse='.
          $this->m_postid.'#'.$this->m_postid.'"
      ><img src="images/minus.gif" valign="bottom"
      height="22" width="22" alt="Collapse Thread" border="0"></a>';
}
else if(!$sublist && $this->m_children)
{
  // we are collapsed - offer button to expand
  echo '<a href = "index.php?expand='.
      $this->m_postid.'#'.$this->m_postid.'"><img src="images/plus.gif"
      height="22" width="22" alt="Expand Thread" border="0"></a>';
}
else
{
  // we have no children, or are in a sublist, do not give button
  echo '<img src="images/spacer.gif" height="22" width="22"
          alt="" valign="bottom">';
}
```

Next, we display the actual details of this node:

```
echo " <a name = $this->m_postid ><a href =
          'view_post.php?postid=$this->m_postid'>$this->m_title -
          $this->m_poster - ".reformat_date($this->m_posted).'</a>';
echo '</td></tr>';
```

We change the color for the next row:

```
// increment row counter to alternate colors
$row++;
```

After that, there is some code that will be executed by all treenodes, including the root one, as follows:

```
// call display on each of this node's children
// note a node will only have children in its list if expanded
$num_children = sizeof($this->m_childlist);
for($i = 0; $i<$num_children; $i++)
{
  $row = $this->m_childlist[$i]->display($row, $sublist);
}
return $row;
```

Again this is a recursive function call, which calls on each of this node's children to display themselves. We pass them the current row color and get them to pass it back when they are finished with it, so we can keep track of the alternating color.

That's it for this class. The code is fairly complex. You might like to experiment with running the application and then come back to look at it again when you are comfortable with what it does.

Viewing Individual Articles

The `display_tree()` call ends up giving us links to a set of articles. If we click one of these articles, we will go to the `view_post.php` script, with a parameter of the `postid` of the article to be viewed. Sample output from this script is shown in Figure 29.7.

Figure 29.7   We can now see the message body for this posting.

This script shows us the message body, as well as the replies to this message. You will see that the replies are again displayed as a tree, but completely expanded this time, and without any plus or minus buttons. This is the effect of the `$sublist` switch coming into action.

Let's look at the code for `view_post.php`, shown in Listing 29.6.

Listing 29.6   **view_post.php—Displays a Single Message Body**

```php
<?php
  // include function libraries
  include ('include_fns.php');
```

Listing 29.6   **Continued**

```
$postid = $HTTP_GET_VARS['postid'];
// get post details
$post = get_post($postid);

do_html_header($post['title']);

// display post
display_post($post);

// if post has any replies, show the tree view of them
if($post['children'])
{
  echo '<br /><br />';
  display_replies_line();
  display_tree($HTTP_SESSION_VARS['expanded'], 0, $postid);
}

do_html_footer();
?>
```

This script uses three main function calls to do its job: get_post(), display_post(), and display_tree().

The get_post() function pulls the function details out of the database. The code for this function is shown in Listing 29.7.

Listing 29.7   **get_post() Function from discussion_fns.php—Retrieves a Message from the Database**

```
function get_post($postid)
{
  // extract one post from the database and return as an array

  if(!$postid) return false;

  $conn = db_connect();

  //get all header information from 'header'
  $query = "select * from header where postid = $postid";
  $result = mysql_query($query);
  if(mysql_numrows($result)!=1)
    return false;
  $post = mysql_fetch_array($result);

  // get message from body and add it to the previous result
  $query = "select * from body where postid = $postid";
  $result2 = mysql_query($query);
```

Listing 29.7   **Continued**

```
  if(mysql_numrows($result2)>0)
  {
    $body = mysql_fetch_array($result2);
    if($body)
    {
      $post['message'] = $body['message'];
    }
  }
  return $post;
}
```

This function, given a `postid`, will perform the two queries required to retrieve the message header and body for that posting, and put them together into a single associative array which it then returns.

The results of this function are then passed to the `display_post()` function from `output_fns.php`. This just prints out the array with some HTML formatting, so we have not included it here.

Finally, the `view_post.php` script checks whether there are any replies to this article and calls `display_tree()` to show them in the sublist format—that is, fully expanded with no plusses or minuses.

Adding New Articles

After all that, we can now look at how a new post is added to the forum. A user can do this in two ways: first, by clicking on the New Post button in the index page, and second, by clicking on the Reply button on the `view_post.php` page.

These actions both activate the same script, `new_post.php`, just with different parameters. Figure 29.8 shows the output from `new_post.php` when we have reached it by hitting the Reply button.

First, look at the URL:

```
http://webserver/chapter29/new_post.php?parent=5
```

The parameter passed in as `parent` will be the parent `postid` of the new posting. If you click New Post instead of Reply, you will get `parent=0` in the URL.

Second, you will see that for a reply, the text of the original message is inserted and marked with a ">" character as is the case in most mail and news reading programs.

Third, you can see that the title of this message defaults to the title of the original message prefixed with "Re:".

Let's look at the code that produces this output. It is shown in Listing 29.8.

Figure 29.8   Replies have the text of the original automatically inserted and marked.

Listing 29.8   **new_post.php—Allows a User to Type a New Post or Reply to an Existing Post**

```php
<?php
  include ('include_fns.php');

  $title = $HTTP_POST_VARS['title'];
  $poster = $HTTP_POST_VARS['poster'];
  $message = $HTTP_POST_VARS['message'];

  if(isset($HTTP_GET_VARS['parent']))
     $parent = $HTTP_GET_VARS['parent'];
  else
    $parent = $HTTP_POST_VARS['parent'];


  if(!$area)
    $area = 1;

  if(!$error)
  {
    if(!$parent)
```

Listing 29.8   **Continued**

```
    {
      $parent = 0;
      if(!$title)
        $title = 'New Post';
    }
    else
    {
      // get post name
      $title = get_post_title($parent);

      // append Re:
      if(strstr($title, 'Re: ') == false )
        $title = 'Re: '.$title;

      //make sure title will still fit in db
      $title = substr($title, 0, 20);

      //prepend a quoting pattern to the post you are replying to
      $message = add_quoting(get_post_message($parent));
    }
  }
  do_html_header($title);

  display_new_post_form($parent, $area, $title, $message, $poster);

  if($error)
  {
    echo 'Your message was not stored.
          Make sure you have filled in all fields and try again.';
  }

  do_html_footer();
?>
```

After some initial setting up, this script checks whether the parent is zero or otherwise. If it is zero, this is a new topic, and little further work is needed.

If this is a reply ($parent is the postid of an existing article), then the script goes ahead and sets up the title and the text of the original message, as follows:

```
// get post name
$title = get_post_title($parent);

// append Re:
if(strstr($title, 'Re: ') == false )
  $title = 'Re: '.$title;
```

```
//make sure title will still fit in db
$title = substr($title, 0, 20);

//prepend a quoting pattern to the post you are replying to
$message = add_quoting(get_post_message($parent));
```

The functions it uses here are `get_post_title()`, `get_post_message()`, and `add_quoting()`. These functions are all from the `discussion_fns.php` library. They are shown in Listings 29.9, 29.10, and 29.11, respectively.

Listing 29.9 **get_post_title() Function from discussion_fns.php—Retrieves a Message's Title from the Database**

```php
function get_post_title($postid)
{
  // extract one post's name from the database

  if(!$postid) return '';

  $conn = db_connect();

  //get all header information from 'header'
  $query = "select title from header where postid = $postid";
  $result = mysql_query($query);
  if(mysql_numrows($result)!=1)
    return '';
  return  mysql_result($result, 0, 0);

}
```

Listing 29.10 **get_post_message() Function from discussion_fns.php—Retrieves a Message's Body from the Database**

```php
function get_post_message($postid)
{
  // extract one post's message from the database

  if(!$postid) return '';

  $conn = db_connect();

  $query = "select message from body where postid = $postid";
  $result = mysql_query($query);
  if(mysql_numrows($result)>0)
  {
    return mysql_result($result,0,0);
  }
}
```

These first two functions retrieve an article's header and body (respectively) from the database.

Listing 29.11   **add_quoting() Function from discussion_fns.php—Indents a Message Text with ">" Symbols**

```
function add_quoting($string, $pattern = '> ')
{
  // add a quoting pattern to mark text quoted in your reply
  return $pattern.str_replace("\n", "\n$pattern", $string);
}
```

The `add_quoting()` function reformats the string to begin each line of the original text with a symbol, which defaults to >.

After the user types in his reply and clicks the Post button, he will be taken to the `store_new_post.php` script. Sample output from this script is shown in Figure 29.9.

Figure 29.9   The new post is now visible in the tree.

The new post is there in the figure, under `Re: using gd? - Laura - 08:28 09/26/2000`. Other than that, this page looks like the regular `index.php` page.

Let's look at the code for `store_new_post.php`. It is shown in Listing 29.12.

Listing 29.12   **store_new_post.php—Puts the New Post in the Database**

```
<?php
  include ('include_fns.php');
  if($id = store_new_post($HTTP_POST_VARS))
  {
    include ('index.php');
  }
  else
  {
    $error = true;
    include ('new_post.php');
  }

?>
```

As you can see, this is a short script. Its main task is to call the store_new_post() func-tion. This page has no visual content of its own. If storing succeeds, we see the index page. Otherwise, we go back to the new_post.php page, so the user can try again.

The store_new_post() function is shown in Listing 29.13.

Listing 29.13   **store_new_post() Function from discussion_fns.php—Validates and Stores the New Post in the Database**

```
function store_new_post($post)
{
  // validate clean and store a new post

  $conn = db_connect();
  // check no fields are blank
  if(!filled_out($post))
  {
    return false;
  }
  $post = clean_all($post);

  //check parent exists
  if($post['parent']!=0)
  {
    $query = "select postid from header where postid = '".$post['parent']."'";
    $result = mysql_query($query);
    if(mysql_numrows($result)!=1)
    {
      return false;
    }
  }
}
```

Listing 29.13 **Continued**

```php
// check not a duplicate
$query = "select header.postid from header, body where
          header.postid = body.postid and
          header.parent = ".$post['parent']." and
          header.poster = '".$post['poster']."' and
          header.title = '".$post['title']."' and
          header.area = ".$post['area']." and
          body.message = '".$post['message']."'";
$result = mysql_query($query);
if (!$result)
{
   return false;
}
if(mysql_numrows($result)>0)
   return mysql_result($result, 0, 0);

$query = "insert into header values
          ('".$post['parent']."',
           '".$post['poster']."',
           '".$post['title']."',
           0,
           '".$post['area']."',
           now(),
           NULL
          )";
$result = mysql_query($query);
if (!$result)
{
   return false;
}

// note that our parent now has a child
$query = 'update header set children = 1 where postid = '.$post['parent'];
$result = mysql_query($query);
if (!$result)
{
   return false;
}

// find our post id, note that there could be multiple headers
// that are the same except for id and probably posted time
$query = "select header.postid from header left join body
          on header.postid = body.postid
                 where parent = '".$post['parent']."'";
```

Listing 29.13 **Continued**

```
                     and poster = '".$post['poster']."'
                     and title = '".$post['title']."'
                     and body.postid is NULL";
  $result = mysql_query($query);
  if (!$result)
  {
     return false;
  }
  if(mysql_numrows($result)>0)
    $id = mysql_result($result, 0, 0);

  if($id)
  {
     $query = "insert into body values ($id, '".$post['message']."')";
     $result = mysql_query($query);
     if (!$result)
     {
       return false;
     }

     return $id;
  }

}
```

This is a long function, but it is not overly complex. It is only long because inserting a posting means inserting entries in the header and body tables, and updating the parent article's row in the header table to show that it now has children.

That is the end of the code for the Web forum application.

Extensions

There are many extensions you could add to this project:

- You could add navigation to the view options, so that from a post you could navigate to the next message, the previous message, the next-in-thread message, or the previous-in-thread message.

- You could add an administration interface for setting up new forums and deleting old posts.

- You could add user authentication so only registered users could post.

- You could add some kind of moderation or censorship mechanism.

Look at existing systems for ideas.

Using an Existing System

There are a couple of noteworthy existing systems.

Phorum is an Open Source Web forums project. It has different navigation and semantics from ours, but its structure is relatively easily customized to fit into your own site. A notable feature of phorum is that it can be configured by the actual user to display in either a threaded or flat view. You can find out more about it at

```
http://www.phorum.org
```

Another interesting project is phpslash. This is a port of the software used to run the Slashdot discussion boards. Although the original software is written in Perl, this PHP version is available. You can get it from

```
http://www.phpslash.org
```

Next

In Chapter 30, "Generating Personalized Documents in Portable Document Format (PDF)," we will use the PDF format to deliver documents that are attractive, print consistently, and are somewhat tamperproof. This is useful for a range of service-based applications, such as generating contracts online.

## 30

Generating Personalized
Documents in Portable
Document Format (PDF)

O<small>N SERVICE DRIVEN SITES, WE SOMETIMES NEED</small> to deliver personalized documents,
generated in response to input from our visitors. This can be used to provide an automatically filled in form or to generate personalized documents, such as legal documents,
letters, or certificates.

Our example in this chapter will present a user with an online skill assessment page
and generate a certificate.

We will explain

- How to use PHP string processing to integrate a template with a user's data to
  create a Rich Text Format (RTF) document
- How to use a similar approach to generate a Portable Document Format (PDF)
  document
- How to use PHP's PDFlib functions to generate a similar PDF document

The Problem

We want to be able to give our visitors an exam consisting of a number of questions. If
they answer enough of the questions correctly, we will generate a certificate for them to
show that they have passed the exam.

So that a computer can mark them easily, our questions will be multiple choice, consisting of a question and a number of potential answers. Only one of the potential
answers for each question will be correct.

If a user achieves a passing grade on the questions, he will be presented with a certificate.

Ideally, the file format for our certificate should

1. Be easy to design
2. Be able to contain a variety of different elements such as bitmap and vector images
3. Result in a high quality printout
4. Only require a small file to be downloaded
5. Be generated almost instantly
6. Be at a low cost to produce
7. Work on many operating systems
8. Be difficult to fraudulently duplicate or modify
9. Not require any special software to view or print
10. Display and print consistently for all recipients

Like many decisions we need to make from time to time, we will probably need to compromise when choosing a delivery format to meet as many of these ten attributes as possible.

Evaluating Document Formats

The most important decision we need to make is what format to deliver the certificate in. Options include paper, ASCII text, HTML, Microsoft Word, or another word processor's format, Rich Text Format, PostScript, and Portable Document Format. Given the ten attributes listed previously, we can consider and compare some of our options.

Paper

Delivering the certificate on paper has some obvious advantages. We retain complete control over the process. We can see exactly what each certificate output looks like before sending it to the recipient. We do not need to worry about software or bandwidth, and the certificate could be printed with anti-counterfeiting measures.

It would meet all of our needs except for attributes 5 and 6. The certificate could not be created and delivered quickly. Postal delivery could take days or weeks depending on our and the recipient's location.

Each certificate would also cost us a few cents to a few dollars in printing and postage costs and probably more in handling. Automatic electronic delivery would be cheaper.

ASCII

Delivering documents as ASCII or plain text comes with some advantages. Compatibility will be no problem. Bandwidth required would be small, so cost would be very low. The simplicity of the end result will make it very easy to design and very quick for a script to generate.

If we present our visitors with an ASCII file, however, we have very little control over the appearance of their certificate. We cannot control fonts or page breaks. We can only include text and have very little control over formatting. We have no control over a recipient's duplication or modification of the document. This is the method that makes it easiest for the recipient to fraudulently alter her certificate.

HTML

An obvious choice for delivering a document on the Web is HTML. Hypertext Markup Language is specifically designed for this purpose. As you are no doubt already aware, it includes formatting control, syntax to include objects such as images, and is compatible (with some variation) with a variety of operating systems and software. It is fairly simple, so it will be both easy to design and quick for a script to generate and deliver.

Drawbacks to using HTML for this application include limited support for print related formatting such as page breaks, little consistency in the output on different platforms and programs, and variable quality printing. In addition, although HTML can include any type of external element, the capability of the browser to display or use these elements cannot be guaranteed for unusual types.

Word Processor Formats

Particularly for intranet projects, providing documents as word processor documents makes some sense. However, for an Internet project, using a proprietary word processor format will exclude some visitors, but given its market dominance, Microsoft Word would make sense. Most users will either have access to Word or to a word processor that will try to read Word files.

Windows users without Word can download the freeware Word Viewer from

```
http://www.microsoft.com/office/000/viewers.asp
```

Generating a document as a Microsoft Word document has some advantages. As long as you have a copy of Word, designing a document is easy. We have very good control over the printed appearance of our documents and a lot of flexibility with its contents. You can also make it relatively difficult for the recipient to modify by telling Word to ask for a password.

Unfortunately, Word files can be large, particularly if they contain images or other complex elements. There is also no easy way to generate them dynamically with PHP. The format is documented, but is a binary format and the format documentation comes with license conditions. It is possible to generate Word documents with a COM object but it's definitely not simple.

Another new possibility you may now consider is OpenOffice Writer, which has the dual advantages of not being proprietary software and using an XML based file format.

Rich Text Format

Rich Text Format or RTF gives us most of the power of Word, but the files are easier to generate. We still have flexibility over layout and formatting of the printed page. We can still include elements such as vector or bitmap images. We can still be fairly sure that the user will see a similar result to us when they view or print the document.

RTF is Microsoft Word's text format. It is intended as an interchange format to transfer documents between different programs. In some ways, it is similar to HTML. It uses syntax and key words rather than binary data to convey formatting information. It is therefore relatively human readable.

The format is well documented. The specification is freely available and can be found here:

```
http://msdn.microsoft.com/library/specs/rtfspec.htm
```

The easiest way to generate an RTF document is to choose a Save As RTF option in your word processor. As RTF files contain only text, it is possible to generate them directly and existing ones can easily be modified.

Because the format is documented and freely available, RTF is readable by more software than Word's binary format. Be aware though that users opening a complex RTF file in older versions of Word or different word processors will often see somewhat different results. Each new version of Word introduces new keywords to RTF, so older implementations will usually ignore controls they do not understand or have chosen not to implement.

From our original list, an RTF certificate would be easy to design using Word or another word processor; is able to contain a variety of different elements such as vector and bitmap images; gives a high quality printout; can be generated easily and quickly; and can be delivered electronically at low cost.

It will work with a variety of applications and operating systems, although with somewhat variable results. On the down side, an RTF document can be easily and freely modified by anybody, which is a problem for a certificate and some other types of document. The file size might get moderately large for complex documents.

RTF is a good option for many document delivery applications, so we will use it as one option here.

PostScript

PostScript, from Adobe, is a page description language. It is a powerful and complex programming language intended to represent documents in a device independent way—that is, a description that will produce consistent results across different devices such as printers and screens. It is very well documented. At least three full-length books are available, as well as countless Web sites.

A PostScript document can contain very precise formatting, text, images, embedded fonts, and other elements. You can easily generate a PostScript document from an application by printing it to a PostScript printer driver. If you were interested, you could even learn to program in it directly.

PostScript documents are quite portable. They will give consistent high-quality printouts from different devices and different operating systems.

There are a couple of significant down sides to using PostScript to distribute documents:

- The files can be huge.
- Many people will need to download additional software to use them.

Most Unix users will be able to deal with PostScript files, but Windows users will usually need to download a viewer such as GSview, which uses the Ghostscript PostScript interpreter. This software is available for a wide variety of platforms. Although it is available free, we do not really want to force people to download more software.

You can read more about Ghostscript at

```
http://www.ghostscript.com/
```

and download it from

```
http://www.cs.wisc.edu/~ghost/
```

For our current application, PostScript scores very well for consistent high-quality output, but falls short on most of our other needs.

Portable Document Format

Fortunately, there is a format with most of the power of PostScript, but with significant advantages. The Portable Document Format (also from Adobe) was designed as a way to distribute documents that would behave consistently on different platforms, and deliver predictable high-quality output on screen or on paper.

Adobe describes PDF as "the open de facto standard for electronic document distribution worldwide. Adobe PDF is a universal file format that preserves all of the fonts, formatting, colors, and graphics of any source document, regardless of the application and platform used to create it. PDF files are compact and can be shared, viewed, navigated, and printed exactly as intended by anyone with a free Adobe Acrobat Reader."

PDF is an open format, and documentation is available from here:

```
http://partners.adobe.com/asn/developer/technotes/acrobatpdf.html
```

as well as many other Web sites and an official book.

Judged against our desired attributes, PDF looks very good.

PDF documents give consistent, high-quality output, are capable of containing elements such as bitmap and vector images, can use compression to create a small file, can be delivered electronically and cheaply, are usable on the major operating systems, and can include security controls.

Working against PDF is the fact that most of the software used to create PDF documents is commercial.

A reader is required to view PDF files, but the Acrobat Reader is available free for Windows, Unix, and Macintosh from Adobe. Many visitors to your site will already be familiar with the .pdf extension and will most likely already have the reader installed.

PDF files are a good way to distribute attractive, printable documents, particularly ones that you do not want recipients to be able to easily modify. We will look at two different ways to generate a PDF certificate.

Solution Components

To get the system working, we will need to be able to examine users' knowledge and (assuming that they pass the test) generate a certificate reporting their performance. We will experiment with generating this certificate in three different ways: two using PDF and one using RTF.

Let's look at the requirements of each of these components in some detail.

Question and Answer System

Providing a flexible system for online assessment that allowed a variety of different question types, various media types for supporting information, useful feedback on wrong answers, and clever statistic gathering and reporting, would be a complex task on its own.

In this chapter, we are mainly interested in the challenge of generating customized documents for delivery over the Web, so we will only build a very simple quiz system.

The quiz does not rely on any special software. It uses an HTML form to ask questions and a PHP script to process the answers. We have been doing this since Chapter 1, "PHP Crash Course."

Document Generation Software

No additional software is needed on the Web server to generate RTF or PDF documents from templates, but you will need software to create the templates. In order to use the PHP PDF creation functions, you will need to have compiled PDF support into PHP. (We'll discuss more about this in a minute.)

Software to Create RTF Template

You can use the word processor of your choice to generate RTF files. We used Microsoft Word to create our certificate template. The certificate template is included on the CD-ROM in the Chapter 30 directory.

If you prefer another word processor, it would still be a good idea to test the output in Word as this is the software that the majority of your visitors will be using.

Software to Create PDF Template

PDF documents are a little more difficult to generate. The easiest way is to purchase Adobe Acrobat. This software will let you create high-quality PDFs from various applications. We used Acrobat to create the template file for this project.

To create the file, we used Microsoft Word to design a document. One of the tools in the Acrobat package is Adobe Distiller. Within Distiller, we needed to select a few non-default options. The file must be stored in ASCII format, and compression needs to be turned off. After these are set, creating a PDF file is as easy as printing.

You can find out more about Acrobat here:

```
http://www.adobe.com/products/acrobat/
```

and either buy it online or from a regular software retailer.

Another option to create PDFs is the conversion program ps2pdf, which as the name suggests converts PostScript files into PDF files. This has the advantage of being free, but does not always produce good output for documents with images or non-standard fonts. The ps2pdf converter comes with the Ghostscript package mentioned previously.

Obviously, if you are going to create a PDF file this way, you will need to create a PostScript file first. Unix users will typically use either the a2ps or dvips utilities for this purpose.

If you are working in a Windows environment, you can also create PostScript files without Adobe Distiller, albeit via a slightly more complicated process. You will need to install a PostScript printer driver. For example, you can use the Apple LaserWriter IINT driver. If you don't have a PostScript driver installed, you can download one from Adobe at

```
http://www.adobe.com/support/downloads/product.jsp?product=44&platform=Windows
```

To create your PostScript file, you will need to select this printer and the Print to File option, typically found on the Print dialog box.

Most Windows applications will then produce a file with a .prn extension. This should be a PostScript file. You should probably rename this to be a .ps file. You should be able to view it using GSview or another PostScript viewer, or create a PDF file using the ps2pdf utility.

Be aware that different printer drivers produce PostScript output of varying quality. You might find that some of the PostScript files you produce give errors when run through the ps2pdf utility. We suggest using a different printer driver.

If you only intend to create a small number of PDF files, Adobe's online service might suit you. For $9.99 a month, you can upload files in a number of formats and download a PDF file. The service worked well for our certificate, but does not let you select options that are important for this project. The PDF created will be stored as a binary file and compressed. This makes it very difficult to modify.

This service can be found at

```
http://createpdf.adobe.com/
```

There is a free trial option for this service if you want to test it out.

There is also a free ftp-based interface to ps2pdf at the Net Distillery:

```
http://www.babinszki.com/distiller/
```

Software to Create PDF Programmatically

Support for creating PDF documents is available from within PHP. Two different function libraries are available, with similar intentions. As they rely on external libraries, neither is compiled in to PHP by default.

PHP's PDFlib functions use the PDFlib library, available from

```
http://www.pdflib.com
```

The ClibPDF functions use the ClibPDF library, available from

```
http://www.fastio.com/
```

Both these libraries are similar. They provide an API of functions to generate a PDF document. We have elected to use PDFlib because it seems to be updated and maintained more regularly.

It is worth noting that neither of these libraries are Free Software. Both permit some non-commercial use without charge, but require a license fee if you intend to provide a commercial service using them.

You can see if PDFlib is already installed on your system by checking the output of the function `phpinfo()`. Under the heading pdf, you can find out if PDFlib support is enabled, as well as the version of PDFlib used.

If you intend to use TIFF or JPEG images in your PDF documents, you will also need to install the TIFF library, available from

```
http://www.libtiff.org/
```

and the JPEG library, available from

```
ftp://ftp.uu.net/graphics/jpeg/
```

On a Unix system, these pieces of software are installed in the usual way, using `configure` and `make`. You will need to recompile PHP with the switch `--with-pdflib`.

On a Windows server, the PDFlib DLL is bundled in the PHP Zip file, so you will just need to uncomment the extension in your `php.ini file`.

Solution Overview

We will produce a system with three possible outcomes. As shown in Figure 30.1, we will ask quiz questions, assess the answers, and then generate a certificate in one of three ways:

- We will generate an RTF document from a blank template.
- We will generate a PDF document from a blank template.
- We will generate a PDF document programmatically via PDFlib.

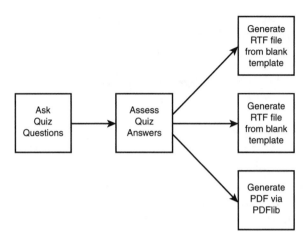

Figure 30.1   Our certification system will generate one of
three different certificates.

A summary of the files in the certification project is shown in Table 30.1.

Table 30.1   **Files in the Certification Application**

Name	Type	Description
index.html	HTML page	The HTML form that contains the quiz questions
score.php	Application	Script to assess users' answers
rtf.php	Application	Script to generate RTF certificate from template
pdf.php	Application	Script to generate PDF certificate from template
pdflib.php	Application	Script to generate PDF certificate using PDFlib
signature.png	image	Bitmap image of signature to be included on the PDFlib certificate
PHPCertification.rtf	RTF	RTF certificate template
PHPCertification.pdf	PDF	PDF certificate template

Let's go ahead and look at the application.

Asking the Questions

The file index.html is straightforward. It needs to contain an HTML form asking the user for his name, and the answer to a number of questions. In a real assessment application, we would most likely retrieve these questions from a database. Here we are focusing on producing the certificate, so we will just hard-code some questions into the HTML.

The name field is a text input. Each question has three radio buttons to allow the user to indicate his preferred answer. The form has an image button as a submit button.

The code for this page is shown in Listing 30.1.

Listing 30.1   **index.html—HTML Page Containing Quiz Questions**

```html
<html>
  <body>
    <h1><p align="center">
        <img src="rosette.gif" alt="">
        Certification
        <img src="rosette.gif" alt=""></p></h1>
    <p>You too can earn your highly respected PHP certification
      from the world famous Fictional Institute of PHP Certification.</p>
    <p>Simply answer the questions below:</p>

    <form action="score.php" method="post">

      <p>Your Name <input type="text" name="name"></p>

      <p>What does the PHP statement echo do?</p>
      <ol>
        <li><input type="radio" name="q1" value="1">
            Outputs strings.</li>
        <li><input type="radio" name="q1" value="2">
            Adds two numbers together.</li>
        <li><input type="radio" name="q1" value="3">
            Creates a magical elf to finish writing your code.</li>
      </ol>

      <p>What does the PHP function cos() do?</p>
      <ol>
        <li><input type="radio" name="q2" value="1">
            Calculates a cosine in radians.</li>
        <li><input type="radio" name="q2" value="2">
            Calculates a tangent in radians. </li>
        <li><input type="radio" name="q2" value="3">
            It is not a PHP function it is a lettuce. </li>
      </ol>

      <p>What does the PHP function mail() do?</p>
      <ol>
        <li><input type="radio" name="q3" value="1">
            Sends a mail message.</li>
        <li><input type="radio" name="q3" value="2">
            Checks for new mail.</li>
        <li><input type="radio" name="q3" value="3">
```

Listing 30.1 **Continued**

```
            Toggles PHP between male and female mode.
    </ol>

    <p align="center"><input type="image" src="certify-me.gif" border="0"></p>

    </form>
  </body>
</html>
```

The result of loading `index.html` in a Web browser is shown in Figure 30.2.

Figure 30.2   `index.html` asks the user to answer quiz questions.

Grading the Answers

When the user submits his answers to the questions in `index.html`, we need to grade him and calculate a score. This is done by the script called `score.php`. The code for this script is shown in Listing 30.2.

Listing 30.2   **score.php—Script to Mark Exams**

```php
<?php
  //create short variable names
  $q1 = $HTTP_POST_VARS['q1'];
  $q2 = $HTTP_POST_VARS['q2'];
  $q3 = $HTTP_POST_VARS['q3'];
  $name = $HTTP_POST_VARS['name'];

  // check that all the data was received
  if($q1==''||$q2==''||$q3==''||$name=='')
  {
    echo '<h1><p align = center><img src="rosette.gif" alt="">
                            Sorry:
                            <img src="rosette.gif" alt=""></p></h1>';
    echo '<p>You need to fill in your name and answer all questions</p>';
  }
  else
  {
    //add up the scores
    $score = 0;
    if($q1 == 1) // the correct answer for q1 is 1
      $score++;
    if($q2 == 1) // the correct answer for q2 is 1
      $score++;
    if($q3 == 1) // the correct answer for q3 is 1
      $score++;

    //convert score to a percentage
    $score = $score / 3 * 100;

    if($score < 50)
    {
      // this person failed
      echo '<h1 align="center"><img src="rosette.gif" alt="" />
                            Sorry:
                            <img src="rosette.gif" alt="" /></h1>';
      echo '<p>You need to score at least 50% to pass the exam</p>';
    }
    else
    {
      // create a string containing the score to one decimal place
      $score = number_format($score, 1);

      echo '<h1 align="center"><img src="rosette.gif" alt="" />
```

Listing 30.2 **Continued**

```
                                        Congratulations
                                        <img src="rosette.gif" alt="" /></h1>';
    echo "<p>Well done $name, with a score of $score%,
            you have passed the exam.</p>";

    // provide links to scripts that generate the certificates
    echo '<p>Please click here to download your certificate as
            a Microsoft Word (RTF) file.</p>';
    echo '<form action="rtf.php" method="post">';
    echo '<center>
            <input type="image" src="certificate.gif" border="0">
            </center>';
    echo '<input type="hidden" name="score" value="'.$score.'">';
    echo '<input type="hidden" name="name" value="'.$name.'">';
    echo '</form>';

    echo '<p>Please click here to download your certificate as
            a Portable Document Format (PDF) file.</p>';
    echo '<form action="pdf.php" method="post">';
    echo '<center>
            <input type="image" src="certificate.gif" border="0">
            </center>';
    echo '<input type="hidden" name="score" value="'.$score.'">';
    echo '<input type="hidden" name="name" value="'.$name.'">';
    echo '</form>';

    echo '<p>Please click here to download your certificate as
            a Portable Document Format (PDF) file generated with PDFLib.</p>';
    echo '<form action="pdflib.php" method="post">';
    echo '<center>
            <input type="image" src="certificate.gif" border="0">
            </center>';
    echo '<input type="hidden" name="score" value="'.$score.'">';
    echo '<input type="hidden" name="name" value="'.$name.'">';
    echo '</form>';
    }
}
?>
```

This script will display a message if the user did not answer all questions or scored less than our chosen pass mark.

If the user successfully answered the questions, he will be allowed to generate a certificate. The output of a successful visit is shown in Figure 30.3.

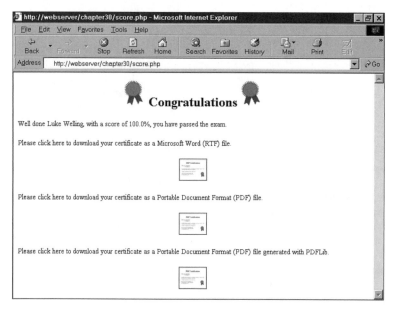

Figure 30.3   `score.php` presents successful visitors with the option
to generate a certificate in one of three ways.

From here, the user has three options. He can have an RTF certificate, or one of two PDF certificates. We will look at the script responsible for each.

Generating an RTF Certificate

There is nothing to stop us from generating an RTF document by writing ASCII text to a file or a string variable, but it would mean learning yet another set of syntax.

Here is a very simple RTF document:

```
{\rtf1
{\fonttbl {\f0 Arial;}{\f1 Times New Roman;}}
\f0\fs28 Heading\par
\f1\fs20 This is an rtf document.\par
}
```

This document sets up a font table with two fonts: Arial, to be referred to as `f0`, and Times New Roman, to be referred to as `f1`. It then writes Heading using `f0` (Arial) in size 28 (14 point). The control `\par` indicates a paragraph break. We then write `This is an rtf document` using `f1` (Times New Roman) at size 20 (10 point).

We could generate a document like this manually, but there are no labor saving functions built in to PHP to make the hard parts, such as incorporating graphics, easier. Fortunately, in many documents, the structure, style, and much of the text are static, and only small parts change from person to person. A more efficient way to generate a document is using a template.

We can build a complex document, such as the one shown in Figure 30.4, easily using a word processor.

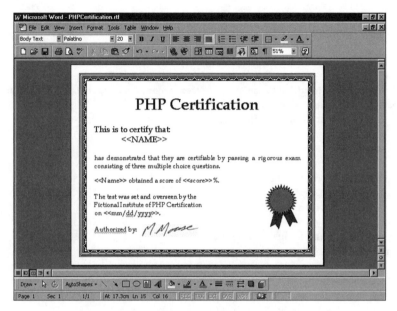

Figure 30.4   Using a word processor, we can create a complex, attractive template easily.

Our template includes placeholders such as <<NAME>> to mark the places where dynamic data will be inserted. It is not important what these place holders look like. We are using a meaningful description between two sets of angled braces. It is important that we choose placeholders that are highly unlikely to accidentally appear in the rest of the document. It will help you to lay out your template if the placeholders are roughly the same length as the data they will be replaced with.

The placeholders in this document are <<NAME>>, <<Name>>, <<score>>, and <<mm/dd/yyyy>>. Note that we are using both NAME and Name, because we intend to use a case sensitive method to replace them.

Now that we have a template, we need a script to personalize it. This script is called rtf.php, and its code is shown in Listing 30.3.

Listing 30.3   **rtf.php—Script to Produce a Personalized RTF Certificate**

```php
<?php
  //create short variable names
  $name = $HTTP_POST_VARS['name'];
  $score = $HTTP_POST_VARS['score'];
```

Listing 30.3 **Continued**

```php
// check we have the parameters we need
if( !$name || !$score )
{
  echo '<h1>Error:</h1>This page was called incorrectly';
}
else
{
  //generate the headers to help a browser choose the correct application
  header( 'Content-type: application/msword' );
  header( 'Content-Disposition: inline, filename=cert.rtf');

  $date = date( 'F d, Y' );

  // open our template file
  $filename = 'PHPCertification.rtf';
  $fp = fopen ( $filename, 'r' );

  //read our template into a variable
  $output = fread( $fp, filesize( $filename ) );

  fclose ( $fp );

  // replace the place holders in the template with our data
  $output = str_replace( '<<NAME>>', strtoupper( $name ), $output );
  $output = str_replace( '<<Name>>', $name, $output );
  $output = str_replace( '<<score>>', $score, $output );
  $output = str_replace( '<<mm/dd/yyyy>>', $date, $output );

  // send the generated document to the browser
  echo $output;
}
?>
```

This script performs some basic error checking to make sure that all the user details have been passed in, and then moves to the business of creating the certificate.

The output of this script will be an RTF file rather than an HTML file, so we need to alert the user's browser to this fact. This is important so that the browser can attempt to open the file with the correct application, or give a Save As... type dialog box if it doesn't recognize the RTF extension.

We specify the MIME type of the file we are outputting using PHP's header() function to send the appropriate HTTP header as follows:

```php
header('Content-type: application/msword');
header('Content-Disposition: inline, filename=cert.rtf');
```

The first header tells the browser that we are sending a Microsoft Word file (not strictly true, but the most likely helper application for opening the RTF file).

The second header tells the browser to automatically display the contents of the file, and that its suggested filename is cert.rtf. This is the default filename the user will see if he tries to save the file from within his browser.

After the headers are sent, we open and read our template RTF file into the $output variable, and use the str_replace() function to replace our placeholders with the actual data that we want to appear in the file. The line

```
$output = str_replace( '<<Name>>', $name, $output );
```

will replace any occurrences of the placeholder <<Name>> with the contents of the variable $name.

Having made our substitutions, it's just a matter of echoing the output to the browser. A sample result from this script is shown in Figure 30.5.

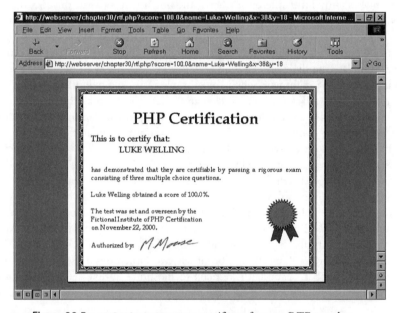

Figure 30.5   rtf.php generates a certificate from an RTF template.

This approach works very well. The calls to str_replace() run very quickly, even though our template and therefore the contents of $output are fairly long. The main problem from the point of view of this application is that the user will load the certificate in his word processor in order to print it. This is probably an invitation for people to modify the output. RTF does not allow us to make a read-only document.

Generating a PDF Certificate from a Template

The process of generating a PDF certificate from a template is very similar. The main difference is that when we create the PDF file, some of our placeholders might be interspersed with formatting codes. For example, if we look in the certificate template file we have created, we can see that the placeholders now look like this:

```
<<N)-13(AME)-10(>)-6(>
<<Na)-9(m)0(e)-18(>>
<)-11(<)1(sc)-17(or)-6(e)-6(>)-11(>
<)-11(<)1(m)-12(m)0(/d)-6(d)-19(/)1(yy)-13(yy)-13(>>
```

If you look through the file, you will see that, unlike RTF, this is not a format that humans can easily read through.

There are a few different ways we can deal with this.

We could go through each of these placeholders and delete the formatting codes. This actually makes fairly little difference to how the document looks in the end as the codes embedded in the previous template indicate how much space should be left between the letters of the placeholders that we are going to replace anyhow. However, if we take this approach, we must go through and hand edit the PDF file and repeat this each time we change or update the file. This is not a big deal when dealing with only four placeholders, but it becomes a nightmare when, for example, you have multiple documents with many placeholders, and you decide to change the letterhead on all the documents.

We can avoid this problem using a different technique. You can use Adobe Acrobat to create a PDF form—similar to an HTML form with blank named fields. You can then use a PHP script to create what is called an FDF (Forms Data Format) file, which is basically a set of data to be merged with a template. You can create FDFs using PHP's FDF function library: specifically, the `fdf_create()` function to create a file, the `fdf_set_value()` function to set the field values, and the `fdf_set_file()` function to set the associated template form file. You can then pass this file back to the browser with the appropriate MIME type, in this case `vnd.fdf`, and the browser's Acrobat Reader plug-in should substitute the data into the form.

This is a neat way of doing things, but it has two limitations. First, it assumes that you own a copy of Acrobat. Second, it is difficult to substitute in text that is inline rather than text that looks like a form field. This might or might not be a problem, depending on what you are trying to do. We have largely used PDF generation for generating letters where many things must be substituted inline. FDFs do not work well for this purpose. If you are auto-filling for example, a tax form online, this will not be a problem.

You can read more about the FDF format at Adobe's site:

```
http://partners.adobe.com/asn/developer/acrosdk/forms.html
```

You should also look at the FDF documentation in the PHP manual if you decide to use this approach:

```
http://www.php.net/manual/en/ref.fdf.php
```

We turn now to our PDF solution to the previous problem.

We can still find and replace the placeholders in our PDF file if we recognize that the additional format codes consist solely of hyphens, digits, and parentheses and can therefore be matched via a regular expression. We have written a function, `pdf_replace()`, to automatically generate a matching regular expression for a placeholder and replace that placeholder with the appropriate text.

Other than this addition, the code for generating the certificate via a PDF template is very similar to the RTF version. This script is shown in Listing 30.4.

Listing 30.4   **pdf.php—Script to Produce Personalized PDF Certificate via a Template**

```php
<?php
  set_time_limit( 180 ); // this script can be very slow

  //create short variable names
  $name = $HTTP_POST_VARS['name'];
  $score = $HTTP_POST_VARS['score'];

  function pdf_replace( $pattern, $replacement, $string )
  {
    $len = strlen( $pattern );
    $regexp = '';
    for ( $i = 0; $i<$len; $i++ )
    {
      $regexp .= $pattern[$i];
      if ($i<$len-1)
        $regexp .= "(\)\-{0,1}[0-9]*\(){0,1}";
    }
    return ereg_replace ( $regexp, $replacement, $string );
  }

  if(!$name||!$score)
  {
    echo '<h1>Error:</h1>This page was called incorrectly';
  }
  else
  {
    //generate the headers to help a browser choose the correct application
    header( 'Content-Disposition:  filename=cert.pdf');
    header( 'Content-type: application/pdf' );

    $date = date( 'F d, Y' );

    // open our template file
    $filename = 'PHPCertification.pdf';
    $fp = fopen ( $filename, 'r' );
```

Listing 30.4 **Continued**

```
//read our template into a variable
$output = fread( $fp, filesize( $filename ) );

fclose ( $fp );

// replace the place holders in the template with our data
$output = pdf_replace( '<<NAME>>', strtoupper( $name ), $output );
$output = pdf_replace( '<<Name>>', $name, $output );
$output = pdf_replace( '<<score>>', $score, $output );
$output = pdf_replace( '<<mm/dd/yyyy>>', $date, $output );

// send the generated document to the browser
echo $output;
  }
?>
```

This script produces a customized version of our PDF document. The document, shown in Figure 30.6, will print reliably on numerous systems, and is harder for the recipient to modify or edit. You can see that the PDF document in Figure 30.6 looks almost exactly like the RTF document in Figure 30.5.

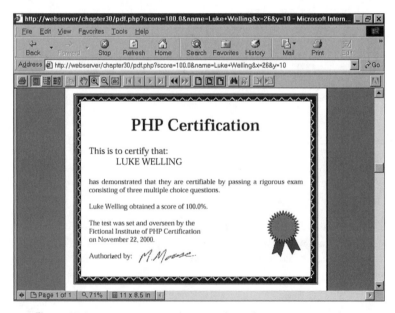

Figure 30.6   pdf.php generates a certificate from an PDF template.

One problem with this approach is that the code runs quite slowly because of the regular expression matching required. Regular expressions run much more slowly than str_replace() that we could use for the RTF version.

If you are going to match a large number of placeholders or try to generate many of these documents on the same server, you might want to look at other approaches. This would be less of a problem for a simpler template. Much of the bulk in this file is data representing the images.

Generating a PDF Document Using PDFlib

PDFlib is intended for generating dynamic PDF documents via the Web. It is not strictly part of PHP, but rather a separate library, with a large number of functions intended to be called from a wide variety of programming languages. Language bindings are available for C, C++, Java, Perl, Python, Tcl, and ActiveX/COM.

Since PHP 4.0.5, PDFLib has been officially supported by PDFlib GmbH. This means that you can refer to either the PHP documentation at

```
http://www.php.net/manual/ref.pdf.php
```

or download the official documentation from pdflib.com.

A Hello World Script for PDFlib

After you have PHP and installed it with PDFlib enabled, you can test it with a simple program such as the Hello World example in Listing 30.5.

Listing 30.5   **testpdf.php—Classic Hello World Example Using PDFlib via PHP**

```php
<?php
  //create file
  $fp = fopen('hello.pdf', 'w');
  if(!$fp)
  {
    echo "Error: could not create the PDF file";
    exit;
  }

  // start the pdf document
  $pdf = pdf_open($fp);
  pdf_set_info($pdf, "Creator", "pdftest.php");
  pdf_set_info($pdf, "Author", "Luke Welling and Laura Thomson");
  pdf_set_info($pdf, "Title", "Hello World (PHP)");

  // US letter is 11" x 8.5" and there are approximately 72 points per inch
  pdf_begin_page($pdf, 8.5*72, 11*72);
  pdf_add_outline($pdf, 'Page 1');
  $font = pdf_findfont($pdf, 'Times-Roman', 'host', 0);
```

Listing 30.5   **Continued**

```
pdf_setfont($pdf, $font, 24);
pdf_set_text_pos($pdf, 50, 700);

// write text
pdf_show($pdf,'Hello,world!');
pdf_continue_text($pdf,'(says PHP)');

// end the document
pdf_end_page($pdf);
pdf_close($pdf);
fclose($fp);

// display a link to download
echo "download the pdf <a href = 'hello.pdf'>here</a>";
?>
```

The most likely error you will see if this script fails is the following:

Fatal error: Call to undefined function: pdf_open() in
/home/book/public_html/chapter30/pdftest.php on line 6

This means that you do not have the PDFlib extension compiled into PHP.

The installation is fairly straightforward, but some details change depending on the exact versions of PHP and PDFlib that you are using. A good place to check for detailed suggestions is the user contributed notes on the PDFlib page in the annotated PHP manual.

When you have this script up and running on your system, it is time to look at how it works.

The first section of the code, including the line

```
$fp = fopen('hello.pdf', 'w');
```

creates a writeable file. It is worth noting that the code here is writing directly in to the current directory even though we have already discussed a number of reasons why it is a bad idea to have your permissions set up to allow PHP to write within the Web tree. The line

```
$pdf = pdf_open($fp);
```

initializes a PDF document using the file we already opened. You can also call pdf_open() without parameters to create a document in memory to be output directly to the browser. In any case, you will need to capture the return value of pdf_open(), as every subsequent call to a PDF function will need it.

The function pdf_set_info() enables you to tag the document with a subject, title, creator, author, a list of keywords, and one custom, user-defined field.

Here we are setting a creator, author, and title. Note that all six info fields are optional.

```
pdf_set_info($pdf, 'Creator', 'pdftest.php');
pdf_set_info($pdf, 'Author', 'Luke Welling and Laura Thomson');
pdf_set_info($pdf, 'Title', 'Hello World (PHP)');
```

A PDF document consists of a number of pages. To start a new page, we need to call `pdf_begin_page()`. As well as the identifier returned by `pdf_open()`, `pdf_begin_page()` requires the dimensions of the page. Each page in a document can be a different size, but unless you have a good reason not to, you should use a common paper size.

PDFlib works in points, both for page size, and for locating coordinate locations on each page. For reference, A4 is approximately 595 by 842 points and U.S. letter paper is 612 by 792 points. This means that our line

```
pdf_begin_page($pdf, 8.5*72, 11*72);
```

creates a page in our document, sized for U.S. letter paper.

A PDF document does not need to be just a printable document. Many PDF features can be included in the document such as hyperlinks and bookmarks. The function `pdf_add_outline()` will add a bookmark to the document outline. The bookmarks in a document will appear in a separate pane in Acrobat Reader, allowing us to skip straight to important sections.

This line

```
pdf_add_outline($pdf, 'Page 1');
```

adds an outline entry labeled Page 1, which will refer to the current page.

Fonts available on systems vary from operating system to operating system and even from individual machine to machine. In order to guarantee consistent results, a set of core fonts will work with every PDF reader. The 14 core fonts are

- Courier
- Courier-Bold
- Courier-Oblique
- Courier-BoldOblique
- Helvetica
- Helvetica-Bold
- Helvetica-Oblique
- Helvetica-BoldOblique
- Times-Roman
- Times-Bold
- Times-Italic
- Times-BoldItalic

- Symbol
- ZapfDingbats

Fonts outside this set can be embedded in documents, but this will increase the file size and might not be acceptable under whatever license you own that particular font under. We can choose a font, its size, and character encoding as follows:

```
$font = pdf_findfont($pdf, 'Times-Roman', 'host', 0);
pdf_setfont($pdf, $font, 24);
```

Font sizes are specified in points. We have chosen host character encoding. The allowable values are winansi, builtin, macroman, ebcdic, or host. The meanings of the different values are as follows:

- winansi—ISO 8859-1 plus special characters added by Microsoft such as a Euro symbol.
- macroman—Mac Roman encoding. The default Macintosh character set.
- ebcdic—EBCDIC as used on IBM AS/400 systems.
- builtin—Use the encoding built-in to the font. Normally used with non-Latin fonts and symbols.
- host—Automatically selects macroman on a Mac, ebcdic on an EBCDIC-based system, and winansi on all other systems.

If you do not need to include special characters, the choice of encoding is not important.

A PDF document is not like an HTML document or a word processor document. Text does not by default start at the top left and flow onto other lines as required. We need to choose where to place each line of text. As already mentioned, PDF uses points to specify locations. The origin (the x, y coordinate [0, 0]) is at the bottom left corner of the page.

Given that our page is 612 by 792 points, the point (50, 700) is about two thirds of an inch from the left of the page and about one and one third inches from the top. To set our text position at this point, we use

```
pdf_set_text_pos($pdf, 50, 700);
```

Finally, having set up the page, we can write some text on it. To add text at the current position using the current font, we use `pdf_show()`.
The line

```
pdf_show($pdf,'Hello,world!');
```

adds the test "Hello World!" to our document.

To move to the next line and write more text, we use `pdf_continue_text()`. To add the string "(says PHP)", we use

```
pdf_continue_text($pdf,'(says PHP)');
```

The exact location where this will appear will depend on the font and size selected. If rather than lines or phrases you are using contiguous paragraphs, you might find the function `pdf_show_boxed()` more useful. It allows you to declare a text box and flow text into it.

When we have finished adding elements to a page, we need to call `pdf_end_page()` as follows:

```
pdf_end_page($pdf);
```

When we have finished the whole PDF document, we need to close it using `pdf_close()`. When we are generating a file, we also need to close the file.

The lines
```
pdf_close($pdf);
fclose($fp);
```

complete the generation of our Hello World document. All we need to do is provide a way to download it.

```
echo 'download the pdf <a href="hello.pdf">here</a>';
```

This example was derived from the C language example in the PDFlib documentation and should provide a starting point.

The document we want to produce for the certificate is more complicated, including a border, a vector image, and a bitmap image. With the other two techniques, we added these features using our word processor. With PDFlib, we must add them manually.

Generating Our Certificate with PDFlib

In order to use PDFlib, we have chosen to make some compromises. Although it is almost certainly possible to exactly duplicate the certificate we used previously, a lot more effort would be required to generate and position each element manually rather than using a tool such as Microsoft Word to help lay out the document.

We are using the same text as before, including the red rosette and the bitmap signature, but we are not going to duplicate the complex border.

The complete code for this script is shown in Listing 30.6.

Listing 30.6 **pdflib.php—Generating Our Certificate Using PDFlib**

```php
<?php
  // create short variable names
  $name = $HTTP_POST_VARS['name'];
  $score = $HTTP_POST_VARS['score'];

  if(!$name||!$score)
  {
    echo '<h1>Error:</h1>This page was called incorrectly';
    exit;
  }
  else
```

Listing 30.6   **Continued**

```
{
  $date = date( 'F d, Y' );

  // create a pdf document in memory
  $pdf = pdf_new();
  pdf_open_file($pdf);

  // set up name of font for later use
  $fontname = 'Times-Roman';

  // set up the page size in points and create page
  // US letter is 11" x 8.5" and there are approximately 72 points per inch
  $width = 11*72;
  $height = 8.5*72;
  pdf_begin_page($pdf, $width, $height);

  // draw our borders
  $inset = 20; // space between border and page edge
  $border = 10; // width of main border line
  $inner = 2; // gap within the border

  //draw outer border
  pdf_rect($pdf, $inset-$inner,
                 $inset-$inner,
                 $width-2*($inset-$inner),
                 $height-2*($inset-$inner));
  pdf_stroke($pdf);

  //draw main border $border points wide
  pdf_setlinewidth($pdf, $border);
  pdf_rect($pdf, $inset+$border/2,
                 $inset+$border/2,
                 $width-2*($inset+$border/2),
                 $height-2*($inset+$border/2));
  pdf_stroke($pdf);
  pdf_setlinewidth($pdf, 1.0);

  // draw inner border
  pdf_rect($pdf, $inset+$border+$inner,
                 $inset+$border+$inner,
                 $width-2*($inset+$border+$inner),
                 $height-2*($inset+$border+$inner));
  pdf_stroke($pdf);

  // add heading
  $font = pdf_findfont($pdf, $fontname, 'host', 0);
```

Listing 30.6   **Continued**

```php
if ($font)
  pdf_setfont($pdf, $font, 48);
$startx = ($width - pdf_stringwidth($pdf, 'PHP Certification'))/2;
pdf_show_xy($pdf, 'PHP Certification', $startx, 490);

// add text
$font = pdf_findfont($pdf, $fontname, 'host', 0);
if ($font)
  pdf_setfont($pdf, $font, 26);
$startx = 70;
pdf_show_xy($pdf, 'This is to certify that:', $startx, 430);
pdf_show_xy($pdf, strtoupper($name), $startx+90, 391);

$font = pdf_findfont($pdf, $fontname, 'host', 0);
if ($font)
  pdf_setfont($pdf, $font, 20);

pdf_show_xy($pdf, 'has demonstrated that they are certifiable '.
                  'by passing a rigorous exam', $startx, 340);
pdf_show_xy($pdf, 'consisting of three multiple choice questions.',
                  $startx, 310);

pdf_show_xy($pdf, "$name obtained a score of $score".'%.', $startx, 260);

pdf_show_xy($pdf, 'The test was set and overseen by the ', $startx, 210);
pdf_show_xy($pdf, 'Fictional Institute of PHP Certification',
                  $startx, 180);
pdf_show_xy($pdf, "on $date.", $startx, 150);
pdf_show_xy($pdf, 'Authorised by:', $startx, 100);

// add bitmap signature image
$signature = pdf_open_image_file($pdf, 'png', 'signature.png');
pdf_place_image($pdf, $signature, 200, 75, 1);
pdf_close_image($pdf, $signature);

// set up colors for rosette
pdf_setrgbcolor_fill($pdf, 0, 0, .4);   //dark blue
pdf_setrgbcolor_stroke($pdf, 0, 0, 0);  // black

// draw ribbon 1
pdf_moveto($pdf, 630, 150);
pdf_lineto($pdf, 610, 55);
pdf_lineto($pdf, 632, 69);
pdf_lineto($pdf, 646, 49);
pdf_lineto($pdf, 666, 150);
pdf_closepath($pdf);
```

Listing 30.6 **Continued**

```
pdf_fill($pdf);

// outline ribbon 1
pdf_moveto($pdf, 630, 150);
pdf_lineto($pdf, 610, 55);
pdf_lineto($pdf, 632, 69);
pdf_lineto($pdf, 646, 49);
pdf_lineto($pdf, 666, 150);
pdf_closepath($pdf);
pdf_stroke($pdf);

// draw ribbon 2
pdf_moveto($pdf, 660, 150);
pdf_lineto($pdf, 680, 49);
pdf_lineto($pdf, 695, 69);
pdf_lineto($pdf, 716, 55);
pdf_lineto($pdf, 696, 150);
pdf_closepath($pdf);
pdf_fill($pdf);

// outline ribbon 2
pdf_moveto($pdf, 660, 150);
pdf_lineto($pdf, 680, 49);
pdf_lineto($pdf, 695, 69);
pdf_lineto($pdf, 716, 55);
pdf_lineto($pdf, 696, 150);
pdf_closepath($pdf);
pdf_stroke($pdf);

pdf_setrgbcolor_fill($pdf, .8, 0, 0);  //red

//draw rosette
draw_star(665, 175, 32, 57, 10, $pdf, true);

//outline rosette
draw_star(665, 175, 32, 57, 10, $pdf, false);

// finish up the page and prepare to output
pdf_end_page($pdf);
pdf_close($pdf);
$data = pdf_get_buffer($pdf);

// generate the headers to help a browser choose the correct application
header('Content-type: application/pdf');
```

Listing 30.6   **Continued**

```
    header('Content-disposition: inline; filename=test.pdf');
    header('Content-length: ' . strlen($data));

    // output PDF
    echo $data;
  }

  function draw_star($centerx, $centery, $points, $radius,
                     $point_size, $pdf, $filled)
  {
    $inner_radius = $radius-$point_size;

    for ($i = 0; $i<=$points*2; $i++ )
    {
      $angle= ($i*2*pi())/($points*2);

      if($i%2)
      {
        $x = $radius*cos($angle) + $centerx;
        $y = $radius*sin($angle) + $centery;
      }
      else
      {
        $x = $inner_radius*cos($angle) + $centerx;
        $y = $inner_radius*sin($angle) + $centery;
      }
      if($i==0)
        pdf_moveto($pdf, $x, $y);
      else if($i==$points*2)
        pdf_closepath($pdf);
      else
        pdf_lineto($pdf, $x, $y);
    }
    if($filled)
      pdf_fill_stroke($pdf);
    else
      pdf_stroke($pdf);
  }
?>
```

The certificate produced using this script is shown in Figure 30.7. As you can see, it is quite similar to the others, except that the border is simpler and the star looks a little different. This is because we have drawn them into the document rather than using an existing clip art file.

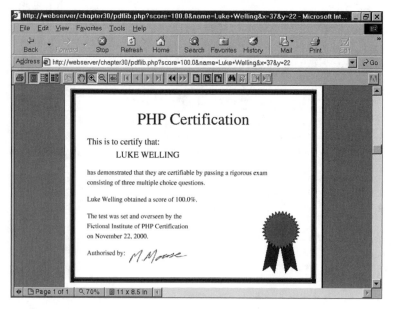

Figure 30.7   `pdflib.php` draws the certificate into a PDF document.

We will look at some of the parts of this script that are different from the previous examples.

Visitors need to get their own details on a certificate, so we will create the document in memory rather than in a file. If we wrote it to a file, we would need to worry about mechanisms to create unique filenames, stop people from snooping into others' certificates, and determine a way to delete older certificate files to free up hard drive space on our server. In order to create a document in memory, we call `pdf_new()` without parameters followed by a call to `pdf_open_file()` as follows:

```
$pdf = pdf_new();
pdf_open_file($pdf);
```

Our simplified border will consist of three stripes: a fat border and two thin borders, one inside the main border and one outside. We will draw all of these as rectangles.

To position the borders in such a way that we can easily alter the page size or the appearance of the borders, we will base all the border positions on the variables that we already have, `$width` and `$height` and a few new ones: `$inset`, `$border`, and `$inner`. We will use `$inset` to specify how many points wide the border at the edge of the page is, `$border` to specify the thickness of the main border, and `$inner` to specify how wide the gap between the main border and the thin borders will be.

If you have drawn with another graphics API, drawing with PDFlib will present few surprises. If you haven't read Chapter 19, "Generating Images," you might find it helpful to do so, as drawing images with the `gd` library is quite similar to drawing them with PDFlib.

The thin borders are easy. To create a rectangle, we use pdf_rect(), which requires as parameters the PDF document identifier, the x and y coordinate of the rectangle's lower left corner, and the width and height of the rectangle. Because we want our layout to be flexible, we calculate these from the variables we have set.

```
pdf_rect($pdf, $inset-$inner,
               $inset-$inner,
               $width-2*($inset-$inner),
               $height-2*($inset-$inner));
```

The call to pdf_rect() sets up a path in the shape of a rectangle. In order to draw that shape, we need to call the pdf_stroke() function as follows:

```
pdf_stroke($pdf);
```

In order to draw the main border, we need to specify the line width. The default line width is 1 point. The following call to pdf_setlinewidth() will set it to $border (in this case 10) points:

```
pdf_setlinewidth($pdf, $border);
```

With the width set, we again create a rectangle with pdf_rect() and call pdf_stroke() to draw it.

```
pdf_rect($pdf, $inset+$border/2,
               $inset+$border/2,
               $width-2*($inset+$border/2),
               $height-2*($inset+$border/2));
pdf_stroke($pdf);
```

After we have drawn our one wide line, we need to remember to set the line width back to 1 with this code:

```
pdf_setlinewidth($pdf, 1.0);
```

We are going to use pdf_show_xy() to position each line of text on the certificate. For most lines of text, we are using a configurable left margin ($startx) as the x coordinate and a value chosen by eye as the y coordinate. As we want the heading centered on the page, we need to know its width in order to position the left hand side of it. We can get the width using pdf_stringwidth(). The call

```
pdf_stringwidth($pdf, 'PHP Certification');
```

will return the width of the string "PHP Certification" in the current font and font size.

As with the other versions of the certificate, we will include a signature as a scanned bitmap. The following three statements

```
$signature = pdf_open_image_file($pdf, 'png', 'signature.png');
pdf_place_image($pdf, $signature, 200, 75, 1);
pdf_close_image($pdf, $signature);
```

will open a PNG file containing the signature, add the image to the page at the specified location, and close the PNG file. Other file types can also be used. The only parameter that might not be self explanatory is the fifth parameter to `pdf_place_image()`. This function is not limited to inserting the image at its original size. The fifth parameter is a scale factor. We have chosen to display the image at full size and used 1 as the scale factor, but could have used a larger number to enlarge the image, or a fraction to shrink it.

The hardest item to add to our certificate using PDFlib is the rosette. We cannot automatically open and include a Windows Meta File containing the rosette we already have, but we are free to draw any shapes we like.

In order to draw a filled shape such as one of the ribbons, we can write the following code.

Here we set the stroke or line color to be black and the fill or interior color to be a navy blue:

```
pdf_setrgbcolor_fill($pdf, 0, 0, .4);  //dark blue
pdf_setrgbcolor_stroke($pdf, 0, 0, 0);  // black
```

Here we set up a five-sided polygon to be one of our ribbons and then fill it:

```
pdf_moveto($pdf, 630, 150);
pdf_lineto($pdf, 610, 55);
pdf_lineto($pdf, 632, 69);
pdf_lineto($pdf, 646, 49);
pdf_lineto($pdf, 666, 150);
pdf_closepath($pdf);
pdf_fill($pdf);
```

As we would like the polygon outlined as well, we need to set up the same path a second time, but call `pdf_stroke()` instead of `pdf_fill()`.

As the multipointed star is a complex repetitive shape, we have written a function to calculate the locations in the path for us. Our function is called `draw_star()` and requires x and y coordinates for the center, the number of points required, the radius, the length of the points, a PDF document identifier, and a Boolean value to indicate if the star shape should be filled in or just an outline.

The `draw_star()` function uses some basic trigonometry to calculate locations for a series of points to lay out a star. For each point we requested our star to have, we find a point on the radius of the star and a point on a smaller circle `$point_size` within the outer circle and draw a line between them. One thing worth noting is that PHP's trigonometric functions such as `cos()` and `sin()` work in radians rather than degrees.

Using a function and some mathematics, we can accurately generate a complex repetitive shape. Had we wanted a complicated pattern for our page border, we could have used a similar approach.

When all our page elements are generated, we need to end the page and the document.

Problems with Headers

One minor thing to note in all these scripts is that we need to tell the browser what type of data we are going to send it. We have done this by sending a content-type HTTP header, for example

```
header( 'Content-type: application/msword' );
```

or

```
header( 'Content-type: application/pdf' );
```

One thing to be aware of is that browsers deal with these headers inconsistently. In particular, Internet Explorer often chooses to ignore the MIME type and attempt to automatically detect the type of file. (This particular problem seems to have improved in recent versions of Internet Explorer.)

Some of our headers seemed to cause problems with session control headers. There are a few ways around this. We have found using GET parameters rather than POST or session variable parameters avoids the problem.

Another solution is not to use an inline PDF but to get the user to download it instead as shown in the Hello World PDFlib example.

You can also avoid problems if you are willing to write two slightly different versions of your code, one for Netscape and one for Internet Explorer.

Extending the Project

Adding some more realistic assessment tasks to the examination obviously could extend this project, but it is really intended as an example of ways to deliver your own documents.

Customized documents that you might want to deliver online could include legal documents, partially filled in order or application forms, or forms needed by government departments.

Further Reading

We suggest you visit Adobe's site if you want to know more about the PDF (and FDF) formats:

```
http://www.adobe.com
```

31

Connecting to Web Services with XML and SOAP

IN THE LAST FEW YEARS, XML (Extensible Markup Language) has become an important means of communication. In this chapter, we will use Amazon's new Web Services interface to build a shopping cart on our local Web site that uses Amazon as a back end. (We will call this application Tahuayo, which is the name of an Amazonian tributary.) We will use two different methods to do this: SOAP and XML over HTTP. We will use PHP's XML (expat) and NuSOAP (SOAP) libraries to implement these two methods.

We will discuss the following topics:

- Understanding XML and SOAP basics
- Using XML to communicate with Amazon
- Parsing XML with PHP's XML library
- Caching responses
- Talking to Amazon with NuSOAP

The Problem

We have two goals with this project:

The first is to for you to gain an understanding of what XML and SOAP are and how we use them in PHP.

The second is to put these technologies to use to communicate with the outside world. We have chosen the new Amazon Web Services program as an interesting example that you might find useful for your own Web site.

Amazon has long offered an associate program that allows you to advertise Amazon's products on your Web site. Users can then follow a link to each product's page on Amazon's site. If someone clicks through from your site and then buys that product, you get a small commission.

The Web Services program enables you to use Amazon more as an engine: you can search it and display the results via your own site, or fill a user's shopping cart directly with the contents of items he has selected while browsing your site. In other words, the customer uses your site until it is time to check out, which he can then do via Amazon.

Communications between you and Amazon can take place in two possible ways. The first way is by using XML over HTTP. If, for example, we want to perform a search using this method, you send a normal HTTP request for the information you require and Amazon will respond with an XML document containing the information you requested. You can then parse this XML document with PHP's XML library and display the search results to the end user.

The second way is by using SOAP. *SOAP* is one of the standard Web Services protocols. It used to stand for Simple Object Access Protocol, but recently it was decided that the protocol wasn't that simple, and that the name was a bit misleading. The result is that the protocol is still called SOAP but it is no longer an acronym.

We will build a SOAP client that can send requests to and receive responses from the Amazon SOAP server. These will contain the same information as the responses we get using the XML over HTTP method, but we will use a different approach to extract the data, namely PHP's SOAP library.

Our final goal in this project is to build our own book-selling Web site that uses Amazon as a back end. We will build two alternative versions: one using XML over HTTP and one using SOAP.

Understanding XML

Let's spend a few moments talking about XML and Web Services, in case you are not familiar with these concepts.

XML is the Extensible Markup Language. The specification is available from the W3C. Lots of information about XML can be found at the W3C's XML site at `http://www.w3.org/XML/`.

XML is derived from SGML (Standard Generalized Markup Language). If you already know HTML (and we assume by this point in the book that you probably do!), you will have little difficulty with the concepts of XML.

XML is a tag-based text format for documents. As an example of an XML document, Listing 31.1 shows one of the responses Amazon sends in response to an XML over HTTP request.

Listing 31.1 **XML Document Describing the First Edition of This Book**

```
<?xml version="1.0" encoding="UTF-8"?>
<ProductInfo xmlns:xsi="http://www.w3.org/2001/XMLSchema-instance"
  xsi:noNamespaceSchemaLocation =
                          "http://xml.amazon.com/schemas2/dev-heavy.xsd">
  <Details url="http://www.amazon.com/exec/obidos/redirect?
     tag=tangledwebdesign%26creative=XXXXXXXXXXXXXX%26
     camp=2025%26link_code=xm2%26path=ASIN/0672317842">
```

Listing 31.1 **Continued**

```
<Asin>0672317842</Asin>
<ProductName>PHP and MySQL Web Development</ProductName>
<Catalog>Book</Catalog>
<Authors>
   <Author>Luke Welling</Author>
   <Author>Laura Thomson</Author>
</Authors>
<ReleaseDate>30 March, 2001</ReleaseDate>
<Manufacturer>Sams</Manufacturer>
<ImageUrlSmall>
  http://images.amazon.com/images/P/0672317842.01.THUMBZZZ.jpg
</ImageUrlSmall>
<ImageUrlMedium>
  http://images.amazon.com/images/P/0672317842.01.MZZZZZZZ.jpg
</ImageUrlMedium>
<ImageUrlLarge>
  http://images.amazon.com/images/P/0672317842.01.LZZZZZZZ.jpg
</ImageUrlLarge>
<ListPrice>$49.99</ListPrice>
<OurPrice>$34.99</OurPrice>
<UsedPrice>$31.95</UsedPrice>
<ThirdPartyNewPrice>$31.75</ThirdPartyNewPrice>
<SalesRank>312</SalesRank>
<Lists>
   <ListId>3KZW1EV9QMB5F</ListId>
   <ListId>22YCO1IGPIZJ3</ListId>
   <ListId>Y2I9B362QXVX</ListId>
</Lists>
<BrowseList>
   <BrowseNode>
      <BrowseName>PHP (Computer program language</BrowseName>
   </BrowseNode>
   <BrowseNode>
      <BrowseName>SQL (Computer program language</BrowseName>
   </BrowseNode>
   <BrowseNode>
      <BrowseName>Web sites</BrowseName>
   </BrowseNode>
   <BrowseNode>
      <BrowseName>Design</BrowseName>
   </BrowseNode>
   <BrowseNode>
      <BrowseName>SQL (Computer language)</BrowseName>
   </BrowseNode>
   <BrowseNode>
      <BrowseName>Sql (Programming Language)</BrowseName>
   </BrowseNode>
```

Listing 31.1   **Continued**

```
            <BrowseNode>
                <BrowseName>Computer Networks</BrowseName>
            </BrowseNode>
            <BrowseNode>
                <BrowseName>Computer Bks - Languages / Programming</BrowseName>
            </BrowseNode>
            <BrowseNode>
                <BrowseName>Computers</BrowseName>
            </BrowseNode>
            <BrowseNode>
                <BrowseName>Programming Languages - General</BrowseName>
            </BrowseNode>
            <BrowseNode>
                <BrowseName>Internet - Web Site Design</BrowseName>
            </BrowseNode>
            <BrowseNode>
                <BrowseName>Database Management - SQL Server</BrowseName>
            </BrowseNode>
            <BrowseNode>
                <BrowseName>Programming Languages - SQL</BrowseName>
            </BrowseNode>
        </BrowseList>
        <Media>Paperback</Media>
        <NumMedia>1</NumMedia>
        <Isbn>0672317842</Isbn>
        <Availability>Usually ships within 24 hours</Availability>
        <SimilarProducts>
            <Product>0735709211</Product>
            <Product>1861003730</Product>
            <Product>073570970X</Product>
            <Product>1861006918</Product>
            <Product>0596000413</Product>
        </SimilarProducts>
    </Details>
</ProductInfo>
```

The document begins with the following line:

```
<?xml version="1.0" encoding="UTF-8"?>
```

This is a standard declaration that tells us the following document will be XML using UTF-8 character encoding.

Look at the body of the document. The whole document consists of pairs of opening and closing tags, such as

```
<ProductName>PHP and MySQL Web Development</ProductName>
```

`ProductName` is an element, just as it would be in HTML. And, just as in HTML, we can nest elements:

```
<Authors>
  <Author>Luke Welling</Author>
  <Author>Laura Thomson</Author>
</Authors>
```

Also like HTML, elements can have attributes. For example:

```
<Details url="http://www.amazon.com/exec/obidos/redirect?tag=
tangledwebdesign%26creative=XXXXXXXXXXXXXX%26camp=2025%26link_code
=xm2%26path=ASIN/0672317842">
```

This `Details` element has a single attribute `url`.

There are also some differences from HTML. The first is that all opening tags should have a closing tag. (The exception to this is that you may have a single tag if you use a special format. If you are familiar with XHTML, you will have seen the `<br />` tag used in place of `<br>` for this exact reason.) In addition, all elements must be properly nested.

The main difference you will have noticed between XML and HTML is that we seem to be making up our own tags as we go along! This is the flexibility of XML. We can structure our documents to match the data that we want to store. We can formalize the structure of XML documents by writing either a DTD (Document Type Definition) or an XML Schema. Both of these documents are used to describe the structure of a given XML document. If you like, the DTD or Schema is like a class declaration, and the XML document is like an instance of that class.

You can read Amazon's DTD for this document here:

```
http://xml.amazon.com/schemas2/dev-heavy.dtd
```

You can read the XML Schema for it here:

```
http://xml.amazon.com/schemas2/dev-heavy.xsd
```

You will not be able to open the DTD file in some browsers, because they will try to parse the DTD as XML and get confused. You can, however, download it and read it in the editor of your choice. You should be able to open the XML Schema directly in your browser.

You will notice that, other than the initial XML declaration, the entire body of the document is contained inside the ProductInfo element. This is called the *root element* of the document. Let's take a closer look:

```
<ProductInfo xmlns:xsi="http://www.w3.org/2001/XMLSchema-instance"
    xsi:noNamespaceSchemaLocation="http://xml.amazon.com/schemas2/
    dev-heavy.xsd">
```

You will see that it has some slightly unusual attributes. These are *XML Namespaces*. We do not need to understand namespaces for what we want to do in this project, but they can be very useful. The basic idea is to qualify element and attribute names with a name-space so that common names will not clash when dealing with documents from different sources.

If you'd like to know more about namespaces, you can read the document "Namespaces in XML Recommendation" at `http://www.w3.org/TR/ REC-xml-names/`.

If you would like to know more about XML in general, there is a huge variety of resources. The W3C site is an excellent place to start, and there are also literally hundreds of excellent books and Web tutorials. ZVON.org is one of the best Web-based ones.

Understanding Web Services

Web services are application interfaces made available via the World Wide Web. If you like, a Web service can be seen as a class that exposes its public methods via the Web. Web Services are now becoming wide-spread, and some of the biggest names in the business are making some of their functionality available via Web Services.

For example, Google now offers a range of Web Services. After you have gone through the process of setting up a client to the Amazon interface in this chapter, you should find it very straightforward to build a client interface to Google. You can find more information at `http://www.google.com/apis/`.

An ever-growing list of public Web Services is available at `http://www.xmethods.net`.

There are a number of core protocols involved in this remote function call methodology. Two of the most important ones are SOAP and WSDL.

SOAP

SOAP is a request-and-response-driven messaging protocol that allows clients to invoke Web Services and allows servers to respond. Each SOAP message, whether a request or response, is a simple XML document. A sample SOAP request we might send to Amazon is shown in Listing 31.2.

Listing 31.2 **SOAP Request for a Search Based on the ASIN**

```
<?xml version="1.0" encoding="UTF-8"?>
<?xml version="1.0" encoding="UTF-8"?>
<SOAP-ENV:Envelope
               xmlns:SOAP-ENV="http://schemas.xmlsoap.org/soap/envelope/"
               xmlns:SOAP-ENC="http://schemas.xmlsoap.org/soap/encoding/"
               xmlns:xsi="http://www.w3.org/2001/XMLSchema-instance"
               xmlns:xsd="http://www.w3.org/2001/XMLSchema"
    SOAP-ENV:encodingStyle="http://schemas.xmlsoap.org/soap/encoding/">
    <SOAP-ENV:Body>
      <namesp1:AsinSearchRequest
               xmlns:namesp1="urn:PI/DevCentral/SoapService">
```

Listing 31.2   **Continued**

```
      <AsinSearchRequest xsi:type="m:AsinRequest">
        <asin >0060518057</asin>
        <tag >your-associate-id</tag>
        <type >heavy</type>
        <dev-tag >your-dev-tag</dev-tag>
      </AsinSearchRequest>
    </namesp1:AsinSearchRequest>
  </SOAP-ENV:Body>
</SOAP-ENV:Envelope>
```

The SOAP message begins with the declaration that this is an XML document. The root element of all SOAP messages is the SOAP envelope. Within this we find the `Body` element that contains the actual request.

This request is an `AsinSearchRequest`, which asks the Amazon server to look up a particular item in its database based on the ASIN, which stands for Amazon.com Standard Item Number. This is a unique identifier given to every product in the Amazon.com database.

Think of the `AsinSearchRequest` as a function call on a remote machine, and the elements contained within this element as the parameters we are passing to that function. In this case, we are passing an ASIN for the Dilbert book *Way of the Weasel*. We also need to pass in the tag, which is your Associate ID; the type of search to perform (`heavy` or `lite`); and the `dev-tag`, which is a developer token value Amazon will give you. The element type tells the service whether we want limited detail (`lite`) or all available information (`heavy`).

The response to this request is very similar to the XML document we looked at in Listing 31.1, but enclosed in a SOAP envelope.

When dealing with SOAP, you will usually generate SOAP requests and interpret responses programmatically using a SOAP library, regardless of the programming language you are using. This is a good thing as it saves on the effort of having to build the SOAP request and interpret the response manually.

WSDL

WSDL stands for *Web Services Description Language*. (It is often pronounced "wiz-dul.") This is used to describe the interface to available services at a particular Web site. If you would like to see the WSDL document describing the Amazon Web Services we will use in this chapter, it is located at `http://soap.amazon.com/schemas2/AmazonWebServices.wsdl`.

As you will see if you follow this link, WSDL documents are significantly more complex than SOAP messages. You would always generate and interpret them programmatically, if given a choice.

If you would like to know more about WSDL, you can consult the W3C Draft at `http://www.w3.org/TR/2002/WD-wsdl12-20020709/`.

At the time of writing, WSDL was not yet a W3C Recommendation so it is still subject to change. This has not stopped developers everywhere from using it enthusiastically. However, like all pieces of the Web Services puzzle, it is subject to change as the whole area is so new.

Solution Components

There are a few parts we will need to build our solution.

Building a Shopping Cart

We will obviously need to build a shopping cart as the front end for the system. We've done this before, in Chapter 25, "Building a Shopping Cart." Because shopping carts are not the main focus in this project, we will use a simplified application. We just need to provide a basic cart so that we can track what the customer would like to buy and report it to Amazon upon checkout.

Using Amazon's Web Services Interfaces

To use the Amazon Web Services interface, you will need to download the Amazon Web Services Developers' Kit. We got it from `http://associates.amazon.com/exec/panama/associates/join/developer/kit.html`. This URL is probably subject to change, however.

You will also need to sign up for a Developer Token. You can do this at the same site. This token is used to identify you to Amazon when your requests come in.

You might also like to sign up for an Amazon Associate ID. This will enable you to collect commission if people buy any products via your interface.

When you download the developer kit, read through it. It comes with documentation on how the interface works, and code samples in a variety of languages, including PHP.

Before you can download it, you need to agree to the license agreement. This is worth reading, as it is not the usual yada-yada software license.

Some of the license conditions that are important during implementation are the following:

- You must not make more than one request per second.
- You must cache data coming from Amazon.
- You must not cache prices for more than one hour.
- You must not cache other data for more than 24 hours.
- You must link every piece of Amazon data back to a page on Amazon.com.

With a hard-to-spell domain name, no promotion, and no obvious reason to use Tahuayo.com instead of going straight to Amazon.com, we do not need to take any further steps to keep requests below one per second.

We have implemented caching to meet the conditions at points 2 to 4. We cache images for 24 hours, and product data (which contains prices) for one hour.

We have chosen to ignore point 5. We want items on the main page to link to detailed pages on our site, and only link to Amazon when complete. This is the way shopping cart applications usually work, and the way that sample third-party applications linked from Amazon's site all work. This leads us to believe that Amazon is not terribly bothered by breaches of this condition. Feel free to make a different decision. An Amazon Web Services staffer indicated that they are aware of the situation, and may review the condition in the future.

Parsing XML

The first interface Amazon offers to its Web Services is via XML over HTTP. This interface accepts a normal HTTP request and returns an XML document. To use this interface, we will need to parse the XML response Amazon sends us. We will do this by using PHP's XML library, which is based on the `expat` parser written by James Clark. This is the same XML parser used by Mozilla. It is a SAX parser. If you want to read more about the PHP XML library, you can look at the PHP Manual or the expat documentation at `http://www.jclark.com/xml/expat.html`.

Using SOAP with PHP

The other interface offering the same Web Services is SOAP. To access them using SOAP, we will need to use one of the various PHP SOAP libraries. At the time of writing, there were three notable PHP SOAP libraries: PHP-SOAP, PEAR SOAP, and NuSOAP.

PHP-SOAP is a C extension to PHP, and will probably become the official SOAP extension. At the time of writing, it was still under development. PEAR SOAP is a set of PHP class files in PEAR that enable you to create SOAP clients and servers. NuSOAP is a set of PHP classes that also enable you to create SOAP clients and servers.

We have decided to use NuSOAP, as it is the library that has the most documentation. It also seems to be the library used by the majority of Amazon Web Services developers using PHP, but this is probably at least in part because Amazon uses this library in its sample PHP code.

NuSOAP is available from `http://dietrich.ganx4.com/nusoap/`. NuSOAP is available under the Lesser GPL; that is, you may use it in non-free applications.

Caching

As we mentioned before, one of the terms and conditions imposed upon developers by Amazon is that data downloaded from Amazon via Web Services must be cached. In our solution, we will need to find a way to store and reuse the data that we download until it has passed its use-by date.

Solution Overview

For this project, we will again use an event-driven approach to writing our code, as we did in Chapters 27 and 28. We will not draw a system flow diagram in this example, as there are only a few screens in the system, and the links between them are simple.

Users will begin at the main Tahuayo screen, shown in Figure 31.1.

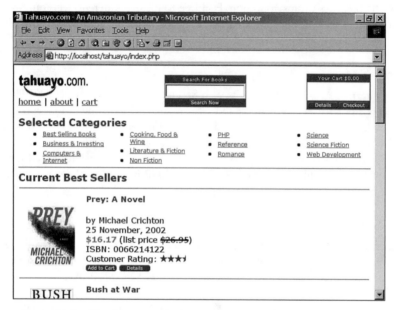

Figure 31.1   The first screen for Tahuayo shows all the main features of the site: category navigation, searching, and the shopping cart.

As you can see, the main features of the site are the Selected Category display and the items in those categories. By default, we are displaying the Current Best Sellers category on the front page. If a user clicks on another category, she will see a similar display for that category.

A brief piece of terminology before we go further: Amazon refers to categories as *browse nodes*. You will see this expression used throughout our code and the official documentation.

The documentation provides a partial list of popular browse nodes. In addition, if you want a particular one, you can browse the normal Amazon.com site and read it from the URL, but there is no way to get a complete list.

Note that there are more books and links to additional pages at the bottom of this page that you can't see in the screenshot. We are displaying 10 books on each page, along with links to up to 30 other pages. This 10-per page value is set by Amazon. The 30-page limit is our own arbitrary choice.

From here, users can click through to detailed information on individual books. This screen is shown in Figure 31.2.

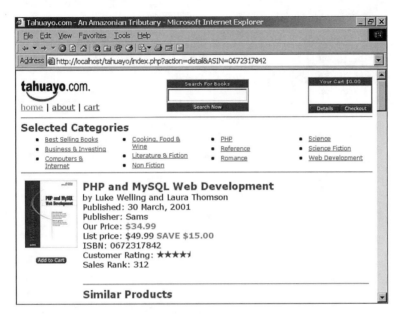

Figure 31.2   Our details page shows more information about a particular book, including similar products and reviews.

Although it does not all fit in a screenshot, we are showing most, but not all, of the information that Amazon sends with a heavy request on this page. We are choosing to ignore parts that are aimed at products other than books and the list of categories the book fits in.

If users click through the cover image, they will be able to see a larger version of the image.

You might have noticed the search box at the top of the screen in these figures. This search will run a keyword search through our site and search Amazon's catalog via its Web Services interface. An example of the output of a search is shown in Figure 31.3.

Although we only list a few categories, customers can get to any book through the search facility and navigating to particular books.

Each individual book has an Add to Cart link with it. Clicking on this or the Details link in the cart summary takes us to a display of the cart contents. This is shown in Figure 31.4.

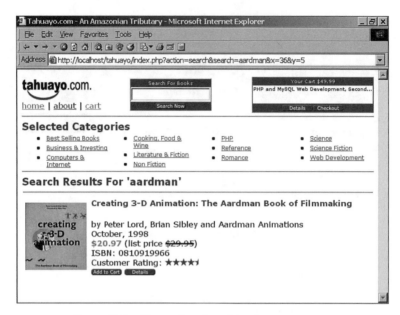

Figure 31.3 The results of searching for `aardman`.

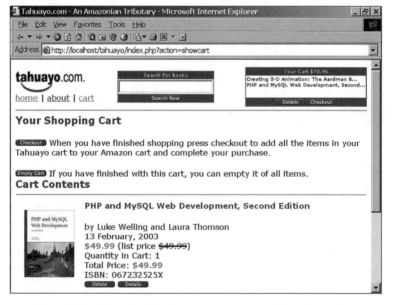

Figure 31.4 From the shopping cart page, we can delete items, clear the cart, or check out.

Finally, when a customer checks out by clicking on one of the Checkout links, we send the details of her shopping cart to Amazon and take her there. She will see a page similar to the one in Figure 31.5.

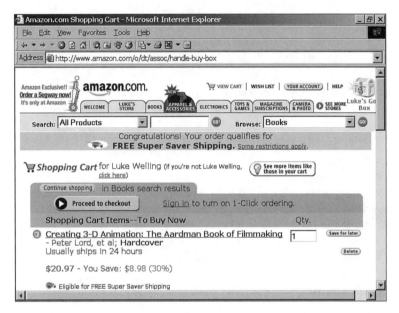

Figure 31.5   The items that were in the customer's Tahuayo cart
are now in her Amazon cart.

You should now understand what we mean by building our own front end and using Amazon as the back end.

Because we have again used the event-driven approach, most of the core decision making logic of the application is in one file, `index.php`. An overview of the files in the application is shown in Table 31.1.

Table 31.1   **Files in the Tahuayo Application**

Filename	Type	Description
`index.php`	Application	The main application file
`about.php`	Application	Shows the About page
`constants.php`	Include file	Sets up some global constants
`topbar.php`	Include file	Generates the info bar across the top of each page and the CSS
`bottom.php`	Include file	Generates the footer at the bottom of each page
`AmazonResultSet.php`	Class file	Contains the PHP class that stores the result of each Amazon query

Table 31.1 **Continued**

Filename	Type	Description
`Product.php`	Class file	Contains the PHP class that stores information on one particular book
`bookdisplayfunctions.php`	Functions	Contains functions that help display a book and lists of books
`cachefunctions.php`	Functions	Contains functions to carry out the caching required by Amazon
`cartfunctions.php`	Functions	Contains shopping cart related functions
`categoryfunctions.php`	Functions	Contains functions that help retrieve and display a category
`utilityfunctions.php`	Functions	Contains a set of utility functions used throughout the application

You will also need the `nusoap.php` file we mentioned previously, as it is required in these files. NuSOAP is in the `chapter31` directory on the CD-ROM at the back of the book, but you might like to replace it with a newer version from `http://dietrich.ganx4.com/nusoap/index.php`.

We will begin by looking at the core application file `index.php`.

Core Application

The application file `index.php` is shown in Listing 31.3.

Listing 31.3 **index.php—The Core Application File**

```php
<?php
//we are only using one session variable 'cart' to store the cart contents
session_start();

require_once('constants.php');
require_once('utilityfunctions.php');
require_once('bookdisplayfunctions.php');
require_once('cartfunctions.php');
require_once('categoryfunctions.php');

// These are the variables we are expecting from outside.
// They will be validated and converted to globals
$external = array('action', 'ASIN', 'mode', 'browseNode', 'page', 'search');

// the variables may come via Get or Post
// convert all our expected external variables to short global names
foreach ($external as $e)
{
```

Listing 31.3   **Continued**

```
  if(@$HTTP_POST_VARS[$e])
    $$e = $HTTP_POST_VARS[$e];
  else if(@$HTTP_GET_VARS[$e])
    $$e = $HTTP_GET_VARS[$e];
  else
    $$e = '';

  $$e = trim($$e);
}

// default values for global variables
if($mode=='')
  $mode = 'books'; // No other modes have been tested
if($browseNode=='')
  $browseNode = 1000; //1000 is bestselling books
if($page=='')
  $page = 1;   // First Page - there are 10 items per page

//validate/strip input
if(!eregi('^[A-Z0-9]+$', $ASIN)) // ASINS must be alpha-numeric
  $ASIN ='';
if(!eregi('^[a-z]+$', $mode)) // mode must be alphabetic
  $mode = 'books';
$page=intval($page); // pages and browseNodes must be integers
$browseNode = intval($browseNode);
// it may cause some confusion, but we are stripping characters out from
// $search it seems only fair to modify it now so it will be displayed
// in the heading
$search = safeString($search);

if(!isset($HTTP_SESSION_VARS['cart']))
{
  session_register('cart');
  $HTTP_SESSION_VARS['cart'] = array();
}

// tasks that need to be done before the top bar is shown
if($action == 'addtocart')
  addToCart($HTTP_SESSION_VARS['cart'], $ASIN, $mode);
if($action == 'deletefromcart')
  deleteFromCart($HTTP_SESSION_VARS['cart'], $ASIN) ;
if($action == 'emptycart')
  $HTTP_SESSION_VARS['cart'] = array();
```

Listing 31.3   **Continued**

```
// show top bar
require_once ('topbar.php');

// main event loop.  Reacts to user action on the calling page
switch ($action)
{
  case 'detail' :
    showCategories($mode);
    showDetail($ASIN, $mode);
  break;

  case 'addtocart' :
  case 'deletefromcart' :
  case 'emptycart' :
  case 'showcart' :
    echo '<hr /><h1>Your Shopping Cart</h1>';
    showCart($HTTP_SESSION_VARS['cart'], $mode);
  break;

  case 'image' :
    showCategories($mode);
    echo '<h1>Large Product Image</h1>';
    showImage($ASIN, $mode);
  break;

  case 'search' :
    showCategories($mode);
    echo "<h1>Search Results For '$search'</h1>";
    showSearch($search, $page, $mode);
  break;

  case 'browsenode':
  default:
    showCategories($mode);
    $category = getCategoryName($browseNode);
    if(!$category||$category=='Best Selling Books')
    {
      echo '<h1>Current Best Sellers</h1>';
    }
    else
    {
      echo "<h1>Current Best Sellers in $category</h1>";
    }
    showBrowseNode($browseNode, $page, $mode) ;
  break;
```

Listing 31.3 **Continued**

```php
}
require ('bottom.php');
? >
```

Let's work our way through this file. We begin by creating a session. We will store the customer's shopping cart as a session variable as we have done before.

We then include several files. Most of these are functions that we'll discuss later, but we need to talk about the first included file now. This file, `constants.php`, defines some important constants that will be used throughout the application. The contents of `constants.php` can be found in Listing 31.4.

Listing 31.4 **constants.php—Declaring Key Global Constants**

```php
<?php
// this application can connect via XML/HTTP or SOAP
// define one version of METHOD to choose.
define('METHOD', 'SOAP');
//define('METHOD', 'XML/HTTP');

// make sure to create a cache directory an make it writable
define('CACHE', 'cache'); // path to cached files
define('ASSOCIATEID', 'webservices-20'); //put your associate id here
define('DEVTAG', 'XXXXXXXXXXXXXX'); // put your developer tag here

//give an error if software is run with the dummy devtag
if(DEVTAG=='XXXXXXXXXXXXXX')
  die ('You need to sign up for an Amazon.com developer tag at<a href =
      "http://associates.amazon.com/exec/panama/associates/join/
      developer/kit.html">Amazon</a>
      when you install this software.  You should probably sign up
      for an associate ID at the same time. Edit the file constants.php.');
? >
```

This application has been developed to use either XML over HTTP or SOAP. You can set which one it should use by changing the value of the METHOD constant.

The CACHE constant holds the path to the cache for the data we download from Amazon. Change this to the path you would like used on your system.

The ASSOCIATEID constant holds the value of your Associate ID. If you send this to Amazon with transactions, you get a commission. Change this to your own Associate ID.

The DEVTAG constant holds the value of the developer token Amazon will give you when you sign up. You need to change this to your own developer tag, or the application will not work. You can sign up for a tag at

```
http://associates.amazon.com/exec/panama/associates/join/developer/kit.html
```

Let's look back at index.php. It contains some preliminaries, and then the main event loop. We begin by extracting any incoming variables that came via GET or POST. We then set up some default values for some standard global variables that determine what will be displayed later on, as follows:

```
// default values for global variables
if($mode=='')
  $mode = 'books'; // No other modes have been tested
if($browseNode=='')
  $browseNode = 1000; //1000 is bestselling books
if($page=='')
  $page = 1;  // First Page - there are 10 items per page
```

We set the mode variable to books. Amazon supports many other modes (types of products), but for this application, we will only worry about books. It should not be too hard to modify the code in this chapter to deal with other categories. The first step in this expansion would be to reset $mode. You would need to check the Amazon documentation to see what other attributes are returned for non-book products and remove book-specific language from the user interface.

The browseNode variable is used to specify what category of books we would like displayed. This may be set if the user has clicked through one of the Selected Categories links. If it is not set—for example, when the user first enters the site—we will set it to 1000. Amazon's browse nodes are simply integers that identify a category. The value 1000 represents the category Best Selling Books, which is what we display on the initial front page.

The page variable is used to tell Amazon which subset of the results we would like displayed within a given category. Page 1 contains results 1–10, page 2 has results 11–20, and so on. Amazon sets the number of items on a page, and we do not have control over this. We could, of course, display two or more Amazon "pages" of data on one of our pages, but 10 is both a reasonable figure and the path of least resistance.

Next, we tidy up any input data we have received, whether through the search box or via GET or POST parameters:

```
//validate/strip input
if(!eregi('^[A-Z0-9]+$', $ASIN)) // ASINS must be alpha-numeric
  $ASIN ='';
if(!eregi('^[a-z]+$', $mode)) // mode must be alphabetic
  $mode = 'books';
$page=intval($page); // pages and browseNodes must be integers
$browseNode = intval($browseNode);
// it may cause some confusion, but we are stripping characters out
// from $search
// it seems only fair to modify it now so it will be displayed in the
// heading
$search = safeString($search) ;
```

This is nothing new. The `safeString()` function is in the `utilityfunctions.php` file. It simply removes any non-alphanumeric characters from the input string via a regular expression replacement. Because we have covered this before, we have not included it here in the text.

The main reason that we need to validate input in this application is that we use the customer's input to create file names in the cache. We could run into serious problems if we allow customers to include .. or / in their input.

Next we set up the customer's shopping cart, if she does not already have one:

```
if(!isset($HTTP_SESSION_VARS['cart']))
{
  session_register('cart');
  $HTTP_SESSION_VARS['cart'] = array();
}
```

We have a few last things to do before we can display the information in the top information bar on the page (see Figure 31.1 for a reminder of what this looks like). A glimpse of the shopping cart is shown in the top bar of every page. It is therefore important that the cart variable is up to date before this is displayed.

```
// tasks that need to be done before the top bar is shown
if($action == 'addtocart')
  addToCart($HTTP_SESSION_VARS['cart'], $ASIN, $mode);
if($action == 'deletefromcart')
  deleteFromCart($HTTP_SESSION_VARS['cart'], $ASIN);
if($action == 'emptycart')
  $HTTP_SESSION_VARS['cart'] = array();
```

Here we are adding or deleting items from the cart as necessary before displaying the cart. We will come back to these functions when we discuss the shopping cart and checking out. If you want to look at them now, they are in the file `cartfunctions.php`. We are leaving them aside for a minute, because we need to understand the interface to Amazon first.

Next, we include the file `topbar.php`. This file simply contains HTML and a style sheet and a single function call to the `ShowSmallCart()` function (from `cartfunctions.php`). This displays the small shopping cart summary you can see in the top right-hand corner of the figures. We will come back to this when we discuss the cart functions.

Finally, we come to the main event-handling loop. A summary of the possible actions is shown in Table 31.2.

Table 31.2 **Possible Actions in the Main Event Loop**

Action	Description
browsenode	Show books in the specified category. This is the default action.
detail	Show the details of one particular book.

Table 31.2   **Continued**

Action	Description
image	Show a large version of the book's cover.
search	Show the results of a user search.
addtocart	Add an item to the user's shopping cart.
deletefromcart	Delete an item from the shopping cart.
emptycart	Empty the shopping cart altogether.
showcart	Show the contents of the cart.

As you can see, the first four actions in this table relate to retrieving and displaying information from Amazon. The second group of four deal with managing the shopping cart.

The actions that retrieve data from Amazon all work in a quite similar way. We will consider retrieving data about books in a particular browsenode (category) as an example.

Showing Books in a Category

The code that is executed when the action is browsenode (view a category) is as follows:

```
showCategories($mode);
$category = getCategoryName($browseNode);
if(!$category||$category=='Best Selling Books')
{
  echo '<h1>Current Best Sellers</h1>';
}
else
{
  echo "<h1>Current Best Sellers in $category</h1>";
}
showBrowseNode($browseNode, $page, $mode);
```

The showCategories() function displays the list of selected categories we see near the top of most of the pages. The getCategoryName() function returns the name of the current category given its browsenode number. The showBrowseNode() function displays a page of books in that category.

Let's begin by considering the showCategories() function. The code for this function is shown in Listing 31.5.

Listing 31.5   **showCategories() Function from categoryfunctions.php—A List of Categories**

```
//display a starting list of popular categories
function showCategories($mode)
{
  global $categoryList;
```

Listing 31.5   **Continued**

```
echo '<hr /><h2>Selected Categories</h2>';

if($mode == 'books')
{

  asort($categoryList);

  $categories = count($categoryList);
  $columns = 4;
  $rows = ceil($categories/$columns);

  echo '<table border ="0" cellpadding ="0" cellspacing="0"
             width ="100%"><tr>';

  reset($categoryList);

  for($col = 0; $col<$columns; $col++)
  {
    echo '<td width = "'.(100/$columns).'%" valign = "top"><ul>';
    for($row = 0; $row<$rows; $row++)
    {
      $category = each($categoryList);
      if($category)
      {
        $browseNode = $category['key'];
        $name = $category['value'];
        echo "<li><span class = 'category'><a href =
                'index.php?action=browsnode&browseNode=$browseNode'>$name
                </a></span></li>";
      }
    }
    echo '</ul></td>';
  }
  echo '</tr></table><hr />';
  }
}
```

This function uses an array called categoryList, declared in the
categoryfunctions.php package, to map browsenode numbers to names. The desired
browsenodes are simply hard-coded into this array. This function sorts the array and displays the various categories.

The getCategoryName() function that is called next in the main event loop is used
to look up the name of the browsenode that we are currently looking at so we can display a heading on the screen such as Current Best Sellers in Business & Investing. It
looks this up in the categoryList array mentioned previously.

The fun really starts when we get to the `showBrowseNode()` function. This function is shown in Listing 31.6.

Listing 31.6   **showBrowseNode() Function from bookdisplayfunctions.php—A List of Categories**

```
// For a particular browsenode, display a page of products
function showBrowseNode($browseNode, $page, $mode)
{
  $ars = getARS('browse', array('browsenode'=>$browseNode,
                                'page' => $page,
                                'mode'=>$mode));
  showSummary($ars->products(), $page, $ars->totalResults(),
              $mode, $browseNode);
}
```

This function does exactly two things. First, it calls the `getARS()` function from `cache-functions.php`. This function gets and returns an `AmazonResultSet` object (more on this in a moment). Then it calls the `showSummary()` function from `bookdisplayfunctions.php` to display the retrieved information.

The `getARS()` function is absolutely key to driving the whole application. If we work our way through the code for the other actions—viewing details, images, and searching—we will find that it all comes back to this.

Getting an `AmazonResultSet`

Let's look at that `getARS()` function in more detail. It is shown in Listing 31.7.

Listing 31.7   **getARS() Function from cachefunctions.php—A Resultset for a Query**

```
// Get an AmazonResultSet either from cache or a live query
// If a live query add it to the cache
function getARS($type, $parameters)
{
  $cache = cached($type, $parameters);
  if($cache)  // if found in cache
  {
    return $cache;
  }
  else
  {
    $ars = new AmazonResultSet;
    if($type == 'asin')
      $ars->ASINSearch(padASIN($parameters['asin']), $parameters['mode']);
    if($type == 'browse')
              $ars->browseNodeSearch($parameters['browsenode'],
```

Listing 31.7 **Continued**

```
        $parameters['page'], $parameters['mode']);
  if($type == 'search')
    $ars->keywordSearch($parameters['search'], $parameters['page'],
                        $parameters['mode']);
  cache($type, $parameters, $ars);
  }
  return $ars;
}
```

This function is designed to drive the process of getting data from Amazon. It can do this in two ways: either from the cache, or live from Amazon. Because Amazon requires developers to cache downloaded data, the function first looks for data in the cache. We will discuss the cache in a few pages.

If we have not already performed this particular query, the data must be fetched live from Amazon. We do this by creating an instance of the `AmazonResultSet` class and calling the method on it that corresponds to the particular query we want to run. The type of query is determined by the `$type` parameter. In the category (or browse node) search example, we pass in `browse` as the value for this parameter—refer to Listing 31.6. If we want to perform a query about one particular book, we should pass in the value `asin`, and if we want to perform a keyword search, the parameter should be set to `search`.

Each of these parameters invokes a different method on the `AmazonResultSet` class. The individual item search calls the `ASINSearch()` method. The category search calls the `browseNodeSearch()` method. The keyword search calls the `keywordSearch()` method.

Let's take a closer look at the `AmazonResultSet` class. The full code for this class is shown in Listing 31.8.

Listing 31.8 **AmazonResultSet.php—A Class for Handling Amazon Connections**

```
<?php
require_once('Product.php');

// you can switch between XML/HTTP and SOAP using this constant set in
// constants.php
if(METHOD=='SOAP')
{
  include_once('nusoap/nusoap.php');
}

// This class stores the result of queries
// Usually this is 1 or 10 instances of the Product class
class AmazonResultSet
{
```

Listing 31.8 **Continued**

```
  var $_browseNode;
  var $_ASIN;
  var $_page;
  var $_mode;
  var $_url;
  var $_type;
  var $_totalResults;
  var $_currentProduct = null;
  var $_products = array(); // array of Product objects
  var $_names = array();
// array of names of the XML nodes we have entered.
// treated as a stack.  Only used during parsing.

  function products()
  {
    return $this->_products;
  }

  function totalResults()
  {
    return $this->_totalResults;
  }

  function getProduct($i)
  {
    if(isset($this->_products[$i]))
      return $this->_products[$i] ;
    else
      return false;
  }


  // Perform a query to get a page full of products from a browse node
  // Switch between XML/HTTP and SOAP in constants.php
  // Returns an array of Products
  function browseNodeSearch($browseNode, $page, $mode)
  {
    if(METHOD=='SOAP')
    {
      // the NuSOAP class generates a lot of notices. Turn them off.
      error_reporting(error_reporting() & ~E_NOTICE);
      $soapclient = new soapclient(
            'http://soap.amazon.com/schemas2/AmazonWebServices.wsdl',
            'wsdl');
      $soap_proxy = $soapclient->getProxy();
      $parameters['mode']=$mode;
```

Listing 31.8   **Continued**

```
    $parameters['page']=$page;
    $parameters['type']='heavy';
    $parameters['tag']=$this->_assocID;
    $parameters['devtag']=$this->_devTag;
    $parameters['sort']='+salesrank';
    $parameters['browse_node'] = $browseNode;

    // perform actual soap query
    $result = $soap_proxy->BrowseNodeSearchRequest($parameters);
    if(isSOAPError($result))
      return false;
    $this->_totalResults = $result['TotalResults'];
    $counter = 0;
    foreach($result['Details'] as $product)
    {
      $this->_products[$counter] = new Product;
      $this->_products[$counter]->soap = $result['Details'][$counter];
      $counter++;
    }
    unset($soapclient);
    unset($soap_proxy);
  }
  else
  {
          // form URL and call parseXML to download and parse it
    $this->_type = 'browse';
    $this->_browseNode = $browseNode;
    $this->_page = $page;
    $this->_mode = $mode;
    $this->_url = 'http://xml.amazon.com/onca/xml2?t='.ASSOCIATEID
                .'&dev-t='.DEVTAG.'&BrowseNodeSearch='
                .$this->_browseNode.'&mode='.$this->_mode
                .'&type=heavy&page='.$this->_page.'&sort=+salesrank&f=xml';
    $this->parseXML();
  }

  return $this->_products;
}

// Given an ASIN, get the URL of the large image
// Returns a string
function getImageUrlLarge($ASIN, $mode)
{
  if( $this->_products[0]->imageURLLarge())
    return  $this->_products[0]->imageURLLarge();
```

Listing 31.8 **Continued**

```
    $this->ASINSearch($ASIN, $mode);
      return $this->_products[0]->imageURLLarge();
}


// Perform a query to get a products with specified ASIN
// Switch between XML/HTTP and SOAP in constants.php
// Returns a Products object
function ASINSearch($ASIN, $mode = 'books')
{
  $this->_type = 'ASIN';
  $this->_ASIN=$ASIN;
  $this->_mode = $mode;
  $ASIN = padASIN($ASIN);

  if(METHOD=='SOAP')
  {
    error_reporting(E_ALL & ~E_NOTICE);
    $soapclient = new soapclient (
          'http://soap.amazon.com/schemas2/AmazonWebServices.wsdl',
          'wsdl') ;
    $soap_proxy = $soapclient->getProxy();
    $parameters['asin']=$ASIN;
    $parameters['mode']=$mode;
    $parameters['type']="heavy";
    $parameters['tag']=$this->_assocID;
    $parameters['devtag']=$this->_devTag;

    $result = $soap_proxy->AsinSearchRequest($parameters);
    if(isSOAPError($result))
    {
      print_r($result);
      return false;
    }
    $this->_products[0] = new Product;
    $this->_products[0]->soap = $result['Details'][0];
    $this->_totalResults=1;
    unset($soapclient);
    unset($soap_proxy);
  }
  else
  {
    // form URL and call parseXML to download and parse it
    $this->_url = 'http://xml.amazon.com/onca/xml2?t='.ASSOCIATEID
                .'&dev-t='.DEVTAG.'&AsinSearch='
                .$this->_ASIN
```

Listing 31.8 **Continued**

```
                       .'&type=heavy&f=xml';
    $this->parseXML();
  }
  return $this->_products[0];
}


// Perform a query to get a page full of products with a keyword search
// Switch between XML/HTTP and SOAP in index.php
// Returns an array of Products
function keywordSearch($search, $page, $mode = 'books')
{
   if(METHOD=='SOAP')
  {
    error_reporting(E_ALL & ~E_NOTICE);
    $soapclient = new soapclient(
         'http://soap.amazon.com/schemas2/AmazonWebServices.wsdl','wsdl');
    $soap_proxy = $soapclient->getProxy();
    $parameters['mode']=$mode;
    $parameters['page']=$page;
    $parameters['type']="heavy";
    $parameters['tag']=$this->_assocID;
    $parameters['devtag']=$this->_devTag;
    $parameters['sort']='+salesrank';
    $parameters['keyword'] = $search;
    // perform actual soap request
    $result = $soap_proxy->KeywordSearchRequest($parameters);

    if(isSOAPError($result) )
      return false;
    $counter = 0;
    foreach($result['Details'] as $product)
    {
      $this->_products[$counter] = new Product;
      $this->_products[$counter]->soap = $result['Details'][$counter];
      $counter++;
    }
    $this->_totalResults = $result['TotalResults'] ;
    unset($soapclient);
    unset($soap_proxy);
  }
  else
  {
    $this->_type = 'search';
    $this->_search=$search;
    $this->_page = $page;
```

Listing 31.8 **Continued**

```
      $search = urlencode($search);
      $this->_mode = $mode;
      $this->_url = 'http://xml.amazon.com/onca/xml2?t='.ASSOCIATEID
                    .'&dev-t='.DEVTAG.'&KeywordSearch='
                    .$search.'&mode='.$this->_mode
                    .'&type=heavy&page='
                    .$this->_page
                    .'&sort=+salesrank&f=xml';
      $this->parseXML();
   }
   return $this->_products;
}


// Parse the XML into Product object(s)
function parseXML()
{
  $xml_parser = xml_parser_create();
  xml_parser_set_option($xml_parser,XML_OPTION_SKIP_WHITE,1);
  xml_set_object($xml_parser, $this);
  xml_set_element_handler($xml_parser,
                          "startElementHandler",
                          "endElementHandler");
  xml_set_character_data_handler($xml_parser, 'cdataHandler');

  if (!($fp = fopen($this->_url, "r")))
  {
    die("could not open XML input");
  }
  while ($data = fread($fp, 4096))
  {
    if (!xml_parse($xml_parser, $data, feof($fp)))
    {
      die(sprintf("XML error: %s at line %d",
                  xml_error_string(xml_get_error_code($xml_parser)),
                  xml_get_current_line_number($xml_parser)));
    }
  }
  xml_parser_free($xml_parser) ;
}


// function to catch callbacks when the XML parser reaches the start
// of a new element
function startElementHandler($parser, $name, $attributes)
{
  array_push($this->_names, $name);
```

Listing 31.8 **Continued**

```
  if($name=='DETAILS')
  {
    $this->_currentProduct = new Product();
  }
  if($name == 'BROWSENODE')
  {
    $this->_currentProduct->_currentBrowseName++;
  }
  if($name == 'CUSTOMERREVIEW')
  {
    $this->_currentProduct->_currentReview++;
  }
}

// function to catch callbacks when the XML parser has data from
// an element
function cdataHandler($parser, $cdata)
{
  $this->_currentName = array_slice($this->_names, -1, 1);
  $this->_currentName = $this->_currentName[0] ;

  switch($this->_currentName)
  {
    case 'TOTALRESULTS' :
      $this->_totalResults = $cdata;
    break;

    case 'DETAILS' :
    break;

    case 'AUTHOR' :
      $this->_currentProduct->authors[] = $cdata;
    break;

    case 'RATING' :
    case 'SUMMARY' :
    case 'COMMENT' :
      @$this->_currentProduct->
         customerReviews[$this->_currentProduct->_currentReview]
         [$this->_currentName] .= $cdata;
      // fields that may contain returns and &s need to be concatenated
      // concatenation will give a notice if they are enabled -
      // hence the @
    break;
```

Listing 31.8 **Continued**

```
    case 'LISTID' :
      $this->_currentProduct->listIDs[] = $cdata;
    break;

    case 'BROWSENAME' :
      @$this->_currentProduct->browseNames[$this->_currentProduct->_
              currentBrowseName] .= $cdata;
      // fields that may contain returns and &s need to be concatenated
      // concatenation will give a notice if they are enabled -
      // hence the @
    break;

    case 'PRODUCT' :
      $this->_currentProduct->similarProducts[] = $cdata;
    break;

    // there are certain keys we are dealing with the
    // children of separately so can ignore
    case 'CUSTOMERREVIEW' :
    case 'AUTHORS' :
    case 'BROWSELIST' :
    case 'BROWSENODE' :
    case 'LISTS' :
    case 'REVIEWS' :
    case 'SIMILARPRODUCTS' :
      //do nothing
     break;

    default :
      @$this->_currentProduct->nodes[$this->_currentName] .= $cdata;
    break;
  }
}

// function to get callbacks when the XML parser reaches an end of element
function endElementHandler($parser, $name)
{
  if($name=='DETAILS')
  {
    //these are no longer required
    unset($this->_currentProduct->_currentReview);
    unset($this->_currentProduct->_currentBrowseName);

    array_push($this->_products, $this->_currentProduct);
```

Listing 31.8 **Continued**

```
    }
    array_pop($this->_names);
  }
}
? >
```

This useful class does exactly the sort of thing classes are good for. It encapsulates the interface to Amazon in a nice black box. Within the class the connection to Amazon can be made either via the XML over HTTP method or the SOAP method. The method it will use is determined by the global METHOD constant we set at the very beginning.

Let's begin by going back to the Category Search example. We use the AmazonResultSet class as follows:

```
$ars = new AmazonResultSet;
$ars->browseNodeSearch($parameters['browsenode'],
                       $parameters['page'],
                       $parameters['mode']);
```

This class has no constructor, so we'll go straight to that browseNodeSearch() method. We are passing it three parameters: the browsenode number we are interested in (corresponding to, say, Business & Investing, or Computers & Internet); the page number, representing the records we would like retrieved; and the mode, representing the type of merchandise we are interested in. The code for this method is shown excerpted in Listing 31.9.

Listing 31.9 **browseNodeSearch() Method—Performing a Category Search**

```
// Perform a query to get a page full of products from a browse node
// Switch between XML/HTTP and SOAP in constants.php
// Returns an array of Products
function browseNodeSearch($browseNode, $page, $mode)
{
  if(METHOD=='SOAP')
  {
    // the NuSOAP class generates a lot of notices. Turn them off.
    error_reporting(error_reporting() & ~E_NOTICE);
    $soapclient = new soapclient(
     'http://soap.amazon.com/schemas2/AmazonWebServices.wsdl',
     'wsdl');
    $soap_proxy = $soapclient->getProxy();
    $parameters['mode']=$mode;
    $parameters['page']=$page;
    $parameters['type']='heavy';
    $parameters['tag']=$this->_assocID;
    $parameters['devtag']=$this->_devTag;
    $parameters['sort']='+salesrank';
```

Listing 31.9 **Continued**

```
   $parameters['browse_node'] = $browseNode;

   // perform actual soap query
   $result = $soap_proxy->BrowseNodeSearchRequest($parameters) ;
   if(isSOAPError($result))
     return false;
   $this->_totalResults = $result['TotalResults'];
   $counter = 0;
   foreach($result['Details'] as $product)
   {
     $this->_products[$counter] = new Product;
     $this->_products[$counter]->soap = $result['Details'][$counter];
     $counter++;
   }
   unset($soapclient);
   unset($soap_proxy);
 }
 else
 {
   // form URL and call parseXML to download and parse it
   $this->_type = 'browse';
   $this->_browseNode = $browseNode;
   $this->_page = $page;
   $this->_mode = $mode;
   $this->_url = 'http://xml.amazon.com/onca/xml2?t='.ASSOCIATEID
               .'&dev-t='.DEVTAG.'&BrowseNodeSearch='
               .$this->_browseNode.'&mode='.$this->_mode
               .'&type=heavy&page='.$this->_page.'&sort=+salesrank&f=xml';
   $this->parseXML();
 }

 return $this->_products;
}
```

Depending on the value of the METHOD constant, this method will either perform the query via XML over HTTP or via SOAP. We will look at each of these separately.

Using XML Over HTTP

We begin by setting a few important class member variables:

- type—The type of search required. We are searching for books within a particular browsenode, so we set the value to browse.
- browse —The value of the particular browsenode we have been passed as a parameter.

- page —The page number that we have been passed as a parameter.
- mode —The type of items we are searching for (for example, books) that we have been passed as a parameter.
- url —The URL at Amazon that we need to connect to in order to perform this type of search.

The URLs that we make our HTTP connections to for different types of searches and the parameters they expect can be found in the Amazon.com Web Services API and Integration Guide in your developer's kit. Look closely at the GET parameters we are passing in here:

```
$this->_url = 'http://xml.amazon.com/onca/xml2?t='.ASSOCIATEID
              .'&dev-t='.DEVTAG.'&BrowseNodeSearch='
              .$this->_browseNode.'&mode='.$this->_mode
              .'&type=heavy&page='.$this->_page
              .'&sort=+salesrank&f=xml';
```

The parameters we need to pass to this URL are as follows:

- t—Your Associate ID.
- dev-t —Your developer token.
- BrowseNodeSearch —The browsenode number you want to search.
- mode —books, or another valid product type.
- type —Heavy or lite (note spelling!). Heavy gives more information.
- page —Group of ten results.
- sort —The order we would like the results returned in. This is an optional parameter. In this case, we have set it to +salesrank because we would like results in sales rank order.
- f —The format. This should always contain the value 'xml'.

Valid sort types are as follows:

- Featured Items: +pmrank
- Bestselling: +salesrank
- Average Customer Review: +reviewrank
- Price (Low to High): +pricerank
- Price (High to Low): +inverse-pricerank
- Publication Date: +daterank
- Alphabetical (A-Z): +titlerank
- Alphabetical (Z-A): -titlerank

After all these parameters are set, we call

```
$this->parseXML();
```

to actually do the work. The `parseXML()` method is shown in Listing 31.10.

Listing 31.10 **parseXML() Method—Parsing the XML Returned from a Query**

```
// Parse the XML into Product object(s)
function parseXML()
{
  $xml_parser = xml_parser_create();
  xml_parser_set_option($xml_parser,XML_OPTION_SKIP_WHITE,1);
  xml_set_object($xml_parser, $this);
  xml_set_element_handler($xml_parser,
                          "startElementHandler",
                          "endElementHandler");
  xml_set_character_data_handler($xml_parser, 'cdataHandler');
  if (!($fp = fopen($this->_url, "r")))
  {
    die("could not open XML input");
  }
  while ($data = fread($fp, 4096))
  {
    if (!xml_parse($xml_parser, $data, feof($fp)))
    {
      die(sprintf("XML error: %s at line %d",
                  xml_error_string(xml_get_error_code($xml_parser)),
                  xml_get_current_line_number($xml_parser)));
    }
  }
  xml_parser_free($xml_parser);
}
```

In this method we are using PHP's XML library, which is based on expat.
We begin by calling the `xml_parser_create()` function. This creates an instance of the
parser and returns a handle to this parser, which will need to be passed to other functions.

We then need to set up a few things in this parser before we can actually parse the
XML document, as follows:

```
xml_parser_set_option($xml_parser,XML_OPTION_SKIP_WHITE,1);
xml_set_object($xml_parser, $this);
xml_set_element_handler($xml_parser,
                        "startElementHandler",
                        "endElementHandler");
xml_set_character_data_handler($xml_parser, 'cdataHandler');
```

The first line sets the parser to skip whitespace (which will save effort). There are a few other options that can be set with this function, but this is the only one relevant here.

The next three lines are used to set up callback functions. We need to tell the parser what to do when it finds elements and character data inside the XML document. The call to `xml_set_object()` tells the parser that the callback functions will be found inside `$this`, the current `AmazonResultSet` object. (If we were just using regular functions rather than class methods, we would not need this function call.)

The call to `xml_set_element_handler()` tells the parser that whenever it finds the beginning of an element, it should call the method named `startElementHandler()`, and when it finds the end of an element, it should call the method named `endElementHandler()`. These are yet more methods we have written inside the `AmazonResultSet` object. These methods are called *callbacks*, and their signature must follow a certain format.

The `startElementHandler()` method must accept three parameters: a reference to the parser, the name of the element that has just started, and an array of the attributes of the element.

The `endElementHandler()` method must accept two parameters: a reference to the parser, and the name of the element that is ending.

The call to `xml_set_character_data_handler()` tells the parser what to do when it encounters character data in the XML document. This will occur when the parser tries to process the actual contents of an element. It should call the method called `cDataHandler()`, also located in the `AmazonResultSet` class. Again, this method must have a certain signature. In this case, it must accept two parameters: a reference to the parser, and the character data as a string. We'll look at the content of these callbacks in a moment.

After setting up all these parameters, we open the file at the URL we received a minute ago, and parse the XML we find there. The parser will work its way through the document, invoking the callback functions as it goes.

Finally, we need to clean up after ourselves by deleting the parser:

```
xml_parser_free($xml_parser);
```

Now, let's see what happens in those callback functions. The three functions are shown in Listing 31.11.

Listing 31.11   **Callback Functions**

```
// function to catch callbacks when the XML parser reaches the start of
// a new element
function startElementHandler($parser, $name, $attributes)
{
  array_push($this->_names, $name);

  if($name=='DETAILS')
  {
```

Listing 31.11 **Continued**

```php
    $this->_currentProduct = new Product();
  }
  if($name == 'BROWSENODE')
  {
    $this->_currentProduct->_currentBrowseName++;
  }
  if($name == 'CUSTOMERREVIEW')
  {
    $this->_currentProduct->_currentReview++;
  }
}

// function to catch callbacks when the XML parser has data from
// an element
function cdataHandler($parser, $cdata)
{
  $this->_currentName = array_slice($this->_names, -1, 1);
  $this->_currentName = $this->_currentName[0];

  switch($this->_currentName)
  {
    case 'TOTALRESULTS' :
      $this->_totalResults = $cdata;
    break;

    case 'DETAILS' :
    break;

    case 'AUTHOR' :
      $this->_currentProduct->authors[] = $cdata;
    break;

    case 'RATING' :
    case 'SUMMARY' :
    case 'COMMENT' :
      @$this->_currentProduct->customerReviews[$this->_currentProduct->_
              currentReview][$this->_currentName] .= $cdata;
      // fields that may contain returns and &s need to be concatenated
      // concatenation will give a notice if they are enabled -
      //hence the @
    break;

    case 'LISTID' :
      $this->_currentProduct->listIDs[] = $cdata;
    break;
```

Listing 31.11 **Continued**

```
    case 'BROWSENAME' :
      @$this->_currentProduct->
          browseNames[$this->_currentProduct->_currentBrowseName] .= $cdata;
      // fields that may contain returns and &s need to be concatenated
      // concatenation will give a notice if they are enabled -
      // hence the @
    break;

    case 'PRODUCT' :
      $this->_currentProduct->similarProducts[] = $cdata;
    break;

    // there are certain keys we are dealing with the children of
    // separately so can ignore
    case 'CUSTOMERREVIEW' :
    case 'AUTHORS' :
    case 'BROWSELIST' :
    case 'BROWSENODE' :
    case 'LISTS' :
    case 'REVIEWS' :
    case 'SIMILARPRODUCTS' :
      //do nothing
    break;

    default :
      @$this->_currentProduct->nodes[$this->_currentName] .= $cdata;
    break;
  }
}

// function to get callbacks when the XML parser reaches the end of an
// element
function endElementHandler($parser, $name)
{
  if($name=='DETAILS')
  {
    //these are no longer required
    unset($this->_currentProduct->_currentReview);
    unset($this->_currentProduct->_currentBrowseName);

    array_push($this->_products, $this->_currentProduct);
  }
  array_pop($this->_names) ;
}
```

By reading through this code, you will see that these three functions populate the class member array $_products with the information contained in the XML document. This array consists of instances of the Product class, which we have created specifically to hold the details of an item. The code for the Product class is shown in Listing 31.12.

Listing 31.12   **Part of Product.php—Storing Data on an Individual Item**

```php
<?php
// This class holds data about a single amazon product
// scalar attributes are all stored in the array nodes
// attributes from the XML document that require special
// treatment have their own array

// if the data came via XML/HTTP, most of the data will be in $this->nodes
// if the data came via SOAP, _ALL_ of the data will be in $this->soap

// This class' main purpose is to provide a common interface to the data
// from these two sources so all the display code can be common
class Product
{
  var $nodes = array();
  var $authors = array();
  var $listIDs = array();
  var $browseNames = array();
  var $customerReviews = array();
  var $similarProducts = array();
  var $_currentReview = -1;
  var $_currentBrowseName = -1;
  var $soap; // array returned by SOAP calls


  // most methods in this class are similar
  // return the XML variable or the SOAP one
  // a single Product instance will only have one or the other
  function similarProductCount()
  {
    if($this->soap)
      return count($this->soap['SimilarProducts']);
    else
      return count($this->similarProducts);
  }
```

This class consists almost entirely of accessor (get and set) functions, so we will not dwell on it here. The main reason this class exists is so that we can conveniently store data from two different sources and access it through the same interface. This means we can take the default output from NuSOAP and an easy-to-parse result from the XML and store them as they come. It also means that our display, cache, and manipulation functions do not need to know what format the data is stored in or where it originated.

Having gone through all this processing to retrieve the data, we now return control back to the getARS() function and hence back to showBrowseNode(). The next step is

```
showSummary($ars->products(), $page,
            $ars->totalResults(), $mode,
            $browseNode);
```

The showSummary() function simply displays the data in the AmazonResultSet, as we see it all the way back in Figure 31.1. We have not therefore included the function here.

Using SOAP

Let's go back and look at the SOAP version of the browseNodeSearch() function. We'll repeat this section of the code here:

```
error_reporting(E_ALL & ~E_NOTICE);
$soapclient = new soapclient(
            'http://soap.amazon.com/schemas2/AmazonWebServices.wsdl','wsdl');
$soap_proxy = $soapclient->getProxy();
$parameters['mode']=$mode;
$parameters['page']=$page;
$parameters['type']='heavy';
$parameters['tag']=$this->_assocID;
$parameters['devtag']=$this->_devTag;
$parameters['sort']='+salesrank';
$parameters['browse_node'] = $browseNode;

$result = $soap_proxy->BrowseNodeSearchRequest($parameters);
if(isSOAPError($result))
return false;
$this->_totalResults = $result['TotalResults'];
$counter = 0;
foreach($result['Details'] as $product)
{
$this->_products[$counter] = new Product;
$this->_products[$counter]->soap = $result['Details'][$counter];
$counter++;
}
unset($soapclient);
unset($soap_proxy) ;
```

There are no extra functions to go through here—the SOAP client does everything for us.

You might not have control over the error reporting setting on your server. If notices are configured to be reported to the browser, the NuSOAP library produces notices, so we've turned it off for now.

We begin by creating an instance of the SOAP client:

```
$soapclient = new soapclient(
                    'http://soap.amazon.com/schemas2/AmazonWebServices.wsdl',
                    'wsdl');
```

We are providing the client with two parameters. The first is the WSDL description of the service, and the second parameter is to tell the SOAP client that this is a WSDL URL. Alternatively, we could just provide one parameter: the endpoint of the service, which is the direct URL of the SOAP Server.

We have chosen to do it this way for a good reason, which is right there in the next line of code:

```
$soap_proxy = $soapclient->getProxy();
```

This line creates a class according to the information in the WSDL document. This class, the SOAP proxy, will have methods that correspond to the methods of the Web Service. This makes life much easier. We can interact with the Web Service as though it were a local PHP class.

Next, we set up an array of the parameters we need to pass to the browsenode query:

```
$parameters['mode']=$mode;
$parameters['page']=$page;
$parameters['type']='heavy';
$parameters['tag']=$this->_assocID;
$parameters['devtag']=$this->_devTag;
$parameters['sort']='+salesrank';
$parameters['browse_node'] = $browseNode;
```

Using the proxy class, we can then just call the Web Service methods, passing in the array of parameters:

```
$result = $soap_proxy->BrowseNodeSearchRequest($parameters);
```

The data stored in $result is an array that we can directly store in our _products array in the AmazonResultSet class.

That's the SOAP version. As you can see, it's a great deal shorter than the XML version, and therefore preferable. But hopefully you've learned something about parsing XML along the way.

Caching the Data

Let's go back to the getARS() function and talk about caching. As you might recall, the function looks like this:

```
function getARS($type, $parameters)
{
  $cache = cached($type, $parameters);
  if($cache)  // if found in cache
  {
    return  $cache;
  }
  else
  {
    $ars = new AmazonResultSet;
    if($type == 'asin')
      $ars->ASINSearch(padASIN($parameters['asin']), $parameters['mode']);
    if($type == 'browse')
      $ars->browseNodeSearch($parameters['browsenode'],
                             $parameters['page'], $parameters['mode']);
    if($type == 'search')
      $ars->keywordSearch($parameters['search'], $parameters['page'],
                 $parameters['mode']);
    cache($type, $parameters, $ars);
  }
  return $ars;
}
```

All the application's SOAP or XML caching is done via this function. We also have another to cache images. We begin by calling the `cached()` function to see whether the required `AmazonResultSet` is already cached. If it is, we return that data instead of making a new request to Amazon:

```
$cache = cached($type, $parameters);
if($cache)  // if found in cache
{
  return  $cache;
}
```

If not, when we get the data back from Amazon, we add it to the cache:

```
cache($type, $parameters, $ars);
```

Let's look at these two functions: `cached()` and `cache()`. They are shown in Listing 31.13. These functions implement the caching Amazon requires as part of their terms and conditions.

Listing 31.13 **Caching Functions from cachefunctions.php**

```
// check if Amazon data is in the cache
// if it is, return it
// if not, return false
function cached($type, $parameters)
{
```

Listing 31.13 **Continued**

```
  if($type == 'browse')
    $filename = CACHE.'/browse.'.$parameters['browsenode'].'.
                '.$parameters['page'].'.'.$parameters['mode'].'.dat';
  if($type == 'search')
    $filename = CACHE.'/search.'.$parameters['search'].'.
                '.$parameters['page'].'.'.$parameters['mode'].'.dat';
  if($type == 'asin')
    $filename = CACHE.'/asin.'.$parameters['asin'].'
                .'.$parameters['mode'].'.dat';

  // is cached data missing or > 1 hour old?
  if(!file_exists($filename) ||
      ((mktime() - filemtime($filename)) > 60*60))
  {
    return false;
  }
  $data = file($filename);
  $data = join($data, '');
  return unserialize($data);
}

// add Amazon data to the cache
function cache($type, $parameters, $data)
{
  if($type == 'browse')
    $filename = CACHE.'/browse.'.$parameters['browsenode'].'.'
                .$parameters['page'].'.'.$parameters['mode'].'.dat';
  if($type == 'search')
    $filename = CACHE.'/search.'.$parameters['search'].'.'
                .$parameters['page'].'.'.$parameters['mode'].'.dat';
  if($type == 'asin')
    $filename = CACHE.'/asin.'.$parameters['asin'].'.'
.$parameters['mode'].'.dat';

  $data = serialize($data);

  $fp = fopen($filename, 'wb');
  if(!$fp||(fwrite($fp, $data)==-1) )
  {
    echo ('<p>Error, could not store cache file</p>');
  }
  fclose($fp);
}
```

Looking through this code, you can see that cache files are stored under a file name that consists of the type of query followed by the query parameters. The cache() function stores results by serializing them, and the cached() function deserializes them. The cached() function will also overwrite any data more than an hour old, as per the terms and conditions.

The function serialize() turns stored program data into a string that can be stored. In this case, we are creating a storable representation of an *AmazonResultSet* object. Calling unserialize() does the opposite, turning the stored version back into a data structure in memory. Note that unserializing an object like this means you need to have the class definition in the file so that the class is comprehendible and useable once reloaded.

In our application, retrieving a resultset from the cache takes a fraction of a second. Making a new live query takes up to ten seconds.

Building the Shopping Cart

So, given all these amazing Amazon querying abilities, what can we do with them? The most obvious thing we can build is a shopping cart. Because we've already covered this topic extensively in Chapter 25, "Building a Shopping Cart," we will not go into deep detail here.

The shopping cart functions are shown in Listing 31.14.

Listing 31.14   **cartfunctions.php—Implement the Shopping Cart**

```php
<?php
require_once('AmazonResultSet.php');

// Using the function showSummary() in the file bookdisplay.php display
// the current contents of the shopping cart
function showCart($cart, $mode)
{
  // build an array to pass
  $products = array();
  foreach($cart as $ASIN=>$product)
  {
    $ars = getARS('asin', array('asin'=>$ASIN, 'mode'=>$mode));
    if($ars)
      $products[] = $ars->getProduct(0);
  }
  // build the form to link to an Amazon.com shopping cart
  echo '<form method="POST"
            action="http://www.amazon.com/o/dt/assoc/handle-buy-box">';
  foreach($cart as $ASIN=>$product)
  {
    $quantity = $cart[$ASIN]['quantity'];
    echo "<input type='hidden' name='asin.$ASIN' value='$quantity'>";
```

Listing 31.14 **Continued**

```
  }
  echo '<input type="hidden" name="tag-value" value="ASSOCIATEID">';
  echo '<input type="hidden" name="tag_value" value="ASSOCIATEID">';
  echo '<input type="image" src="images/checkout.gif"
                            name="submit.add-to-cart"
                            value="Buy From Amazon.com">';
  echo ' When you have finished shopping press checkout to add all the
        items in your Tahuayo cart to your Amazon cart and complete
        your purchase.<br />';
  echo '</form>';

  echo '<a href = "index.php?action=emptycart"><img
          src = "images/emptycart.gif" alt = "Empty Cart" border = 0></a>
        If you have finished with this cart, you can empty it of all items.
        <br />';
  echo '<h1>Cart Contents</h1>';
  showSummary($products, 1, count($products), $mode,  0, true);

}

// show the small overview cart that is always on the screen
// only shows the last three items added
function showSmallCart()
{
  global $HTTP_SESSION_VARS;

  echo '<table border = 1 cellpadding = 1 cellspacing = 0>';
  echo '<tr><td class = cartheading>Your Cart $'
.number_format(cartPrice(), 2).
      '</td></tr>';
  echo '<tr><td class = cart>'.cartContents().'</td></tr>';

  // form to link to an Amazon.com shopping cart
  echo '<form method="POST"
              action="http://www.amazon.com/o/dt/assoc/handle-buy-box">';
  echo '<tr><td class = cartheading><a href =
                          "index.php?action=showcart"><img
                          src="images/details.gif" border=0></a>';
  foreach($HTTP_SESSION_VARS['cart'] as $ASIN=>$product)
  {
    $quantity = $HTTP_SESSION_VARS['cart'][$ASIN]['quantity'];
    echo "<input type='hidden' name='asin.$ASIN' value='$quantity'>";
  }
  echo '<input type="hidden" name="tag-value" value="ASSOCIATEID">';
  echo '<input type="hidden" name="tag_value" value="ASSOCIATEID">';
```

Listing 31.14 **Continued**

```php
  echo '<input type="image" src="images/checkout.gif"
              name="submit.add-to-cart" value="Buy From Amazon.com">';
  echo '</td></tr>';
  echo '</form>';

  echo '</table>';
}

// show last three items added to cart
function cartContents()
{
  global $HTTP_SESSION_VARS;

  $display = array_slice($HTTP_SESSION_VARS['cart'], -3, 3);
  // we want them in reverse chronological order
  $display = array_reverse($display, true);

  $result = '';
  $counter = 0;

  // abbreviate the names if they are long
  foreach($display as $product)
  {
    if(strlen($product['name'])<=40)
      $result .= $product['name'].'<br />';
    else
      $result .= substr($product['name'], 0, 37).'...<br />';
    $counter++;
  }

  // add blank lines if the cart is nearly empty to keep the
  // display the same
  for(;$counter<3; $counter++)
  {
    $result .= '<br />';
  }
  return $result;
}

// calculate total price of items in cart
function cartPrice()
{
  global $HTTP_SESSION_VARS;
  $total = 0.0;
```

Listing 31.14 **Continued**

```
  foreach($HTTP_SESSION_VARS['cart'] as $product)
  {
    $price = str_replace('$', '', $product['price']);
    $total += $price*$product['quantity'];
  }

  return $total;
}


// add a single item to cart
// there is currently no facility to add more than one at a time
function addToCart(&$cart, $ASIN, $mode)
{
  if(isset($cart[$ASIN] ))
  {
    $cart[$ASIN]['quantity'] +=1;
  }
  else
  {
    // check that the ASIN is valid and look up the price
    $ars = new AmazonResultSet;
    $product = $ars->ASINSearch($ASIN, $mode);

    if($product->valid())
      $cart[$ASIN] = array('price'=>$product->ourPrice(),
                     'name' => $product->productName(), 'quantity' => 1) ;
  }

}


// delete all of a particular item from cart
function deleteFromCart(&$cart, $ASIN)
{
  unset ($cart[$ASIN]);
}


? >
```

There are some differences about the way we do things with this cart. For example, look at the addToCart() function. When we try to add an item to the cart, we can check that it has a valid ASIN and look up the current (or at least, cached) price.

The really interesting thing here is this question: When customers check out, how do we get their data to Amazon?

Checking Out to Amazon

Look closely at the `showCart()` function in Listing 31.14. Here's the relevant part:

```
// build the form to link to an Amazon.com shopping cart
echo '<form method="POST"
      action="http://www.amazon.com/o/dt/assoc/handle-buy-box">';
foreach($cart as $ASIN=>$product)
{
  $quantity = $cart[$ASIN]['quantity'];
  echo "<input type='hidden' name='asin.$ASIN' value='$quantity'>";
}
echo '<input type="hidden" name="tag-value" value="ASSOCIATEID">';
echo '<input type="hidden" name="tag_value" value="ASSOCIATEID">';
echo '<input type="image" src="images/checkout.gif"
            name="submit.add-to-cart" value="Buy From Amazon.com">';
echo ' When you have finished shopping press checkout to add all the items
      in your Tahuayo cart to your Amazon cart and complete your purchase.
      <br />';
echo '</form>';
```

The checkout button is a form button that connects the cart to a customer's shopping cart on Amazon. We send ASINs, quantities, and our Associate ID through as POST variables. And hey presto! You can see the end result of clicking this button in Figure 31.5, back at the beginning of this chapter.

The resulting page will look a little different if the user does not have an Amazon cookie stored on his machine allowing Amazon to identify him, but the end result is the same.

One difficulty with this interface is that it is a one-way interaction. We can add items to the Amazon cart, but cannot remove them. This means that people cannot browse back and forth between the sites easily without ending up with duplicate items in their carts.

Installing the Project Code

If you want to install the project code from this chapter, you will need to take a few steps beyond the norm. After you have the code in an appropriate location on your server, you will need to do the following:

- Create a cache directory.
- Set the permissions on the cache directory so that the scripts will be able to write in it.
- Edit `constants.php` to provide the location of the cache.
- Sign up for an Amazon developer tag.
- Edit `constants.php` to include your developer tag and, optionally, your Associate ID.

- Make sure NuSOAP is installed. We have it inside the Tahuayo directory, but you could move it and change the code.
- Check that you have PHP compiled with XML support.

Extending the Project

There are lots of fun things you could do to extend this project:

- You could expand the types of searches that are available via Tahuayo.
- Amazon also has an XSLT Web Service that you might like to experiment with.
- In Amazon's Web Services How-To, there are links to innovative sample applications. Look at these for more ideas:

    http://associates.amazon.com/exec/panama/associates/ntg/browse/-/567634/

Shopping carts are the most obvious thing to build with this data, but they are not the only thing.

Further Reading

There are a million books and online resources available on the topics of XML and Web Services. A great place to start is always at the W3C. You can look at the XML Working Group page:

http://www.w3.org/XML/Core/

and the Web Services Activity page:

http://www.w3.org/2002/ws/

just as a beginning.

VI

Appendixes

A

Installing PHP and MySQL

APACHE, PHP, AND MYSQL ARE AVAILABLE FOR many combinations of operating systems and Web servers. In this appendix, we will explain how to set up Apache, PHP, and MySQL on a few server platforms. We'll cover the most common options available for Unix and Windows 2000.

Topics we will cover in this appendix include

- Running PHP as a CGI interpreter or as a module
- Installing Apache, SSL, PHP, and MySQL under Unix
- Installing Apache, PHP, and MySQL under Windows
- Testing that it's working: `phpinfo()`
- Adding PHP and MySQL to Microsoft Internet Information Server
- Adding PHP and MySQL to Microsoft Personal Web Server
- PEAR Installation
- Considering other configurations

Our goal in this appendix is to provide you with an installation guide for a Web server which will enable you to host multiple Web sites. Some sites, like in the examples covered, require Secure Socket Layer (SSL) for e-commerce solutions. And most are driven via scripts to connect to a database (DB) server and extract and process data.

Many PHP users never need to install PHP on a machine, which is why this material is in an appendix rather than Chapter 1. The easiest way to get access to a reliable server with a fast connection to the Internet and PHP already installed is to simply sign up for an account at one of the thousands of hosting services or hosting service resellers that litter the globe.

Depending on why you are installing PHP on a machine you might make different decisions. If you have a machine permanently connected to the network that you intend to use as a live server performance will be important to you. If you are building a development server to build and test your code on, having a similar configuration to the live server will be the most important consideration. If you intend to run ASP and PHP on the same machine, different limitations will apply.

Running PHP as a CGI Interpreter or Module

The PHP interpreter can be run as either a module or as a separate CGI binary. Generally, the module version is used for performance reasons. However the CGI version is sometimes used for servers where a module version is not available or because it enables Apache users to run different PHP-enabled pages under different user IDs.

You might also choose to use the CGI version because the easy-to-use Windows installer uses this version.

In this appendix we will primarily cover the module option as the method to run PHP in a Unix environment, and the CGI method with Windows systems.

Installing Apache, PHP, and MySQL Under Unix

Depending on your needs, and your level of experience with Unix systems, you might choose to do a binary install or compile the programs directly from their source. Both approaches have their advantages.

A binary install will take an expert minutes and a beginner not much longer, but it will result in a system that is probably a version or two behind the current releases and a system configured with somebody else's choice of options.

A source install will take a few hours to download, install, and configure, and it is intimidating the first few times you do it. It does, however, give you complete control. You choose what to install, what versions to use, and what configuration directives to set.

Binary Installation

Most Linux distributions include a preconfigured Apache Web Server with PHP built in. The details of what is provided will depend on your chosen distribution and version. We will have a brief look at version 8 of Red Hat's distribution.

One disadvantage of binary installs is that you will rarely get the latest version of a program. At the time of writing, Red Hat 8.0 includes packages to install Apache 2.0.40, PHP 4.2.2, and MySQL 3.23.52; all of these products are slightly out-of-date and are missing bug fixes that the source distributions will include. Depending on how important the last few bug fix releases are, this might not be a problem for you.

A bigger potential problem is that you have to use an Apache 2.0 http server. This will certainly give you some advantages, but depending on your attitude to risk, it might be wise to wait a little longer while more of the PHP extension libraries are modified to be thread-safe.

The biggest issue is that you do not get to choose what options are compiled into your programs. The killer for readers of this book is MySQL.

You can very quickly get a working Linux/Apache/PHP setup using Red Hat 8.0 using the packages provided. A few steps that can be done through the GUI should have you underway. The problem with this approach is that the PHP binary that Red Hat provides was compiled without MySQL support.

A valid approach might be to install the RPMs, then only reinstall the parts that need reinstalling to repair the system. In the case of Red Hat 8, this probably means recompiling just PHP. If you want to try this, follow only parts of the instructions we give for a full installation from source code.

The most flexible and reliable path to take is to compile all of the programs you need from their sources. This will take a little more time than installing RPMs, so you might choose to use RPMs or other binary packages when available. Even if binary files are not available from official sources with the configuration you need, you might be able to find unofficial ones with a search engine.

Source Installation

Let's now install Apache, PHP, and MySQL under a Unix environment. First, we need to decide which extra modules we will load under the trio. Because some of the examples covered in this book use a secure server for Web transactions, we will install an SSL (Secure Socket Layer) enabled server.

Our PHP configuration will be more or less the default setup but will also cover enabling the following two libraries under PHP.

- cURL
- PDFlib

These are just two of the many libraries available for PHP. We are including them so you can get an idea of what it takes to enable extra libraries within PHP. Compiling most Unix programs follows a similar process.

You usually need to recompile PHP after installing a new library, so if you know what you need in advance, install all required libraries on your machine and then begin to compile the PHP module.

Our installation will be done on a Red Hat 8.0 Linux server, but will be generic enough to apply to other Unix servers.

Let's start by gathering the required files for our installation. We need these programs:

- Apache (http://www.apache.org/): The Web Server
- OpenSSL (http://www.openssl.org/): Open Source toolkit that implements the Secure Sockets Layer
- Mod_SSL (http://www.modssl.org/): Provides an Apache module interface to OpenSSL
- MySQL (http://www.mysql.com/): The relational database
- PHP (http://www.php.net/): The server-side scripting language

- `http://curl.haxx.se/`: Client URL library functions
- `http://www.pdflib.com/pdflib/download/index.html`: Library for generating PDF documents on-the-fly

We will assume that you have root access to the server and that you have the following tools installed on your system.

- Perl (Preferably a recent version)
- gzip or gunzip
- gcc and GNU make

When you are ready to begin the installation process, you should start by downloading all tar file sources to a temp directory. Make sure you put them somewhere with plenty of space. In our case, we chose `/usr/src` for the temporary directory. You should download them as root to avoid permissions problems.

Installing MySQL

We are going to do a binary install of MySQL. This will automatically place files in various locations. The directories that we chose for the remainder of our trio are the following:

- `/usr/local/apache`
- `/usr/local/ssl`

You can install the applications in different directories by changing the prefix option before installing.

Let's begin! Become root by using `su`.

```
# su root
```

and enter the user root's password. Change to the directory that you have stored the source files in, for example

```
# cd /usr/src
```

MySQL is currently recommending that people download a binary of MySQL rather than compiling from scratch. It is believed that there are problems with certain versions of the C compiler gcc.

We downloaded the following RPMs from mysql.com:

```
MySQL-3.23.53a-1.i386.rpm
MySQL-devel-3.23.53a-1.i386.rpm
MySQL-client-3.23.53a-1.i386.rpm
MySQL-shared-3.23.53a-1.i386.rpm
```

If you intend to run the MySQL client and server on this machine, and to compile MySQL support into other programs such as PHP, you will need all of these.

The following command will install all parts:

```
#  rpm -i MySQL*
```

Now it's time to create the mysql tables, start the server and give the root user a password. Make sure you replace new-password in the command below with something of your choice; otherwise, new-password will be your root password.

```
#  mysql_install_db
#  safe_mysqld &
#  mysqladmin -u root password 'new-password'
```

You can verify that MySQL is working by running some simple tests. The output should be similar to what is shown here:

```
#  mysqlshow -p
Enter password:
+--------------------+
|  Databases         |
+--------------------+
|  mysql             |
+--------------------+
```

When you install MySQL, it will automatically create two databases. One is the mysql table, which controls users, hosts, and DB permissions in the actual server. The other is a test DB. You can check your database via the command line like this:

```
# mysql -u root -p
Enter password:
mysql> show databases;
+--------------------+
|  Database          |
+--------------------+
|  mysql             |
|  test              |
+--------------------+
2 rows in set (0.00 sec)
```

Type quit or \q to quit the MySQL client.

The default configuration of MySQL allows any user access to the system without providing a username or password. This is obviously undesirable.

The final compulsory piece of MySQL housekeeping is deleting the anonymous user. Opening a command prompt and typing the following lines will accomplish that.

```
# mysql -u root -p
mysql> use mysql
mysql> delete from user where User='';
mysql> quit
```

You will then need to type

```
mysqladmin -u root -p reload
```

in order for these changes to take effect.

Installing PDFlib

If you do not want to use PDFlib to create PDF files as discussed in Chapter 30, "Generating Personalized Documents in Portable Document Format (PDF)," you can skip this section.

Note that PDFlib creates shared objects intended for specific versions of PHP. You may need to wait for PDFlib to catch up if you are installing a new version of PHP.

To extract the contents of the PDFlib archive, type:

```
# gunzip -c pdflib-4.0.3.tar.gz | tar xvf -
```

PDFlib has many configure options. Type

```
./configure -help
```

for details. As PHP binding is enabled by default, the only flag we will give it is a path prefix to specify the directory where we want the files to be installed.

To install, we took the following steps:

```
./configure --prefix=/usr/local/pdflib
# make
# make install
```

We will not use PDFlib directly, so we will come back to it later once PHP is running.

Installing cURL

The cURL library is available as source code or as binaries precompiled for a range of platforms. We chose the source download. If you do not intend to use cURL (see Chapter 17, "Using Network and Protocol Functions"), you can skip this section.

The first step is to uncompress the archive:

```
# bzip2 -d curl-7.10.2.tar.bz2
# tar xvf curl-7.10.2.tar
```

The next step is to enter the cURL source directory and configure, make, and install the software.

```
# cd curl-7.10.2
# ./configure
# make
# make install
```

We will need to mention it again to link it to our PHP install, but that is all that is needed to install the library.

Installing PHP

You should still be acting as root, if not *su* back to root.

Before we can install PHP, you need to have Apache preconfigured so that it knows where everything is. You will come back to this later in the section when you set up the Apache server. Change back to the directory where you have the sources.

```
# cd /usr/src
# gunzip -c apache_1.3.27.tar.gz | tar xvf -
# cd apache_1.3.27
# ./configure --prefix=/usr/local/apache
```

Okay, now you can start setting up PHP. Extract the source files and change to its directory:

```
# cd /usr/src
# gunzip -c php-4.2.3.tar.gz | tar xvf -
#  cd php-4.2.3
```

Again there are many options with PHP's `configure` command. Use `./configure --help=short` to determine what you want to add. In this case, we want to add support for MySQL, Apache, PDFLib, and cURL.

Note that the following is all one command. We can put it all on one line, or as we have here, use the continuation character, backslash (\), to allow us to type one command across multiple lines to improve readability.

```
# ./configure --with-mysql=/usr \
            --with-xml --with-apache=../apache_1.3.27 \
            --with-curl=../curl \
            --enable-shared-pdflib
```

Next, make and install the binaries:

```
# make
# make install
```

Copy an ini file to the `lib` directory:

```
#  cp php.ini-dist /usr/local/lib/php.ini
```

or

```
# cp php.ini-recommended /usr/local/lib/php.ini
```

The two versions of `php.ini` in the suggested commands have different options set. The first, `php.ini-dist`, is intended for development machines. For instance, it has display_errors set to On. This will make development easier, but it is not really appropriate on a production machine. When we have referred to a php.ini setting's default value in this book, we mean its setting in this version of php.ini. The second version, `php.ini-recommended` is intended for production machines.

You can edit the php.ini file to set PHP options. There are any number of options that you might choose to set, but a few in particular are worth noting. You might need to set the value of sendmail_path if you want to send email from scripts. You might want to consider whether to have register_globals on or off.

It's time to set up OpenSSL. This is what you will use to create temporary certificates and CSR files. The --prefix specifies the main installation directory.

```
# gunzip -c openssl-0.9.6g.tar.gz | tar xvf -
# cd openssl-0.9.6g
# ./config --prefix=/usr/local/ssl
```

Now make it, test it, and install it:

```
# make
# make test
# make install
```

We will configure the mod_SSL module and then specify it to be a loadable module with the Apache configuration.

```
# cd /usr/src/
# gunzip -c mod_ssl-2.8.11-1.3.27.tar.gz |tar xvf -
# cd mod_ssl-2.8.11-1.3.27
# ./configure --with-apache=../apache_1.3.27
```

Note that we can add more Apache modules to the Apache source tree. The optional --enable-shared=ssl option enables the building of mod_SSL as a DSO 'libssl.so'. Read the INSTALL and htdocs/manual/dso.html documents in the Apache source tree for more information about DSO support in Apache. It is strongly advised that ISPs and package maintainers to use the DSO facility for maximum flexibility with mod_SSL. Notice, however, that Apache does not support DSO on all platforms.

```
# cd ../apache_1.3.27
#  SSL_BASE=../openssl-0.9.6g \
   ./configure \
   --enable-module=ssl \
   --activate-module=src/modules/php4/libphp4.a \
   --enable-module=php4 \
   --prefix=/usr/local/apache \
    --enable-shared=ssl
```

Finally you can make Apache and the certificates, and then install them.

```
# make
```

If you have done everything right, you will a message similar to the following:

```
+----------------------------------------------------------------------+
| Before you install the package you now should prepare the SSL        |
| certificate system by running the 'make certificate' command.        |
```

```
| For different situations the following variants are provided:        |
|                                                                      |
| % make certificate TYPE=dummy     (dummy self-signed Snake Oil cert) |
| % make certificate TYPE=test      (test cert signed by Snake Oil CA) |
| % make certificate TYPE=custom    (custom cert signed by own CA)     |
| % make certificate TYPE=existing (existing cert)                     |
|        CRT=/path/to/your.crt [KEY=/path/to/your.key]                 |
|                                                                      |
| Use TYPE=dummy    when you're a  vendor package maintainer,          |
| the TYPE=test     when you're an admin but want to do tests only,    |
| the TYPE=custom   when you're an admin willing to run a real server  |
| and TYPE=existing when you're an admin who upgrades a server.        |
| (The default is TYPE=test)                                           |
|                                                                      |
| Additionally add ALGO=RSA (default) or ALGO=DSA to select            |
| the signature algorithm used for the generated certificate.          |
|                                                                      |
| Use 'make certificate VIEW=1' to display the generated data.         |
|                                                                      |
| Thanks for using Apache & mod_ssl.       Ralf S. Engelschall         |
|                                          rse@engelschall.com         |
|                                          www.engelschall.com         |
+----------------------------------------------------------------------+
```

Now you can create a custom certificate. This option will prompt you for location, company, and a couple of other things. For contact information, it makes sense to use real data. For other questions during the process, the default answer is fine.

```
# make certificate TYPE=custom
```

Now install Apache:

```
# make install
```

If everything went well, the message that you should see is something similar to this:

```
+------------------------------------------------------+
| You now have successfully built and installed the    |
| Apache 1.3 HTTP server. To verify that Apache actually |
| works correctly you now should first check the       |
| (initially created or preserved) configuration files |
|                                                      |
|   /usr/local/apache/conf/httpd.conf                  |
|                                                      |
| and then you should be able to immediately fire up   |
| Apache the first time by running:                    |
|                                                      |
|   /usr/local/apache/bin/apachectl start              |
|                                                      |
```

```
| Or when you want to run it with SSL enabled use:        |
|                                                          |
|   /usr/local/apache/bin/apachectl startssl              |
|                                                          |
| Thanks for using Apache.        The Apache Group        |
|                                 http://www.apache.org/  |
+----------------------------------------------------------+
```

Now it's time to see whether Apache and PHP are working. However, we need to edit the `httpd.conf` to add the PHP type to the configuration.

`httpd.conf` **File—Snippets**

Look at the `httpd.conf` and add or uncomment the following lines. If you have followed the previous instructions, your `httpd.conf` file will be located in the `/usr/local/apache/conf` directory. The file has the `addtype` for PHP 4 commented out. You should uncomment it at this time, so it looks like this:

```
# And for PHP 4.x, use:
#
AddType application/x-httpd-php .php
AddType application/x-httpd-php-source .phps
```

Now we are ready to start the Apache server to see whether it worked. First, we will start the server without the SSL support to see whether it comes up. We will check for PHP support, and then we will stop the server and start it with the SSL support enabled and see whether we got everything working.

The `configtest` will check whether the configuration is set up properly:

```
# cd /usr/local/apache/bin
# ./apachectl configtest
Syntax OK
# ./apachectl start
   ./apachectl start: httpd started
```

If it worked correctly, you will see something similar to Figure A.1 when you connect to the server with a Web browser.

> **Note**
> You can connect to the server with a domain name or using the actual IP address of the computer. Check both cases, to ensure that everything is working properly.

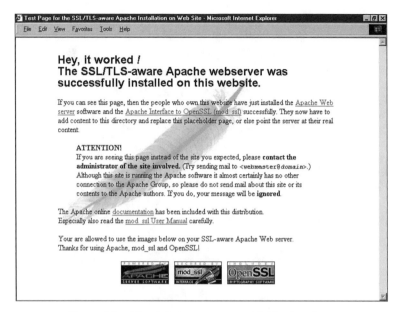

Figure A.1   The default test page provided by Apache.

Is PHP Support Working?

Now we will test for PHP support. Create a file with the name of `test.php` with the following code in it. The file needs to be located in document root path, which should be set up by default to `/usr/local/apache/htdocs`. Note that this is dependent on the directory prefix that we chose initially. However, this could be changed in the `httpd.conf`.

```
<?php phpinfo(); ?>
```

The output screen should look like Figure A.2.

Is SSL Working?

Okay, now we are ready to test for SSL. First, stop the server, and restart with the SSL option enabled:

```
# /usr/local/apache/bin/apachectl stop
# /usr/local/apache/bin/apachectl startssl
```

Test to see whether it works, by connecting to the server with a Web browser and selecting the `https` protocol, like this:

```
https://yourserver.yourdomain.com or http://yoursever.yourdomain.com:443
```

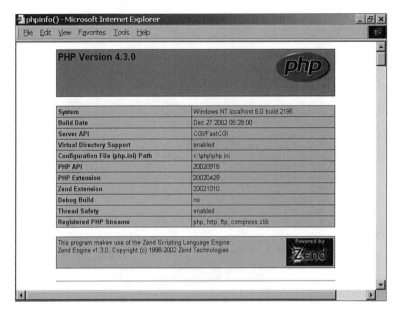

Figure A.2   The function phpinfo() provides useful
configuration information.

Try your server's IP address also, like this:

```
https://xxx.xxx.xxx.xxx or http://xxx.xxx.xxx.xxx:443
```

If it worked, the server will send the certificate to the browser to establish a secure connection. This will make the browser prompt you for accepting the self-signed certificate. If it were a certificate from a certification authority you're your browser already trusts the browser would not prompt You. In our case, we created and signed our own certificates. We didn't want to purchase one right away. We wanted to ensure that we could get everything working properly, first.

If you are using Internet Explorer or Netscape, you will see a padlock symbol in the status bar. This tells you that a secure connection has been established. The icon used by Netscape is shown in Figure A.3.

Figure A.3   Web browsers display an icon to indicate the page you
are viewing came via an SSL connection.

Final Steps

In order to use the PDFlib shared object, and any other modules you installed in this way you will need to complete a few more steps.

Copy the file libpdf_php to PHP extensions directory. This will probably be

```
/usr/local/lib/php/extensions
```

Add the following line to your php.ini file:

```
extension = libpdf_php.so
```

Installing Apache, PHP, and MySQL Under Windows

With Windows the installation process is a little bit different because PHP is set up either as a CGI (php.exe) script or as an ISAPI module (php4isapi.dll). However, Apache and MySQL are installed in a similar fashion to the way they are installed under Unix. Make sure you have the latest operating system service patches applied to the machine before you begin the Windows installation. In particular, if you are using Windows NT make sure you have service patch 3.

You should start by downloading all the latest source files to a temporary directory with ample space. For our installation we used c:\temp\download as our temp directory.

If you have a slow network connection you may prefer to use the versions from the CD, but they are likely to be a version or more out of date.

The install files we are using here are

```
mysql-3.23.52-win.zip
apache_1.3.27-win32-x86-no_src.msi
php-4.2.3-Win32.zip
```

Installing MySQL Under Windows

The following instructions were written using Windows 2000. If you are using Windows NT or XP the steps will be very similar. If you are using one of 95, 98 or Me, the parts directly interacting with MySQL will be the same, but parts interacting with the system will differ.

Let's begin by setting up MySQL. Assuming you have already downloaded all the required files, begin by unzipping MySQL zip file to the temp directory and run the *Setup.exe* program. The installer is a standard InstallShield wizard and should look like many other installers you have seen.

Choosing Typical Install in the wizard will not ask any questions other than where you would like MySQL installed. The directory where MySQL will install itself by default will be the c:\mysql directory. You can move it to a different directory if need-ed, after it's fully installed, but if you do you will need to take some extra steps to keep everything working.

If you move MySQL and intend to run the MySQL executable, `mysqld`, you must tell it where everything is by supplying command line options. Use `C:\mysql\bin\mysqld --help` to display all options. For example, if you have moved the MySQL distribution to `'D:\programs\mysql'`, you must start `mysqld` with: `'D:\programs\mysql\bin\mysqld --basedir D:\programs\mysql'`.

If you move it and are running it as a Windows service, you need to create an ini file called my.ini and place it in your main Windows directory. Your ini file will have content something like this:

```
[mysqld]
basedir=D:/programs/mysql/bin/
datadir= D:/programs/mysql/data/
```

In the NT/2000/XP setup, the name of the MySQL server is `mysqld-nt`, and it will normally be installed as a service. A service is a program that runs constantly in the background intended to provide services to other programs. They usually run automatically when you start the machine, which will save you the effort of having to start them each time.

You can install the MySQL server as a service by going to the windows command prompt and typing this:

```
cd c:\mysql\bin
mysqld-nt -install
```

The response you should get is

```
Service successfully installed.
```

Now you can start and stop the MySQL service from the command line with:

```
NET START mysql
NET STOP mysql
```

Note the executable's name is mysqld-nt, but the service's name is just mysql. If you run NET START mysql you should see the following message:

```
The MySql service is starting.
The MySql service was started successfully.
```

After the server has been installed, it can be stopped, started, or set to start automatically using the Services utility (found in Control Panel). To open Services, click Start, point to Settings, and click Control Panel. Double-click Administrative Tools, and then double-click Services.

The Services utility is shown in Figure A.4. If you want to set any MySQL options, you must first stop the service, and then specify them as *startup parameters* in the Services utility before restarting the MySQL service. The MySQL service can be stopped using the Services utility, or using the commands NET STOP MySQL or mysqladmin shutdown.

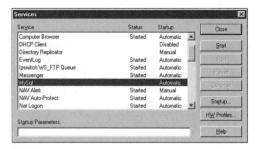

Figure A.4   The Services utility allows you to configure the services running on your machine.

To test whether or not MySQL is working, you can execute the following commands:

```
C:\mysql\bin\mysqlshow
C:\mysql\bin\mysqlshow mysql
C:\mysql\bin\mysqladmin version status proc
```

The first command (`mysqlshow`) should give you a list of databases. When installed, MySQL automatically creates two databases named `mysql` and `test`. The database `mysql` will be used for storing the permissions and access to the server. The database `test` is not required, but gives you a safe place to execute commands to see if things are configured correctly.

The second command (`mysqlshow mysql`) will show you the tables in the mysql database.

The third command (`mysqladmin version status proc`) will tell you about the current status of MySQL.

The default configuration is not really ideal. There are a few loose ends we need to attend to:

- Setting your PATH
- Deleting the anonymous user
- Setting the root password

Setting Your PATH

MySQL comes with lots of command line utilities with varying degrees of usefulness. None of these are easy to get at unless the MySQL binary directory is in your PATH. The purpose of this environment variable is to tell Windows where to look for executable programs.

Many of the common commands you use at the Windows command prompt, like `dir` and `cd`, are internal and built into cmd.exe. Others, like `format` and `ipconfig`, have their own executables. It would not be convenient to have to type C:\WINNT\ system32\format if you wanted to format a disk. It would not be convenient to have to type C:\mysql\bin\mysql to run the MySQL monitor.

The directory that the executables for your basic Windows commands, like format.exe, reside in is automatically in your PATH, so you can simply type format. In order to have the same convenience with the mysql command line tools, we need to add it.

Click Start, and choose Settings, Control Panel. Double-click System and go to the Advanced tab. If you click the Environment Variables button, you will be presented with a dialog box which allows you to view the environment variables for your system. Double-clicking PATH will allow you to edit it.

Add a semicolon to the end of your current path to separate your new entry from the previous one then add `c:\mysql\bin`. When you click OK, your addition will be stored in the machine's registry. Next time you restart the machine, you will be able to type `mysql` rather than `C:\mysql\bin\mysql`.

Deleting the Anonymous User

The default configuration of MySQL allows any user access to the system without providing a username or password. This is obviously undesirable.

The first thing we want to do is delete the anonymous user. Opening a command prompt and typing the following lines will accomplish that.

```
c:\mysql\bin\mysql
use mysql
delete from user where User='';
quit
c:\mysql\bin\mysqladmin reload
```

The anonymous user is now gone.

Setting the root Password

Even the superuser account, root, has no password yet. To set this user's password type these lines:

```
c:\mysql\bin\mysqladmin -u root password your_password
c:\mysql\bin\mysqladmin -u root -h your_host_name password your_password
```

You should find that tasks that previously required no username or password will now fail without this information. Attempting to run

```
c:\mysql\bin\mysqladmin reload
```

or

```
c:\mysql\bin\mysqladmin shutdown
```

will now fail.

From now on, you will need to use the `-u` flag and provide a username, and the `-p` flag to tell MySQL that you have a password, as in this example:

```
c:\mysql\bin\mysqladmin -u root -p reload
```

If you type this command MySQL should now prompt you for the root password that you just set.

If you need more information, please refer to the MySQL Web site, `http://www.mysql.com`.

We are now ready to install Apache under Windows. Let's begin!

Installing Apache Under Windows

Apache 1.3 and later is designed to run on Windows NT, 2000, and XP. The installer will only work with the x86 family of processors, such as Intel's. Apache also runs on Windows 95, 98, and XP but these have not been tested. In all cases TCP/IP networking must be installed. Make sure you use the Winsock 2 library if you decide to install it under either Windows 95 or 98.

We downloaded this file: `apache_1.3.27-win32-x86-no_src.msi`.

This file contains the current version (within the 1.3 hierarchy) for Windows, without source code, packaged as an MSI file. MSI files are the package format used by the Windows installer.

Unless you have a really elusive bug, or want to contribute to the development effort, it is unlikely that you will want to compile the source code yourself. This single file contains the Apache server ready to be installed.

Double-clicking the file you downloaded to start the process.

The installation process should look familiar to you. As shown in Figure A.5, it looks similar to many other Windows installers.

Figure A.5   The Apache installer is easy to use.

The install program will prompt you for the following:

- The network name, server name, and administrator's email address. If you are building a server for real use, you should know the answers to these questions. If you are building a server for your own personal use, the answers are not particularly important.

- Whether you want Apache to run as a service. As with MySQL, it is usually easier to set it up this way.
- The installation type. We recommend the Complete option, but you can choose Custom if you wish to leave out some components such as the documentation.
- The directory in which to install Apache. (The default is `C:\Program Files\Apache Group\Apache`.)

After you choose all these options, the Apache server will be installed and started.

Apache will be listening to port 80 (unless you changed the Port, Listen, or BindAddress directives in the configuration files) after it starts. To connect to the server and access the default page, launch a browser and enter this URL:

`http://localhost/`

This should respond with a welcome page similar to that shown in Figure A.1, and a link to the Apache manual. If nothing happens or you get an error, look in the `error.log` file in the `logs` directory. If your host isn't connected to the Internet, you might have to use this URL:

`http://127.0.0.1/`

This is the IP address that means localhost.

If you have changed the port number from 80, you will need to append `:port_number` on the end of the URL.

Note that Apache *cannot* share the same port with another TCP/IP application.

You can start and stop the Apache service from your Start menu: Apache adds itself under Programs->Apache HTTP Server. Under the "Control Apache Server" heading you will see that you can Start, Stop, and Restart the server.

After installing Apache, you might need to edit the configuration files that live in the `conf` directory. We will look at editing the configuration file `httpd.conf` when we install PHP.

If you need to enable Apache with SSL in Windows, you should follow the excellent FAQ at

`http://tud.at/programm/apache-ssl-win32-howto.php3`

but be aware that it is not for the faint-hearted.

Installing PHP for Windows

There are a couple of different ways to do this. You can either install it manually, or use the InstallShield installer. You have a choice of downloads at the PHP site.

Using the installer makes it amazingly easy and will give you a working PHP installation but with no modules installed. Installing manually is also pretty simple and gives you a full set of modules. The choice is yours, but we recommend you use the manual approach as you will need many of the different modules as you work your way through this book. We will discuss both installations.

Using InstallShield

The installer comes as an executable file. Begin by stopping your Web server, and then double-click the installer to run it.
The installer will ask you if you would like to use the standard or advanced setup.

The standard setup will ask you very few questions: It will ask you what directory to install to, where your mail server lives, what your email address is, and the type of web server you have.

The advanced setup will also ask you

- If you want to create backups during the installation
- Where you would like uploaded files to be placed
- Where you would like session data stored
- What error reporting level you would like
- What file extensions you would like Apache to recognize

Manual Installation

Begin by unzipping the Zip file to the directory of your choice. The usual location is c:\PHP, and we will use this in the following explanation.

1. In the main directory you will see a file called php.exe, and one called php4ts.dll. These are the files you will need to run PHP as a CGI. If you would like to run it as a SAPI module you will need to look in the directory c:\PHP\sapi and copy the relevant DLL file to C:\PHP. If you are using Apache, the file is called php4apache.dll for example.

    The SAPI modules are faster and easier to secure; the CGI version allows you to run PHP from the command line. Again, the choice is up to you.

2. Copy the contents of c:\PHP\dlls to your Windows system directory. This will be C:\winnt\system32 on Windows NT or 2000 or C:\windows\system32 on Windows XP.

3. Move the directory c:\PHP\mibs to c:\usr\mibs.

4. Set up a php.ini configuration file. PHP comes with two prepared files: php.ini-dist and php.ini-recommended. We suggest you use php.ini-recommended. Make a copy of this file and rename it php.ini. Place your php.ini file in the '%SYSTEM-ROOT%' directory. This is usually c:\winnt or c:\winnt40 on Windows NT or 2000, or c:\windows on Windows XP.

5. Edit your php.ini file. There are many settings in it, most of which can be ignored for the time being. The settings you need to change now are

    - Change the extension_dir directive to point to the directory where your extension DLLs reside. In the normal install this will be C:\PHP\extensions. Your php.ini will therefore contain

    ```
    extension_dir = c:/php/extensions
    ```

- Set the doc_root directive to point at the root directory that your Web server serves from. This is likely to be

```
doc_root = "c:/Program Files/Apache Group/Apache/htdocs"
```

if you are using Apache, or

```
doc_root = "c:/Inetpub/wwwroot"
```

if you are using IIS.

- You can also choose some extensions to run. We suggest at this stage that you just get PHP working; you can add extensions as needed. In order to add an extension, look at the list under "Windows Extensions". You will see a lot of lines such as

```
;extension=php_pdf.dll
```

In order to turn this extension on, you can simply remove the semicolon at the start of the line (and do the opposite to turn it off). Note that if you want to add more extensions later, you should restart your Web server after you have changed php.ini in order for the changes to take effect.

Close and save your php.ini file.

6. If you are using NTFS, make sure the user that the Web server runs as has permission to read your php.ini file.

Adding PHP to your Apache Configuration

You may need to edit one of Apache's configuration files. Open up the file httpd.conf in your favorite editor. This file is typically located in the c:\Program Files\Apache Group\Apache\conf\ directory. Look for the following lines:

```
ScriptAlias /php/ "c:/php/"
AddType application/x-httpd-php .php
Action application/x-httpd-php "/php/php.exe "
```

If these lines are not there, add them at the end of the file, save it, and restart your Apache server.

Adding PHP and MySQL to Microsoft IIS and PWS

This section will cover how to add PHP and MySQL support to IIS with the ISAPI (php4isapi.dll) module. (You can also install it as a CGI, but we strongly recommend you use the ISAPI module as it is faster.) It assumes that you have followed the steps in either the "Using InstallShield" or "Manual Installation" sections. The main difference is that the doc_root configuration directive is likely to be "c:/Inetpub/wwwroot".

Once you have done that, you need to start the Microsoft Management Console (which may appear on your system as the Internet Services Manager). If you have NT this can be found in the NT4 Option Pack. If you have 2000 or XP it can be found in the Control Panel under Administrative Tools.

Once this is open, you should see a tree view of services on the left side. Right-click the Web server (usually called Default Web Server) and select Properties.

You will be shown the Properties dialog box. This contains quite a lot of information but we only need to change a few things.

Under Home Directory click the Configuration button. Under App Mappings, select Add to add PHP. It will ask you for an executable. Supply the full path to the location of php4isapi.dll (probably c:\php\sapi\php4isapi.dll if you have followed these instructions). There is also a box labeled Extension in which you should type .php. You also need to have the Script Engine box checked. Click OK.

If you want to be able to do HTTP Authentication (which we cover in this book) you should also look under ISAPI filters. Select Add. You will be asked for a filter name—type PHP—and an executable—supply the full path to the php4isapi.dll file as above. Click OK.

Close the Properties dialog by clicking Apply.

You should now stop (or check that it is stopped) and restart the Web server. You can do this from the Management Console/Internet Services Manager by right-clicking on the Web server and choosing Stop. You can restart in the same way by selecting Start.

Let's Test Our Work

Start your Web server and test to ensure that you have PHP working. Create a `test.php` file and add the following lines to it:

```
<? phpinfo(); ?>
```

Make sure the file is in the document root directory (typically c:\Program File\Apache Group\Apache\htdocs under Apache or c:\Inetpub\wwwroot under IIS) and then pull it up on the browser, as follows

```
http://localhost/test.php
```

or

```
http://your-ip-number-here/test.php
```

If you see a page similar to that shown in Figure A.2, you know that you have PHP working.

PEAR Installation

PHP 4.3 is supposed to come with the PEAR package installer. At the time of writing, the Linux version installs automatically, but the Windows version did not include this. If you are using Windows or an earlier version of PHP (from 4.1 to 4.2.3) you will need to download the package installer separately. You can obtain this from

```
http://go-pear.org
```

There is exactly one script at that site. Save it as go-pear. You need to run this script through PHP from the command line. Go to the command line and type

```
php go-pear
```

The go-pear script will ask you a few straightforward questions about where you would like the package installer and the standard PEAR classes installed, and will then download and install them for you.

At this stage you should have an installed version of the PEAR package installer. You can then simply install packages by typing

```
pear install package
```

where *package* is replaced with the name of the package you wish to install.
To get a list of available packages, type:

```
pear list-all
```

To see what you have installed currently try

```
pear list
```

To install the MIME mail package used in Chapter 28, "Building a Mailing List Manager," type:

```
pear install Mail_Mime
```

The DB package mentioned in Chapter 10, "Accessing Your MySQL Database from the Web with PHP," is installed automatically, but to make sure you have the newest version you can type

```
pear list-upgrades
```

If there is a newer version available type

```
pear upgrade DB
```

At the time of writing it was difficult to get the PEAR package installer working on Windows. If the above procedure does not work for you, we suggest you try downloading PEAR packages directly rather than via the installer.

To do this, go to

```
http://pear.php.net/packages.php
```

From here you can navigate through the various packages available. For example, in this book we use Mail_Mime. Click through to the page for this package and click Download Latest to get a copy. You will need to unzip the file you have downloaded and put it somewhere in your include_path.

You should have a c:\php\pear or similar directory. If you are downloading packages manually we suggest you put the packages in the pear directory tree. PEAR has a standard structure so we suggest you put things in the standard location—this is where the installer would put them. For example, the Mail_Mime package belongs in the Mail section so in this example we would place it in the c:\php\pear\Mail directory.

Other Configurations

You can set up PHP and MySQL with other Web servers such as Omni, HTTPD, and Netscape Enterprise Server. These will not be covered in this appendix, but you can find information on how to set them up at the MySQL and PHP Web sites:

```
http://www.php.net
```

and

```
http://www.mysql.com
```

respectively.

B

Web Resources

THIS APPENDIX LISTS SOME OF THE MANY resources available on the Web, which can be used to find tutorials, articles, news, and sample PHP code. These are just some of the many out there. Obviously there are far more than we could possibly list in one appendix. And many more that are popping up daily as the usage of and familiarity with PHP and MySQL continues to increase among Web developers.

Some of these resources will be in different languages like German or French or something other than your native language. We suggest using a translator like `http://www.systransoft.com` to browse the Web resource in your native language.

PHP Resources

PHP.Net—`http://www.php.net`—The original site for PHP. Go here to download all the sources of PHP and for a copy of the manual.

ZEND.Com—`http://www.zend.com`—The source for the ZEND engine that powers PHP 4. A portal site that contains forums, articles, tutorials, and a database of sample classes and code that you can use. A must see.

PHPWizard.net—`http://www.phpwizard.net`—The source of many cool PHP applications like phpMyAdmin; an excellent front end GUI for Managing MySQL Servers. You can also find tutorials on PHP at this site.

PHPBuilder.com—`http://www.phpbuilder.com`—The portal for PHP tutorials. At this site, you will find tutorials on just about anything you can think of. Site also has a forum and message board for people to post questions.

DevShed.com—`http://www.devshed.com`—Portal type site offers, excellent tutorials on PHP, MySQL, Perl, and other development languages. A must see for newbies.

PX-PHP Code Exchange—`http://px.sklar.com`—A great place to start. Here you will find many sample scripts and useful functions.

The PHP4 Resource—`http://www.php-resource.de`—A very nice source for tutorials, articles, and scripts. The only "problem" is that the site is in German. We recommend using a translator service site to view it.

WeberDev.com—`http://www.WeberDev.com`—Formerly known as Berber's PHP sample page, this site grew and is now a place for tutorials and sample code. The site targets PHP and MySQL users, and covers security and general databases.

HotScripts.com—`http://www.hotscripts.com`—A great categorized selection of scripts. The site has scripts in various languages like PHP, ASP, and Perl. It has an excellent collection of PHP scripts. Updated very frequently. A must see if you are looking for scripts.

PHP Base Library— `http://phplib.sourceforge.net` —A site used by developers for large-scale PHP projects. Offers a library with a lot of tools for an alternative session management approach, as well as templating and database abstraction.

PHP Center—`http://www.php-center.de`—Another German portal site used for tutorials, scripts, tips, tricks, advertising, and more.

PHP Homepage—`http://www.php-homepage.de`—Another German site about PHP with scripts, articles, news, and much more. Has a quick reference section.

PHPIndex.com—`http://www.phpindex.com`—A nice French PHP portal with tons of PHP related content. Site contains news, FAQs, articles, job listings, and much more.

WebMonkey.com—`http://www.webmonkey.com`—A portal with lots of Web resources, real world tutorials, sample code, and so on. The site covers design, programming, back end, multimedia stuff, and much more.

The PHP Club—`http://www.phpclub.net`—The PHP Club offers many resources for PHP beginners. The site has news, book reviews, sample code, forums, FAQs, and many tutorials for beginners.

PHP Classes Repository—`http://phpclasses.upperdesign.com`—A site that targets the distribution of freely available classes written in PHP. A must-see if you are developing code or your project will be composed of classes. Nice search functionality, so you can find stuff easily.

The PHP Resource Index—`http://php.resourceindex.com`—Portal site for scripts, classes, and documentation. The cool thing about this site is that everything is nicely categorized, which can save you some time.

PHP Developer—`http://www.phpdeveloper.org`—Yet another PHP portal that provides PHP news, articles, and tutorials.

Evil Walrus—`http://www.evilwalrus.com`—A cool-looking portal for PHP scripts.

Oodie.com—`http://www.oodie.com`—Provides lists of free PHP hosting service providers and scripts.

e-gineer—`http://www.e-gineer.com`—Articles, scripts, and a knowledge base of common questions and answers.

Source Forge—`http://sourceforge.net`—Extensive open source resources. Source Forge not only lets you find code that can be useful, but it also provides access to CVS, mailing lists, and machines for Open Source developers.

Codewalkers—`http://codewalkers.com/`—Contains articles, book reviews, tutorials, and the amazing PHP Contest where you can win stuff with your new skills. They have a new code contest every two weeks.

PHP Developer's Network Unified Forums—
`http://forums.devnetwork.net/index.php`—Discussion of all things PHP related.

PHP Kitchen—`http://www.phpkitchen.com/`—Articles, news, and PHP advocacy.

Postnuke—`http://www.postnuke.com/`—A frequently usedPHP content management system.

PHP Application Tools—`http://www.php-tools.de/`—A set of useful PHP classes.

MySQL and SQL Specific Resources

The MySQL site—`http://www.mysql.com`—The official MySQL Web site. Provides excellent documentation, support, and information. A must-see if you are using MySQL.

The SQL Course—`http://sqlcourse.com`—Provides an introductory SQL tutorial with easy-to-understand instructions. Allows you to practice what you learn on an online SQL interpreter. Advanced version is provided at `http://www.sqlcourse2.com`.

SearchDatabase.com—`http://searchdatabase.com`—Nice portal with lots of useful information on DBS. Provides excellent tutorials, tips, white papers, FAQs, reviews, and so on. A must-see!

Apache Resources

Apache Software—`http://www.apache.org`—The place to start if you need to download the source or binaries. The site provides online documentation.

Apache Week—`http://www.apacheweek.com`—Online weekly magazine that provides essential information for anyone running an Apache Server or anyone running Apache services. A must!

Apache Today—`http://www.apachetoday.com`—A daily source of news and information about Apache. Users must subscribe to post questions.

Web Development

Philip and Alex's Guide to Web Publishing—`http://philip.greenspun.com/panda/`—A witty, irreverent guide to software engineering as it applies to the Web. One of the few books on the topic coauthored by a Samoyed.

Index

D

documents

personalized, 705-710

structure, content management systems, 558

DoS (Denial of Service), 278

doubleval() function, 248

downloading

Amazon Web Services Developers' Kit, 746

files, FTP servers, 371-372

FreeType library, Web site, 388

GIF (Graphics Interchange Format), Web site, 389

jpeg-6b, FTP site, 388

PostScript Type 1 fonts, FTP site, 388

t1lib, 388

do_html_header() function, 536, 606

draw star() function, 736

drawing

data, code, 408-410

figures, 404-412

images, with scripts, 390

text on images, 391-393

variables, code, 407

drawing functions, parameters, 392

DROP DATABASE statement, 220

DROP INDEX index syntax, 219

DROP PRIMARY KEY syntax, 219

DROP privilege, 187

DROP TABLE statement, 220

DROP [COLUMN] column syntax, 219

dropping, databases or tables, 220

DTD (Document Type Definition), XML, 743

Dubois, Paul, 258

dynamic content, 18-19

dynamically loading extensions, 434

dynamically produced inline images, 395

E

e-commerce Web sites, 261

adding value to goods or services, 268

authentication, 275

cutting costs, 269

online brochures, 262-264

orders for goods or services, 265-268

privacy policies, 266

providing services and digital goods, 268

risks, 269-272

Secure Electronic Transaction standard, 280

security

authentication, 282-283

backing up data, 290-291

Certificate Signing Request (CSR), 289

Certifying Authorities (CAs), 287

compromises, 281

Denial of Service (DoS), 278

digital certificates, 287-288

digital signatures, 286-287

encryption, 284-286

errors in software, 279-280

exposure of confidential data, 275-276

firewalls, 290

hash function, 286

importance of stored information, 274

log files, 289-290

loss or destruction of data, 276-277

modification of data, 277-278

passwords, 282-283

physical security, 291-292

repudiation, 280-281

Secure Web servers, 288-289

security policies, creating, 281-282

threats, 274-281

strategies, selecting, 272

user interface design, 267

e-gineer Web site, 814

e-mail, 358

error messages, calling undefined functions, 130

error reporting levels, **465-468**

error suppression operator, **34-35**

errors

  401 errors (HTTP), 306

  error reporting levels, 465-468

  exception handling, 468-471

  logic, 462-463

  programming, 455-463

  runtime, 457

    database interaction, 459-461

    functions that don't exist, 458-459

    input data, 462

    network connections, 461-462

    reading/writing files, 459

  software (security threats), 279-280

  syntax, 456-457

  triggering, 468

escapeshellcmd() function, 323, 354

escaping characters, 102

eval() function, 430-431

evaluating strings, 430-431

Evil Walrus Web site, 814

exception handling, 468-471

exec() function, 352

executable content (stored data), 323

execution operator, 35

exit language construct, 431

exit statement, 49

expanding threads (Web forum application), 682-685

expand_all() function, 685

EXPLAIN statement, 251-254

explode() function, 88-89, 103, 365

exploits, BUGTRAQ archives Web site, 344

exporting public keys (Gnu Privacy Guard), 326

extended syntax, 216

extends keyword, 152

Extensible Markup Language. *See* XML

extensions

  loading, dynamically, 434

  Shopping Cart application, 553

  Warm Mail application, 620

  Web forum application, 703

extensions (filename extensions), require() statement, 120

extract() function, 92-94

extract_type parameter (extract() function), 93

F

f file mode, 55

f parameters, 771

FastTemplate Web site, 451

fclose() function, 60, 346

fdf create() function, 722

fdf set file() function, 722

fdf set value() function, 722

FDF Web site, 722

Fedex Web site, 268

feof() function, 62

fgetc() function, 64

fgetcsv() function, 62-63

fgets() function, 62

fgetss() function, 62

fields

  scope, 243

  tables, 170

  user file (HTML form), 339

figures, drawing, 404-412

File Details view, 349

file modes, 53

file paths from directories, 347

FILE privilege, 188, 248

File Transfer Protocol (FTP), 365, 374

  anonymous login, 368

  filetime() function, 370

  file_exists() function, 370

  FTP transfer modes, 372

  ftp_connect() function, 369

  ftp_fput() function, 372

S

W

X-Z

Developer's Library

Essential references for programming professionals

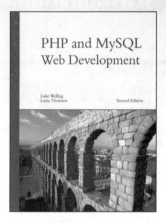

PHP and MySQL Web Development

Luke Welling
Laura Thomson

ISBN: 0-672-32525-X
$49.99 US/$77.99 CAN

Cocoon

DEVELOPER'S HANDBOOK

Lajos Moczar
Jeremy Aston

ISBN: 0-672-32257-9
$49.99 US/$77.99 CAN

MySQL

Paul DuBois

ISBN: 0-7357-1212-3
$49.99 US/$77.99 CAN

OTHER DEVELOPER'S LIBRARY TITLES

PHP
DEVELOPER'S COOKBOOK

Sterling Hughes
Andrei Zmievski

ISBN: 0-672-32325-7
$39.99 US/$59.95 CAN

PHP Functions
ESSENTIAL REFERENCE

Zak Graent
Graeme Merrall
Torben Wilson
Brett Michlitsch

ISBN: 0-7357-0970-X
$49.99 US/$74.95 CAN

PostgreSQL
DEVELOPER'S HANDBOOK

Ewald Geschwinde
and Hans–Jürgen
Schönig

ISBN: 0-672-32260-9
$44.99 US/$67.95 CAN

mod_perl
DEVELOPER'S COOKBOOK

Geoffrey Young
Paul Lindner
Randy Kobes

ISBN: 0-672-32240-4
$39.99 US/$62.99 CAN

PRICES SUBJECT TO CHANGE

DEVELOPER'S LIBRARY

www.developers-library.com

What's On the CD-ROM?

The book's companion CD-ROM contains full versions of PHP, MySQL, Apache, several graphics libraries, files containing the code listings in the book, and the entire book electronically in PDF format.

Windows

Appendix A describes setting up Apache, MySQL, and PHP on a Windows platform. We have included Windows versions of these products on the CD-ROM.

Apache 1.3.27 is in the Software\Apache\Windows\Binary directory. Double-click on `apache_1.3.27-win32-x86-no_src.msi` to launch the Apache installer.

MySQL 3.23.54 is in the `Software\MySQL\Windows\Binary` directory. Double-click on `SETUP.EXE` to start the MySQL installation program.

PHP 4.3.0 is in the `Software\PHP\Binary` directory. You can use the simplified installer (`php-4.3.0-installer.exe`) which will configure PHP for use with MySQL but lacks options and modules, or you can extract the full package (`php-4.3.0-Win32.zip`) and follow the instructions in the Readme file within the Zip file to configure PHP for your particular system.

Several graphics libraries and a PDF library (PDFlib) are available for your use in the `Libraries` directory. You can use WinZip or an unarchiver of your choice to extract the code to your computer.

Linux/Unix

Many Linux distributions and some Unix workstations are already configured with Apache, MySQL, and PHP. Appendix A describes setting up Apache, MySQL, and PHP on a Linux or Unix workstation if you need to install them. Source code for Apache, MySQL, and PHP and binary installers for MySQL on Linux are included on the CD-ROM.

The source code for Apache 1.3.27 is available in `Software/Apache/Unix/Source`. If you have GNU tar available use `httpd-1.3.27.tar.gz`. Otherwise use `httpd-1.3.27.tar.Z`.

Binary installers for MySQL 3.23.54a for Linux are in `Software\MySQL\Unix\Binary`. If your Linux system uses the RPM manager to install software, use `MySQL-3.23.54a-1.i386.rpm` to install the server portion of MySQL and use `MySQL-client-3.23.54a-1.i386.rpm` to install the client portion of MySQL. If your Linux system does not use the RPM manager to install software, use `mysql-3.23.54a-pc-linux-i686.tar.gz` to install the client and server portions of MySQL.

The source code for MySQL 3.23.54a for Unix is at `Software/MySQL/Unix/Source/mysql-3.23.54a.tar.gz`. Solaris users should download GNU tar to extract these files because of a bug within Solaris' version of the tar program.

The source code for PHP 4.3.0 is at `Software/PHP/Unix/Source/php-4.3.0.tar.gz`.

Several graphics libraries and a PDF library (PDFlib) are available for your use in the `Libraries` directory.